THE
ENCYCLOPEDIA
OF
PRACTICAL
BUSINESS

THE ENCYCLOPEDIA OF PRACTICAL BUSINESS

By the Editors and Experts
of Boardroom® Reports

BOARDROOM® BOOKS

THIRD PRINTING

Library of Congress Cataloging in Publication Data
Main entry under title:

Encyclopedia of Practical Business

Includes indexes.
1. Business — Addresses, essays, lectures.
2. Finance, personal — Addresses, essays, lectures.
I. Boardroom® Reports, Inc.
HF5356.B65   658   79-25507
ISBN 0-932648-08-8

CONTENTS

TABLE OF CONTENTS

4 • COMPUTERS

5 • CREDIT MANAGEMENT

6 • EXECUTIVE SKILLS

7 • EXECUTIVE TRAVEL

12 • MAINTENANCE AND ENERGY

13 • MANAGEMENT STRATEGIES

14 • OFFICE MANAGEMENT

15 • OWNING A BUSINESS

16 • PERSONAL BUSINESS

17 • PERSONNEL MANAGEMENT

18 • POINTS OF LAW

19 • PRODUCT DEVELOPMENT AND MARKETING

20 • PURCHASING AND INVENTORY

21 • REAL ESTATE

26 • TAXES

27 • TIME MANAGEMENT

ADVERTISING

1

ADVERTISING

How to Cut Waste from Ad Expenditures

• Stop running so many different ads. Most advertisers prepare and pay for far too many ads and commercials. They are acutely aware of every ad they run, so they think the public is, too. It takes three or four insertions just to get to the point where most people note—let alone read—a company's first ad. What to do instead: Find the best-selling message. Instead of spending money to prepare second, third, and fourth versions, put the saved dollars into more insertions. Famous ad man Rosser Reeves summed it up: "My job is to stop my clients from changing their ads."

• Don't run any ad that fails to stand out. Paste a copy of the proposed ad into a newspaper or magazine. Let someone thumb through it. Ask them what they remember. If your ad isn't one of the two or three best remembered, it's too dull, i.e., it's not worthwhile.

• Stop paying for space you don't need. Buying one column less than a full page is a smart move, because it usually gets you editorial mat-ter on the same page, adding to the readership. Ten-second television spots can be even more effective than "30s," if the product story is simple.

• Offer a free booklet, a free trial, or put a phone number in every ad or commercial. Reason: Compare the effectiveness of one station or publication with another. Any station or publication that doesn't deliver its share of inquiries should be cut.

• Take advantage of seasonal and quantity discounts. Once you are convinced that a station or publication reaches your best potential customers, negotiate for discounts on the basis of frequency or season or category. Speak personally to a representative of the station or publication. Tell him you're prepared to buy a considerable schedule if the buy is attractive. Works better than placing an impersonal, automatic buy.

• Maybe you shouldn't be advertising in the first place. Advertising without "news" is sheer waste. Better to put your money into improving your product or service, even if it means postponing all advertising until such time as there is something worth talking about.

Source: Gerald Schoenfeld, Gerald Schoenfeld, Inc., 341 Madison Ave., New York 10017.

Questions to Ask a Prospective Ad Agency

• Is our account likely to be profitable enough for you to put forth your best efforts?

• Which copywriter and artist will really work on our account? (Ask to see samples of their work.)

• What has been your experience and success in advertising products or services marketed the way our company's are?

• How do you suggest the effectiveness of the advertising be measured?

• Which of your clients can we call for more information?

Source: *The 27 Most Common Mistakes in Advertising* by Alec Benn, AMACOM, 135 West 50 St., New York 10020.

Prospect Should Remember the Product, Not the Ad

Most advertisers and their advertising agencies believe the following:

• Our advertisements must compete with thousands of other advertisements.

• Therefore our advertisements must get attention.

• Therefore our advertisements must be different.

This reasoning is false, according to Rosser Reeves, former chairman and chief operating officer of Ted Bates & Co., one of the largest advertising agencies in the world, and now head of Rosser Reeves, Inc. A better line of reasoning would be:

• Our product must compete with thousands of other products.

• Therefore, our product must get attention.

• Therefore, our product must look different.

This applies especially to industrial products. Take the machine-milling ad that showed a beautiful, big picture of a crew rowing a shell, their oars flashing in perfect precision. Somewhere in the copy, the writer linked the precision of the crew to the precision of the milling machine. Reeves criticizes this technique. The product has nothing to do with rowing; the ad's job is to make the milling machine fascinating.

• Clients should ask these questions of their advertisements: What gets the attention: the ad, or the product? What does the reader remember about the product? Has the product been made exciting?

Before Okaying a TV Commercial

• Does the script have a clear start and finish to separate it from the rest of the TV programming? Without a distinctive introduction, it gets lost in the clutter of other commercials.

• Is there a "key visual" that will stick in the mind of the consumer?

• Arty shots and tricky camera angles can leave viewers disoriented; the viewer who doesn't understand what he's looking at simply turns away.

• Watch the casting. Build commercials around one, two, or three basic characters; crowds are confusing.

• Does the TV campaign tie in with print, package design, and point of sale? It should.

Source: Harry Wayne McMahon, McMahon, Criswell, Escondido, CA 92025, in *Advertising Age*.

Smart Ways to Buy Radio Ad Time

• Don't buy from combined figures on audience ratings. Get the station's breakdown of those figures by age group. Most stations lump the 18-49 age group together for sales purposes. But if your company is selling home improvement products, the rock station, with all of its 18-49-group listeners under 23 years of age, isn't the place to spend your advertising dollars.

Beware of ratings that are distorted by temporary promotions which are timed to increase audience during ratings periods. Tip-off: Too-dramatic gains.

• Choose the type of station most appropriate

to your purpose. The rock station is a good place to recruit young people. Top middle-of-the-road stations are good for product selling. FM stations used as background music in offices and plants reach that captive industrial audience.

• In choosing the time at which your spots are to be aired, don't overlook lower-cost weekend radio. The weekend audience is less predictable, but it's there.

If your dollars are going to buy more expensive "drive time," specify when the ad will run.

Why? Actual commuter rush hour is generally 7 to 9 a.m., but radio stations often charge prime drive time rates for ads run from 6 to 10 a.m.

• Save high costs of buying during special broadcast by buying ad "adjacency" which runs immediately before or after show.

Source: Walter G. Young, vice president of John E. Hayes Co., in *Industrial Marketing.*

Cut-Rate TV Time

Smart marketers are constantly on the lookout for the media business version of distressed merchandise. In television, it's commercial time that some advertiser has dropped out of at the last minute. Or time that could not be sold in advance.

Most likely places to find bargains: Late night movies, low-rated specials and reruns. Commercial time on these programs can be bought at the last minute, cheaply. Just push.

Important for negotiating: Contrary to what many station managers tell unwary local advertisers, television is a supply and demand medium, with hardly any fixed rates at all.

How Often to Advertise

Results of recent market research: Ads scheduled to run close together (known as blocks or flights of ads) are often more effective than ads run separately throughout the year.

How it works: If running a campaign of 12

ads, say, schedule one weekly for each of four consecutive weeks, then three in consecutive weeks several months later, then another three in consecutive weeks two months later, and the final two ads in consecutive weeks at year's end.

Source: Dr. Edward Strong, Tulane University, writing in *Journal of Advertising Research,* 3 E. 54 St., New York 10022.

Alternatives to Big Ad Campaigns

Resist the temptation to put big dollars in the standard media instead of working out difficult marketing problems.

Sure, television has clout. But does your product need to spend that kind of money? Does it need that kind of exposure? (It may be appropriate for Alka Seltzer—but for steam engines?)

Start with the selling situation. If your company depends on its own salespeople to move product to 5,000 wholesalers, it may well be smarter to forget media altogether right now, and instead spend the money to push the sales force. Get the best. Give them real and enthusiastic support.

Too often, companies put most of their advertising budget into a big media splash, then, if there's some money left, they send reprints to the company's salespeople.

Analysis might show that broad-based media aren't awfully important for the way your product is bought. In some cases, better results can be obtained from a carefully planned trade show exhibit.

Or, money could be better spent by offering customers a money-back guarantee. It probably won't cost much, and it will make a good impression of quality product and consumer concern.

• Another idea: Perhaps it would pay to send "demonstration vehicles" around the country, providing a very personal and timely delivery of your new product and your sales message.

• Public relations: Another way to promote inexpensively. Perhaps your agency could arrange group press conferences, bunching several clients with *semi*-similar products, giving editors useful exposure for their time. Important that there be a news angle or something meaningful

to say about *each* product. It is important to keep faith with the editors and not let them down.
Source: Leif Juhl, Juhl Associates, 529 S. Second St., Elkhart, IN 46514.

Mistakes in Setting an Advertising Budget

Some common pitfalls that can hurt results:

1. Budgeting based on a percentage of sales: This can accelerate a downward sales spiral.

2. Budgeting the industry average: Not a good way to increase share of market.

3. Spending as much as a major competitor: This assumes he knows what he's doing, which may not be the case; it also assumes all other things are equal, almost never the case.

A better way: Decide goals first, campaign next, cost last. Then adjust goals and campaign to fit resources. Important: Draw contingency plans to change campaign quickly as results come in. That provides full flexibility to take advantage of market surge, avoids overspending if market sags.

Designing a Small Ad That Gets Attention

• Outline the ad with a heavy border or design to set it apart from its competition.

• White space can be used effectively to draw attention to the message.

• Important: Try a gripping headline (one *large* word—or two).

• Use a distinctive logo.

• Build visual movement toward the center of the ad. Symmetrical balance makes for attractiveness.

• Develop continuity with a similar treatment in ads over a period of time.

Don't think of the ad as being alone on a page. Consider the competition. Be defensive *and* aggressive.
Source: Herbert Greenwald, promotion consultant, 521 Fifth Ave., New York 10017.

Outdoor Advertising Knowhow

• Driver needs about 150 feet of reaction time for every 10 miles per hour of vehicle speed. So 30 mph needs 450 to 500 feet; 60 mph, 900 to 950 feet.

• Height of letters should be six inches for every 10 miles per hour of vehicle speed. So 30 mph needs 18-20 inches; 60 mph, 36-38 inches.

• Overall size of sign should be letter height squared times number of letters, plus 40% more for borders.

Get Results from Your Yellow Pages Ad

As big a business as the Yellow Pages has become, hardly any advertisers take advantage of all the opportunities presented and the low rates. (They're still low, even though they've been rising—and directories proliferating.)

Ways to make the Yellow Pages work better for your company:

• Use multiple listings.

• Advertise prominently under broadest category applicable. List in all categories covering specific services or products in your line. List in the trademark ads of national advertisers identifying authorized dealers.

• Make your listing stand out: Pay the small extra charge for an extra line or two of information. Better yet: Take a box ad listing *specifically* what your company provides.

• Use referral ads under other headings referring to your big display ad.

• List major services offered, brands carried.

• Highlight special features: Evening/weekend/24-hour/one-day service, free parking/estimates/pickup and delivery, credit cards honored, collect calls accepted. Give toll-free number if you have one.

• Include a map or description of your location (e.g., opposite the shopping mall, next to City Hall).

• Size implies reliability, length of time in

business suggests trustworthiness, photo of the building indicates solid status.

Technical tips: Vary type sizes, use full lines to create a neat, unified appearance; use simple illustrations for best reproduction results, place them on a diagonal to get maximum attention.

Advice: Take listings in directories for nearby communities, privately published directories.

Advertising Traps

Beware of special issues of magazines, so overloaded that ads may get lost.

Watch ad agency closely for signs of financial problems. If the agency goes bankrupt, the advertiser might have to pay his bills *twice*. Decision in the landmark Lennen & Newell case: Client paid its agency for TV time, but the money was used for other bills. The agency later went under and the network is now suing several clients for its money; some have settled out of court. One case was settled for $50,000 on a $400,000 claim that court had rejected. Reasons: To avoid costs, time investment of appeal.

Retailer warning: Carefully check any advertising provided by suppliers. The retailer can be held legally responsible for misleading or fraudulent claims.

Don't get shortchanged in TV advertising when audience is smaller than promised. As television audiences decline, especially during daytime hours, stations compensate advertisers with additional spots, free.

Replying to inquiries generated by an ad? By the time prospect gets your reply he may have forgotten what it was that interested him. So include a copy of the ad. (Or incorporate it into your sales literature.)

Secrets of Direct Mail

Direct mail is generally misunderstood. It's often mistrusted by advertising agencies, which have pretty much left the field to a few experts.

Dick Benson is one of the experts. The 30-year veteran of Time Inc., American Heritage, and years of consulting leads advanced seminars on the subject. His advice:

Forget the traditional advertising concepts of cost per thousand mailing pieces. Cost per order is far more important. That can often be improved by raising the cost per thousand, not shaving it.

Also important to measure: Cost per paid order (some mail-order respondents are deadbeats). And cost per converted order (the second order is considered a conversion; once prospect has bought twice, he's much easier to sell again).

• Be prepared to spend as much after an inquiry has been received as before.

Think of the first sale as getting the prospect to raise his hand and say he's interested. Advertisers typically spend much more to get people to express interest than they do to follow through on that interest. However, few agencies understand the importance of follow-through, because there's not enough in it for them.

• Caution: Direct mail can unsettle the company's normal procedures. Salespeople may resent or fail to put forth best effort for prospects enticed into showroom by "bribe" (free book, free package of seeds, etc.). However, some "bribe," premium, or incentive (trial offer, special price for limited time, supply limited) is imperative to give prospects a reason for taking action now.

• Be careful of "free" merchandise up front. Make people pay a little. Often the premium, free copy, or whatever can be used as an incentive for payment.

• Elementary point often overlooked in trying to tell prospects how good product is: Always mention the rewards of buying the product, what it will do for them.

• Direct marketing is easiest where purchase involves fun or pure enjoyment (as opposed to work). Being first on the block to own something also has strong appeal.

• Direct marketing is not a substitute for other advertising. It would not be cost-efficient for large-scale image or awareness campaigns. But do use it to test relative pulling power of different premium offers.

• Other applications: (1) Pricing a new product. Salesmen may give misleading advice based on industry tradition or on competitive factors. Find out what the public really will pay. (2) Selling unique products. (3) Poorly distributed products.

• Avoid direct marketing when the product is relatively inexpensive. Avoid items so heavy that shipping costs are excessive. There are exceptions: Example: Grapefruit marketing operation where shipping added greatly to normal costs, but customers perceived the product as being worth the extra price.

Running a Mail-Order Ad

In newspapers, Sunday spots usually produce significantly better than daily ones. *Positioning:* Pages 1, 3, and 5 are excellent in national magazines. Pages 2 and 3 are good in newspapers. Top of the page is better than the bottom.
Source: John Caples, B.B.D.O.

To get maximum response to a coupon ad, concentrate on improving these areas:
• Visual impact. Most conspicuous: Rectangular coupon located in lower corner of page, surrounded by dashes, which suggest cutting (dots don't).
• Headlines. Easiest to read: Familiar combinations of words in familiar sequences. True even of long headlines. Use upper- and lower-case type—easier to read than all caps.
• Art. Most effective: Familiar objects in familiar patterns. *Clever* artwork usually fails to get the message across. It distracts the reader and the message gets lost.
Source: Bob Stone of Stone & Adler, Chicago, in *Advertising Age.*

Before You Rent a Mailing List

Two kinds of lists can be used for direct marketing:
• Compiled lists: A list of names developed from published sources, such as directories, membership lists, professional associations, etc. Strength: May be best way to identify specific type of customer for the product. Weakness: No evidence the listed name ever bought anything by mail, a big factor in getting a profitable response.

• Response lists: Names of individuals, companies, organizations that have bought a product (book, equipment, magazine) or a service (attended a seminar on a particular subject) related to the one your company sells. Strength: Prospects have defined themselves as interested in the area and as being able and willing to *buy* by mail. Weakness: May not be able to identify qualified list for your company's product.

Both kinds of lists are available from list brokers. For information on brokers, write to: Direct Mail/Marketing Association, 6 E. 43 St., New York 10017.

Costs: Compiled lists run about $25 to $30 per thousand names. Qualified lists average about $40 per thousand, but range from $25 to $100. The broker's fee comes out of this charge (usually it amounts to approximately 20% of the list rental cost).
Source: Walter Prescott, president, Prescott Lists, 17 E. 26 St., New York 10016.

Mail-Order Strategy for Retailers

• Offer merchandise different from what is available in the store. Credit customers won't order as much through the mail if they can pick up that merchandise in the store. Use different buyers to assemble mail-order line.
• Don't allow customers to exchange mail-order merchandise in stores.
• Allow two or three years for venture to turn a profit. Don't expect results overnight.
• Run tests using store name versus different mail-order name in market area outside of retail store's territory.
• Accept national credit cards to increase out-of-town response.
Source: Maxwell Sroge, Sroge Company, 303 E. Olive St., Chicago 60611.

Timing a Direct Mail Campaign

Best months: January and August (except for week before Labor Day). Best days to reach recipients (if delivery time can be controlled): Tuesday, Wednesday, and Thursday. Avoid weekends and the day after a holiday.

How to Write Better Sales Letters, Product Brochures

When selling a product or service by mail, include a strong covering letter that:
- Seizes the reader's attention quickly.
- Establishes a bond of friendly mutual self-interest.
- Tells positively and without apology how the product or service will help the reader.
- Refers to a brochure and/or reply form, describes the offer or deal.
- Pushes for immediate action on an order or sales inquiry.

Then, in the product brochure that accompanies the letter, include the following:
- What the product does and how it works.
- A list of the ways the product can benefit the reader.
- A comparison of the product with the competition, using charts, illustrations, tables.
- Technical specifications.
- Testimonials of satisfied users.
- Commonly asked questions about the product, with clear factual answers.
- The guarantee and how it can be ordered.

Quick test for a sales letter: Substitute competitor's name for yours. If letter fits them just as well, rewrite it.

Source: Ed McLean, in *Direct Marketing Copy* newsletter, 1280 Saw Mill River Rd., Yonkers, NY 10710.

A Boardroom Guide to Advertising Media

	Metropolitan newspapers	Suburban newspapers	City/local magazines	Local radio
Description	Broad information and entertainment. Usually respected and well read.	Highly localized news of social events and community services. Very uneven in quality.	Concentrated coverage of trendy, social events. Slick but uneven in quality.	Highly varied, from hard rock to all news, easy listening to country and western. A flexible medium.
Advertisers	Cars, cigarettes, travel, foods, liquor, furniture, retail stores, services.	Local stores (TV repair, florists, druggists). Many advertisers cross over from metro dailies.	Liquor, hi-fi/stereo, entertainment, cars, restaurants, records, photography.	Banks/S&L's, department stores, cars, restaurants, furniture stores, supermarkets, appliances.
Audience	69% of all adults read yesterday's paper. Stronger among better educated (82% of college grads), older, more affluent consumers.	Higher-income, better educated. Frequently very similar to general newspaper audience. Strong concentration among housewives.	Upscale, affluent, upper middle class.	Varies by station. Highest among youth. 90% of 18-24 yr. olds; 77% of 55-64 yr. olds. Individual stations have specialized pieces of this total.
Markets	Concentrated in more populous counties. Heaviest exposure in northeast and central regions of U.S.	Suburban communities around urban centers.	Most large and many medium-size cities. Better magazines concentrate in major cities.	All markets. Major urban centers have up to 30 or 40 stations. Smallest cities have a handful.
Cost	Varies by market. Cost of covering a major city effectively with a ¼-page ad in each of its newspapers: $4,000-$20,000. Medium city: $500-$750. Small city: $200-$500.	Considerably less expensive than metro dailies but often with good reason. Prices range from over $1 a line to just pennies.	Extremely varied. $600 a page in Albuquerque. $6,050 in New York. And everything in between.	Inexpensive on station-by-station basis. $20,000-$40,000 to cover major markets effectively, $1,000-$5,000 in smaller cities.
Best way to use	Wide coverage of markets when more than name identification is needed. Good for conveying information on products and companies.	Pinpointed coverage of specific communities. Good for tie-ins with local store promotions.	Adds a touch of class, develops strong awareness among chic trend-setters.	Highly selective exposure among pinpointed audiences. Name identification, musical tie-ins, on-air personalities.
Disadvantages	Rising cost. Nonselective audience. Limited appeal to younger markets. Declining readership.	Frequently poor editorial quality. Uneven readership. Limited exposure.	Varies by market. Some are strong, some weak. Advertising clutter.	Fragmented audience. Limited information-delivering capacity. Advertising clutter.

Designing a Catalog

• Display the best-selling products in the most prominent spots: the front and back covers (outside and inside), the centerfold, pages 1, 2, and 3, and opposite the order form.

• Use special offers, discounts, deadlines, premiums, and other inducements for quantity orders—and quick responses.

• Provide for telephone ordering. Take advantage of impulse responses and the appeal of faster delivery time.

• Guarantee customer satisfaction, state it prominently throughout the catalog.

• Keep typeface simple. Avoid fancy lettering (interferes with readability).

• Use subheadings often. Break up solid blocks of copy to help readers who want to skim.

• Design the layout in pairs of facing pages, never a single page at a time.

• Order form: List the products according to warehouse sequence to enable order picker to fill orders with minimum backtracking and error. (Or, set up warehouse according to the list.)

Seven Ways to Cut Printing Costs

• Buy paper from paper wholesalers and jobbers, and let them deliver it to the printer (average saving: 10%). Buy only 3% extra if using sheets, 6% extra if rolls.

• Use higher-grade, lighter-weight paper instead of lower-grade, heavier-weight paper.

• Prepare work to be printed, using red acetate (called "rubylith") to show exactly where photos and drawings should be placed. Use overlays to show second and third printing colors. Taking these steps reduces chances of error in the

Local television	Outdoor (billboards)	Direct mail	Cable television	Yellow Pages
Mass audience. High visibility. Ubiquitous medium for instant exposure of pictures and ideas.	Highly visible, mass medium. Obtrusive. Limited applications for many companies.	The second largest medium (newspapers are first). Considered junk mail by most consumers, but is often effective.	Newly developing, very uneven medium. Strong potential. Highly localized. Generally repeating TV fare.	Mass medium, reaching most users and owners of telephones. Strongly supported by phone company advertising.
Cars, restaurants, stores, record offers, you-name-it.	Packaged goods, photographic, cars, liquor, tobacco, any mass market products and local retailers.	Anything that can be sold by getting a consumer to answer a mailer.	*Much like suburban newspapers:* Local stores, adventuresome national advertisers, services and restaurants.	Almost all retail and service businesses.
Broad, whole family. Varies by time of day. But TV is the medium to use to reach *everyone.*	Anybody who goes outside. Age, income, sex vary by location. But, like TV, outdoor medium is used to cover the world.	Completely controlled. Direct mail lists are available to cover almost any conceivable market.	Generally upper-income.	Almost everyone who's a prospect.
At least three TV stations in most cities. One in smaller towns.	Anywhere there are cars and highways. Concentrated on major arteries and around larger cities.	Controlled by the mailer.	Concentrated in rural markets, but is penetrating major cities. 20% of all homes are wired for cable. Growing in importance.	There is a Yellow Pages directory in every market.
Very expensive. $150,000 for minimum schedule in medium-size market. Up to $750,000 for larger markets.	For a strong showing, reaching 89% of the people: An average of 14 would cost $4,000 a month in Albuquerque and $23,500 in Boston.	Average cost to rent 1,000 names is $30. Cost of the whole mailing can run $200-$400 per 1,000.	Much cheaper than commercial television. Costs vary widely across the country.	Directories are published by different phone companies in different markets with varying standards and rates. A two-inch in-column listing runs $341/yr. in Albuquerque and $984/yr. in Boston.
Broad exposure. Product demonstration. Name identity.	Name and image identification. Broad awareness.	Personalized, pinpointed marketing.	A highly localized medium, especially suited to pinpoint geographic marketing.	Primary usefulness is in catching consumers when they are looking to buy.
Cost is prohibitive. Difficult to break through threshold of awareness.	Limited ability to convey product information. Inability to narrow audience.	Antagonistic consumer attitudes. No editorial environment.	Still in infancy. Uneven from market to market. Low viewer involvement for many systems. Poor editorial environment.	Not a *dynamic* selling medium. Has to be thought of differently. Must give full service details in ad to maximize value.

printing shop, and means that the printer has to do less work.

- Written agreement or contract with the printer should include separate prices for plates, makereadies, press time, wash-ups, author's alterations, overruns, additional ink charges, delivery, and, if needed, bindery and proofs.

- If one printer is to be used for series of jobs, have him draw up a table of standard charges so that the cost of any future work can be easily projected.

- Get effect of two-color printing on a small catalog at a lower cost by mixing one-color and two-color pages. For eight-page catalog, use two-color on the front and back cover and on pages four and five. Use one-color on pages two, three, six, and seven.

- Four-color printing can be imitated by printing in magenta (reddish blue) plus cyan (bluish green) on yellow paper.

Source: Center for Direct Marketing, 3 Sylvan Ave., Westport, CT 06880.

Successful Press Releases

- Good material for releases includes new products, achievements, prizes, promotions or additions to the staff, findings from company research (that don't give away company secrets), speeches, participation in community activities by employees. (For local pickup: News about people.)

- Develop a mailing list of newspapers and trade journals. Two sources: (1) *Editor and Publisher Yearbook*, (575 Lexington Ave., New York 10022, $30) lists newspapers by city. In most local libraries. (2) *Writer's Market* (sold in most bookstores and available from Writer's Digest, 9933 Alliance Rd., Cincinnati 45242, $14.95) has a complete up-to-date list of trade, technical, professional, and consumer publications.

- Print up the press releases on 8½ " × 11 " paper. Use a simple heading in the upper right-hand corner. It should say *Press Release,* then the name and address of the company, and the name and phone number of the individual to contact for more information.

- Start the press release copy at least one-

quarter of the way down the first page. (Leave wide margins for editors to write in any instructions to their staff.)

- Get everything important (who, what, where, when, how, and why) in the beginning. Then give details of increasing importance, so that the least important information is last. (Don't save the punch line for the end.)

- Write a tight headline. Editors may or may not use it. But it's worth a try.

- Using pictures: Tape a piece of paper on the back of the photo (5 " × 7 " black and white glossies), with a caption that explains clearly what (or who) is in the picture. Don't ruin the photo by writing on the front or back, or taping anything to the front side.

- Best product photos: Most business magazines prefer black and white, sharp detail, simple background, emphasis on the product itself (not a model) and its use. Ideal: Show relative size of product, too. When introducing a line, present a representative range. Note: To parlay a newsworthy product announcement into a cover story, offer to supply color transparencies.

Sales Promotion Budget: Is It Under Control?

Danger sign to watch for: Rapidly escalating trade allowances, couponing, premium, other promotions, cutting sharply into profits. Management should be answering some questions before reaching to match the competition's latest offer.

- Last year's promotion costs: Were they within budget? Budgeted as a percentage of sales or specific share of ad budget? Did the company wind up cutting ad outlays to finance unanticipated promotions? Are real total costs known? Example: Is loss of revenue from temporary price reductions, special labeling, cost of additional product in bonus packs being charged to promotion, or to production, packaging, and other operations?

- Planning: Have promotion programs been tied to longer-term brand and product strategies? Designed to induce trials, get shelf space for a new product? Or designed to hype an old one that's losing market share, or simply to top competitor's efforts? (No one wins a promotion war.)

• Coordination: Were promotions tied in with national/local advertising campaigns to maximize market share impact? Are ad agencies, field sales managers, others involved in planning promotions, coordinating them with long-term strategies? Or are they strictly the province of the product manager?

Effectiveness: Were couponing, premium, and other efforts pretested to get the maximum response from specific regional markets? Were they selected for age, income, special interest groups? Were alternate programs tested? Were customers drawn from another company brand? Did coupon or premium offer have a negative effect on brand loyalty or prestige?

• Are trade allowances actually going into displays, advertising, price reductions, other incentives that reach the consumer? Are dealers policed to be sure performance requirements are met?

• Are more frequent, more costly promotions cutting seriously into profits? (Reminder: A $1 per case allowance on an item contributing $3/case to profits has to increase sales 50% to be self-liquidating.)

• Are couponing, premium, other promotions really appropriate to your line and image?

Picking Trade and Consumer Incentives

The soundest and most risk-free promotion item is more of whatever the consumer is buying. A product's quality and value are already perceived. The seller doesn't have to convince the consumer. Also, it's the most measurable reward since the consumer quickly can figure the value of getting two for the price of one, or 12 oz. for the price of 8 oz.

Next best is a related product. (Examples: Plastic styling comb with a can of hair spray, or a free toothbrush with toothpaste.) But beware of trade attitudes. A retailer may resent losing toothbrush sales because of toothpaste promo-

tion. This problem is multiplied when a giveaway item is something with a long shelf life or purchased infrequently. Then he may lose customers for months to come.

Important: When retailers will bear brunt of a promotion, they should at least be compensated —or they'll find ways to hurt your company. If the giveaway will deprive them of 50 cents in revenues, for instance, give them 25 cents.

Other forms of compensation: Increased ad allowances, display allowances, special profit or better payment terms during life of deal.

Sometimes just the promise of advertising that will build the traffic is enough. It's also possible to put merchandise in on consignment. Guarantee to take back unsold merchandise.

Each industry has its own unique standards relating to the size and type of promotion allowances to retailers. Often salesmen can help here by talking to trade and observing competition.

But try not to get caught up in an escalating promotion war with competition. Just meeting it is usually enough.

Industrial selling: This field has special disciplines. Aside from merchandise rewards (that are illegal if used to "bribe" the purchasing agent), there are many service incentives (such as special packing to meet customer requirements, or more convenient or economical shipping arrangements). Extending payment terms from a normal 30 days to 60 or even 90 days can be a tremendous incentive. That's especially useful if it means that the wholesaler or retailer doesn't have to pay for deal items until a deal is over. Again, price incentives are always effective with regular buyers.

Timing strategy: Avoid establishing a regular promotion pattern. If the trade is tuned into a promotion timing, it's natural that they'll hold off buying at the regular price.

Same goes for consumers. And here, if promotions are too consistent, there's also the risk of losing the product's dignity.

Best tactic: Vary approach. Offer two for the price of one in the spring and 15 cents off in the fall. Don't always do things the same way.

What to expect from promotion: Remember, promotions are by definition short-term. With, say, two promotion offers a year, representing 15%-20% of the promotion and advertising budget, expect a sales kick of perhaps 10%-11% while promotion is going on. But that will level off to a much more modest (2%-3%) increment in future sales. Same thing happens when selling ahead of price increase is announced. It's a great trade-loading device but you mortgage future sales. Expect slower orders in following months.

For those and other reasons, the best promotions involve greater sales of regularly priced merchandise along with the deal. Example: Retailers normally buy 24 cases. Offer them some cut-rate or free merchandise if they take 36 cases of regularly priced merchandise. Now the cost of the promotion has been made up. Sales at regular markup have been increased, and what's more, if retailers misuse promotion merchandise (that is, tear apart a twofer and sell items separately), it hasn't hurt the manufacturer.

When a promotion backfires (trade resistance, consumer indifference or aversion) the usual remedy is to go deeper in terms of discounts, stretched-out payment terms, and advertising and display allowances. May be better to pretest promotions on trade, consumer focus groups.

Be cautious about promotion deals that involve unusual-shaped special packaging. This often makes product inappropriate for normal shelving. That may mean better positioning on aisle gondola while promotion is hot, but becomes a problem later, perhaps requiring pickup of leftovers by manufacturer. If a deal is going over big in one state or at one chain, but not another, consider pulling merchandise from slow mover and offering it to better merchandiser. Even with transportation costs this might pay.

What to Look For in an Industrial Ad Manager

The most important credentials that a candidate must have:
- An interest in working in industrial communications. Don't settle for someone who'd rather be on the consumer side. If a candidate thinks industrial advertising is second-rate, his work will fulfill that prophecy.
- A definite point of view about how industrial

advertising should sell products and convey the character of the company. He must understand the need for sales materials, mail programs. He should be able to spend time with distributors and with the field sales force. The applicant doesn't have to be creative but must be able to recognize good creative work.
- Key requirement: A strong positive attitude about the company and its products.

Source: William J. O'Connor, executive vice president, Source Inc., Chicago, in *Advertising Age.*

Guidelines on Comparative Ads

Notwithstanding the continuing argument over whether comparative ads work (squaring off your product against your competitor's in the ad), here are guidelines for keeping out of trouble with the advertising industry's self-policing agency (and possibly the Federal Trade Commission):

1. Is our product's superiority provable under usual conditions of use? Example: If we claim superior traction for our tire based on a dry test track, will the same superiority hold true on wet, slippery surfaces?

2. Have we refrained from implying overall superiority on the basis of a single advantage or a limited group of advantages? Example: If we claim superiority in the removal of oily grease stains, are we implying overall superiority for our detergent even though it isn't demonstrably superior with respect to waterborne stains, perspiration stains, safety for colors?

3. Are we comparing grades within our product line with a competitor's truly comparable grade? Example: In claiming that our tire wears longer, are we comparing our top-of-the-line to our competitor's bottom-of-the-line tire?

4. Are the descriptions meaningful to the consumer? Example: If we compare the price of our car on the basis of specified "extras," are we ignoring other equally desirable, but different, extras which our competitor includes in his price?

5. Is our comparative demonstration fairly presented? Example: If two polishes are being

demonstrated side by side, are they both being applied according to label directions? Are the lighting conditions identical?

6. Are we exaggerating the consumer benefit? Example: Our diet soft drink has two calories, our competitor's has four; if we say "50% fewer calories," does this give the consumer meaningful information or exploit a trivial difference?

7. Do the test results support all claims made or implied? Example: Even if laboratory tests show that our pet food contains more protein than our competitor's, are we trying to use the tests to imply overall nutritional superiority?

8. Will most people be able to achieve the test results in actual use? Example: If our floor wax shows a better shine when demonstrated against a competitor's, is there a special preparatory action that has to be taken before applying our polish which is not mentioned in the ad?

9. In selecting media for comparative advertising, are we allowing enough time or space to tell the story adequately? Will consumers be misled by getting only part of the message in a 30-second commercial or a small print ad?

BUSINESS
PSYCHOLOGY

Successful Negotiating Gambits

Reading the Poker Face

Games Employees Play

Dealing With Lateness

Criticizing People

Emotional Outbursts in the Office

How to Assert Authority

2

BUSINESS PSYCHOLOGY

Psychological Gambits of Successful Negotiators

First item for negotiation: The agenda. Businessmen rarely use the agenda as a negotiating point. The agenda can force a quick decision or permit a patient exploration of the facts. It determines what will be said and, perhaps more important, what will not be discussed.

Pertinent considerations in drawing up an agenda:

• An agenda isn't a contract. If either party doesn't like it, change it, even after talks have begun.

• Accept the other's agenda only after careful analysis. Look for things he left out deliberately.

• Make sure the discussion schedule allows time to think about the issues.

• Refuse to permit items that are considered nonnegotiable to be discussed. This is an early show of resolve.

Measure opponent's authority: Does he have real authority to make a deal? This may not be as easy as asking him. Have him describe his au-

thority as clearly as possible. Inquire how long it takes to get an approval cleared. Be prepared to walk out if you are subjected to last-minute authority changes. Test them.

Countertactic: Don't state your authority unless pressed hard. Even then, don't be too clear about it. The less the other person knows about you the better.

Answering opponent's questions: Remember, the best answer may be no answer. Never answer until the question is clearly understood. Do not hesitate to answer only part of the question if you do not want to give a full answer. Make the other party work for answers. Get him to clarify his question. (This may also give clues about his strategy or negotiating goals.) Allow the other person to interrupt—it gives you more time.

Never elaborate. A full and complete answer may be foolish, even harmful to the cause.

Catch-22 of negotiating: "Dumb is smart and smart is dumb." It is not always smart to be decisive, brilliant, quick, fully knowledgeable or totally rational. You'll probably get more concessions and better answers if you are slow to understand, less decisive, and slightly irrational. Unfortunately, most businessmen find it hard to say, "I don't know," or, "Will you tell me that again?"

Negotiating techniques: Use tact in challenging an opponent's position, introducing facts or arguments that prove him wrong. Aim to save an opponent's face, avoid hostility:

• Find as many areas of mutual agreement as possible, set them up in a position that emphasizes community of interest and agreement. Then petition basic points in his position with which you disagree.

• Lead your opponent into examining your counterposition—never try to demolish his case. "Based on your assumptions, I'd agree, but aren't we overlooking—?" "We seem to be on the same track except for—; let's get our engineers together." "Your data's open to several interpretations; here's a special study that really seems to clarify the matter."

• Place the blame for errors and oversights on past policies, data-processing systems, outside consultants, bad data sources—anybody but the person opposite you.

• Deadlock: Because it is one of the most dreaded situations in negotiating, deadlock is a powerful tool for the negotiator who uses it consciously. Buyer and seller are softened up after deadlock. Both are more willing to compromise —especially if a face-saving way out is found.

• Smokescreens: Useful to delay a decision or cloud an issue. Some typical smokescreens: Detailed exploration of some unimportant procedure or process; letting a poor speaker handle a complicated explanation; getting hungry all of a sudden; reading a complicated regulation aloud; introducing a new proposition that starts everything all over.

Super smokescreens: Confuse to a point where nobody knows what's happening. Use with care. How to construct one: Put a new man in charge of the negotiations. Generate a bigger issue. Provide loads of detailed information that must be endlessly studied. Get good publicity. Start a lawsuit. Set up a committee. Write new procedures or rules. Deny that a problem exists.

How to say no without ruffling feathers: Pin the blame for the negative answer on somebody (or something) else. That "something else" could be a superior, company policy, government regulation, manufacturing standard, etc.—but not yourself. Lack of authority can provide a powerful negotiating tool.

Choice to the other side: Accept the deal within the limitations, or devise a way around them (and possibly wind up with no deal).

How to make concessions without coming off the loser:

• Get the other party to put all his demands on the table first (and keep yours to yourself). Don't be baited into item-by-item negotiations and concessions until you know all his demands.

• Never be the first to make a major concession. When your opponent makes one, don't assume you have to make an equal one.

• Get something in return for each concession you make.

• Conserve your concessions—give a little at a time, make your opponent work for it.

• Don't hesitate to say no to a key demand. Say it often enough, effectively enough so the other party knows you mean it.

• Don't agree to "split the difference." Try for 70-30, 60-40 first.

• Don't be afraid to back off from a concession you've already made; but never try to back off once the deal's concluded.

• Keep track of all concessions made. Take notes on yours and the other party's.

Source: Chester L. Karrass, Center for Effective Negotiating, 2066 Westwood Boulevard, Los Angeles 90026.

Breaking a Deadlock

Deadlocks are common to all negotiating. But Americans have more deadlocks than others. Reason: Greater ego involvement. Antidotes: Learn how to walk away from a deal and walk back graciously. Tactics:

• Change the shape of money (size of deposits, length of pay periods, etc.). It can work wonders in breaking up a negotiating logjam.

• Postpone difficult portions of an agreement for negotiation later.

• Share risks. Willingness to share unknown losses or gains may aid lagging talks.

• Change the atmosphere from competitive to

cooperative. Involve people with similar backgrounds. Example: All engineers or all operations people.

• Change the base for a percentage. Smaller percentage of larger base or larger piece of smaller base. A more predictable base may push things back on track.

• Add options: They can be real or implicit. Even options that are unlikely to be taken may still sweeten an otherwise questionable deal.

Another route: Change the members of the negotiating team. This always favors the team making the change. A new person can retreat from previous concessions, introduce new arguments, delay agreements, or change the very nature of discussions. Major benefit: The opposing team feels obligated to bring the new member up to date. There's a good chance that greater concessions will be granted in the process. Recommended: Change the team only to achieve specific goals.

Games Negotiators Play to Keep Opponent Off Balance

Experienced negotiators use some bargaining ploys designed to intimidate and outmaneuver the opposition. Five of the most common and how to counter them:

• Bargainer "sums up" what the other party has just said but slants it so that it's favorable to his own argument. Countermove: Politely but firmly correct the "summary." Don't let the discussion move on until the slanted version has been laid to rest and an accurate one substituted.

• Two bargainers play the "Mr. Bad Guy/ Mr. Good Guy" game. The first one is unreasonable and abusive. The second is nice and polite, trying to win the opponent's confidence as an ally, and get him to compromise. Countermove: Disregard the acting. Don't take the "bad guy" seriously. Don't compromise with the "good guy" because he seems so reasonable.

• Bargainer simply stares after opponent has finished speaking instead of responding. Silent stare is supposed to intimidate opponent into speaking again, possibly taking a softer line be-

cause of nervousness. Countermove: Don't stare back. Don't say anything. Examine papers, jot down notes, look busy and unconcerned until the starer breaks the silence.

• Bargainer launches a "fit" that's supposed to convince the opponent that he is pushing too hard. Countermove: Disregard the yelling, make no concessions because of it.

• Negotiator makes a sudden additional demand after an agreement has supposedly been reached. Pushes for it so the agreement won't be "spoiled." Countermove: Decline the demand politely. Let the other party be the one to "spoil" the agreement; he probably won't.

Source: *Chronolog,* Box 456, Orinda, CA 94563.

Spot the Unspoken Thought Behind the Poker Face

Watching people's actions can bring you a lot closer to the truth than merely listening to what they say (which might be a coverup). This is the "science" of kinesics, or "body language." It can be very revealing. Some outward expressions of inner feelings:

• Openness: Open hands, unbuttoned coat.

• Defensiveness: Arms crossed on chest, crossing legs, fistlike gestures, pointing index finger, "karate" chops.

• Evaluations: Hand to face, head tilted, stroking chin, peering over or playing with glasses, cleaning glasses, cleaning or filling a pipe, hand to nose.

• Suspicion: Arms crossed, sideways glance, touching-rubbing nose, rubbing eyes, buttoned coat, drawing away.

• Insecurity: Pinching flesh, chewing pen, thumb over thumb, biting fingernail, hands in pockets.

• Cooperation: Upper body in sprinter's position, open hands, sitting on edge of chair, hand-to-face gestures, unbuttoning coat.

• Confidence: Steepled hands, hands behind back, back stiffened, hands in coat pockets with thumbs out, hands on lapels of coat.

• Nervousness: Clearing throat, "whew" sound, whistling, smoking, pinching flesh, fidgeting, covering mouth, jiggling money or keys, tugging ears, wringing hands.

• Frustration: Short breaths, "tsk" sound, tightly clenched hands, wringing hands, fistlike gestures, pointing index finger, rubbing hand through hair, rubbing back of neck.

• SOS: Subordinate may send out nonverbal clues that he needs help but is unwilling to ask for it. Example: Supervisor asks employee if he needs help and the verbal answer is no. But other signs such as uneven intonation of voice, wringing of hands, poor body posture, or failure to make eye contact could be clue that the real answer is yes.

And some apparently acquiescent verbal expressions that really mean "no":

• "Yes, but . . ."
• "I don't know why, but . . ."
• "I tried that, and it doesn't help."
• "Well, to be perfectly honest with you . . ."
• "But it's not easy . . ."
• "I know, but . . ."
• "I don't remember."

Managing a Valuable But Abrasive Employee

• When he disrupts office or group, make it a point to talk it over with him privately and quietly as soon as possible—keeping in mind that his abrasiveness stems from his vulnerability and drive for perfection.

• Report observations on his behavior uncritically in these discussions. Ask him how he thought others felt about what he did or said. Also ask if that's the result he wanted. Ask, too, how he might better get the response he wants. Describe to him how his co-workers actually did react to him.

• Point out that, in order to reach his goals, he must improve his relationships and that management is willing to help. Stress his value to company and his need to change.

• Avoid impulsive attack. But let him know his behavior is annoying.

• Never counterattack (when he becomes defensive), merely state observations of his beha-

vior. Stress value of compromise and impracticality of the all-or-nothing stance.

Important: Don't assume he is aware of his problem. Tell him, in writing if necessary, that he won't be promoted unless he changes.

Source: Harry Levinson, Levinson Institute, Cambridge, MA, in *Psychology Today.*

Overcoming Inability to Delegate

Advice to the executive who runs too tight a ship, holds fast to all managerial authority, even usurps control that subordinates normally exercise over their own jobs: Experiment!

Changing management posture requires time, discipline, major adjustments in personal attitudes and emotions. But it's worth the effort, in terms of improved productivity by subordinates. Steps to take:

• Assess compulsion to control. Possible fears: (1) Being overshadowed by talented subordinates; (2) subordinates are inadequate; (3) results won't be acceptable to your superiors. Assess the impact on your position (you wind up doing subordinates' work instead of, or in addition to, your own). Assess the impact on your staff (erosion of initiative, decision-making capacity, productivity).

• Don't try to change overnight. Just delegate a single task you could handle superbly—one involving managerial authority (representing you at a meeting, responding to a request from top management) to the individual who could best handle it. Choose a task that doesn't threaten your ego (if he fails, you won't lose face; if he succeeds, he still won't outshine you). Outline it adequately. Leave the rest up to him. Be available for consultation. Resist the chronic temptation to hover, overmonitor, or do the job over. Offer as much praise and as little criticism as possible on completion of the job.

• Assess the performance—and your reactions. Did you pick the right person? Was his performance reasonably satisfactory? Could you call on him again—with greater confidence than before? Did the experience build his self-esteem?

Do you feel you gained (or lost) managerial control by "letting go"? Did you gain valuable assistance, time for a more important task?

• Repeat the experiment with other staff members (even if the first was a disaster) until you've really assessed their capacity to take on responsibility, freed yourself for higher-level activities, increased their productivity (and gained the confidence and control you need).

Games Employees Play

Bothered by subordinates who come for assistance or advice and then systematically shoot down all the suggestions? Actually, they're playing a little game that inflates their egos by "proving" (to themselves) that they're better than you. Tactic: When you recognize that he's "playing" again, turn the tables. Say you're flattered that he has come for advice but feel he's in a better position (because of his experience) to come up with ideas. You, of course, will be more than willing to critique them for him.

How to Help the Ones Who Weren't Promoted

Don't make assumptions about how the people who didn't get promoted feel. Find out.

Best way to find out: Ask each one to express his feelings directly about the situation. The individual's response may indicate what being passed over will do to his job performance and how best to deal with the situation.

Counseling advice: Avoid emphasizing negative factors—why the person was passed over.

Try to get those who were passed over to focus on new goals—a new performance target or a future promotion.

Warning: Don't stop dealing face-to-face with these people on the mistaken assumption that this will give them time to cool off. Instead, they will think that there is no further interest in their performance (or in them).

How to Reprimand Employees Without Humiliating Them

Effective ways to turn negative, humiliating employee reprimands into tactful, constructive criticism:

• Give employee an alibi for mistake. Use the "I know, but . . ." approach. Example: "I know you've had a lot of paperwork lately, but these forms . . ."

• Take the blame for not preventing the mistake from happening. Example: "It's my fault for not mentioning this problem sooner, but . . ."

• Place the blame on conditions beyond his control. Example: "I know these federal regulations seem to complicate things, but . . . ."

• Point out the benefits that come from the mistake. Example: "The way those reports were lost makes me think we should do something about our delivery system."

• Best time to dispense employee criticism: Early in the day and early in the week. Day-end fatigue can exaggerate criticism. The employee who is reprimanded just before his weekend begins goes home in a bad state of mind and blows discussion out of proportion by stewing about it all during the weekend.

For best results, time remarks so there's another chance to talk with employee before end of day. A casual conversation—even a few words—after several hours will assure him that feelings toward him haven't changed, that his job isn't in jeopardy, and that there is confidence in his ability to resolve the problem.

Source: Herman Harrow, Envirotech Corp., in *Sales & Marketing Management.*

Criticizing Sensitive People

• Before meeting with the person, decide precisely what should be said. Writing it out helps.

• Don't allow the person to use the meeting to talk about all his troubles. Some of this may be necessary, but don't let it get out of hand. Constantly bring the discussion back to the main topic, without arguing or being contentious.

• Don't get brought down to the level of the other person's emotions. At the conclusion of the meeting, be sure he understands what was said. Ask him about the changes he'll make.

How to Deal With the Chronically Late

Destructive lateness, the chronic kind that puts friendships, marriages and jobs in jeopardy, is only one small part of a larger personality picture. The person may, for example, be rebellious. Not coming to work on time is just one form of resistance. Other signs: Difficulty in accepting orders. Often says he (or she) is being pushed around. Or the employee may be overly passive and feel justified in not being able to cope with everyday difficulties.

What the employer can do:

• After continued attempts fail, call the offender in and say, "I've used all my skills as a manager to resolve this problem. Will you tell me what I need to do for you to come in on time?" No matter how long it takes, wait for the employee to answer. And listen sensitively to what's being said. Don't accept any reiteration of excuses.

• If the outcome of this initial discussion isn't satisfactory, move on to phase two. Say: "If you continue coming in late, what measures do you think would be reasonable for me to take?" Again, wait for an answer. Based on the reply, negotiate a contract. (Example: Late twice in one month, lose two hours' pay. Late four times in a month, two days' suspension. Late four times or more, termination of employment. This assumes, of course, that there are no established union rules for disciplinary action.)

Avoid accusatory questions. The objective is to let the employee take the initiative in setting guidelines to solve the problem. (Or admit that he is not prepared to solve it.)

Timing: Do not attempt the discussion while angry. Calmness is essential.

Source: Gisele Richardson, 4134 Dorchester West, Montreal, Quebec 1T3 Z1V1.

When a Subordinate Comes In with a Personal Problem

Listen. Many times, that is all you need to do to be helpful. A survey of employees by behavioral scientists at York University in Toronto, Canada, found that only 3% wanted the manager to take over the problem. One in seven just wanted the supervisor to listen. But 13% of the managers thought they were being asked to take some action.

• Remember that the problem is the subordinate's, not yours. Don't take it over. Don't get sucked into emotional involvement with the other person's personal problem. Don't impetuously offer help.

Instead: Question the person who comes to you before you start to make declarations. By questioning instead of declaring, you give the other person a chance to define the problem and explore options without being sidetracked by your point of view.

Wait until you hear a direct request for action. Then, if you must do something, state what you will and won't do. This will avoid misunderstandings later. Some problems, though, need time to solve.

Convincing Reluctant Employees That Job Must Be Done

Some time before a problem must be resolved, begin pressing gently toward a solution. Offer alternatives.

Example: A new supervisor was told that the workers wouldn't work overtime. But one job had to be completed within four days and would require overtime to meet the deadline.

First day: While cleaning up for lunch, the supervisor casually asked some of the workers if they thought the job could be completed on time, mentioning that it would cost the company something if it was completed late. That afternoon the supervisor said that he was staying late to check on the part of the job that was already completed.

Second day: In the morning, he mentioned that the customer had called, inquiring whether the job would be ready. He said he told the customer it would be ready and asked the workers if they thought so, too.

At the end of the day, he told the workers that the deadline was getting near and wondered if some of them could work a few hours extra that night, or whether it would be easier if they worked the next night.

Third day: Almost all workers volunteered to work overtime.

Note: This same tactic works just as well with managers and executives as it does with workers or subordinates.

Source: Dr. Mortimer R. Feinberg, in *OBI Interaction,* 666 Fifth Ave., New York 10019.

Defusing Hostility in Rivals and Subordinates

Never make an enemy if you can avoid it. The business world is too small. An enemy today may be your superior tomorrow. In some situations, that rule may be hard to follow.

Example: You and your colleague are under consideration for a promotion. You get it. He either quits or stays on and hates you. How to defuse that hate and get his cooperation: Follow the primary rule of getting power as quickly as you can, only this time confer the power on your colleague who is now your subordinate. Share some of your power with him, give him new responsibilities, and thus a reason to be beholden (and loyal) to you. Otherwise he'll wait for the appropriate time and stab you in the back.

Another example: When firing someone, take the onus off yourself. Don't limit the failure to his shortcomings—make it a mutual shortcoming, including the organization's failure to meet his needs. And then give him time and support in finding a new job. He'll emerge unscarred (that's important), and you'll remain his friend.

Source: Michael Korda, vice president and editor-in-chief, Simon & Schuster, New York.

How Not to Be Put on the Defensive

Criticism from fellow workers or superiors on the job can escalate if you react defensively. How to avoid this instinctive reaction:

• Paraphrase an accusation as a way of slowing down reaction time and giving the accuser a chance to retreat. Accuser: How come that report isn't ready? Can't you ever get your work done on time? Response: Do you think that I never get my work done on time?

• Describe in a tentative fashion what appears to be the other person's psychological state. In response to a scowling superior, say: I'm uncomfortable. I don't understand what your frown means.

• Ask for clarification. Accuser: This proposal isn't what I asked you to design at all. Response: Is nothing in the proposal acceptable?

• Use a personal response to assume responsibility. Accuser: This is entirely wrong. Response: I guess I didn't understand. Can I review the instructions again?

Source: Gary P. Cross, management consultant, Cross Names & Beck, Box 5198, Eugene OR 97405, in *Personnel Journal.*

Calming Emotional Outbursts in the Office

Don't attempt to settle emotional problems right away. Try to prevent the situation from blowing up. Several possible ways to do this:

• An apology or statement from a key executive, like, "I'm really sorry that happened," may calm things down. It's helpful, even if the cause isn't related to anything the executive did.

• Don't say anything at all. Letting the other person blow off steam may be all that's needed in many situations.

• Agree wherever possible. If the charged-up person is right about some things, you can absorb some of his anger by agreeing immediately on those things. But if he's totally wrong, then say so calmly.

• Exercise authority if things can be postponed till cooler heads prevail. State that you will talk about the issue at hand on a given date.

What you shouldn't do:
- Joke or laugh about it.
- Cut in or try to shout down either side.

Getting Your Ideas Accepted at Meetings

1. Don't be the first presenter.
2. Never present your best idea first. The energy level is too high at the beginning of a meeting, so you are apt to get clobbered.
3. Never be enthusiastic about your idea. Presenting it modestly, even doubtfully, disarms hostile forces.
4. Be courteous to the ideas of others and you may get the same treatment.
5. Don't count on friends or best buddies.
6. Don't present your ideas too slickly. If you do, your opponents will get suspicious and seek even its slightest faults.
7. Listen carefully to comments on preceding ideas for clues to a negative response to something in your idea.
8. Don't be the first (or last) to arrive. Don't sit too close to the table. Don't drink too much water. (It may be mistaken for a hangover—or illness.)

When Harmony Isn't Productive

Beware of too much harmony in your organization. Consider these findings:
- Groups that have been together a long time tend to perform less well as time goes on because they develop a feeling of too much security.
- Groups in which the individuals get along with each other best may start spending more time getting along and less time working.
- The most satisfied employees are the most difficult to change.
- Groups that get along harmoniously aren't

going to give an executive much trouble. But— they aren't going to give him much help, either. Conflict often results from—and in—new approaches and fresh ideas.

Seek the understanding of those affected by your decisions. But don't expect to ever be able to eliminate all resistance to them.

Source: *Judgment in Administration,* by Ray E. Brown, McGraw-Hill, New York.

Asserting Your Authority

- The act of giving orders frightens most people—even a boss. People are afraid the person receiving the order will simply say no. That fear stifles many personal relationships.

How to deal with that fear: Begin small. Pick a situation where there's good reason to think the person will be agreeable. Just in case, be ready with a fallback position. The knowledge that you have a fallback position already worked out provides the courage to give the initial order.

- Once you graduate to the big challenge, you'll discover a curious response from others: Most people do. That is, if you express your power position at the outset, most people will not go along because they would rather not have a confrontation. After all, they think, if he wants it that much, he's obviously ready to battle for it. Although they don't know that you have a fallback position, they are ready to concede your power.

- In a conversation, some people have great difficulty breaking in to state their position. If that's a problem, the easiest solution is to give the person you're talking to a very clear signal that now it's your turn. Examples: Put your hand on his shoulder. Look away from him and say something like, "Well . . ." Or take off your eyeglasses and direct them at the other person. Such simple actions, when done clearly and distinctly, assert your entry into the conversation.

- Where to sit at a meeting: Close to and facing in the same direction as the most important person there. Then, if the Great Man fires out criticisms, they'll be aimed at the person sitting opposite and facing him. The assembly, in the meantime, sees the criticism coming from your direction.

• When an expert tries to put you down: He will usually try to awe you with his superior knowledge and jargon. Counter with a request for him to repeat what he just said in your terms, because you can't understand him. If the explanation isn't sufficient, make the request again. In time, he'll be brought down to a working level where you two can make contact.

• The ability to say nothing: That's one of the strongest power plays. The Orientals have the technique perfected. Unless the other person really holds all the cards—at which point it's wise not to play games—delay always works. And delay means not feeling you have to respond to every offer. Silence often produces an even better offer—before you open your mouth. Silence, after all, hints at rejection without shouting no at the other person.

Source: Michael Korda, author of *Power! How to Get It, How to Use It,* Random House, New York

Controlling Meetings with the Right Questions

Questions to ask to get discussion started: What do you think about this problem? What has your experience been on this type of problem? Can anyone suggest the kinds of facts we ought to have at this stage?

To draw more participation: How does what we have been saying so far sound to those of you who have been thinking about it? What other phases of the problem have we missed covering?

To limit the overactive participant: You have made several interesting statements; does someone else want to add to them or modify them?

To orient the discussion: Where do we stand now in relation to our goal?

To keep the discussion moving: Do you think we have spent enough time on this phase of the problem? Can we move on to another part of it?

To press for a decision: Am I right in thinking that we agree on these points? (Follow with a brief summary.) What have we accomplished up to this point? We seem to be moving toward a de-

cision now, so should we consider what it will mean if we decide this way?

Avoid questions which complicate an issue or mislead the group members. Also avoid those which might limit the group's thinking by taking away from of their latitude.

Source: *How to Be a More Creative Executive* by Joseph G. Mason, McGraw-Hill, New York.

Being a Mentor

The most effective way to develop a subordinate is to become a mentor. This involves:

• A mutual agreement, based on genuine personal affinity, to engage in a teacher-subordinate relationship.

• The mentor's ability to structure learning situations that suit the particular needs of the subordinate and that help build confidence.

• Daily informal contact, as well as instructional dialogue.

• The mentor's willingness to be open with information received from above—first, to prepare the subordinate for moving up the company ladder and, second, to encourage the subordinate to be open about problems.

Source: James Clawson, Harvard Business School.

Five Ways to Improve Performance-Rating Systems

All employee performance evaluation systems suffer "score inflation" sooner or later. Often it's because raters believe that high scores make subordinates and departments look good.

The time for a change is when average performance scores move near the top range:

To make ratings realistic again:

1. Change rating scales, categories, and names of categories. Usually this is only a temporary solution.

2. Set quotas for the highest rankings. Limit the top 5% rating to no more than 5% of employees, for instance.

3. Use behavioral scales. These award points

for traits desirable for each type of job rather than for general performance.

4. Bring in outside raters. This increases objectivity, but removes managers from evaluation process.

5. Measure performance strictly by success in meeting management-by-objectives goals. The drawback is that this system makes no judgment on the value of the goals to the employer.

Source: *The Personnel Administrator*, 30 Park Dr., Berea, OH 44017.

Public Speaking

Pick five or six people in the audience who really seem to be responsive, and maintain eye contact with them for the rest of the speech. This creates a personal rapport, and the resulting "lift" for the speaker often brings the rest of the audience along.

Increasing Cooperation Between Departments

Friction between specialized departments is not inevitable. Good managers avoid conflict.

Three biggest mistakes:

• Passing the buck. When one manager pushes his department's slip-ups onto another department, he quickly earns a reputation that destroys future cooperation.

• Failing to make the right friends. Service departments such as personnel, industrial relations, and maintentance handle conflicting priorities by taking care of "friends" first and "enemies" last, if at all. Not getting on the good side of these managers is a big mistake.

• Offending experts: Know when in-house advisers are giving opinions, and when they're issuing orders. They are easily offended and are likely to take their complaints directly to top management.

Psychological Moment to Quit for the Day

There's a virtue in knowing just when to quit work for maximum productivity the next day. Examples:

(1) Stop on a high note—helps promote eagerness to get back to things the following day.

(2) Stop at a point of accomplishment. Promotes satisfaction, and makes it easier to relax overnight and come in fresh in the morning.

(3) If forced to stop when stalled with an unsolved problem, write it down. Think it through overnight. Come in with a new approach the next day.

(4) Have a logical starting point at which to resume in the morning. That reduces start-up time. Especially useful after weekend or holiday.

CAREER STRATEGIES

Sizing Up a Job Offer

How to get a Big Raise

Job Hunting

Handling a Head Hunter

How to Quit

Office Politicking

Hard Work & Other Success Secrets

Losing Gracefully

3

CAREER STRATEGIES

How to Evaluate a Job Offer

Questions you must ask (yourself and the recruiter) to increase the chance that you land in a job that offers opportunity for promotion, mobility, power, personal growth:

• Who's in the job now? What is the average length of time people stay in the job? Where do they go? How old do people get to be in that job? How to find out: Often, a recruiter won't answer directly, or doesn't have the information. Ask to talk to people holding the same or similar jobs. Get the information from them. What you want to know: How other people in the company think about the job. If they think the job is dead-end, don't consider taking it. You may think you can overcome and be the "pleasant surprise." But chances are excellent that you will fail. First, you will have to boost your own credit and then you will have to boost the stature of the whole job function—almost an impossible task. Look around some more.

• Will the job give me a chance to know other people in the organization doing lots of different jobs? Will I represent the department (or group or section, etc.) at meetings with people from other parts of the organization? If the job is in the field, do I get much chance to meet with managers from headquarters? What you will want to know: That the job has lots of visibility—with other departments and with higher levels of management, if possible. Beware of too much autonomy: Working on your own too much can be the kiss of death for upward movement if no one else gets to know you and your ability.

• Is this job in an area that solves problems for the company? Where there is trouble and crucial decisions are going to be made? What you want to know: That there's a sense of danger. Those are the best jobs for getting power (and promotions) fast. Also, the most risky, of course. But jobs in safe areas where everything is going well offer a slower track to promotion. Advice: A small company may offer the best chance to be in this position.

What to beware of: If the interviewers won't answer questions about mobility, visibility, etc., the job probably doesn't have much. If they don't like your asking questions or asking to talk to other people in the organization, that's a very bad sign. They may not like people who speak up, ask questions—and probably won't offer you much chance to shine.

Source: Dr. Rosabeth Moss Kanter, *Men and Women of the Corporation,* Basic Books, New York.

First Things to Do on a New Job

When you change jobs, even if your mission is complete reorganization, ease in quietly.

• Get to know your staff. Know who gets things done, who doesn't. How, and how well.

• Learn before you leap. Ask questions, solicit advice, don't be afraid to lean on staff in areas you aren't familiar with. Look to making small changes that require teamwork and cooperation, enable you to gauge subordinates, inspire their confidence in you as a learner as well as a leader. Cultivate the dissenters (they care—and usually have something worth listening to). Beware of quiet acquiescers; they may be waiting for you to make the first move.

• Review your predecessor's records, correspondence, information flows for insight into his priorities, management methods, innovative successes and failures, problem-solving techniques. Be sure you know the realities of your job before you discard his approaches.

• Clarify interdepartmental relationships as rapidly as possible. Look for access or admission to policy and planning committees, pertinent task forces, or other company groups that help give you perspective on overall goals and operations, insight into how your reorganization ideas could affect other departments.

For a Better Starting Salary

First, find out what the potential employer expects to pay and what the company can afford. Get some idea of what the range is before negotiating for the maximum.

• The real problem: Raising the salary ques-

tion at the wrong time. Avoid discussing salary until the interviewer has a complete picture of your qualifications.

• Cite potential benefits to the employer. Emphasize profit contributions to past employers (e.g., innovative ability, managerial experience, cost-cutting effectiveness, etc.). Be specific in terms of dollars whenever possible.

• Ask for time to think it over, while simultaneously conveying enthusiasm about the prospects and eagerness to start. No good organization will withdraw an offer because an applicant thinks he or she is worth more than was offered.

• Explain that after reviewing the costs of a job change, personal situation, and other considerations, the numbers still present a problem. Offer to meet the prospective employer halfway.

Point to remember: A whole range of benefits may be negotiable. Examples: Company car, stock options, deferred payment plans, etc. A comprehensive contract can be as important as salary. General rule: Anyone making over $40,000 a year should consider asking for a contract. Be particularly firm if the organization: (1) Exhibits any instability. (2) Is a candidate for a takeover or merger. (3) Is in financial difficulty. (4) Is family owned. Note: Termination agreements are sometimes substituted for employment contracts. Common provisions: Severance pay of six months' (or more) salary, relocation expenses, professional outplacement assistance, and the extension of insurance benefits for one year after termination.

Source: Robert Jameson Gerberg, president, Performance Dynamics, 400 Lanidex Plaza, Parsippany, NJ 07054.

Comparative Pay of Top People

Second in command is usually paid about 75% of the chief's salary and bonus. Number three's figure is 60%. Surprisingly enough, these ratios apply regardless of industry, location, or size, according to The Conference Board. Exception: When president and chairman are two different people. Second-ranked executive earns 80% of the top man's compensation.

How to Negotiate a Big Raise

The best way to get a sizable raise is to start campaigning for it on the day you're hired. Don't talk dollars then, of course, but it's important to set up standards of performance that will be the basis for future wage negotiations with your new boss. If possible, find out if there are ways you can influence the standards so that your strongest qualities are rewarded.

In gauging the company's position, find out:
- Pattern of raises for your type of job.
- Extent to which pay is part of a fixed budget process.
- How much autonomy your boss has in granting raises.
- Business conditions in the company and in the industry.

Don't let your request be treated in an offhand manner. Make a date with your boss to talk just about money, and if he puts it off, persist.

Key to successful negotiation: Narrow down obstacles until the supervisor is holding back because of one major factor ("Things are tough this year"). Let him cling to that, but in the process make sure he assures you that your performance has been excellent. Then attack the main obstacle ("Are things really that bad?"), pointing out that your capabilities should be rewarded in any case.

Unless you're quite sure of your ground, don't threaten to quit. Even if you are a ball of fire, the boss may welcome your departure because he's scared of you.

Source: *How to Negotiate a Raise,* by John J. Tarrant, Pocket Books, New York.

Who Gets Promoted First

The four most important factors:
- How top management feels about the person who recommended the promotion.
- The exposure and visibility of candidate to those in higher management.
- Background, education, work experience.
- How well candidate performs in present job.

Job-Hunting Tips

- If company's ad lists a phone number or address, employer is eager to fill job quickly. If box number is used, the employer is prepared for a lengthy search.
- Impeccable credentials are often overshadowed by a sloppy resume. Common errors: Inaccurate typing, misspellings, bad grammar, poorly reproduced copies.
- Keep your resume short. One page is still best. What to do with lengthy, move-filled career? Eliminate all itemization of jobs held more than 15 or 20 years ago. Just describe them briefly under a single heading such as "Earlier Employment."
- Job interview pitfalls: Questions like "What is your greatest weakness?" or "What features of this job interest you least?" Employers do not expect total candor, and applicants who are totally honest about their shortcomings are at a disadvantage in getting the job.
- Write your own resume. Interviewers can spot the canned formats of professionally prepared resumes. Tip: Avoid the common error of starting the resume by describing your career objectives. It limits your possibilities.
- Usually better to talk too much than too little at interviews. Most people equate wordiness with motivation, involvement, and leadership qualities.
- Clues that an interview went well: (1) Interviewer did most of the talking. (2) Salary and benefits were brought up toward the end of the interview. (3) Interviewer talked about inviting you back to meet other staff members.
- After an interview that goes well, immediately prepare for the next one. Most hunters sit back in relief that the interview went well and look further only when they know they've failed. Answer more ads, write a new letter, do some job prospecting, retailor your resume. Best time to tackle more job-hunting is when self-confidence is highest (especially if the job seeker is currently unemployed).
- Best fields for the woman executive: Personnel, accounting, sales, engineering, marketing, administration, data processing, public relations, and systems analysis. Companies hiring most women managers: Retailers, banks, credit

agencies, brokerage houses, health-related businesses, insurance, food, and chemicals.

• Job prospects for executives over 50 are getting better. Lower birthrate during Depression years has produced fewer candidates. And those executives are less and less willing to sacrifice to move up. The best older candidates have stable work histories, have changed jobs a few times, but not too frequently.

How to Make a Good Impression When a Recruiter Calls

• Don't be afraid to listen. (Always call back to be sure it's a legitimate call.)

• Don't ask how your name came up (try to convey the impression that this happens fairly frequently).

• Be crisp, businesslike, helpful. If you aren't interested, recommend a friend.

• Don't allow yourself to be interviewed over the phone; insist on a personal interview if you want to pursue the matter.

• Never give away anything about your present position or employer.

• Never offer any criticism of the company or hint you're dissatisfied in your present job.

Mistakes That Spoil Career Chances

Many fully qualified executives make it through elaborate early screening procedures only to stumble during final interviews.

Five common mistakes made by applicants for CEO positions:

• Careless language. Avoid hackneyed phrases, timeworn cliches, and ''cute'' jargon. All of these make you sound trite, petty, or just not big enough in stature for a top job.

• Covering one's own mistakes by passing the buck for previous failures to someone else. The

truth usually catches up. It's far better to be objective about strengths and weaknesses.

• Being overly critical of current employer. Creates a counterproductive atmosphere and demonstrates a lack of constructive, positive thinking.

• Coming on too strong, thus seeming too aggressive or arrogant to be compatible CEO. Related problem: Demanding perks or pressing premature, preconceived solutions to company's problems in an early interview. Equally bad: Sounding too timid or reserved (signs of weakness), or adopting such a casual approach that answers indicate a ''what-the-hell'' attitude.

• Poor grooming. Amazing as it seems, some top executive candidates still show up with dandruff on their collars or unshined shoes. Don't wear the same suit for several different interviews, even if it is your most flattering.

Additional tips: Watch what you say and do in social chitchat with interviewers, too. It pays to find out everything possible about the company and the interviewers beforehand.

Eleven Most Common Reasons Job Applicants Aren't Hired

1. Too many jobs. Employers are suspicious of changes without accompanying career advancement.

2. Reluctance of applicant or spouse to relocate if necessary.

3. Wrong personality for the employer.

4. Unrealistic salary requirements.

5. Inadequate background.

6. Poor employment record.

7. Unresponsive, uninterested, or unprepared during the interview. (Being ''too aggressive'' is not a serious handicap.)

8. Negotiations with employer handled improperly.

9. Little apparent growth potential.

10. Long period of unemployment.

11. Judged to be an ineffective supervisor.

Source: National Personnel Associates.

Why Executives Quit

More executives switch jobs for better advancement prospects than for higher pay. Nevertheless, 81% of those who move receive a better compensation package.

Major reasons for changes, other than salary:
- Too little responsibility or freedom.
- A slow-moving boss.
- Personality clash with managers with more seniority.

Source: Survey by National Personnel Associates, 1100 17th St., NW, Washington, DC 20036.

How to Leave a Job

When quitting to take another job, it's often tempting to get pent-up gripes off your chest. Especially if the employer has ignored some of your best ideas or failed to recognize and reward your talents and achievements.

Yielding to that temptation can be a serious mistake. Remember: Every job becomes part of your permanent reference, for better or for worse.

No matter how frustrating or unfair the experience, leave it in good spirits. Dwell on the positive reasons for leaving (the chance to get new, needed exposure, a once-in-a-lifetime opportunity, etc.).

In talking about a previous job, the phrases "excellent experience" or "learned a lot" cover a great deal of ground. Leave the impression that you would be pleased to be working there still, except for this marvelous chance to take on a new challenge.

Strategy: Even if your mind is made up to leave, it doesn't hurt to talk over a new offer with the current boss. This leaves an upbeat impression that you respected his advice.

Recommended: Beware of exit interviewers who try to draw out candid opinions on the old organization, problems with supervisors, and your real reasons for leaving. References are likely to be better if you keep emphasizing the positive right to the end.

Source: Robert Lear, Columbia University Graduate School of Business.

Top Business Schools Rated

The best business school, according to 85 business school deans answering a survey, is Stanford, leading by a fairly good margin. Just about tied for second place were Harvard and the University of Chicago, followed by Sloan (MIT) and the Wharton School.

Status of Occupations

Recent survey by a UCLA sociologist of the occupations considered most prestigious:
1. University professor
2. Physician
3. Lawyer
4. Dentist
5. Head of big business
6. Accountant
7. Business executive
8. High school teacher
9. Veterinarian
10. Clergyman

Harvard Business School reports that 1977 MBA graduates averaged $22,595 in starting pay (the figure was $20,060 in 1976). The best-paying starting jobs were in the management consulting field, with a median salary of $27,000.

Others: Electronics machinery manufacturers, $22,500; investment bankers, $22,000; and jobs in commercial banks, $20,800.

Executive Profile

A study of 3,500 top executives revealed these facts:
- Average 1979 compensation: $116,000 annually.
- Education: 85% with college degrees, 34% with MBAs (mostly from Harvard).
- Marital status: 95% are married (11% have been married more than once).
- Average work week: 53 hours.
- Factors in their success: Ability to get re-

sults, integrity, responsibility, ability to get along with others.

- Nonessentials: Good connections, appearance, social ability, job-hopping (75% have worked for three or fewer companies).
- Best skills to have: Finance and marketing. General management is a distant third.

Source: University of Southern California Graduate School of Business, for Korn/Ferry.

Characteristics of Successful Entrepreneurs

- Oldest (or only) child.
- Started work young (ran a teenage or preteen business).
- Launched first real company at 35 years of age or younger because of desire not to work for someone else.
- Earned a master's degree but quit before getting a Ph.D.
- Creative, sets realistic goals, calculates risks carefully, has difficulty in delegating.
- A high ego and a need for achievement which can be traced to relationship with a father who was usually self-employed. Another key relationship: An unusually supportive spouse.

Source: Joseph R. Mancuso, Center for Entrepreneurial Management, 311 Main St., Worcester, MA 01608.

Winning at Office Politics

Believing that hard work alone will lead to recognition and success is a common career mistake. Fact: Your boss determines whether you are a success. And he may also be in a position to define what successful performance is.

Rule 1. Find out what the boss expects.

- It's not necessary to change your life to fit in with an organization. But find out before joining the company whether you can fit in. If you don't fit, or can't, don't take the job. Maybe you're a loner and the company stresses teamwork. Maybe long hours are required, and you want time for your own activities. You'll either be unhappy,

passed over when it comes to promotions, or let go one way or another.

- Learn about the values of an organization by listening to what the interviewer stresses. Make every effort to talk to present employees.

Rule 2. Once you are in the organization, knowledge is power. Build an information network. Identify the people who have power and the extent and direction of it. Title doesn't necessarily reflect actual influence.

- Find out how the grapevine works. Don't neglect secretaries as a source of information. (Women too often make this mistake.) Gossip goes on anyway, so make use of it.
- Develop good internal public relations for yourself. Let higher-ups know, through memos or the grapevine, when you have completed a project. Trade shows, community newspapers, and public speaking engagements also can bring attention to your accomplishments.

Rule 3. Find a mentor, a trusted counselor. Four types are useful:

- Information mentor, who tells you where the skeletons are buried, and how to avoid becoming one. Could be the boss's secretary who tells you with a raise of the eyebrow that the boss is in no mood to hear your ideas today.
- Peer mentor, who can help as long as you're not competing directly.
- Competitive mentor. One who is in the same type of job at another company. That person can often clue you in on what's happening in your own company before it's common knowledge.
- Retiree mentor. Often the best kind. Former employee has little stake in the organization and can give you honest advice.

Note: A mentor can be a man or a woman. The women who have male mentors may run into some difficulty. Co-workers may see the relationship as a sexual one rather than business-oriented. But that's the risk you have to take. As long as you and your mentor understand where you stand, it should work out.

Mentors must be carefully sought out at trade shows, company meetings, etc.

Basic rules for office politicking:

- Don't make enemies without a very good reason. You can't always be certain of where the power will flow next.
- Avoid cliques. Keep circulating in the office.

Become known as someone who can work with everyone.

- If you must fight, fight over something that's really worth it. Don't lose ground over minor matters or petty differences.

- If you shoot, shoot to kill. If you only wound, your victim will be able to get back at you some day.

- Don't take office politics personally. Office politics are impersonal, just as are muggings. If you get mugged, it's because you happened to be there, not because it was you. Losing at office politics just means you didn't fit in. It doesn't mean you're a personal failure.

Source: Marilyn Moats Kennedy, Career Strategies, 2762 Eastwood St., Evanston, IL 60201.

Psychology on the Job

Past or present trouble dealing with parent can affect your career. Frequent problem: The individual's time-honored responses to the parent who wanted him (her) to grow and succeed, subconsciously sought to keep that child dependent. There's a counterpart ready to undermine similarly in every company. If you work for one, you'd better learn to spot the ploys that are used to keep you dependent.

Here are the key parent and boss ploys:

Belittlement: Your parent thought three A's and two B's were good, but surely you could do better. (Your boss says that report you produced on the double for the top brass was good, but why did it take so long? Why wasn't it better written?)

- Martyrdom: Dad told you to go have a good time, he'd mow the lawn. When you came back he claimed exhaustion, but he was so glad you had fun. (The boss rewrote the report over the weekend himself. He didn't want to ask you to work overtime.)

- Emasculation: You *could* take the family car to the ball game, but why bother—we'll take you and pick you up. (The boss tells you to implement a new prodedure you suggested and then issues orders changing it without consulting you about it.)

- Fake dependency: Mom has you write all

her checks for her: You're so much better at figures than she is. (Your superior blocks your transfer to a managerial position: You're the best estimator he has—how could he manage to function without you?)

- Fear of success hampers people who work diligently toward a goal, but goof just when it is at hand. It often stems from having a controlling mother who kept her child dependent by doing things for him/her. And it can generate life-long fear that accomplishment will result in abandonment. Women often have the additional fear that competence will alienate men. Recognizing this pattern of behavior can avoid a critical misstep.

Those who habitually respond to these traps with feelings of guilt, obligation, inadequacy, or stifle feelings of inner rage while yielding to the punishment, should ask themselves why they need the approval of others so badly.

Advice: Recognize the ploys for what they are: The immature side of another human being. Appeal to the mature side: Call the bluff, state the facts, don't attempt to avoid a showdown.

Don't compensate by "overparenting" subordinates. If you can't retrain the secretary who thinks you're better than she is at finding the typos and the missing files, replace her.

Source: Dr. Howard Halpern, *Cutting Loose: An Adult Guide to Coming to Terms with Your Parents,* Simon & Schuster, New York.

Beyond Working Hard: Seven Success Secrets

The first step in becoming a success in almost any organization is to be convinced that it's okay to achieve success. It's okay to be ambitious, to be rich, to look out for oneself. It does no good to deny those feelings.

- Step 1: Develop self-confidence. Everybody does some things well. List yours. Concentrate on them. View them as precious commodities. Recognize that you have talents and skills that are ingredients of success. Forget your bad points entirely.

- Step 2: Concentrate your energy. Working long hours isn't necessarily the same thing. Having the desire to get things done is. One way to focus energy: Split up your day into the smallest possible segments of time. Treat each segment as independent and get each task done one at a time. This will give you the feeling of accomplishment and will fuel your energy.

• Step 3: Take responsibility. A person must be willing to accept personal responsibility for the success of his assignments, for the actions of people who work for him, and for the goals he has been given and has accepted. Seize responsibility if it is not handed over easily. There are always company problems that are difficult to solve and that nobody has been assigned to—take them for starters.

• Step 4: Exhibit leadership. Ask questions and take action instead of waiting to be told. Listen to other people's problems and link their ambitions to your goals. Then deliver what you promise.

• Step 5: Nurture self-control. Don't speak or move hastily. Don't let personal emotions color decisions that must be hard and analytical. If you must speak out emotionally or resolve an inner conflict, talk to yourself, alone, even if it sounds like madness. Act out a difficult situation in your mind or out loud—it will reduce your anxiety. And before taking a major action, ask yourself, "What's the worst that can happen?" Let that guide your next step.

• Step 6: Display loyalty. No matter how disloyal you feel, never show it. Show loyalty to your boss, your company, your employees. Be positive about yourself and about others. Never run anybody down.

• Step 7: Convey a successful image. Move decisively—walk fast and purposefully, with good posture. Look as if you are on the way to something rather than moping along as if you had nothing to do.

When you are sitting, don't slump. Sit upright and convey alertness. Choose a chair of modest dimensions. A large chair makes you look small and trapped. The chair should have a neutral color and be of a material that doesn't squeak or stick to your body. Avoid large lunches—they deprive you of energy. Successful people tend to eat rather sparingly.

Source: Michael Korda, author of *Success! How Every Man and Woman Can Achieve It,* Random House, New York.

Mid-Life Crisis or Opportunity?

Executives face a critical period when they reach their 40s, and it can be a period of trauma or opportunity. So says Prof. Daniel J. Levinson of the Yale University School of Medicine, author of *The Seasons of a Man's Life.* *

Of the four occupations studied (executives, hourly workers, biologists, writers), Levinson found that the most frustration is felt by middle managers of typically (pyramid) structured corporations: They feel they will not succeed or rise higher.

The crucial mid-life transition is rooted in the executive in his late 30s. At this age, success means climbing higher in the corporate structure, getting his own business established, acquiring more power and money, and finally reaching a position by around age 40 which will enable him to climb beyond that. So by age 40 he must reach the top of one ladder and move over to the bottom of another.

• These goals, which he's set for himself much earlier (often by his late teens), have a magical quality. He may muse: "If I make it, I will realize my youthful dreams and live happily ever after. If I fail, I won't have anything."

It's either total success or total failure.

Ambition peaks at this time of life. Occupational success is viewed as the main evidence of manhood.

This psychological turning point usually lasts five or six years. Levinson refers to the mid-life transition as the mid-life crisis only when this period is particularly painful.

What precipitates the transition? A promotion—or the failure to get it—that the executive interprets as a key event. He may have had a number of promotions, but this one at around age 40 carries greater emotional weight. Sometimes the event is connected with his marriage, family, religion, or politics. The death of a relative or close friend is for some the trigger to a transition (or crisis).

Even if the event is a success, Levinson says, in most cases the executive doesn't perceive it as adequate success. Within five years or so, he

*Alfred A. Knopf, New York.

learns that the success doesn't bring him the eternal joy of his youthful dreams.

He begins to question what he wants, to question the ladder he's on. Does he really want to be president of his company? He finds that he doesn't really know much about himself, outside of his job.

He may realize that he doesn't know very much about his children. Also, he questions his marriage. Is this marriage what he wants for the next 20 or 30 years? Characteristic of this questioning is the acknowledged fact that extramarital relationships usually peak in the late 30s and the early 40s.

At this point, many executives decide to retire early to teach or do something that they feel has greater social value than their present work.

How can the mid-life transition be handled? Some men build on what they had before. For others, struggle is natural, and they successfully face the process of uprooting themselves. Still others remain in business, but take off in a broader, more satisfying direction.

Levinson believes that the mid-life crisis can be minimized through awareness of conflicts.

One man may become alcoholic or suicidal. Another may be convinced that he has failed as a husband and father. Some may feel they've been in the wrong occupation all their lives or have been working in ways that are wrong for them. They become frightened, but they go on living and struggling for something better.

The transition can be characterized by two opposite extremes: One man can go through the period blithely, unchanged; another will fall apart. Neither extreme is good. This is the time for personal growth and increased self-knowledge. It is the foundation for the rest of a person's life.

Vital Skills of a Good Boss

1. He keeps informed. Knows where to go in the organization for reliable information. Keeps open a range of pipelines both inside and outside the company. Often bypasses the chain of command. He continually checks on his subordinates' perceptions of their problems.

2. He focuses on the key issues—those which the boss alone can handle (or handle best), those which the organization may not yet appreciate as significant, those which actually threaten the survival of the organization.

3. He knows how hard and how far to push the organization. Pushing too far merely provokes irritation.

4. He gives a sense of direction. Even if company's strategy falters, the boss must have in mind a clear concept of where to take the organization. He must be able to translate the concept into language appropriate to each level of the organization.

5. He discerns opportunities and relationships in the stream of operating decisions. Since the most innovative elements of overall strategy may evolve from opportunities presented during day-to-day operations, it is crucial that the boss not become insulated.

Source: *Good Managers Don't Make Policy Decisions* by H. Edward Wrapp, professor of business policy, Graduate School of Business, University of Chicago.

How to Deal With a Bad Decision

The way to handle the embarrassment of having made a bad decision: Admit it and move on to the next project.

Don't spend the time needed to solve current problems explaining past failures.

Guidelines to losing gracefully:

• Admit the mistake immediately. Don't try to force your assistants to continue an unworkable or obviously inefficient idea in an effort to save face. Those responsible for carrying out the impractical idea won't be fooled and you'll lose their respect.

• Don't look for scapegoats. The code of management calls for its members to assume blame in proportion to their authority. This does not mean the top executive should not hold individual employees responsible for their failures. It does mean that he must be prepared to shoulder the blame for the errors that are made by those under him.

• Think back to people that you respect: Chances are, a good bit of that respect can often be traced to the times they were wrong and said so promptly.

• Don't try to salve your own feelings by clouding another person's victory. If his way has proven the best way, admit it and apply it. Accepting his victory gracefully earns his goodwill.

• Don't look for excuses like outside interference, bad breaks, circumstances beyond control. When alibis become habitual, deficiencies are never corrected, because they're never recognized as problems in the first place.

• Don't forget a mistake. After admitting it, analyze it objectively, and try to learn from it.

COMPUTERS

4

COMPUTERS

To Buy or Not to Buy

Rules of thumb to help the company make the computer decision:

• Annual cost of a computer, for depreciation, maintenance, supplies, installation, is approximately 30% of its purchase price.

• Total cost of operating a computer is roughly three times the annual hardware cost. It includes staffing, program amortization, electricity, air conditioning, overhead, software maintenance, and the like.

• Thus, annual cost of running a computer is about 90% ($3 \times 30\%$) of the purchase price.

Economics should be the first concern. Intangible benefits may come later, but if the cost-benefit analysis doesn't come out in management's favor, neither will other benefits. Guideline: Computer should be able to displace annual costs roughly equal to its purchase cost, in order to make a profit for its owner of 10% or better.

Remember: It's better to be conservative. Computer costs have a way of increasing far beyond the user's wildest estimates.

To determine what costs the computer could displace, study the organization. Steps to take:

• Define objectives of the information systems change being studied. Competition? Economies? More accuracy? Better information?

• Identify areas in the organization which lend themselves to computer use. Rapid information needs, high volume, and complex calculations are some of the characteristics that help to spot these areas. High clerical costs, heavy customer complaints, and poor service are others.

• Define information needs. What does each department need in order to operate? In order to manage?

• Forecast future needs—five to eight years out. A computer ordered today won't be truly operational for at least a year. Then it needs to earn its amortization for four to seven years. So the system must meet the needs of the organization well into the future.

• Study alternatives. Which way can these needs be met? Service bureaus, facilities managers, time-sharing systems, and in-house facilities all have advantages and disadvantages. (Consultants can help here.)

• Intangibles. If the economics are in line,

then list the intangibles. There are benefits and limitations to each alternative.

There are no easy answers to the questions. But, as with all business problems, there are intelligent ways of finding business solutions. Don't become infatuated with hardware or technology. Remember that computers are tools in the hands of skilled businesspeople. They cannot make up for a lack of management skills.

Source: Dick H. Brandon, Brandon Consulting Group, Inc., 1775 Broadway, New York 10019.

Guidelines for a Small Business Computer

All the much-heralded promises of computer-reduced overhead and improved efficiency are within the reach of every business today with the advent of the small and inexpensive business computer.

A company, division, department, or branch can justify buying its own computer if its gross sales run at least ten times the machine's cost. And since small business computers run from as little as $10,000 to $75,000, the purchase of a small computer is not difficult to justify.

Another way to determine need: Compare the current budget for payroll processing, inventory maintenance, etc., against the cost of a computer. A $36,000 machine costs about $600 a month, amortized over five years. Add another $150 or so a month for maintenance. Total computing costs: Less than $800 a month. If the payroll for doing the job manually runs more than twice that amount, consider a computer.

More numbers worth noting: Manual processing of a statement or an order costs about $2.50 each. Having the job handled by an outside computer service runs $1 apiece or less. The small in-house computer may be able to process those same documents for 25¢ each.

Warning: Hidden costs. Software may turn out to be as expensive as the computer itself.

• Make sure all costs—complete software, maintenance, training of company personnel—are clearly spelled out in advance and in writing.

• Make sure the company can switch over to a newer, more powerful machine without having to change software or add completely new peripheral devices (terminals and printers).

• Another must: The company should also be able to take advantage of any price reductions the manufacturer posts within a specific time after the computer has been ordered. Minimum guarantee: At least until delivery of the machine.

• What to look for in a machine (and the software package):

• Make sure the machine can produce an auditing trail (an automated summary of transactions). This helps guard against embezzlement or human error by allowing an auditor or internal manager to retrace steps of a transaction. Software should also be able to generate an accounts receivable report that breaks out 30-, 60-, and 90-day past due accounts.

• The machine should be capable of producing backup files in case it is damaged by fire, vandalism, etc. (These files should be stored away from the computer site.)

Before buying: Talk with other companies that have bought the same machine the company is considering. Ask them about installation, operating, or service problems with the manufacturer. Advice:

• If the salesperson cannot provide customer references, find another manufacturer.

• Shop around. In the highly competitive small systems market, a number of manufacturers have recently come out with low-cost machines aimed at the first-time computer user. Leaders: Data General, Wang Labs, IBM, Hewlett Packard, and Digital Equipment. Talk to several before making the choice. Suggestion: See if a retail store has opened up in the area. These outlets often carry a variety of computer lines. They will frequently offer big concessions in terms of service and training to get the company's business.

• Don't buy a newly designed model. The risks are too high, even with well-established manufacturers.

• Insist that the manufacturer agree to test the computer after installation and train the company's staff to operate it. Important: Manufacturer should also assume responsibility for converting the company's old files to the computer.

• Have the accountant evaluate the lease/purchase trade-off. First-time customers often buy their systems outright because of the low cost, the investment tax credit, and depreciation. However, some computer vendors are now offering attractive lease agreements.

• Make sure all the manufacturer's promises are incorporated into the purchase contract. That contract should be thoroughly reviewed by a lawyer, financial manager, and perhaps by an outside data-processing consultant.

Test of a Good Computer Program

Whether you lease or buy a software package, these are key contract considerations:
• Does it work with your computer?
• Does it work with your data?
• Does it perform in the expected time?
• Does it produce the output you expect?
• Is it reasonably error-free?
• Is the documentation (the program's service manual) quality up to or beyond your standards?
• Vendor's financial stability: Although the package may work when delivered, you may be dependent on the vendor's survival for maintenance, enhancements, or upgrading to newer hardware. Therefore, obtain vendor's financial statements and contractually obligate him to supply them continuously. Do not make a down payment until the vendor has delivered the usable package and its documentation. If vendor is unwilling to give the original (source) program code, ask him to escrow it with an independent agent (e.g., local bank).
• True package ownership: If the package wasn't developed by the vendor marketing it, you as the user may be liable to the true owner, especially if it was fraudulently obtained. A warranty of ownership, with indemnification by the vendor (and a strong financial statement) will overcome the problem.
• Rights to improvement: You, as user, should have the right to access *all* program corrections, upgrades, improvements, etc., at a price no higher than that charged all others, or the differential in selling price between what you

paid and what new users are now paying. Errors, of course, should be corrected at no charge.
• Precaution: When buying a new software package, make sure the contract specifies that designers will be around to debug the programs after implementation.

What's Needed from a Computer System

One major source of conflict between client customers and computer service companies is the lack of a clear-cut agreement about what is expected from computer system. Management should spell out needs in specific detail before signing a contract. Otherwise, the result could be costly changes and legal disputes.

Typical problems:
• Contract promises an accounts receivable aging report. One is delivered—but with no breakdowns. The client had expected to be informed which specific accounts were 30, 60, or 90 days in arrears.
• Company system is built around a one-digit product code which breaks down when the company introduces its tenth product. Dilemma: Eliminate the product or revamp the system at a cost of over $100,000.

Signing a Third-Party Lease

When acquiring a big-ticket item like a computer, the buyer should weigh the alternatives: Direct purchase, installment purchase, direct rental, and third-party lease. Third-party leasing has major advantages over the others, under certain conditions.

There are several forms of third-party leases offered by reputable leasing firms, financial organizations, or banks.
• Risk lease: Generally short-term, with the risk of re-leasing on the owner (lessor), who won't recover his money during the period of the

lease. The owner assumes that the value of the item at the end of the lease (or the re-lease value) will exceed his cost and profit requirements. Consider this type of lease if your company's requirements are relatively short-term (two to four years).

• Payout lease: Usually longer-term, with the total payments covering the owner's financial requirements. The value at the end of the lease may belong to the user (lessee) or the owner, depending on the agreement. Consider this type of lease if your requirements are firm for five years or longer.

• Leveraged lease: A form of either of the above, in which the owner borrows the principal part of the financial requirements, counting on the tax advantages inherent in ownership (the investment tax credit, accelerated depreciation, sales tax write-offs), and uses the credit of the user as a guarantee for the loan. This method provides the lower cost of money to a user, although it generally transfers the tax advantages to the owner. A leveraged lease is more commonly used for a longer-term lease, when the lease can be used as collateral.

Advantages of a third-party lease:

• The monthly cost to the user will be lower than with other methods.

• The tax advantages can be passed on to a high-bracket taxpayer.

When preparing or reviewing the lease agreement, alert your lawyer to these points:

• Attorney-in-fact clause. The user should retain *all* rights to deal with the vendor (even though the owner is the contract signatory with the vendor). The owner should appoint the user as his attorney-in-fact, for purposes of negotiating or obtaining benefits and rights under the lessor-vendor contract.

• Right to dispute taxes. One of the incidents of ownership is the obligation to pay taxes on the equipment—primarily property tax, but possibly also sales tax, use tax, or excise tax. The owner will be charged for these taxes, and normally passes the charges on, which makes the user liable, without the right of protest. A contract clause should be included, giving the user the right to object to the payment of such taxes without being in default.

• Quiet enjoyment. As long as lease payments

continue, the user should have the right to use the equipment undisturbed. Lessor (owner) bankruptcy or failure to meet the obligations on the equipment, or other act of the lessor should *not* endanger the user's rights.

• Purchase option. It may be desirable for the user to have the right to purchase the system at the end of the lease, or at any time, at a defined price. This may be a disadvantage, however, and tax counsel should be consulted.

• Early termination option. The user should have the right to cancel the lease at any time, naturally at a penalty, and probably with significant notice.

• Tax credit pass-through. If the user has an independent contract for maintenance with the equipment vendor, this is not a problem. However, some leasing companies will include maintenance as part of the deal. In that case the user should have protection with respect to price, quality, source, response time, and possibly the right to take it over.

• Rights to assign. The user may wish to be able to "sublet" or assign the lease to another related party. The owner might want a similar right.

• Rights to upgrade or add. The user should be able to add or change equipment with a *common* lease expiration date, at whatever rates or costs are in effect.

Some items to be avoided in negotiating a third-party lease:

• Reduction of limitation of liability. Owner will want to limit liability, perhaps only to a few payments.

• User refurbishment. The lessor might want the user to pay for "any needed" refurbishment on termination.

• Risk of loss. Should be with the owner (the lessor) and insurance premiums should be paid by him.

• Floating interest rates. On a leveraged lease, the subordinated financing may be subject to a floating interest rate. The lessor may wish to pass this on. If so, the user should obtain the right to cancel or refinance if the rate is increased, and to obtain a reduction if the prime interest rate goes down.

Source: Dick H. Brandon, Brandon Consulting Group, Inc., 1775 Broadway, New York 10019.

Choosing a Computer Service Bureau

Here are some basic risks to be aware of if computer chores are handled by a service bureau —and some suggested remedies, which should be included in the contract signed with the bureau.

• Financial responsibility. A number of service bureaus have gone bankrupt, and in some cases such failures have resulted in government or creditor impoundment of equipment and media (tapes, disks, or cards). User data on the medium is irretrievably lost. But even if the data is returned, it may be temporarily unusable if the bureau's programs aren't available.

Remedy: Deal with financially strong service bureaus. Contractually require quarterly copies of their financial statements. Cover ownership of data, programs, tapes, disks, and cards in the contract to protect them from impoundment.

• Ability to correct errors. A service bureau prepares your paychecks and mails them directly to your employees. If there's an error, who's liable? Probably the bureau is, if you can collect.

Remedy: Same as above— pick a bureau with financial strength. Also, don't abdicate responsibility for the accuracy of the bureau output. Check it. Sign the checks at your office. Institute your own controls.

• Lowballing. A service bureau in desperate need of business prices your job on an "incremental cost" basis, giving you an unrealistically low price. If their business improves, the squeeze is on, and your data or programs are held for ransom for service price increases. The bureau may argue that the programs are its property and may demand a "transfer fee" to release the data.

Remedy: Get multiple bids before signing. Be sure that the question of program ownership is resolved in the contract.

• Confidentiality and security. You ask the bureau to print a confidential list of your most important customers. By coincidence, a programmer for your principal competitor, testing a program at the bureau, uses a work-file containing this list, and realizes what he has found. Or he finds the carbon sheets "deleaved" from your multipart paper and notes that by holding it up to the light he can read the entire list. Or someone

sells or uses your data or mailing list. Or he determines through your data that your earnings are up (or down) and then buys (or sells) your stock accordingly.

Remedy: For all confidential data, obtain all work-files, carbons, and the like. Establish security procedures and inspections contractually. Execute confidentiality clauses with all employees of the bureau. Also be sure to provide backup storage on your site for all key files in case of accidental loss or destruction.

Why Facilities Management Contracts Don't Work

No matter how bad the situation may be in a company's own data-processing operation, a worse solution might be to turn the whole EDP department over to an outside company under a facilities management contract. What the outside contract will promise: Either to set up a new EDP operation or take over an existing facility and run it on-site or off-site for a fee. (Much different from a service bureau which just provides a specific service, such as payroll, accounts receivable, etc.)

Beware of promises by the facilities manager that it can do the EDP job for no more than it's costing the company now. This means the outside firm will have to squeeze its own profit (20% is not uncommon) out of the operation. It's not likely that most companies' data processing *could* be made that much more efficient. More likely: Service will be reduced in ways that are not quickly apparent.

Caution: It can be dangerous to hand over vital company records to an outsider. And it's especially troublesome if disputes arise later. The contractor may even refuse to give back the company records. In one case, the service company had possession of the master tape listing all the receivables of a large company. They wouldn't return it until the client, who had many serious complaints, paid up.

There's no assurance that the system will be handled by experts. Slick sales representatives may give the impression that they could solve all the company's problems. But the people actually assigned to the account may be raw recruits, no better than the company could hire on its own.

Advice: Use a turnkey operation, where the company retains ownership, Negotiate a comprehensive contract (*see following article*).

Final caution: Biggest service companies (EDS, Computer Sciences, Bradford, On Line Systems) prefer to work with very large companies and organizations. Smaller companies have more leverage working with smaller service companies. (Especially if the company's account is 80% of the facilities operator's business, or if it operates on companies premises.) But getting an advantageous contract can be a hollow victory if the service firm isn't capable of carrying it out, or if it goes broke.

Source: Dick H. Brandon, Brandon Consulting Group, Inc., 1775 Broadway, New York 10019.

Traps in Ordering a Complete Computer System

An increasing number of companies that never used a computer are considering a "turnkey" system—that is, a complete package including hardware and (presumably) custom-tailored software.

There are traps in buying such a turnkey system. What to know—and what to avoid:

• It's cheaper to buy a complete system than the separate parts. Reason: Investment tax credit (currently 10%) is applicable to both hardware (the computer and its mechanical/electrical accessories) and software (the mathematical program; logic). Bought separately, software isn't usually subject to the credit.

• The vendor, a "systems" house or software house, obtains a considerable hardware discount. Worth negotiating for part of it.

• The user can use accelerated depreciation on both hardware and software, or arrange for lease financing of the entire package.

• Be aware that the time schedule laid out by the vendor is almost always too optimistic, and is geared to hardware delivery (typically 90-120 days) and not to software development time, which could be considerable longer.

• Vendors often underestimate the work or

problems involved. Quality may be lowered to prevent out-of-pocket loss—or ways may be found to charge the user for even minor adjustments to the system.

Steps to take to protect your company:

• Deal with reputable "systems" organizations. Check them out independently of any hardware vendor recommendations.

• Obtain bids from at least three such organizations. Be wary of bids that are extremely low or very high.

• The software costs should be separately stated somewhere in the proposal. Generally, software should cost about the same as the hardware. (This, of course, varies with the appplication, the amount of its standardization, etc.)

• Write a careful, comprehensive contract. The contract is the most important document you will prepare in the entire relationship. It should be reviewed by a lawyer who has experience with computer contracts.

Source: Dick H. Brandon, Brandon Consulting Group, Inc., 1775 Broadway, New York 10019.

Effective Computer Maintenance

The need for rapid and foolproof computer maintenance is increasing. As more and more systems, even small ones, are being used on-line (terminals directly connect users with the system), equipment failure and lengthy downtime create havoc in daily business operations that depend on machine interaction (order entry, shop scheduling, customer inquiry, reservations, and banking).

The solution can be a tightly written maintenance contract that assures reliability from a vendor who provides rapid response and full maintenance service and parts.

With a rented computer, maintenance is typically part of the rental contract. Negotiating leverage is relatively limited.

Choices when computer is owned (after initial fee service warranty period expires):

• Purchase maintenance from the original manufacturer under a maintenance contract.

• Buy maintenance from an independent

maintenance company. (Leaders: Comma and the RCA Service Company, Sorbus.)

• Self-maintenance is only economically justified for a large user. (Expect to pay around $20,000 a year for a trained computer maintenance engineer, plus the expense of spare parts and tools.)

Contract alternatives: Most use the original manufacturer.

• Time and materials contract. Normal rates are $40-$50 per hour, including travel time. The expense discourages use of the service.

• Full-service contract. This is really a form of insurance.

What to get in a contract:

• Define expected reliability and try to get vendor to guarantee it. Ideal: 98%-99% uptime guaranteed. Negotiate as part of purchase.

• Normal and maximum response time to a service call request.

• Vendor's guarantee to continue to perform maintenance for the expected life of the machine.

• Price protection (or limit on the price escalation).

• Eliminate clauses which give the vendor the right to refurbish the machine at the company's expense.

• Push for a lemon clause: This is an agreement by the vendor to replace a component that seriously affects operating reliability or that fails often.

• Store some key spare parts and circuit cards on company's site.

Source: Dick H. Brandon, Brandon Consulting Group, Inc., 1775 Broadway, New York 10019.

User's Report on Small Computers

IBM 5110.
    Advantages:
• Easy to use.
• Dependable.
• Service readily available.
    Disadvantages:
• Users are generally unhappy with the display screen. The limitations of 64 characters per

line can cause substantial problems in writing and debugging programs.

Running time for solving a standard scientific/engineering problem: 30 minutes.

Wang 2200 VP.
    Advantages:
• Outstanding abilities for large, complex calculations.
• Numerous features (Example: 32 special function keys) which give programmers a great deal of control and versatility.
    Disadvantages:
• Weak in file handling. Most users with high data management requirements have to overcome problem by having a customized program made for them by a software house.
• Repair service: Mixed reviews.

Running time for same problem fed the IBM 5110: 2 minutes.

Datapoint 1170.
    Advantages:
• Good for companies that need a small computer for a number of different purposes. It's easy to retrieve information. It's easy to manipulate information stored in its memory.
• Wide variety of Datapoint software available.
    Disadvantages:
• High math functions are not wired into the machine. They must be software implemented.
• Repair personnel sometimes fix symptoms of machine breakdown, rather than causes.
• Relatively complicated to use.

Running time for the same problem fed the other two machines: 38 minutes.

Randal RDS 100.
    Advantages:
• Good for general business use. Basic package includes software package for accounting, payroll, inventory, and record-keeping purposes.
• Reliable hardware.
    Disadvantages:
• Quality of installation assistance and maintenance support varies from distributor to distributor.
• Users who place a high priority on speed report the system is slow.

Running time for solving a standard scientific/engineering problem: 14 minutes.

Sperry UNIVAC.

Advantages:

• Flexible software.

• Memory, external storage, and data base capacities can easily be expanded.

Disadvantages:

• Expensive.

Running time for solving a standard scientific/engineering problem: 12 minutes.

Q1 Lite Microcomputer System.

Advantages:

• Corporation is quick to respond to user's questions and problems.

• Programming language used on the Q1 Lite, PL/1, is an easy one.

Disadvantages:

• The Q1 Corporation is new, and has yet to build a solid track record.

Running time for solving a standard scientific/engineering problem: 7 minutes.

Hewlett Packard System 45.

Advantages:

• Truly portable system with a built-in thermal printer.

• Users report little downtime.

• Comprehensive and powerful BASIC language and CRT-graphics capability.

Disadvantages:

• Weak on supporting software.

Running time for solving a standard scientific/engineering problem: 4½ minutes.

Texas Instruments FS990/10.

Advantages:

• Cost-effective for users who are technically knowledgeable.

• Particularly suited for scientific environments.

• Scientific volume discount to original equipment manufacturers (OEMs).

Disadvantages:

• Users who expect the ''complete package approach'' might feel uncomfortable.

Running time for solving a standard scientific/engineering problem: 6½ minutes.

Digital DEC PDP-11V03.

Advantages:

• A powerful and reliable system at a cost-effective price.

• Software upward-compatible with Digital's larger equipment.

Disadvantages:

• OEM must supply many support services unavailable from Digital.

• Support services received mixed reviews from users.

Running time for solving a standard scientific/engineering problem: 15 minutes.

Source: Hillel Segal, president, Association of Computer Users, P. O Box 9003, Boulder CO 80301.

How to Buy a Used Computer

A new generation of computers has bumped a number of older machines onto the second market. There are plenty of computers available at bargain prices. Most used machines are four to seven years old and still have a life expectancy of at least five years before they become inoperable or obsolete. Caution: Used computers are as risky to buy as used cars unless proper precautions are taken.

What to do:

• Determine the kind and class of machine needed. What kinds of applications will be run? How big a machine and how much memory will be required? What kinds of peripheral devices will be necessary? How much can the company afford to spend?

• Then start shopping around. How to do it: (1) Read used computer ads in trade publications like *Computer World* and *Electronic News.* (2) Talk to several dealers in the company's area to see what they're offering, or might be able to acquire. (3) Place an ad and deal directly with the original owner rather than through a dealer.

If the company decides to work through a dealer, check the concern out thoroughly.

• Most important: Get business and customer references.

• Make sure the dealer has clear title to the computer that's being sold.

• Insist that the dealer guarantee in writing to provide spare parts for the machine. Make sure (by asking dealer's customers) that there is adequate technical support available.

• The purchase agreement should include

penalties and/or the right to cancel the order if the dealer runs late on delivery.

• Buy a used computer "installed and delivered." It costs more this way but it's usually worth the difference. Reason: Moving and setting up equipment can be risky and time-consuming. With an installed price, however, the dealer assumes the risk.

Taxes: Check out the tax ramifications of the used computer. The company should be able to obtain an investment tax credit (10% of the cost up to $100,000), but it may not be able to depreciate a secondhand machine. Recommended: Talk to the company's accountant or lawyer before signing any agreement.

Financing: Same deals as with new equipment. Common length of payment contract: Seven years, as long as machine is not too old.

Software: Get assurance from the dealer (and, if possible, the manufacturer) that the necessary software will be available. Since these machines have been on the market for some time, software in most instances is proven. It should be easily obtainable from the manufacturer at a nominal charge. A few computer concerns, however, charge significant amounts for the software that goes with their gear.

Service warning: If the computer is bought directly from the original owner, buy only IBM gear. Reason: Most other vendors charge a heavy service fee to service secondhand equipment. IBM, however, provides ongoing maintenance at a nominal rate for most of its machines as long as the service agreement is still in effect.

Upgrading: Try to find a used machine that can be traded in on new equipment in the future.

Manning problem to anticipate: The best programmers and operators don't like to work on older machines. Labor costs may actually be higher with a used machine than with a new one.

The Electronic Revolution

As the telecommunications industry grows, costs have continued to decline relative to the traditional forms of communication. Outlook: In three years it will be as cheap or cheaper to send communications by facsimile over telephone lines than it will be to mail a letter. And it's already much faster. At worst, delivery will be made overnight.

What businesses should do: Beware of purchasing telecommunications equipment that takes more than three years to pay for itself in savings. The state of the art is changing so fast that equipment could become obsolete in that time. Some electronic products, due to labor-saving benefits alone, currently offer payback a less than a year.

Sound strategy: Rent equipment from AT&T short-term (ideally a 30-day lease) and be ready to make a long-term commitment when one technology becomes dominant.

More suggestions:

• Designate someone now to research different telecommunications equipment. Conventions are a good place to start.

• Re-examine the industry every six months or so to keep pace with changing technology.

• Because the independent equipment industry is young, many small firms are vying for leadership. To avoid a commitment to a firm vulnerable to a shake-out, it's wise to get a D&B, check with tradespeople, banks, and customers to make sure it is sound.

For telecommunications investors: Keep portfolio diversified. Gambling on one firm is risky because shake-outs may loom ahead. By distributing investment among several firms, the chances are better that one of them may turn out to be a big winner within five years.

What to look for in a telecommunications firm: Good management. Don't be dazzled by exotic technology.

Some smaller firms may have good prospects: Avantek, Inc., California Microwave, Inc., Plantronics, Inc., ROLM Corp., Frequency Sources, Inc. Scientific-Atlanta, Inc., MCI Communications.

Larger firms with bright prospects: Northern Telecom and Harris Corp. AT&T, which so far has concentrated on telecommunications services instead of equipment, could also be a good long-term play.

Source: Cliff Higgerson, electronics analyst, Hambrecht & Quist, 235 Montgomery St., San Francisco 94104.

Protecting Computer and Software

• Keep duplicate disks and tapes of important data in a separate location. Update frequently. Duplicating takes very little computer time. It protects against operator errors and machine malfunctions that erase data and against fires or thefts that can destroy data.

• Install shock impact detector. Costs under $10, warns of vibrations and impacts that can cause malfunctions and/or unintended erasures.

• Clean area regularly. Keep paper clips, staples, cigarettes, food, and other potentially harmful items out of the computer room.

• Use floor wax that doesn't need buffing to avoid airborne particles that can affect equipment.

• Keep temperature at constant 68°-72°F. Install humidifier to keep humidity above 36% and avoid machine static.

• Install fire and smoke detectors. Keep fire extinguishers handy. Cost: As little as $125-$200 for small setup. Make sure extinguisher is rated for electrical fires.

• Computer fire protections: Avoid dry chemical or all-purpose fire extinguishers. They leave solid chemical deposits that are difficult to remove and may render electronic equipment useless. Remove dust or lint from printers daily. Vacuum space under the raised floor every few months. Store all flammable liquids in safety cans outside computer room.

CREDIT
MANAGEMENT

The Tactful Turndown

How to Get Credit Information

Spotting a Customer in Trouble

Definition of Collecting Efficiency

Collecting on the Telephone

Self-inflicted Credit Problems

Defenses Against Slow Payers

Handling Disputed Payments

5

CREDIT MANAGEMENT

How to Get Credit Information from Banks

Checking credit ratings can be tricky, but a customer's bank will usually supply useful information. It's a good idea to work through your own bank, and have them get the information from the customer's bank.

Do-it-yourself inquiries are okay, but know what to ask, what kinds of answers to expect.

Best questions: (1) How long has customer had account? (2) Average balance? (3) Customer's credit rating with bank? (4) Does customer have a loan? (5) If so, how much? (6) Is it secured? (7) What kind of security? (8) When is the loan due?

Always start by telling bank why information is being requested. Stick to facts. Don't comment on the customer himself.

Banks will answer most questions fully, hedge on size of account and customer's credit rating. Size usually described as "upper four figures," "lower five figures," etc. The vaguer the answer, the more likely rating isn't good.

Formula for Assessing Credit Risk

The essence of credit sales is the trade-off between increased sales and increased collection costs. Credit sales can be increased infinitely in most businesses simply by liberalizing credit arrangements. But the increased sales become unprofitable when the costs of collection exceed the profit margin on the swollen sales. Therefore, a balance must be sought.

The most commonly used financial ratio for assessing short-term credit risks is the ratio of current flow to current liabilities. A better ratio, however, is cash flow to total debt. (Cash flow is approximated by adding depreciation expense to net income and subtracting the sum of purchases of fixed assets and dividends.) The ratio will vary by industry, but a ratio of 1:4 may be an expected average. (For public companies, this data is easily obtainable. For privately owned firms, the creditor must ask the customer to provide that information.)

In general, a credit policy should be based on

the typical credit terms in the industry, and businesses should expect to meet the terms provided by others in the industry. Customers who are poor credit risks require stricter terms. Here is a way to formulate a sound credit policy, based on the five C's of credit: Character, capacity, capital, collateral, conditions.

• Character: The probability that a customer will try to honor his obligations is measured by his payment history.

• Capacity: The length of time the concern has been continuously in the black.

• Capital: Measured by the financial position of the firm as indicated by total assets, total net worth, or the debt-to-equity ratio.

• Collateral: Represented by assets the customer may offer as security.

• Conditions: The state of the economy and the industry in which the customer operates.

EXAMPLE OF CREDIT SCORING

Character					Points
Subjective Measure	Excellent 5	Good 3	Fair 1	Marginal 0	☐
Capacity					
Years of profit	15+ 5	10-15 4	5-10 3	2-5 2	2 or less 1	start up 0	☐
Capital					
Debt/Equity Ratio	0-.10 5	.10-.25 4	.25-.50 3	.50-.75 2	.75-1.00 1	1+ 0	☐
Collateral					
Type	Mortgage 5	Securities 4	Pledge Receivables 2	None 1	☐
Conditions					
Sales Growth in Customer's Industry	Growth in past 4 quarters 5	Growth in past 2 quarters 4	Stable in past 2 quarters 2	Decline in past 2 quarters 0	☐
				Total Score	☐

How to score: Assign points in each rating category, then decide what cutoff point you want to establish. The sum of these points provides the customer's credit score.

Aging accounts is also a useful technique, because it directs attention to the most troublesome areas. Also useful would be analysis of payment history by customer class or category.

Checking a Customer's Credit with Supplier

Basic procedure for getting useful answers:

• Send a personal letter telling why information is being requested. Enclose stamped reply envelope.

• Make your questions specific. How long has

the supplier been doing business with customer? Terms? Line of credit? Promptness of payment? Current situation? If behind, how much? For how long? What kind of credit risk is account?

• Most important: Ask the supplier for names of other businesses that deal with the customer—in case customer has handpicked his references.

Before Giving Credit to a Company Just Starting Out

• Is it a corporation, a partnership, or a sole proprietorship? Who are the principals?

• What is the business experience of the company's principals?

• What was their initial investment?

• How experienced is the management?

• What are the company's total assets? How much is secured by loans on equipment?

• Which equipment or other fixed assets are secured?

• How much initial inventory will the company have to order?

• What are projected sales for the next year?

• What does the balance sheet look like?

Source: *Credit and Collections: A Practical Guide* by Rick Stephan Hayes, CBI Publishing Co., Boston.

Guidelines for Setting Up Company Credit Policies

Credit policies should be determined by three things: Competition, market position, and corporate priorities.

Credit should be freely extended and easy to get when:

• The company's overhead is high and sales volume is necessary.

• The company is trying to establish new accounts or create a market.

• The industry is hotly competitive.

• The company is holding a heavy inventory.

• Demand for company products is temporary or declining.

Management can afford to put more restrictions on credit and reduce its risk when: (1) Demand for products exceeds production. (2) Overextended financial situation already exists. (3) Company's products are either unique or recognized as superior to the competition's.

Rule of thumb: Credit policy should not be so tight that profits lost on denied sales exceed dollars that might have been lost to bad debts. Common error: Using a too-complicated credit-checking procedure on all new accounts. This slows orders and irritates salespeople and customers. Better way: Perform a check only on orders above a prudent predetermined amount. Smaller amounts are put through immediately.
Source: *Successful Business,* 505 Market St., Knoxville, TN 37902.

Extending Credit to Customer's Subsidiary

When selling to a subsidiary of a solid company, don't extend credit without checking how strong the subsidiary itself is. If it collapses, the parent probably isn't legally required to make good and pay its bills.

What to do: If proof of good financial condition of the subsidiary is impossible to get, ask the parent corporation to guarantee payment.

Spot Customers on Their Way to Financial Trouble

What to watch for:
• A dramatic and unexplained increase in the number and size of orders. Possible significance: Other suppliers are becoming wary and your company is getting business normally earmarked for them. Or the customer is trying to lay in a stock of supplies while it still can.
• Postdated checks or delayed payments. Be especially wary when delays are caused by ostensibly trivial questions about such things as billings and work order numbers.
• Abrupt change of banks. The customer may be shifting its checking accounts from a bank where it has an outstanding loan in order to

avoid a bank freeze on its operating funds.

Commonsense tactic: Keep an eye on industry trends and use them to guide credit policies. For example: A manufacturer supplying the building trade might want to tighten credit when housing starts to decline.
Source: *Small Business Report,* 550 Hartnell St., Monterey, CA 93940.

Writing Good Collection Letters

Effective collection letters are polite, straightforward, and concise. Ideas that might apply to your company's particular situation:
• Always include the date, debtor's name and address, a description of the merchandise involved, the amount due, and a self-addressed reply envelope.
• Address letters to a named individual. Don't address the Accounts Payable Department or some other anonymous entity.
• If the goods were shipped in response to an oral or telephone order, don't mention this in the letter. It may tempt the debtor to deny that the order was placed.
• Appeal to the customer's reputation, sense of fair play, self-interest, or fear of legal problems. Escalate these appeals as the collection series progresses. (Avoid form letters late in series.)
• Send the letters in close sequence. Keep the debtor's attention with changes in letter format.
• Successive letters should be signed by executives of increasing rank (assistant collection manager, manager, president). Intersperse with telegrams or phone calls.
• Use certified mail, return receipt requested.
• Encourage the debtor to respond, even if he can't pay in full.
• Imprint envelopes with "address correction requested" so the post office will supply a forwarding address if the debtor has moved.
• Maintain intensity of the collection effort. If the debtor has several creditors, chances are the most insistent will be paid first.
Source: *Credit and Collection: A Practical Guide* by Rick Stephan Hayes, CBI Publishing Co., Boston.

Using the Phone to Boost Bill Collection

Super-tough telephone collections, never pleasant, can be more effective than letters—if properly planned.

How one company does it: Person-to-person call to the individual responsible for paying bills. The caller gives own name only, not company's. (Frequently, he gets through to the right person where an ordinary collection call would not.) He insists on finalizing the terms of payment during the phone call and follows up immediately with a letter "confirming" arrangement. This approach is limited to cases where cost of call doesn't exceed 1% of overdue amount.

If the debtor keeps ducking call, the caller leaves a full message—reason for call, amount owed and for how long, all other facts—no matter who's on the other end of the line. The "message" usually embarrasses debtor into paying, calling back, or accepting future call to work out terms of payment.

This is a high-pressure tactic. Misused, it can raise legal problems if caller isn't careful. Callers should be briefed in advance to avoid personal slurs on debtor, any other statements that could lead to legal liability. It's a good idea to check with attorney and work out a standard "script."

When the Check Is 'In the Mail'

Follow up with a telegram saying, "Thorough search shows no record of payment. Stop payment on previous check and send new check for $_____ at once."

Self-Inflicted Credit Problems

• Are too many credits being issued? Slow payments are often linked to legitimate customer grievances. An increase in the volume of credit memos can point up production or shipping problems. It might also uncover the need for higher-level review before any credit is issued.

• Are customers allowed to take cash discounts after allowable time has expired?

• How quickly are orders processed? A good part of the collection cycle could represent the time it takes an order to be shipped. Tightening up lead times can also keep business from going elsewhere.

Source: *How to Increase Profits with Cost Management* by Carlton D. Richardson, Duquesne Publishing Co., 209 Douglas Court, Moorestown, NJ 08057.

Leniency Can Cost a Creditor His Rights

Problem: An agreement provides that the entire amount of a loan becomes due if a single payment is late. But the payments are constantly late and the creditor accepts them without complaint. Many courts have held that the creditor, by its leniency, gave up its rights to strictly enforce the terms of the contract.

How to change the pattern and get compliance with the payment schedule: Send the buyer a written notice that lateness will no longer be allowed. By giving notice that the contract will be strictly enforced in the future, the creditor can regain rights that it may have given up.

Source: 24 UCC Reporter 044.

Defend Your Company Against Slow-Paying Customers

First, understand the real cost of slow-pay accounts. Expense is not limited only to the fact that money tied up in accounts receivable could be earning greater return elsewhere in the business. Other costs:

• Not every company can borrow more from a bank to finance slow pays. It may have to go to secured financing or to factoring, which can cost more than twice as much as bank financing.

• Lost sales. If a customer respects a company and pays its bills on time, single orders might be smaller but, in the aggregate, orders might be greater. Most customers deal with more than one supplier. If they owe one supplier, they buy from another supplier.

• Tics up time and effort of high-level executives, who very often wind up getting into the act of collecting from key accounts.

Recognize the first clue that a problem is developing: A change in the paying habits of a customer, especially a good customer that the company tends to treat leniently. If a 30-day customer goes to 40 and then to 60 days, or starts making promises, on-account payments, or says the mail is slow, take action quickly.

What to do: Make a business risk decision. How much should the company gamble in hope of keeping the customer? Consider cutting down the line of credit immediately. It reduces risk and lets customer know you really mean business.

Review credit records of the customer but don't rely entirely on so-called objective sources of information (Dun and Bradstreet reports, trade association reports, etc.). They are useful for background and as indicator (not 100% accurate) of whether there are secured liens and lawsuits against the company. But relying on them as sole information source is dangerous.

Call the company's bank or factor directly and ask for an opinion. A company that grants credit based on a story instead of on facts will get hurt sooner or later.

Collection guide. First-line, basic system is a series of letters, triggered by computer if possible, and phone calls that get made automatically when payment is late.

Get the right reports to upper management so action is taken immediately. What's needed:

• Aging of receivables into accounts that are 1-30, 31-60, 61-90 days old and over.

• Make certain that sales to a chain are totalled. Many accounting and computer systems list sales to branches separately so company doesn't recognize how much credit has been extended to one customer.

• Flag on-account and skipped payments.

• Most important: Procedure that alerts sales department to any collection problem. Stop shipments, or at least hold them until a new credit decision is made.

Salespeople can be excellent collectors, too, despite the general opinion that they are wrong for the job. Train them to pick up a check and write an order in one friendly visit.

Aggressive collecting. Discounts can work. But they probably have to be steep to be effective. It's common to offer a 2% discount for payment within ten days.

For tough collections, turn to legal help. Strike a deal with the company lawyer to send out two form letters to certain slow-pay customers as part of his regular retainer. Negotiate fees with lawyers and with collection agencies. They will say that a certain percentage of collections is standard, but most will accept less for sizable collection (for instance, 10% for collections over $25,000).

Most debtors think notes carry more legal weight than unsecured open accounts. So take a series of notes from a customer whenever possible. But don't fall into the trap of letting a customer buy terms from you with a sale.

Other techniques:

• Send someone out to pick up a promised check. Even a cross-country plane trip to pick up a $25,000 check may be worthwhile.

• Consider a settlement. A quick 5% to 15% off the bill may be cheaper than a lawyer or collection agency fee in the long run. The money is in hand and the problem is off the books and out of the minds of managers and the credit department. (Real deadbeats often counterclaim when a case goes to court anyway, and wangle a costly settlement then.)

Source: Malcolm P. Moses, 3428 S. Hewlett Ave., Merrick, NY 11566.

What to Do When a Customer Goes into Bankruptcy

Unsecured creditors needn't give up hope of collecting something. But it will take time and effort to collect.

The theory of bankruptcy, of course, is to let

the debtor start over. Once the bankruptcy petition is filed, unsecured creditors must file their claims with the referee—or court-approved trustee—and wait.

The assets, if any, will eventually be sold and the proceeds distributed to creditors. Their claims are then discharged. If the bankrupt later gets back on his feet, creditors have no legal right to press those claims.

But there are exceptions. Certain claims aren't affected by the filing of bankruptcy. They can still be pressed, maybe even during the proceedings. They are:

• Secured debts. Creditors with secured debts can immediately liquidate collateral and keep the proceeds (up to the amount owed). If the proceeds aren't enough, they have an unsecured claim for the balance. That claim then becomes part of the bankruptcy proceedings. There's still a chance of getting something along with other unsecured creditors.

• Claims of creditors who relied on inaccurate financial information submitted by the debtor in order to get credit. Debts that were incurred by "fraudulent" means, though, aren't dischargeable. However, a creditor may be required to prove that he relied on the false statement.

• Unsecured debts not listed by the debtor in his bankruptcy petition. If the bankrupt fails to list your company as a creditor, you won't share in what other creditors get. But after discharge from bankruptcy, your claim isn't discharged. You can still collect, or try to.

• Court judgments, if they arose out of personal injuries.

In addition, the following claims are also not dischargeable:

• Penalties and fines levied by courts and government agencies.

• Taxes assessed within three years of the filing of the bankruptcy petition. (Taxes incurred more than three years before the filing date are discharged by the bankruptcy proceeding.)

• Payroll taxes withheld or penalties imposed on "responsible" officers of the corporation for late payment of payroll taxes.

Some hard work and digging may increase the assets available for distribution to creditors. Example: The debtor gave away assets to members of his family within one year of filing. The trustee may be able to recover them for the creditors, but if they were sold for fair value, they probably cannot be recovered.

Similar reasoning applies if the debtor paid old bills just before filing bankruptcy. He may have been trying to give preferential treatment to some creditors. In this case, the cutoff is four months before the bankruptcy filing.

It may take some close questioning to turn up these things. The referee is supposed to raise these questions. If he doesn't, the creditors have a right to pursue it at the creditors' meeting. Of course, if your diligence turns up something, all creditors will benefit, not just your company.

When a customer files bankruptcy and lists your company as a creditor, you will be notified of the meeting of creditors. You may be inclined to write off the debt and not bother with the meeting. Most creditors don't bother; they assume there will be no assets to distribute except for secondhand furniture.

But it might pay to go—or to send your lawyer. Bankruptcy doesn't discharge all debts.

Source: Edward Mendlowitz, CPA, Siegel & Mendlowitz, 310 Madison Ave., New York 10017.

Creditor Safeguards

Controls that creditors should insist on when allowing the insolvent company to reorganize:

• The stock of the debtor corporation placed in an escrow account until the agreed-on payment of what is due has been made.

• Resignations of directors, officers, and key employees held in escrow.

• Stop-loss provisions set up to terminate the plan and permit takeover of the debtor by creditors if the company situation deteriorates.

• Limits on both salaries and fringe benefits of debtor company executives and stockholder-employees.

• Prohibition against or a limitation on dividends or other distributions.

• Restrictions on acquisition or expansion of fixed assets.

• Limits on new borrowing, whether it is secured or unsecured.

• Financial reports required at designated intervals to the creditors' committee or its counsel.

• Require the debtor to retain accountants designated or approved by the creditors' committee until full settlement under the plan has been made.

Source: *Insolvency Accounting* by Robert Weiner and Roger W. Christian, McGraw-Hill Book Co., New York.

For Quick Recovery of Goods

Suppliers who have shipped goods to a company shortly before it declares its insolvency have a big advantage over other creditors as a result of a recent court decision.

What to do: Sellers have to move as soon as they know of the insolvency. Wire the company, rescinding the sales agreement and demanding return of the goods. Under the Uniform Commercial Code, that demand takes precedence over other creditors'.

Advantages: Close to 100% recovery. And no waiting for trustees to sort through assets and liabilities.

Caution: If the returned goods have lost value, this action wipes out the seller's right to levy loss claims against the bankrupt company.

PFA Farmers Market v. Wear, W.S.C.A., Eighth, 8/29/78.

Quick Measure of Collection Efficiency

Daily Sales Outstanding (DSO) gauges efficiency of the credit department's collection.

How it works:

Pick a time period—usually one business quarter. Divide total credit billings by 90 (days) to get the average daily credit billings. Example: Total credit billings of $300,000 divided by 90 days equals an average daily credit billing of $3,333.

To calculate DSO: Divide the accounts receivable balance at the close of the period (on the 90th day) by the average daily credit billing. Example: Closing balance of $100,000 divided by average daily credit billing of $3,333 equals DSO of 30.

What it means: On average, the outstanding credit billings during that period equalled 30 days' worth of sales.

To measure efficiency of collections:

• Compare DSO against company's collection policy. If terms of sales require customers to pay within 30 days, a DSO of 30 is fine. But 45 or 60 is a danger sign. Rule of thumb: The DSO should not exceed 1.33 of the period specified in the terms of sale (e.g., if the terms of the sales are 30 days, the DSO should not exceed 40 days). Warning: Any longer period indicates collection procedures should be strengthened.

• Compare current and past DSOs to spot trends toward longer collections. Take corrective actions as indicated.

• Compare company's DSO to competitior's to measure relative efficiency. Data is available from *National Summary of Domestic Trade Receivables,* Credit Research Foundation, 3000 Marcus Ave., Lake Success, NY 11042.

Source: *Credit and Collections: A Practical Guide* by Rick Stephan Hayes, CBI Publishing Co., Boston.

Billing Procedures That Speed Collections

• Always process high-dollar invoices quickly. (Still better: Process all invoices quickly.)

• Bill separately for each shipment. Waiting to combine different shipments into one invoice saves paperwork but isn't worth the slowdown in collections, or the increase in risk.

• Submit progress bills for work in process.

• Consider using special delivery for very large invoices to underscore the importance of prompt payment.

• Know big customers' monthly cutoff dates for paying bills. Make sure invoices are sent well enough in advance of the cutoffs to avoid another month's delay.

Source: Edwin Lederman, partner, Laventhol & Horwath, 1845 Walnut St., Philadelphia 19103.

How to Handle Disputed Payments

The creditor can preserve a claim by writing *Under protest and without prejudice* above the endorsing signature. The Uniform Commercial Code (1-207) says those words will protect the creditor's right to continue to demand a larger amount.

Certification: The seller should not have the check certified and then add the under-protest wording. A court has ruled that certifying a check constitutes acceptance as payment in full, even though the under-protest language was added later.

403 NYS 2d 1012, 24 UCC Reporter 11.

Collecting Accounts Before Closing a Business

When you're liquidating a division or an entire business, it's important to recover the maximum amount of receivables in the least time and with the least expense possible.

First, before your customers become disenchanted with you, verify accounts' correctness via an auditor's statement or a brief letter requesting confirmation of balance.

When announcing the closing, formally notify customers by mail (ask legal staff for help), using certified letters where contracts call for it. If you have long-term agreements with some, try to have another firm take over the business, or, where possible, the entire account.

Review status of all accounts with salespeople during termination interviews, retaining some personnel for collection work or to act as valid witnesses in any court cases that materialize.

If you are unable to collect 100% of the cash due, accept partial payment plus installment note, and waive interest on subsequent payments if you must (except in some cases of default). Be sure the note is payable in your city, so that it will be easier to file a suit if you have to . (Only resort to a suit if all else fails. Litigation is costly and time-consuming.) Settle for less than 100 cents on the dollar if that seems to be the only way to collect anything.

Where possible, call on debtors jointly with the sales rep. He knows the account's status and can rebut any false claims. Obtain promise of payment in writing, if necessary, but try for full payment first.

Follow up installment notes systematically— by phone when they're missed. Be sure the customer knows that a tight collection procedure is in operation even though the business is closing. Keep records of all conversations and meetings with debtors as well as copies of correspondence and transactions.

Traps in Credit Reporting

Giving incorrect information on a customer to a credit bureau can open a company to expensive libel suits. But caution can protect a firm. Credit reports are given a "conditional privilege" in the federal courts. Just showing that a mistake was made, even if it stemmed from negligence, isn't enough for the subject of the false report to collect damages. But a customer who can show malice will collect. That means that if there is a history of acrimony with a particular account, it should be flagged for special examination before any information is given out regarding it. Recklessness can be interpreted by judges to amount to malice. Don't let bad credit reports become so routine that there's a chance for sloppiness to creep into reporting to the credit bureau. One store was socked with a $300,000 jury award recently, because it reported a check had been returned for insufficient funds when in fact the bank had sent the check back—twice—because the store forgot to endorse it.

EXECUTIVE
SKILLS

How to Write Better

Making an Effective Speech

Speedreading; Pros and Cons

Delegating Work

How to Retreat From a Contract

Assembling a Good Team

Successful Chairmanship

6

EXECUTIVE SKILLS

Writing Better Reports, Letters, Memos

Plan the format of the business letter or memo in advance. The writing itself won't take long after the plan is clear. Include the following (in this order):

• An eye-opener—a first sentence that arouses interest. Most important: State the point. Recipient of the letter or memo should not have to figure out why he's being written to. The same rule applies to report writing. Summarize the report at the very beginning. It should contain: (1) Findings. (2) What they mean. (3) Recommendations.

• Next step: Supportive data to bolster the opening point. Where many supportive details are involved, list them by number or with an introductory bullet (•) to make the letter or report easier to read.

• Indicate the significance of the opening point. Highlight the implications of what's being proposed.

• Suggest action. This section should motivate the recipient to respond. Example: Please let us know by February 15 what you think about this. Or, Let's have a meeting on the subject next Thursday at 10 a.m. The advantage of the motivational ending: Stimulates action and avoids hackneyed, formal conclusions that say nothing. For sales letters: This section should provide the opening for a continuing relationship. (I'll be in touch with you around February 7. Or, I will call to set up a meeting.)

How to use this technique for an internal memo to correct employee's habit of taking irregular lunch hours:

• The eye-opener: We're setting official times for employee lunch breaks.

• Supportive data: We've found in the past that many people are leaving offices uncovered and telephones unanswered because of irregular lunch hours. Please choose a specific time, from 12 to 1 p.m. or 1 to 2 p.m., whichever is most convenient for you.

• Significance: Specific lunch hours will allow us to work more efficiently and thus to increase productivity.

• Motivational conclusion: Please let us know

by June 1 what time you'd prefer having lunch.

• In letters, be conservative about salutations. People receiving letters with creative salutations (I'd like to have the pleasure of meeting with you, Mr. Jones) are often put off by the artificiality. Such salutations sound too much like the openers on promotional pieces. Rule: Stick with the old-fashioned Dear So & So.

For a clear, easy style:

• Dictate the message and then leave it alone once it's on paper. Don't think how to say it, just say it. Principle: Write as you speak.

• Use "you" psychology. Examine the letter after writing it and try to change *I* and *We* to *You*. Reason: The reader operates on the what's-in-it-for-me principle. Another device: Use the person's name in the body of the letter.

• Avoid hackneyed expressions that mean nothing. (Please be advised that, Enclosed please find.) Just say: Here is the report.

• Keep paragraphs short. Paragraphs that say too much and go on too long tend to turn readers off. Ideal: One thought per paragraph. Keep sentences short, too.

Recommended: Be yourself. Attempts to copy the style of others will result in strained, ineffective communication.

Source: Dr. Roger E. Flax, Motivated Learning Center, 2165 Morris Ave., Union NJ 07083.

Using Plain English

Simplicity is more effective than verbosity in memos and business letters:

Verbal overkill	Equivalent word
in the event that	if
with the exception of	except
at a later date	later
in a timely manner	promptly
at an early date	soon
has the capability to	can
sufficient quantity of	enough
by virtue of the fact that	because
the manner in which	how
at this point in time	now

Source: *Sales Manager's Bulletin*, 24 Rope Ferry Rd., Waterford, CT 06386.

Making a Speech

Type the last line of each page on the top of the next page.

Don't have the speech typed in all capital letters. Word recoginition is easier when normal upper- and lower-case letters are used.

Have speech typed in triple space.

Don't hyphenate words.

Memorize important points. Then the eyes can lift from text to look directly at your audience when these points are being made. Memorize both opening and closing lines.

Write the words "slow down" in large letters at top of each page. That compensates for general tendency to speak too rapidly.

Don't staple speech manuscript. Allow completed pages or large cards to be casually (and noiselessly) slid off to the side.

Underline the last three words of sentences or long phrases as cues to look up.

Use a slant-top lectern so manuscript can be read by lowering your eyes only slightly—but not your head.

Don't worry about your hands. Putting them in your pocket does not aid in relaxing. Hold them behind your back if you don't need them to illustrate a point.

When gesturing (always a good idea), keep a finger or pencil on the line being read so the place won't be lost. Gesture with your other hand.

Lean closer to the audience when sharing a personal or intimate thought. Stand straight or move slightly back to be more formal. The same movements can be used when you are speaking while sitting.

Before answering a question, stop and think. Frame the principal thought of your answer before starting to speak. Personalize the answer, using anecdotes and actual personal experiences.

When your remarks are scheduled for the end of a program, have two versions ready, one regular length and the other much shorter. If the program runs long, go with the short one. Audience response will be better.

The speaker who writes on a blackboard or easel pad as a visual aid should keep it on his left (when facing the audience) if right-handed (and on right if left-handed). This way, he won't turn his back on the audience or block what's written.

Impromptu Speaking

Best advice: Prepare well in advance for the possibility of being called upon "to say a few words." Have a short speech ready.

When more is required:
- Focus on the subject and the occasion.
- Refer to what was said by the previous speaker(s).
- State the problem in detail and suggest a solution for it.
- Compare advantages and disadvantages.

Important: Never begin your remarks by apologizing. And remember: Impromptu does not mean unprepared.

As Others Hear You

Face the corner of a room, cup your ears with your hands and speak. You'll hear a good approximation of how you sound to others. If your voice pitch is too high, try relaxing your jaw. That will relax your vocal cords as well and lower your voice.

Making Good Telephone Impression

Tape some telephone conversations and note how many "ahs," "ers," and "ya knows" are said. Try to eliminate these verbal pauses. Speak in sentences or complete phrases. Then be silent when pausing or thinking. In conversations without those hesitations and sounds, callers will receive a more positive image.

Your Business Photographs

- Have two sets of photos on hand: Formal for business announcements, informal for feature articles about you and your company. All photos should be 5" x 7". All should be printed for reproduction.
- Don't bother with color prints, unless your photo is likely to be used on TV.

How to prepare for the picture-taking session:
1. Dress as you would for an important business meeting. Men should wear dark suits with little or no pattern, and a shirt in a muted color. Women should wear clothes that suit their complexions, and avoid clothes that draw attention from their eyes.
2. The camera will exaggerate fatigue, so get a good rest before being photographed. Schedule your picture-taking session for the morning.
3. Allow a week for a haircut to grow out before having pictures taken.

Selecting the right photographer:
- Choose a photographer by his samples, not his credentials. Remember: A photographer skilled at portrait work may not be good at taking candid shots.
- How much should you pay? A moonlighting newspaper photographer will probably charge $50-$125 for candids done in your office. A well-known freelance photographer may charge $300 or more for the assignment.

Studio portraits will range anywhere from $100 to $2,000, depending on the reputation of the photographer and area of the country.

If you can, buy the negatives. New prints can be made from old ones, but quality suffers, and it's illegal (the photographer is legally protected against pirating of his work).

To keep up with changing styles, have a new business photo taken once every five years.

Source: Peter Silver, producer, Sound Concepts, Inc., 30 Hazel Terrace, Woodbridge, CT 06525.

Speedreading: Fact vs. Fiction

What to be wary of:
- Any system that guarantees increased reading speed. The International Reading Association is on record against "speed" reading, and its members are not allowed to guarantee that a student will ever read at any particular level. The most deceptive thing about a guaran-

tee: It gives a false sense of confidence to the individual with low verbal skills. If you don't start out with basic skills, you will not learn them in speedreading.

• Anyone who suggests that you can read 900 or 1,000 words a minute. Impossible, except when reading extremely easy material. Average reading speed is around 250 to 300 words per minute. Some reading specialists claim 600 to 800 is maximum for good reading comprehension. When reading speed is blown out of proportion, look elsewhere for your lessons.

How reading can be speeded up:

• Preview material. Skim for key words and phrases. Then decide which memos, reports, surveys, business and professional journals you should keep to read.

• Read flexibly. Most experts believe learning to read flexibly is the real key to speedreading. A fast look is valuable when you need to get through repetitious material that doesn't require you to take in every word. It is also helpful when you're trying to locate a specific fact or phrase. Adjust to a slower reading tempo when the information on the subject is unfamiliar.

• Constant use. It's necessary to keep good reading habits sharp.

Source: Dr. Charles Shearin, president, Vicore Inc., 2009 N. 14 St., Arlington, VA 22201.

Important Reading

Use a transparent marker to highlight key concepts and phrases. Important materials should always be read twice: First, to sort out what's important and mark it; second, for retention.

Source: *Chronolog,* Box 456, Orinda, CA 94563.

Learning How to Remember

Contrary to the conventional wisdom, memory doesn't work like a muscle. You can't exercise your way to a perfect memory. But you can learn

tricks and techniques that can give you a far better memory than you'd believe.

Chunking: That's the basic technique for short-term memory improvement. It's quite easy, and most people with good memories do it all the time. How it works: Grouping apparently isolated facts, numbers, leters, etc., into chunks. Thus, the series 255789356892365 turns into 255 789 356 892 365.

Sleep and remembering: There is some evidence to indicate that things learned just before sleep are retained better.

Spacing: Don't try to memorize by swallowing the whole thing down in one gulp.

Three-hour study marathons are useless because the mind gets weary and ten-minute spans leave too much time between memory efforts. Try 1½-hour spans for learning. But everyone has to do a bit of experimenting to see what time period is best for you.

Reciting: Provides a kind of feedback to the learner as you literally hear (in addition to seeing) the words. It also forces you to organize the material in a way that is natural for memory improvement.

Story system: A very effective way to remember some obviously unrelated objects. Just make up a silly story, using each of the objects in the story. Thus, if you want to remember the words *paper, tire, doctor, rose, ball,* try this story:

The *paper* rolled a *tire* down the sidewalk, and it hit the *doctor,* knocking him into a *rose* bush, where he found a *ball.*

Source: Kenneth L. Higbee, author of *Your Memory: How It Works and How to Improve It,* Prentice-Hall, Englewood Cliffs, NJ.

Guidelines for Delegating Work

• Never take work back. When subordinate raises a problem, talk it out on the spot. Memos simply burden the delegating executive with the responsibility of response while the subordinate does nothing.

• Set an arbitrary limit (hours per week) on how much time to spend with staff on tasks that have been delegated. Insist that staff make appointments in advance to talk about these areas. Discourage frivolous requests for help.

• Be specific in issuing instructions and deadlines. Instead of "Think about that problem this week," try, "Bring me five alternate solutions by Monday."

• Advise, consult, support, encourage, channel, and coordinate, but never do the delegated work. If one subordinate can't handle it, give it to someone else.

Source: *Execu*Time,* Box 1138, Newington, CT 06111.

Who Gets Which Task

One of the important decisions to make in delegating is whether better results will be produced by an individual or a group.

Guidelines for making that decision:

• Generally, individuals are better at creative tasks. (Examples: Designing technical components, writing computer programs, coming up with new alternatives.) If, however, the problem requires bringing together various bits of information (developing business strategy or evaluating new products), groups are superior, provided that the group members work well together.

• Advantages of group work: Greater total knowledge and information. Great variety of approaches. Increased acceptance of the final decision and reduced communications problems when the decision is implemented. Disadvantages: Pressure to conform and accept a popular solution too quickly. Time constraints because of the necessity of many meetings.

• If task to be done requires setting goals, the best people to do the job are those who will be responsible for meeting the goals.

• Warning: Don't insist that people whose jobs are largely independent work together as a team merely to encourage teamwork.

• Commitment is important. If implementation of a plan depends on a key group's commitment, it's best to involve that group in drawing up the plan. They then have a personal stake.

Source: John J. Sherwood, Purdue University, and Florence M. Hoylman, Organizational Consultants, Inc., West Lafayette, IN, in *Supervisory Management,* 135 West 50 St., New York 10020.

Making Sure Directives Are Understood

• Get feedback. Ask a few employees: "How would you explain this memo to someone working under you?"

• Invite questions. "Which areas of the memorandum seem to need more explanation?"

• Pursue implications and applications. Ask: "What effect do you think this will have?" Or, "How do you think this will affect our day-to-day operation?"

Source: Dr. Mortimer R. Feinberg, management consultant, 666 Fifth Ave., New York 10019.

Assessing Your Performance As a Manager

Managers are often unsure of their own management skills. One of the best ways to assess them: Take a very hard look at the behavior of the subordinates who report to you. The differences between what subordinates do when they are skillfully led and what they do when top management is poor are usually unmistakably clear.

Signs of good management:

• Subordinates do not seem timid about referring questions to the boss or asking his advice on difficult problems. At the same time, they are quite willing to make decisions on their own.

• When subordinates disagree, they say so. Rarely do they say yes and mean no.

• Subordinates show initiative in responding to unanticipated events. They also don't follow orders to the letter if it means destroying the original objective.

• The boss can express ideas without fear that they will be interpreted as orders. But when he gives an order, he finds that subordinates are responsive.

• Differences among subordinates over technical issues do not lead to personal acrimony, jealousy, and backbiting. Another good sign: No cliques and factions. The same individuals are not always lined up together every time.

• Subordinates are not tense and anxious

about the top person's authority, and when he meets them they appear to be relaxed with him.
Source: Dr. Leonard R. Sayles, Columbia University School of Business.

Getting Your Opinion on Record

An effective manager who is forced to implement a policy he strongly disagrees with should get his contrary views on the record. Several techniques can be used.

• Confirming memo: Lets top management know its authority is accepted even though the implementing manager is in disagreement. A single sentence will do. (Do not send carbons around the company, but keep one copy in a personal file.)

• Objecting memo: Put objections as well as recommendations in memo form. This tougher tactic may work but it is riskier.

• Memo to the file: Dated memo stating that on such and such a day executive was ordered to do something. Save it for backup; don't use it simply to say "I told you so."

• Over the boss's head memo: It's certain to make waves. To be used only when executive is certain his boss's mistake could produce a major disaster. The writer clearly puts his job on the line with this one.

• Sometimes an involved third party (a client, sales manager, supplier, or ad agency) can convince upper management of a mistake when staff cannot. But this can be tricky. The implication is that the boss is too stupid to understand the danger without outside pressure being applied.
Source: The Effective Manager, 210 South St., Boston 02111.

Four Ways to Get Out of a Tough Contract

What to do when committed to an unfair, tough contract, where sticking to the terms would be very expensive:

• Try to renegotiate it, offering or withholding future business as a lever. If locked into buying at a painfully high price, try to extend the term or increase the quantity in exchange.

• Some contracts aren't legally enforceable as written—simply because circumstances have made legal enforcement of them unreasonable.

• Look at the whole relationship with the other party, not just at this contract. Try to find a counterclaim to use in negotiating.

• If your company bids on a contract and through error bids too low, you are not necessarily locked into the price. It's often possible to get out without a penalty. Case in point: A contractor miscalculated and bid $200,000 too low. When he tried to rescind, after the customer accepted the bid, the customer sued, arguing that the contract should be enforced unless it would threaten the contractor's solvency. The court let the contractor off the hook. It thought the mistake was big enough to make the contract unconscionable, even though the contractor's survival wasn't in danger.
Source: *Baltimore County* v. *Ruff*, Maryland Ct. of Appeals, 7/18/77.

Getting Ahead in a Company

• Avoid routinization. Tasks that are highly predictable and routine have little power. Retain leeway to do your own thing. Be unpredictable. Instead of passively accepting external requests, change the assignment to make it more exciting or professionally challenging.

• Gain visibility by innovating. Seek approval for new products. Sell new markets. Find important problem areas that have not been attacked successfully. Move into areas seen as critical by the top management. Examples: Dealing with government, key customers, outside suppliers. These tend to be nonroutine and unpredictable. They heighten visibility and add power. Note: Critical areas change. The trick is to move into the right area at the right time—and then move out before it's taken for granted by management.

• Position the department to minimize the

necessity to defer to others. And increase the frequency with which other managers must defer to your department. How to do it: Stress the special training and experience the group provides, the unique factors (special jargon) that make it inappropriate for the department's work to be checked by nonspecialist "laymen." Add activities that make the department more autonomous, less dependent on others. It's even better to add functions that make it necessary for other groups to get your department's clearance before they can go ahead.

• Advance the department's location on the decision chain. Try to place yourself in the earliest possible stages. In purchasing, for example, it's preferable to contribute ideas in the early design stages rather than to simply be handed a list of specifications that might present buying problems. Add research and similar activities that suggest innovation, increase autonomy.

Don't expect the department's efforts to increase autonomy and power to go unopposed. Other departments will be doing the same thing, maneuvering for earlier work flow positions, getting rid of routine functions, etc. Winning depends on who has the most facility with tactics and relationships.

Be Known as an Expert

Improve your chances for promotion and attract outside job offers by displaying expertise and calling attention to yourself.

Some ways to do it:

• Write for publication in a key trade journal.

• Join an association of peer professionals. Know your counterparts and their superiors in other companies. Get yourself elected and officer of the association.

• Develop a speech about your work and offer to talk to local groups and service clubs.

• Teach a course in a community college.

• Write letters to the editor of trade journals, commenting on or criticizing articles that they publish in your field.

• Have lunch with your company's public relations people. Let them know what your department is doing. They need good internal contacts to help them understand the company's operations—as well as the important work that you're up to.

• Use vacation time to attend conferences and seminars.

• Write to experts, complimenting them (when appropriate) on their work and their articles. Whether or not they reply, they'll be flattered and they'll probably remember your name.

Source: Errol D. Alexander, president, Profiles, Inc., Vernon, CT.

Putting Together a Good Business Team

A truly effective group is characterized by a balanced diversity of personalities. Some rules of thumb:

• "Think-alikes" don't make the best teams. Neither does similarity in working habits or priorities. Conflict, in fact, may be desirable.

• Self-confident and fast-moving, decisive-leader types and creative people usually need the support of thoughtful, meticulous, slower-moving individuals willing to do research, work out details, and see the jobs through once essential decisions have been made.

• Profit-oriented types need the check provided by socially oriented teammates capable of articulating the human or public relations impact of decisions and policies on employees, customers, shareholders, and the general public.

• The fact that neither may initially respect the other's orientation needn't detract from productivity—or preclude harmony. Behavior studies, in fact, suggest that lack of respect (or active dislike) for highly dissimilar individuals declines (or reverses) when conflicting personalities are thrown together in work situations that require both accommodation and extended interaction.

• Alternatively, familiarity sometimes breeds dislike, even contempt, for working partners who were initially linked (and sought) for similarity in outlook.

Source: Tom Tyler and David O. Sears of the University of California, in *Journal of Personality and Social Psychology.*

Running a Business Meeting

If you have to run meetings—of staff members, trustees, committees—the following techniques may be useful:

• Pick the proper-size room, since physical facilities are crucial. If the group can't fit comfortably, see, hear, and breathe, the meeting will fail. It's worth the money to seek outside premises, but try to avoid hotels or other facilities that have many meetings at the same time. Your people may lose a lot of time finding their way through crowds or waiting for elevators.

• Check the sound system, lighting, projection equipment, and ventilation far enough in advance so there is time to get backups and replacements if necessary. Check on seating, tables, water, ashtrays.

• Be sure that those who aren't invited to a meeting know that it's because there's no need for them to be there. And make sure that everyone who ought to be present is invited.

• The purpose of a meeting should be an exchange of ideas and information. This requires structuring and planning: Who is to speak, on what, for how long. Those making presentations should be briefed well in advance to make sure their talk will generate discussion. Adequate time should be allowed for audio and visual aids. But don't get carried away by technology—it can boomerang in the hands of inexperienced people. Be sure that slides, tapes, charts, and other materials are really essential, and that they're properly cued into presentations.

Source: Charles Bleich, vice president, Committee for Economic Development, 477 Madison Ave., New York 10022.

How to Be an Effective Chairman

• Anything contributed to a meeting should be thought of as a contribution from the group as a whole and not from one individual member of the group. Don't tag an idea with the name of the person who suggested it. Avoiding such labeling removes each member's ego from his contribution and makes the discussion freer and much more constructive.

• Handling nitpickers: Don't ignore or put them down irritably. Say, "I'm glad you brought that up. How do you suggest we avoid the problem?"

• If an employee has difficulty expressing himself, don't respond with, "What you are trying to say is . . ." Instead, try, "That's a good point, the idea that . . ." and go on to restate the idea in a better form.

• When a decision is to be made, be suspicious of agreement that comes too quickly. Individuals in a decision-making group shouldn't change their minds just to avoid disharmony. Their reasons for disagreement should be drawn out and considered by the group, since the synthesis of everybody's reasoning may be valuable in strengthening a group decision.

• Side discussions: If two participants are carrying on a private conversation, direct a question to one of them. But make the question clear and simple so as not to embarrass him. Alternative: Restate a previously expressed suggestion and then ask his opinion. This should reinvolve the disrupter in the meeting.

• To dominate a meeting as chairman, sit at the end of a long table. Use blackboards or other visuals to help sell a viewpoint. To be even more authoritative, adopt a training session format: Committee seated at a U-shaped table facing your small table at the open end of the U.

• To get more participation from a group, sit on the long side of a long table—or choose a round table arrangement.

• Question and answer sessions: Tell the speaker and audience in advance that there will be a Q & A session after the speech.

Allow at least ten minutes for questions.

Prevent anyone from monopolizing the floor by pointing to three people to ask questions, one after the other.

Defuse a loaded question by immediately interrupting to correct an inaccurate premise in the question.

Repeat and paraphrase all questions.

Stop the questions before they peter out. Accept the final question while several hands are still raised.

• Closing a meeting: The worst way to end a

meeting is to announce, "We've just got time for one more question." The leader then has no control over whether the final question will be of general interest, and can be answered simply or will require a lengthy explanation. Better way: Restate the objective of the meeting and summarize your main points.

Avoiding the Overload Syndrome

Getting overburdened with obligations can lead to serious anxiety and depressions. A prime cause of the overload syndrome is outside pressure to accept too many work or volunteer obligations.

Another factor: The initial receptiveness of certain personality types to taking on tasks. People who are so inclined are particularly prone to guilt feelings.

Symptoms of overload syndrome:

• Fear that the additional responsibilities taken on (which suddenly seem overwhelming) won't be met.

• Inability to make decisions.

• Difficulty in communicating with family.

• Isolation. The manager begins to discard usual recreational outlets and exercise habits on the grounds that there is no time.

How to manage overloading: Ideally, avoid it in the first place.

What it takes to say no:

• A clear awareness of priorities.

• A willingness to accept temporary feelings of guilt.

Source: *The Psychometabolic Blues,* Woodbridge Press, Box 6189, Santa Barbara, CA 93111.

Running a Brainstorming Session

Brainstorming sessions work for developing creative ideas, breakthroughs on problems that your staff's best efforts aren't solving. Important: Recognizing what brainstorming is—and isn't. It's not just another special meeting or debating session. It's intended to assemble a group of informed people, stimulate lateral thinking, link unrelated ideas to create new ones, break the ruts people get into with straight-line, logical approaches.

Structuring a successful session:

• Define problems in writing, in advance, to participants with enough background information so they're understood. State each problem with a note of urgency: Failing product X has to be repositioned; operating costs have to be cut 20%; a marketing regulation must be dealt with. Make it clear that "anything goes." You are soliciting fresh, untried ideas; never mind about feasibility at the beginning.

• Include participants from a range of fields so marketing can be built on production ideas, etc. Do not invite negative thinkers.

• The chairman's job: Redefine each problem as it is considered; maintain a relaxed, humorous tone; keep the ball rolling with ideas if participants lag; outflank negativists; re-express ideas to give them simple, clear meaning.

• Take notes or, more in keeping with its nature, tape the session.

• Don't limit brainstorming sessions to managers and professionals. Hold them with office workers and blue collar people who often see company problems and possibilities with simplicity, clarity, and irreverence.

Source: Bob Stone of Stone & Adler, 150 North Wacker Dr., Chicago 60606, in *Advertising Age.*

Brainstorming Do's and Don'ts

• Don't criticize ideas. Participants are asked to express any idea, however impractical, ridiculous, time-consuming, or expensive, without fear of putdown. The idea's evaluation comes later.

• Don't compliment. Kind words lead people to focus only on merits of the praised suggestion instead of considering them all.

• Don't ask questions. That, too, focuses

group's attention on a single suggestion.

• Encourage ''piggybacking'' to expand the number of ideas. Pride of authorship only gets in the way of a successful session.

   • Best group size: Four to seven members.

   • Set a time limit in advance.

   • All ideas should be recorded. An idea may sound better the second time around.

To break the ice for inexperienced brainstormers, provide an absurd sample problem to consider for two to five minutes. Example: You have been cast ashore on a deserted South Pacific island with only a leather belt. How can the belt be used to aid in your survival? Nonbusiness problem breaks the tension, dissipates inhibitions, and gets the participants accustomed to a freewheeling exchange.

When Not to Use Brainstorming

The technique does not work for problems that require value judgments of any kind; broad or general business problems; complex problems; problems that have only one solution or right answer; or problems that have a limited number of very specific answers.

EXECUTIVE
TRAVEL

Mixing Business and Pleasure

Budget Air Fares

The Corporate Airplane

Dealing With Car Rentals

Outwitting Hotel Thieves

How to Cope with Jet Lag

"Duty-free" Shopping

Where to Eat

|7|

EXECUTIVE TRAVEL

Trips Mixing Business and Pleasure

Don't lose perfectly proper tax deductions. Here are the rules:

• If the trip is primarily for business, it's proper to deduct all the transportation expenses, plus meals and lodging for business days. Example: Leave Wednesday night, return home Monday night, spend Thursday, Friday, and Monday on business, weekend with friends. Since business took three out of five days (more than half), travel there and back can be deducted, plus three days' meals and lodging.

• If the trip is primarily personal, none of the travel can be deducted. Living expenses are deductible only for the part of the trip devoted to business. Example: The executive takes his family to San Diego for a ten-day vacation. While they are there, he spends three days on business in Los Angeles. He can't deduct any of the expenses of the main trip, only his own expenses on the L.A. business trip.

• The rules are tougher for travel outside the U.S. by owner-stockholders, top executives, and the self-employed. If the trip takes more than a week and more than 25% of the time is personal, then travel expenses must be allocated. Thus, if a foreign trip is 60% business, deduct only 60% of travel. (But if a domestic trip is 60% business, deduct 100% of transportation.)

One company recently beat an IRS challenge that certain expenses were really personal and social rather than business by producing charts that showed the corporation's growth paralleled increased expenditures for dinners and similar kind of activities.

Deducting a Wife's Trip to Convention

One way it's been done: A bank required its employees who went to annual conventions of the industry to take their wives as registered participants. At these conventions, executives fraternized with other bankers and regularly dis-

74

cussed such mutual problems as loans, investments, and leveraged transactions. Wives entertained and socialized with other bankers and their spouses. The Internal Revenue Service argued that the wives' attendance was not necessary to the employer's business activities. But a court rejected the argument, ruling that the conventions were working sessions and not vacations. The employer had found the presence of spouses was so useful in fostering good working relations with other companies that executives were instructed to bring their wives. An expenditure qualifies as a necessary expense when it is appropriate and helpful to the taxpayer's business, and such was the case here.

Warning: Don't overreact to this important decision. Note that here we are dealing with a customary industry practice. Also: (1) The executives were obliged to bring their spouses. (2) None of the executives involved was a major stockholder in the corporation. (3) There were both individual and group activities on the program. (Be sure to keep a copy of the printed program for the revenue agent.)
Source: Bank of Stockton, T.C. Memo, 1977-24, 1/31/77.

Business Use of Personal Car

Big tax savings are possible depending on which way auto costs are figured. Alternatives:

(1) Calculate the IRS-allowed mileage.

(2) Calculate the actual cost, including depreciation.

It's best to do the calculation both ways to see which one is better in any particular year. And it's okay to switch back and forth from one year to another.

Mileage method: This involves less bookkeeping. The deduction is 20 cents a mile for all business driving up to 15,000 miles, and 11 cents over 15,000. Tolls and parking may also be deducted, but not parking-violation tickets.

If the mileage method is used, oil, gas, repairs, insurance, and the cost of the car—including interest—may not be deducted as business expenses. But interest on your car payments and

sales tax on a new car may still be deducted as personal deductions itemized on Schedule A.

The mileage allowance method isn't good for an older car. If depreciation was taken in any year and the car has lived out its estimated useful life, only 10 cents a mile can be deducted.

Another catch: If in earlier years you took deductions for accelerated depreciation or additional first-year depreciation, then the mileage method cannot be used at all.

Actual cost method: If the car is used only for business, this is simply the total of all actual out-of-pocket expenses plus depreciation. If it is used both in business and for personal use:

• Figure out percentage of mileage driven for business.

• Deduct that percentage of all expenses including depreciation.

• Deduct 100% of all tolls and parking on business trips.

Tax Status of Travel Reimbursement

An employee who is away from home overnight doesn't have to report any reimbursement for expenses for meals, lodging, and local travel—provided the employer limits the reimbursement to $44 a day and requests substantiation and adequate accounting (time, place, and business purpose of the expenditure).

If employer reimbursements are in excess of this amount, the employee may deduct expenses above the standard rate only when he can meet the usual travel and entertainment substantiation requirements.

Deduct Travel to Check On Investments

Investors can deduct expenses of travel, including foreign travel, to check on investments in real estate or business

Keep careful records, though. Expect IRS to

be skeptical. A diary should clearly show how much of trip was spent inspecting properties and how much time was personal and recreational.

Important: IRS can challenge any transaction that doesn't have a serious business purpose, but appears to be only an effort to avoid taxes. And investment-hunting trips aren't deductible.

Budget Air Fare on Quick Business Trips

Businessmen making frequent trips to the same destination don't always have to pay full fare, even if they don't stay at their destinations long enough to qualify for budget tickets.

How to qualify for excursion fares: Combine outgoing flights on early trips with returning flights on later trips to meet minimum stay requirements and earn reduced rates.

Example: A businessman travels regularly between New York and Chicago. In September, his schedule will be:

Leave	Return
9/4	9/7
9/11	9/14
9/18	9/21
9/25	9/28

Ticket for these trips in the following manner:

Leave New York	Return to New York
9/4	9/14
9/11	9/21
9/18	9/28

Reverse one ticket, asking for travel from Chicago:

Leave Chicago	Return to Chicago
9/7	9/25

Source: Florence Margolius, Pierre's World of Travel, 2314 Monroe Ave., Rochester, NY 14618.

Discounts for Business Travelers

Your company may be overpaying for business travel if it doesn't take advantage of the 10%-20% business discounts offered by many hotel, motel, and auto rental chains. Not usually advertised but available if applied for in advance on company letterhead.

When and How to Buy a Corporate Airplane

Yes, owning a corporate plane is an ego trip, admits Leon H. Sicular, New York insurance executive and pilot, but it can also be a smart business investment.

Sicular cites the time he finally won an audience with a potential client in New York, only to find he couldn't get a commercial flight up from Florida. He flew his own plane, through terrible weather, but did manage to keep the date just before the prospect took off for an extended European trip. The payoff: Sicular landed the account, and the firm's commission on it was enough to pay for a new twin-engine plane.

Most likely candidates for corporate aircraft: Companies that frequently send out teams of executives within a radius of 500 miles. A company plane eliminates unproductive waiting time. It also provides a very private working environment, so travel time isn't wasted.

Where to start: There are a number of services (including some advanced by plane manufacturers) to help determine the feasibility of owning a company plane. Tip: Start by analyzing the company's travel vouchers for the past 12 months. A good reference is the *Feasibility/Justification Study Kit* ($2) put out by Business and Commercial Aviation Magazine (Westchester County Airport, Hangar C-1, White Plains, NY 10604). Also available: An annual *Planning and Purchasing Handbook* ($5)—same source—that compares business aircraft.

Another good source: National Business Aircraft Association (One Farragut Square South, Washington, DC 20006), representing plane-owning businesses. Ask for their *Recommended Standards Manual* ($25, refundable if you join NBAA). It covers just about everything a novice needs to know. NBAA can also provide names of local aircraft consultants.

Beware of optimistic estimates on range and

carrying capacity. Meeting the advertised range often requires carrying so much fuel that there's little room left for passengers or luggage.

Whether piloting the plane yourself, hiring a full-time pilot, or using one who has been professionally screened by a service organization, be aware that continuous training is required to maintain proficiency.

Safety: It's a good policy to do more than is legally required on pilot training and plane maintenance. Owner-pilots can probably get by with a private license. They should also have multi-engine and instrument ratings.

Common mistake: Buying more plane than is needed. For business trips under 500 miles, speed is not crucial. Making the distance in 15-20 minutes less doesn't justify extra expense.

Better: Start small, with perhaps only 80% of desired capacity, and trade up.

Good choice for a first plane: Piper Aztec, not the fastest or the most expensive. It's a good workhorse that can be operated and maintained on a reasonable budget. And it can be landed on a short (2,000 feet) runway. Faster, more expensive planes in the light twin-engine category: Beech E55 Baron, Cessna 310, Piper Aerostar.

Where and how to buy: Even if the company can afford to lay out the $170,000-$200,000 for a new well-equippped light twin-prop, it's wise to look into the used market. There is an *Aircraft Dealers Bluebook*. Another source to check: Trade-A-Plane ($9.50, Roy Stone, Crossville, TN 38555).

Dealers and distributors often have "demonstrators" with low mileage and in near perfect condition. These might go for 25%-30% off list. Try to get the full warranty. Never buy a used plane without a thorough examination by a trusted mechanic. Get the logs for each engine and the airframe.

Private Plane Deductible, and So Is the Pilot

If business expenses seem extravagant, the Internal Revenue Service may try to disallow the deductions. How case comes out depends on whether or not the court thinks that the expense was reasonably necessary in the conduct of the business.

In one case, a shopping center developer kept a private plane and pilot available on standby basis to take prospective tenants to the property and back with minimum time loss. IRS said okay for actual flying time but not for the plane's standby: That was extravagant and unnecessary. But since the standby costs were necessary to offer the service, a court overruled the IRS.
Palo Alto Village v. *Comm'r.,* 9th Cir., 12/19/77.

Safeguarding Hotel Reservations

• Best way: Pay in advance by check or major credit card.

• When reservation is made, ask hotel for a written confirmation. It's not foolproof, but it improves chances.

• If a regular visitor to that city and hotel, get to know the hotel manager. The personal contact will help.

Another hotel tip: If it's necessary to extend stay longer than planned, remember that a hotel cannot evict a guest if he's paid his bill or established credit.
Source: Steven Moran, Midtown Hotel, 220 Huntington Ave., Boston 02115.

What Car Rental Agencies Don't Explain

• If you damage a rented car, it can cost you more than you expect. The first $350 is now on you. The deductible used to be $100, but most chains quietly raised it recently. Best bet: Avoid the increased risk by paying a $3.50-a-day fee. Or get your car from a dealer who rents as a sideline. His rates are lower. The deductible is usually still $100.

• Pay traffic tickets you get when driving a rented car. Many rental companies give the police your name, address, and your home state license number if the car you rented gets a ticket. You risk being picked up as a scofflaw when you get back home.

• Liability insurance: Be wary if the car rental agency asks for the name of your auto insurance company. Chances are they're giving you only secondary liability insurance coverage. That means their insurance company won't pay until your own insurance is exhausted (and your own premiums will go up after you have an accident in a rented car).

Protecting Luggage on Plane Trip

• Place name- and business-address tags on the inside and outside of each bag. (Don't use home address. It can be a tip to a burglar that your home is empty.) If necessary, the airline will supply you with tags. Remove all tags from previous trips. (Confusion could send your luggage to the wrong destination.)

• Place a note inside each bag, listing the detailed itinerary of your trip. This way, if lost bags are found, they can be sent ahead to the next stop.

• Get to the baggage-claim area as soon as possible after landing. This minimizes chance of someone walking off with your luggage.

• If your luggage doesn't show up at the baggage-claim area, notify baggage-service personnel immediately.

• Carry on the plane such items as medicine, jewelry, and anything else small that might be difficult to replace.

• Insurance: While the U.S. government recently increased (from $500 to $750) the amount per bag that airlines can be held responsible for, consider additional insurance where your luggage and its contents are worth more than the maximum. "Extra valuation insurance" is sold at the check-in counter. Or get an all-risk policy from your regular insurance broker, which covers loss or damage to baggage, along with death payment and medical coverage in the event of illness or accident. Your homeowner policy may cover luggage too.

Outwitting Hotel Thieves

• Don't use a "pickproof" lock on hotel room drawers. That lets the burglar know precisely where your valuables are.

• Good place to hide things in hotel room: Under the rug under the bed. If it's difficult to get to, it will also be difficult for burglar to get to.

• Don't drop off your room key at the desk while you're away. Hold on to it until you are ready to check out.

• Request the duplicate room key.

• When you go out, leave a light and/or the TV on in the room.

• Whenever you leave your car, lock it and take your valuables with you. If parking in a garage that has an attendant, don't leave the key to the trunk.

• Don't put all your cash or traveler's checks in one place or one pocket. Although traveler's checks will be replaced, there is inconvenience and delay involved.

Avoiding Jet Lag

• Don't change your watch or your habits for brief stops.

• Stay at an airport hotel with 24-hour food service and a quiet room.

• Schedule meetings soon after you arrive if you get there before end of your normal working day. Example: An executive regularly flew from California at 8 a.m. to the East Coast, arriving at 5 p.m., New York time. He knew from experience that he'd have problems "getting started" the next morning, so he scheduled his meeting at 6 p.m., just after he arrived, since it was only 3 o'clock for him.

• For longer stays, be fully rested before departure. Don't rush to the airport. Plan arrivals as close as possible to your normal time for going to sleep. Don't take pills or alcoholic beverages. They hinder the deep sleep vital to recharging yourself mentally.

• If time permits, don't plan important hard work for the first or second day of a long trip.

• When traveling, wear comfortable, loose

clothing and shoes. Exercise during the flight. Isometrics, etc. Don't overeat or drink heavily.

• If crucial work must be done immediately after arrival, precondition your mind and body to the destination's time zone for several days before the trip.

• Travel fatigue is different from jet lag. Travel fatigue results from long periods of exposure to ozone and airplane cabin pressure, dehydration, and inadequate nutrition complicated by alcohol. Symptom: Persistent dry cough. Prevention: (1) Avoid alcohol. (2) Drink at least eight ounces of fluids per hour during flight. (3) Suck on honey-glycerine lozenges. Treatment: Use a humidifier in the bedroom after a long trip.

Traveler Beware

• You shouldn't pay the 8% federal tax on air fare if you're flying from one U.S. city to another U.S. city in order to catch a flight to another country. Tell the ticket agent about the foreign flight. You may have to show the agent the foreign ticket.

• When to turn down travel bargains: If super cut-rate tickets are offered by a travel agent (or even an acquaintance), be aware that they are probably stolen. The airlines are using computers to track down these illegal tickets. The user faces the embarrassment and inconvenience of confiscation, detainment, even legal action.

• First-class air travel: Not worth the 30% premium unless the flight is going to last more than four hours.

• Precaution when paying for a charter tour: Make out check to escrow bank account, usually found in small print in tour operator's brochure. Put destination, dates, and other details on the face of the check. Write *For Deposit Only* on the back. Reasons: Tour operator must deposit check in that account. Purchaser is protected against cancellation of the trip, failure of the tour operator or travel agent. If travel agent objects to this procedure, find another.

• Boarding the wrong plane: Airline regulations allow for reimbursement of air fare to passengers who accidentally board the wrong flight. The refund also covers the return flight. Note: Passenger may have to pay the round-trip price and then later apply for what the airlines call a futile flight refund.

• Don't fly within 12 hours after dental work. The change in atmospheric pressure can cause severe pain.

• Airline price increases: Domestic airlines exempt tickets from fare hikes if the fare has already been paid.

• Best tourist-class seats on a 747: Rows 11 through 18. Good visibility and smoother ride. For nonsmokers: Reserve a seat at least five rows in front of smoking section for smoke-free air. Extra leg room: Sit in first row of a section or just in back of exits.

• Preventing Montezuma's revenge: University of Texas Medical School researchers have discovered that the primary ingredient in Pepto-Bismol (subsalicylate bismuth) can help to prevent the most common traveler's ailment. A group of new students in Mexico received four tablespoons of the medication four times a day (for 21 days). Others were given a placebo. Diarrhea developed in only 14 of 62 students on medication versus 40 of 66 students on the placebo.

• Don't buy travel insurance at airports. Coverage is much more expensive and rates vary from city to city. Buy directly from insurance company.

Packing to Avoid Wrinkles

• Suits: (1) Lay jacket on bottom of valise, sleeves flat, pointed diagonally toward center of jacket below bottom button. (2) Place top half of pants across top of jacket, flat and lined up on creases. (3) Fold bottom of jacket over top of pants. (4) Fold bottom of pants across top of jacket. Crisscrossing provides extra cushion.

• Shoes, shoe trees, other heavy objects: Pack along sides on bottom. Helps keep suits from shifting.

• Shirts: Remove laundry cardboard and stack, alternating collars. Place each stack in plastic bag to reduce shifting. Then place over suits.

• Underwear: Fold in thirds and put in plastic bags over shirts. Same with lightweight sweaters, pajamas, handkerchiefs.

• Socks and belts: Rolled and then used to fill spaces or shoes.

• Ties: Fold neatly. Place where there'll be no weight on top of them.

• Toilet kit: Goes on top for easy access.

Other hints: Unpack upon arrival, even if only overnight; hang garments in bathroom while showering to steam out minor wrinkles without losing time.

Source: *Gentleman's Quarterly* magazine, 488 Madison Ave., New York 10022

Using Credit Cards Overseas

Use of credit cards in foreign countries can produce savings on currency conversion. Credit card companies convert at the wholesale rate, which is 3%-5% better than individuals pay. Diners Club and Carte Blanche pass full benefit along to cardholder. Visa and American Express pass along most of it. Master Charge keeps it all, so the cardholder gets no benefit.

Be aware that you're speculating in foreign exchange—though it's rarely with really big dollars. The charged item will cost more if the dollar falls between purchase date and preparation of bill. It will cost less if the dollar rises.

How to Keep Out of Trouble with U.S. Customs

• Get a receipt for everything you buy abroad no matter how inexpensive. Even if it's purchased at a local bazaar or flea market, get something in writing. A scrap of paper with a foreign name or stamp and any legible receipt is admissible proof of a transaction.

• Make sure local sales taxes are listed sepa-

rately on invoices. Taxes on purchase are not subject to duty.

• List items first that have the highest rates of duty so they will come under the $300-per-person exemption. Always list clothing under the legal exemption to avoid high duty (up to 42%). Jewelry should also be ranked up high on the exemption form. It should always be declared if it was purchased abroad, even though it's been worn. Items with relatively low rates of duty (about 7%): Cameras, radios, and perfume.

• When you leave the U.S., give Customs officer a list of any foreign-made items you are taking with you, like a Japanese camera, Swiss watch, etc. Otherwise, when you re-enter the country, Customs officials will assume that these items were just purchased abroad. They may charge full duty on them unless a certificate of registration is produced.

• Traveling from so-called developing countries: Recently enacted Generalized System of Preference rule lets you bring in normally dutiable items duty-free from 98 countries and 40 dependent territories. (Details: *GSP & The Traveler,* available at all U.S. Customs offices.)

Tipping Guide

Restaurant tipping guidelines from restaurateurs Vincent Sardi (of Sardi's) and Tom Margittai (co-owner of the Four Seasons):

• Waiter: 15% of the bill (not including tax).

• Captain: 5%. Note: If diner writes tip on the check, the waiter gets it all, unless the diner specifies how it is to be split. (Example: Waiter $5, captain $2.)

• Headwaiter who seats diners: $5 or $10 or more at intervals for regular patrons. He should be tipped in cash.

• Sommelier: 10% of the wine selection or 5% if the wine is expensive. $2 or $3 is a good tip.

• Bartender: $1 minimum or 15% of check.

• Hatcheck: 50 cents to $1 per couple.

• Restroom attendant: 50 cents.

• Doorman (to get taxi): 50 cents normally. $1 in bad weather or rush hour.

• Other staff at a restaurant that is regularly

used should be tipped once or twice a year: Hosts, switchboard operators (where the restaurant provides telephone service).

• Nightclubs: Headwaiter should get $2-$10 per person, depending on the impression the party host wishes to make on his guests. (Higher tip usually ensures better service.)

Other tipping:

• Limousine service: 15% to the driver. If a service charge is included in the bill, tip an additional $5.

• Hotels: Valet, room service, bartender should get about 50 cents, depending on amount and quality of service. Bellboy: 50 cents per bag. Chambermaid: $1 per day.

• Sports arenas and racetracks: A $5 tip to an usher as you ask, Are there better seats available? will often give you and your guests access to unused reserved seats.

Tipping Overseas

When leaving the U.S.: Tip skycaps 25 cents-50 cents a bag, sometimes a little more, depending on weight and distance carried.

On a package tour: Even if tips are "included," employees may not know it, so play it safe. Bellhops: 25 cents a bag. Waiters: No tip necessary if it's a different one each meal. But if it's the same waiter for the whole day, a dollar or two on the first day with the promise of the same at the end will usually guarantee top service. *Tour Manager's Guide:* $8 per person per week, $12 for 10 days. Local guides: 30 cents per person for a half day; 50 cents for a full-day tour.

On a cruise: If employees pool tips (ask the steward), $30 per person per week with an extra 15% of the tab for bartenders, hairdressers, and the like. If they don't pool, $1.50 per day for cabin steward and waiter, 75 cents for the busboy. If the ship has a no-tipping policy, $5-$10 to the waiter at the end of the cruise is probably what's expected.

Touring on your own: Depends on the city and country. In Athens, 18 cents-25 cents (6-8 drachmas) each time the doorman hails a cab for you; $2-$5 a week for the concierge of a hotel; 30 cents per bag for the bellhop, $3 per person per week for the chambermaid. In Paris or London, considerably more.

In restaurants: Usually there's a 15% service charge, so no tip is necessary. But round off the total to the nearest whole currency denomination (don't add more than 5% to the bill).

Don't Be Misled by 'Duty-Free' Shopping

Basically, only $300 worth of merchandise can be brought into the U.S. duty-free. $600 is duty-free on purchases made in the U.S. Virgin Islands. Aside from this, you may have to pay duty on anything above these limits that you bring back from your trip.

The duty referred to in the "duty-free" signs means no duty (or perhaps taxes) imposed by that country on the goods you buy. It doesn't mean free of U.S. duty.

Two types of duty-free operations abroad: (1) Those at Shannon Airport in Ireland and at DeGaulle Airport in Paris. These are segregated "free zones" accessible only to those who have cleared Customs. Travelers there are considered to be out of the country. (2) Shops in the Caribbean, including U.S. Virgin Islands.

Choosing the Right Vacation Cruise

Focus on a cruise with a compatible group of people. People over 60 generally take longer cruises. People on summer cruises are usually 15 to 20 years younger than those on winter cruises.

Compare capacity of the ship's main lounge to number of passengers. If lounge is relatively small, there will be uncomfortably fast meals and guests will scramble for seats at entertainment performances.

Avoid seasickness by choosing a cabin as close to the center of the ship as possible, on the middle deck, off the main corridor.

Getting VIP Treatment on a Cruise Ship

First, get the word to the shipping line that you rate A-1 treatment. This can be done by your travel agent writing the shipping line. Or you might have the public relations director of your firm write with the same message. This one-two attack is bound to get your name starred for VIP treatment when you come aboard. That could include dinner at the captain's table, an invitation to the captain's special cocktail party, or perhaps flowers and assorted gifts in your cabin. Also, of course, the more expensive your cabin accommodations are, the better treatment you will generally get.

Make sure to get a good seat in the dining room. Usually, that means in the center, close to the captain's table. Go over the dining room plan in advance of your trip with your travel agent and pick out the two or three tables you want. Then ask the agent to see if he or she can reserve the table for you in advance. If that can't be done, make sure that as soon as you go aboard ship, you visit the maitre d' and tell him what you want—with a $20 tip.

It's desirable to have an early talk with your dining room captain and waiter. Ask them what the chef's specialties are. Order those far in advance for your dinners later on the cruise. See if you can order such items as Chateaubriand, crepes suzette, special souffles, scampi, lobster, Caesar salad. These items usually can be ordered on most cruise ships. The trick is to know what the kitchen is good at; give the chef time to prepare them.

Give the dining room captain $20 and let him know there's more for him if the service is excellent. Also give the dining room waiter, in advance, half the amount you would normally tip him at the end of the cruise and indicate he'll get at least as much more for top-notch service. (Reasonable tip: $5 per day per person.)

Your room steward is the man who can get you all sorts of snacks, like fruit, cheeses, sandwiches, iced tea, and ice cream—almost any time of day or night. Ask him what is available, and if there is a best time to order these items for your cabin. If you want ice cream at 11 p.m. every night, tell him in advance, so he can plan accordingly. Also, give him half the tip in advance and let him know that good service will bring a reward.

If you want to impress your friends, invite them to the ship for a bon voyage party. It can be quite elegant but remain inexpensive. Make all the arrangements through the shipping company. The ship will usually supply setups, soda, and hors d'oeuvres at a very modest price. Expect to bring your own liquor when the ship is in port, but you can easily buy a few bottles from a local liquor store and bring them aboard.

The steward can serve drinks and other items to your guests in your cabin. If your crowd is large enough, ask for a section of one of the public rooms.

You can play expansive host by holding nightly parties while cruising, and it won't be too costly. The ship's staff will help you with parties in your room or in a public room at a fraction of the cost of a party in a hotel ashore. The liquor costs are minimal. Setups and other items often come free, as do canapes and other party snacks. You also usually get the service of waiters and bartenders at no cost (but you provide the tips).

Gambling Junket: The Real Cost

People who enjoy gambling in somewhat more than modest amounts should consider the many "free" junkets offered by most Las Vegas hotel-casinos. If a person is known to be a high roller, chances are he already knows about these all-expense-paid trips to the Nevada resort, because the casinos recruit such players for their junkets.

But a person who has not established such a reputation can get the free RF&B (Vegas hotel talk for room, food, and beverages) by calling or visiting the offices of various Las Vegas hotels situated in major cities. Although these offices are also there to book rooms and tours for people who are willing to pay their own way, they serve to steer the big shooters to Vegas on the free, chartered flights that arrive every day.

There's no trick to getting aboard, except that the junketeer must show a willingness to risk, though not necessarily to lose, substantial sums of his own cash.

How much? A topflight hotel-casino such as the M-G-M Grand or Caesar's Palace wants the first-time junketeer to come with at least $5,000 to bet. (That's for the player and a spouse or friend.)

But, as one junket manager put it: "People go there with the idea of beating the casino without playing—eating the gourmet food in the half-dozen restaurants, having the room with the sunken tub, drinking all that free booze. But they don't want to put their money at any peril. So the guy takes $500 worth of chips, thinks nobody is looking, gives his wife $400, she runs to the cashier's window, and he puts the $100 in his pocket. But that won't work, because everybody in a casino is watched by stickmen, croupiers, pit bosses, and cameras. It's all recorded on his markers and—through the ceiling—on film or tape.

"So if he tries to pull that, it goes on his record: Stiff! Don't invite again."

It's strictly business. The obligation of the junketeer is purely to give the house the opportunity to win his money.

Some casinos will settle for less than the $5,000 minimum. But depending on the length of stay and the quality of the hotel, that amount could vary. Some don't even ask to hold the money but settle for a look at a checkbook or savings account passbook to establish that the player is good for the agreed-upon amount.

Once a player becomes known as a heavy bettor, he will usually find (1) that he is in demand for free trips to other casinos, including those in the Caribbean, Monte Carlo, and (2) that he won't have to put up his own money but can get credit up to a limit from a casino.

Typically, play works this way: The player deposits his money with the casino on arrival, then goes to whatever game he wants to play. At such front-rank establishments as the Grand, he is expected to buy at least $500 worth of chips at a time. He gets the chips by identifying himself to the croupier and signing a marker against his deposit, just like in a bank. These markers become the record of his style of play.

Players are rated A, B, or lower. But below C +, the player won't be asked back. An A − rated player is strictly black-chip from the shoulder. In Vegas parlance, that means he bets at least $100 (black chips) on his opening bet (from the shoulder). A C + bettor bets $50 from the shoulder and never much less later on.

What shows your pattern and therefore your reputation is the opening bet style. A small initial bet that produces winnings and subsequent bigger bets doesn't rate a player highly. "He's playing with our money," says the junket manager. "If he bets $25 of his own but $100 of the house's, there's nothing wrong with that. But that's not what it's all about."

What it is really about, is the house getting a chance to win the player's money. The casino doesn't provide the $300 or $400 a day worth of food, drink, lodging, and entertainment for fun. If a player wins by betting big with his own money, that's fine. He'll look kindly on the premises, tell his friends at home about it, and almost certainly come back and allow the odds to work themselves out.

As long as a player with a plunger reputation can afford to keep coming back, he is assured of all kinds of extra-special treatment. Every first-rate hotel has a Resident Host or equivalent, a kind of concierge who arranges restaurant and show reservations (the best seats). All the big hotels have reciprocal arrangements.

Best gambling: Craps and baccarat offer the best shot that Las Vegas casinos give. They take the smallest percentage and are easiest to play. Blackjack is the game for those with a sharp eye and a good memory. Worst bets: Keno, roulette, and slot machines (in that order). Atlantic City roulette odds are better than Nevada houses but not as good as French casinos. But the best blackjack is in Las Vegas, the worst in Atlantic City. Best craps rules are in Great Britain.

Business Breakfasts in New York

Business breakfast meetings are a New York tradition. They add needed hours to the day and allow attendees to function at their freshest. The most popular spots are at the top hotels:

• Carlyle Restaurant (The Carlyle), 35 East

76 St. (744-1600). International art crowd and top business executives meet at this quiet, elegant uptown spot. Breakfast is served from 7 to 11 and peaks around 8:30. For reservations call Eddie or Pierre.

• The Conservatory (The Mayflower), Central Park West at 61 St. (265-0060). Special buffet breakfast includes choice of omelette, fruit salad, and homemade Danish. Continental breakfast also available from 7 to 10:30.

• Edwardian Room (The Plaza), Fifth Avenue and 59 St. (759-3000). One of the city's most elegant spots. The crowd peaks at around 8, but breakfast is served from 7 to 11. A la carte menu with reservations an absolute must. Another good breakfast meeting spot at the Plaza: The Palm Court, where the menu and service are less formal. Service from 7:30 to 10:30.

• King Cole Room (The St. Regis Sheraton), Fifth Ave. and 55 St. (753-4500). Breakfast served from 7 to 11. Lounge service until noon. Busiest time: 8:30 to 9. Because of the large size of the room, reservations are not essential.

• Le Petit Cafe (The Sherry Netherland), Fifth Ave. and 59 St. (355-2880). Continental breakfast and full menu breakfasts served from 7 to 11. Reservations recommended for a good table with a view of Central Park.

• Le Restaurant (The Regency), Park Ave. and 61 St. (759-4100). Top spot in the city for business breakfasts. Service from 7 to 11. Busiest time: Around 8:30. Some of the best rolls and buns in town. Must call for reservations.

• Rose Room (The Algonquin), 59 West 44 St. (840-6800). Central midtown location. Excellent food. A la carte menu from 7:30 to 11:30. Busiest time: Around 9. Reservations essential.

• Yellowbird Room (The Pierre), Fifth Ave. and 61 St. (838-8000). A quiet, luxurious and relatively unknown room serving a la carte breakfast from 7 to 11:30. Call for reservations.

Dining Out in Boston

Boston's restaurants offer more than traditional New England cooking. Besides usually excellent seafood, they provide a variety of good quality American as well as continental fare.

Outstanding:

• Ritz Carlton Hotel, main dining room, 15 Arlington St., 536-5700. Most elegant place in town. Overlooks Boston Common. Specialties: Chicken diablo, sweetbreads, and lobster whiskey.

The next best:

• Anthony's Pier Four, 140 Northern Ave., 423-6363. Huge harbor-side popular eating place, generous servings. Specialties: Fresh seafood, popovers.

• Cafe l'Ananas, 281a Newbury St., 353-0176. Small, elegant, and charming. International menu, with different countries' cuisines served on a rotating basis.

• Cafe Budapest, Copley Square Hotel, 90 Exeter St., 734-3388. Hungarian charm and music to match. Specialties: Veal goulash, chicken paprika, Wiener schnitzel, cherry soup, and Dobos torte.

• Cricket's, Faneuil Hall Marketplace, 227-3434. Informal nautical atmosphere with brick walls, wood beams, and butcher blocks. A recent addition to the market area. Specialties include original dishes such as orgasmic mud pie (coffee ice cream, chocolate cookies, and whipped cream).

• The Empress, Hyatt Regency Hotel, 575 Memorial Dr., Cambridge, 492-1234. Magnificent view of the skyline and the Charles River and a wide assortment of elegant Chinese dishes. Specialties: Cold seafood, winter melon soup, Manchurian veal roast, Peking duck.

• Joseph's, 279 Dartmouth St., 266-1502. Under the same ownership as Locke-Ober, this smaller restaurant is a bit more formal and less crowded. Specialties: Sole Marguery, rack of lamb, and duckling.

• Locke-Ober Cafe, 3 and 4 Winter Pl., 542-1340. An institution in the city going back to 1875. Ask for seating in the Grill. Specialties: Lobster Savannah, filet mignon, and oysters and clams Winter Palace.

• Maison Robert, 45 School St., 227-3370. Really two restaurants (located in the former Old City Hall): Bonhomme Richard upstairs and Ben's Cafe on the lower level. The former more classic, the latter simpler. Specialties: Veal and lamb dishes.

Dining in Toronto

• Copenhagen Room, 101 Bloor Street West. Midcity. An attractive luncheon spot. Scandinavian buffet. Specialties include fish soup with shrimp and asparagus, herring in curry sauce, dilled salmon.

• Fingers Restaurant, 1240 Bay St. Opulent setting with a French accent, favorite spot with the local "in" crowd. Specialties: Seafood, game, crepes, omelettes.

• Le Chateauneuf (Harbor Castle Hilton), 1 Harbor Square. On the shore of Lake Ontario, elegant French Provincial decor. Specialties: Steak a la Moscovite, partridge, scampi flambe.

• Noodles, 60 Bloor Street West. Very modern and sleek, with pink neon lighting that makes everything and everyone look great. Specialties: French pasta and Italian classics, iced cucumber soup.

• Prince Arthur Room (Park Plaza Hotel), 4 Avenue Road. Very posh, excellent service. Specialties: Roast beef, Dover sole, eggs Benedict.

• Troy's Restaurant, 31 Marlborough Ave. Quiet grace charms diners in two intimate rooms. Specialties: Coquilles St. Jacques, veal, rabbit, fresh fish.

• Truffles (Hyatt Regency Hotel), 21 Avenue Road. Excellent French cuisine and ambience. Specialties: Ringneck pheasant Perigourdine, escargots au champagne, chicken a la Kiev.

• Winston's, 104 Adelaide St. West. Art Nouveau setting with plush upholstery, Tiffany-type lamps, murals, soft music. Specialties: Shrimp wrapped in sole, rack of lamb, duckling, zabaglione.

Favorite Places to Eat in San Francisco

• Le Club, 1250 Jones St. Specialties include saddle of lamb, duckling with Cointreau sauce, poached salmon, and a variety of souffles. Very elegant.

• Trader Vic's, 20 Cosmo Place. The menu is extensive, including Manchurian lamb stew, Tahitian-style double pork loin, and barbecued salmon.

• Blue Fox, 659 Merchant St. Elegant dining room. Specialties: Tortellini Veneziana, mousseline de poisson, duckling flambe, piccata di vitello.

• Agadir, 746 Broadway, Moroccan menu. Diners sit on leather hassocks around low tables. Specialties: Lentil soup, tajines of chicken or lamb, couscous, and pastilla.

• Tadich Grill, 240 California St. One of the city's best eating places. Excellent fish. Many meat favorites such as corned beef and cabbage, pot roast, tongue. They take no reservations, so a long wait is inevitable.

• The Mandarin, Ghirardelli Square, 900 N. Point St. Handsome, with grace and elegance. Try Mongolian firepot, smoked teal duck, beggar's chicken, prawns a la Szechuan.

• L'Etoile (Huntington Hotel), 1075 California St. Very swank. Fresh flowers, gleaming crystal and silver. Specialties: Poularde etuvee champenoise, quenelles maison, noisette d' agneau.

• Fournou's Ovens (The Stanford Court Hotel), 905 California St. Specialties: Beef, duck, rack of lamb.

Where to Eat in New Orleans

• Antoine's, 713-717 Rue St. Louis. Perhaps the best-known New Orleans restaurant. This venerable favorite, now under the direction of the fifth generation of restaurateurs, is just as good as ever. Specialties: Famed oysters Rockefeller, oysters Foch, chicken Rochambeau, tournedos marchand de vin, and lamb chops maison d'or.

• Brennan's, 417 Royal St. Don't miss breakfast here, a tradition known around the world. Try a Sazerac, the local drink. Follow it with all the breakfast favorites: Eggs Sardou, French bread, bananas Foster. Also excellent for lunch or dinner.

• Broussard's, 819 Conti St. A lovely restaurant known for serving topflight Creole food.

Specialties: Breast of chicken ratatouille, squab Louisiana, duck Nouvelle Orleans.

• Caribbean Room (Hotel Pontchartrain), 2031 St. Charles Ave. The best hotel meal in town. Very elegant atmosphere. Regional cooking, with such specialties as crab Remick, shrimp saki, soft-shell crabs, and their own mile-high ice cream pie.

• Commander's Palace, 1403 Washington Ave. (Run by a branch of the Brennan family.) Specialties: Turtle soup, shrimp Creole, jambalaya, stuffed merlin, and red beans and rice.

• Elmwood Plantation, 5400 East River Rd. Old plantation in a suburb of the city. Specialties: Traditional southern dishes, oysters, red snapper, roast whole baby pheasant, veal stuffed with oyster dressing.

• Galatoire's, 209 Bourbon St. Very busy. No reservations. Great for fish, served in simple but friendly atmosphere. Specialties: Pompano, shrimp remoulade bouillabaisse, crepes maison.

• Le Ruth's, 636 Franklin Ave. Modest surroundings, but excellent service and food. Reservations are essential far in advance. Specialties: Crabmeat St. Francis, potage Le Ruth, soft-shell crabs, trout, tournedos.

• Louis XVI, 892 Toulouse St. Small, elegant, and expensive. Specialties: Terrine, cream soups, watercress and mushroom salad, roast rack of lamb.

Dining Out in Washington, D.C.

The nation's capital isn't renowned as the center of haute cuisine. However, there are some excellent French, Italian, and other ethnic restaurants worth a visit. Some good choices:

• Apana, 3066 M St., N.W. Georgetown restaurant with excellent service, Indian food. Specialties: Lamb Bhuna, brandied sirloin cubes with pureed spinach, salmon marsala.

• Le Bagatelle, 2000 K St., N.W. Garden setting, excellent quality food. Specialties: Rockfish flambeed with Pernod, venison, tournedos Rossini, pheasant.

• Cantina d' Italia, 1214-A 18th St., N.W.

One of the finest northern Italian restaurants in the country. Specialties: Fricasseed rabbit, paglia e fieno (spinach spaghetti and very thin regular spaghetti in bechamel sauce).

• The Empress, 1018 Vermont Ave., N.W. A landmark for superior Chinese food. Specialties: Mandarin and Szechaun dishes, Peking duck.

• Jean-Pierre, 1835 K St., N.W. The favorite of Washington's establishment and a mecca for French cooking, in a tavern setting. Specialties: Coulibiac de saumon, quenelles.

• Le Lion d' Or, 1150 Connecticut Ave., N.W. Traditional French cuisine, elegant setting. Specialties: Foie gras en croute, chicken vinaigre, pigeon mousse.

• Sans Souci, 726 17th St., N.W. Famous dining spot where politicians, journalists eat. Specialties: Shad roe, crabmeat pancakes, chicken tarragon en croute.

• Tiberio, 1915 K St., N.W. Elegant modern decor, excellent food. Specialties: Lamb in cream, superb veal and pastas.

Where to Dine in Los Angeles

• Bernard's (Baltimore Hotel), 515 South Olive St. Elegant style. Poached bass bearnaise, lobster in red wine sauce, salmon steak with green peppercorns, kiwi sherbert.

• Perino's, 4101 Wilshire Blvd. Somewhat out of favor with the flashy crowd, but still a splendid place. Consomme bellevue, squab with bacon, breast of pheasant perigourdine.

Beverly Hills:

• Ma Maison, 8368 Melrose Ave. Hollywood style French but maybe the best in town these days. Gigot and all the fish dishes are great, also homemade sherberts.

• Palm, 9001 Santa Monica Blvd. Very popular, like its New York counterpart. Good expensive steak and lobster, reasonably priced lunches, casual service.

• Dar Maghreb, 7651 Sunset Blvd. Palatial North African decor and food. Try couscous, b'stilla, squab, rabbit.

• L'Hermitage, 730 North La Cienega Blvd. A

simulated French country house with real first-rate French food, including lobster salad, duck in medoc, chicken au poivre vert.

• Scandia, 9040 Sunset Blvd. Remarkable Scandinavian menu that's hard to pick anything but winners from.

• Chasen's, 9039 Beverly Blvd. Reliable to topflight food, service, celebrities. Hobo steak, chicken pot pie, imported Dover sole, oysters.

• The Bistro, 246 North Canon Drive. Inspired by a set from Irma la Douce, it's as near to real French as you'll find in the area. Stars of movies, music. Excellent classic French menu.

• Dan Tana's, 9071 Santa Monica Blvd. Good Italian food and celebrity crowd, worth the long wait at the bar that seems inevitable even with a reservation.

• Polo Lounge (Beverly Hills Hotel), 9641 Sunset Blvd. Best quality hotel food any time of the day or night, expensive but fun to watch the greats and the phonies on the phone.

• The Saloon, 9390 Santa Monica Blvd. A tavern atmosphere. Stuff like hot breads, chili, steaks. Pleasant, reasonable.

• Mr. Chow's, 344 N. Camden Dr. Big-time movie and rock music people love the masterful Mandarin dishes.

Century City:

• Harry's Bar & American Grill, 2020 Avenue of the Stars. Supposed to be a replica of Harry's in Venice. Good, reasonably priced Italian food in an easy atmosphere.

Eating in Style in Chicago

• Le Perroquet, 70 E. Walton Pl. Luxurious, sophisticated ambience. French cooking with accent on new cuisine minceur (lighter sauces, less butter, flour). Specialties: Venison with chestnut puree, lobster bisque, lamb orientale.

• Jovan, 16 E. Huron St. Intimate setting, best quality foods available. Specialties: Fish soup provencale, pate de campagne, salmon mousse.

• Chez Paul, 660 N. Rush St. Two luxurious dining rooms with fireplaces in an exquisite old

mansion. Specialties: Veal Normande, filet de boeuf a la Colbert, saumon en croute.

• Maxim's de Paris, 1300 N. Astor St. A franchise of the original French restaurant, outstanding food, very high prices. Specialties: Crepe veuve joyeuse, tournedos Rachal, filet of sole Albert.

• The Bakery, 2218 N. Lincoln Ave. Award-winning, festive atmosphere. Specialties: Beef Wellington, roast duckling with cherries, roast pork stuffed with sausage.

• Cricket (Tremont Hotel), 100 E. Chestnut St. Same ownership and decor as the 21 Club in New York, with similar menu. Excellent but expensive.

• The Ritz Carlton Dining Room, Water Tower Place at Michigan Ave. Lush, formal room at one end of the hotel's lobby with view of gorgeous indoor gardens. Specialties: Game including partridge, venison, pheasant, saddle of antelope.

• The Cape Cod Room (Drake Hotel), 140 E. Walton Ave. Most famous seafood restaurant in the Midwest, superb quality, cozy atmosphere. Specialties: Bookbinder soup, crab amandine, enormous variety of fresh fish.

• The Ninety Fifth, Michigan and Chestnut Aves. Best view of the city from the 95th floor of the John Hancock Center. Specialties: Rack of lamb, seafood dishes.

Enjoying Japan While on Business

It's not as expensive as you've heard it is. It's not cheap, either. New York, Chicago, Houston, and Los Angeles prices are about the same as Tokyo's. Other major cities, such as Osaka, are more reasonable.

Room rates: Large singles in first-class western-style hotels range from 15,000 yen ($75*) per night in the tower of Tokyo's giant New Otani (reputed to be Japan's finest) to under 10,000 yen for a small single at the Nagoya Castle. Peak-season rates are slightly higher.

*Approximate exchange rate as of early 1980: 15,000 yen/$75; 10,000 yen/$50; 1,000 yen/$5; 500 yen/$2.50

Second-class hotels, in the western mode, cost less. Use these as a base for appointments, rather than braving dense traffic in a taxi to get there from a better hotel across town.

Traditional Japanese inns are becoming hard to find, and are expensive. Those who want to "go native" for a night may spend 15,000 yen for the privilege. The baths at those inns are a great experience, though. (The Japanese rinse themselves first, lather up, scrub clean outside the tub, and then climb in to soak.)

Business entertainment: Japan is an expense-account culture. That's where scare stories on prices come from. Be prepared to spend upward of 40,000 yen to wine and dine clients at top Tokyo night spots. At some restaurants, if the waiter thinks you look well heeled, the tab goes up. This is considered a perfectly acceptable way of redistributing income. Especially enjoyable: Shabu-shabu (available in U.S., too). Diners get thin slices of vegetables and raw meat to cook in boiling water right at the table. After that, noodles are added to the water (which has been turned into a flavorful broth from the meat) to make a delicious soup. Allow two to three hours.

Night life: Tokyo's Gray Line franchise runs tours of theaters, geisha houses, and "westernized" Japanese restaurants. In Kyoto, don't miss the fantasy lights and fireworks of nighttime cormorant fishing. Typical night tours in Japan begin with a meal at seven and return by a sedate 10 or 11 p.m. Typical dinner-plus-tour cost: Under 10,000 yen.

On your own at night: Tokyo vistors will be disappointed at the lack of bright lights. Japan's energy crisis is more severe than the U.S.'s.

Casual dining: Prices for an American or Japanese-style breakfast run 800 to 2,000 yen, typically 1,200 yen in hotels. Lunch: 450 yen to 2,000 or more. Lowest prices are for hole-in-the-wall local restaurants. Hotel lunches can go to 4,000 yen (almost $20) or more for American-style food. Fast food: Lunch at McDonalds or Kentucky Fried Chicken: 600 yen.

What to buy: Silk kimonos, 20,000 yen and up; yakudas (light cotton robes used as pajamas in Japan), 2,000 yen; ceramics (Kyoto is good for this; concentrate on designs not commonly imported into the U.S.); cloisonne and damascene jewelry (prices, at 1,000 to 30,000 yen and higher, are no bargain, but the selection is broader than in the U.S.).

Prints and original watercolors are available at reasonable prices. Cost of a 2-by-4-foot watercolor on gilded silk, unmounted, at Kyoto's Handicraft Center: 35,000 yen ($160). Original art (including limited-edition prints) can enter the U.S. duty free if it is signed by the artist or has the artist's "chop mark."

What to avoid buying: Japanese electronics (generally cheaper if purchased in the U.S.); cameras (they're cheaper in the U.S., too, especially through big-city mail-order houses); Noritake china (U.S. selections are adequate and Japanese prices, plus shipping, are higher).

Travel tips: The famed Bullet Train is amazingly comfortable. But there is little room for two-suiters except in the first-class "green cars" and reservations are necessary. In Kyoto, permits are required to tour some of the best gardens; obtain them well ahead of time (in the United States if possible). Visas are free for Americans; allow 30 days for processing.

Language: Hire an interpreter for negotiations unless you're sure that language will not be a problem. A prime source for interpreters is the American Chamber of Commerce in Japan (ACCJ), Tokyo.

For more information: Japan National Tourist Organization offices (45 Rockefeller Plaza, New York 10020).

Making the Most of Your Time on a Business Trip

There are four areas where it is possible to reduce "wasted" travel time: (1) In preparation for the trip; (2) at the airport/railroad station; (3) at the destination, on business; (4) returning and getting back to work.

The more preparation that can be done in advance, the better.

Clothing lists are a big help. Have lists for cold, hot, temperate climates. Lists for five-day, two-week, one-month trips. Lists for one-city trips (long stay, laundry facilities), five-city trips (one day each, no time for laundry services).

Goal: Packing should become automatic, take no more than ten minutes.

Luggage: Most people store luggage in inaccessible places. This is a mistake. Luggage should be easy to get at so that packing isn't put off until the last minute. Use the new fabric luggage that has no internal structure. Advantages: It's light, easy to use. Can be folded neatly into its own envelope and put on a shelf or in a drawer. Disadvantages: It must be packed full or clothes will wrinkle. And it may puncture or tear more easily than sturdier conventional luggage.

Travel toiletries kit should be used only for travel. It should be checked and refilled after each trip, so that it can be packed automatically.

At the airport/railroad station, expect and plan for delays. Use the time to get work done, catch up on reading and correspondence, make phone calls. People who don't work well in strange or noisy surroundings should use this time to talk to others, read for pleasure, do crossword puzzles, or sleep. Some executives save their light reading for business trips.

At the destination, carry-on luggage is an advantage. Get a cab while others are still waiting at the baggage carousel.

Itineraries are crucial: The executive should take two copies (one is for the hotel desk at his destination), leave one with his spouse, another with his secretary. What it should include: Local telephone numbers of people being met (their office and home numbers, if possible). Caution: Schedule enough travel time between appointments, especially in a strange city.

Returning and getting back to work: To facilitate getting back into the usual daily rhythm, try to return home in late afternoon or early evening so that it's as though it were at the end of a normal working day. Or very early in the morning, to get the feeling of starting the day. Returning in the middle of the day can produce disorientation.

To minimize time lost in readjusting to office routine, pick up a project that has been left unfinished on desk. If possible, it should be relatively easy and the executive should have good feelings about it.

Source: Stephanie Winston, author of *Getting Organized,* W.W. Norton & Co., New York.

FINANCIAL MANAGEMENT

Choosing the Right Bank

How to Get a Bank Loan

Tricks that Banks Play with Interest

Mistakes Borrowers Make

Alternatives to Bank Loans

Loans from Insurance Companies

How to Get a Higher Credit Rating

8

FINANCIAL MANAGEMENT

Choosing the Right Bank

Contrary to what most managers believe, monthly charges for maintaining a commercial bank account aren't all the same. In fact, because of the differing fees and, more important, the differing ways the fees are calculated, the total month-end charge can vary by as much as 150%. And again, depending on how fees are calculated, the amount necessary to keep on no-interest deposit to cover these fees can also vary by about 150%.

Here is the essential information either to (1) shop for a bank or (2) negotiate with a present banker to see if some adjustments in his methods —or yours—could cut costs, reduce no-interest balances, or even provide more "free" services for your company.

What banks charge: Most large banks have "activity charges" for each of over 100 different services. Examples: Charges for each deposit, each item in the deposit, stop-payments, overdrafts, returned checks, coin transactions, credit checks, lock box services, etc. While these charges are generally the same for all customers

in a particular bank (except for an occasional volume discount on some items), banks have different ways of calculating these items. And the charges can vary widely from bank to bank.

There is an even larger variance in the way banks calculate your basic balance. That's important, because it bears directly on all your charges. The earnings credit on balances maintained is used to offset these charges. Most banks use one of two methods to figure credits:

1. Using the simple method, the bank allows, as an earnings credit, an amount, say, 10 to 30 cents per $100 of average balance maintained in a given month (at the high end 30 cents, i.e., the equivalent of 3.6% interest). Charges are then subtracted from the earnings credit. If the difference is positive, the account is profitable, and no charge appears on the monthly bank statement —but the bank "pockets" the "profit." If the difference is negative, the customer pays the net amount as a service charge. Most banks will let customers see a breakdown of the "profit" in their account if asked. A few banks even send out a detailed breakdown if a customer is billed.

2. A second method used is to multiply the ac-

count's average monthly balance by a monthly interest rate. In many cases, the average collected balance is first reduced by the bank's percentage reserve requirement set by the Federal Reserve. The net result of this method is also a dollar amount of "earnings" the account has produced and is used as a credit to offset charges in the account. The interest rate is normally related to the Treasury bill rate, the Federal Reserve discount rate, or the prime rate. In each case the rate is divided by 12 to make it monthly.

The variance in earnings credit can be sizable. Much depends on whether the bank deducts a percentage of the average balance for its reserve requirement. Large banks deduct as much as 16.5%, and very small banks as little as 7.5%.

Another difference: The method of computing average balances. Banks often use average collected balance, which isn't the same thing as the current balance. For example, a large check deposited in your (Chicago) checking account drawn on a New York bank is probably included in your current balance almost immediately. However, if the check were drawn on a bank in a small Texas town it might take your bank seven working days to clear it. Thus, that money becomes part of your collected balance only when your bank considers it has collected the funds—and that varies from one bank to another.

So if you choose a bank only on the basis of how it handles the credit and charges to your commercial checking account, the optimum bank will have:

• Low charges on a per-item basis.

• Low reserve requirements or, better still, omission of this factor in the computation of credits.

• High "interest rate" applied to balances.

• Short period for calculating collected funds or, better yet, use of the average current balance.

Obviously, it may be hard to find a bank that stands out in all these respects. You should look for the trade-offs that are pertinent to your unique business.

If you prefer to pay monthly charges rather than maintain sufficient balances to cover them, you would want a bank with low charges—so it's not very important to you how the bank calculates your earnings credit. But if you elect to maintain balances to cover the charges, you may

find that a bank with relatively high charges is still your best bet, because of the fact that it has a more advantageous method of giving you credit for your balances.

Obviously, it doesn't make sense to choose a bank solely on costs and credits. There are more important criteria: Convenience, a good relationship with your banker, etc. But once you've selected your bank and understand how the credits and charges on your account are figured, you have the knowledge you need to handle your account to your advantage. For example, if you have traditionally had large balances, you have two options: You can keep just enough to cover what you normally run in charges, but not much more. In fact, you can work with the bank to get your excess funds switched into a savings account that will earn interest.

Or you might use the fact that you have substantial balances whose earnings generously cover your charges to seek special treatment from the bank: A better interest rate on your next loan, perhaps, or even a couple of tickets to the bank's box at the football or basketball games. If you have the flexibility, you might use more bank services. Unless you make use of those credits in some way, they are lost. Once you know how your bank balances are handled, you can make sure it's for your own best interests.

LIFO vs. FIFO: Choosing an Inventory Account System

SWITCHING TO LIFO

For companies whose costs for raw materials and components are rising—and will probably continue to rise—consider the switch from FIFO (first-in, first-out) to LIFO (last-in, first-out). It will save tax money.

How it works: Suppose a manufacturer has raw material cost of 40 cents per unit and sells the product for 80 cents per unit. Gross profit: 40 cents. Then material cost moves up to 50 cents and the selling price is raised to $1.

But there's still some 40-cent raw material in

inventory. Under FIFO, the material bought first (at 40 cents) would be used first. This would produce a gross profit of 60 cents: $1 selling price less 40 cents material cost. So there's a large apparent increase in gross profit, but much of it results from higher inventory values caused by inflation. The company pays income taxes on these higher profits.

Under LIFO, the material bought last would be used first. Gross profit would be 50 cents per unit ($1 selling price less 50 cents material cost). LIFO means lower reported profits and lower income taxes.

Background: To understand FIFO, visualize a factory receiving raw materials and components at the front door. They move along an assembly line and then the finished goods are shipped out the back door. The raw materials received first are used first.

LIFO, by contrast, is like a coal pile. Arriving shipments of coal are dumped on top of the pile and taken off the top, too. Coal delivered in the morning may be used in the afternoon; meanwhile, the coal at the bottom of the pile won't be used for a long time—if at all.

There's another difference. With LIFO, the older and lower-cost material remains in inventory. Thus, the inventory value shown on the balance sheet will be understated in an inflationary period.

Who should use it: LIFO isn't right for every company, but it probably should be considered by companies that expect material cost to continue rising and never drop.

Keep these points in mind:

• Changes in accounting methods normally require consent of IRS. The consent is pretty much automatic for the change from FIFO to LIFO. However, it's very difficult to get consent to change back. If your company makes the change, be prepared to stick with it.

• If the company uses the LIFO method in filing its tax returns, it must also use LIFO in compiling its financial statements.

• If market value of inventory drops below cost, LIFO doesn't permit writing down inventory to market value. (FIFO does.) And in the year of changing to LIFO, it might be necessary to write some inventory up, if it was written down in previous years.

STAYING WITH FIFO

LIFO is an effective way to reduce taxes and improve cash flow—this is important—in an inflationary environment.

But LIFO does something else which isn't good for many companies. It creates an artificially low inventory valuation. Reason: At the time of the switchover, the firm's inventories in effect are frozen at the then existing level. They are carried in "layers" of historical cost on the books. Increases in inventory thereafter are brought in as new layers.

LIFO thus reduces not only the income statement but the balance sheet as well. This combination makes it tough for some firms, especially smaller, growing ones.

When companies go to the bank for a loan, the banker looks at the bottom line. In this case, he sees smaller profits. He also sees a smaller net worth and working capital. Thus, LIFO can have the effect of reducing a company's creditworthiness. And credit is the lifeblood of a company that is expanding and finding it difficult to keep up with increasing receivables, payables, and inventories.

LIFO tends to lock firms into very tight Internal Revenue Service restrictions and requirements. The general rule that applies is simple: Whatever you do for tax purposes, you also have to do for accounting purposes.

That means firms can't supplement the LIFO statement by giving the banker another set of so-called "real" figures showing inventories at replacement value or average cost. Nor can they send to their own executives a report showing real cost of goods sold. If so, IRS can take the firm off LIFO.

The penalty: For tax purposes, the firm will have to go back to FIFO, average cost, or some other method that values the inventory nearer market cost. That can hurt badly if the company isn't in a position to product the increased taxes that will result.

Remember: From a tax standpoint, LIFO is a form of tax deferral. At some point or another, the taxes on the increased value of the inventories will have to be paid. The question that always has to be considered in thinking about LIFO is the timing of these payments. Possible trigger: A drop in inventories. If a reduction in the level of inventories occurs from one year to the next, this in effect forces out an old "layer" (or layers) of inventory purchased at low prices several years before. Bad results:

• Paying up the taxes on the gain in value can be very costly.

Example: A small company gets a big order at the end of the year that would reduce its year-end inventory sharply. It knows it can't replace the inventory for several months because of supply shortages. But dipping down into one or two old inventory layers will trigger extra taxes. Is that a sufficient reason for the company to turn down the substantial order?

• Caution: LIFO can be very rough on companies that are in volatile industries, where there are apt to be sharp runups and rundowns in inventory levels.

Another LIFO timing trap: Deferred tax has to be paid after the firm has grown from a very small firm and is in a higher tax bracket. Warning: If and when the business is sold, the tax finally comes due. (Though not if it's a tax-free exchange of stock.)

Other LIFO negatives that make FIFO a more attractive choice:

• For companies growing at a steady but slow pace, LIFO usually provides only a one-time saving. First year gives substantial savings but after that they are minimal.

• Bookkeeping is expensive, especially for small companies.

• Artificial nature of the LIFO inventory data makes it harder for the average executive to rely on financial reports to match cost with price. As a result, he falls back on hunches and thus makes mistakes.

Source: Mary A. Mead, partner, Seidman & Seidman, Grand Rapids, MI, and Edward Mendlowitz, Siegel & Mendlowitz, 310 Madison Ave., New York 10017.

Monitoring Financial Strength

Most companies are careful about their costs, profit margins, and capital investments. But they have only a vague notion of how financially strong they are. Key: Monitor the few simple and basic ratios and compare them with financial standards.

In most companies there are three main elements to watch:

• Liquidity—the ability to pay debts as they come due.

• Leverage—the mix between debt and equity capital in the business.

• Profit—the overall effectiveness of the business firm.

When all three of these elements are strong, a firm can withstand occasional setbacks and take advantage of good opportunities. If it is weak in one area, strength in the other two can make up for it.

Essential ratios to watch:

• Liquidity. (1) Current ratio: Current assets ÷ Current liabilities; (2) Quick ratio: (Cash + Receivables) ÷ Current liabilities. (3) Liquidity ratio: Cash ÷ Current liabilities.

• Leverage. Asset ratio: Total assets ÷ Total liabilities.

• Profit. Return on Investment (ROI): Annual net profit ÷ Equity.

How to analyze the numbers:

Statement ($ millions)

	1979	1980
Cash (incl. liquid investments)	$ 4.2	$ 5.1
Accounts receivable	8.8	11.6
Current assets	28.8	37.5
Total assets	39.4	52.5
Current liabilities	9.6	20.3
Total liabilities	20.2	31.7
Equity	19.2	20.8
Profit for the year	2.8	3.5
Sales for the year	55.0	72.0

Ratios

	1979	1980
Current ratio	3.00	1.85
Quick ratio	1.35	0.82
Liquidity ratio	0.44	0.25
Asset ratio	1.95	1.66
ROI	14.60%	16.80%

The ratios show an excellent level of profit but a significant drop in liquidity and increased leverage.

Final step: Compare ratios to accepted standards applied to most companies (except financial institutions and utilities):

Current ratio—2.0   Asset ratio—2.75
Quick ratio—1.0   ROI—12%
Liquidity ratio—.4

Source: *Analyzing Financial Statements* by James E. Kristy, Books of Business, Box 113-A, Buena Park, CA 90621.

Strategies for Business Slowdowns

• Watch for warnings from government economists and scale down the basis of estimates for corporate federal income tax payments even if the effects of a recession are not yet apparent to the company.

• Eliminate or reduce, where possible, fixed charges. Example: Under a percentage lease, there is an automatic reduction if the "measuring rod" dips (that is, rent declines if sales dip). Monitor all such arrangements and adjust payments accordingly.

Reduce or omit dividend payments. In addition to smaller profits to be shared with stockholders, such a change constitutes documented fear of the consequences of recession and is an acceptable defense against any imposition of the accumulated earnings tax by the Internal Revenue Service.

• Consider a switch to the Asset Depreciation Range system (ADR). It permits a corporation to adjust its depreciation each year according to income. The company then can decide annually on the depreciation rates to be applied to assets acquired during that year. This may be 20% higher or lower than the normal guidelines for an asset. In a poor income year, when deductions are not needed, use of this system would allow part of the depreciation deduction to be saved for a higher-income year.

• Instead of making cash outlays for new equipment, evaluate the merits of repairing the old. Reason: Repairs are deductible if they really are aimed at maintaining equipment in its original operating condition. They are *not* deductible if they substantially increase the life or usefulness of assets. Consider the trade-off between a present repair deduction and higher depreciation deductions in the future if new equipment is bought.

• Avoid the temptation to buy attractively priced used equipment. Unless new equipment is bought, accelerated depreciation methods, such as a double declining balance, may not be used in all future years. In addition, part of the investment credit will be unavailable. Another potential problem with used gear: Very likely a casualty-loss deduction would be denied because the requirement of suddenness for a casualty loss may be unprovable.

• Think one step beyond the sale of business property that is not being used because of the recession. It can mean a depreciation recapture that will increase taxes in the year of sale.

• Time the company's expenditures to avoid deductions in years when they aren't needed. Examples: Repainting the plant, refurbishing executive offices, advertising.

• Protect the compensation of key executives. Problem: Poor business means that deductions for executive compensation are likely to be disallowed as unreasonable by IRS. Defense: Accumulate data to prove that the officers aren't responsible for the bad showing. Show that they actually do more work than ever because of the dismissal of other executives. Show, too, that more work is required of them in order to develop new sources of income. Another angle: Show that competitors are doing even worse in the recession because they don't have these same valuable executives.

• Review the stock-option program. In bad times, stock options actually provide a negative incentive. Employees who find the options useless because the stock is purchasable on the market below the option price may move. Alternatives: (1) Non-cash incentives (such as a new title) or (2) inclusion in an executive profit-sharing plan.

• Change the company's retirement program to a deferred profit-sharing plan. Payouts would be at the normal retirement age. When business is bad, the profits which must be contributed to the fund automatically are lessened or are eliminated entirely.

• Review employee fringe-benefit plans. Often they've been adopted as incentives or devices to counter what competitors may have been offering. But if business is off and employees are nervous about their jobs, there probably won't be much objection to discontinuance of educational reimbursement plans, funding of the workers' softball team, or other nonessential fringes.

• To raise cash for operating expenses, maturing bonds, etc., enter into a sale-and-leaseback arrangement for buildings or major equipment. This can also improve the appearance of the balance sheet, which is important to bankers and trade creditors.

• Reduce interest on bond indebtedness. Try to recapitalize from bonds into stock. Since this can pose a tax problem to bondholders, consider a tax-free recapitalization from the existing bonds into other bonds of the same principal amount, bearing much lower interest rates. This offer could be made attractive to the present stockholders by adding features to the new bonds, such as making them convertible or having stock warrants accompany them.

• Review the company's charitable contributions policy. The deduction is limited to 5% of income, not sales. Caution: Declining or nonexistent profits could create a serious impact in this area.

• Recession probably means firing some employees, who will then claim unemployment insurance. The payments may seriously affect the company's unemployment insurance rate. Considerations: Drop people who will have the smallest benefit claims against the company's account, persons who are likely to find other work first, those with the lowest compensation or the shortest working time with the company. Recommended: Audit claims against the company's account carefully. What to look for: Were the claimants really trying to find work? Were they fired for cause? Such reasons could delay or even disqualify the payments of claims which may hurt the company's state-tax rate.

• Perhaps the corporation hasn't had a loss in many years. Get familiar with the loss-carryover rules and opportunities.

• If the corporation has a substantial loss, management now may have something very desirable to sell which is more marketable than its inventory or other assets—a net-operating-loss carryover. There's little to risk in selling a company so that another corporation can use the carryover. Problems with the IRS about the allowance of the carryovers are the buyer's headache, not the seller's.

• Bad-debt write-offs are deductible only in the year that a debt actually becomes bad, not when the company is prepared to recognize that worthlessness exists. So by year-end, be certain to see whether there has been an identifiable event which would set up the timing for a claimed tax deduction.

Analyzing the Balance Sheet: Four Simple Ratios to Use

Few firms use the information available on their balance sheets to best advantage. The ratios described here help managers to evaluate their company's financial postiion, as well as to compare the company with others in the same field (assuming, of course, that their financial data are available).

$$\frac{\text{Allowance for Depreciation}}{\text{Gross Plant and Equipment}}$$

This ratio gives an approximation of the age of the company's plant—the higher the ratio, the more fully depreciated the plant. Thus, if Company A's ratio is 0.75, and Company B's is 0.5, it can be assumed that Company B has a more modern plant.

This ratio excludes land, which isn't depreciable. Also, care should be taken to make certain that both companies use the same depreciation method, and similar asset life.

$$\frac{\text{Net Plant, Property \& Equipment}}{\text{Long-Term Debt}}$$

It is usually assumed that a company finances current working capital requirements with short-term loans, and its physical plant through long-term financing. As long as this ratio exceeds 1:1, the depreciated value of the plant is more than the long-term debt. If the ratio falls below this, the company is using long-term debt funds to finance current operations. This situation is considered a questionable financial practice.

$$\frac{\text{Long-Term Debt}}{\text{Total Capitalization}^*}$$

This ratio is commonly referred to as the debt-equity ratio. This is probably the most important indication of a firm's long-term financial health. The higher the ratio, the more vulnerable the firm is to unfavorable swings in business, because interest and amortization payments absorb an ever greater portion of both available earnings and cash flow.

In evaluating this ratio, lenders look for a maximum value, depending on the nature of the firm's business. Financial companies, for instance (e.g., leasing, personal finance), can be comfortable with a 75% debt, 25% equity ratio. In these companies, the assets are mainly pledged to lenders, and cash flow isn't subject to the swings found in industrial firms. Industrial companies, on the other hand, normally look to 40% debt, 60% equity as maximum.

$$\frac{\text{Common Shareholders' Equity}}{\text{Common Shares Outstanding}}$$

The result of this ratio is the book value per share of the outstanding common stock, one of the conventional factors in the stock valuation.

In evaluating two firms, one of which purchases its assets, while the other leases the same types of assets, the balance sheet and income statement of the firm that leases should be adjusted to a purchase basis. Then the two firms can be compared on an equal basis.

*Long-term debt plus shareholders' equity.
Source: Merwin Leven, The Flintkote Co., 1351 Washington Blvd., Stamford, CT 06902.

Business Diagnosis Formulas Every Manager Should Know

Here are a series of ways to analyze a firm's capital position if it has been declining and you want to identify the causes and find correctives.

• Be sure there are no changes in the statements you are studying that are attributable to changes in accounting practices, i.e., change in inventory valuation from LIFO to FIFO.

• When comparing two different time periods, be sure to allow for any seasonal factors, and always use the same basis for measurement. If an average inventory figure is used, calculate turnover in one period; don't use opening inventory as a basis in the following period.

• Compare trends rather than just one period. A decline in working capital between two periods could be an extraordinary occurrence. But a trend of a year or more indicates the probability of a basic problem.

Current ratio (working capital ratio): In the analysis of working capital, this is the basic analytic ratio used:

$$\frac{\text{Current Assets}}{\text{Current Liabilities}}$$

This ratio describes a firm's ability to meet its short-term liabilities. As a rule of thumb, a 2:1 ratio is considered desirable.

Quick ratio (acid test ratio): Measures a company's immediate liquidity:

$$\frac{\text{Cash } + \text{ Marketable Securities } + \text{ Accts. Recvble.}}{\text{Current Liabilities}}$$

A ratio of at least 1:1 indicates that the firm is in a highly liquid position.

The following ratios measure the factors that make up working capital, and are useful in determining the reasons for changes in a firm's working capital position.

Cash to sales ratio: This ratio can be expressed either as a percentage derived from cash divided by net sales, or a percentage derived from dividing net sales by cash. The latter gives dollars-of-sales per dollar-of-cash. Either figure permits measurement of the amount of cash balances a company requires to maintain its sales level. In computing, excess cash should not be included in the calculation. Seasonal factors must be considered in a comparison of different periods.

Days' receivables outstanding:

$$\frac{\text{Accounts Receivable}}{\text{Net Sales}} \times 30^*$$

As the days' receivables outstanding increases, so does the working capital needed by

*If using monthly sales. When using annual sales, the multiplier would be 365.

the firm. An increase can also indicate that a greater number of the firm's customers are becoming delinquent in paying, or that sales efforts have resulted in longer terms than usual being given on sales.

This ratio can also be applied to accounts payable, where an increase in days' outstanding would indicate a reduction in working capital requirements. A decrease could indicate a change in suppliers' terms, or an overzealous accounts payable department, which is paying invoices long before they are due.

Inventory turnover:

$$\frac{\text{Net Sales}}{\text{Inventory}}$$

This is the most widely used and most important of all the ratios used in analyzing working capital.

In most firms, inventory represents the single largest working capital item. Its efficient control is usually a major factor in the profitability of these firms.

The higher the number of inventory turns per year, the greater the efficiency of inventory management. The efficient firm is reducing the amount of inventory required in order to maintain sales volume. A decrease in inventory turnover is a warning that it's time to examine existing inventory for slow-moving or obsolete items. Or it could be time to check for overstocked conditions.

The use of the above ratios gives management insight into the key relationships that exist between the operating and the financial aspects of the firm. Aim: Using these relationships to increase efficiency and profitability.

How Much Working Capital Is Enough for Growth?

Is your company's working-capital position strong enough to support an increase in sales volume—such as when a major sales campaign is planned?

• The first item to consider: How much inventory increase will be necessary to ensure that products are available? Use the inventory turnover ratio. If sales volume had been $1,000,000, and inventory levels averaged $250,000, then inventory turns over four times a year (net sales divided by inventory).

If the sales budget calls for a sales increase to $1,250,000, then inventory would have to increase by $62,500, to $312,500. Calculation: $1,250,000 ÷ $312,500 = 4.

• Accounts receivable also can be expected to increase as sales volume increases. By using the *days' receivables outstanding ratio*, one can estimate the increase that can be expected.

If a firm has $1,000,000 in sales, and average receivables of $150,000, it has a receivable collection period of 54.75 days ([accounts receivable ÷ net sales] × 365). If volume is increased to $1,250,000, receivables increase by $37,000, to $187,500. Calculation: ($187,500 ÷ $1,250,000) × 365 = 54.75 days.

• As sales increase, so does the amount of cash the company must have on hand for general operating purposes. This is usually expressed in the cash to sales ratio. If average cash balances of $100,000 were needed to maintain a $1,000,000 sales level, then $125,000 would be needed if sales increased to $1,250,000.

• Offsetting some of these increases is the fact that, as sales rise, so do accounts payable. These are measured in the same way as accounts receivable. So, if 36.5 days' payables outstanding is normal, a sales increase from $1,000,000 to $1,250,000 will increase payables by $25,000.

To summarize, we find that an additional $100,000 of working capital is necessary to support a $250,000 increase in sales:

Cash	$25,000
Inventory	62,500
Accounts receivable	37,500
Accounts payable	(25,000)
Total	$100,000

If the company pays 10% interest for short-term borrowing, then an additional expense of $10,000, pre-tax, should be considered in determining the cost of the sales increase.

The financial planning that goes along with the sales planning must provide for the $100,000 in extra funds. Otherwise, the firm can find that it doesn't have sufficient cash on hand to pay its current obligations. The increased cash flow from sales usually cannot be expected until one or two months after goods are sold, and all suppliers and employees must be paid before then.

Also useful: Construct a chart that can be used to estimate when these funds will be required, so that the firm's financial officer may have them available when needed.

	Month 1	Month 2
Cash	$12,500	$12,500
Accounts receivable		37,500
Inventory	62,500	
Accounts payable	(25,000)	
Funds Required	$50,000	$50,000

In Month 1: Inventory must be increased to provide goods for the sales program. Payables are also increased as raw materials are purchased for manufacture of goods. The cash item is then estimated to increase equally in both months.

In Month 2: When the goods are sold, the accounts receivable will increase, and the remaining cash is then committed.

If, along with increased sales, it is possible to improve operations by increasing inventory turnover, or by reducing days' receivables outstanding, then the cost of the increase in sales can be reduced accordingly.

Important: Costs incurred for additional working capital for a sales promotion campaign are a direct cost of that campaign.

How to Use Break-Even Analysis

If a competitor forces a 5% price cut in a product line, how many more units must the company sell to earn the same profit? And how many units of a new product must be sold before it can break even?

The way to solve these and other profit/cost/volume problems is by using simple break-even analysis techniques.

Key to analysis: Identify costs that vary with volume (variable costs) and separate them from those that are unaffected by volume (fixed costs).

• Variable costs. Direct labor, raw materials, supplies, and selling expenses based on volume are all a direct function of volume. If it costs $10

in direct labor to produce one unit, then it should cost $100 to produce 10 units. The same formula applies to raw materials and supplies.

• Fixed costs. Supervisory labor, real estate taxes, fire and casualty insurance are all examples of costs that are unaffected by volume changes. A $10,000 real estate tax is considered an unchanging expense if one to 100 units are produced.

• Variable-fixed costs. Not entirely dependent on volume, but are not entirely fixed. Power costs, for instance. Where there is a demand charge plus an energy charge, the demand segment can be treated as a fixed cost, while the energy portion is treated as a variable. Telephone, maintenance, and some other costs have a fixed portion plus a variable portion. They must be examined and allocated out on as realistic a basis as practical.

PRODUCT COST DATA

Fixed Costs	Amount
Real estate taxes	$10,000
Supervisory labor and administration	3,000
Insurance	2,000
Other	5,000
Total Fixed Costs	$20,000

Variable Costs	$ per unit
Direct labor	$1.50
Raw materials	3.00
Supplies	.50
Total Manufacturing	$5.00
Selling Commission	1.00
Variable Costs Per Unit	$6.00

Setting a price: To sell the product in this example at $10 per unit, $4 per unit is available to offset fixed costs:

Selling price/unit	$10
Less: Variable costs/unit	6
Available for fixed costs and profit unit	$ 4

Figuring break-even volume: To recover the $20,000 in fixed costs, 5,000 units would have to be sold.

$$F/(S - V) = B$$
$$\$20,000/(\$10 - 6) = 5,000 \text{ units}$$

F = Total fixed costs; S = Selling price; V = Variable cost per unit; B = Break-even volume.

How to figure the effect of price change: Use the same break-even formula to ascertain the effect of changes in selling price on the break-even volume. Example: If the selling price of product goes down to $8 a unit, the break-even volume will be 10,000 units. $20,000/ ($8-$6).

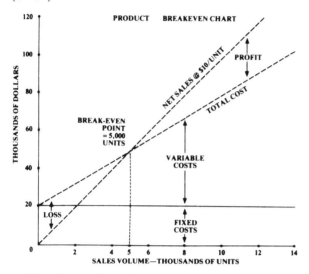

The above chart shows only the $10 per unit sales price. Other prices can be drawn on the chart—or overlaid.

Projecting sharp increases in volume: Be careful not to exceed the capacity limits assumed in the fixed cost determination. If it is necessary to pay overtime, additional supervisory or administrative costs, or rent additional production or warehouse space, a new fixed cost level is reached. That figure should be used in the break-even calculations.

Note: In determining both fixed and variable costs in periods of high interest rates, it can be useful to include interest on plant facilities in the fixed costs and changes in working capital in the variable costs.

Profiting from 'Bank Float'

Most companies underestimate their checking account balances by at least 30%, according to a consultant in cash management. The corporation doesn't estimate the float and doesn't know at any given moment what checks haven't cleared yet. Learning to analyze and monitor the float can mean extra earnings with little effort.

What to do: Make a six-month study of outgoing checks to major suppliers (chances are 80% of dollars paid go to 20% of vendors). Check each one's float pattern, then estimate how long new checks will take to clear, have money on deposit only as needed.

When Bank Must Honor Bounced Check

It could be possible to collect a bounced check if the bank waits more than 36 hours to reject it. The Uniform Commercial Code provides that a check presented to a bank for payment today must be rejected by midnight tomorrow or the bank has to make good on it, even if the account has insufficient funds.
Woodform Bank. v. *Blake*, Ky. App., 3/11/77.

Faster Use of Incoming Checks

● Bank lock box. Have customers send checks to bank's postbox. Saves time lost in sorting incoming mail, making up deposits, getting them to bank. Also, banks pick up checks to process them several times a day. Some banks even do it around the clock.

● Concentration accounts. Customers send payments to the company's local office for deposit in a branch of the company's bank. Headquarters' account is credited the same day.

● Mail pouches. Best for distant customers who write big checks drawn on their home banks. The check is sent directly to the local airport in a special container. A messenger service picks up the check at the destination and takes it to the interbank clearinghouse, crediting the company's account quickly.

● Wire service. Useful for moving large sums

from bank to bank when the company's bank does not have local branches located near the regional offices.

• Easy way often overlooked: Make a copy of each check as soon as it is received. Reason: Checks can then be deposited immediately in the bank without waiting for processing. One company that does this has eliminated costly overtime caused by heavy payments on the first of the month.

• Useful technique: Use customer's remittance envelope, which already includes name, postmark date, to record check number, invoice number, control number, discount data, attachments, and other information that must be posted later. Meanwhile, check is in the bank.

Depositing Canadian Checks

Double-check the discount taken by U.S. banks when checks from Canadian customers are deposited. Common problem: Discount is taken when checks are credited to company's account. Then checks go to foreign desk of the bank, which takes the discount again and sends along a debit memo.

Best Way to Get a Loan from Your Bank

• Prepare a loan proposal. Include amount of capital needed, type of loan (long- or short-term, revolving credit line), terms (secured, unsecured, endorsed, guaranteed), desired interest rate, and proposed pay-back schedule.

• Clearly explain purpose of loan.

• Show company fundamentals. Include cash flow and operating projections, balance sheets and income statements for past three years, collateral, inventory, fixed assets, life insurance, marketable securities, listing and aging of accounts receivable.

• Provide related nonfinancial information.

Show business strategy, data on company's industry and its position in that industry. Also: List trade suppliers for references.

Some Banks Are Better Than Others for Getting a Small Business Loan

Try taking your firm's loan request to a bank that is working with the Small Business Administration's new secondary market program. About 1,400 banks* are now doing it. The new program greatly multiplies the bank's lending ability, increasing the possibility that your company's loan will get considered.

How the secondary market works: Bank gets a line of credit from the SBA. Ninety percent of each loan made to a company under SBA program is guaranteed by the U.S. government. The bank then sells that 90% portion (or packages several loans and sells them together) to a broker. Result: Bank has that amount of money back again to lend.

The broker, in turn, sells the loan to an insurance company or pension fund, which picks up a 100% government-guaranteed instrument that pays 9% or more.

*For names of local banks that are in SBA program, write Office of Public Information, Small Business Administration, 1441 L St. N.W., Washington, DC 20416.

Tricks Banks Play with Interest Rates

Banks teach their loan officers a number of strategies to get an extra ¼% or even ½% from borrowers. Recognize some of their tricks:

• Doing the negotiating at the bank, which is familiar territory to the banker, intimidating to the borrower.

• Not mentioning the rate at all, but simply filling it in on the note.

• ''Since you need the money today, let's write

it up at X%. Then we can talk later about changing it.'' The banker hopes you'll never bring it up again. He certainly won't.

• Flat statement: ''The rate for this type of loan is X%.'' (Never true except for small consumer loans. There is always room to negotiate.)

• Postponing the rate discussion as long as possible, hoping borrower will weaken under deadline pressure.

• Ego-building. Bank president stops by during negotiations.

• Talking constantly about how little the interest costs after taxes. And comparing it with finance company rates, secondary mortgage rates, or the cost of equity capital.

The banker looks at the company's account as a package, including loans, average balances maintained, and fees for service. Borrower options: Trade off higher average balances for a lower interest rate on borrowings, or vice versa.

The borrower is at a disadvantage because he probably negotiates a loan only once a year or less, while the banker spends full time at it. So prepare carefully for negotiations.

Good tactics for the borrower:

• Ask interest rate question early—in your office, not his. Don't volunteer suggestions.

• Negotiate everything as a package—rate, repayment schedule, collateral, compensating balances. Banker's strategy will be to try to nail down everything else and then negotiate interest rate when the borrower has no more leverage and no room to maneuver.

• Be prepared with an expression of surprise and shock, even rehearse it before a mirror. React that way when the banker mentions the interest rate, no matter what the figure is.

Source: Lawrence T. Jilk, Jr., executive vice president, National Bank of Boyertown, Pa., in *The Journal of Commercial Bank Lending.*

Mistakes Borrowers Make

Desperate as a company may be for money, it's extremely important not to give the lender more security than absolutely necessary.

A loan officer obviously needs some kind of a lien to show his superiors. The less the security interest, the stronger the relationship with the lender will be.

• Key points: (1) The lender is in effect a partner. (2) The more given in security, the greater the commitment the borrower should seek.

• Common mistake borrowers make: Automatically agreeing to the lender's loan request. It isn't always necessary to say yes or no. There is usually something in between. It's to the company's advantage to explore all possibilities.

• Example: Offer a lien on inventory but not receivables; on plant, furniture, fixtures (all requiring time to dispose of); on contract rights; or some combination of these.

• The worst thing to sign over is receivables. They mean quick cash. They are also the easiest thing for the lender to collect. The lender collects—and the business is ruined.

• Inventory, however, is good for a lien. Even though it may turn out to be virtually worthless, it looks good in the loan file for the loan officer to show his superiors.

On the other hand, resist giving *all* inventory as security. Some can be rapidly converted into receivables, often by selling to a competitor.

From borrower's standpoint, it is best to offer things that will take months, even years, for lender to collect. That time may mean the life-and-death difference for the company. Even if it is necessary to sign over receivables, try to sign over only a percentage of them, retaining the rest to keep business running.

When lender asks for a personal guarantee, be careful not to sign away everything—and don't have your wife as a co-signer.

Here's where you need a smart lawyer:

Wording: There's a difference between a guarantee of payment and a guarantee of collectibility. If you guarantee payment, the lender is legally entitled to get his money fast. In some cases, one also forfeits the right to countersue the lender when there is a serious misunderstanding. A guarantee of collectibility, on the other hand, requires the lender to take all of the company's assets and liquidate them before coming after you. In a privately owned company, this gives one valuable time and may save personal assets so that the firm can survive and start over.

• Don't overlook the possibility of limited

guarantees. Think of the guarantee as basically an indication of good faith. Agree to perhaps $50,000 on a $1 million loan. But don't be deceived by lenders' disclaimers about enforcing personal guarantees. When push comes to shove, they will.

Typically, borrowers are enthusiastic, sometimes overoptimistic. Even if company avoids serious trouble or bankruptcy, realize that over a five-year period, 40%-50% of companies have a bad year. Maybe a big customer goes sour and it takes time to recoup that loss. Or payments start coming in late and cash flow becomes a problem.

The only defense is a continuing frank, friendly relationship with lenders. The best time to take banker out to lunch is when things are going well. Always keep lenders informed about business and upcoming problems. The uninformed lender tends to overreact in times of surprise or crisis. The better he understands your business (the fatter his file, etc.), the stronger the case he can make for your company with his superiors. It's harder to say no to someone you know.
Source: Arthur Malman, Esq., Brown & Malman, 299 Park Ave., New York 10017.

Alternatives to Borrowing from Bank

A company may be able to borrow more from a commercial finance or factoring company than it can from a bank. Of course, the interest rate will be higher, too.

Here's how such organizations work and how your company can borrow from them:

Commercial finance companies: A company might borrow 75% to 85% of the value of receivables (excluding those that are past due). Or it might borrow 50% to 70% of the value of raw material inventory or work in process. Most commercial finance companies don't like to lend on plant and equipment, but a few specialize in this activity.

They usually take a lien on the assets they lend against. Banks, however, generally make unsecured loans based on the company's general credit and balance-sheet strength. The bank probably won't lend more than 50% or 75% of the company's net worth, but the finance company may lend several times the net worth if sufficient assets are pledged to secure the loan.

Commerical financing is usually done on a revolving basis. That means that the loan is reduced as receivables are collected or other assets liquidated. Then it can be increased again as the pledged assets increase. Some commercial finance companies will consider making three- or five-year term loans secured by plant and equipment if the company is also borrowing on a revolving basis against current assets.

Interest rates usually float—from 3½ to 6 percentage points above bank prime rates. If the same borrower went to the bank, it would probably pay 1 to 2 points over prime, but the difference is less than it seems. Banks usually ask for compensating balances, so the bank's effective interest rate is higher than its stated rate. And the bank may insist on lending for 60 or 90 days, even though all the money isn't needed for that long. The commercial finance company calculates its interest charges daily.

A possible way to get a lower rate: Ask the commercial finance company to bring in a bank to take half the loan. If the finance company charges four points over prime and the bank two points over prime, the borrower pays a blended rate of three points over prime. Sometimes the entire transaction can be done in the bank's name, so that nobody knows the company is borrowing from a commercial finance company.

Such knowledge can generate problems. If a company uses commercial financing, some people will think it's in financial trouble. This is less true than it used to be. Some very large listed companies use commercial financing for seasonal needs. (Usually a company's customers aren't notified of the commercial financing. But Dun & Bradstreet will pick the information up, and the lien on the assets will probably be entered in public records.)

Factoring: In this approach, a factoring company signs on to perform a package service—for lending, credit management, and protection against credit losses. How it works:
• The factor makes credit investigations of the company's customers.
• The factor takes over all approved receiv-

ables and pays the company face value for them a few days after the due date. This is called maturity factoring.

• The factor assumes all collection problems and all credit losses on approved receivables. Thus, the factor, in effect, provides credit insurance to the company.

• The factor charges a fee—usually between ¾% and 2%—of receivables collected.

• In addition, the factor is willing to lend money to the company by paying for the receivables in advance of the due date. This is called discount factoring. The factor will discount receivables by subtracting from their value an interest amount (usually an annual rate 2½-4 percentage points over bank prime rate).

• The company's customer is notified that the factor has acquired his obligation and he is asked to send payment directly to the factor.

Factoring is commonly used in the textile and apparel fields, where there is no stigma attached to it. It is also being used somewhat more in furniture, shoes, plastics, and hardware and by wholesalers and importers.

How to find commercial finance companies and factors: Write to National Commercial Finance Conference, One Penn Plaza, New York 10001, for a free copy of *Roster of Membership*. It includes names and addresses of over 150 commercial finance and factoring firms throughout the country.

Business Loans from Insurance Companies

Don't overlook the possibility of long-term borrowing from an insurance company. Companies of all sizes are doing it. Insurance lenders usually don't care whether a company is public or not.

What insurance company lenders look for: They examine financial statements and credit standing very closely. Most want a borrower to have at least $5 million of net worth, but some will consider lending to a company with a net worth of $2 million.

Size of loan: Many don't like to lend less than

$3 million. A few will make $1 million loans. (Very few go down to $500,000.)

Some of the largest insurance companies are the best for smaller companies to talk to. Prudential, biggest in the world, has lending offices in 12 cities. It has loan specialists actively looking for companies that want to borrow. Equitable, third largest, is looking actively, too. Both will lend sums from $750,000 up.

Some companies go through investment bankers. Wall Street firms can place a loan faster because they know whom to call. Also, they may get slightly better terms for the borrower by shopping around.

But those Wall Street firms' fees run at least $40,000, often much more, when the deal is completed. (They usually get expenses plus a few thousand if it isn't.)

To avoid fees, borrowers can go directly to insurance companies.

Here's how to do it: Have an informal exploratory conversation first, to get an idea what's possible before spending time and money on a detailed loan proposal. Most insurance companies, but not all, are willing to have this kind of informal preliminary talk, maybe even on the telephone.

Every major insurance company has a mortgage department and a bond department. Consider talking to either or both, depending on your company's needs.

Mortgage loans collateral: Insurance companies are interested in lending on factories, warehouses, and large retail stores. They don't like lending on a group of small stores or fast-food outlets. They especially don't like single-purpose buildings (not easily usable by other types of businesses).

They very rarely will lend more than 75% of value. Mortgage loan maturity: 20 to 25 years, occasionally longer. Usually the lender has the right to call (demand repayment) at the end of 15 years. The borrower has to pay the legal fees of the lender.

If there's already a mortgage on the property, insurance companies probably won't lend more and take a second mortgage. They might consider a larger loan that pays off the existing one, but this could cost prepayment penalties and maybe a higher interest rate. Few insurance companies will lend mortgage sums of less than $1 million.

Unsecured private placement loans: Insurance company bond departments make unsecured loans only to companies with good credit standing. They usually require agreement that plant and equipment won't be pledged to some other lender.

Loans of this type are negotiated directly between the borrower (perhaps with a broker involved) and one or a few insurance companies. They are not registered with the Securities & Exchange Commission as a public offering (hence the use of the term *private placement*).

Insurance companies usually want borrower to have at least $2 or $3 of net worth (equity capital) for every $1 borrowed. Sometimes, but very rarely, they will consider a heavier debt percentage, or a weaker credit. Then they may want stock or warrants together with a high rate of interest.

Typical terms: Final maturity 12 to 15 years; repayments starting in third or fourth year and spread equally over remaining life; interest rates 9%-11%; borrower pays lender's legal fees.

Borrowing Out-of-State

Firms that lend money or sell on credit to customers in another state are bound by that state's maximum interest rate law, even though the lender or selling company has no offices or employees there.

524 F. 38, F. 2d 745, F. 2d 1159, 425 US 943.280.

When Adding New Capital Is a Mistake

Raising the productivity of a company's work force increases its sales and, thus, its profits. But high productivity is especially crucial for the company that is capital-intensive.

An ongoing study of the experiences of 1,800 businesses shows that the worst combination for

a company (in terms of profits) is low productivity and high capital investment.

A company that is very investment-intensive has to keep its productivity high (producing more than $48,000 in sales per employee) if it is to be most profitable. Even then, the company will not be as profitable as the firm with low productivity and low investment.

RELATION OF PRODUCTIVITY TO INVESTMENT INTENSITY

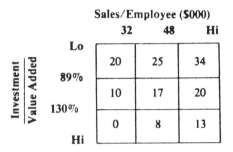

The chart above indicates dollar sales per employee (horizontal line) and (vertical line) the amount of investment it takes to produce one dollar of added value (the amount by which a company upgrades raw material before selling the final product). The numbers within the squares are return on investment. A low-productivity company that is achieving a 20% return on investment will cut its profit rate in half if it increases the intensity of its capital investment by any significant amount.

Source: Dr. Sidney Schoeffler, director, Strategic Planning Institute, 1 Broadway, Cambridge, MA 02142.

Raising Capital Through an ESOP

An Employee Stock Ownership Plan (ESOP) can be the best (or even the only) way for a small, closely held company to raise equity capital. And ESOPs are being actively encouraged by government policy. But consider the disadvantages, too, before starting one.

The pluses:

• The ESOP can borrow money to buy company stock. Company then makes tax-deductible contributions to the ESOP as a profit-sharing plan for employees. The ESOP uses the cash to repay the loan. In effect, company gets a tax deduction for additional capital.

• The ESOP can also buy stock from present stockholders. Example: Buy from estate after a stockholder dies. Or if an owner simply needs money and wants to sell some stock without bringing in an outside interest.

The minuses:

• Government red tape and constantly changing regulations.

• Potential liquidity problems when employees leave or retire and receive their stock. They'll want company or ESOP to buy it back right away. Could be a problem if cash is short.

• Expense of putting a valuation on the stock (and the company) at least once a year.

• Stock ownership is extended outside the family. (But shares are usually voted by management appointee.)

• There's no assurance of better employee attitudes and improved productivity. If employee relations were poor before, they'll probably stay that way.

• Employees may have too many eggs in one basket. If the company gets into real trouble, they might not only lose their jobs but see their retirement nest egg wiped out, too.

For information on ESOPs and TRASOPs, write Employee Stock Ownership Council, 11661 San Vicente Blvd., Los Angeles 90049.
Source: Ron Ludwig, Esq., partner, Ludwig & Curtis, 114 Sansome St., San Francisco 94104.

How to Postpone Estimated Tax Payments

A business may be able to improve its cash position by postponing estimated income tax payments. This works especially well for businesses that earn large profits late in the year.

General rule: Corporations and other businesses must make four estimated income tax payments during the year. The payments usually should total at least 80% of the total tax that is due, or the IRS will assess penalties for underpayment.

The opportunity: But the total estimated payments may be much less than 80% if the business loses money in the early part of the year or makes more than half of its profits in the second half. That's because the rules permit each estimated payment to be based on income earned in the most recent quarter. The estimate does not have to reflect improved profits that are expected later in the year.

Thus, if a business breaks even or loses money in the first half, it doesn't have to pay any estimated tax until the fourth quarter. That payment can be as little as 20% of the estimated tax due for the year. If it breaks even or loses money in the first quarter, it can make only two estimated tax payments, totaling 40% of the tax due, in the third and fourth quarters. Profits in the last two months can be ignored in calculating the estimated payments.
Rev. Rul. 76-563, Letter Rulings 7801005 and 8812040.250.

Legal Ways for a Company to Hold Back Payroll Tax

It's not necessary to pay the entire amount due of corporate payroll taxes (FICA and federal withholding) on deadline (three business days after the 7th, 15th, or 22nd of the month, depending on paydays). Alternative: Hold back 10% of the tax bill for as much as 70 days (only 90% is due immediately). Another possibility: Consider switching paydays. Employers paying on the 15th of the month must deposit taxes by the 18th, but if payday is on the 16th, taxes are not due until the 25th. Caution: Evaluate the risk of unhappy employees if payday is changed.

Paying Employees' FICA Tax Can Save Employer Money

Companies with rapid labor turnover (those hiring large numbers of seasonal employees or women who are working to supplement their family's income) may be able to reduce their Social Security contributions by paying employees net rather than gross salaries.

A net payment method is permitted by the Social Security Act: (1) Company pays 100% of its employees' Social Security contribution instead of 50%. (2) Employees take correspondingly lower salaries. Result: The company's payroll shrinks, so the total amount of Social Security collected to cover the company's employees in the future shrinks, too. Savings are modest, but they more than offset the cost to the company of paying 100% of the Social Security tax due.

Example: A company that adopts the net pay method owes $76 less Social Security for every worker earning $10,000 a year.

Companies with a stable work force may also benefit from the net pay method. However, there's a potential problem. The arrangement does not alter workers' take-home pay, but it does reduce official salary levels. Thus, if a company's fringe benefits are pegged to salary levels, workers may oppose the new system.

In considering net pay, remember that by 1987, Social Security tax will rise to 14.3%, and be paid on maximum salary of $42,000 instead of $22,900. So savings from the net pay method will increase, too.

Source: Michael F. Klein, partner, Price Waterhouse & Co., 153 East 53 St., New York 10022.

Postponing Interest Deductions to Next Year

If this has been a bad year and next year's income will probably be no better, it may be desirable to postpone interest deductions.

How to do it: Debtor reaches agreement with creditor that this year's loan payments are applied to principal. This agreement would override the usual rule that debt payments are applied first to interest, with any remainder going to reduce principal.

Creditor may be willing, because this postpones interest income to next year, just as it postpones interest deduction for the debtor.

Note: It's not permitted to do the reverse and

prepay interest so as to move deductions from next year to this year. Prepaid interest isn't currently deductible.

Mason v. *U.S.*, Dist. Ct., N.D. Cal. 7/13/78.

Are You Overpaying State and Local Taxes?

Correct company tax strategy depends on understanding the allocation formula used to calculate what percentage of a company's federal taxable income should be taxed by state and local governments.

Three factors to consider that relate within and outside the state:
• Sales.
• Payroll.
• Property.

How calculation is made: For each factor, the company's figures for the state are compared with its figures nationally (or internationally). Example: Company has 80% of its property (including inventory) in the state, 60% of its payroll, and 40% of its sales. State tax allocation is 180% (80% + 60% + 40%) divided by 3, or 60%. State taxes are levied on 60% of firm's federal taxable income. Exception: New York State counts sales twice and divides by 4. Results for the same example would be 220% and 55%.

First step in tax planning: Qualify the company to allocate. Usual state criteria is to have at least one other regular place of business (plant, warehouse, or sales office regularly maintained by company employees) in some other state. (No longer necessary in New York under a 1978 law.)

California and Illinois have "throwback rules," meaning that shipments which originate from a plant or warehouse in those states and go to a state where they are not taxed are then taxed in California or Illinois. To get around this: Move finished goods from plants in these "throwback" states to warehouses in non-tax states pending final sale to customers.

Separate sales income from manufacturing income when a large proportion of sales is made to customers located in high tax states such as New York. Reason: Usually, the numerator in state tax allocation formulas is determined by where shipments go rather than where they originate.

How this strategy works: If a company manufactures products in a Texas plant (no income tax) but sells most of its output in New York (or any other high tax state), it could greatly improve the bottom line by setting up two companies: (1) A New York sales company would then buy its product from (2) the Texas manufacturing company, at a price that generates a manufacturing profit in Texas. The New York company would then sell the product for slightly more than it paid, earning a sales profit.

Result: The Texas company's higher manufacturing profits are then beyond the reach of New York State. And even if the New York company's profits are 100% taxable (unlikely, since there would probably be some sales elsewhere), the company's taxable income there is much smaller without the manufacturing profits.

When building or renting new facilities, property and payroll factors become important to tax strategy. Comparative tax burdens of one state versus another become crucial. If one state, for example, has not only an income tax but also a personal property tax on both manufacturing machinery and inventory, it is obviously less appealing than a state that imposes the tax only on inventory. Still more appealing: State that exempts both machinery and inventory. Most attractive: State that has no personal property tax. Avoid states which impose "throwback" taxes.

Another consideration (much more important than generally realized): Level of a state's individual taxes for company officers.

Source: Tax Accountant Stephen J. Epstein, Richard A. Eisner & Co., 380 Madison Ave., New York 10017.

Ways to Show a Credit Bureau Your Company Deserves a Higher Rating

It's not necessary to live with a poor credit rating. Steps may be taken to convince the rating services that your firm deserves an upgrading.

The key is to be aggressive. Tell your story to the services if you believe it has merit. Many of the rating categories overlap—especially in the middle ranges. Thus, your company may easily fit into a higher range than the one it has been assigned. The intangibles, the reasons behind the ratios, make the difference. It's important that you put these factors—quality of management and long-range planning—into the best perspective.

What to do: Keep in touch with the rating services. Make regular presentations using top executives (including the boss). Emphasize how the firm is positioning itself for the future. Explain why store assets may not appear on balance sheets. Help the rating services to know and understand the business. Point out special advantages, such as able leadership and tight cost control program.

Additional pointer: Present future plans as realistic projections. Plot alternatives; discuss management depth, market leadership, and how the firm has taken advantage of its position (if not a leader, can it react quickly to changes).

Hold a practice session to throw unanticipated questions at executives. (Ask your investment banker for help here.) Evasiveness or lack of preparation can hurt you. Also a drawback: Gimmicky accounting techniques. Expect queries about how you're preparing to react to current trends and future economic problems.

Note: The services pride themselves on consistency. If you can show that your ratios compare well with those in the next higher category, you might get a boost. Or, if you're about to be downgraded, stress that your ratios have held steady or are moving up.

The communication shouldn't be one-way. Ask the services for feedback. You may discover that by making a few changes, you can move to a higher category.

Source: *Institutional Investor.*

Inflation Arithmetic

If prices rise 8% a year, they double in 9 years. At 10%, they double in 7.3 years. At 12%, in 6.1 years, and at 15%, in exactly 5 years.

INSURANCE

Alternative to Blue Cross-Blue Shield

Business Interruption Insurance

Insuring Receivables

Company Insurance for Retirees

Life Insurance that Saves Taxes

Little Known Insurance Bonuses

When to Drop Collision Coverage

Insuring a Boat

9

INSURANCE

Before Buying Policy Through a Broker

Insist that he provide a certificate of insurance—a type of "malpractice insurance" for brokers. Make coverage obtained through him contingent on such a certificate. If the broker, through an error, fails to follow through on a "binder" or omits some critical detail which affects the coverage, at least you can collect via the broker's own coverage.

Reducing the Cost of Employee Medical Benefits

Once you grant an employee benefit, it's very hard to take it back. Even if you have no union contract to contend with, a pullback could devastate your employees' morale. How to trim benefit costs without such consequences:

• Announce to your staff that, given escala-

ting medical costs, you've arranged to increase major medical insurance limits to some higher level. If the lifetime level is now $25,000, boost it to $100,000. The higher limit won't cost you a cent, in most cases. All it requires is some negotiation with your insurance carrier. If your insured group is very small (less than a dozen people, say), you may have to push this point hard with the carrier—or you may have to shop for a new carrier. But with a little perseverance, you can get the higher limit with no extra premium payment.

Be aware that, if you wish, you could even get the increase to $250,000 or even unlimited—also with no extra premium. But resist too large a jump; save that for the next go-round.

• Also let your employees know that, due to a decline in profits (if that's the case), you simply must reduce cash outlays. Thus, while they are getting more coverage with the higher limit, you must ask them to pay, say, the first 20% of their medical bills up to some level. Your broker or carrier will advise you of the various insurance formulas and their impact on premium savings.

Resist the temptation to ask the employee to

pay for part of his insurance premium. If he has to pay that money up front, he'll be anxious to "get it back" by trying to stay in the hospital a bit longer, selecting some elective medical treatment that he would otherwise not bother with, etc. If, however, he must pay a small portion of the actual charges rather than the insurance program, he'll be more circumspect.

• Extend the waiting period for new employees to be eligible for medical benefits from 30 days to, say, 90 days, especially in high-turnover jobs. Impact: A decline in premiums. Research shows that many people take a job specifically for the medical benefits—housewives especially. With the longer waiting period you'll eliminate (or sharply reduce) such applications. That will trim not only your present premium but your future ones as well.

• Consider, too, asking employees to pay for all or part of the additional coverage for their dependents. That step alone could cut those insurance costs in half.

Alternatives to Blue Cross-Blue Shield

Blue Cross-Blue Shield is no longer the only game in town. In health benefits, as in every other service a company buys, it makes sense to get bids from other suppliers.

Possible alternatives:

• Group practice plans and independent practice associations, commonly known as Health Maintenance Organizations (HMOs). They will give a company a bid on providing a total health care package for employees, including visits to doctors as well as hospitalization.

• Group practice plans hire doctors on salary, run their own hospitals, have excellent record for keeping costs under control. That's how they can offer more service than Blue Cross at the same or lower rates. (Best known is the Kaiser Foundation Plan in Oakland, California.)

• Independent practice plans are basically groups of physicians. They provide services in individual offices rather than a central clinic.

Federal law now requires companies employ-

ing 25 or more to offer their employees a chance to join a Health Maintenance Organization if a request is made to the employer by an HMO that's qualified under federal standards.

• Other insurance companies: Most major life insurance companies offer hospitalization insurance in competition with the Blue Cross. Premiums vary and there's room to negotiate. Policies vary widely, too. Some provide only administrative services and little or no insurance. (Employer is billed for full cost of claims paid.)

• Self-insurance: Payments are made into self-insurance reserve funds and can be tax deductible.* That's not the case with all kinds of self-insurance. Recomended: Reinsurance umbrella to protect against major catastrophe or abnormal flood of claims.

• Cost control: Reducing hospital use may produce even bigger savings than shopping around for insurance, according to John van Steenwyk of Martin E. Segal Co. (730 Fifth Ave., New York 10019), actuaries and employee benefit consultants. Some of the techniques van Steenwyk suggests: Second surgical opinion, same-day surgery, advance approval required for hospital admission, use of convalescent facility (cheaper than hospital), home care with visiting nurse.

*Under Section 501(c)(9) of Internal Revenue Code.

Get a Better Deal on Group Insurance

Companies buy group benefit insurance believing that premiums represent the total cost. But it does not always work that way. When insurers reject claims, employers frequently have to pick up the tab (as if they were self-insurers).

Trouble comes from three directions:

(1) Union contracts usually define an employee the same way the Taft-Hartley Law does to include people who are on leave of absence, on strike, or on layoff. But insurance contracts usually provide for benefits to individuals currently at work. Expectations of the employees and the insurers are not always the same.

(2) Another semantic problem: The layman

tends to think of an untoward incident as an "accident." But insurance regulations and court decisions usually exclude injuries that are foreseeable because of a criminal or reckless course of conduct. Example: A person injured while resisting arrest or for driving while drunk may not be covered by an insurance policy.

(3) Medical benefit plans usually exclude cosmetic or elective procedures. But opinions may differ as to what is necessary. Recent cases:

• One employer had to pay for the removal of a wart because, in some instances, warts develop into malignancies.

• Another employer had to pay for a transsexual operation because the arbitrator ruled that it was necessary to correct a "gender dysphoria syndrome" in the employee.

Management's customary line of defense: The matter is not the company's problem. The employee should sue the insurance company. But this defense is almost always struck down by arbitrators. Reason: Employers usually want a free hand to shop around for what they consider to be the best deal. Therefore, they must make good if employees do not get what they were led to expect they would be entitled to by the terms of the union contract.

The best course is to get the union's agreement that a particular policy satisfies obligations under the contract. If a specific policy is named in the contract, it will be persuasive evidence that the employer has done all that was required of him. Another approach: Companies that do a substantial amount of business with the insurance company may have enough clout to compel the carrier to pay arbitration awards, even after initially rejecting claims. This will save the cost of self-insurance, although it will not save the cost of the arbitration.

Insuring Leased Property

Don't overlook improvements and betterments clause. Make sure it covers improvements made both by landlord and tenant, in amount equal to at least 80% of improvement's value.

If insured for less than 80% of value, coin-surance clause limits recovery to the same percentage of loss that face amount of policy bears to property's actual value.

Standard fire insurance covers property loss only. Tenants must get business interruption and leasehold insurance to cover other losses caused by destruction of leased premises.

Collecting a Business Interruption* Insurance Claim

Points to bear in mind when seeking to collect a claim: Don't ask the adjuster, hired to assess the loss, to compute the claim. He doesn't know enough about the facilities. What the company should do: Make realistic calculations in order to avoid delays in settling the claim.

Important: Property damage must interfere with or prevent the insured from realizing a profit from his business. Material and noncontinuing costs not incurred while a plant is shut down must be deducted from the profit calculation.

Example: If the plant could produce 200 units of a product worth $300 a unit during the period of shutdown, the loss isn't automatically $60,000. The shutdown might save the company material costs of $50 a unit plus $20 a unit in noncontinuing costs, bringing the value of each unit down to $230—or a total loss of $46,000 in product value.

Traps to avoid:

• Don't use an automatic formula, developed for a claim at one plant, as a pattern for subsequent claims at other sites.

• Don't farm out all the audit or accounting work to an outside firm. It's essential that an employee who understands how the business operates be involved.

• Don't let an adjuster leave the site of the damage before a responsible company manager

*When fire or other damage forces the plant or store to close temporarily, business interruption insurance pays the company its profits lost during the shutdown. The full amount of lost sales, though, can't be collected. When it makes its claim, the company must subtract the cost savings (material not used, labor not paid) from lost sales.

makes a thorough review with him of the situation and they both come to some agreement on the facts.

• Be aware that most insurance will cover payroll expense of key employees who stay at home during a loss period, unless those employees are assigned to work in other parts of the company during that time. The insurance company may then assume that the company was getting value received for the work done, and exclude wage payments from its calculations of losses.

Source: *Business Insurance,* 740 Rush St., Chicago 60611.

Buying Credit Insurance on Receivables

Credit insurance—where the insurance company guarantees payment of all receivables—sounds like a good idea.

But most businesses will find that credit insurance isn't worth what it costs. It doesn't really give the company very much protection.

The credit insurance companies won't quote a fixed rate (so much per dollar of receivables). Instead, they examine receivables and past bad debt losses. Then they negotiate a deductible. The premium covers insurance on receivables over that amount.

The point is that the deductible will usually be about equal to average bad debt losses in past years. And the premium (usually 1/10% - ¼% of company's annual sales) is probably too high for the protection it offers. Still, it might be useful in cases where a company had three or four customers that account for most of its business.

What to Tell Insurance Broker

It's important to explain details about company operations to the insurance broker to avoid danger that major risks will be left uncovered.

Company's risk manager should volunteer information. Don't wait for the broker to ask,

because he may not know the right questions.

One thing the company should never tell the broker: How much it's willing to pay for insurance coverage.

The broker's job is to negotiate with the insurance carrier for the most coverage at the fewest premium dollars. If he knows a deal is acceptable to the company, he may settle for it rather than negotiating further to improve it. Remember: The broker is usually on a percentage commission. He earns more if the premium is higher.

Exception: If there's only one insurance source, such as Lloyd's, the best negotiating strategy is to make an opening offer after the company and broker compare notes on needs—and on costs.

Source: *Business Insurance,* 740 Rush St., Chicago 60611.

Company Insurance for Retired Executives

Executives don't have to lose their life insurance coverage when they retire and drop out of the company's group life plan.

What to do: The company and the exec can put aside money during his working years for after-65 coverage.

Two ways it can be done:

Split-dollar insurance. The company buys an ordinary policy on the executive's life and owns the policy. Each year the company pays the part of the premium equal to that year's increase in the cash value of the policy. The executive pays the balance of the premium (usually about what term insurance costs).

The policy provides that if the executives dies, the company gets the cash value back. The rest of the proceeds go to the beneficiary.

Results: In early years, most of the proceeds go to the beneficiary. Later, most of them go to the company.

The executive isn't getting any compensation that he has to pay taxes on. Premiums aren't deductible by the company, either.

The company can elect to borrow the amount of the premiums and deduct the interest. If it borrows from the insurer, the company must pay the first year's premium. (Individuals who borrow must pay four out of the first seven year's premiums.)

When the executive retires, he can start paying the whole premium. Then the company's share of the proceeds stops going up. Or he can pay the company the cash value. That's a big cash outlay, but he can borrow most of it from the insurance company.

Another possibility: The executive gives up his rights to the policy when he retires. The company continues to pay the premiums and receives the proceeds, tax-free, when he dies. But the company can elect to keep only the amount of money it has paid out in premiums. The rest is paid to the executive's family (taxable income). Or since the payment is deductible, it may pay considerably more without any added cost. (Twice as much if it's in the 50% bracket.) Example: $100,000 policy. The company retains the cash value of $40,000. It has an additional $60,000 tax-free. If it pays $120,000 to the executive's family, tax-deductible, its after-tax cost will be that same $60,000.

Retired life reserve. A company that has a group policy makes regular, tax-deductible payments into a trust fund. Earnings in the fund accumulate tax-free.

At retirement, the money put aside (plus interest earned) is used for a one-time premium payment providing continued full coverage for life. Example: 45-year-old executive is given a $100,000 death benefit after 65. Firm pays $39,000 (tax-deductible) over 20 years.

Payments that are made into the trust fund during working years do not constitute income to the executive.

Source: Leon H. Sicular, CLU, Leon H. Sicular Associates, 350 Fifth Ave., New York 10001.

Check the Credit Rating of an Insurance Company

Life insurance is regulated by state, not federal, regulations. Consumer protection varies around the country. Twenty-five percent of 458 U.S. insurance companies are domiciled in Ari-

zona, 10% in Texas. Both states have low requirements for capitalization. Bankruptcy disasters could leave beneficiaries with worthless policies.

Solution: Check out insurer's capitalization, reputation, credit-worthiness before buying policy. Prime source: *Best's Review,* Anbest Rd., Oldwick, NJ 08858. Lists all domestic insurers with data necessary for proper choice. Be wary if company isn't qualified to sell in New York, which has very tough standards.

Single Payment Life Insurance with Tax Shelter

This plan is worth considering for the executive who wants a mixture of life insurance, investment opportunity, and tax savings. What it offers:

• Complete safety of principal.
• Liquidity. Get money back without penalty after one year.
• Moderate income.
• Income tax shelter.
• Possible estate tax shelter.
• Life insurance protection that increases over the years.

Single premium life insurance is a whole life policy paid for by one lump-sum premium at the time the policy is taken out. Many companies offer such policies up to age 75, although in order to be insured the individual must pass a physical examination.

Cash values, death benefits, and dividends increase over the years.

Example:

$10,000 Single Premium Policy
for 54-Year-Old Man

Year	Annual Tax-Free Dividend	Cash Value	Death Benefit
2	$395	$ 9,875	$13,580
5	425	10,630	13,690
10	481	12,033	14,250

Tax advantage: Dividends and increases in cash value are completely free from income and capital gains taxes. Exception: If dividends are collected in cash, they'll be taxed after about 19 years, because by that time the accumulated dividends will be equal to the original lump-sum premium paid.

Borrowing against the policy: IRS will not permit interest payment deduction if individual borrows to make the lump-sum payment on this tax-advantaged insurance investment.

Cash value of the policy is good collateral, however. Policyholder can borrow against a policy and then deduct the interest payments. If policy is given away to the beneficiary, that person may borrow against it. (But the original purchaser may not.)

Disadvantages: Income and cash value buildup are lower than with other investments that don't provide insurance protection.

Joint Life Insurance Covering Group of Execs or Stockholders

Several stockholders of a closely held company need insurance to buy the stock of the first one who dies. But buying several policies can be a very expensive proposition.

One way to do it: Joint life insurance covering the group of stockholders and/or executives. Premiums run as much as 40% less than individual policies on every member. And they're based on the average age of the group. When the first death occurs, policy pays off and terminates. But survivors usually have the option to convert to whole life (if they are under 65) without taking a physical.

Another approach is called joint life exchange of insureds. Instead of one policy on the group, it's a collection of individual policies, with premiums that are considerably lower and based on average age. Upon the first death, all surviving policyholders get their cash value back. Beneficiaries of deceased get policy amount minus cash values paid to others. Then survivors can start over with new joint policies (that means more commissions, though). And they can add new members to the group.

How Much Life Insurance You Need

After the death of its principal income-producer, a family requires 75% of its former after-tax income to maintain its standard of living, according to a recent Citibank report, and at least 60% to get along at all.

Here is the amount of life insurance (in terms of annual earnings multiples) needed to provide this income at different ages (taking into account Social Security benefits and assuming the insurance proceeds were invested to produce an after-inflation return of 5% a year, with the entire principal consumed over survivor's life expectancy).

Present Age	YOUR PRESENT EARNINGS				
	$15M	$23.5M	$30M	$40M	$65M
25 years					
75%	4.5	6.5	7.5	7.5	7.5
60%	3.0	4.5	5.0	5.0	5.5
35 years					
75%	6.5	8.0	8.0	8.0	7.5
60%	4.5	5.5	6.0	6.0	6.0
45 years					
75%	8.0	8.5	8.5	8.0	7.5
60%	6.0	6.5	6.5	6.0	6.0
55 years					
75%	7.0	7.5	7.0	7.0	6.5
60%	5.5	5.5	5.5	5.5	5.0

While the chart shows insurance needs, it would be more useful to say that it shows captial requirements. Those requirements can be met by life insurance or through savings and investments, employee benefits, or inheritance. Thus, to the extent that the independent capital resources are built up, insurance needs diminish.

Example: An individual aged 55 with earnings of $40,000 and a net worth of $240,000, instead of requiring insurance in the face amount of $280,000, could get by with $40,000 in life insurance coverage.

How Much Fire Insurance You Need

Be sure the amount of your home fire insurance policy is at least 80% of the replacement value of your house. Most standard homeowners policies will pay the full value of the policy only if that value is 80% or more of the replacement value of the house. If coverage is below 80%, the maximum payment is limited to the replacement value minus a depreciation charge (usually quite large).

Insurance You May Not Know You Own

- Homeowners policy usually covers stolen purses and wallets, lost luggage, and property taken in car break-in. Also covers many offbeat accidents. Example: The damage to power mower borrowed from neighbor. Also: Trees, shrubs, fences, or tombstones damaged by vandals or motor vehicles. Property lost or damaged while moving.
- $25,000 travel life insurance if the ticket is bought on American Express, Diners Club, or Carte Blanche card.
- American Automobile Association (AAA) members have automatic hospital and death benefits if hurt in a car accident.
- Many clubs and fraternal organizations have life and health benefits.
- It's possible to collect twice on car accident injuries, once through health insurance and again through medical payments provision of auto insurance.
- Family health policies usually cover children away at college. Check before buying separate policies for them.

Life Insurance If You Can't Pass a Physical

Can't pass the life insurance physical? Don't give up on getting insurance—there may be a way.

Find an agent who knows his way with insurance companies. Their standards vary on overweight, blood pressure, smoking, other medical conditions. Example: Six-foot middle aged man weighing 270—many companies would add big surcharge to the standard premium for his age. But one company will insure him with no surcharge at all.

The agent's job is to find the exceptional company, know how to present the application in the most favorable light. Few agents do this well. You've got to insist agent shop for you.

If an individual policy isn't available (or only at very high cost), group policies normally cover everybody, regardless of medical history.

Besides company employees, group policies can be found in clubs, fraternal orders, religious orders, volunteer fire department. It may pay to join a club just for the group insurance. The saving on the premium is usually more than the cost of the dues.

Another possibility: Guaranteed issued policies. These take account of special medical impairments and provide that if death occurs in the first two years (or maybe three), the insurance company refunds the premium with interest. But after that you have full coverage.

Source: Frank J. Crisona, attorney and principal of the Crisona Agency, 100 Ring Road West, Garden City, NY 11530.

When to Drop Auto Collision Coverage

Consider dropping collision coverage if car isn't financed (or if lender will agree). Save the premiums instead.

How costs work out for car owner in 50% bracket:

- Collision insurance for three years on luxury car costs approximately $1,350.
- Driver can deduct collision repairs after first $100. Assume two accidents in three years, total repairs $2,500. Deduct $2,300; tax saving (50%) $1,150. Plus $200 nondeductible equals $1,350: Same as cost of insurance premiums.
- If the self-insurer deposits amount of premiums into savings account, he will have $1,500 at end of three years (less tax on interest).

Odds are in driver's favor to self-insure. Caution: Risk remains. Should only be taken if driver has enough cash reserves to handle repairs of major collision.

Boat Insurance Guidelines

• The policy should cover ice, freezing, and racing damage.

• Include protection and indemnity coverage. A boat can be sued much like a corporation ashore. Personal homeowners insurance won't protect it from confiscation to satisfy an award against it.

• Policy should cover use of the boat in all planned geographic areas.

• Ask about discounts based on owner experience, Power Squadron courses, automatic fire-extinguishing systems, diesel engine, etc.

Insurance Traps and Opportunities

• Fire or burglar alarm should entitle the owner to a reduction in insurance premiums. The saving on homeowner's premiums is about 2%-10% a year. Addition of a smoke detector should lower premiums another 3%.

• Bargain policy picks up when major medical runs out. Cost of really complicated illness today can exceed major medical coverage. Solution: "Excess" major medical policy with deductible equal to maximum benefit under your current plan. Cost: Can be as low as $136 per year at age 45 for million-dollar policy with $10,000 deductible. Features to shop around for: Guaranteed renewability; five-year benefit period; coverage of children from birth to age 18 or 21; payment of "reasonable" or "usual" hospital costs rather than specified daily rate.

• Save on title insurance. Many title insurers have a special reissue rate for property on which they've written a policy within the past five years. Advantage: A full title search is not necessary. Savings can be considerable. Companies usually don't mention the special rate unless a customer asks for it.

• Poor lock can lose insurance claim. Most insurers won't pay if lock was opened by key (even if it was a stolen key).

• Collecting when insurance company says no. Even insurance agents and claims investigators are sometimes unaware of the policy's full coverage. Claimant who's told he's not covered should always ask to speak to the disclaimer's manager. If the answer is still no, there is plenty of time to check with lawyer.

INVESTMENT STRATEGIES

What to Look For

Reading the Ticker Tape

Spotting a Good Low-Priced Stock

How and When to Sell Short

Protecting Paper Profits

Ways to Call Tomorrow's Market

Using Discount Brokers

Investment in Art

10

INVESTMENT STRATEGIES

Dividend Reinvestment Plans

Some 1,000 corporations now offer stockholders special inducements to reinvest their dividends. What an investor should know about such offers:

• Some companies offer a 5% price discount. Buying additional stock this way eliminates brokerage commissions. (A few plans have a small service charge.)

• Stockholder may be able to invest additional cash, saving more on commissions and price discounts.

• Provides investment discipline for those who would otherwise fritter away small amounts.

• New feature: The agent for the plan will hold original shares for safekeeping and send a regular statement to the stockholder.

• Tax treatment: A recent private ruling* by the IRS states that administrative service charges and brokerage fees subsidized by company reinvestment plans may be treated as additional dividend income to the investor. This ruling will

*7830104, July 24, 1978.

certainly be challenged by the corporations offering such plans.

• Reinvested dividends are still subject to income tax. ($100 dividend exclusion could partially offset income tax consequences. If some shares are put in a spouse's name, the exclusion is boosted to $200.)

Important: Dividend reinvestment plans should only be considered by an investor with a high degree of confidence in the future outlook of the issuing company.

Source: Robert Ferris, Georgeson & Co., 100 Wall St., New York 10009.

Getting Around the Minimum on Money Market Certificates

To get the high yield on the six-month money market certificates offered by banks and savings and loans, a minimum purchase of $10,000 is required. Investors can still get the good return even if they lack the $10,000 minimum by borrowing the difference from the institution issuing the certificates. Standard charge: 1% above the certificate yield on amount borrowed. Earn full certificate yield on the $10,000 purchase.

When to Avoid Bond Mutual Funds

Bond mutual funds, either corporate or municipal bonds funds, are probably not a good deal unless the management fee charged by the fund is very low (½% or less). They do provide diversification, but for most investors, buying the bonds directly through a broker is cheaper. One-time sales commission on a purchase of $25,000 worth of bonds is about $125. Fund annual management fees can be as much as $250/year on same-sized purchase.

Source: *The Only Investment Guide You'll Ever Need*, by Andrew Tobias, Harcourt Brace Jovanovich, New York.

Before Buying Municipal Bonds

Find out whether the interest is exempt from state as well as federal income taxes. (It can make a big difference in New York and Massachusetts, among others.)

Generally, the state and local agencies in each state can sell bonds with interest exempt from that state's, and federal, income tax. In New York, bond interest paid by any governmental agency within the state is exempt from federal, New York State and City income taxes.

Municipal bonds can be bought by individual issues, in unit trusts, or in mutual funds, which work like any mutual fund.

In a unit trust, the promoters buy one batch of bonds. The customer owns a piece of that particular batch, and there will be no charges. He gets his principal back piecemeal at various times as the various bonds are paid off. If he wants to sell

his unit trust shares, it may be difficult. He may have to take a discount in the process.

Municipal Bond Insurance

Investors who own $50,000 or more worth of tax-exempt bonds may be able to protect their investments with insurance. If the state or local government or agency defaults, the insurance company will pay the interest and principal.

Annual premiums start at about 0.1% for the highest quality general obligation bonds, backed by the full credit of the governmental unit. They can go as high as 0.9% for lower quality bonds or some revenue bonds.

Insurance isn't available at all on some issues. And the insurer demands higher quality bonds if asked to insure only one security rather than a mixed portfolio of bonds.

Once issued, the policy is guaranteed renewable at the same premium for the life of the bonds.

Idea: Instead of buying the safest bonds, consider lower quality issues plus insurance. Example: Switch from Aaa-rated issues yielding 5% to Baas yielding 6% or more. The gain might be an extra 1% or more in yield by paying .2%-.3% in premiums.

Insurance doesn't cover a drop in market price. In a default, the investor may have to hold bonds until maturity to get principal back.

Source: MGIC Indemnity Corp., MGIC Plaza, Milwaukee, WI 53201.

Interest Not Deductible If Loan Pays for Tax-Exempts

The Tax Code [Section 265(2)] is very specific about barring the deduction of interest on debt incurred (or continued) to buy or carry tax-exempt investments.

IRS can apply this rule in an extremely broad

manner, and will disallow deductions whenever an individual borrows money (including broker margin loans) to finance investments in any stock, bonds, or real estate while he still has the tax-exempts in his portfolio. Exceptions:

• If the investment in tax-exempts is less than 2% of the taxpayer's investment portfolio.

• If the borrowing is in connection with the needs of an active business.

• If the borrowing is for personal reasons (such as a home mortgage or high-ticket consumer goods), as a general rule.

Caution on home borrowing: Mortgage interest was disallowed when an individual took out the mortgage 13 months after having acquired the home for cash, and then bought tax-exempts that amounted to two-thirds of the face value of the mortgage.

A tax court ruled that this situation should be distinguished from the more usual one of individual owning a mortgaged home who may on occasion purchase tax-exempt securities.

Effect of losing the deduction: The full amount of interest paid is disallowed when there is direct evident that the borrowing was done to invest in tax-exempts. Otherwise, the amount disallowed is determined by the formula:

$$ab/c$$

a = Total interest on all indebtedness.

b = Average amount of tax-exempts held during the year.

c = Value of individual's total assets.

The result is adjusted for debt not subject to disallowance to any extent under IRS guidelines.

Example: $10,000 investment in tax-exempts yields $600 a year, tax-free. If cost of borrowing $10,000 ($750+) is disallowed, the individual has a net loss of $150 + on his investment.

Taking Advantage of Favorable Capital Gains Rules

Long-term capital gains are back in style. Once again the best way—perhaps the only way—to build wealth is to acquire valuable prop-

erties (business, stocks, real estate, collectibles) and hold on to them for many years, perhaps for generations. That's the way all the great American fortunes have been built, and probably most of the smaller ones, too.

Background: For many years, long-term gains were taxed at half the rate that applied to other income. And the absolute maximum tax rate on long-term gains was 25%, even for those in the highest tax bracket (70%).

But that wasn't all. The best part of the old system was that if the property passed by will to the next generation, the capital gain would never be taxed at all.

That's the way it was until 1969, when Congress started increasing the tax bite on long-term gains. Hardest hit: Executives with large earned incomes who also realized long-term gains. In some situations taxes took as much as half of the gains.

Then in 1976 Congress went even further. It took the first steps toward taxing capital gains that were passed on in estates.

Now the trend has reversed.

• Capital gains tax rates are now better than they were before 1969 for most taxpayers.

• For all taxpayers they are better than they were on October 31, 1978. Not a little better, but much better. The maximum tax on long-term gains is now 28%, no matter how large the gains or the other income, either earned or unearned.

The 1978 tax law made six important changes in taxes on capital gains. Five of the six were tax reductions:

• Only 40% of long-term gains are subject to tax, rather than 50% as before. This reduced the tax for everybody, from the highest brackets down to the lowest.

• The untaxed part of capital gains is no longer subject to the add-on minimum tax on tax preference items.

• Long-term gains no longer can "poison" earned income subject to the 50% maximum tax. In most situations, this very important provision helps high-salaried people who also have capital gains. (How it works: There's a maximum tax rate of 50% on earned income. But, under the old law, every dollar of the untaxed half of capital gains had the effect of excluding a dollar of earned income from the 50%

ceiling, which meant that it could be taxed as high as 70%. This provision has now been repealed.)

Note: The combined effect of these three changes means that the maximum rate on long-term gains is now 28%, even for those in the top bracket (70%).

• Persons over 55 can sell their homes and realize up to $100,000 of long-term gains absolutely tax-free (only once in a lifetime, though).

• The carryover basis provisions of the 1976 law have been changed as a result of the Windfall Profit Act of 1980. These provisions would have taxed heirs on capital appreciation after 1976 of property owned by decedents. (The heirs would not be taxed when they inherited the property, but later if and when they sold it.)

These dramatic reductions in taxes on long-term gains will have major effects upon investment planning. Biggest change: Wealthy executives won't lose as much money investing in dubious shelters.

What to look for in investment planning:

• Equity in a sound business that prospers and grows.

• Good stocks of solid companies.

• Well located, income-producing real estate. Maybe vacant land, too.

Some collectibles may be good, but that's less certain. Ownership produces no income and involves some expense (insurance, safekeeping, appraisal or assay fees). And the investor often has to buy at a retail price and sell at a wholesale price. It could take up to five years of appreciation to make up that gap.

Revise thinking about executive compensation. There should be less emphasis on untaxed perquisites (it's getting harder to find them, anyway). More important now: stock purchase plans, stock options, and pension and profit sharing plans that will eventually make lump-sum distributions.

Cash deals are more attractive than ever for owners of smaller companies who want to sell out. There's less reason than ever for them to be acquired by a larger company in a tax-free exchange of stock. More likely result: Staying independent.

There's more incentive to buy good stocks

now. And there will be less reluctance to sell and take profits.

Outlook: There's no assurance that Congress won't change the rules again. Best guess: Capital gains changes made in 1978 will stand, because they appear to have widespread popular support, especially from millions of homeowners who have seen their homes double and triple in value. In conjunction with the other tax benefits available to homeowners, capital gains opportunities have made home ownership possibly the most widely used tax shelter available.

Reading the Ticker Tape

Popularly traded issues like IBM and gambling stocks show distinct tendencies during the course of the day. Reason: Traders tend to buy and sell at certain hours. Astute investors can take advantage of these patterns:

• Day traders often buy early in the morning or on evidence of overall stock market strength that day. If the market is weak, traders will sell short at the earliest opportunity. Positions on the New York exchange are normally equalized between 3:30 and 3:45 p.m. there.

• On stronger days, expect temporary weakness in the issue at about 3:30 when most traders close out their long positions. Buyers should try to place orders during this period. Sellers should wait until just near the close when prices often recover. (Another point of market weakness is between noon and 1 p.m.).

• On weaker days, short sellers should expect some price recovery at about 3:30 p.m. when traders are covering their shorts.

Why a Stock's Price Sensitivity Is Important

Some stocks tend to rise more rapidly in a rising market and fall more rapidly during a market decline. (Market technicians call them high-beta stocks.) Others are less price volatile (low-betas). The higher the beta, the more the potential reward to the investor who assesses the market's direction correctly. And the greater the risk when the investor makes a mistake.

How to identify a stock's beta: Use the quality ratings in *The Standard & Poor's Stock Guide.* Research indicates that there is a very close correlation between quality rating and beta: The higher the quality rating, the lower the beta (and the less the stock's volatility).

Source: *Financial Analysts Journal*, 219 East 42 St., New York 10017.

January: An Early Predictor of the Stock Market

January stock prices have been an excellent predictor of direction stock prices will go for the rest of the year. When prices rise on Wall Street in January, odds are they will end the year higher. When prices fall in January, odds favor a weak market for the rest of the year.

No need to wait until the end of January, either, for an early bead on market action. The first five days of January alone have had almost as strong a predictive value as the entire month.

• Since 1950, there have been 19 years in which the Standard & Poor's Index declined during the first five days of January. The market showed a loss for the entire year in seven of those years. Declines during this period showed up during both 1977 and 1978.

Source: *The Stock Traders Almanac*, Hirsch Organization, 6 Deer Trail, Old Tappan, NJ 07675.

When to Turn Down a Tax Shelter

Stephen D. Oppenheim, partner in the accounting firm Oppenheim, Appel, Dixon & Co. (1 New York Plaza, New York 10004), reviews hundreds of tax-shelter deals a year for wealthy clients. His advice:

After 15 years of this work, I'm not sure tax shelter investments, per se, make investors any wealthier. I believe the evidence is that those people who are always looking for a tax shelter "deal" would have been wealthier if they paid their taxes and invested their funds more prudently. Owners of businesses should be among the most wary of tax shelter investments. Since they usually receive the bulk of their income as earnings, subject to 50% maximum tax, many shelters just don't have much to offer.

Four commonsense rules to follow:

1. The farther away from home the investment is, the worse it usually is. When a California oil and gas deal is being sold in New York, begin wondering why it's being marketed so far away. There are an awful lot of wealthy people in between. Why won't those who are closer to the deal touch it?

2. The smaller the minimum unit of investment, the worse the investment. With a really good situation, it's easy to raise $100,000 to $200,000 per investor. These are sophisticated investors who know what they're doing and have experts around looking for deals and reviewing them, too. As the unit comes down, it's promoted to less and less sophisticated individuals, people who are less willing to pay someone to look over the deal.

Another negative feature of small-unit offerings: Large percentage taken by promoters in finders fees, management fees, general partners' compensation, etc.

General rule: A deal with a $50,000 minimum investment is probably more than twice as good as one with a $25,000 minimum.

3. The better the anticipated tax deduction, the worse the deal. For really solid investments, it shouldn't be necessary to promise five-to-one writeoffs (deducting as expenses a sum five times the actual cash investment). People go into the deal confident they will make a lot of money on it. Tax deductions are just icing on the cake—not the substance of the transaction itself.

Warning: Any deductions taken in excess of cash contributions as a liability come back to the taxpayer or his heirs somewhere, somehow, sometime. A tax-shelter deal is nothing more than a postponement of tax liability—and that liability may turn up just when it is needed least.

4. The better the promised economics, the

worse the deal. If someone comes to you promising to quadruple your money—or better—in a short period of time, you've got to ask why he isn't begging or borrowing all the money he can to put in the deal himself rather than urging you in. For deals like that, wealthy people would be standing in line at the door, and smaller investors wouldn't stand a chance.

Beware of the glamorous tax shelter you hear about at a party. The bulk of transactions come from "a friend." Many people hear about them at cocktail parties where alcohol has already lowered resistance, turned off the thinking process. In my experience smart businesspeople's IQs deteriorate geometrically as the tax-deduction multiple goes up. They hear about a two-for-one deal and they're operating at about half their level; a four-to-one deal, they're at 25%; and when you talk to them about a five-to-one multiple, you're dealing with a functional imbecile. The most useful advice I can give a client is to say: The deal just isn't that good.

An even worse way to hear about a tax shelter is through an advertisement.

Check out technical details of a deal with a real expert. Get assurance from your lawyer that the documents you sign actually make you a limited partner (where your loss is limited to the size of your investment), not a general partner (unlimited liability). And it's often desirable to get an opinion from a lawyer or accountant that the tax considerations in the papers are at least defensible.

But don't substitute the professional's judgment for your own on whether the deal makes good business sense. Think of the money being invested as a capital contribution to a business, not as a tax deal. Take the same steps you would to examine a business decision. If it's an apartment house deal, check the projections of the vacancy rate and the rent. Have someone go around adjacent blocks and ask to rent an apartment. See how many are available and at what rent. If it's a gas-drilling deal, ask your fuel supplier whom you can talk to at the firm that supplies him. Ask if the projections make sense.

If businesspeople would just take these simple steps it would stop them from going into many deals. And that would be right.

What most tax shelter investors overlook: Investigate the quality of the people making the tax shelter offer. That's the single most important piece of information an investor should have in hand before deciding.

Have your lawyer check out the credentials and background of any lawyers involved.

Ask for specifics. Ask your accounting firm to give you a report on the CPAs involved in putting together the offering. What kind of companies or industries do they work for? Have they been involved in any serious problems?

And don't forget to look into the credentials of consultants connected with the offer. Ask them for the names of companies and individuals they've worked for in recent years.

How Professionals Spot a Low-Priced Stock That Is Ready to Bounce Back

Value has little to do with telling a good company from a bad company. A top-quality large company which is selling at a high price/earnings multiple is less attractive than a lesser-quality company which is selling at a depressed price in terms of its past and future earning power, working capital, book value, and historical prices.

What to look for:

• Stocks that have just made a new low for the last 12 months.

• Companies that are likely to be liquidated. In the liquidation process, shareholders may get paid considerably more than the stock is selling for now.

• Unsuccessful merger candidates. If one buyer thinks a company's stock is a good value, it's possible that others may also come to the same conclusion.

• Companies that have just reduced or eliminated their dividends. The stock is usually hit with a selling wave, which often creates a good buying opportunity.

• Financially troubled companies in which another major company has a sizable ownership position. If the financial stake is large enough, you can be sure that the major company will do

127

everything it can to turn the earnings around and get the stock price up so that its investment will work out.

Opportunities, also, in stocks that are totally washed out—that is, situations where all the bad news is out. The stock usually has nowhere to go but up.

How to be sure a stock is truly washed out:

• Trading volume slows to practically nothing. If over-the-counter, few if any dealers are making a market.

• No Wall Street research analysts are following the company any more.

• No financial journalists, stock market newsletters, or advisory services discuss the company.

• Selling of the stock by company's management and directors has stopped.

Signs of a turnaround:

• The company plans to get rid of a losing division or business. If so, be sure to learn whether the company will be able to report a big jump in earnings once the losing operation is sold.

• The company is selling off assets to improve its financial situation and/or reduce debt.

• A new management comes on board with an established track record of success with turnaround situations.

• Management begins buying the company's stock in the open market.

• Also, be sure to follow the Form 13d statements filed with the SEC. (A company or individual owning 5% or more of a public company must report such holdings to the Securities and Exchange Commission.) If any substantial company is acquiring a major position in a company, it's possible a tender offer at a much higher price is in the wind.

Source: Robert Ravitz, director of research, David J. Greene & Co., 30 Wall St., New York 10005.

How and When to Sell Short

Short selling opportunities develop even during bull markets. Most such markets are interrupted at least once by a severe decline.

Suggestions for profitable short selling:

• Sell only heavily capitalized issues with a low outstanding short interest. They are less like-

ly to be subject to a short squeeze (sharp rallies caused by many short sellers rushing to cover and too few shares available).

• Cover short sales during moments of market weakness. Take advantage of market declines that are stimulated by bad news to cover into periods of weakness. Warning: Do not wait for a rally to cover shorts. What the pros do: Cover short sales just before weekends in case favorable news triggers sharp Monday rallies.

• As an alternative to selling short, consider the purchase of puts (selling an option contract at a stated price on or before a fixed expiration date).

• A stock that is sold short can decline by only so much, but there's no limit on how much it can rise. Result: Short selling bucks the odds because the ultimate risk is always greater than the potential reward. Place stop loss orders to cover when the short sale goes against you by more than 10%-15%.

• Sell short stocks that show definite signs of overhead resistance (areas of heavy trading in that stock just above your short selling level) on their charts. Such areas tend to impede upside progress.

• Do not sell those short issues that have just made new highs. Wait for definite signs of weakness before selling short.

Source: *Personal Finance*, Kephart Communications, 901 North Washington St., Alexandria, VA 22314.

Questions to Ask Before Buying Utility Stocks

Utility stocks, more than most issues, are purchased for reliable income by conservative investors who may require current income from investment holdings. Here are some guidelines which may help avoid unpleasant surprises:

• Is the utility located in a state with favorable regulatory climate? Some states make it very difficult for utilities to pass along rising costs to consumers; some states are more permissive. The typical state will generally grant the utility approximately two-thirds of the rate increase requested. It will usually require approximately one year following such requests to provide the necessary authorization.

• The utility should have ample earnings from which to pay interest on any bonds outstanding. Utility companies are generally heavy borrowers of capital for expansion. Should a cash flow bind develop, dividend payouts may have to be suspended, since bondholders hold first call on company assets. Earnings for the company should amount to at least 2.5 times the interest payments due on corporate notes; preferably more. In considering any stock for its dividends, make certain that earnings are ample to cover projected dividend payouts.

• The price of the shares should be no lower than book value if the company has plans to issue more shares. Otherwise, shareholder equity will be diluted by such distribution.

• The company shouldn't pay out too high a percentage of earnings in dividends. Approximately 65-70% is average. The lower a percentage of earnings in dividend payout, the more protected the dividend.

• Check the balance sheet for excessive debt and for favorable asset-to-liability ratios.

Your broker should be able to provide the above information either via in-house research or access to Standard & Poor's ratings of corporations and corporate debt.

Source: *Electric Utilities 1977*, Prescott, Ball & Turben, 900 National City Bank Building, Cleveland.

Stock Options As an Alternative to Buying on Margin

Aggressive investors who think the market will advance often buy options instead of buying stock on margin.

Advantages:

• The choice of options avoids margin interest charges, which can be very high when the prime rate is high.

• There's a much smaller loss if the stock drops sharply.

• If the stock goes up as expected, the profit

will be almost as big as with buying on margin.

Disadvantages:

• Loss to the investor is larger if the stock doesn't move at all.

• Profits will be taxed as a short-term gain rather than long-term.

How the transactions compare:

• Margin: Buy 100 shares at 80. Put up $400 and borrow $4,000 from the broker at 12½% or so. Interest cost: $500/yr. Result: If stock goes to 100 in a year, the net gain (after commissions) is about $1,400 (plus dividends received). If it goes down to 60, the net loss is about $2,600 (less dividends received).

• Options: Pay about $800 for a call option to buy 100 shares at 80. Invest the remaining $3,200 to earn interest. Result: If the stock goes to 100, profit is about $1,300 including interest earned. (It's a short-term gain, though, since no options are available for as long as a year.) If the stock drops, no matter how far, the loss will be about $700. The amount of this loss could be cut by selling the option before it expires. Note: Even if the stock stays at 80, the option transaction still loses about $700 (cost of option less interest earned).

How Options Traders Make Money in a Declining Market

Trading in listed puts is available on five option exchanges (Puts: The right to sell shares of a specified stock at a specified price until a specified date).

Puts provide a way of selling stock short in hope of a market decline, without the risk of severe loss usually associated with short selling.

How puts work: Suppose XYZ Corp. is selling at $50 and you can purchase a January-50 put on the options exchange for $350. The put entitles you to sell 100 shares of XYZ at 50 until the expiration of that option in the following January.

If XYZ were to decline to, say, 40, at or before the expiration of the option, an option conveying the right to sell the shares at 50 would be worth

$1,000 (the $10 difference times 100 shares). The profit would accrue immediately to the option holder, who could exercise the option on shares that he could purchase on the open market at $40. Since the option buyer paid $350, his gain would be $650, or 186% on a stock that declined by 20%.

Of course, if XYZ rose or stood still through the life of the option, the option would expire worthless, resulting in a 100% loss. However, the maximum risk to the short seller using the put would be $350, the cost of the obligation.

Using puts with call options (the right to buy a specified stock at a specified price until a specified date) provides some interesting opportunities for mathematically oriented investors. Straddles (using puts and calls) can produce profit regardless of the direction of market movement, provided underlying common moves away from its start price by a certain amount.

Example: Assume XYZ at 50 again, the listed put selling for $350 (3½) and the listed call, strike-50 (the price at which the option is exercised), January expiration, also selling at 3½. Instead of purchasing the put alone, you purchase both. Here are the workouts at different prices of XYZ at the expiration of both options.

Price XYZ	Put Value	Gain (Loss)	Call Value	Gain (Loss)	Net
70	0	− 350	20	+ 1650	+ 1300
65	0	− 350	15	+ 1150	+ 800
60	0	− 350	10	+ 650	+ 300
55	0	− 350	5	+ 150	− 200
50	0	− 350	0	− 350	− 700
45	5	+ 150	0	+ 350	− 200
40	10	+ 650	0	− 350	+ 300
35	15	+ 1150	0	− 350	+ 800
30	20	+ 1650	0	− 350	+ 1300

The position shows a profit as long as XYZ moves beyond the 43-57 price range, a 14% movement in either direction from 50.

It's possible to profit on both sides of a straddle. Example: If XYZ first rises to 60 and then falls to 40, you might sell or exercise your call at a profit into the rise and then sell or exercise your put for an additional profit into the fall. However, in practice, one side or the other of a straddle is usually exercised, not both.

Straddles are best purchased after the market has rested within a trading range for some time and you expect a breakout but are uncertain of the direction. And, of course, you should purchase an option only when option premiums (the price of options) are running below normal.

How to Buy a Stock at Less Than Its Current Price

• Select issues of interest that have listed puts available.

• Sell listed puts in the amount of shares that you might wish to purchase. Emphasize puts that are slightly out of the money (exercise price below the current market price of shares).

If the stock falls to the exercise price of the put, you will have purchased your shares at lower than the current price. If not, you will have pocketed the put premium free and clear.

Example: Stock X was recently selling at 28½, at which time a July-25 put was selling at 5/8. If you owned Stock X at the time, you might have sold one July-25 put for each 100 shares you had planned to purchase. If Stock X was to decline to 25 or below, the put might be exercised, and you would be obligated to purchase the shares at 25—an effective cost of 24 1/8 since you had previously received 5/8 of a point from the put. If the stock were to remain above 25 through the period before the option's expiration, you would receive the premium free and clear as a profit.

Alternate strategy: If put premiums are low, you might, as an alternative, purchase the shares immediately, and also purchase a put to protect against loss. If the market declines in the near future, you could sell your put at a profit.

A Way to Protect Paper Profits

There's a way to safeguard paper profits against the stock market dropping without selling out entirely. It's called covered-option writing. How covered-option writing works:

Sell short one 100-share call option* for every 100 shares of stock owned. If the stock goes down, the option will go down, too. Then there'll be a profit when the investor buys it back at a loss, or when it expires worthless. If the stock goes up (providing more paper profits), the option will go up, too. The investor must then buy it back (that's a cash loss, not a paper loss). Otherwise, the option will be exercised, which means he's forced to sell the stock at the option exercise price.

The technique is a bit complicated, but many brokers are familiar with it and will guide the investor. Be aware that this is a strategy for uncertainty. If an investor feels sure the market will drop, he probably should sell his stocks outright.

Points to remember: Covered-option writing gives only limited downside protection. If the market drops faster than 10% in six months (which could happen), this program loses money. And the cost of getting this protection is that the investor gives up most of the additional profits he'd make if the market goes higher.

Also, commissions are high, especially on one or two options. (Example: One option at 3 ($300); the commission is $25 to sell and another $25 to buy back.)

*An option to buy 100 shares of stock at a fixed price within a specified time limit; nine months is the maximum.

How to Tell When a Fast-Rising Industry Is Topping Out

Typical pattern: Initial price gains attract wide public speculative interest which finally gives way to sharp price declines. The declines often trap unwary investors.

How to recognize when such groups may be topping out prior to a sharp price drop:

• The industry group already has had a very sharp runup.

• Very heavy trading volume. Stocks in this group dominate the list of most actively traded stocks.

• Near the top of the rise, the stocks gain and

lose in violent price swings. But little ground is gained in the process.

• Price/earnings multiples for the group soar far above historical norms.

• Heavy short selling appears. Early short sellers of the stocks are driven to cover by sharp rallies. Their covering of shorts adds fuel to late rallies within the group. (Short sellers who enter the picture later, however, are likely to be amply rewarded.)

Trading tactics that work for professionals: Extreme caution first and foremost. Close stop-orders are placed on any long and/or short positions taken. Short sales are entered into only after these issues have shown signs of fatigue and of topping out, and then only after recent support levels have been broken. Wait for a clear sign that the uptrend has ended before selling out.

How Bear Market Rallies Can Fool You

Bear market rallies are often sharp. They're fueled, in part, by short sellers rushing to cover shares. However, advances in issues sold short often lack durability once short covering is completed. Details:

• Bear market rallies tend to last for no more than five or six weeks.

• Bear market advances often end rapidly—with relatively little advance warning. If you are trading during a bear market, you must be ready to sell at the first sign of weakness.

• The first strong advance during a bear market frequently lulls many analysts into a false sense of security, leading them to conclude that a new bull market is underway. The majority of the bear markets don't end until pessimism is widespread and until the vast majority is convinced that prices are going to continue to decline indefinitely.

• Although the stock market can remain ''overbought'' for considerable periods of time during bull markets, bear market rallies generally end fairly rapidly, as the market enters into ''overbought'' conditions. An ''overbought'' condition occurs when prices advance for a short

131

time at a rate that can't be sustained.

One way to predict a decline—using the advance-decline line as a guide: Each day, compute the net difference between the number of issues that rise on the Big Board and the number that decline. A ten-day total of the daily nets is then maintained. During bear markets, be careful when the ten-day net differential rises to +2,500 or more, and be ready to sell immediately once this figure is reached and starts to decline. The decline will usually indicate that the advance is beginning to weaken.

Formula for Calling Tomorrow's Market

Here is a short-term composite indicator useful for calling the direction of the market over the next trading session or two. Total score of at least 3 out of possible 5 points indicates that the market will rise tomorrow. Results are not perfect, but the composite's batting average has been very high.

Index	Score
Change in Direction: *Standard & Poor's 500 Composite Index.*	1, if the index is up for the day.
(Usually on newspaper financial pages.)	
Short Term Trading Index (TRIN): Measures volume in advancing issues as a proportion of volume in declining issues.	1, if the closing TRIN is below 1.00.

$$\text{TRIN} = \frac{\text{No. of Issues Up}}{\text{No. of Issues Down}} \div \frac{\text{Up Volume}}{\text{Down Volume}}$$

(Data for TRIN and TICK available quickly from stockbroker.)

Index	Score
Net Upticks vs. Net Downticks at Close (TICK):	1, if the market closes with a plurality of upticks.
Volume:	1, if trading volume exceeds the previous day's.

Index	Score
Favorable Market Periods:	1, if tomorrow will be the last trading day of a month or one of the first four trading days of a new month. Or: 1, if the day before a holiday. Or: 1, if tracking market cycles and the *Wall Street Journal's* daily 15-18 day trading cycle chart shows that the market lies within the first 5-6 days.

Source: Murray M. Kimmel, Herzfeld & Stern, East 210, Rt. #4, Paramus, NJ 07652.

Spotting the Bottom of a Bear Market

Here's how sophisticated investors recognize that a bear market is near its last phase:

• Downside breadth increases. That is, market declines become broader, including even stocks that had been strong before. More issues are making new lows.

• ''Oversold'' conditions (periods in which the market seems to decline precipitously) extend for longer periods of time. Technical recoveries are relatively minor.

• Pessimism spreads, but analysts and bullish advisories still discuss ''bargains'' and ''undervalued issues.''

• Stocks continue to be very sensitive to bad news. The market becomes very unforgiving of poor earnings reports and monetary difficulties.

• Trading volume remains relatively dull. Prices seem to fall under their own weight, the result of a lack of bids rather than urgent selling.

Important: The bear market isn't likely to end until pessimism broadens into outright panic, and until public and institutional selling become urgent.

Some of the most reliable nontechnical signals that the bear market is over:

• When the mass media begin to headline the

fact that the stock market is hitting its bottom.

That's when *Time* and *Newsweek,* and the TV networks, warn of even lower Dow levels. When those reports appear regularly, wise investors know the bottom has already passed.

When a Stock Is Likely to Change Direction

A simple tool to determine when a stock is likely to change its direction (either up or down) can be useful for short-term traders and for fine-tuning buy and sell decisions on any portfolio.

How to track a stock:

• Measure the difference between the latest price of the stock and its price two days earlier. Run a tab on the two-day change. Example:

Price, XYZ Corp.		Two-day change
Day 1	$15.00	0
Day 2	16.25	0
Day 3	16.00	+ 1.00
Day 4	18.00	+ 1.75
Day 5	19.00	+ 3.00
Day 6	19.25	+ 1.25

• Buy signal: Whenever the two-day change exceeds the highest level recorded by this indicator over the previous two days. (Day 5 above.)

• Sell signal: Whenever the two-day change falls below the level of the previous two days. (Day 6 above.)

Source: *New Concepts in Technical Trading Systems* by J. Welles Wilder Jr., Windsor Books, Box 280, Brightwaters, NY 11718.

Early Signals That the Market Is Taking a Turn

Significant stock market moves—whether short-term, intermediate, or long-term—usually follow this pattern: Three well-defined waves, each interspersed with a corrective or reactive move. This is called the two-follows-three rule.

If the major market trend is up, this series of three swings is likely to be followed by two declines before the uptrend resumes. Avoid the temptation to renew purchases following the first of these two declines.

If the prevailing trend is down, anticipate three down-legs, each followed by two up-moves. During bear markets, be certain to sell into the second of these two legs and to avoid new purchases until the third of the well-defined down-legs is complete.

The rule applies to shorter-term swings during intermediate moves, as well. During an intermediate advance, each short swing will consist of three defined waves, and will be followed by two reactions.

Another signal is the three-week rule. It may help in short-term market forecasting.

If the stock market hasn't made a new high within a three-week period, expect a short-term market decline. There's a possibility of an intermediate decline, too.

If the stock market hasn't fallen into new low ground, below the previous low point, within a three-week period, a market advance usually follows.

For safety's sake, give the three-week period an extra day or two before drawing conclusions.

Three Ways to Spot a Market Decline Before It Starts

Strong market moves frequently end in one- or two-day reversal spikes. Those spikes often provide advance warning of significant market turning points. Here are signs that show when a market decline may be coming:

• The market will rise sharply in the morning on very high volume running at close to 15 million shares during the first hour of trading.

• From 10:30 a.m. (Eastern time) on, the market will make little or no progress despite heavy trading throughout the day.

• By the end of the first day, almost all the morning's gains will have been lost, with the market closing clearly toward the downside. Occasionally, this process will be spread over a two-day period.

Steps to take: When you see the pattern, either sell immediately or await the retest of the highs that were reached during that first morning. Such a retest often takes place within a week or two, on much lower trading volume. This may prove to be the last opportunity to sell into strength.

The patterns seen during one-day reversals occasionally take place early in intermediate advances, with the backoff representing a test of previous lows. If such action appears prior to significant market gains, do not sell. Rather, buy during any near-term weakness. The market will probably resume its rise.

However, if such a trading pattern occurs following a period of several weeks or months of rising prices, the odds increase that a genuine one-day reversal is occurring. Then you must take protective action.

Pointers from Professional Traders

• If the market has already risen for five to six weeks, it is almost always too late to make new purchases with safety. Possible exception: The first months of a fresh bull market.

• Strongest short-term market periods: Last trading day of each month and first four trading days of the subsequent month. Days before holidays often show good market strength, too.

• If a stock has not made a new high within a five- to six-week period, there is a good chance that its intermediate trend is about to turn down.

• If a stock fails to make a new low five to six weeks after a decline, there's a good chance its intermediate trend is about to turn up.

• Count the weeks from one significant market bottom to another and from one significant market top to another. Strong market advances often start at intervals of from 20 to 26 weeks. Severe declines often start at same intervals.

• Before buying preferred stocks of blue chip companies, investors should consider the current reality that the same company's bonds may yield more. This is surprising, because the bonds are safer. Some high-grade preferred stocks yield ¼% or ½% less than bonds of same company. Commissions on bonds are lower, too.

• When convertible bonds in your portfolio are called for redemption, write directly to the company chief executive and ask: "Is there any material information I need in order to make an informed decision whether to turn in my bonds for cash or convert them to common stock? Please reply in writing."

• Source of latest information on public companies: Copies of 10-Ks, 10-Qs, 8-Ks, proxies, prospectuses, annual reports. National Investment Library, 80 Wall St., New York 10005.

An Expert's Questions Before Buying a Stock

Investment adviser Gerald Appel offers this checklist for making stock purchases. He wants a yes answer to just about every question before taking a long position in a stock.

• Is the price/earnings ratio of the stock (price divided by latest 12-month earnings) well below the price/earnings ratio of the average listed issue?

• Have earnings of the company been rising at a steady rate over a period of years, preferably at a rate exceeding the rate of inflation?

• Has the company had a recent history of steadily rising dividend payouts?

• Has the stock recently risen above a clearly defined trading range that lasted for at least five weeks?

• If not, has a recent sharp decline ended with the stock trading on extremely high volume for that issue, without the price falling further?

• Have insiders of the company purchased more shares of the company than they have sold?

• Has the company recently purchased its own shares on the open market?

• Has the stock remained relatively undiscovered by the advisory services and brokerage houses? (One sign that an issue is near the end of a rise is that many advisory services suddenly begin to recommend its purchase.)

Guidelines for Investing in Closed-End Funds

A closed-end fund is like a mutual fund, in that it invests in a number of other securities. But unlike mutual (or open-end) funds, it doesn't constantly sell new shares and redeem shares at net asset values. Rather, the shares of a closed-end fund trade in the open market, just like other stocks.

Closed-end funds enable an investor to buy a widely diversified portfolio of stocks, bonds, or convertible bonds at a large discount from their actual market value. Reason: Most funds sell at a 15%-30% discount from net asset value. (Net asset value is computed by dividing the total number of shares of the fund into the current market value of the securities that make up the fund's portfolio.)

Advantage in a rising market: Closed-end funds generally outperform other securities. As securities in the portfolio rise, the discount from net asset value tends to shrink. Thus, the value of an individual investor's shares often tends to outpace the market.

Advantage in a declining market: If shares in a fund are purchased at a heavy discount from net asset value, a decline in its portfolio should have relatively little, if any, effect on the price of the fund's shares.

Criteria for selecting the right closed-end funds:

• Find out the fund's discount from net asset value over the last year. Good buy: Shares that sell at 5% below their normal value. For a conservative investor: 10% below the normal discount would be even better.

• Be selective. Some funds are selling at a heavy discount for a good reason. The assets in the portfolio may be illiquid or unmarketable.

• Don't buy a fund "at the market." These funds can be fairly volatile. Instead, put in the order to buy at a specific price.

• Avoid funds with by-laws that require a supermajority of shareholders (usually two-thirds) to change the fund's status from a closed-end fund to an open-end fund. Reason: If a fund becomes open-end, the shareholders get an immediate stepup in the value of some 20%-30%, depending on the actual discount of the fund from net asset value.

How to hedge with closed-end funds: Buy a stock fund and then sell naked (uncovered) options against the largest holdings in the fund.

• If the stock market declines: Options will make a lot of money, while the closed-end fund may not decline at all because it is already selling at a large discount from net asset value.

• If the stock market rallies: Gain in the price of the fund should more than offset losses in the options.

And you might consider using closed-end funds to invest pension funds of a small company rather than paying fees to an outside money manager.

Source: Thomas J. Herzfeld, executive vice president, Bishop, Rosen & Co., Inc., 7800 Red Rd., South Miami, FL 33143.

How to Spot a Small Growth Company

The long-running strength of the American Stock Exchange Index has regenerated broad investor interest in small companies. Two analysts with exceptional performance records tell how they spot potential way ahead of the market.

Bob Detwiler, partner of Fechtor, Detwiler (53 State St., Boston 02109), looks for a company headed by a hard-driving entrepreneur. He insists on knowing management on a personal level. Specifics that he looks for:

• Unconventional managers willing to take risks. Ideal: A chief executive who surrounds himself with people who complement his abilities and personality. Worst: A dictator who has yes-men on all sides.

• Talented key team: Strong chief financial officer, marketing manager, research director. Executives who can and do play devil's advocate to the boss's ideas.

• Focus on where the company is going rather than where it has been. Be sure that the company is spending heavily from current revenues on the development of new projects.

• A company that is in a period of healthy

135

transition. Good sign: Rising earnings after several years of flat results due to heavy R&D and marketing expenses.

What to avoid:

• Companies that are run by lawyers. In order to grow, a young company needs a chief executive who is willing to take risks. Such an approach, unfortunately, is anathema to most legal minds.

• A management that responds to tough questions in a vague way.

Charles Allmon, publisher of *Growth Stock Outlook* (4405 East/West Highway, Bethesda, MD 20014), describes his technique as "aggressively conservative." He looks for industries, then companies in them, that will be around for a long time. He doesn't try to assess the quickly changing fortunes of high-technology companies. Allmon looks at the company's balance sheet first. He wants to find:

• Current ratio (current assets to current liabilities) of 2:1 or better, a large amount of cash, and little debt. Keep a wary eye on long-term lease obligations, which are, in effect, a form of indebtedness. Learn how heavy such obligations are and whether they will put an undue burden on the financial resources of the company.

• No recent accounting changes that artificially boost earnings.

• Inventories accounted for on the most conservative basis (LIFO rather than FIFO).

• Fast inventory turnover.

• Small number of shares outstanding. This will prevent institutional investors from taking a position in the stock, which can be disastrous if they decide to sell all at once.

Allmon also wants to see a return on equity of at least 17% and profit margins that are high in relation to industry norms.

Two measures growth stock investors often overlook:

• The company's tax rate. Be sure that if the company is paying less than the usual 48% tax rate, an increase in the rate isn't likely for several years. A big tax bill could wipe out any earnings gains for the year.

• Company annual reports for four to ten years. See if actual results lived up to management's predictions.

When Not to Pay a Stockholder's Commission

It's not necessary to use a broker and pay a commission to make a gift of stock. Or if a sale of stock is negotiated privately.

How to transfer stock ownership to another person:

• Enter the other person's name, address, and Social Security number on the back of the certificate.

• Sign the back of the certificate and have the signature guaranteed by a commercial bank.

• Send it by registered mail to the transfer agent, whose name is on the certificate.

Allow two to six weeks for the other person to receive the new certificate. There will be no charge, although in some states the seller, or donor, has to pay a small transfer tax. It's a good idea to phone the bank first to find out its procedure and also the exact address of the stock transfer department.

Using Discount Brokers

How much can be saved? Discount brokers generally charge 35% to 85% less in commissions than full-service houses. Savings are particularly good on trades involving large numbers of shares.

Example: An individual has $15,000 to invest. If he buys 300 shares at $50 each, full-service house will charge about $230, discounter will charge about $110. If he buys 3,000 shares at $5 each, full-service house will charge about $400, discounter about $135.

Another point: People taking orders get no commissions, so there's no incentive to persuade an investor to do something he doesn't want to do. Discounters generally don't give investment advice. Otherwise, confirmations, monthly statements, and account insurance are generally the same for discounters as they are for full-service brokerage firms.

Who should use discounters? Investors who don't want or need advice from brokers. Among them are the following:

- Investors liquidating market holdings.
- Beneficiaries of estates who are moving inheritance from stocks and bonds to other kinds of investments.
- Employees whose only holdings are stocks in the companies they work for, who sell these stocks occasionally to pay bills.
- Lawyers, accountants, and other professionals who believe their personal contacts and own market analyses make for better guidance than what brokers are offering.
- Retired persons or other investors with free time to do their own market research.

Who should not use discounters?

- Investors interested in commodity trading. Discount houses handle stocks, bonds, and options only.
- Those with less than $2,000 to invest. Savings on discount commissions at this level do not outweigh the plus of free advice from full-service houses.
- Individuals getting into the market for the first time, with no experience.

Idea: Keep accounts at both full-service and discount houses.

Source: J. Bud Feuchtwanger, Financial Consultant, 161 E. 91 St., New York 10028.

How to Place Orders with a Stockbroker

Most investors are familiar with the basic forms of execution orders which they may give to their stockbrokers—limit orders (orders to buy and/or sell at the best available price), and stop loss orders (orders to buy and/or sell at the best available price if specified price levels are crossed). But far fewer investors are familiar with some of the other instructions. Examples:

- Fill or kill orders. These are either executed immediately or canceled. The investor wants to buy and/or sell immediately, in light of current market conditions. He does not wish to leave an open order which may be executed at some point when market conditions change adversely.
- Clean-up basis. Buy an amount of stock at the asked price only if the purchase "cleans up"

all available stock at that price. If the order is executed, the investor has reasonable assurance that no other heavy seller exists at the price range at which he purchased the shares. Result: The price is unlikely to drop rapidly.

- Not held. The investor provides the floor broker with full authority to use his judgment in the execution of the order. In a rapidly moving market, an alert floor broker may be able to secure a more advantageous price. But if the floor broker makes an error in judgment, the investor has no recourse.
- All or none. When buying or selling multiple lots, the investor requests that his entire position or none be sold at a limit price. He can often save on commissions by trading in large lots. The specialist is prevented from marking down the investor's shares in a series of partial executions.
- Short, short exempt. If the investor holds securities or bonds which may be converted into common stock, he can sell short the amount of stock into which these convertible issues may be converted without waiting for an uptick. To do this, he places a "short, short exempt" order. Advantages: The market for many convertible securities is thinner than the market for the underlying common. He will often get superior executions by selling the common short and then turning the convertible security into common, which is then employed to cover the short sale.

Source: Irving Waxman, R.F. Lafferty & Co., 50 Broad St., New York 10004.

When a Merger Is Bad News for Bond Owners

Mergers and tender offers generally represent good news to common stock holders of the company being approached. However, under certain conditions, holders of convertible bonds and convertible preferred shares or warrants can get hurt in the deal.

Here is how to protect yourself in any of these possible situations when the news of the merger discussion becomes known:

- If the convertible bond is selling at no or little premium over its actual conversion value (that is, value if converted into common shares), it's best to do nothing until the deal is announced. Reason: If a tender offer is made either in cash or stock, the convertible will rise equally with the common to reflect the value of the offer. You will be in position to simply sell your bonds or to convert them, using the common shares received to participate in the tender offer.

- If the bonds are selling well above conversion value: Assess the chances of a tender offer being made in cash. If that happens, the bond could lose value.

Example: You own convertible bonds, priced at $500, which can at the moment be converted into $300 worth of XYZ Corp. common. Such bonds are selling at a 67% premium over conversion value, but may rise in price in the future if the underlying common rises substantially.

If the buyer, ABC Corp., offers to tender in cash, and if the offer comes to $400 worth of stock per bond, that's less than the current selling price of the bonds. In such a situation, the bond will, in effect, lose its convertibility into equity, trading thereafter as a straight bond. There is a fair chance that the bond will soon drop in price.

Indicated action: Consider selling the convertibles immediately.

- A more favorable situation occurs if ABC Corp. offers its own shares for shares of XYZ. Since the tendering company is usually stronger than the takeover candidate, the convertible holder may benefit from holding bonds convertible into ABC. Where a merger for shares is offered, it often pays to hold the convertibles or to convert and tender.

Source: *The Value Line Options & Convertibles*, 5 E. 44 St., New York 10017.

Getting Financial Information on Over-the-Counters

Investors in smaller companies may not receive regular financial reports showing how the company is doing. What to do first:

- Ask for latest annual and quarterly financial statement.
- Find out if there is a recent proxy statement.
- Ask to be sent all future information.

If no response, try contacting broker-dealers who make a market in the company's stock, suggests Manhattan lawyer Dan Brecher. They are required to have the reports available. (To find market-makers, contact your regular broker or check *National Quotation Bureau* publications in the public library.)

If these steps don't work, write directly to the Securities and Exchange Commission, 500 North Capitol St., Washington, DC 20549. Advise SEC that company is not complying with regulations requiring it to provide financial information to stockholders.

Tax Advantages of Series E Savings Bonds

Savings bonds (Series E bonds) have a tax advantage that makes them worth looking into. The income tax on the interest can be either paid every year or postponed until the bonds are cashed in, and it's the bondholder's choice.

The government regularly extends the maturity date and continues to pay interest. Some people still hold bonds that were supposed to "mature" in the 1930s. This policy isn't likely to change.

Many working adults postpone the tax. When they cash the bonds, they'll pay tax on a big chunk of interest. But by that time they'll probably be retired and in a lower bracket. And they can cash a few bonds every year to spread out the tax. If the bonds are left in the estate, it's possible to continue postponing the tax.

Another approach: Make gifts of bonds, or cash to buy bonds, to minor children. Then make the decision that the interest will be reported every year. (But there won't be any tax unless the child receives more than $1,000 per year in interest.) To do this, be sure to file a tax return for the child the first year and report the interest. This must be done, even though the return isn't required, to show that the decision was made to report the interest currently. Once interest is reported, it must be reported every year. You can't switch back to postponing it.

Important: Check issue date before cashing Series E bonds. Several months' interest is lost if they're cashed before six- or twelve-month anniversary, because interest is credited only every six months. Buy them late in the month. Interest is credited from first day of month of purchase.

Before You Invest in a Business

Any investor, even a small one, can do the kind of analysis that two of Wall Street's most sophisticated security analysts do for the nation's major institutional investors. Robert Olstein and Thornton O'glove sell their *Quality of Earnings Report* for fees running into five figures a year in security transaction commissions. They don't forecast the market or recommend buys, sells, or holds. They critique the financial statements of hundreds of major corporations, looking for troubles. And they find them.

When they have a question about a company, the first thing they do is call the company for an answer. Individual investors have an advantage over professionals here: Corporate executives are less wary of them, more likely to answer straight rather than evade or smooth-talk. Steps to take:

• Look for such financial statement peculiarities as deviations from trends, inconsistencies, especially between stockholder reports (annual and quarterly) and filings with the SEC (10Ks, 10Qs, proxy statements, prospectuses, etc.) that companies must provide (usually on request).

• Focus on big deviations between the financial reports and the tax returns. No outsider, not even a shareholder, can see a tax return. But corporations must reconcile deviations between the two sets of books in their SEC 10K filings. They must explain the significant differences between tax costs in financial statements and what's actually paid to IRS. Key items: Deferred taxes, differences between effective tax rates and statutory rates because of depletion allowances, investment tax credits, offshore tax credits,

DISC benefits, etc. Example: Corporation's reported earnings went from 93¢ to $1, but 5¢ represented deferred taxes. Significance: Real earnings growth may have been only 2¢—not 7¢.

Inventory figures are crucial: The turnover ratio changes, but also the mix of raw materials, work in process, finished goods. Look at these figures to see if there are buildups of finished goods, maybe signifying plans to cut production, or increases in raw materials without increases in work in process, maybe meaning there's a worrisome production problem.

Accounts receivable: What's happening to allowance for doubtful accounts? Worry if the ratio to receivables is up or down. Could mean they are expecting trouble if it's up or manufacturing false earnings if it is down. Another key number worth figuring can be number of days of sales in the receivables total, indicating level of activity compared with previous years.

Accounts payable: Are they stretching out payments? Why? Are there credit problems?

Sources and uses of funds statement: How is company's liquidity, financing situation?

Income statement: Look at ratios of marketing costs, R&D costs, cost of goods sold, etc., compared with trends. Is it controlling its expenses at past rates or losing control? Did changes in trends penalize earnings? Increase them? Deviations in either direction are worth following up with calls to management (play the bumpkin; you may get better information).

Every stockholder ought to ask himself and management: If I see problems cropping up in financial statements, I need more reason for owning this stock than I needed before.

Protection for Investors in Small Businesses

Deductions of stock losses against ordinary income are generally limited to $3,000. But it's possible to deduct up to $25,000 (or $50,000 on a joint return) when the loss is an investment in a small business company organized under Section 1244 of the Internal Revenue Code.

Important condition: The stock must have

139

been issued under a plan which "specifically states, in dollars, the maximum amount to be received for the stock." In a recent case, the investor lost the deduction because the plan mentioned only number of shares, not value.

What to do: Before investing in stock of a small business company, have counsel check the exact language of the plan under which the stock was issued.

Mogab et al. v. *Commissioner,* 70 T.C., No. 19, 5/15/78.

Investment Traps to Avoid

• Eighty percent of those who speculate in commodities lose. If more than luck is involved in winning (and that's not certain), then those who have the best chance are the big food companies that have worldwide sources of inside information. On the other hand, if trading commodities is just a form of gambling, recognize that fact and stay away from it.

• Coins: Many services offering gold and other coins (usually silver dollars) actually charge far more than an investor would pay at a typical coin dealership. Tip: Before purchasing via mail order, you should comparison-shop. One information source: Coin hobbyist magazines, available at many newsstands, carry advertisements which list current prices.

• Gold: A number of gold plans offer gold in a form which is either: (1) A commodity option to buy gold (but these are often unsupported by any ability of the issuer to honor the contract if the price of gold rises sharply). (2) The equivalent of a conventional gold futures contract.

In the futures type of program, the investor is asked to put up a "deposit" and is given the right to take delivery of gold at some future date or to liquidate his "right" should gold rise in price. What's wrong with the deal: (1) Such promotions often charge much higher commissions than an investor would pay for a simple commodity contract executed through a major brokerage firm. (2) The deposit the investor has to put up often exceeds the margin normally required for a gold futures contract.

Other problems: The policing of such contracts and the ability of promoters to meet obligations is questionable. And token amounts of gold, delivered to small investors, aren't as easy to resell as promoters would have potential investors believe.

Guidelines for Investing in Diamonds

Diamonds are complex—no field for tyros looking for a safe investment.

• Risks: In the open market, diamond prices fluctuate as supply and demand conditions change. Invest only funds not needed for three to five years. Based on historic price trends, that's how long it takes for the wholesale price (at which an investor sells) to catch up with the retail price (at which he buys). Thus, even if prices continue steadily upward, it may take three years or more to break even.

• Selecting diamonds for an investment: If liquidity is the most important consideration, buy the same grades that jewelers do. That is, diamonds worth less than $2,000 (roughly the maximum amount most people are willing to pay for an engagement ring).

High-liquidity diamonds should have a GIA (Gemological Institute of America) color grade not lower than J. (K and lower grades have traces of yellow visible to the naked eye.) The GIA clarity grade should be VS (very slight imperfection) or SI (slight imperfection—might be visible to the naked eye).

For maximum appreciation, buy high-quality diamonds, which are rarest. Top grade is D (pure white) Flawless (no imperfections). Also accepted as high quality are diamonds with color grades down to about F and clarity grades down to VVS (very very slight imperfection). They're sold through major jewelers, diamond investment firms, and auction houses as well as through private investors.

• Check the reputation of a firm carefully before doing business. Get the name of the firm's banker and ask him about the company's financial strength. Also check the firm's Dun & Bradstreet report. Ask the local Better Business Bureau if it has received any complaints about the company. And shop around before choosing your firm. Markups range from 20% to 100%. Ask diamond investment firms, jewelers, and diamond brokers (who sell to jewelers) what they would charge for a diamond of a specific weight, cut, color, and clarity.

• Insist on a grading certificate from a major independent laboratory. Don't rely solely on a certificate from the seller. There's always the temptation to overgrade. The difference between two grades can mean hundreds (or thousands) of dollars.

Diamonds graded by the Gemological Institute of America are more easily salable than diamonds graded by any other laboratory, and they can command a 15%-20% premium. Other laboratories whose certificates are widely accepted: American Gemological Laboratories, United States Gemological Services.

Terms of sale:

• Avoid margin plans. Some firms have misappropriated investor funds.

• Prompt delivery. If diamonds are ordered by phone or mail, the contract should specify that the diamonds will be sent within ten days after the firm receives good funds.

• Satisfaction guarantee. Thirty days is a reasonable guarantee period, although not every firm offers that much. Use the guarantee period to check whether the diamond that was ordered matches the diamond that was received. The guarantee should remain in force even though a laboratory report is received after the guarantee period has expired.

Have the diamonds reappraised every six months. The longer the delay, the greater the uninsured risk. Use an appraisal firm linked via computer to diamond cutters and dealers across the country.

Three such firms: Analytics, Inc., 645 Fifth Ave., New York 10022. Independent Jewelry Appraisers, 2100 West Look South, Houston 77027. United States Gemological Services, 201 Civic Center Dr. East, Santa Ana, CA 92701.

Best ways to follow news affecting diamond investments: *Diamond Registry Bulletin*, 30 West 47 St., New York 10036. *Precious Stones Newsletter*, Box 4649, Thousand Oaks, CA 91359.

Book Collecting: A Time-Tested Hedge Against Inflation

As with other investments, book values act according to the laws of supply and demand. But unlike stocks, the supply of first editions can't ever increase. Over the years, quality books almost always appreciate in value. In addition, like art, books offer a return in aesthetic pleasure above and beyond monetary investment.

Investors who know what they're doing often have collections that appreciate in value by 20% annually.

Four principal ways to invest:

• First edition classics. Collecting these books is much like collecting art masterpieces. You are competing against professionals and prices are very high. The likelihood of finding bargains is remote. Unless you become an expert (or can retain one) and have a lot of money to invest, it's probably a better idea to put your money in other types of books.

• First edition nonclassics. Try to anticipate which of today's first editions will be highly valued in the future. Because these books are not yet classics, the investor risks only the book's current market price. Advice: Look for authors or subjects you like. If the book doesn't appreciate, at least you have an enjoyable item. Longshot: The number of hardcover books sold each year has been declining. It's possible that sometime in the future, hardcovers themselves may become a valuable investment.

• Specialize in books by or about one author or subject. By choosing a slightly unusual author or topic, one can build a valuable collection even though it isn't in first editions. And the cost isn't exorbitant.

• Book clubs. These make for a much less time-consuming way to collect. You don't have to have great hunches or compete against professionals. But you must be sure to join the right club. The only club one collector, Louis Ehrenkrantz, recommends is The Limited Editions Club (551 Fifth Ave., New York 10017). Because it prints only 2,000 copies of the 12 books it puts out each year (a member is required to buy all 12 at $60 apiece), each book is automatically a rare book. It also gets top artists to illustrate them. (Picasso and Matisse have illustrated books, which have appreciated from the $10 selling price at the time to between $1,500 and $2,000 each.) They are all autographed by the authors or artists. So the books appreciate on the basis of the writer and/or the artwork. Bindings, printing, and paper are all the best and the subjects are usually well chosen. Membership is limited to 2,000, however, so you may have to be put on a waiting list.

Caution: The Limited Editions Club has been in business for 50 years and has many imitators, none of which matches its track record.

Basic guidelines:

• Only invest if you love books. Book collecting is not a sure thing for everyone, and an investor must get pleasure from his books in noneconomic ways.

• Don't follow the crowd. If you decide to collect books by or about an author or subject, be sure to avoid the obvious choices. Shakespeare and the Civil War are two examples of subjects that are so popular and widely printed that it's unlikely most collections will appreciate. Just about everything that came out during the Bicentennial year (coins, stamps, books) is worth little. But don't take it as a rule of thumb that you should be scared off by large first printings—if you have a hunch a book will be famous in the future, demand can eventually overtake supply.

• What percentage of your portfolio to invest: No more than 10%. Someone with more than $100,000 to invest annually should not exceed $10,000.

Forgeries: A serious problem with first edition classics (and another reason the nonprofessional book collector shouldn't invest in them). It's impossible for a nonexpert to tell whether a book is genuine or not. Antiquarian Book Sellers Association of America (50 Rockefeller Plaza, New York 10020) will help direct you to experts who can identify forgeries. But sometimes even the experts are fooled.

Care of books: Proper care is essential to preserve valuable books, but it need not be a burden. Some basic information:

• Where to store them. In a bookcase that is protected from direct sunlight. Sunlight fades the print and can cause the printing to transfer.

• Temperature and humidity. The room should be cool and not too dry. Overheating warps books and yellows the pages.

• Bookworms are not a serious problem. If they turn up, seal the book in a large plastic bag with some paradichlorobenzene mothballs for a month. Be careful not to let the mothballs touch the book itself.

• Other rules. Dust the books regularly. Use bookmarks. Never lay a book face down—that cracks the binding.

Source: Louis Ehrenkrantz, Rosenkrantz, Ehrenkrantz, Lyon & Ross, New York.

Buying Antique Rugs

Unlike many antiques that can be bought, used, and then sold at a profit, Oriental rugs require special care. Even with the best of care, the wrong rug in the wrong place can be destroyed. (A major law firm paid $20,000 for a delicate antique Kerman and was surprised when it didn't stand the wear of the main conference room.) Some things to consider:

• Never buy an Oriental rug that needs repairs. Repairs are costly.

• Resale of antique rugs is difficult because of the dealer's spread. Basically, the retailer wants a 100% markup. So a rug bought at auction for $1,000 might double in retail value in five years, but it still will fetch only $1,000 from a dealer. If sold at an auction, the gallery takes 20%. However, the cost of trucking, cleaning, and cataloging must be deducted from the selling price of the rug.

• There are profits to be made, but antique rug selling is no game for amateurs.

Investing in Art

Year-end is the worst time to buy from an art dealer. Best time is May and June, when dealers seek to wind down inventory for the end of the business year. In the summer, many dealers travel to Europe on buying trips or go on vacation. They would prefer to have sold most or all of their art before departing. As a result, they are likely to be more receptive to lower offers from collectors than they would be otherwise. Be prepared to pay immediately upon acceptance of your offer.

Source: *The Investor's Guide to the Art Market,* The ARTnewsletter, 122 E. 42 St., New York 10017.

Stamp Collection Investment Traps

Novice stamp investors can be easy marks for swindlers. Counterfeiting and altering stamps does take place.

A couple of pointers: First, keep in mind that retail stamp prices in catalogs are close to what you may pay, but not the price you would get if you sell. The dealer's markup amounts to at least 15% to 20%.

Second, if you invest in new stamps, you probably will have to hold them 20 to 40 years to get sizable appreciation. Most smart money is invested in classic stamps, those issued between 1840 and 1900.

What to do: Find a reputable dealer and ask him to help you fashion an investment collection. If you are concerned with the authenticity of a stamp, invest a small sum—usually 1% to 5% of the value—and get a certificate of authenticity issued by one of the many philatelic societies that exist in most major cities.

Or, you might buy on extension, asking the seller for a written agreement to refund your money if the stamp proves to be a fake or if it turns out it has been doctored.

LABOR RELATIONS

When a Union is Organizing

When a Lost NLRB Election is O.K.

Dealing with Union Activists

Signs of Organizing

Disciplining a Union Steward

Filing an NLRB Complaint

Traps of Arbitration

How to Curb Wildcat Strikes

11

LABOR RELATIONS

How Unionization Affects Company Profits

The profits, or return on investment, of a unionized company become more vulnerable as its share of a particular market increases.

That's the finding, according to Dr. Sidney Schoeffler, head of the Strategic Planning Institute (1 Broadway, Cambridge, MA 02142), a nonprofit think tank that runs continuing series on the effects of business variables.

How unions, market share impact return on investment

		Employees unionized		
		1%	50%	Over 50%
	Lo			
		10	15	13
Relative	26%			
Market		21	22	19
Share	63%			
		39	38	29
	Hi			

The chart shows how return on investment varies with the percentage of employee unioniza-

tion (read vertically) and the percentage of market share (read horizontally).

Don't be misled by the term market share: It doesn't necessarily imply a big, nationwide business. Market share can be measured locally or with a narrow product segment.

A drop-off in profitability doesn't happen because the union has forced a rapid rise in wages. Compensation rises at the same rate for unionized and nonunionized firms.

The real reason unionization affects profits is that it lowers productivity. The amount of value added to a commodity per employee is less in heavily unionized companies than in nonunion companies.

Dr. Schoeffler says that unionization can mean shorter work hours or more restrictive work rules, which limit a company's ability to adjust its work force as needed.

Companies with a low (below 26%) or a medium (from 26% to 63%) share of a particular market aren't hurt by heavy unionization as much as companies with major (more than 63%) market share.

Those major-share companies lose 10 points of

profitability as they move from nonunionization (1% column) to heavily unionized (over 50% of employees).

What's Allowed When a Union Tries to Organize

If a union starts an organizing drive at a company, there are a number of things that can and should be done about it.

The most important thing: Don't give up without a fight. Unions aren't all powerful. They often lose an election.

And it's not true, as many may think, that employer's hands are tied by the labor laws when it comes to union organizing. Some things are prohibited, but there are many steps that can legally and properly be taken to try to persuade employees not to sign union cards and to vote against the union if there's an election.

The best way to keep a union out: Treat employees fairly. That doesn't mean the company has to give away the store to do it. Wages, fringe benefits, and working conditions don't have to be better than competitors' or better than those of other employers in the area. But they should be competitive.

What is essential is good two-way communication between workers and their immediate supervisors. When this is missing, employee dissatisfaction runs high—one of the biggest reasons that unions succeed. The worker's impression of the company and its management depends almost entirely on the supervisor whom he takes orders from and deals with every day. To the worker, the foreman is the company.

Very common is a situation where the worker thinks his supervisor plays favorites in handing out job assignments and recommending promotions, as well as in demanding performance or in overlooking mistakes. That worker is sure to vote for the union.

Foremen and other lower-level supervisors should understand the importance of their role in forming employee attitudes. It won't work if line supervisors themselves don't have good morale. Consider starting a training course for line su-

pervisors. Warning: A course of this kind can be resented as a waste of time by the supervisors if not accompanied by good two-way communication up the line.

When a union organizing drive starts, there are certain things an employer is legally not permitted to do:

• Make threats of any kind, such as to take away benefits or close the plant and move if the union wins.

• Promise new benefits on condition that the union loses.

• Grant wage increases or other improved benefits, since this could be interpreted as anti-union move, unless they were planned before the drive started.

What the employer may do during the organizing drive:

• Talk to employees in large or small groups or one-to-one.

• Place messages in the pay envelope or on the bulletin board, or send letters to homes.

• Explain the advantages of working there compared with other places.

• Say that better money benefits can only come if company survives and prospers, and if it does they'll probably be achieved with or without the union.

• Tell the truth about the union, such as officers' salaries, official charges of corruption. Articles about union corruption from responsible publications are probably okay, too.

The big problem is workers who don't care. Their attitude: A union won't do any harm and it might do some good, so might as well vote for it. (Or they don't bother to vote.) It's important to emphasize to workers the disadvantages of having the union:

• Dues. They won't go down, will probably increase in years to come.

• Loss of personal freedom. They will be forced to go along with majority of members; submit to decisions made somewhere else, perhaps even another geographical area.

• A third party present in discussing grievances with employer.

• A strike that the worker may not want. It could be called by the international union. The issue may not even involve the particular plant, but the worker will lose pay anyway.

How Workers Lose Money on Raises Won by Striking

An effective way to show workers how much a strike costs them: A chart using a range of possible hourly increases and showing how long after a strike it would take to make up the loss.

Example: An employee who takes home $200 a week after deductions.

Length of strike	Hourly wage gain	Time it takes to make up lost wages
2 weeks	20¢	50 weeks
	30	33 weeks
	40	25 weeks
4 weeks	20	1 yr., 48 weeks
	30	1 yr., 14 weeks
	40	50 weeks
10 weeks	20	4 yrs., 42 weeks
	30	3 yrs., 10 weeks
	40	2 yrs., 21 weeks

Unmasking Union Tactics

Protect the company against unionization by periodically informing employees about their rights in resisting organizing efforts. One of the most frequently misunderstood organizing vehicles is the union authorization card. Be certain employees understand these points:

• The union argues that the cards are used only for the purpose of getting an election. What they don't say is that cards may be used to try to obtain certification of the union without an election if more than half the workers in the unit sign.

• Organizer says the cards are confidential and the employer will never know who signed. Point out that if the organizer needs to prove he has a majority or if management initiates legal challenge to validity of cards, management has the right to examine the cards.

• The card is a legal application for membership in union and can bind signer to dues, fees, and union by-laws immediately.

• The union can use signed authorization cards to call a strike at any time after the cards are signed (even before election is held), and signers are commited to strike, no matter what their intentions were when they originally signed the cards.

• It is very difficult, if not impossible, to get a card back once it has been turned in to the union.

• Signing a card in no way commits an employee to vote for union representation if an election is held. Ballots are secret.

Source: *The Hughes Report* (on Practical Employee Relations for Non-Union Organizations), 33 W. 60 St., New York 10023.

NLRB Union Election Rules: A Company That Loses May Still Win

Most American companies do not have unionized employees. As a result, managements are inexperienced in dealing with union organizing drives. They don't know what to expect. It's easy to overlook lawful countermeasures or run afoul of National Labor Relations Board rules.

But the law is explicit and management should know what to expect when a union organizing campaign begins.

The law provides for this sequence of events:

• Union organizers solicit authorization cards from employees to authorize the union to represent workers in dealing with the company on wages, hours, and working conditions. An employer should never start negotiating terms of an agreement prematurely at this point.

• When 30% of the members of a bargaining unit have signed authorization cards, the union can petition the NLRB for an election. But if more than 50% of the employees sign authorization cards, the NLRB may grant the union representation status directly, bypassing an election altogether. The company, however, can still insist on an election if there is a doubt that cards were signed by an informed and uncoerced majority of employees.

• Once the union's petition is filed, the NLRB sends a copy to the employer with a request for a list of employees and job classifications. The list must include names and addresses of employees in the bargaining unit requested by the union.

- The NLRB then calls a meeting to see if the union and the company agree on what makes up the bargaining unit (department, etc.) and the date of election. If the employer disagrees, the NLRB regional office will make a decision, which is appealable.
- The election usually takes place about three weeks later. Union and management meet beforehand to inspect the polls and voting eligibility list. Each side may post two observers at the polls to challenge ineligible voters. Challenged ballots are sealed and their validity is checked by an NLRB agent if the vote is close.
- The losing party can file objections within five working days after an election. Objections ruled on by the NLRB local regional director may be appealed. If the company is still not satisfied, it can refuse to bargain with the union and fight charges the union brings through the NLRB, or it can take the case to the U.S. Court of Appeals. Many companies lose an election but never sign a union contract anyway, because bargaining is effectively delayed so long that the union loses strength.

How a Union Can Bluff You into Recognizing It

Don't recognize a union merely on assurances that a majority of employees have joined, or even on a offer to show signed cards.

- Signatures may have been obtained by coercion, misrepresentation, or even forgery.
- Cards may have authorized the union only to ask for an election.
- Cards may have been signed several months earlier and no longer represent the current wishes of employees.

If the employer promises to recognize a union on a showing of majority support, the NLRB may compel recognition without an election if it is satisfied that the cards are valid. Further, the employees will not have heard the employer's point of view during a pre-election campaign.

Company Strategy for Tipping Scales in Union Election

There are many ways to reduce the risk of unionization—provided they are started before the union drive begins. But this is a very tricky area and expert labor counsel must be consulted every step of the way. Here's one approach:

Create favorable bargaining units, the group of employees who vote on whether to join a union at all. The larger the unit, the harder it is to organize, and the more it costs the union to try. The chief test of what is a unit is "community of interest": Similarity of wages, hours and working conditions; physical proximity of employees; common supervision, interchange of personnel; relatedness of employee functions in the production line.

Remember that every one of these factors is directly controllable by the employer.

Discharging the Union Activist

The National Labor Relations Board won't let a company get away with firing an employee on the pretext of his performance when the real reason is his union activity. But that doesn't mean the company can't fire an employee for good cause even though he's been a union activist. Common problem: A worker may get into trouble for his job performance and then claim he is being disciplined for his union activities. But that strategy won't work if the reason for the discharge is sound.

In a recent case, a newly hired mechanic tried to get the union in the shop to enforce its contract with the company more effectively. Management took away the activist worker's privileges, such as drinking coffee at his workbench. But he was fired only when he was caught smoking near a can of flammable solvent. The NLRB upheld the firing. Its ruling:

The mere fact that an employer may desire to

149

terminate an employee because he engages in protected activity does not, of itself, establish the unlawfulness of a subsequent discharge. If an employee provides an employer with sufficient cause for his dismissal by engaging in conduct for which he could have been terminated in any event, and the employer discharges him for that reason, the fact that the employer welcomed the opportunity to discharge does not make it discriminatory and therefore unlawful.
Fikse Bros., 98 LRRM 1141; *Propak Corp.* v. *NLRB,* 98 LRRM 2946.

Signs of Undercover Union Organizing

• Busyness during breaks instead of people relaxing.
• New groupings emerging with new leaders.
• Small gatherings of employees in unusual areas of the plant or office.
• Sudden increase in questions about company policies and benefits.
• Former employees coming by and talking to workers.
• Complaints and demands for rights by groups of employees made in a miltant way.
• Changes in workers' attitudes from friendly to uncommunicative.
• Unpopularity of once popular employees.
• Claims of loyalty by new employees.
Source: Alfred T. DeMaria, Partner, Clifton, Budd, Burke & DeMaria, New York, in *The Hughes Report,* 33 W. 60 St., New York 10023.

Past Practice Guidelines

If your company is forced into arbitration over a grievance that appears to have no contractual justification, chances are the union's case will be that the company is bound not by the contract but by past practice.

Sometimes arbitrators are persuaded by the past practice argument. Some guidelines:
• The past practice must be clear and consis-

tent. Occasional lapses won't count if they can be explained satisfactorily.

Example: A company had the right to insist that employees work overtime in turn. But this right wasn't forced on an unwilling worker when there was someone else who would take his place. On a later occasion, the management refused to take no for an answer when no substitute was available. An arbitrator ruled that occasional leniency didn't constitute a waiver of the company's right under the contract.
• A practice can be no broader than the circumstances that gave rise to it.

Example: In its old location, a company had room in its parking lot for all employees. On moving into a more congested part of the city, however, it no longer had off-street space for vehicles. Since the contract didn't mention parking privileges, the company didn't have to give employees a parking allowance, an arbitrator ruled.
• The existence of the practice must be known to management and the union.

Example: When a plant manager discovered that a supervisor in a remote area of the plant was letting his crew sign out ten minutes early, he put a stop to it. The early quitting practice in that one location wasn't binding, an arbitrator wrote, because there was no "mutuality." The only people in the plant who knew about it were the local supervisor and the members of his particular crew.
• The practice must have been in effect long enough to create an expectation that it will continue.

Example: Because the company had, for at least ten years, let employees leave a few hours early the day before Christmas, union negotiators never bothered to ask for this privilege to be included in the contract. An arbitrator said the practice could not be discontinued on short notice. However, once the union knew that the employer wanted the practice stopped, it was on notice to bring the issue up in negotiations or acquiesce in the future.

Warning: Don't ignore morale factors. If management is asserting its rights for the first time or making decisions that its employees might find hard to take, give as much notice and as full an explanation as possible.

When a Union Steward Can Be Disciplined

Under the law, union stewards are permitted to argue vigorously against company policies. But personal abuse directed at supervisors can make the steward vulnerable to discipline.

To win such a case, management must show the supervisor stayed cool during the dispute.

An arbitrator recently upheld an official warning to a steward who called the foreman a "dummy" and threatened to make life tough for him. Other employees were within sight and hearing. A controlling fact was that the foreman maintained "a high standard of civility."

Unionizing Executive Secretaries

The National Labor Relations Board concedes that employees privy to confidential management information cannot join unions, but the board defines confidential narrowly. Thus, secretaries privy to the company's books or market plan, for example, can sign up. An exception: Those actually privy to management policies with respect to labor relations.
Springhill Bank & Trust Co., 238 NLRB No.17.

When an NLRB Complaint Can't Be Filed

Employees are expected to exhaust their private remedies (the grievance procedure of union contracts) before the NLRB will examine alleged labor law violations.

There are exceptions (as stated recently by the Fifth Circuit Court of Appeals in Dresser Industries, 97 LRRM 2579):

1. The union wrongfully refused to process the grievance.

2. The employer's conduct constituted a repudiation of contractual procedures (making it impossible for the employee to use the grievance procedure).

3. Filing of a grievance would be futile because the worker's complaint was against the union, as well as the employer, and he would have to argue his case before a body that was stacked against him.

When the Insurer Insists a Union Driver Can Be Removed

A truck driver covered by a union contract can't be fired or transferred to a nondriving job merely because an insurance company threatens not to renew a policy unless the company complies. But it is possible to take action if done the right way. Rules to follow:

• Investigate the facts. Don't assume the driver was at fault without getting a police report or some objective evidence. A statement by the operator of the other vehicle in an accident is self-serving, and should be discounted.

• If the company driver was not at fault, or if his accident record was otherwise good, look for another insurance company. Search for alternative coverage. This will help convince the arbitrator that the company did not let an outsider dictate personnel policies.

• The fact that rates may go up after the accident is not by itself justification for discharge or transfer of the driver. There is a possible exception if a change in rates would have a truly catastrophic impact on the company.

• If the driver's license is suspended, the company must remove him from a driving job. But it can let him operate vehicles again when the suspension is lifted.

• Discharge or suspension stands a better chance of approval by an arbitrator if the action follows company rules. Typical rule permits discharge after a third chargeable incident in a 12-month period.

Note: These are good rules to follow in non-union establishments, as well. The same issues might arise in an EEOC or court action if the driver can invoke the Civil Rights Act.

Who Is a Supervisor?

Giving an employee a little responsibility doesn't necessarily make him a supervisor under the National Labor Relations Act. One senior technician made work assignments and had authority to rearrange the layout of the shop. The company considered him a supervisor and felt justified in firing him for participating in union activity. But the court held that he didn't exercise independent judgment on the job and was merely an intermediary between management and workers, not a supervisor.

Traps of Arbitration

Companies writing arbitration clauses into union contracts should be aware of two catches in the arbitration process that make it increasingly less effective as protection against litigation than it was at one time.

• Does public law have precedence over a private contract written before the law came into existence? This has been an increasingly muddy area ever since the first civil rights laws were passed. When an arbitrator rules for company on an issue involving, say, seniority, the union may go to the courts. Occupational Safety and Health Administration made the problem worse. Now we have legislation banning mandatory retirement before 70. What next?

• Likelihood is increasing that an employee may bring legal charges of "unfair representation" if the union fails to bring a grievance to arbitration. Or even if the union does and the arbitrator finds in favor of the company. It's a difficult charge for the employee to prove. But more and more cases of unfair representation are being taken to court by employees with a real (or fancied) grievance.

As a result, many arbitration proceedings are dragged out interminably as arbitrators and legal counsel bend over backward (at high cost) to remove any pretext for further legal action.

The best advice to employers is to retain a law firm that has experience in arbitration proceedings and also closely follows impending federal legislation in a wide spectrum of regulatory fields.

Source: Morris Stone, former vice president, American Arbitration Association.

Checking on the Union

Whether the union's already in the company or trying to get in, here's good advice: Know as much about it as possible. In planning strategy, it's very valuable to know what experiences other employers have had with this union, what cases it has won and lost.

Where to get that information (or ask your lawyer to get it):

• The Department of Labor in Washington has copies of all union constitutions and by-laws, also Form LM-1 and LM-2, which give names and salaries of union officers and details of structure and operations of both local and international unions. Write Department of Labor, 200 Constitution Ave., N.W. Washington, DC 20210.

• The Department of Labor may have copies of union contracts in force with other employers. They don't have them all, because filing is not mandatory, but it's worth asking.

• Cases fully replorted and indexed by NLRB (1717 Pennsylvania Ave., N.W., Washington, DC 20570); Commerce Clearing House, Inc. (1120 Ave of the Americas, New York 10036), and Bureau of National Affairs, Inc. (1231 25th St., N.W., Washington 20037).

• Labor Arbitration Reports published by American Arbitration Association (140 W. 51 St., New York 10020) and by BNA.

• Labor Cases, reporting service of court cases covering labor (CCH).

These services are expensive, but lawyers have access to them.

From these and other sources, find out what

152

other companies have been organized by the union that's trying to organize the plant. Call those companies, get tips on what the union people are like and where they are vulnerable.

New York labor lawyer Henry P. Baer* says many employers find that having a union doesn't make that much difference in wage rates, since they have to pay competitive wages to keep good people anyway. The biggest disadvantage: Rigid union rules that restrict flexibility on job assignments and transfers, and require that seniority be followed absolutely with no recognition of individual merit.

• Indicated action: Fight hard for maximum flexibility while keeping rigid work rules to a minimum. Be sure to have a "zipper" clause: Any rights not specifically granted the union in contract are reserved to management.

Offer the union a provision that all grievances and controversies not resolved internally will go to binding arbitration. Tell the union you're willing to surrender this much control to an independent third party (the arbitrator), but you want a no-strike agreement for the length of the contract in exchange.

If the union calls a strike over an issue that

*Skadden, Arps, Slate, Meagher & Flom, 919 Third Ave., New York 10022.

could have been arbitrated, it may be possible to get a federal court injunction against the strike. (This is one of the rare cases where an anti-strike injunction is possible.) And it may also be possible to collect money damages from the union if it calls a strike during the contract term in violation of its no-strike agreement.

How to Curb Wildcat Strikes

A clear and enforceable no-strike clause should say: "In the event of any strike or concerted stoppage of work, the union shall declare publicly that the strike is unauthorized, and order its members to resume normal duties notwithstanding the existence of a picket line."

The last part of the clause prevents union officers from announcing that a stoppage is "unauthorized," but then supporting employees who refuse to cross the unauthorized picket line. It also prevents union leaders from evading responsibility by claiming that a stoppage is a "sympathy" strike that's not barred by the terms of the contract.

MAINTENANCE AND ENERGY

Prolonging Machine Tool Life

Cleaning in Plants and Offices

Replacing Cars and Trucks

Smart Tire Maintenance

After a Collision: Fix or Replace?

Saving Truck and Tractor Fuel

New Construction that Saves Energy

Easy Energy Savers

12

MAINTENANCE AND ENERGY

Preventive Maintenance

Waiting for breakdowns is expensive and dangerous. That policy increases machine wear and damage, lowers production efficiency, increases scrap rate, and—in extreme cases—shuts down production lines.

Solution: Identify maintenance priorities.

1. Critical: Takes priority over everything else. Failure to react immediately can be dangerous. (Example: Leaking gas line.)

2. Demand: Not critical but not routine, either. Must be performed as soon as possible but need not break into work routines. (Example: Security gate is stuck so must be kept open, causing a backup as identification is checked. Should be fixed before end of the work shift or day.)

3. Preventive: Most easily ignored, and most in need of management. Problem: When machinery is running well, production management will not give it up. But the more machines are used to meet tight production schedules, the greater the danger of a major breakdown.

When preventive maintenance is needed:

• Increased downtime of equipment. (Might

have been avoided by analyzing recent history of breakdowns.)

• Increased amount of machine setup time. (May be indication that machine tolerances need analysis.)

• Increased scrap rates because of poor machine performance.

• Machine problems detected only after breakdowns.

• Inventory being built up to guard against machine failures.

Preventive maintenance is repetitive and can be scheduled. Examples: Lubrication, inspection, overhauls, tool replacement.

Managing a preventive maintenance program:

• Use maintenance crew to produce machine downtime records and cost files instead of letting them wait around for next emergency.

• Train manpower and purchase needed materials in advance.

• Isolate production areas where things can be fixed quickly and cheaply. Leaking hydraulic systems, for example. Replace hoses, couplings, and valves twice a year at minimum cost, whether necessary or not. Much cheaper than waiting for a breakdown.

• Schedule downtime for routine maintenance for off-hours (after hours, during vacation, summer or seasonal shutdowns).

Ways to Prolong the Life of Expensive Plant Tools

• Don't operate machines faster than the manufacturer's recommended feeds and speeds.

• Post cost information for each tool. Awareness by workers of the high cost prompts more careful use.

• Post records of average tool life so employees using them know how long they should last.

• Tool grinding and sharpening should be performed only by authorized personnel, accountable for tool usage in their departments.

• Limit authority for requisitioning and issuing new tools to one or two people.

• Keep machines clean and in good operating condition.

• Periodically check used and discarded tools for possible salvage or use in other departments.
Source: *Financially Speaking,* General Motors Education and Training, 1700 West Third Ave., Flint, MI 48502.

When to Use Outside Cleaning Contractors

It's not always cost-efficient to have company staff clean the plant or office. The first step in determining who should do cleaning is to pin down exactly what is being done, by whom, and at what cost.

Best to have special cost analysis to pull together all items, including Social Security, worker's compensation, overtime, supplies.

• The analysis will bring realization that maintenance is an expensive element of running a business. Maintenance decisions should not be left to people with no maintenance expertise.

Nothing is ever 100% clean, and it is usually

not cost-justified to strive for small increments at the upper levels. Cleanliness can be related to a productivity level (thousands of feet per hour) to predict exactly what level can be obtained for a certain cost. Each company must determine its own requirements and special circumstances.

• Where to get help: Professional cleaning services can help in this analysis. (There are also independent consultants.) Check with Buildings Owners and Managers Association for good cleaners. Also, Yellow Pages listings will include many small entrepreneurs ("mom and pop" operations) that offer personalized service. The small ones may not be professionally competent to deal with unusual materials or circumstances. Best to seek out members of Building Service Contractors Association. Membership assures at least a minimum of experience.

It's also wise to ask other building owners or plant managers about their cleaning contractors. This is a service business, and even a big national contractor may or may not offer good service in a particular geographical area.

Considering all the expenses, it's generally more cost-effective to use a contractor than to have an in-house staff.

Don't overlook possible union problem. Maintenance people are unionized. If your company isn't, and has no labor or industrial relations experts to negotiate contracts, a better deal might be arranged by contractor with more clout. This would save the company from having to unionize just one operation.

Security poses a problem. Where extreme security or secrecy is required, it may pay to use in-house people. Contract firms, though, can provide bonded (for extra fee) and security-cleared personnel. Good contract services closely monitor routine of employees, can focus on which one was probably involved with any disappearing merchandise. Note: Plant security guards tend to blame cleaning people and vice versa, while another employee might be the real culprit. One technique: Lock cleaning people in, let them out only through security desk.

What to check for in office cleaning: Obvious dust balls or tendrils hanging down from corners take weeks or months to develop and indicate extreme neglect.

Subtler signs of deteriorating cleaning quality:

157

Dust, nothing ever moved on desk, and wastebaskets that haven't been emptied. Try placing a small object under wastebasket when leaving for a few days. That's when cleaners are likely to "snipe" (skip offices).

Contract fees vary from cost plus (for companies with some level of in-house maintenance capability) to a fixed price, where all cleaning needs are taken care of for a set monthly fee. Some services will also work on a cost-plus-incentive-fee basis, sharing benefits from productivity improvements with the customer.

Maintenance Tips

• Keep oil tanks from rusting inside by adding emulsifying pellets or liquids to suspend any water in the oil. Sources: Plumbing supply stores and fuel-oil suppliers.

• Soap savings: Powdered soap gets 260 hand washes per pound. Cake soap ground into flakes gets 390 per pound. Liquid soap dispensed as liquid, 595 per gallon. Liquid soap dispensed as lather, 1,950 per gallon.

• Cheaper flashlight batteries are best buy for most uses. Lowest-cost carbon-zinc batteries have excellent "bounce-back" after intermittent use for brief periods. Don't buy alkaline batteries (which cost more than twice as much) except for long, continuous use (as with portable radios).

How to Minimize Flood Damage

Flooded basements can be good. If flood reaches your property, water inside will equalize underground pressure outside and prevent collapse of basement walls. Don't pump out basement until flood recedes.

If you have no second floor: Remember, water inside a building often gets no higher than two or three feet. Use high shelves for valuables (including furnace motor).

Keep underground fuel tank full. Otherwise it can buoy up to the surface, causing foundation walls to collapse. (If no fuel is available, fill tank with water.)

When a Flat Roof Leaks

One solution: ¾-inch insulation boards applied in layers that taper toward drains. Sand the edges of layered boards to make slope relatively smooth. Place capping layer of boards on top with a final layer of bitumen to waterproof the assembly. Payoff: No more leaks and improved insulation, resulting in lower fuel bills.

Trading in Company Cars and Trucks

For high-mileage drivers (30,000 to 35,000 miles a year), it's best to trade in annually. Any auto driven that much has no resale value after three years.

A truck fleet replacement schedule should be based on maximum mileage limits or specific age, whichever comes first. Recommended replacement intervals:

• Vans, pickups, and light duty cab/chassis: 65,000 miles or 40 to 42 months.

• Step and cut-away vans and most medium duty trucks: 80,000 miles or 50 months.

• Heavier medium duty, heavy duty trucks and associated equipment: Review on a unit by unit basis.

Source: Peterson, Howell and Heather, P.O. Box 2174, Baltimore 21203.

Replace Tires at Right Time of Year

Increase tire life by about 25% or more by simply installing new tires in the fall rather than in the spring. Here's why: Tires are thickest and run hottest when when new. If some of the tread is worn away during the winter, the tire will run cooler during summer, last longer.

Other factors that wear out tires faster: Each 10 pounds of underinflation will increase tire temperature 30%. Each 20 miles an hour over 50 raises tire temperature 40%. Each 10% of overload increases tire temperature 30%.

Smart Tire Maintenance

• Bald spots: Wheels should be balanced and shock absorbers checked.
• Heavy wear on one edge: Realign wheels.
• Disproportionate wear on both edges: Keep air pressure higher.
• Heavy wear in center: Keep pressure lower.
• ''Feathering'' of ribs: Realign wheels.
Source: National Car Rental System, Inc.

After Collision: Repair vs. Replace

• Determine the clean, adjusted-for-mileage value of the car according to a recognized wholesale guide (such as the *Automotive Market Report,* Automotive Action Publishing Co., 1101 Fulton Bldg., Pittsburgh 15230).
• Divide the repair estimates (made by at least two reliable garages) by the adjusted wholesale value. Result: The replacement percentage. Example: Average repair estimate: $1,600. Clean, adjusted-for-mileage value according to AMR: $3,212. Replacement percentage = 49.8% (1,600 ÷ $3,212).
• If replacement percentage runs 25% or less, repair the unit. 40% or more, replace the unit. Between 25% and 40%, make a repair or replace decision.

Also take into account:
• Economic cost of extensive downtime for major repairs. (Remember, parts for current model year cars are usually in short supply early in the model year.) Include cost of a rental car,

availability of a pool car (least expensive alternative), or cost of reimbursing the driver for using his personal car.
• Visible repairs diminish resale values. Small dents can be hammered out without affecting resale value. But large damaged areas should be replaced to make the repair less visible at the time of resale.
• Possible bad effects on morale of the driver of an extensively repaired vehicle.
Source: Peterson, Howell & Heather, fleet management consultants, P.O. Box 2174, Baltimore 21203.

Saving Truck and Tractor Fuel

• Wind deflectors over cab: Fuel savings of 1.5% to 4.%.
• Smooth sides on trailers instead of exterior posts: Fuel savings of about 1%.
• Radiator shutters that keep engine coolant temperature at 195°: Fuel savings about 1.5%.
• Synthetic lubricants: Fuel savings over 3%.
• Temperature-controlled drive for cooling fan: Fuel savings vary from 2% to 8%.
• Lower exhaust back pressure: Fuel savings of 2.5%.
• Lower restriction on air intake system: Fuel savings more than 1%.
• Longer trailer (48 feet instead of 45 feet): More cargo can be moved with little increase in fuel consumption.
Source: *Commercial Car Journal.*

Heat Savers

• Insulation: The best kind is fiberglass batts. Blown-in insulation is risky; rock wool settles; cellulose can be a fire hazard; foam shrinks.
• Storm window coatings: Polyurea coating is best on wood frames because it adheres well and is able to shrink and expand when temperature changes. Polyester and acrylic coatings are best on aluminum because of superior resistance to

159

chipping, scratching, and the effects of weather.

• Easiest way to recirculate warm air: Old-fashioned ceiling fan (especially if the ceiling is high). The fans are simple to install, inexpensive to run, and require little maintenance.

• Nighttime thermostat fallacy: Although thermostat setback does save energy in "thermally light" structures (such as houses built of wood), it can be an energy waster for "thermally dense" structures, larger buildings made with lots of concrete or stone. Because of all the energy absorbed by such structures, raising the temperature back to a comfortable 68 °F in the morning actually costs more than holding it level all night.

• Increase fuel savings by planting foundation shrubs to create dead air space next to the house. During the winter less heat escapes. During the summer insulation is increased. Best bets: Evergreen trees and shrubs planted close together. Multiple rows are even more effective.

Reducing Power Consumption

• One 100-watt bulb gives more light than two 60-watt bulbs and uses less power.

• Fluorescents last six to ten times longer than incandescents and use one-third to one-fifth the power.

• Energy and money are saved every time an unneeded incandescent light is turned off. With fluorescent lamps, the story is different. They wear out when turned on and off frequently. However, if you are going out to lunch for an hour or so, you save by turning off fluorescents.

• Light bulbs: Double the light from fluorescent fixture just by changing dirty or yellow lenses. Best replacement: Vacuum metalized parabolic lens.

• Big-space lighting: New high-pressure sodium systems can substantially reduce energy consumption, increase production, and lower costs for warehouses and manufacturing facilities. Added benefit: Improved worker performance.

• Schedule peak electricity demand for times when rates are lower. If a particular plant opera-tion takes up a substantial amount of energy, try to schedule it for the second or third shift if time-of-day rates are available.

• Keep overall lighting to a minimum. Use work-directed light instead. Considerable air-conditioning power is used each summer just to offset the heat generated by lighting.

Designing New Construction to Save Energy

• Tinted double-glazed windows.

• Computerized energy management systems that analyze peak-hour use and regulate off-peak consumption.

• High-efficiency lights (some with polished parabolic reflectors) that provide the same illumination using half the wattage.

• Heat recovery systems to redirect excess heat into cold areas instead of venting it.

• Insulated glass curtain walls that reflect heat in summer (to lessen cooling loads) and insulate from heat loss in winter.

• Windows in high-rise buildings that can be opened for natural cooling in appropriate weather and for natural light.

• Square-shaped building and thicker, concrete-backed walls.

• All-concrete construction can produce savings on heating and cooling (because of concrete's slow reaction to temperature fluctuations compared to glass). These savings can offset initially higher construction costs.

• Shallower, 12-foot floor-to-floor height.

• Important: A two-story building costs less to heat than a comparable size one-story building.

Easy Energy Savers

• A preheating system for processing furnace. There are two types: (1) A regenerative heater that uses rotor to transfer heat from outgoing flue-gas to incoming airstream. It's simple to install and maintain, but occasionally air can leak into the gas, cutting efficiency. (2) A recuperative preheater that transfers flue-gas heat via a convection coil and heat-transfer fluid with little or no air leakage. Disadvantages: It can be hard to maintain, as well as a potential fire hazard.

• Hydraulic power for hand-held tools. Advantages: Cheaper to add hydraulic circuits to existing hydraulic systems (i.e., in vehicles) than to add large compressors. Hydraulic systems are not as bulky as compressors (important if tools must be transported to field jobs). And tools run quietly, have no electrical circuitry.

Energy Reclamation

New systems tap waste heat of cooling condensors on air conditioners, freezers, refrigerators, to help meet space-heat and hot-water requirements. Payback periods range from less than one year for hot-water heating to almost five years for large water- and space-heating capabilities. As energy costs escalate, these payback periods will shorten.

Source: *Heating/Piping/Air Conditioning,* 600 Summer St., Stamford, CT 06904.

MANAGEMENT
STRATEGIES

Turning a Company Around

Reappraising M.B.O.

Better Cost Control

Make or Buy?

Training Young Managers

When to Get a New Accountant

Coping with a Labor Shortage

Business Espionage

13

MANAGEMENT STRATEGIES

Turning a Company Around

Don't think cost cutting. Think profit improvement. The difference isn't just semantic. Cost cutting (substituting, trimming, etc.) is negative; profit improvement is positive—areas that contribute more to profits, that lead to the type of business which is better over the long run, producing healthier growth.

How to begin: By asking yourself what's essential to the success of the business. Then ask each executive—both senior and middle management—to make a list of all his activities and projects. Have him rank each in order of importance and estimate the time involved. Then review it with him.

You are likely to uncover some disturbing things: (1) His sense of priorities may not mesh with yours. (2) He may be following an old business plan and somehow may not have made the conversion. (3) He may be putting too much time in so-called "maintenance" duties which should be taken over by a clerk, but which he held onto because it was a project he initiated. (4) He may not be a good planner.

Or you may find how excellent that person really is. Don't expect this work review to be taken by your staff without suspicion. First, it represents a change, and no one likes change. Everyone feels a bit insecure about it. Secondly, it could be taken as a direct critical assault on their abilities. In fact, if not handled with understanding, count on losing some of your better, independent-minded people.

How to get around the problem: Present the review as a shared experience—something you and your subordinate should go over together. You should invite him to help you review your own list of priorities. The reasoning to use: I want my staff to get closer, to develop more of a cooperative spirit and to move closer into the circle of management. If it's conducted with understanding, the review could leave an executive feeling quite good.

Beware of trying to make big, bold changes in one step. They are difficult to manage and rarely get implemented. A better way: Decide what you want to do, pick out a small area to develop, and test the idea. Then, as results are achieved on the limited basis, plan and extend it to broader

164

areas. Set a timetable for implementation and monitor the progress.

How to track goals: This is fundamental, yet it's clearly one of the major omissions by most businessmen—they don't know how to monitor the objectives they and their subordinates establish. Here's a simple way to do it:

1. Select the objective and assign a person to be fully responsible for it. Have him draw up a formal action plan, charting, the steps that are needed to implement it, who will be responsible for each, and how long each will require.

2. Each week (or month, depending on the goal timetable) the executive in charge should mark on the chart in a different color pen how far the idea has progressed, matched up with the original plan. If the plan falls more than, say, two weeks behind schedule, the person's superior should be alerted. Exhibit the chart at all regular planning meetings.

Danger of overselling: The executives will quickly learn not to underestimate the time for a project to be fulfilled. They know they are being monitored each step of the way.

But when the plan is initiated, be sure the goal isn't actually too low. Be sure these four things are in every plan: (1) A specific goal, (2) time limits, (3) result-oriented schedule (measured by dollar savings, output gain, etc.), and (4) realism. Too often, recommendations go through without itemized plans, and the result is nearly always disaster.

Budget overview: Too frequently, budget cutting is used only in a crisis situation—and when used that way, it almost always is an across-the-board slice. Progressive companies make budget review an integral part of their planning process. Basic to this planning is zero-base budgeting. The idea isn't new, and most chief officers will tell you how great it is, but few ever use it.

When preparing a budget, instead of putting in an automatic increase for each line, start from zero. Pose these questions: What is the worst thing that could happen if we don't budget anything for this? And what would probably happen? You may find that, using this fresh thinking, some significant budget cuts are possible, and some old assumptions may go by the board.

Source: Joseph Eisenberg, president, Profit-Improvement, Inc., management consultants, New York.

Appraising Long-Term Business Performance

• Plot each of the following against sales volume for the past five years: Net earnings, operating earnings as a percentage of sales, return on investment, rate of inventory increase, and receivables.

• Next, plot what the company's corporate goals were for each of those factors for the past five years.

• Compare the resulting charts for a rapid review of how company performance matched management goals. But the charts are not the final word. If the firm did not meet its self-imposed goals, find the reasons behind the failure. Things may not be as bad as they look.

For another view, plot earnings over five years versus gross national product in constant dollars. What the comparison shows: The portion of earnings that came from just being part of the American economy. Rule of thumb: A true growth company should grow about twice as fast as the GNP.

• If a manager can't get enough information to plot the suggested graphs, this in itself probably means the company has problems. The implication is that management doesn't know enough about its own business.

• If the charts show a downward trend over an extended period, that's another insight. Management is out of touch with reality and is not managing by performance.

Early Signs of Company Decline

For the most part, business warning signals don't jump up and demand to be heeded; the manager has to seek them out. Things to watch:

Market share: Has it been falling or staying flat? That's the critical sign, because it monitors the foundation of the business. If your competitors aren't publicly owned, sufficiently accurate information is frequently available from your industry association, local bank, or Dun & Bradstreet. It's not even unheard-of to trade that sort of information with competitors. The aim: Find out whether your relative position has been changing.

Sales: Be wary about settling on sales volume as a measure of market penetration. Nearly every company grows somewhat (don't forget to cancel out inflation), but that kind of growth may be camouflaging the worst problem: Dropping market share. Check to see if your sales have risen, not just year to year, but when compared with others in your industry. Don't accept excuses that it's too hard to compare your firm's result with others. Sure, there are differences, but you can still establish a frame of reference.

Profits: This is the hardest comparison to make. Again, for nonpublic firms, some reasonably good figures are available from your industry association or from your banker.

Debt structure: What's been happening to your debt? Is it getting bigger in absolute and relative terms? Does the bank force you into shorter-term loans as your credit rises?

Management turnover: Are you having succession problems? Turnover of the smart, young executives? Is there a real second-in-command? How about a third-in-command? Is there a narrow age distribution of your top people—all in their 50s or 60s? (They should be spread between mid-30s and 60s.)

Reinvestment: Track the investment schedule on plant and equipment and maintenance. If there is a dollar decline, that's a bad sign.

None of these situations occurs overnight, but they will show up as a clear trend over time.

Companies that get into trouble generally have much in common:

• A climate that's clearly against change or new ideas; a let's-leave-things-alone feeling.

• The top person does everything himself. If there is a middle management, they're given little real responsibility. That's a sign the top person lacks managerial skills, so he can't get the company over the hump.

• A general attitude that nothing can be learned from the competition. Officers don't belong to trade associations or attend association meetings. A belittling of others' new products.

Source: John Harris, Booz Allen & Hamilton, management consultants, New York.

Basic Business Planning Techniques

The forecast method relies on periodic market research to identify current needs, desires, demands, and changes. Then, based on the results of research, the forecast method predicts future occurrences.

Advantage: Assures that external market factors will be taken into account.

Disadvantage: Doesn't allow for other factors that could affect the plan (such as social, technological, and political changes).

The extrapolation method uses past experience to predict the future.

Advantage: It's easy to apply. Example: To come up with this year's sales quotas, add 10% to last year's actual sales.

Disadvantages: Builds errors of the past into the system. Does not allow for changed market or new environment where real growth opportunities may lie.

The strategic planning method identifies future opportunities for growth to anticipate needs.

Advantage: Considers external variables that may adversely affect growth so that alternative strategies can be developed to neutralize their impact.

Disadvantages: Expensive, time-consuming, requires high level of skill and sophisticated analysis. Not necessary for single-line businesses.

Source: *Planning Commandments,* by Jack Bologna, MBO, Inc., Box 10, Westfield, MA 01085.

Keeping Business Planning in Touch with Reality

Chief problem with most company planning is that it concentrates on financial projections and rarely takes a tough look at outside pressures on the company.

Result: Plans aren't very useful, are often ignored after being developed. Also, the planning process is a time-wasting exercise that makes use of only a fraction of the knowledge and abilities of the company's managers.

Solution: Open Planning—open up the planning process. One company that took this advice even involved the union in planning for an old plant and succeeded in making major improvements in job classifications (without hostile bargaining). Open Planning in a brand new plant resulted in streamlined management (three instead of six layers) and a team system among the workers that has kept unit production costs half that of other plants making the same products under more conventional management.

How to practice Open Planning: Bring together a group of managers (maximum—12) responsible for business planning (representing a variety of skills and responsibilities) for three days of intensive work away from the office.

Take some time to establish that the reason for the planning session is the survival of the organization—not merely better sales.

Ask: What are the expectations, pressures, opportunities coming from outside the company that affect its operations significantly? List all responses on big sheets of paper that are hung on the wall. Expect conventional answers (''competition''), but press for the less obvious ones that some may be experiencing but not the others. Time for this exercise: Four to five hours.

Do the same exercise to list internal pressures and opportunities.

Ask a tough question: How would you describe the way managers spend most of their energy in this company? Example: It took two hours for one group of managers to realize that most of their time was spent dealing with confrontations: Young vs. old, women vs. men, technical vs. nontechnical.

Use the lists around the wall to define what expectations and pressure from both inside and outside the company aren't being matched by efforts, energy, attention of management.

This ends the first day of work.

Begin the second day by asking everyone to define what will happen to the company in three years and in five years if nothing different is done. Outline the scenario on new sheets.

Break up the group into twos or threes. Have each subgroup think up the most daring alternative futures for the company—if it could change anything it wanted in the company. When the groups reassemble, list all the ''ideal'' plans.

The whole group, then, should debate the pros and cons of each scheme.

As the debate continues, catalog all issues that arise into three categories: Agreed (all think the issue should be tackled); disagreed (tempers are frayed, but no agreement seems possible); gray areas (nobody feels knowledgeable enough to make a firm decision).

Final step: Take all the ''agreed'' items and decide as a group who does what and when on each item. Example: We need a new raw materials laboratory because we are losing money on raw materials quality. Who should handle that or find the right person to be in charge of it?

For the ''gray areas,'' work out a system for information-gathering, research to clarify issues. Make people responsible for this task, too. (Hire a consultant, use an MBA candidate as summertime employee to work on the problem, etc.).

Caution: Open Planning is useful and effective only in a company where managers feel they can be candid and share information without being threatened. And follow-up is essential: Make sure the group meets again in three to four months (and continues to meet) to monitor changes, verify who did what, reassess plans.

Source: G.K. Jayaram, senior consultant, Arthur D. Little.

Management by Objectives: a Reappraisal

The concept of Management by Objectives (MBO) is as old as scientific management itself—and is a valuable tool for all. The central role of the manager is to be a goal attainer and problem solver. Thus, the manager who has to be taught how to perform this role in an extended, expensive course was never a manager—nor is his boss if he failed to recognize this.

Well-run organizations set goals that get reached by parceling them out to managerial units which employ two management principles: Feedback and reward. In addition, they keep checking performance to determine which workers fail to meet established standards, and deal with it by either further job training or disciplinary measures. MBO usually adds the participation of subordinates in establishing these standards, discussing results, getting explanations and future commitments.

In many organizations, however, managers become nonachievers, perceiving their role as simply defenders of the status quo. Their prime priorities become ensuring that nothing is done that might be a source of embarrassment or make them open to criticism; proving some outside or uncontrollable force is at fault when real problems arise. Examples: "Our performance is off because of absenteeism; the equipment is down because the workers you hire these days are unmotivated; we didn't get the order out because the parts didn't arrive on time."

Managers who are aggressive in perceiving and attacking problems (not defensively rationalizing them) can cope with an unexpected breakdown in a positive manner—they get repairs made or shift production as quickly as possible; they handle late deliveries of parts by improvising or by sending a truck out to get the parts from another vendor.

More subtle aspects of the manager's role: It requires somewhat more ingenuity to conceive of targets to motivate supervisory staff and workers in nonproduction operations, where there is no visible output. Possibilities: Aim for quicker response time to outside requests for information or reports, better assimilation of new sources of market information, etc. The manager must develop clear objectives that permit problem solving on a continuous basis.

The extraordinary popularity of MBO indicates that many organizations have lost the elementary insight into the essential functions of a manager. Their managers go through the motions of managing by living up to set procedures, e.g., watching time clocks, granting everyday personnel requests, selecting replacements when someone quits—focusing on minor elements while not seeing the "big picture."

Costly programs with attractive packages and procedures (sort of paint-by-number sets) to reinstitute the traditional managerial functions are unnecessary. Once corporate objectives are ascertained and competent managers hired, MBO becomes a natural function.

Source: Dr. Leonard R. Sayles, professor of management, Graduate School of Business, Columbia University.

Profit Centers and ROI: Use and Misuse

The concepts of profit centers and return on investment are indeed valuable management tools. But they're often used incorrectly. Result: They produce results quite the opposite of what was intended. The results often work against the corporation's best interests, both in the long and short term.

• The Profit Center: Profit centers create "rat-holes" in transfer pricing—the price that one profit center (division) will charge another for goods or services. Naturally, if both divisions are gauged by their independent results, the "seller" would want to get the highest price, the "buyer" would want the lowest. Result: Often bitter squabbling and rarely a cooperative effort.

If you diagnose that symptom, you must first ask whether the profit center concept should be used at all in your business. The more integrated a company (the more dependent each branch is on each other branch), the less reason to break it into profit centers.

Problems that come up: (1) Pressure to sell a component or service to the outside world at one price and in-house at another price. (2) Pressure to buy the component from the in-house source, even though it's possible to get better items faster or cheaper—or both—elsewhere.

If a division has a choice, it would rather not buy components in-house, even if the sister division can offer a slight price advantage. Reason: An outside supplier almost always provides better service. Arm's-length dealing gives the buyer more leverage.

When a company organizes in divisions, it frequently makes a policy statement on how one division will treat another in the customer/supplier relationship. But, no matter what is stated or written, the reality is that friction develops, strong pressure exists for a division to buy in-house at less than the best prices, delivery schedules, etc.

If the chief executive officer steps in to mediate a dispute between division heads, he will find guideline-setting won't work. He will have to get involved in the details of each dispute, make a heavy time investment, and risk alienating one or both of the division managers by polarizing the situation.

Prescription: Establish a single manager (be sure he's an off-line person) as a mediator. Let him get involved in the details, and give him the responsibility of deciding what action will benefit the whole corporation, not just one division.

If a chief officer hears that one division is trying to make a sharp change in transfer-pricing arrangements, that's a good advance indication that the division is running into problems. The division manager will try to take the "corrective" action in an effort to straighten out the problem before his financial reports get up to top management.

• Return on Investment (ROI):

Most firms use ROI in some form to measure a unit's achievements. But their use of it is so rigid that results are often counterproductive.

Consider the formula: ROI = Profit/Investment.

If the division is faced with a decline in profits (for any reason), and it's being monitored for its ROI, it will frequently move to reduce the investment as a short-term solution to its drooping ROI. But the short-term solution may lead to disaster—such as failure to invest in maintenance or new equipment.

Example: A division suddenly faces a competitor's new product, which is grabbing a bigger share of the market. If the division tries to offset the losses by dropping its research for new products, advertising, etc., it may generate a short-term improvement, but over the longer term it's just getting into deeper trouble.

The same negative result could occur if a company uses some sort of budgeted profit plan for a profit center. The manager, fearing he's not meeting his budgeted goal, reduces some other variable, which may produce long-term problems, just to prop up the short-term numbers.

The real shortcoming, naturally, isn't in profit centers or in return on investment; it's in the too-rigid use of them. It's when top management limits its assessment of a division by such narrow measurements that companies get into serious trouble, even though they think they are following smart management practices.

Source: John Dearden, professor of accounting, Graduate School of Business, Harvard University.

Four Steps to Better Cost Management

Cost-reduction programs are the most talked about but least effective method of cost management. The very concept implies that management has already let operations get fat. Usually it's more effective to start with a cost-elimination technique first.

It's amazing how much energy can be wasted trying to reduce costs on functions or products that should have been eliminated in the first place.

Basic elements of cost management:

1. Cost avoidance. Postpone spending wherever possible. (But not if the postponement would cause an increase later. Example: Necessary equipment maintenance.)

2. Cost prevention. All new projects, staff additions, other actions and programs should be thoroughly evaluated both in advance and as they proceed. Don't spend the money unless they're sure to meet objectives.

3. Cost elimination. Do away with operations that aren't profitable or only marginally productive. Could be a product, a whole plant, or an outmoded procedure. Every company has a few "sleepers" and "sacred cows." Get rid of them.

4. Cost reduction. Set measurable goals and monitor them. The worst mistake you can make is to enforce across-the-board percentage cut in costs. It's unfair, impractical, and, in the long run, ineffective.

Why Costs Get Out of Control

• Empire-building managers. Owners and managers with entrepreneurial skills usually base decisions on profitability, but a professional manager is more apt to worry about his own survival. It's hard to find entrepreneurial managers because they want to be doing their own thing.

• Keeping up with the latest technology. Often fostered by a chief executive. Sure sign: Any technology put in without full cost/benefit analysis. Most likely example: Computerization without solid rationale. Computers introduce supplementary equipment (CRTs, green screens, etc.) and a potential horde of systems analysts. Expense is virtually unlimited.

• Low-yield activities. Departments or functions that have outlived their usefulness. Problem: Management adds operations to respond to new needs but fails to cut back on unnecessary operations.

• Deadwood. Don't ask department head to justify function. Instead, ask other parts of the company that use its services. Find out if use is marginal. Example: Comptroller may be providing complex analyses that are never used.

• Uneven work distribution. Check to make sure that departments have enough valuable things to do and are not padding the job. Ask every department head for a list of the services that his department provides, and the people and costs associated with each service. Make decision to keep or eliminate services based on assessment of service's usefulness and end-user evaluation of performance.

Source: Joseph Eisenberg, president, Profit-Improvement, Inc., management consultants, New York.

Productivity Campaigns That Boomerang

Despite some of the highest pay rates and the best working conditions in history around the world, productivity of American workers is stalled and quality of output is low. At the same time, inflation is putting greater pressures on managers to increase productivity. What is being done about this problem, and what should (and should not) be done?

A veritable army of management consultants, industrial engineers, and behavioral scientists are giving advice, but the plain truth is that while management is treating employees better, it's not making much better use of labor's abilities.

Though there are many valid approaches to the subject of productivity, it's clear that conventional wisdom isn't working. Job enrichment, a technique for expanding job responsibilities and

getting the worker more involved, has failed to live up to its initial promise. For one thing, it discounts the importance of financial rewards. While the idea of tying pay to productivity is well accepted among executives, only about a quarter of U.S. workers are in fact on some form of incentive plan.

The major stumbling block, however, is in both management and worker attitudes. Typically, today's business system will operate almost perfectly to demotivate instead of motivate workers. Even when unintentional, productivity increases generally result in smaller crew sizes, displaced workers, and, perhaps, even layoffs. Workers fail to perceive any self-interest in working either harder or "smarter."

The upshot is that workers correctly perceive management efforts to increase productivity in a negative way. Management, sensing their antagonism, responds with even more sophisticated control systems designed to operate in that hostile environment. And the workers increasingly direct much creative ingenuity to circumventing those controls.

To defeat this vicious cycle and obtain worker cooperation for productivity improvement, managers must do two things: (1) Recognize and reward employee performance, and (2) eliminate practices that in effect penalize employees for making progress.

Almost everybody agrees that linking workers' pay to their performance and productivity gains results not only in higher productivity, but in greater job satisfaction as well. Most plans haven't worked too well, however, either because they failed to give enough targeted incentive or because management defeated the plan.

One recent plan that seems to be getting good results is Improshare (which stands for Improved Productivity Through Sharing), the brainchild of Mitchell Fein,* an industrial engineer.

The key to the success of a sharing plan, says Fein, is management's willingness to accept the employees' cooperation, and to share responsibility with them in implementing ways to raise output. This goes counter to basic authoritarianism management philosophy.

Other long-smoldering management problems finally get solved (or are alleviated) as work-

*202 Saddlewood Dr., Hillsdale, NJ 07642.

ers' interests begin to parallel management's. For example: When workers become concerned about the total output (Fein's plan assures this by counting only finished shippable product), many former impediments and logjams magically disappear, as does much previous waste. Because workers are now concerned with their output and careful of spoilage, droves of quality control inspectors are no longer necessary. Somehow there are fewer shortages and less machine downtime. ''There is enormous know-how and creativity in the work force that today operates against management,'' says Fein.

Group vs. individual incentive plans. The traditional management rationale favors individual incentives, and those only for some individuals. This, says Fein, alienates workers who are excluded and also causes covered workers to maximize their earnings at any cost. His goal is to involve all workers, including nonproduction people such as material handlers, maintenance people, inspectors, shipping clerks, and other workers who are normally eliminated from productivity calculations, at least partly because it's so difficult to measure productivity in their areas.

A complementary approach to productivity is taken by Dr. Leonard R. Sayles, professor at Columbia University School of Business. He focuses on restructuring the organization of a work force. Instead of automatically grouping together employees with similar job titles or ''functions,'' the manager should look at what people actually have to do in their relationships with one another if the work is to flow smoothly and with coordination. The arrangement may bear absolutely no resemblance to the organization chart or to elaborately designed procedures. Workers circumvent them when it's necessary to get the job done, anyway.

Having established what the actual working relationships are, the manager puts those people who must coordinate tasks under a common supervisor. The ultimate example of this is similar to the ''task force'' approach used to develop the atomic bomb and many defense projects. In civilian life, it's increasingly reflected in organization by product manufactured or service rendered, rather than by process or function.

Organizing work into groups with relatively autonomous tasks is the best way to develop group responsibility and internal leadership. But avoid putting large numbers of people who are doing the same work in a single department, even if that would mean more efficient work scheduling and use of equipment, particularly if the work itself is unchallenging, or personnel difficulties are likely to multiply. Typing pools or departments filled with hundreds of draftsmen or engineers doing identical tasks also have serious morale problems. In more than one company, such a department is called Siberia.

Equally damaging to morale and productivity is excessive physical distance. This almost invariably reduces opportunities to cooperate. If floor layouts cannot be revised to bring groups together, you may have to devise special procedures (e.g., committees meeting formally or informally). In larger companies, coordination or liaison specialists such as product planners may be needed to get engineering, manufacturing, and sales to work together, modifying their efforts for the common good. Training programs can also help to bridge the gap between different groups, showing engineers, for example, how to communicate with accountants.

Make-or-Buy Decisions

In deciding whether to contract out or have the work done in-house, cost may be a first consideration—but it should never be the only one or even the main one in certain cases.

Other factors:

• Size of job. A major construction job may require staff and equipment capabilities that aren't easily available in-house.

• Need to complete job quickly. Often less downtime when contractors move in with large staff to complete job quickly and efficiently. On the other hand, employees who work with a specialized piece of equipment every day may be much more efficient that outside contractors in a job that involves that piece of equipment.

• Job with rigid specifications and a need for guarantees. Guarantees on outside contractors' work means unsatisfactory work gets redone. It might also be easier on management to be a

171

tough and demanding buyer of short-term outside contractor's crews than to rely on company employees with tenure and job security. The manager can push outside workers harder than inside employees without fear of grievances or walkouts.

• Need for stable work force. Company with dramatic seasonal or temporary peaks might be better off hiring outside contractors to fill peak needs. Putting them on staff would involve layoffs (and more problems) when the peak passes.

• Type of work to be done. Major construction often has to be contracted out; maintenance work seldom does.

• How busy in-house employees are. If job requires workers with particular skills (e.g., machinists) and those company workers have a large backlog of in-house work, contracting out becomes more attractive. If in-house workers are idle and probably will remain so for the next few months, it might be better to give them a job, even if it will take them longer (or even cost more) than contracting out.

• Probability of antagonizing the unions. Advance notice to employees of work that is being contracted out can alleviate some problems. But if in-house union employees are irritated enough by outside contracts, they can run up substantial costs—by such tactics as work stoppages, interfering with outside contractor's crews, and slowdowns that affect total plant production. If union employees want the contracted-out work themselves—and are able to perform—it might be cheaper to let them do it, even if apparent cost of contracting out, in dollars, seems to be less.

Reassure in-house employees when work is contracted out. Make sure that one contractor doesn't become a "fixture" in the firm. Set quotas on amount of work contracted at any particular time so that the insiders don't feel outnumbered. Change contractors at intervals (to emphasize the competitive, tenuous nature of the contractor's relationship to the firm).

Be aware that tax benefits may be available for contracted-out work and not to in-house projects. Check it out with accountant.

An often-overlooked service of outside contractors: They provide a valuable comparison for evaluating internal costs. The competition of an outside contractor can help keep internal costs in line. If outside contractors' estimates are consistently less than costs of doing the same job in-house, it's a sign that in-house operations need some streamlining and fat-cutting.

Source: Drs. Margaret Chandler and Leonard Sayles, Columbia University.

When to Lease Equipment and When to Buy It

• By leasing rather than buying, the company may have to give up the "residual" value, or permanent ownership, of the equipment and the chance to continue using it long after it's paid for. When the lease runs out, it will cost more to replace it because of inflation; probably much more if it's eight to ten years from now.

One way around that is to make a deal that allows the user to buy the equipment for some nominal amount at the end of the lease, but the monthly rental will be as much as 20%-25% higher on that kind of deal. IRS doesn't consider that a true lease, so the leasing company loses major tax benefits and has to charge more.

• When to consider leasing: The company is short of cash. No down payment, thus, less cash is required the first year. Whether there's more or less cash required over the lease term depends on the particular deal. Have accountants compare cash outlay over the years on buying vs. leasing.

Leasing also makes sense where the company doesn't want to own the equipment permanently. Examples: It might be worn out or need constant repair by the end of the term, so it's just as well to replace it. (Many people lease cars for this reason.) Or it might be obsolete by the end of its lease and it's better to replace it with a newer model. This is common with data-processing equipment.

Sometimes the user wants other services provided by the leasing company, such as accounting or faster repair service. Some large companies lease fleets of cars and trucks, even though they could easily afford to buy them, in order to get the fleet management services, such as controlled maintenance and simplified costing.

Leasing may be wise if the company has been losing money for several years. It might have to forgo the tax benefits of ownership if it doesn't expect to be profitable soon enough to take the tax deductions on a carry-forward basis.

Example of tax benefits: On a $100,000 piece of equipment, there would be a $10,000 investment tax credit in the year of purchase. That's a credit directly against the income tax, so it's worth much more than a deduction. Tax-deductible depreciation might be $10,000 a year straight-line or up to $20,000 the first year, then a declining amount if other methods are used.

If the user of the equipment has such large losses that it can't take advantage of the tax benefits, it can, in effect, trade them to the leasing company in exchange for a lower rental rate. In a lease transaction, the leasing company is the owner, and so it always takes the depreciation. It may also take the very valuable investment tax credit.

• When leasing companies take investment tax credit as well as depreciation, they often make substantial concessions on interest rates.

When to Stop Fact-Finding and Make a Decision

• When the facts coming in seem to duplicate each other.

• When the facts are not really usable.

• When the cost of gaining any additional information will be higher than the possible value of the information. It's impossible to have all the facts pertaining to a problem. There comes a time when a decision must be made on the basis of the facts in hand.

Quick Course in Decision Theory

Decision theory is a technique for organizing information. The technique can be applied to any type of management decision, but some of the more popular applications are in new product introductions, investment decisions.

Example: In February, Johnson arranges a weekend ski trip from New York to Vermont. His passengers don't reserve places; they simply show up Saturday at a specified place. Johnson charges $30 for the round trip. Each Wednesday, he must contract for vehicles for the trip. He can rent buses for 20 to 80 passengers. If he selects the wrong size, he cannot hire more buses or cancel those he hired. A small bus rents for $300; a large one for $500.

Payoff matrix: The heart of a decision theory analysis is a payoff matrix. It has three elements: Actions, states of nature, and payoffs.

Actions: The first step is to specify the actions under consideration. For Johnson, they are the numbers and types of buses he must contract on Wednesday. He has four possibilities: (1) Hire one minibus. (2) Hire two minibuses. (3) Hire three minibuses. (4) Hire one big bus.

In practice, specifying the various actions may be difficult. To a marketing manager planning a new product strategy, each action might consist of product specifications, price, advertising budget, media schedule, and distribution channel. An action is composed of values for all variables over which decision maker has control.

States of nature: Then specify the variables over which the decision maker has no control. These are known as the states of nature. One would be weather: If there is snow in Vermont, more people will go. Again, Johnson has two possibilities: (A) No new snow before Saturday—20 people show up. (B) Ten inches of snow fall before Saturday—80 people show up.

	States of Nature	
Actions	A (no new snow)	B (new snow)
1—1 minibus		
2—2 minibuses		
3—3 minibuses		
4—1 big bus		

In real life, there are other variables which must be considered: Actions of competitors, the business cycle, legal developments, etc.

Payoffs: The payoff matrix contains a row for each action and a column for each state of nature. Each combination of possible action and a possible state of nature determines a possible payoff to the decision maker.

Johnson's payoff is defined as the difference between his revenue and costs. In some analyses, payoffs may be sales revenue, return on investment, market share, etc. The relationship between payoff and the actions and states of nature is known as the payoff function. It may be a known accounting relation or it may be necessary to estimate it with statistical tools or even base it on hunches.

For Johnson, the payoff function is:

$$P = \$30S - C$$

where P = Net profit, S = Number of skiers transported by the buses, and C = Cost of hiring the buses.

Suppose Johnson hires one minibus (action 1) and ten inches of snow fall between Wednesday and Saturday (state of nature B). Then:

$$P = \$30 (20) - \$300 = \$300$$

Although 80 people showed up on Saturday, Johnson's decision to hire just one minibus constrained him to accommodate only 20 people. Note also that, in this example, one is dealing only with monetary profits. In fact, those 60 disappointed people may represent a real cost to Johnson which somehow should be included in the payoff. But if attention is restricted to monetary payoffs and all payoffs are calculated, the matrix looks like this:

States of Nature

Actions	A	B
1	$300	$ 300
2	$ 0	$ 600
3	− $300	$ 900
4	$100	$1,900

At this point, the decision maker can list alternative actions and evaluate them under all possible conditions. Also, he can eliminate those actions that are inadmissible, i.e., one wouldn't choose them under any circumstances.

For example, consider action 2 in Johnson's payoff matrix. Regardless of the state of nature that occurs, action 4 yields a higher payoff than action 2. (Action 4 is said to "dominate" action 2.) Since action 2 is clearly inferior to action 4, one can remove action 2 from consideration. For similar reasons, action 3 is inadmissible. Action 1, however, is admissible, since if there is no new

snow, it returns a higher payoff than action 4.

By recognizing inadmissible actions, we may now simplify the decision problem:

States of Nature

Actions	A	B
1	$300	$ 300
4	$100	$1,900

After the construction of a payoff matrix and the removal of inadmissible actions, decision theory focuses on selecting that action which is "best." For the moment, define "best" as highest dollar payoff.

Which action is best depends on which state of nature occurs. If A occurs, action 1 is best. If B occurs, action 4 gives a higher payoff. Therefore, the choice of action depends on what one knows about what will or might occur.

Decision theory embraces four situations: (1) Decisions under certainty, (2) uncertainty, (3) risk, and (4) conflict.

Certainty: In this case, one knows for sure which state of nature will occur. Example: Johnson knew there was absolutely no chance of new snow; that state of nature A had to occur. So he would simply take action 1 and hire a minibus. In real-world situations, decisions under certainty aren't so simple. The short-term production scheduling problem of a refinery may be classed as a decision under certainty—available resources, prices, costs, and technology can be assumed fixed (known). What makes that problem difficult is that there may be thousands of possible actions, each a different production schedule, and complex management science technique may be required to select the best.

Uncertainty: Such a decision is characterized by ignorance of which state of nature will occur. In between are decisions under risk, the most common. One way to select an action under those circumstances is to weigh the payoffs by the probabilities of the states of nature. Such an average is known as an expected payoff.

Example: If there were a 20% chance of B occurring (and, thus, an 80% chance of A), then:

Expected payoff of action 1 = (0.8)($300) + (0.2)($300)
= $300

Expected payoff of action 2 = (0.8)($100) + (0.2)($1,900)
= $460

Conflict: This occurs when the states of nature

are actually under the control of someone else. Example: In a new-product decision, competitors' actions may play a large role in the states of nature. (When one is making a decision against a thinking opponent rather than fate, additional concepts must be used to select the best actions. These approaches are known as game theory.)

Where to Find Help for Employees with Emotional/Family Problems

Speak to your local medical advisor. Or write to one of the national specialist organizations:
- Family Service, 445 East 23 St., New York 10010.
- Association of Marriage Counselors, 270 Park Ave., New York 10017.
- National Council on Community Mental Health Centers, 2233 Wisconsin Ave. N.W., Washington, DC 20037.
- Psychiatric Services for Children, 1701 18th St. N.W., Washington, DC 20009.
- Society for Autistic Children, 169 Tampa Ave., Albany, NY 12208.

Training Young Managers for Top Jobs: Three Methods

- Understudies. Manager trains his eventual successor.

Problems: Deciding whether to have only one understudy (which may discourage other people) or several (which may create too much rivalry). Dilemma: Choosing early provides more opportunity to observe but may discourage those not chosen and demoralize them.

Advantage: The system needs very little control or systematization.

Disadvantages: The understudy must wait until boss moves on before advancing. In some departments there may be several highly qualified people, some of whom will get passed by.

- Rotation. The manager goes from job to job, always learning new ones. The rotation may be planned and coordinated, or unplanned.

Advantages: Provides challenging work that produces generalists who see overall company viewpoint, can deal with others, and make decisions. It brings new viewpoints and fresh ideas into departments, and offers a better opportunity for a manager to succeed. He doesn't have to stay in a dead-end department or under a boss with whom he doesn't get along.

Rotation also allows flexible use of managers, allowing company to fill needed gaps quickly to respond to sudden surges in business. Eliminates the problems of a fellow worker suddenly supervising those he has worked with as equals.

Disadvantages: It can be very costly in terms of relocation expenses, time spent by the relocated manager learning new jobs. Hinders basic change. Managers may only make changes with short-term payoffs to make himself look good. Developing longer-term innovations gets passed-by. Unfair to the manager who starts slowly, but may be very capable.

The focus is on an adequate performance. That discourages risk-taking. The training forces the manager to rely on subordinates for help. Subordinates, subjected to frequent changes of managers, lose respect for manager, become independent, resist attempts to change things. Result: Frequent changes produce little real change.

Manager's loyalties are reversed. He should be representing subordinates. Instead, he is more loyal to his superiors who provide him with the promotions and job changes.

- Special broadening assignments. Manager is assigned tasks above his current level of authority. He may work on his own or in a committee, with others on his level or with higher-level executives, or as an assistant to a superior.

To be effective, these assignments must be worked on directly under the supervision of the higher-level executives who will evaluate the manager's work. The work must be difficult, requiring more than adequate solutions, to allow real talent to be demonstrated. Also, it must cover several departments and involve long-range planning.

Advantages: It locates managers who have the

capabilities for higher-level jobs involving long-range planning and innovation. In lower-level jobs those capabilities are generally not needed and, therefore, not used or demonstrated. In addition, use of special broadening assignments reduces a manager's dependence on his superior, and provides higher-level executives with fresh ideas and suggestions.

Source: *Managing Human Resources,* by Leonard R. Sayles and George Strauss, Prentice-Hall, Englewood Cliffs, NJ.

Making Your Accountant Earn His Fee

Many successful business people are unsophisticated about accounting, and feel out of their depth when dealing with outside CPAs.

• Don't be afraid to ask questions. The accountant is essentially conservative—and should be, both for his own sake and the client's. To protect himself against liability, and to keep client from getting into financial or tax trouble, the accountant may not volunteer information about possible alternative accounting treatment that the client may be ignorant of.

• Ask what the alternatives are. A lot of accounting is highly judgmental. There are usually more ways than one to treat expenses, accruals, reserves, valuations, etc.

• Tactics when preliminary figures are drawn up: Don't panic, no matter what the numbers show. The accountant may not have explored all the angles. Take each of the figures and ask for other ways, better ways, to handle them.

• Reserves. Are they adequate or not? Accountants usually take a conservative position here, and justify it by saying that a conservative stance this year will help the company in the future. Management is more inclined to worry about next year when it comes and to look into the next year's alternatives then.

• Depreciation methods and inventory valuation. Discuss and understand the choices. Under certain circumstances, substantially different financial results occur when different kinds of methods are used.

• Many accountants are inclined to think that

dropping a few hints will get their message across when they sound a warning. Clients, on the other hand, have a habit of hearing what they want to hear and not heeding such warnings. Make your accountant spell out his hint so that there can be no possible misunderstanding.

• Smaller clients of big accounting firms often do not realize that they can talk with the top partners simply by asking to. Don't be afraid to contact the senior partner if things aren't going right. It isn't necessary to wait until something goes wrong to talk things over. Talk with the top person at least once a year and explain what your company needs.

Time to Get a New Accountant

• When options are never presented during tax preparation. Be especially suspicious of accountants who always take the tax collector's side or don't seem sensitive to the company's special circumstances. Remember, there's nothing illegal about tax avoidance. Firms that never tangle with the IRS may be too conservative.

• When turnover of accounting personnel is so great that the company is, in effect, paying for training CPA firm's employees. Get a guarantee that both the accountant who does most of the work and the supervising partner will handle the company's affairs for a minimum period of two to three years.

• When CPA personnel don't measure up to your company's own hiring standards.

• When CPA is unwilling or unable to offer advice on typical management problems that may not be strictly related to taxes or the audit. Most good accountants, whether in small or large firms, can be helpful in planning, instituting controls, analyzing profitability, etc., as well as offering tax and financial advice. CPAs with too narrow a focus probably are not serving the company well.

Useful: One small firm that will do the dirty work, and a larger firm for special consulting (corporate structure, industry yardsticks, etc.).

Worse than no advice is advice that is too glib.

Beware of any accountant who never has to look anything up.
Source: *Harvard Business Review,* Boston, MA 02163.

How to Use Consultants

When a consultant is being considered for an assignment, conduct a detailed interview. If the consultant seems rigid (he has the answer before he has the problem), it's a good clue to keep looking. Some consultants ask to be paid for these interviews. There is no fixed rule on such payments. It depends on how hungry the consultant is or how much potential he sees in your company's business.

If the consultant wants a contract that ties together both the diagnosis and the solution, be wary. By linking the two, you guarantee that his bias will guide him into finding a particular problem (which he believes he can solve). Rather, insist that he be paid a fixed hourly fee for the diagnosis. On average, a good diagnosis for a company that is physically situated in one location and in which everyone is accessible takes about two weeks.

You should require progress reports—not to "look over his shoulder" and second-guess him, but to be ready to offer any extra assistance or information he may need.

Make it easy for the consultant to learn as much as possible about the company. The more he knows, the better the chance of a workable solution to the problem.

If the consultant's report isn't clear, get an explanation. All too often, consultants couch their comments in jargon (to protect themselves, since the jargon is often just a way of saying nothing specific). Insist that the report be in clear, everyday business language and that it be easily understood.

Some consultant troubles:

• It takes an unusual consultant to tell a client what he doesn't want to hear, especially if their future business relationship depends on his saying yes. So he fudges the risk analysis, picks the rosiest-looking market potential, and estimates low on expenses and capital needs.

• The company seeks out the best consultant for a particular problem. He's internationally known. Once hired, the manager who brought him in feels relieved and contentedly leaves the problem in the hands of the expert.

At the extreme, the manager's critical thinking becomes paralyzed—after all, who can question the top person in the field?

• The manager determines that he has a "problem." Actually, he does not know what the real problem is—he's nearly always getting the "problem" confused with "symptom." He finds a consultant who specializes in that "problem." And before the initial interview is over, the consultant whips out a complete solution (which, he contends, has worked marvelously for scores of other clients).

The logic for using the prepackaged solution is hard to refute. Why reinvent the wheel?

The truth, however, is that rarely are corporate problems so similar that prepackaged solutions work. The symptoms may be similar, but not the causes.

• Only upper-management people are consulted during the problem-definition (diagnosis) stage of the assignment. This is done intentionally by the client in order to avoid bogging the expensive consultant down in a mass of extraneous data; data that the lower-level staff might thrust on him if allowed.

Result: The consultant will have serious trouble finding the real problem—and may actually believe that the problem, as interpreted by top management, is the one that needs treatment. A self-fulfilling prophecy.

When Muddling Works

Most companies are compulsive about planning. But planning often puts a company into a managerial straitjacket. Here is an alternative:

Planning and reality are worlds apart, and managers often don't take this into account. What was so carefully planned comes out differently—and much later than was originally intended.

The problem: Plans don't respond to essential

changes. What was true when the plans were laid out (taste, facts, business tempo) becomes less true as time elapses.

The alternative: Muddling through. Here, muddling doesn't mean indulging in sloppy thinking. Instead, it's what Charles Lindblom of Yale University called adaptive planning: Don't put plans on such a single, unalterable track that reality and the need to change are ignored.

Most plans fail to meet expectations—on timing, benefits, and/or costs. Here's why:

• To get an idea adopted by the company, an executive must push the positive side and understate the negative. Result: Benefits are exaggerated and costs are underestimated.

• Managers need supporters around them. They attract those with similar thinking, repelling those with different views. Thus the overestimated, unrealistic plan is psychologically induced and organizationally encouraged. And efforts to restore reality are rejected as negativism or lack of cooperation.

Interdependent systems: Success of a new dry cleaning process, for example, might well depend on several interdependent factors. They might include the kinds of fabrics used, methods of manufacture and design, available equipment, competitive processes, and varying consumer taste with respect to aesthetics.

If the development of the process takes a significant period of time, it's more than likely that one of the these elements will change. When one or more factors change, the end result may be significantly affected and the entire plan may have to be revamped.

Foreseeing change is hard—if not impossible. So keep plans adjustable. Keep competition among planners keen. Let fresh ideas put pressure on old plans. Force planners to stay sensitive to reality. Resist creating isolated planning groups (big, inflexible plans). Question new data that may be created just to prove the prophecy.

Organizational momentum:

• Don't be afraid to devote time to putting out fires and to so-called remedial decisions. Work step by step.

• Don't work too hard to avoid differences.

• Resist efforts to agree on absolute goals. Accept satisfactory solutions. Don't demand optimal ones for each situation.

• It's essential to aim at the broad target. Let middle management have a chance to muddle.

• Reason: Muddling induces adaptive thinking and a pragmatic approach. The staff can recognize differences between variations from plan and original premises (which are acceptable) and real deviations (which change the foundation upon which the plan is built).

How to Limit Bureaucracy As a Company Grows

Most companies do become more "bureaucratic" as they grow, but it's not inevitable. Some understanding of what causes this frustrating "hardening of the arteries" can help prevent the disease.

The basic problem is the natural routinization of work within every group as it seeks to become more "businesslike" and "organized," developing regular rhythms that can be controlled to gain efficiency.

The trouble is that each operating unit develops its own routines—routines that may not jibe with those developed by other operating units. In fact, one may actually inhibit another operating unit from satisfactorily doing its job.

As management tries to bridge the gaps created by individual units, they often fight back by stiffening or adding to their routines so that the flow of work is increasingly hampered by authorizations, threats, etc.

Management's natural tendency then is to put some specialist over all of the operating units. This may accomplish more professional or cost-efficient standards of performance. But, as more and more specialists work their way in, they tend to become sources of approval and control, requiring still more time to get anything done. There are now many more levels of authority; managers need more help in dealing with new sources of control—preparing justifying reports, etc.—so managerial staffs also tend to expand.

Finally, as the helping specialists themselves become serious sources of constraint, management is driven to hire expediters—and the whole process begins again.

How to fight this insidious cycle: Start by training managers to prevent excessive rigidification of routines by introducing continuous change. Keep every department a little off balance. An organization of many independent, predictable routines may sound good, but in a dynamic world there are always many reasons why the "master plan" cannot be followed. Prepare every operating unit to shift gears as necessary to keep the whole organization's work flow moving. Plan to restrict the number of specialists on the payroll as much as possible. And keep checking them to be sure they haven't converted their job from one of giving advice and service to one of control and rule-making. There will always be new problems, perhaps requiring the aid of new specialists. Resist the temptation to build them into the system permanently.

When an 'Indispensable' Employee Leaves

A common cause of large company setbacks and small business failures is the loss of a key employee when there's no one groomed to take over. Here are the steps to take to protect against that possibility:

• Make a list of all employees with major responsibilities and special know-how.

• Next to each name, summarize the probable impact of the sudden departure or prolonged absence of that person. Include a cost estimate.

• Add the name of the person who would step into the job. Analyze what that person would have to learn to do the job as well as the person who's gone.

• Start preparing the potential successor with more work in the weakest areas. The program should be gradual to avoid alarming the key employee or raising false hopes of speedy action.

• Use key employee's vacations to field-test his substitute's readiness to step in when needed. Adjust training accordingly.

Source: Moustafa H. Abdelsamad, director of Graduate Business Studies, Virginia Commonwealth University, and Alexander T. Kindling, president, Automatic Mfg. Co., in *Advanced Management Journal,* American Management Associations, Trudeau Rd., Saranac Lake, NY 12983.

Which Economic Indicators to Watch

By simply following the indicators reported in the financial press and watching for the same signals as the economists do, anyone can spot the signs that mean the caution flag should go up.

The five indicators to watch:

• Total employment. Released on the first or second Friday of the month. The number of people employed reflects labor demand. Thus, it's more meaningful as a recession indicator than the unemployment rate (reflecting labor supply) which is released the same day and usually gets more attention in the media. The total number of employed rose by an average of 350,000 per month from mid-1977 through most of 1978. Then in December it rose by only 100,000. If it continues to rise by less than 100,000, that's a negative signal.

• Monthly retail sales. Published about the tenth of the following month. It takes a sales increase of 0.6%-0.7% month-to-month just to stay even with inflation. If the increase in dollar sales is less than that, it means that unit sales have actually declined. And if retail sales in dollars actually decrease month-to-month, showing that unit sales have dropped sharply, that's a strong negative indicator.

• Industrial production index. Issued about the 15th of the following month. This index measures physical production, not dollar sales. If the industrial production index declines, that's a negative signal. But it may be a negative signal if it rises, too. Here's why: Suppose industrial production rises while retail sales for a month are up less than 0.5% in dollars, which means no real change in unit sales. That shows that the factories are producing more goods than the stores are selling. Which means that inventories are building up. Sooner or later, production will have to be cut back in order to bring inventories into line.

• Personal income. It's released about the 18th of the following month. Since it's measured in dollars, it should go up by at least 0.6% per month just to stay even with inflation. Any smaller increase is a negative signal, showing that buying power is falling.

• Consumer price index. This is the principal

fever chart of inflation. Compare it with retail sales and personal income for the same month to determine whether those indicators are staying even with the inflation rate or falling behind it.

These five are what economists call coincident indicators. They do not forecast the future, rather they tell what is happening in the present. Figures that are released this month tell what happened last month.

Why not use the highly publicized leading indicators? Because they just are not dependable. They sometimes give a false negative signal and predict a recession that doesn't happen. Even when the signal is right, there's no way of knowing how soon the turn will come. It could be as little as three months or as much as nine months.
Source: Dr. Irwin Kellner, economist and senior vice president, Manufacturers Hanover Trust Co., 350 Park Ave., New York 10022.

Ways to Defend the Company Against a Labor Shortage

Hiring a good secretary, a good machinist, a good technician, and even a good maintenance person is getting harder. The spotty labor shortages plaguing many companies right now are a preview of troubles to come—first symptoms of a long-term problem no business will be able to avoid. Causes: Too few trained workers and a changing population mix (fewer young workers).

Policies and procedures are needed to cope successfully with the current personnel pinch incorporated into standard personnel practices.

Now is the time for managers to develop new recruitment, training, and layoff policies. That's the consensus of economists and top personnel managers in five major cities: Atlanta, Chicago, Houston, Los Angeles, and Pittsburgh.

Recruitment: There are no panaceas. It pays, though, to consider some new tactics that companies have tried to ease the people pinch:

• Break away from conventional classified ads. Radio turns out to be highly effective in some parts of the country. Different times, pro-

grams, and stations reach different types of workers. It's also highly flexible and cheaper than most businesses think. Possible sometimes to barter company products (especially if they're consumer goods) for time. Call in competing local station reps for a fast education. Advertise in different places in the newspaper. The sports page or page 2 could be good.

• Involve current employees as recruiters by offering them an incentive. One formula that worked: $100 bonus for a referral if the new worker stays on the job for 90 days.

• Hire from outside the traditional skill pool. Science and math teachers have the skills to handle many technical jobs, and unemployment among teachers is high. Studies show that coaches, phys ed teachers, and ex-jocks of all sorts tend to make excellent salespeople.

• Part-timers. Recruit a reserve force of eager and experienced part-time workers from among the company's own retirees. Recruiting is easier now that retired workers can earn up to $4,500 a year without forfeiting Social Security benefits.

• Review job specs. Many have become unrealistically inflated. Companies usually demand a typing speed of 50 words per minute, but often what they really need is a bright, eager person who can type four letters a day. Another false spec: Requiring a junior college degree for an entry-level job when manual dexterity, minimal technical aptitude, job experience, common sense, and reliability are all that's needed.

Training. Conference Board economist Audrey Freedman lays the blame for the skilled worker shortage right at business's doorstep. Companies didn't develop a skilled labor force when they could—and should—have trained it, she says. A trade-off to consider: Invest money in finding and training people all over again after a layoff. Or spend the money to hold on to them through a slowdown. Discover a way to supplement the unemployment benefits of skilled, technical, professional, and managerial employees who are temporarily not needed on condition that they come back to the company. Might keep them from moving away to find work or taking a permanent job with a competitor. But arrangements must be cleared with local unemployment people to ensure that they don't jeopardize the worker's normal benefits.

Another tactic: Rotate available work, say every other week or two weeks per month, among laid-off employees. Once again, exact mechanics must be checked out with local unemployment office to avoid forfeiture of benefits.

Layoffs. On the record, many executives now claim that the surprise and severity of the current labor shortage makes them more cautious about future layoffs. Some say that if a recession is mild, they won't cut back on skilled workers at all. But the experts don't believe them. Dr. Marvin Kosters, economist with the American Enterprise Institute who has tracked the long-term rise in U.S. labor costs, contends there is no reason to believe companies won't handle layoffs in a slowdown just as they have in the past, by laying off highly trained workers. His forecast: A big increase in labor costs that will eat into profits.

First-line supervisors who have had job slots unfilled for weeks or even months are now very reluctant to fire incompetent or lazy workers. The problem spreads when other workers see what they can get away with. Expect deteriorating product quality and rising reject rates.

Controlling Arbitration Costs

The costs of arbitration are still within control of the parties involved. Biggest direct charge is the arbitrator's fee of $200/day or more during the hearing and for each day of studying the record and writing an opinion. Even in a fairly simple matter, count on at least one day of study for every day of hearing.

Most arbitrators bill for a full day even when the work takes only a few hours. Travel time and expenses are also tacked on. Briefs and transcripts are sometimes required more out of habit than necessity.

In order to cut costs:

• Pick the arbitrator much more carefully. Choose one experienced in the kind of problem under arbitration. The less time spent educating the arbitrator at the hearing, the fewer days of hearing-room time and study time.

• Get together with the other party before the hearing and agree to stipulate as many facts as possible. Don't waste time filling the record with technical details such as seniority dates, wage rates, and other undisputed facts.

• If both sides want to control costs, ask the arbitrator to write a brief opinion. The message will be clear: Both sides expect a modest bill.

• Don't quote precedents unless they are really necessary and pertinent. The arbitrator will feel obligated to look up citations. That takes time and costs money.

• Schedule hearings near the plant (on company premises, if the union will agree) so witnesses can be called from their jobs only for the time they are needed. Schedule hearings to start early, take short lunch breaks, and make the arbitrator work a full day for the fee.

• Finally, take one last look at the case before going into the hearing. If the outcome is predictable, settle in advance. But give the arbitrator plenty of notice if you settle, or he'll bill you for the day anyway. Note: Once a case is started with AAA, the administrative fee must be paid even if an arbitrator has not yet been selected. Although this may seem to be a needless expense, it serves to encourage early settlement.

Source: Morris Stone, former vice president, American Arbitration Association.

Cost Management Principles

• Develop a cost-conscious attitude in top managers and their subordinates.

• Place responsibility for costs where they actually are incurred. Others can advise and assist, but cost improvements must be made where the cost occurs. Lower-level supervisors, for example, can have a heavy influence on costs.

• Make certain managers and supervisors know what their costs are and how they influence the profits of the company.

• Motivate employees to improve costs. Best method—recognition of achievement.

• Use the existing organization to bring costs under control. Consultants, teams of auditors, management committees, and the like can help. But unless the organization becomes cost conscious, results will only be temporary.

Source: *How to Increase Profits with Cost Management,* by Carlton D. Richardson, Duquesne Publishing Co., P.O. Box 85, Moorestown, NJ 08057.

New Manager's Doldrums

Problem: Getting used to being responsible for other people's work. What to do: (1) Let the new manager know that he must get others to produce. (2) Have him evaluate the strengths of each staff member and make specific recommendations for increasing output. (3) Reinforce his efforts by checking back periodically and by encouraging him to develop subordinates who can be depended on.

Help Managers Cope with Change

A manager who is reacting to very dramatic changes in his daily operations and his responsibilities usually goes through five distinct psychological phases:

• Denial. Claims the change won't work in the department because the work is too creative.

• Anger. Refuses to institute the changes. Often ends up in a shouting match with the boss over the inappropriateness of the new methods.

• Bargaining. While feeling that the new methods will not work, says he's willing to try if he can have additional budget.

• Depression. Sits around feeling sorry for himself and fantasizing about changing jobs.

• Acceptance. Confronted with the inevitable and the need to relieve frustrations, slowly accepts the idea that there is no escape, that he might as well accept the new methods.

Recommended: The top manager who recognizes these stages as natural and temporary will be better prepared to help associates gradually accept the change.

Similar stages will accompany any massive

change, whether it be a switch to management by objectives, or to zero-base budgeting, or a company-wide conversion to word-processing office systems (in which managers lose their personal secretaries).

Source: Dr. Russell A. Johnston and Dr. Guy J. DeGenaro, Virginia Commonwealth University, in *Administrative Management.*

Using Field Personnel in Headquarters Projects

Bringing field employees into headquarters to work on a thorny company problem is a good way to eliminate the "us and them" feeling field people often have toward those in company headquarters.

Occasional headquarters assignments give field personnel an opportunity to:

• Become familiar with headquarters staff.

• Demonstrate their ability and resourcefulness to headquarters staff.

• Challenge problem-solving ability. They are more able to concentrate on problem because they are removed from "home" distractions.

• View problems from corporate perspective.

• Provide corporate executives with new perspective on field problems.

Source: *Administrative Management.*

How Business Can Use Political Clout

Political action committees (devices by which officials of a company can pool their campaign contributions for maximum flexibility and impact) are still a good way to make political weight felt. But so many businesses are getting on the bandwagon that the rules are being tightened. It is estimated that a new PAC is formed every business day. Key revisions:

• Unions are increasingly demanding that line workers be allowed to have payroll deductions go into a union-packed political campaign chest. They have the right to get such a checkoff if management is contributing to a fund.

• Costs of asking stockholders and executives to work for the election or defeat of a particular candidate have to be reported to the Federal Election Commission if they go over $2,000 per election. (It's legal to spend $1,999 in the primary and to spend another $1,999 in the November election.)

• Expenses involved in drumming up support for (or opposition to) legislation having a direct effect on business can no longer be deducted on income tax returns as a cost of doing business.

Despite the changes, though, more political involvement is well worth the time and effort. Washington's intrusion into business decisions isn't going to end. Having lawmakers who will listen to management's side of a controversy is a real asset for a company.

How to Communicate Effectively

Effective oral communication skills are needed to be a persuasive manager, get others to change actions and decisions. Basics:

Be sure that you have the subordinate's full attention before beginning the conversation.

• Pick a time and place free from noise and interference (preferably a conference room or your office). Don't expect anyone to follow your reasoned argument against a background of ringing phones, noisy machinery, or during a less than private business lunch.

• Look directly at the other person. Keep your body alert and erect, even if sitting, to reinforce seriousness of your message.

• Ask questions to be sure he's really listening—not absorbed in a personal crisis or anxious to catch the 5:15. Might be best to postpone the discussion if it's clear that he's distracted.

Prepare what you say with the care that goes into a good memo and the salesmanship that goes into a good pitch.

• Use hard facts.

• Anticipate objections. Be prepared to offer solutions as you go along.

• Be specific about the assistance, funds, or action you want.

• Aim to reach the other person's specific commitment.

• Use clear, simple, direct language. Don't lose him in a burst of technical jargon that can leave him confused, unwilling to admit ignorance—and determined to say no.

Encourage a postive response.

• Beware of religious, political, or sexual references that could turn the other person off completely or provoke hosility.

• Avoid glib comebacks to objections. Pause, speak slowly and deliberately in reply to make it clear that you've considered his viewpoint carefully.

• Watch your body language. Are your body and face saying what you want them to say? Never crowd the other person.

Very important: Don't use oral communication on a sensitive or complex matter in order to avoid the hard work of thinking out the issues and writing a memo.
Source: Alan Jay Weiss, Kepner-Tregoe Inc., in *Supervisory Management,* AMACOM, Trudeau Rd., Saranac Lake, NY 12983.

Which Government Agencies Cause the Most Problems

The White House polled senators and congressmen to find out which foul-ups they got the most complaints about. The agency most often cited for demanding excessive paperwork from business was the Occupational Safety and Health Administration. Most inefficient: Postal Service, Civil Service Commission, Farmers Home Administration.

The lawmakers say they have trouble checking on the current status of cases at Small Business Administration, Internal Revenue Service, Office of Worker's Compensation, Immigration and Naturalization Service.

The best places in Washington to get fast, accurate answers: Defense Department, Veterans Administration, Passport Office, Social Security Administration.

Crank Consumer Complaints

How to deal with those handfuls of consumerists who have no justified claims, hold grudges, write silly complaint letters to FTC or other agencies?

Don't get excited. Write a polite letter; it will probably solve the problem.

Consumer agencies are supposed to act on complaints; that's their job. So don't be too concerned if they send a form letter. In many cases they'll do nothing further; they know it's a crank as well as you do.

If the agency seems to be taking the complaint seriously, call them up or drop in to see them. Explain why the complaint has no substance. They'll listen, and since they have more cases than they can handle, they'll probably drop it.

Help from Congressmen

Most managers of medium-size businesses are important enough in their own region to get through to their congressman when they really want to. But often the telephone calls don't produce results. Here's how to make the contact work out, based on the advice of an effective business lobbyist (a former congressman).

• Keep the call brief. Most congressmen actually talk to 75 or more persons a day. They are always pressed for time.

• Get to the point. Don't hesitate to ask for what you want.

• Be specific. Outline just who within a particular agency is causing the trouble with what rule. If much detail is involved, send relevant documents ahead of time.

• Don't hestitate to spell out the negative impact of a new law or regulation on your company's business. The idea of the call isn't to plead the public interest but to let your representative in Washington know the personal impact of what is happening in his area.

• Arm him with information he'll need about who opposes your company's stand and why. If the opposition should surprise him later, there's a good chance that he may back off.

What to Tell All Employees

A very useful handbook of conduct that one executive distributes to new employees:

• My primary goals are to make this company bigger and more profitable while enjoying it in the process. Your goals should be compatible with these.

• Creativity: You do not get an ''A'' simply by solving all the problems within your jurisdiction. An integral part of your job is to identify new opportunities and recommend creative ways to take advantage of them.

• One of your primary jobs is to keep me out of trouble.

• Asking questions: It is your responsibility to understand all of the ''rules'' relating to your job—that is, how you succeed and how you fail. If anything of significance is unclear, you have an obligation to ask questions. Ignorance is no excuse in this case.

• Remembering: Through whatever method you find successful, you must remember items of importance or those requiring some sort of action. This includes requests made to you in writing as well as oral orders made in passing. If you can do this without writing, you have a better memory than I.

• Overtime: Routine, substantial overtime is neither necessary nor desirable. On the other hand, almost any level of overtime is mandatory if that's what it takes to get a particular job done.

• Your problems: I will try to be sensitive to your problems, but it is your specific responsibility to tell me about the important ones. I do not expect to have to draw them out of you.

• Job offers and contacts with competitors: I expect you to look after your own personal interests, but I also expect to be informed of all discussions related to outside employment and all contacts with competitors.

• Dress is important because it creates a perceived image with outsiders and it sets an example for others in the company. I expect professional consideration of both facts.

• Surprises are bad. Unless they are good. But even if they are good they should not be very big, because that would probably mean you should have known about them sooner.

• Errors of commission: I prefer errors of commission to errors of omission. Sometimes it is best to do something even if it is wrong.

The preceding items are important to me. They are intended to be fundamental enough so that they will be important to you also. If any of them are unclear or objectionable to you, please discuss them with me.

Source: J. Clifton Lundberg, executive vice president, PRC Technical Applications, McLean, VA.

Changing from Autocratic to Participative Management

One-man shows and entrepreneurs often fail to realize the tremendous importance of both strategic planning and regular reviews of performance, including their own. Every company chief must spend a few days every year with his key people and review from scratch the whole mission and concept of the business. They should analyze their strengths and weaknesses as an organization. Then decide where they want to go over the short, medium, and long range. Get alternate approaches to achieving those objectives. And develop an action plan.

Plans cannot be formulated without a hard-headed analysis of how the past year's performance fell short. Perhaps the disappointments were caused by a critical lack of personnel, a sagging distribution system, or misdirected use of advertising and promotion funds. Without a review of the past, future results are not likely to be much better. Participatory communication often reveals that not everybody is pulling in the same direction. Once common objectives are understood and set down, it's much easier to reach them.

Equally important for the chief executive: Make a personal review and analysis of the job performance of each member of the executive team. This can't be done properly on the spur of the moment—"Come on in, Joe, and let's discuss your performance." Instead, plan it well in advance. Measure each performance against previously established targets. And it should be on a regular basis, no less than once a year, preferably each quarter.

Most important, though, it that everyone, from the #1 man down, first evaluate his own performance. Nobody knows it better than the individual. And, almost without exception, executives will set a higher standard for themselves than could ever be imposed autocratically from above. (Many times, the boss will have to reassure penitent vice presidents that they are doing better than they think.)

Same goes for corporate objectives. Sales targets set by the participants themselves are, if anything, apt to err on the high side. Here it may be necessary to adjust the aspirations downward to more realistic, attainable levels.

Switching from autocracy is easiest, of course, when a new boss takes over. An example of how to turn things around:

A new product team comes in for a decision on whether the widget should be red, green, or blue. Resist the temptation to hand down a verdict. Ask for recommendations. Perhaps they favor red, and enumerate their reasons. But they also admit that the outside design consultant's choice was blue, and there is a small minority group within the company making a case for green.

At this point, the boss's best course of action is not to make a decision. Instead, it is to encourage the group in developing more information. Whatever one may think of outside design consultants, expert opinions cannot be dismissed out of hand. And the maverick who pushed for green is considered one of the brightest in the department. Why does he want green?

Whatever the final decision, it won't (and shouldn't) be because "the boss likes red." It should be the result of thoughtful analysis and participation by all those responsible for making sound judgments.

Source: Robert W. Lear, visiting professor, Columbia University Graduate School of Business.

Leadership Checklist

• Have I spelled out what's expected in terms of results? Should I discuss these results with my subordinates?

• Have I told employees where they stand?

- Do employees understand how to do the work?
- Do I give employees adequate support?
- What have I done or not done to cultivate positive relationships?
- Do employees know why their jobs are important, how they fit into the overall company structure and the effects of poor performance?
- Are employees kept informed on what is going on in the department and the company? (Not just need-to-know items but nice-to-know.)
- Do employees have adequate freedom in which to work?
- Are employees too often put in a defensive position regarding performance?
- What have I done to get employees mentally and emotionally involved in their jobs?
- Have employees been allowed to participate in setting goals and deciding means of achieving them?
- Have good aspects of performance received adequate and periodic recognition?
- Have I shown adequate concern for the employees as individuals? For their personal goals?
- Am I willing to listen to employees and give them a chance to implement ideas and suggestions?
- Have I ever consciously assessed employees' strengths and weaknesses with the idea of structuring work to capitalize on those strengths?
- Are employees adequately and reasonably challenged?

Source: Burt K. Scanlan, professor of management, University of Oklahoma, in *Personnel Journal,* 866 West 18 St., Costa Mesa, CA 92661.

Improve the Company's Hot Line

Quality control programs continue to deteriorate. The shopping public is generating more complaints. Some manufacturers are improving their hot line systems (special telephone number to handle complaints). They're making them a good deal more than a public relations gesture. Many record the complaints, analyze them, and have the marketing department follow up. The use of form letter replies is being cut way back. Does your company have a hot line? Test it to gauge relations with the public.

Business Espionage

How business uses dirty tricks to get competitors' secrets:

- Interviewing and questioning competitors' employees about a "job opening" that doesn't exist.
- Negotiating with a competitor for a license, with no intention of taking it.
- Bribing the competitor's suppliers and employees.
- Planting an employee on the competitor's payroll.
- Using private investigators.

A survey by *Industry Week* magazine found only 5% of business managers willing to admit (without signing the questionnaire) that they had knowingly used unethical tactics. But 70% admitted winking at dirty tricks carried out by subordinates.

One manager said: "If he's a good marketing research man, ethics won't stop his research for vital information on a competitor."

Junior Boards of Directors

A junior board of directors is a proven way to develop young executives, improve communication among all managers, and provide fresh source of new ideas at one major corporation.

The technique in use for 50 years:

- Each division or subsidiary has its own board, which is autonomous and free to investigate any company activity (except salaries and wages).
- Board members serve a six-month term, then rate each other's performance. The 20% with lowest ratings are dropped and new members elected to fill their places.

- Members are nominated by a special membership committee of the junior board and elected by the full board. Each board member is paid a monthly fee and gets an extra two weeks of vacation.

- The board must be autonomous and self-perpetuating. This eliminates undue influence by top management and reveals the most promising young executives. Re-election by peers is important in identifying standout leaders.

- Unanimous board endorsement of an idea is followed by presentation to the corporate board of directors.

The payoff lies in the hundreds of ideas that have saved the corporation money and have streamlined operations.

Source: *Dun's Review*, 666 Fifth Ave., New York 10019.

What Businesses Are Asking Accountants Today

- Pensions and profit-sharing. How to maximize tax benefits for individuals and companies through pension and profit plans, despite the complications caused by ERISA.

- Electronic data processing (EDP). Smaller firms that have thus far computerized only their payrolls are ready to extend their EDP operations to other areas of the business. Questions: What should go on the computer (or minicomputer)? Rent or buy? Use a service bureau? Or time-share?

- State taxes. Getting to be a bigger and bigger headache. Potential savings here could be greater than on federal taxes.

- Tax shelters. Now that IRS has closed many loopholes, clients are hunting for new ones. Use an accountant to help assess soundness of the promised tax angles.

- Long-term debt. Growing companies wonder about timing and costs. The CPA is called in as a diagnostician to look at cash flow projections, budgets, net worth—and offer an opinion.

- Restructuring the corporation. The founding generation asks: How can we be assured that our capital won't be frozen in the firm? And the younger generation asks: How can we be assured that the new net worth being created by our efforts will be passed along to us?

- Acquisition opportunities. CPA evaluates financial record of potential candidates.

- Selling the business. Potential buyers are putting together offers in such ingenious packages that owners who hadn't thought seriously about selling before are being tempted.

Source: Richard Eisner, Richard A. Eisner & Co., CPAs, 380 Madison Ave., New York 10017.

OFFICE MANAGEMENT

How Long to Retain Records

Capitalizing on the Telephone

Before Hiring an Answering Service

Eleven Ways to Cut Mailing Costs

Pros and Cons of Word Processors

Setting up a Conference Room

How to Streamline Files

Growing Plants in the Office

14

OFFICE MANAGEMENT

How Long to Retain Business Records

Refers to General Ledger only. Supporting journals and entries that summarize cash receipts and disbursements, sales, returns and allowances (deductions from sales), purchases of material, labor and overhead costs, method and computation used to evaluate inventories and cost of sales, depreciation and amortization of assets, general and administrative expense, etc., should be treated as accounts payable invoices and credits.

190

INVENTORY AND COST RECORDS

MANUFACTURING

PAYROLL, RELATED RECORDS

PERSONNEL

Source: *Records Retention,* Ellsworth Publishing, P.O. Box 3162, Evansville, IN 47331.

Getting Fast Repairs from the Phone Company

If the phone company doesn't react quickly enough, there are steps you can take to get them moving.

After going through the usual channels (i.e., calling the service or business office) and still not getting satisfaction, ask to speak to the local division manager or vice president. (It's good to call now to get his name for future reference.) Tell him that your phones are out of service. That's the specific phrase that will get the fastest response. Insist that the outage is more than an inconvenience; it's a critical business necessity to get service restored quickly. For that, the phone company will probably authorize overtime work, if necessary.

Determining How Many Incoming Phone Lines You Need

Telephone companies offer a busy or blocked-line study, free of charge. It determines whether a subscriber has enough incoming lines. General rule: Lines are adequate if no more that 2% of callers get busy signals on the first try.

Arrange for a study on days when phone traffic is expected to be heavy. If possible, get an hour-by-hour breakdown of busy signals.

Then have the switchboard keep a record of the total number of calls received hour by hour. (Use this to calculate the percentage of busies since the phone company only reports the number of busy signals.)

Reading the results: If less than 2% busies are reported, the company may be paying for too much incoming capacity. It should consider removing one trunk line, making a new study, and then repeating the process until the busies increase to 2%.

If more than 2% busy signals are logged, the company may have too little incoming capacity. Repeat study to verify the results, then get the telephone company to add trunk lines until the busies drop to 2%.

Special problem: Study shows that busies are 2% or less, but customers are complaining that they get a lot of busy signals. They're getting a busy exchange signal, something not covered by the study; it's caused by too many telephone company subscribers sharing the same exchange number. If the phone company is uncooperative, file a formal complaint with the state telephone commission stating that the company isn't providing the proper grade of service. Caution: It can take months, sometimes years, to modernize exchange facilites to eliminate "exchange busy" problems. The only alternative may be to change the company's phone number so that calls come in through a different exchange, one that is not overcrowded.

Source: *How to Cut Costs and Improve Service of Your Telephone, Telex, TWX, and other Telecommunications* by Frank K. Griesinger, McGraw-Hill, New York.

Direct-Dial Overseas Calls

Callers can dial 64 countries without the assistance of an operator. The rate for direct dial is 10% to 42% less for calls made during daytime business hours. International direct distance dialing (IDDD) saves time, too, since no operator assistance is required at either end.

Limitations: Older telephone exchanges are not equipped for IDDD. Tell the operator the caller wants the IDDD rate but the exchange is not equipped for direct dialing. The lower rate should be charged. Other points: IDDD rates are not applicable to calls made from coin stations. And they don't apply to collect or credit-card calls or calls billed to a third number.

AT&T publishes booklets giving specific instructions on using IDDD to each of the countries involved. Ask the telephone company for a complete set.

Cost-saving tips:

• U.S. three-minute minimum applies to most international calls originating here. But many other countires use a one-minute, one-second, or message-unit costing system. Cut costs by having the company's overseas offices call the U.S. at agreed-upon times to take advantage of lower charges.

• Consider monetary rates of exchange when deciding where calls should originate.

• International calls that are placed after 5 p.m., before 5 a.m., and on Sunday also save money. (The rate depends on where the call originates, not its destination.)

Buying Your Own Phones

It has become legal to purchase your own telephones, return present instruments (which are really rented) to the phone company, and maybe even save money on the deal. How to go about it:

First, tell the telephone company business office you want to buy your own phones and stop paying a monthly rental charge for them. The company may want to sell you the instruments you're now renting; get prices, but don't act yet.

Visit the telephone company phone store (if there is one in your area) or business office to see what instruments and colors it has. Compare these with what's available in independent stores, which frequently sell unusual decorator models in addition to the same phones the telephone company offers.

If you don't buy phones from Bell, the Bell System will continue to service the phone lines, but it will impose a substantial charge if trouble on the line is caused by a non-telephone company phone. However, chances are slim that service problems will develop on instruments made by first-line manufacturers such as Western Electric, ITT, Stromberg Carlson, GTE, and Northern Telecom.

Be sure phones that are purchased have a Federal Communications Commission registration number stamped on the housing, indicating they have been certified. Notify the phone company of plans to connect FCC-approved phones to their lines.

If additional jacks are required, they must be installed by the telephone company. Only the instruments themselves may be purchased, and plugged into the phone company's lines. The Bell System is installing a new type of jack that isn't compatible with four-prong plugs. But adapters are available in electonics and phone-supply stores.

If you assume that phone rates will continue increasing at about 6% a year, you can evaluate the cost of owning your own phones to see how long it takes to break even. Remember, there's no charge by the phone company for removal of telephones.

Source: Frank Griesinger, president, Frank K. Griesinger & Associates, Inc., 1412 Superior Bldg., Cleveland 44114.

Buying a Switching System

Growing numbers of private vendors are offering new, computer-controlled (CBX) telephone switching systems, competitive to Bell System equipment.

Before any purchase, investigate these important features:

• Can data also be transmitted over the wires?

• Cost of maintenance. Can company people be trained to do in-house maintenance?

• Vendor's response time on major and minor breakdowns.

• The number of conversations which can be handled simultaneously (by total system and by each subsystem down to individual extensions.).

• Credit on return of surplus equipment.

• Guarantee that repair parts will be available.

• Will vendor make periodic traffic studies free?

• Added cost for wiring existing physical plant to capacity.

• Who will negotiate with Bell System for removal or purchase of cabling already in building?

To make the best decision on what capabilities to build into switching system, ask each vendor for a glossary of terminology in addition to the standard literature that accompanies the product. The glossary describes the functions of each feature of the equipment clearly and simply, without sales puffery.

Alternatives to WATS Line

Southern Pacific Communications (SPC), Microwave Communications (MCI) and ITT-Corporate Communication Services (ITT-CS) —the specialized private common carriers—now offer service in many cities that resembles AT&T's WATS (Wide Area Telecommunications Service).

Advantages:

• Simultaneous conversations. A WATS line allows only one conversation at a time. But the microwave carriers establish multiple circuits in each city that they serve. The result: As many simultaneous conversations as are needed.

• Lower cost. The carriers measure a call in tenths of minutes. WATS is charged in full minutes and tenths of hours. If the person called is not there, the private carriers bill only for the 20 seconds it takes to find that out.

• Itemized billing. The monthly bill lists all calls dialed, with costs shown for each. SPC even provides individual billing codes. Up to 99 persons receive bills showing calls they dialed. Extra cost: $10 monthly for all 99 codes.

• Off-peak rates and quantity discounts. MCI offers a 40% discount on traffic over 60 hours, 85% after 240 hours. Both MCI and SPC offer substantially reduced rates after working hours. They are much cheaper than direct-dialing at the AT&T's 35% discounted "evening" rate. Employees can call from distant cities that are on the networks.

Where WATS has the edge:

• Limited geographic coverage. SPC serves 55 metropolitan areas (29 more will be added before the end of 1979). MCI: 46. ITT-CS: 28. WATS can cover any telephone in the U.S. For many calls to a specific distant city, a "foreign exchange" line rented from AT&T may be less expensive if employees will wait for line availability. A "tie line" to a specific switchboard in a distant city may give 24-hour, seven-day service to that particular organization at even lower cost.

• Dialing ease. With AT&T, caller dials the company one- or two-digit access code for WATS, sometimes an extra "1," the area code and the telephone number. Total: 12 or 13 digits.

In contrast, the private carriers require 22 to 25 digits. One remedy: Automatic dialers to compress distant numbers frequently called.

How to comparison-shop: Make a list of cities called frequently. See if common carriers cover these areas.

Private common carrier rates will be less per minute than any direct-dialed long-distance call. Substantially less than either station-to-station or person-to-person "operator assisted" calls. They are probably less than usage of 25 hours or less on a WATS "measured time, 10-hour minimum" circuit.

When to stick with WATS: If the company

uses 6,000 to 8,000 minutes of conversation per month on a "full business day" WATS line, or uses it on second shifts, after business hours, or on weekends, the cost per minute probably will be less than that of the private carriers. Also, if many calls go to smaller cities and rural areas not served by the private carriers, companies may still be able to fully justify WATS.

When you don't need a WATS line: Don't consider it unless current long-distance toll calls are at least 125% (preferably 150%) of the estimated cost of the WATS line. There's always some monthly overflow from WATS to toll calls when WATS circuits are busy. Overlooking this is the most common cause of disappointment with WATS line savings.

How to Pick the Best Toll-Free System

Consider all the options before establishing a way that customers or employees can call the office toll-free. The choices:

Collect calls. Advantage: They can be made at any time from any telephone. Disadvantages: (1) Customers may hesitate to call collect when a competitor offers a toll-free 800 number (which is faster to get). (2) Cost is higher. Collect calls are billed at high operator-handled rates. There's a three-minute minimum.

Foreign exchange service (FX). Example: Company has a New York City telephone number for its Cleveland office. New York customers call that number. Advantage: Customer pays only for a local call. Company pays monthly circuit charge on a mileage basis for unlimited usage. Employees can also use the line to call any telephone in the New York metropolitan area. Disadvantages: Only one conversation is possible at a time. If the company releases the number to employees, outgoing calls to New York may block incoming customer calls.

Suggestion: Telephone company can make the FX circuit work only one way—inward.

Private hot line. Usually desk-to-desk service. The customer picks up the telephone and it rings in the manager's office.

AT&T system cost: A mileage charge, plus the cost of two local connections Service is full-time. Western Union cost: Measured services with a minimum charge based on a rate for each 1/10 minute, plus instrument rental cost.

Advantage: Immediate connection and speedy service for an important customer. Disadvantage: Each circuit serves only one distant location.

Off-premises extension. Company can install one station of its headquarters telephone system at a branch office. By dialing three or four digits, any telephone in the system can be reached. Another application: Circuit could also be given to an important customer who calls many different people at company's headquarters.

Cost: Company pays local station rental charge, plus mileage cost to destination for full-time usage.

Disadvantage: One conversation at a time. Buttons on telephones at the distant end limit the number of people who can use the circuit.

Tie line. Circuit connects company switchboard or switching equipment with distant switchboard or switching equipment. All stations at headquarters and in distant office have access to the line.

One call at a time. But circuit can work simultaneously in both directions if you wish.

Remote call forwarding (RCF). AT&T is heavily promoting this new service, available in cities that use an electronic switching system (ESS) in central offices. The company rents an RCF seven-digit local number in the city from which management wants to receive toll-free calls. The number may be listed in the city directory. Or it may be left unlisted (the company informs customers and employees about the new service). Callers dial a low-cost local call. Receiving company is billed for RCF calls at relatively inexpensive direct-dial long-distance rates.

Advantage: Many simultaneous calls at low monthly rental cost for a special number (average $16).

Disadvantage: Separate number rental required for each distant city. For a company with a large volume of inward traffic, inward WATS 800 service will be less expensive.

Important If the company is using Zenith or Enterprise special four-digit directory numbers, and is in a city where RCF service is now available, change immediately. RCF and inward WATS have made the popular Zenith and Enterprise special numbers obsolete.

Inward WATS. Offers both inward and outward service. Circuits cover all states. (A separate circuit is needed for the state where the company's office is.)

For the continental U.S. a 600-minute inbound package costs about $245 monthly, or less, depending on location. Overtime is billed at $18.31 (or less) per hour, measured in 1/10 hour increments. For larger requirements: A package of 240 hours is available for $1,675 (or less).

Cost-saver: If nationwide inward WATS service is not needed, there are five regional WATS bands to pick from. Advantage: Relatively low circuit cost for simultaneous conversations. Consider full business day, 240-hour circuit, if traffic justifies capacity. Properly loaded, it produces very low cost-per-minute toll-free calling.

Rules of thumb:

• For relatively few calls from a specific city, use RCF rather than collect calling. Direct-dial rates are much less expensive than operator-handled, three-minute-minimum collect calls.

• For many calls from diverse locations, investigate FX and inward WATS.

Source: Frank K. Griesinger, president, Frank Griesinger & Associates, Inc., 1412 Superior Bldg. Cleveland 44114.

When Not to Use the Phone

Transmitting a short written message from New York to Los Angeles by the next day (including labor and prorated equipment rental) can be cheaper than phone—mainly because the average phone call is seven minutes long, even when the actual message is very brief.

Telex . . . . $ .66
TWX $1.00
Mailgram, dispatched by Telex or
    TWX telprinter $1.66
Mailgram, telephoned to Western
    Union's 800 number $3.27
Telegram, dispatched by Telex
    or TWX teleprinter $6.20

Night Letter, dispatched by Telex
    or TWX teleprinter $5.78
Telegram, telephoned to Western Union's
    800 number $8.43*
Night Letter, telephoned to Western
    Union's 800 number $7.48*
Express Mail, taken to post office and
    picked up there . . . . $5.88 to $6.38
Express Mail, taken to post office
    and delivered . . . . $7.98 to $8.48
*Includes $3 for hand delivery.

Taking Phone Messages

A busy switchboard operator can't take messages and give out information at the same time. Designate another company employee (perhaps a veteran who knows company policy and has time on his hands) to whom time-consuming calls and questions can be routed.

Common switchboard error: An operator issues progress reports on busy lines without giving the caller time to respond.

Message-taking mistakes: (1) Time of call not noted; the message doesn't tell you whether you've already spoken to caller. (2) Initials of person taking message omitted; time is wasted tracking person down if the message is unclear.

Phrases to avoid: "He's not in yet." "He's not back from lunch yet." "He's gone for the day."

What should be said: "I'm sorry, he's away from his desk. May I have him return your call, or can someone else help?"

Before You Hire an Answering Service

The right answering service at a branch office can increase your company's capacity to receive incoming orders and improve customer service. Problem: Many services are understaffed and the operators poorly trained. Those with the largest ads in the Yellow Pages may be the worst.

How to pick a good one:

• Visit the service's offices (without an appointment) to observe the operators' manner. Are they pleasant? Do they try to be helpful to callers? Do they allow phones to ring more than three times before picking up? If many lights are flashing on an individual operator's switchboard, callers may be made to wait, then given hurried treatment.

• Ask the supervisor how messages are stored. Each customer should have a folder for incoming messages. Ask how often the folder is reviewed to be sure messages are picked up. Will the service call to relay messages? How do they handle emergencies if a caller really has to reach the company?

Advice: Request names of three users of the service in businesses similar to yours. Ask the customers if they're satisfied.

Once the service is selected, don't leave the answering response up to the discretion of the operators. Tell them exactly what they should say in order to personalize their response. For the best service: Call them when the office will be empty. This helps to ensure that your calls will be picked up on the first ring.

Alternative: Use an answering machine. They're good.

Source: Frank Griesinger, president, Frank Griesinger & Associates, Inc., 1412 Superior Building, Cleveland 44114.

Time Differences

Business telephone calls made abroad should be placed when people are most accessible. Here is a guide to the time in some key foreign cities when it is noon in three major American cities:

	Noon in New York	Noon in Chicago	Noon in L.A.
Buenos Aires	2 p.m.	3 p.m.	5 p.m.
Honolulu	7 a.m.	8 a.m.	10 a.m.
London	5 p.m.	6 p.m.	8 p.m.
Mexico City	11 a.m.	12 p.m.	2 p.m.
Montreal	12 p.m.	1 p.m.	3 p.m.
Nassau, Bahamas	12 p.m.	1 p.m.	3 p.m.
San Juan	1 p.m.	2 p.m.	4 p.m.
Sydney	4 a.m.	5 a.m.	7 a.m.
Tel Aviv	7 p.m.	8 p.m.	10 p.m.
Zurich	6 p.m.	7 p.m.	9 p.m.
Following Day			
Tokyo	2 a.m.	3 a.m.	5 a.m.

Handling Telephone Complaints

Let the customer have his or her full say without interruption. Murmur an occasional word of sympathy or say, "Oh, I see." Admit a mistake (if there was one) and apologize for it. Make adjustment immediately, if possible. Even a partial adjustment handled promptly and courteously will create more good will than a full adjustment that is slow—or handled rudely.

Cutting Payroll Costs

The true cost of a payroll includes the clerical processing effort as well as salaries and fringes. Here are four ways to shrink clerical costs:

• Reduce the number of paydays. Go from weekly to biweekly or from biweekly to monthly. Another possibility: Monthly pay for management and biweekly for hourly workers. Benefit: Achieves savings while minimizing inconvenience to lower-paid workers.

• Stagger pay time by department. This won't reduce clerical costs but can eliminate problem of work coming to a standstill just before paychecks are distributed. It helps avoid production delays due to extended lunch hours when all employees are out of the office or plant standing in line at the bank.

• Use a time clock to record overtime hours only and cut out paperwork under normal working conditions.

• Use window envelopes so the name on the check shows through. Saves time of retyping names on envelopes.

Source: *Cost Reduction from A to Z* by Lindley R. Higgins and Ruth W. Stidger, McGraw-Hill, New York.

The Split Bonus

Split the annual bonus into two payments. Give one at year-end and one later next year. The divided bonus offers several advantages:

• Employees get feedback on performance at shorter intervals. The company can reward or penalize without waiting full 12 months.

• The company can retain the option to cut second payment if business turns down. (Make it clear that this is a possibility.)

• Employees get another cash transfusion just as the vacation season begins.

How one company did it: Management labeled the second bonus Christmas in July. Results: Mid-year performance has improved. Turnover rate of employees was also reduced.

Source: *The Best of OBI Interaction,* Organizational Behavior Institute, 666 Fifth Ave., New York 10019.

Moving Mail Through the Post Office Fast

Use white envelopes and cartons to speed mail. For some unknown reason, postal employees move them faster. Large envelopes with green-diamond borders are even better for first-class mail. All postal employees respond to that symbol.

Eleven Ways to Cut Mailing Costs

• Check mailing scales regularly. Put nine pennies on the scale. They should weigh exactly one ounce.

• Consider using microfiche or microfilm for bulky catalogs or detailed instructions that must be mailed regularly. Costs much less to mail, and savings quickly pay for initial investment in equipment.

• Be sure company reports and bulletins that are mailed out are printed on both sides of the paper to cut down on weight.

• Use certified mail instead of registered mail unless the item must be insured. Certified rates are one-third of registered rates.

• Use third class when a large number (over 200) of identical items must be mailed out.

• High-volume mailers should question the value of parcel insurance. If what is mailed isn't very valuable, it may cost less to drop the insurance and pay for claims.

• A real bargain from the Postal Service: Its stamped, printed envelopes, especially if a company usually buys 5,000 envelopes or less.

• Fold all correspondence into standard business-size envelopes whenever possible. A single sheet in a large 9-by-12-inch envelope not only costs more to mail but also takes longer to be delivered.

• Continuing postage error: Paying 15¢ per ounce for first-class mail over one ounce. The rate is only 13¢ for each additional ounce.

• Spoiled postage imprints, stamps, or cards are redeemable within one year at 90% of the original cost.

• Don't use special delivery to large metropolitan areas, or to large companies which pick up their mail, or to post office box numbers.

Wrapping a Package the Right Way

Seal a sturdy carton with six strips of two-inch-wide plastic tape (not masking or cellophane tape, which tear easily): a strip across the center of top and bottom and each open edge on flap ends. Don't just go to the ends. Go a few inches around. Have an address label inside so that if outside label is lost or defaced, the package can be opened and sent with second label. Don't use brown paper or string; they only increase chance of loss if paper tears and label rips off or the string unties and gets caught in a sorting machine.

Choosing a Fire-Resistant Safe

Paper burns at 350°F. Computer tape and microfilm decompose at 150°. Most fires reach 1,000° in the first few minutes and can go much higher. Expensive solution: Duplicate all vital records off premises. Much cheaper alternative:

Fire-resistant storage. Look for safes with the Underwriters' Laboratories classifications:

• A Class A safe withstands 2,000° for four hours before interior temperature reaches 350°. Class B, 1,850° for two hours. Class C, 1,700° for one hour.

• Protect tape and film by suspending a data safe inside a Class A safe. The sealed compartment will maintain moisture-free 150° or less as long as outer safe holds.

• Fire-resistant safes are not burglar-proof. To combine theft and fire protection, place the fire-resistant safe inside the regular one.

• Fire safe must be new. It should be replaced after each fire, because exposure to fire uses up insulation.

Source: *Office and Office Building Security* by Ed San Luis, Security World Publishing Co., 2639 So. La Cienega Blvd., Los Angeles 90034.

Before You Buy a Calculator

Here are five factors that many buyers overlook, distracted by deciding what kind of mathematical capabilities the calculator should have:

• A display that shows as many digits as are needed.

• A display that is big and bright enough to be read without strain under actual office lighting.

• If the calculator prints, the type of paper it uses should be easily available in local stationery stores.

• Adequate length and coverage of warranty. Are there pick-up and delivery charges for repairs?

• Dealer that can handle most repairs in the office (or in its own shop). Avoid sending machine to factory for every repair.

Before You Buy a Word-Processing Machine

Word-processing systems can speed up the mechanical production of typing letters, reports, etc.—and at lower cost. But unless care is taken in selecting equipment and applications, the system may not be cost-effective.

Major questions to ask if you're thinking about acquiring a processing system:

1. How much of the material do you really need quickly—in fact, the same day?

There's no question that word processors are fast. Some are almost five times faster than regular typing. But don't forget, before that speed can be attained, a typist has to enter the material into the system. Thus, for some typing jobs, the inherent speed of the machine is offset by the need to "input" the text. The speed is valuable in repetitive typing from text entered once, and in creating letter-perfect text from drafts with light editing.

2. How many times do your documents go through the draft stage?

This is often the critical question. The machine's biggest plus is its ability to handle corrections and spew out a finished copy with inserts and deletions. (Low-cost machines can handle that function on a limited scale; higher-priced machines have a nearly unlimited ability to include such changes.) In some operations, where editing of major reports is a big part of the operation, the word processor could be a big asset. But if the raw material goes through only one draft, say, the asset may be marginal.

3. How often is the text repeated?

In law offices, where many paragraphs or even whole pages must be "edited" into contracts, the word processor is great. But if you're just making exact copies of a letter, you may be better off printing the letter and then typing in the name and address. Done right, it's hard to tell it from a personally typed letter.

Where and when word processors are best:

Their biggest impact is in situations where major redrafts are necessary and where large sections of text must be edited into the document. The simplest word processor lacks the sophistication to handle such heavyweight editing functions. The more complicated models can do the job. But be aware that not only are such models more expensive but some require extensive training for the operator.

For such a machine to be potentially cost-effective, it may have to be set up in a separate word-processing center, where a well-trained operator is functioning full-time. Once you move in that direction, there is a need for supervision to ensure that the work is collected, done, and distributed in a timely way.

But full-time typists get bored, and boredom can become resentment. If efforts aren't made to assure the typist of a sense of valuable participation in your company's work, high turnover and low productivity may offset any gains from the word-processing machines.

Use by secretaries: If the machine is of the simplest variety, it can offer a few time-saving advantages. If it's a sophisticated machine, a secretary will probably not use it enough to offset the cost involved.

Word processors are frequently a status symbol for the executive and his secretary. It's important to realize this when considering a system. Remember, a typical secretary spends only a fraction of the day using a typewriter. Despite the razzle-dazzle promises of the word-processor salesman, it's sometimes hard to pin down the dollar savings or advantages. In the typical office situation, the biggest savings are speed (how much do you really need?) and convenience (do you really care if the secretary has to type the letter twice?)—and they're hard to quantify.

If a secretarial office can clearly demonstrate the need for such a machine, turn to the least sophisticated models, which electronically link a typewriter to a magnetic-tape memory device. Even then, the move should be made cautiously.

In trying to calculate time saved with word processors, remember that if the system does not save 20% of typing time (net), and if your secretary only types 20% of the time (the average), the net saving is really very minor.
Source: Dr. Richard E. Heitman, senior vice president, Arthur D. Little, Inc., Cambridge, MA.

Realistic Expectations from Office Automation

Firms planning to automate their secretarial staffs should brace themselves for a surprise. The immediate benefit will not be cost savings through greater productivity. Real benefits are more likely to be an improved work environment that will have its payoff in important ways—but in the future.

The most meaningful immediate benefit: Not the application of word processing itself, but the planning process that goes into it.

Two points to consider: (1) Who uses what secretarial functions. (2) How the needs of the department or unit can be met by reorganizing secretarial work.

Continuing benefit: If the reorganization is properly carried out, it will open up career paths for the secretarial staff that have never been there before. It provides an incentive to attract a better grade of job applicants. This could be very important as changing population patterns and new jobs opening up for young women reduce the flow of qualified candidates.

• The clustering of word processors and secretaries creates new training ground for managers. A cluster of four to seven secretaries is headed by a coordinator (about equivalent in pay to today's executive secretary). Several clusters are managed by a supervisor—a new job.

• Secretaries who demonstrate ability move up this ladder into professional and managerial positions. Typical next step: Budget analyst.

Other benefits:

• The cluster arrangement is flexible so secretaries can develop different skills, concentrate on what they like doing best, or vary routine.

• Under the one-to-one system of secretarial staffing, only senior professionals and managers usually have full secretarial help. Cluster systems make more secretarial aid available to juniors.
Source: Allan Z. Loren, senior vice president, INA Corp., 1600 Arch St., Philadelphia, PA 19101.

How to Choose an Office Carpet

Carpeting can be a major investment. It should be chosen with an eye to fiber, construction, maintenance, static control, probable traffic —not just color. Some points to check:

• If one type of carpet will be used throughout

the whole office, pick the one best suited to heaviest use.

• Nylon and acrylics are more durable than wool, but they don't look as good.

• Low, dense, level loops wear best. They also make it easier to move carts, chairs, etc.

• Fiber and color choice should include the carpet's ability to hide signs of soiling. Most fibers can be treated chemically to increase soil-hiding (and soil-repellent) qualities. Treatment should be strong enough to stand up to heavy-duty cleansing agents in regular cleaning.

• A static control system should be built into the yarn, especially if wool or nylon. Spray-on antistatics are not as effective and attract dirt.

• Fiber should be treated for flame resistance.

Chairs for Desk-Bound Executives

• Backs: Should be straight at the shoulder level to prevent neck strain, slightly convex where they touch the spine. Small of the back should fit snugly into the chair back.

• Seats: Opt for a hard one, slightly contoured to the buttocks (soft cushions roll up around and put pressure on joints).

• Arm supports: Firm, softly padded, at least two inches wide.

• Height: Be sure it's adjustable—get the height that's right for you.

• Look for back- and position-adjustable chairs that let you move forward, tilt backward, sit upright for posture changes that rest and relax if you're sitting for hours at a time.

Setting Up a Conference Room

Best table design for a meeting room is U-shaped. All participants have a clear view, if seating is limited to the outer rim. The open end can be used by a small audience.

When planning any conference room:

• Leave at least three feet between the outer edge of table and the wall to give participants room to get in and out of chairs. Four to five feet is best. More than eight feet is unsettling.

• Exits should be at side or rear of room to allow people to come and go without disturbing others.

• Leave 10-15 feet in the front of the room, or open end of the horseshoe, for blackboards, easels, audio-visual screens.

• Best height for the ceiling is about 12 feet. Less makes the room seem cramped if the meeting is large. More than 15 feet causes acoustical problems.

• The room should be about 25′ × 35′ for meetings of 15 to 25 people and 45′ × 50′ for groups of 26 to 45 people.

Source: *Management Development Through Training* by Charles E. Watson, Addison-Wesley, Reading, MA.

How to Handle Rush Periods

• Don't force people to work faster than usual. Require that they work at a normal rate. Pushing harder produces more errors.

• Don't cancel breaks. Rotate them so everybody gets a break at some time.

• If extra people are added, put them to work doing easy, routine tasks. If possible, don't take on inexperienced workers in rush periods. They will tie up regular workers with questions.

• Be sure working areas are as comfortable and pleasant as possible. Spartan conditions do not boost productivity.

• Do not implement new ideas or time-saving innovations in the middle of a rush period. Try them later.

Source: *Electrical World.*

Growing Plants in the Office

More plants die of kindness than of neglect. If yours grow poorly no matter how much you do for them, you may be doing too much.

A really good decorative plant can cost as much as a typewriter and may last almost as long, given proper care. No rules can guarantee perfect plants, but this list of do's and don'ts should help.

Watering: Most plants grown in offices are kept too wet. This causes roots to rot. Leaves turn yellow and fall. Trouble is compounded when office workers misinterpret symptoms and try to help plant by watering more.

Corrective action: Prior to watering, poke finger several inches into soil. If damp, leave alone. If dry, water thoroughly until excess water runs out drainage hole at bottom. Then let plant dry out so air can reach roots. Most big plants will be ready for more water in about seven days. Establish one day a week as time to tend plants. Put one person in charge and warn rest of staff to keep hands off.

Caution: Never grow plant in pot without drainage hole. Never let water collect in saucer under pot. Don't be in a hurry to repot a plant. Most do best in pots that look small. A pot too big for the plant stays wet too long. If you're not sure that the plant needs water, it probably doesn't.

Light: Most foliage plants don't need strong sun; some are harmed by it. Very bright light from unobstructed north window is perfect. If window is sunny, move plant back a little to where direct sun is minimal but light is still strong. Plants at window tend to grow toward light, so move quarter turn each time you water.

Artificial light: Fluorescents commonly found in offices are good for tall plants. A little additional light from window helps.

Brightness test: When hand is between light and plant, shadow should be fairly sharp.

Temperature: Plants don't need as much heat as people think. They're comfortable when people are (68°-72° by day, somewhat cooler at night). If heat goes off when office is closed, plants do well, provided temperature doesn't drop below 50°. Summers, when air conditioning stops at night, can be hard on plants.

Caution: Keep plants out of direct air flow from radiators and air conditioners. The cooler the room, the less often plants need water.

Plant food: Too much is worse than none at all. Feed only when plants are visibly growing. Suggestion: No food in winter. Around Wash-ington's Birthday, start adding soluble plant food to every watering at one-eighth strength recommended on label. Stop feeding on Columbus Day.

Good office plants: Stick to those that don't require much humidity. Big indoor trees—Ficus, Dracaena, Schefflera. Vines—Philodendron, Pothos, Wandering Jew, Spider Plant (available in hanging pots with attached saucers).

Plants to avoid: Ferns look great at first but soon fade; watering is tricky and humidity need is high. For ferny look, try Asparagus Sprengeri in bright window. English ivy gets bugs; use Swedish ivy or grape ivy instead. Palms are temperamental; for a good substitute, try yuccas. They make excellent indoor plants if kept dry enough. No sun needed. Water every two to three weeks; more in summer but less than other plants.

Magnificent and foolproof: Try a few Bromeliads (pineapple family). Start with an Aechmea Fasciata: leaves covered with incredible patterns of silvery white; blooming stalk of fantastic blue and pink; usually sold in bloom but spectacular even without it. Don't water soil. Just keep water in "cup" formed by base of leaves. The brighter the light, the better the color.

Plants for poor light: Chinese evergreen (Aglaonema); cast-iron plant (Aspidistra); snake plant (Sanseviera).

But poor light doesn't mean darkness. Too dark for reading is too dark for plants. And the less light, the less water.

Keeping plants attractive: Vines tend to get scraggly with stems too long and leaves too far apart. When this happens, don't be afraid to prune stems back at least halfway. Best place to cut is at a leaf node (even if leaf is gone, you can spot the bump where it grew). New leafy stems will grow from the node. If new leaves on Philodendron are too small, plant needs more light. Once a year, prune indoor trees, but only those with leaves that grow from branches, not if leaves are borne on single trunk.

Care of new plants: Resist temptation to "baptize" plant by watering unless you're sure it's dry. Don't panic if plant loses leaves while settling into new home.

Shopping for plants: Biggest plants suffer most when moved to new surroundings. Smaller ones are a safer investment; adjust fast, last longer. If the goal is long-term value instead of immediate grandeur, buy lots of three-foot plants instead of a few six-footers.

No-work gardening: The job of caring for office plants can be contracted out to a specialist. Plant stores and garden centers in many parts of the country will send a person once a week to water, feed, prune, and do anything else required. In some cities it's possible to rent indoor plants from dealers who take care of them and replace any that get into trouble.

Important: Never buy a plant, no matter how much you like it, without knowing what it is. Ask for botanical name (common names may vary and overlap). Look up care in a reliable plant book. Then decide if plant is for you. Good book for use in office or home: *The Apartment Gardener* by Florence and Stanley Dworkin, New American Library, New York.

Fastest Way to Send Money by Western Union

A VISA or Master Charge card, plus a telephone, permits the holder to send up to $300 at a time via Western Union's toll-free number, 800-325-6000, day or night. (In Missouri the number is 800-342-6700.) The total amount that can be sent depends on the individual's credit limit on the card.

The recipient should be able to pick up the cash within two hours if the distant office is open. (There are 8,100 Western Union offices and agencies in the 48 contiguous states.) Charges will appear on the next VISA or Master Charge statement.

A company that needs to send money regularly to employees (such as stranded truck drivers) can open a Commercial Money Order account with Western Union. Up to $5,000 can be sent at a time. Telex or TWX terminal can be used to make the money order request.

For details, contact your local Western Union marketing representative.

Best Office Light

Natural light from windows is ideal for office workers. The worst office light: Flat, uniform fluorescent ceiling lights. Light with no variations produces monotony, boredom, restlessness, frequent breaks. Too much or too little light can produce headaches and short tempers.

It's best to vary office light during the day, using window blinds or curtains or alternating overhead lights and desk lamps. Besides providing light, office windows can also help reduce eye strain, because viewing objects at a distance relaxes eye muscles.

For offices with no windows, the use of wall lights instead of overhead lights will create a spacious feeling similar to the effect of windows.

Cutting Costly Paperwork Blunders

A typical invoice costs $1 in overhead to process, but can cost as much as $40 in overhead to correct after being mailed with a mistake on it.

Ways to eliminate errors:

• Some mistakes can be avoided by redesigning clerical material. For example, use different colors for easy identification of various forms.

• Put the person in the right job, rather than treating all nonmanagement personnel interchangeably. Develop sufficient office flexibility to switch the new clerks around for several weeks to find the best job fit. By taking the trouble to match people and jobs carefully, the company lets clerical employees know that they will be held personally accountable for their work. The company can thus demand higher standards of performance from them.

Discuss errors so they become part of the learning experience, rather than a critique or attack. Talk about mistakes immediately after they're detected or when a similar task is assigned. Ask employee's help in analyzing the mistakes and for ideas on reducing or preventing them in the future.

Source: William Exton, Jr., William Exton & Associates, management consultants, New York.

202

How to Streamline Files

Some sure signs your company files need streamlining: Frequent additions to filing equipment and clerical staff; slow retrieval; files bulging with old materials. Steps to take:

• Inventory your files—all of them. Establish record titles for all materials and correspondence held in all departments and central files; how long held; how many copies.

• Establish how long your company should hold certain records. Precaution: Review all materials scheduled for destruction personally before discarding them.

• Pare files vigorously. Usually as much as 30% of materials currently held can be discarded and another 20%-30% can be sent to records storage.

• Safeguard the few documents vital to running the business in event of fire, flood, or the like. Include charters, deeds, pension and tax records, patents, accounts receivable. Proper location: Fireproof, waterproof cabinet, safe, or vault, with duplicates in off-premise location.

• Create a centralized records storage area. If possible, arrange to have it supervised by one person with responsibility for filing, retrieval, and eventual destruction.

Simple Office Economies

Use the clean side of old forms.

Reuse large envelopes received in the mail.

Cover old file-folder tabs with labels.

Log long-distance calls.

Eliminate telephone extensions and lines that get little use.

Keep office supplies in a controlled area (locked room or cabinet).

List supplies needed for a year and get bids on total amounts.

Offer awards for cost-cutting ideas and group efforts. In addition to saving money, the award system boosts morale.

Source: *Information Management*, Box 3414, Sioux City, IA 51102.

OWNING
A BUSINESS

To Incorporate or Not to Incorporate

The Right Board of Directors

Organizing Under Subchapter S

Simplifying Corporate Succession

How to Sell Out

Tax Traps When Buying or Selling

Sizing Up an Acquisition Opportunity

Adding a Business Partner

15
OWNING A BUSINESS

Mistakes Commonly Made by Successful Entrepreneurs

• The ego trap:

People who have built up a business from scratch have much to be proud of. However, their biggest fault is that they are too proud of it. In a number of firms, the boss's ego stands in the way of:

1. Hiring competent middle managers and assistants to oversee employees.

2. Handing over full responsibility to a subordinate in certain areas.

3. Developing a staff to continue the business after he dies.

The problem takes many forms. A subtle one: The boss limits his staff to "adequate" people—no one really superior (to him, that is). The entrepreneur often rationalizes this by saying that small firms can't compete with big companies for top managers, so he must make do with what's available.

Clues that the boss is fooling himself:

Length of service and loyalty become the key reasons for promotion to higher positions, rather than ability or drive.

The boss is doing everything, not just managing. He continually steps in to fix and correct problems as they arise.

"Little" problems (manufacturing bottlenecks, late deliveries) are brushed aside or dealt with before any facts are generated or options considered.

• The fixed overhead fallacy:

CPAs hear this all the time: "Sure, we 'bought' that piece of business by giving them a very low price—but it's profitable. That incremental rise in my production doesn't cost us much. Our overhead is paid for already. It's a good way to get a new customer and keep our production lines running at full steam."

But when a customer places an order on price alone, it's difficult to step the price up later. The customer isn't apt to stay with you when you raise your price later to its "normal" level. And it's a rare businessman who has really figured out his incremental costs in raising his production just a little to meet this new demand. Frequently the incremental cost is higher than he

206

calculated in his head. He may discover, after a careful accounting, that he should have just cut back his operation and let the opportunity go.

• Caveats on acquisitions:

Most businessmen make one or more of these mistakes when acquiring another business:

When the acquisition is for a customer list, they rarely ask themselves whether it would be cheaper to hire the best salesmen and have them work the competitor's territory. Also, if they do buy the firm, how do they know for sure that its customers will be as loyal to them? It's not uncommon for a person who's selling a business to lean on his friends to get a temporary boost in volume.

Buying a firm with a good spurt in profits—without checking to see whether the profit jump was due to real operating efficiencies, the ad budget was suddenly sliced, or maintenance was trimmed back. As obvious as it may seem, this checkup is often overlooked.

Buying a firm that makes a product and has a service about which very little is known. It's very expensive to learn on the job when you're the boss. And if you keep the old management, it's easy to forget that once the deal is consummated, management's attitude changes—even in a payout deal.

Source: Jerome Zanar, partner, Laventhol & Horwath, CPAs.

To Incorporate or Not to Incorporate

If the business earns between $50,000 and $100,000 per year before taxes, take another look at the pros and cons of incorporating, rather than operating as a partnership, sole proprietorship, or a Subchapter S corporation.

Reason: Low corporate tax rates, especially on income between $50,000 and $100,000. Most closely held corporations now have an effective tax rate that is less than 25%.

Tax disadvantage of the corporation: Double taxation. First, there's the corporation income tax and then, when dividends are paid, the stockholders pay a second tax. And if the corporation tries to avoid the second tax by keeping the profits in surplus and not paying dividends, it may be hit with a tax on excess accumulated earnings (that is, if the amount involved is more than $150,000, and it is not earmarked for a good business purpose).

Many business owners are in the 43% bracket, at least, on personal income (taxable income of $35,200 for a couple). And 50%-60% brackets are not unusual, especially when state and local income taxes are added to the federal income tax.

Thus, it may be better to leave some after-salary profits in a corporation and have them taxed at 17%-30%, rather than take out a larger salary or dividends and pay 50%-60%. If the corporation is then sold or liquidated at a profit, the tax will be at the lower capital gains rate (with a 28% maximum).

Other advantages:

• Tax-deductible profit-sharing and pension contributions can be larger. Example: If the owner draws a salary of $100,000, a corporation could contribute $25,000 to retirement plans. But if the business is a partnership, the maximum contribution would be $7,500. (Exception: A defined-benefit plan might permit larger contributions for partners in their 50s.)

• Other fringe benefits are more liberal, too. Example: Group life insurance premiums on coverage up to $50,000 per person for business owners are deductible by corporations but not deductible by partnerships.

Source: Norman H. Cohen, partner, Langer, Beaudet, Cantor & Cohen, 2 Park Ave., New York 10016.

Going Public: It Is Now Easier, Faster, and Cheaper

The SEC's Form S-18 applies to underwritings of up to $5 million. It is available to any domestic or Canadian company that is not yet filing under SEC reporting requirements. Benefits of using Form S-18:

• Cheaper. As much as 50% lower accounting fees and 30% lower legal fees than required under regulation S-1. That translates into savings of roughly $50,000-$60,000 per offering.

• Quicker. Three to five months vs. six to eight months.

• Easier. Form S-18 can be filed with regional SEC offices as well as in Washington.

Like the still simpler Regulation A (which can be used for filings up to $1.5 million), Form S-18 requires only a narrative discussion. Financial statements can be prepared in accordance with generally accepted accounting principles, rather than the much more complicated Regulation S-X financial filings required under S-1 registration statements. And preparation time can be reduced to as little as one month vs. the two and one-half to four months needed to get an S-1 registration underway.

Source: Dan Brecher, attorney, 230 Park Ave., New York 10017.

Board Meetings, Minutes, Other Corporate Technicalities

Don't neglect all the formalities of board meetings, even though they seem to be useless ceremonies, especially when the company is owned by the same few people who run it and see each other every day. It's possible to keep the formalities to a minimum, but they shouldn't be eliminated entirely.

Why the formalities are needed: If the corporation doesn't "act like one," creditors could claim that it's really a partnership in disguise, and push to hold the owners personally liable for the debts of the corporation. And minority stockholders might sue directors for failure to carry out corporate duties.

Also, directors could be personally liable for unpaid wages in certain cases, and for failure to withhold taxes and pay them to IRS. And there could be personal liabilities under OSHA and the Employee Retirement Income Security Act.

Be sure to take these minimal steps:

• Formal stockholder meeting at least once a year, with proper notice (or waiver of notice) to elect directors. Have proper documentation of

meeting notice or a waiver, minutes, and (if necessary) proxies. Stockholders can also act by majority written consent in some states; but, again, the action should be documented.

• Board should meet regularly with proper notice or waiver. Probably at least four times a year. At one meeting have directors formally nominate and elect officers of the company.

• Keep the minutes of board meetings. Record time and place, who was present, noting a quorum. Be aware that directors can't use proxies; can't vote or be counted for quorum unless physically present. Exception: Some state laws permit board meetings by telephone if all directors can speak to and hear one another.

• Minutes should say something like "There was discussion of the business of the corporation and results of operations during the latest quarter." Shows the directors are acting like directors, keeping informed about what officers are doing. Be sure to mention major happenings, fires, strikes, lawsuits. Avoid forecasts.

• Remember where there are some minority or nonmanagement shareholders, the directors have a fiduciary duty to keep themselves informed about what's happening and to exercise some degree of supervision over officers of corporation. If they don't, they could be sued by stockholders.

For very "private" corporations a different approach is possible. New corporation codes in about 15 states provide for a "close corporation," in which shareholders may agree to dispense with boards and board meetings and manage the business directly. But even here, careful records of the shareholder action must be kept to preserve the protection that is afforded by the corporate entity.

Source: Robert Green, partner, Green, Sharpless & Greenstein, 1 Rockefeller Plaza, New York 10020.

How a Board of Directors Should Be Made Up

A board chairman who is someone other than the company chief executive poses special problems. Unless he is intimately familiar with the daily operation of the company, he'll have trouble formulating a meeting agenda. And if he is present on a day-to-day basis, how can he help but run the company?

Eliminating company employees from the board separates the company policy-making body from the people who carry out the policy. Result: Low morale and confusion in implementing policy decisions.

One advantage of having insiders on board is that they know the company business and cannot be as easily beguiled as outsiders by an eloquent but fallacious boardroom presentation. Also, they can be assembled quickly for a board meeting on an urgent matter.

Caution: Eliminating all nonemployees from the board lessens the pressure on management to explain and defend its actions. Outside members are much more likely to be critical of management proposals than are members who are part of company management.

The presence of outsiders on the board reassures bankers, customers, and stockholders that their interests are being represented.

Ideally, one-third of the members should be outsiders. Because they have other demands on their time, it will be easier for outsiders to miss meetings. An outsider who finds himself the only one on the board feels like an ineffective token and is unlikely to remain with the board.

Pros and Cons of Subchapter S

Basically, a Subchapter S corporation is one that generally does not pay federal income taxes. Instead, the shareholders include the income or loss on their personal returns in proportion to their stock holdings. Tax is paid on undistributed income as of the last day of the taxable year (similar to the way partners are taxed on profits). Distributions during the year (called dividends) are taxed as of the date paid, except if made during the first 2½ months of the year, and they are deemed to be distributions of the prior year's undistributed taxable income.

Disadvantages: Profits taxed to the shareholder that are not distributed within the 2½-month period after the end of the year may be locked into the corporation. Result: Tax may be triggered for the year it is finally distributed.

Furthermore, Subchapter S income is not subject to the 50% tax ceiling on earned income. In a single-owner corporation, where one person does all the work but doesn't take out his salary, the tax rate can go up to 70%. If a partnership, or if the owner paid himself a salary, the principal might only be subject to the 50% tax.

If the firm's income is high enough, it might be desirable for the corporation to pay tax instead of the individual. The corporation's tax bracket is effectively 18.5% on the first $50,000 profit. A taxpayer in the maximum bracket would be paying 50% if he gave himself the entire income as salary. Of course, a regular corporation pays a second tax on retained money, but this happens many years forward and can be taxed as a capital gain. In addition, creating retained earnings in a regular corporation builds up the capital base of the corporation.

Where the investment is substantial and losses are anticipated the first year or two, a Sub-S corporation is a useful vehicle. The losses would be deductible by the shareholders immediately. They could thereby recover a portion of their investment in the first year through tax savings.

A company with an accumulated earnings problem could use the Sub-S election to advantage. Dividends paid within 2½ months after the end of the year are deemed to be dividends paid out of the prior year's accumulated earnings. The amount is subtracted from any "unreasonable accumulation" for purposes of assessing the penalty. Additionally, this dividend counts toward the current year's Sub-S income distribution. By making a Sub-S election for the year in which payment is made, the penalty will be avoided and amounts will be taxed only once.

The Sub-S vehicle is also ideal for diverting income to younger or lower-tax-bracket family members. Stock interest can be given to infants, unlike the case of most partnerships.

The 1978 tax law eased Subchapter S requirements: Up to 15 stockholders are permitted. A married couple counts as one stockholder. And the election can be made at any time during the tax year, or up to 75 days after the tax year ends.

Reducing the Tax Bite When Transferring Control to Next Generation

When owners of closely held companies transfer their shares to children, taxes may take a big chunk of the value of the company.

Recaptalizing the company can reduce the tax burden by:

- Freezing the value of the present shares.
- Letting all future company growth benefit the next generation without gift or estate tax.

How it works: Suppose the company is worth about $2 million, and it is 100% owned by a man and wife in their 50s. The only capital stock is common shares. The company is recapitalized, with $2 million worth of preferred stock and $10,000 worth of new common exchanged for the owners' original common shares.

Then they give all the new common stock of the recapitalized company to their children or grandchildren.

Tax effects:

- Common has such small value that there's little or no gift tax.
- Parents' exchange of old common stock for new preferred is tax-free. Cost basis of the new preferred (for future capital gains tax purposes) is the same as it was for the common.

The new preferred should be callable (redeemable) by the company at par or face value. Result: Its face value will be fixed. As the company grows, all of the increased value will benefit the children who own the new common stock.

Cautions on preferred stock:

- Should probably have a realistic dividend rate, such as 8%. Otherwise, IRS might claim the preferred is worth less than face value, thus there's a big gift to the children.
- To avoid making the dividend requirement too big a burden on the company, provide that dividends are noncumulative. Thus the company can pay them in good years and skip them in bad years, without any obligation to make them up later.
- The preferred stock should have voting rights to ensure that the parents continue to control the company. Since common has the voting rights also, set the exact number of new preferred and common shares according to how much voting power the parents want to give their children.

- Get an advance ruling approving the transaction. IRS won't rule on the value of the preferred, but it will rule on other aspects of the transaction.

Another idea: A father buys a $2 million life insurance policy and gives it to his children. When he dies, they receive tax-free $2 million, and can use it to buy the preferred stock from his estate or his widow.

Source: Herbert Paul, partner, Touche Ross & Co., 1633 Broadway, New York 10019.

Pension Plan Can Favor an Owner Without ERISA Penalty

Defined benefit pension plans with retirement at 55 are useful for closely held companies with a few owner-officers in middle years and most other employees younger. In that situation, a very high percentage of the pension contributions will benefit the owner-officers. Yet it doesn't violate ERISA by disciminating in their favor.

Under ERISA, contributions to a pension plan are not tax deductible if the plan discriminates in favor of senior officers. So, many pension plans set aside a fixed percentage of each employee's pay (7% is common). This is called a defined contribution plan.

Defined benefit plans work differently. A benefit that will be paid at retirement age is set first. (Often a percentage of salary during final five years, minus expected Social Security.) Then an actuarial calculation is made as to what amount must be put aside each year in order to pay that benefit.

Amounts funded vary widely according to the employee's age and salary level. They will be very high for executives who are middle-aged and highly paid when the plan starts. And they will be especially high if a 55-year retirement age is used.

How it might work: A typical plan takes into

account length of service and expected Social Security benefits.

Tax Deductible Contributions and Expected Pension Benefits
(annual)

	Jr. Mgr.*	Sr. Mgr.*
Age when plan begins	26	46
Present salary	$20,000	$60,000
Annual company contribution to defined contribution plan (7%)	1,400	4,200
Defined benefit plan, retirement at 65		
Annual contribution	560	8,963
Annual benefit at retirement	8,767	32,646
Defined benefit plan, retirement at 55		
Annual contribution	1,058	25,388
Annual benefit at retirement	6,613	24,772

*Both started working at age 24.

Disadvantage: Much more expensive for the company, so it's not a step to be taken without careful study.

Source: Robert D. Paul, Martin E. Segal Company, 730 Fifth Ave., New York 10019.

Disability Income Protection for Owners

Most employee benefit packages don't cover prolonged disability. The employee loses income, the company loses his services.

For the sole proprietor, it can be even worse. The business may never recover.

The company could deduct premiums on disability insurance if all employees were covered, but not if a plan covered top officers alone.

One solution: Company buys a disability policy, with benefits payable to the company itself for loss of services if the executive is unable to work. Then it pays the benefits to him. The premiums are not deductible, and thus the insurance payments received by the company aren't tax-able income. But the benefits paid to the executive are a deductible expense by the company.

An individual disability income policy might be worth considering. Insurance companies, sensing a major new source of business, are sharpening their pencils and competing more aggressively. Rates have come down, may come down further.

Points to consider on an individual policy:

Take the longest waiting period (before payments start) to get the lowest premium, maximum protection per dollar.

Be sure the policy is guaranteed renewable to age 65.

Look for a provision to buy additional protection, if necessary for inflation protection, without another physical exam.

Remember that insurance payments are tax-free. Buy only enough insurance to match after-tax income.

Check the fine print as to what happens if disability is partial or if you are able to do some work but not in your present field of activity.

The policy should waive premiums during disability.

Closely Held Corporation as a Tax Trap for the Owner

If a closely held corporation receives 60% or more of its income from nonoperating sources such as investment, personal service income (e.g., personal consulting fees), or rent (in most instances), any undistributed income may be subjected to the 70% personal holding company tax. This applies if at any time in the last half of its taxable year more than 50% of the stock is owned, directly or indirectly, by or for not more than five individuals.

An unsuspected trap: Company has six stockholders. Then an executive dies and the company buys his stock. Or he retires and sells his holdings back to the company or to another stockholder. Now, with only five stockholders, the company has a problem.

What to do: Make certain that at least some of the shares of a person who retires or dies are purchased by some unrelated party. (Or increase the number of shareholders or the amount of operating income.)

When IRS Disallows Corporate T&E Deductions

Corporations often have agreements requiring officer-shareholders to repay expenses that have been disallowed as deductions by the Internal Revenue Service. In some circumstances, these agreements work as an effective tax loophole to reduce the tax burden on both the company and the officer. But not always.

How they work: The corporation has $10,000 of travel and entertainment expenses disallowed. All of these expenses were incurred by the officer-shareholder. Result:

• Corporation in 46% bracket pays an additional $4,600 in taxes.

• Officer-shareholder is deemed to have received a dividend. Federal tax on the $10,000 can be as high as 70%. Assuming the shareholder is in the maximum tax bracket of 50% but earns sufficient income to place him in a 60% normal bracket, he pays $6,000 tax on the $10,000 disallowed amount.

• Total combined tax burden for shareholder and company is $10,600 on the disallowance of $10,000.

How to avoid this double tax penalty: Corporation has an agreement with the officer-shareholder that any amounts disallowed as deductions by the IRS are considered to be loans to the shareholder that must be repaid. Result: Shareholder deducts the amount of repayment on his individual tax return. In effect, he recaptures the tax previously paid on the constructive dividend. This is a good technique when the taxpayer has sufficient means to repay the loan to the corporation.

Problem: When officer-shareholder does not have his own funds and has to rely on the corporation to supply the cash for the repayment.

• Example: Shareholder has to repay $10,000 loan to company incurred as a result of disallowed expenses. In the 50% bracket, he needs an additional salary of $20,000, which means an additional tax liability of $10,000.

• Corporation gets $20,000 deduction for the salary. In the 46% bracket the saving would be $9,200 in taxes.

• Officer repays $10,000 to the corporation and gets a $6,000 tax refund.

• Total additional taxes: $800.

Sounds like a good method for a closely held corporation. But this type of transaction can lead to other problems:

• It may trigger an unreasonable compensation problem. With the company in the 46% tax bracket, it is probably paying as generous a salary to the officer-shareholder as its tax advisers think can be substantiated. The additional $20,000 salary might trigger IRS challenge.

• $10,000 repayment to the corporation might eventually be taxed to the shareholder either as a dividend or as a capital gain. Only exception: If the corporation was formed before 1977 and the shareholder died thereafter.

• $10,000 is added to the company's accumulated earnings and profits. This could cause a problem if IRS determines that the company has an unreasonable accumulation of earnings.

Suggestion: Before rushing into repayment agreements, consider the overall consequences. It might be best to pay the taxes now.

Source: Edward Mendlowitz, CPA, Siegel & Mendlowitz, PC, 310 Madison Ave., New York 10017.

When Owner Contributes Company Stock to Charity

Anyone can avoid capital gains tax by making a direct charitable contribution of stock. But a 100% shareholder can do even better.

Method: A 100% shareholder makes a charitable contribution of stock. The company then redeems the stock from the charity, returning the shareholder to 100% status.

Result: The shareholder deducts as a charitable contribution the amount it costs the corporation to redeem the stock. The tax saving is cash to the shareholder.

Here's a comparison of what the shareholder

would net from a $100,000 dividend, versus what he would derive from giving a charity stock worth the same amount.

	Dividend Paid	Stock Contribution
Shareholder's additional income	$100,000	0
Shareholder's additional charitable contribution	0	$100,000
Tax cost (savings) at 65% tax bracket	65,000	($65,000)
Net cash to shareholder	35,000	65,000

Moral: In this case, it's $30,000 better to give than to receive.

Some cautions:

• Control of stock given to charity must be relinquished. What's more, there must not be any preplanned arrangement whereby the corporation will redeem stock immediately after contribution. A charity, however, usually has little interest in being a minority shareholder in a private corporation.

• The contribution must be made to a qualifying charity. Certain private foundations are excluded, for example.

• The value of the stock must not exceed 30% of the shareholder's adjusted gross income for the year.

Although IRS in the past has fought this type of transaction (and consistently lost in the courts), it now permits it.

Another attraction: There are a number of charitable organizations that will accept the stock, redeem it, and hold the funds for later distribution to other designated charities. This permits a substantial contribution without immediate pressure to decide on a specific charity.
Source: Edward Mendlowitz, CPA, Siegel & Mendlowitz, 310 Madison Ave., New York 10017.

Simplifying Corporate Succession

The best way to guard against possible corporate chaos that might result from the sudden death of the owner or manager is a sealed letter. The envelope should specify "for whose eyes only" and the letter should be safeguarded so that it can never fall into the wrong hands.

In the letter, summarize all the strengths, skills, potential, and weaknesses of each likely successor. In addition, give your reasons for including certain candidates in the running and excluding others.

The ultimate value of this document lies in its complete candor and its sensitive, personal appraisals. It has no legal validity, but can give invaluable help to the chairman, the executive committee, or whoever is charged with assuring effective continuity of power. Note: The letter should be revised annually and redated if no changes are made.
Source: *Management Practice*, Main, Jackson & Garfield, Inc., 535 Fifth Ave., New York 10017.

How to Sell Your Business

First, clean up the company—financially and organizationally. Eliminate assets that aren't business-related. Put a stop to nonproductive expenses. Clean up contingent liabilities. The buyer doesn't want a company with a "dirty" balance sheet.

Review complex, age-old agreements with family-owners and employees, to make sure they don't hinder the negotiations.

Consider having the financial statements certified; it makes the buyer more comfortable. Three years of audited results are usually needed to be useful.

Review supplier and customer agreements (or lack of them). Any potential problems? Does one supplier (or customer) control too large a portion of your business? If so, consider diversification. Few buyers, unless the situation is unique, are willing to go into a deal like that. Your years of trust don't matter to the buyer. Ditto with leases: Are they "clean"—at arm's length?

Review employee relations. Are there any contracts with key people that could present problems? Is there one person the buyer can't afford to lose? Decide early what to do: Tie up that key employee with a good contract? Offer stock? Offer a share of the sales price? Do nothing?

213

Whatever you do, don't ignore the situation: It could kill a deal.

Don't go to old friends for advice—unless they have real experience. If your lawyer or accountant lacks specific acquisition experience, find someone else to handle this deal for you. It's complicated—and it's probably the biggest deal you've ever been involved in.

People you might want to discuss it with: Merger/acquisition broker, experienced accountant, lawyer, investment banker, or regular banker.

The price is often a hard number to come up with. Get the experts to advise you. Avoid pulling a number out of a hat. It must be tied to something firm.

You might find a comparable public company and relate your price to that firm's price/earnings ratio. Or your advisers may be able to learn the sales price of a firm in your field—and relate that price to your asking price.

If you don't have backup management, get it. It's a rare buyer who'll acquire a company without it. Most entrepreneurs who sell but remain on to run the company are gone within three to five years for many reasons. Buyers know it and demand experienced backup management before they will sign.

Aside from the balance sheet and profit and loss statements, the buyer will want to know how you are maintaining the business: Internal procedures, controls, five-year forecasts, equipment inventory, lines-of-business accounting, divisional breakout, etc. The more the better.

Details on pay scales and fringe benefits are a sticky area, not just for the executives, but the clerical, sales, and blue-collar employees, too. Often, informal agreements have led to very complex (and inconsistent) pay structures. Problems arise when a new boss tries to straighten out the complexities.

Not infrequently, state and federal wage/labor laws are being violated (improper overtime, no differentials between the shifts, discrimination, and the like).

A typical way to find the buyer is to contact sources listed above as advisers. Alternative: Make a list of those who you and your associates know are potential buyers: Competitors, suppliers, customers, related businesses, and so on.

Your list will probably be a better one than your adviser's.

Agree to let an adviser conduct a "fishing expedition" but without disclosing your company's name. Secrecy is important: It could harm relations with customers, suppliers, employees if news of the sale got out prematurely.

There's no easy answer to whether you should tell your customers, suppliers, and employees ahead of time. Usually, secrecy is the best policy. If any of them is a key to your success, it's best to disclose your plans confidentially.

Don't expect to be able to keep your plans a secret for long. You can't repeatedly identify visiting executives who come to look over the facility as bankers, insurance agents, etc. People will catch on soon.

The first meeting with a potential buyer should be social. Avoid talking dollars. If he asks, answer; but don't force it. Let him learn about you and your business before you tell him what price you want.

Smart sellers pull some "dirty linen" out right up front. That's usually a show of good faith. Over the longer run, don't try to hide anything that could be a problem. It's bound to come out eventually, and it will either kill the deal or you'll wind up being sued.

Possible surprise: When you tell the potential buyer about your "problem," he may say it's not serious or he may offer you advice on solving it. Perspective: It's better to frighten off a buyer early if that issue is important to him. In that case, you've saved lots of time and money.

When you get to talking price, expect this question from the buyer: How did you come up with that number? It's a clever question. It puts you on the defensive, forces you to qualify your position, and gives him a chance to pick your response apart. So you must be ready—with solid accounting and good reasoning.

Single biggest error made by sellers: Setting an unrealistically high initial price. If too high, the buyer may just want to forget it—figuring that you're not the kind of person to try to do business with.

Every seller gets cold feet at the moment of decision when the contract is ready for signing. So be ready for that reaction, too.

Source: Source: Bertram Frankenberger, Haskins & Sells.

Tax Traps When Buying or Selling a Business

Watch out for the tax consequences of good will (the part of the price paid for a going business that exceeds the net fair market value of the tangible business assets).

Problem: The Internal Revenue Service does not recognize good will as a deductible expense.

Solution: If the excess can be termed part of ''a covenant not to compete,'' it's completely deductible (to be amortized over the period of the agreement).

Seller's interest is the reverse. Receipts for good will are taxed at capital gains rates. Those for noncompetitive covenant are taxable as ordinary income. Splitting the difference 50-50 may be the wrong compromise when it favors seller over buyer. Most equitable answer: Adjust the purchase price to even out net after-tax effects. And don't forget that an installment deal reduces the seller's tax burden by spreading it over several years.

Avoid IRS problems by specifying exactly what both sides want in the sale contract. IRS generally will go along. Such contracts normally provide some form of noncompetitive covenant.

Make sure the contract also spells out allocation of other components of the price. Don't allocate more to depreciable property (trucks, machinery, etc.) than fair market value. That part of transaction may require payment of sales taxes. Allocation to the covenant is probably the simplest, clearest, and quickest way to get maximum deduction.

Alternative: Where customer service contracts are transferred, good will can apply on a per-item basis to the individual contracts. As contracts are terminated, this cost can be deducted. It can take longer than a covenant to get deductions, but still provides a way to write off the good will cost.

Another cost: Leasehold purchase. Used when a specific site, such as a retail store, carries the good will. Purchase price should allocate good will cost to purchase of leasehold. Then cost can be amortized over the life of the lease, since the asset's value falls to nothing at termination.

Important: Unnecessary inclusion of covenant not to compete, as when seller is retiring, can transform part of the proceeds of sale from capital gains into ordinary income. IRS reasoning: The covenant is deemed to be worth something to the seller, but what he's selling (i.e., his right to compete with the buyer) isn't a capital asset. So whatever portion of the sales price is allocable to the covenant isn't a capital gain. The Court of Claims agreed.
Proulx v. *U.S.*, #381.74, Ct. Cl. 2/21/79.

Selling a Company for Cash Without a Big Tax

There comes a time in the life of many closely held corporations, and even some publicly held ones, when the controlling shareholders begin to feel locked into their investments. They would like to cash in without having to pay to the tax collector as much as 28% of the appreciated value of the company they built up. Here is a tax-wise way to achieve this goal:

What kind of company would be a candidate for this tax-saving idea? It must be:

• A healthy one with good earning prospects.
• One that is controlled by a few shareholders.
• One whose stock is undervalued in the marketplace.

The procedure: The corporation agrees to sell all the assets (factory, machinery, customer lists, good will, etc.) and the liabilities of the company for cash. The sale price for the assets must be lower than their tax basis (original cost minus depreciation). That produces a tax loss for the sellers, which is guaranteed by the buyers. With the tax loss in hand, the sellers are more apt to give the buyer some price concession.

Note that the stock hasn't changed hands. The shareholders have sold only the assets. They keep their stock in a corporation that has no assets except cash.

Now, with that hard cash, the corporation converts into an investment firm. It buys a diversified portfolio with the cash—anything from stock or real estate to other companies.

Potential problems: The selling company

becomes a personal holding company. It must distribute its earnings at least annually or face a heavy personal holding company penalty tax.

• There is also the problem of double taxation—income taxed once at the corporate level and again when distributed to shareholders as dividends. The personal holding company status makes distributions mandatory, precluding the use of the corporation as a tax shelter.

Ways to minimize the dual taxation problem: Use of the 85% dividends-received exclusion by the corporation, which should invest in tax-free securities, low-dividend-paying growth stocks, and tax shelters.

• The buyer's guarantee of a tax loss also creates a potential problem. The seller could be viewed as increasing the sales price and thus reducing the anticipated loss. And payment of the guarantee would appear to be taxable income.

The model for this technique will be found in the Big Bear Stores Co. proxy statement dated July 24, 1976, on file with Amex and the SEC. The technique has also been used with unlisted, closely held companies, although there is a more difficult problem in determining the value of the company.

Selling Out to a Foreign Buyer

The typical European investor is in the market for a company with assets of $3 million to $10 million and about $10 million to $30 million in sales. Best profile: Privately owned, and owner wants to stay on to manage the company.

Acquisitions may be either on an assets or stock basis, depending on the capital gains tax situation created by the transaction. Installment sales (29% down payment and the balance over five years or more) frequently offer the preferred structure. Bank financing (both U.S. and foreign) is usually involved, particularly when balance sheet financing is feasible and the buyer can leverage his investment.

A European buyer may outbid a U.S. company for two reasons:

• Currency exchange rate favors Europeans.

• Advantageous way that European tax laws allow companies to write off good will (the difference between book asset value of the company and the selling price). In the current market, good will can account for some 25% to 50% of the purchase price of a company.

Another advantage: Europeans can offer the seller expertise in starting or expanding an international business. Most small and medium U.S. companies know very little about export. But they have products or services that can sell overseas, which the European parent firm can often develop. Very attractive prospect for the seller who makes a profit-sharing deal with the buyer.

Owner-managers can usually negotiate excellent incentive contracts to stay with a successful business. Reason: Buyer is generally unfamiliar with business terms and conditions in the U.S. He invests to learn. He wants to diversify assets out of the European economy, protect holdings against creeping socialism at home, and get a foothold in the massive U.S. market. He looks on the former owner of the business here as the best asset manager of his investments that he can find. Role of trusted adviser may be far more satisfying for former owner who stays with the business than the position he would have if he sold out to an American company, especially a big conglomerate.

What to expect from negotiations: Frustrations. European buyers sometimes don't understand that in looking for good small and medium companies in the U.S., they are up against hot competition from scores of eager, canny buyers. They think they can pick and choose. Result: They procrastinate. (It generally takes most European investors about a year to get the feel of the U.S. business climate before they make their first deal.)

Other negotiating hurdles:

• The openness with which most U.S. business firms treat (or are obligated to treat) financial and marketing information generally upsets European prospects.

• American and European managers usually differ widely on how to handle employee relations. The prospect of bargaining with American trade unions also baffles some foreigners.

Source: Michael Morrell, Michael W. Morrell & Co., Inc., 152 East 78 St., New York 10021.

Tax-Free Swaps

Tax-free exchanges of like businesses or investment properties can postpone capital gains tax. If the current value of the two properties isn't exactly the same, the difference can be made up in cash. The party getting cash pays tax on it, but not on the rest of the deal.

Common problem: One party wants to swap but the other wants to sell. A compatible third party must be found. Here's how one group of businessmen did it:

The owner of the Baltimore Colts wanted to dispose of the team and buy the Los Angeles Rams. He wanted to swap to save $4.4 million in capital gains tax. But the owner of the Rams wanted to sell, not swap.

The Colts' owner found a third party willing to buy the Colts. The third party bought Rams for cash, then swapped with Colts' owner. The Rams' owner got cash. The Colts' owner got his swap. The third party acquired the Colts.

The same approach can also be used where existing facilities and land are swapped for facilities that have been constructed especially for the exchange.

Caution: The whole deal can be disallowed if formalities aren't followed exactly. Expert legal counsel is a must. An advance IRS ruling is often advisable. Reminder: A swap doesn't eliminate taxes—it merely postpones them until the business is sold or transferred.

Source: *Business Acquisitions Desk Book with Checklists and Forms,* by F.T. Davis, Jr., Institute for Business Planning, Inc., Englewood Cliffs, NJ.

Before Okaying Acquisition

The failure rate of acquisitions is very high. About 50% do not reach expectations, according to informed estimates. There are certain obvious mistakes that should be avoided. If they are, the chance of the merger or acquisition being successful goes up significantly. Questions to ask:

• Is the decision to acquire chiefly a response to the fact that the competition is doing it? Every decision to acquire should be based only on the company's own growth needs and capabilities.

• Is the acquisition being considered simply as a reaction to an idea? Intermediaries (brokers, investment bankers, lawyers, etc.) who frequently present interesting acquisition candidates to chief executives are often unfamiliar with the specific technical and management needs and capabilities of the acquiring company. Management time and energy spent in reacting to proposals is probably better spent clarifying overall business strategy for growth, including the question of acquisitions.

Is there a member of management, or an outside adviser, who understands the operations of the prospective acquisition well enough to identify less obvious problems? It is very important to eliminate poor candidates quickly.

• Who will competitors be? The share of market projections will depend on what competitors the acquisition faces. The larger the combined company's market share, the more of a leader it can be in setting prices, market strategies, etc. Best opportunity to consider: Buy into a market that is fragmented, if possible, not one with one or two strong market leaders.

Special acquisition strategy for a smaller company: Management capabilities are usually narrower and more specialized, thus less able to provide expertise in a number of different industry areas. Acquisitions should not stray far from home.

Source: William Kirschenbaum, Neuberger & Berman, 522 Fifth Ave., New York 10036.

Realistic Acquisition Guides

• Current after-tax return on capital more than 12%, preferably over 15%.

• Earnings history without major cyclical swings.

• Market for products growing at least 10% per year.

• Major firm in its market or geographical area. Strong brand or market franchise.

• Not dependent on single supplier, customer, or product (unless it happens to have a very strong patent position).

Acquisitions: Cash vs. Stock

Cash deals are subject to capital gains tax when the cash is received by the seller. But though cash deals are taxable, they are best when there are doubts about the buyer's solvency—or when the stock doesn't suit seller's investment criteria or estate planning.

Minimize taxes by treating the deal as an installment sale. Buyer receives no more than 30% of purchase price the first year. The remaining cash is spread out over a specified number of years, reducing the overall capital gains tax.

- Business risk. Will the buyer be able to pay? In an installment deal, the seller is just as tied to the fortunes of the buyer as if he had taken stock instead of cash.

- Purchasing-power risk. Present value of $1 million is much more than the same amount paid out from 1980 through 1987. Seller should keep in mind the net amount he will sell for, discount future dollars, and negotiate from that position.

For the buyer, paying cash is more expensive than issuing treasury stock or new preferred, but it can have advantages:

- When companies are nearly equal in size and a stock deal would dilute the buyer's control of company.

- If the buyer wants the tax advantages that stem from being able to take depreciation on a larger sum (the cash payment) than on the seller's tax basis (usually below the selling price). The buyer can do this only on an all-cash deal.

The seller should take stock only when the stock of the acquiring company is an attractive investment on its own merits. Advantages of a stock deal:

- Defers capital-gains liability. Can shift it to the next generation if the stock is left to seller's heirs.

- Good chance of lower capital-gains taxes in future years.

Installment-sale strategy in stock deals: Also takes advantage of any future easing of capital-gains taxes. Seller has much more flexibility than with a cash deal on what to sell and when. Disadvantage: Vulnerablity to vagaries of the stock market.

When buyer should use stock:

- To conserve cash.

- When company stock is selling at a high price/earnings multiple.

- For the seller: Cash is taxable when received if stock makes up at least 50% of total (making the deal a merger). Stock is not taxable until sold.

- For the buyer: A hybrid deal is treated like a stock deal. Buyer loses the advantage of getting stepped-up depreciation of seller's assets. He can't pick up half the advantages for paying half cash. It's not a good choice unless buyer is afraid of diluting his present stock interest.

Source: Robert Willens, Peat, Marwick & Mitchell, 1025 Connecticut Ave. N.W., Washington, DC 20036.

Deducting Acquisition Expenses

A mistake made too often by acquisition-minded companies: Assuming that all expenses incurred in the search for a suitable company are tax deductible. Not so, if these expenses were related to a trade or business in which the firm was not already engaged and no successful acquisition was made.

What can be deducted: Expenses for attorneys to draft purchase agreements and any other costs of an effort to complete the purchase of a specific business or investment.

Revenue ruling 77-254.

Buying a Business Without Down Payment

For many, the idea is just a fantasy, but for a growing number of entrepreneurial managers, it's a practical solution to a long-held wish: Buying the division or business department from the parent company.

The idea: Buying the business operation with little or no down payment. The method is called leveraged buy-out—and it's gaining increased attention from financial people and would-be entrepreneurs. Here's how it works:

A new corporation is created that purchases

the division by borrowing up to the hilt against the divisions's assets. It might borrow 80% of the value of receivables, 60% of inventory, and 60%-75% of land, buildings, and equipment. If it isn't possible to borrow the full purchase price (plus working capital that the new company may need), the selling company may take back a subordinated note for part of the purchase price.

Many lenders are willing to finance leveraged buy-outs, even where the new owner-managers don't have much cash to invest, if the division had a good track record and if they believe management is strong. Their reasoning: If execs did a good job working on salary, they'll probably do even better as owners.

The best sources for this kind of borrowing are the selling companies themselves. Some banks are becoming active, too. And equity capital or subordinated loans may be obtained from venture companies (their terms are tough, though).

It's a way for good managers, now on salary, to build a personal fortune. If the new company does well, their stock holdings should become very valuable in a few years.

Managers of divisions who are thinking about going on their own should consider these points:

• Lenders will want ironclad assurance that the management team will stay. They'll probably ask for five-year employment contracts and expensive life insurance on top officers.

• Lenders will insist on a pledge of all assets and will supervise operations very closely. Management may find itself restricted, may have to go to finance company for permission to do anything new. (One disappointed owner said, "All I did was change bosses.")

• Because the load of debt is so heavy, lenders may insist on personal guarantees of loans by owner-managers and their wives. That means the house, the bank account, and all personal assets are on the line.

• Risks are high, too. Managers are so dazzled by the chance to be independent that they sometimes fail to analyze the company's future dispassionately. It's a good idea to review the company and industry outlook with an experienced adviser whose thinking isn't colored by personal involvement.

Source: Dan Brecher, attorney, 230 Park Avenue, New York 10017.

Finder's Fees for Merger Acquisition

If a merger deal is arranged by an investment banker or finder, you should expect to pay a percentage of the total amount of the deal as a fee. The fee is negotiable and should be agreed upon in advance.

Many finders will quote what has been called the "Lehman formula" of 5% on the first million dollars, 4% on the second million, 3% on the third, 2% on the fourth, and 1% on the rest. That works out to $150,000 on a $5 million deal and $200,000 on a $10 million deal.

That's the standard formula. But it can be negotiated down. Many deals are done for less. If there are finders on each side, they will work out the fee split.

Before Starting a New Venture

When starting a new venture, don't assume it will succeed.

Ask instead: What can be done with this plant or building if the project fails? What if the market disappears? What if the price drops to the point where it's unprofitable to continue? What if the production skills aren't there? What are the alternatives?

And most important: What are the recovery prospects?

• Make sure to have realistic cost estimates on how long it will take to really get the production line on stream. Most people understand fixed costs, and maybe even variable costs, but many ventures die of underfinancing because of failure to understand true working capital requirements of a new venture.

For one thing, accounts receivable are no more than that. Vendors and salaries must be paid in cash. And be sure to allow for the element of time.

It's best to think in terms of escalating costs. Those fixed at $1.00 in planning stage may become $1.07 next year and $1.10 the year after that. Most planning errs on the side of underestimating costs. They must at least allow for inflation.

Other considerations:

• Isolate sensitive variables: No more than four variables may account for as much as 90% of costs. Isolating them can provide important insight for costing the production mode. Analyze pilot project experience and try to extrapolate costs that will also apply in production stage.

• Look for ways to telescope or multiply production for greater efficiency.

Before going ahead, management should be given options (e.g., 400% greater production would reduce losses from 5% to 4%). Management then decides whether the one-point increment is worth tooling up for.

• Check production model reproducibility. For example, there may well be technological problems in volume production that weren't encountered in the research model. Electronic mechanisms may have to replace manual devices; monitoring equipment may be needed.

Other problems: Larger facilities will present new dimensions in security (fencing, lighting), cleaning, purchasing, storage, materials handling, accounting. All will become large-scale, ongoing functions.

Many jobs that were cheerfully performed by professionals during the research phase must be routinized, downgraded for performance by foremen and blue-collar workers.

Particular sticking points:

Accounting. Must be set up with controls so that variations from predetermined costs and unexpected problems can be immediately identified and remedied

Quality control. Many problems don't appear until production reaches larger numbers. Also, typical production personnel may not be as sensitive to problems as are scientists who guide research project.

Research. Should not end with production model, but must continue at higher yields. And with equipment that is often different from that used in a research model.

When moving pilot or production some distance from research location, various considerations of transferability come up.

Some of the more obvious: Local market requirements, land and construction costs, availability of materials, personnel skills.

• Less obvious are process considerations (Is water available in sufficient quality and quantity?), facility maintenance (if one pump goes out will production have to shut down?). Also take into account the availability of spare parts, electrical skills, security.

Final step: Planning and scheduling implementation. And here's an area where it's critical to take a pessimistic approach. Cost for delays. They are almost inevitable. Ask questions about possible contingencies; have alternate courses of action and sources of supply ready in order to deal with them. Best to put one full-time person in charge of this step, but remember, no plan is any good without controls.

Source: Norman Kobert, Norman Kobert & Associates, P.O. Box 21396, Ft. Lauderdale, FL 33335.

Disclosure Requirements for Franchise Sellers

• Seller's past business experience, bankruptcy and litigation record.
• Prior year's certified balance sheet.
• List of all fees that have to be paid to run the franchise.
• Limits on right to resell.
• List of ten closest franchisees in the same chain.

Adding a Business Partner

Two of the prime ways to bring a new partner into firm: (1) You receive 70% (or so) of net income the first year and the new partner receives the balance. Each following year you reduce the difference until you are each drawing 50%. (2) You each draw a fixed amount monthly. In addition, every four months you each **draw a sum** from the surplus (above a minimum **balance**) proportionate to the amount of **business that** each has brought in.

Tax Strategy When Owners Split Up a Corporation

The owners of the corporation decide to cease doing business together. Reasons vary: They have a dispute about operations. One wants to retire. One wants to set up another business. Problem: There is a substantial amount of accumulated earnings in the firm, which could result in high capital gains taxes upon liquidation of the business.

One option: Make the corporation into a personal holding company, which defers payment of taxes on the accumulated earnings. If the shareholders have common investment ideas, this solution will work.

Best way to allow each owner complete flexibility with no tax disadvantages: Split the corporation by distributing its assets to some newly formed corporations, each owned 100% by a shareholder of the liquidated company.

How it works:

• X corporation has been engaged in business as a general wholesaler for the last five years. The stock of X is owned equally by A (president) and B (general manager), who are not related to one another.

Serious disputes between A and B as to expansion, marketing channels, and discount policy create a situation where the parties are so antagonistic that the normal operations of the business are serously affected.

Solution: 50% of the operating assets and related liabilities are transferred into a new corporation (Y) in exchange for all the stock of Y. Stock in corporation Y is distributed to owner B solely in exchange for the surrender by B of all his X stock. (The same procedure is followed by owner A, using still another newly formed corporation.)

• Result: No income is realized by the shareholders until the successor corporations liquidate or make a distribution.

Important requirement: The IRS must be convinced that the distribution of assets is undertaken for reasons germane to corporate business problems and is necessary for continuation of the business.

If the owners anticipate that a business will be winding down, the split-up should be made while there is still a viable operating entity. If this is not possible, it might pay to continue the business long enough to qualify for the business purpose requirement.

Source: Edward Mendlowitz, CPA, Siegel & Mendlowitz, 310 Madison Ave., New York 10017.

Lowest-Cost Financing for Pollution Equipment

Urgent advice to firms that have been hit by an administrative order to clean up pollution: Don't make a move before examining the project through a local pool of tax-exempt pollution-control bonds backed by the Small Business Administration. A company can miss out on assistance if it starts ordering pollution-control equipment or begins construction before it files application to get into the program.

Who qualifies: (1) Any firm that can show a bona fide need to build a pollution-control facility, (2) has had three profitable years out of the last five, and (3) falls under the SBA's definition of a small business—which varies with the kind of industry.

Advantages of a tax-free program: Through the tax-free bond market, a small- or medium-size firm can finance a $100,000 to $5 million pollution-control project at an effective rate of 6¼% to 6½% over a period of from 20 to 30 years. Additional costs: SBA insurance fee, 3½% of the total of principal plus interest and application and processing fees (paid once, not annually). Legal fees, escrow costs, and printing can add up to another 1%, but will probably come to less.

SBA-guaranteed financing covers 100% of costs (from design through construction and financing). Firm can either own the facility outright or lease it back from the agency. Payback is in level monthly payments (like a mortgage) over the 20- or 30-year period.

It's best for a company to start with a bank that knows the company's finances and business. It will act as the firm's sponsor—speed up things as detailed information is called for by the agencies, and put the company in touch with an investment banker to arrange pool.

Source: Raymond L. Roton, Montgomery, Alabama office of Robinson-Humphrey Co., Inc., investment bankers, 2 Peachtree St., N.W., Atlanta 30303.

'Pooling' Reduces Costs

Giant industry doesn't consider itself too large to pool its technology and production facilities to reduce costs and thus win larger markets. Yet few small-to-medium size manufacturers pool, even though their small size can free them from the possibility of antitrust action. A notable exception is the furniture industry (mattresses, too), where small producers abound. Often five (or more) manufacturers cut costs by pooling shipping, production facilities, sales forces, etc.

New Definition of Interstate Commerce

It's a mistake to think a company can ignore a federal regulation because it's not in interstate commerce. The definition of interstate commerce has been stretched so far that it includes almost every business. For example, a small plastering firm was held to be in interstate commerce and thus within OSHA jurisdiction because it bought material and equipment outside the state and used the telephone and the mails interstate.

Marshall v. *Anchorage Plastering,* C.A. 9, No. 75-2747, 2/2/78.

Make the Company Gift Deductible—and Tax-Free to Recipient

Opportunities to make tax-free (and deductible) gifts to business associates and employees are more prevalent than most executives realize.

Here's how to make a gift that benefits both the donor and the recipient.

Business gifts:

● Deductible up to $25 per person per year. Additional costs of wrapping, mailing, and delivery are not counted. But the limit also includes gifts made indirectly to customers (via a spouse, for instance).

● Advertising premiums on which the company's name is permanently imprinted are not counted toward the $25 limit if the item costs less than $4.

● Records are important. Keep receipts for the purchase of the gifts, a mailing list, and even thank-you notes received.

Gifts to employees:

● Up to $5,000 may be paid to an employee's spouse as a death benefit. Technically it is not a gift, so the $25 limit doesn't apply. And the spouse doesn't report the death benefit as income if all these conditions are met:

Payments were made to the spouse of the deceased employee, not to the executive's estate.

Company derived no economic benefits from the payments. Payment was made out of affection, respect, admiration, or charity.

Spouse had never performed any services for the company for which compensation could be anticipated.

Services of the deceased employee had been fully compensated during his life. It's important to avoid suggestion that the gift payment represents accrued vacation or sick pay.

● Prizes and awards can be tax-free gifts to employees if they are made primarily in recognition of past achievements in religious, charitable, scientific, educational, artistic, literary, or civic fields. Employees are not required to give the award to the charity or organization. They may keep it as a tax-free bonus. Make sure that employees are selected without any action on their part to enter a contest. They also cannot be required to render substantial future services to the company as a condition of receiving the prize or award. The award should have nothing to do with the employee's performance at work. (Suggestion and merit awards are taxable.) The amount should appear reasonable enough to preclude a challenge by IRS.

● Awards to employees for length of service or

safety achievements are taxable to the employees with a $100 deduction limit to the employer. Instead, give a bonus to the employees, since that is fully deductible.

Perks as gifts:

• The Revenue Act of 1978 permits an employer to pay for educational expenses of his employees. To be eligible for a deduction, the company payments on behalf of an employee must be made according to a written plan. Benefits to principal shareholders are limited. But payments that qualify are tax-free to the employee.

• Premiums on group-term life insurance policies can be paid for employees by an employer. Up to $50,000 in coverage is tax-free to the employee. Premium for coverage in excess of $50,000 is still deductible by the employer, but a portion must be included in the employee's taxable income. (The cost to the employee is extremely small.)

• Legal services provided to an employee are tax-free if the company has a qualified group legal service plan. The legal services can be made available to the employee's spouse and dependents. Also, employer contributions to the plan are deductible.

Source: Randy B. Blaustein, J.D., tax manager, Siegel & Mendlowitz, CPAs, 310 Madison Ave., New York 10017.

PERSONAL
BUSINESS

Divorce and the IRS

Cutting College Costs

Used Cars Mechanics Like Best

Choosing a Moving Company

How to Buy Caviar

Heating the House

Office Exercises and Relaxation

Understanding Hospital Talk

16

PERSONAL BUSINESS

When Husband and Wife Both Have Substantial Incomes

Husbands and wives who each have sizable personal wealth or income should handle their financial affairs differently from other couples. Prime areas:

Savings and investments. It's probably advisable for them to have most of their assets in individual rather than joint ownership (except the home). Reasons:

• They may have different philosophies and approaches to saving and investing. And even if there are no differences now, they may develop in later years.

• Each spouse will probably want to favor his or her own family if property is to be willed to relatives other than children and grandchildren.

Life insurance. Probably a good idea for spouses to give their life insurance policies to each other. That removes life insurance proceeds from taxable estate. Each should pay premiums on the policy on the other spouse's life. Giving

over the policy is a reportable gift if it has a value of more than $3,000. Do this as early as possible before the cash value builds up. Generally no gift tax problem with term life, including group term policies paid for by the employer.

• Policies should not be willed to each other. That defeats original purpose of keeping the insurance proceeds out of the estate.

Further complication arises if one dies, wills policy on the other's life to a trust for children, but surviving spouse is trustee. In this situation, some courts have held that the spouse, as trustee, has incidents of ownership in the policy on his or her own life. Thus, the proceeds are included in estate of surviving spouse. Advice: Don't make spouse a trustee if the trust assets include a policy on the spouse's life.

State and local income tax. The couple should probably file those returns separately. Most states use the same tax rates for single and married people. Filing separately produces a lower total tax, since one income isn't piled on top of the other to reach the higher brackets.

Federal income tax. In most cases, joint federal returns should be filed. Federal rates for

226

married couples filing jointly are the lowest available. The rates for marrieds filing separately are the highest (even higher than those for singles).

However, in certain situations there could be a saving by filing separate returns. Make calculations both ways to see which is better under these circumstances:

• One has large medical deductions and the other doesn't. The nondeductible part of medical bills (equal to 3% of adjusted gross income) will be less if filing separately.

• One has municipal bonds and the other has interest deductions for money borrowed to carry investments. On a joint return the interest deductions might be disallowed.

• One has realized capital gains and the other losses. The tax advantage of long-term gains is lost if they are offset by losses. And the tax advantage of losses (using them to offset ordinary income) is lost if they are offset by gains.

Source: Norman H. Cohen, Esq., Langer, Beaudet, Cantor & Cohen, 2 Park Ave., New York 10016.

Divorce and the IRS

Two basic tax principles to keep in mind:

First, periodic alimony payments over many years are tax deductible. However, no other payments are deductible. (Possible exception: Child's medical bills, if the husband properly claims the child as a dependent.)

Second, if the husband deducts the alimony, the wife must declare it as income.

Child support, lump-sum payments, wife's legal fees, premiums on life insurance policies owned by the husband—all these are not deductible by the spouse paying them. And they need not be reported as income by the spouse who received the payments.

In the still common case among executives where the husband has a large taxable income and the nonworking wife has little or none, it probably makes sense to make all the payments as alimony rather than something else. The result is to shift income from the husband's high bracket to the wife's lower bracket. It's essential to prepare carefully several alternative plans,

varying the mix among alimony and other types of payments, and figuring the available income from each after taxes. Keep in mind that:

Usually the parents can decide between them who will claim the children as dependents. Thus, the father probably can claim them even if they live with the mother. Of course, only one can claim them.

A parent having a child living with him or her may be able to file as a tax-favored head of household by claiming that child as a dependent.

Conceivably, both parents might have head-of-household status. This could happen if the younger children stayed with the mother, but an older child—away at college full time—stayed with the father when home on vacation.

Child support normally stops when the kids become independent. Alimony often goes on until the wife remarries.

If it's agreed that the husband will pay for the wife's divorce lawyer, add the estimated cost to the alimony. Thus, get a deduction for the amount. But don't forget it's income to the wife in that case.

Sometimes child support can be paid as alimony by providing that the alimony is reduced when child becomes self-supporting.

Saving Taxes by Shifting Income to the Children

Most wealthy families can realize major tax savings by transferring income from high-bracket parents to low-bracket children. If the children have no income now, they will pay no taxes at all on the first $1,000 of transferred income ($1,100 if they receive at least $100 of dividends). On higher amounts they'll probably pay taxes at a much lower rate than their parents.

And the parents may still be able to claim the children as dependents, even though they have income of their own.

Ways to transfer income to children:

• Let them work in the family business, either full-time or part-time. In this case, the child pays no income taxes on the first $3,200 of earnings. And wages paid are fully deductible by the business. Important: The child must really work, and the pay must be in line with what is paid to other employees for similar work.

• Make gifts of securities or other income-producing property, or of money to be used to buy such assets. Up to $1,000 of income will be completely tax-free ($1,100 if it includes at least $100 of dividend income). If the child is too young to handle the gift in a responsible way, the gift can be made to a custodian or to a trust.

• Make a temporary gift of securities or other income-producing property that will revert back later to parents' ownership. This is done by using a short-term trust (often called a Clifford trust). Generally, the trust must last for at least ten years.

Under Internal Revenue Service rules, support includes food, lodging, clothing, medical and dental bills, medical insurance premiums, tuition, charitable donations, transportation, and recreation.

Parents' contribution to support can include: (1) Reasonable value of food and lodgings furnished at home. (2) Value of the room maintained year-round for the child's use when at home. The child's own income has to be included in the calculation only if it's actually used for support.

Gift tax consequences: There's generally no gift tax effect on gifts of up to $3,000 in any one year from an individual (or up to $6,000 to each child from a married couple). But the gift has to be a present interest (the child must have free access to the money).

Parents Supported by More Than One Child: Who Takes Deduction?

When brothers and sisters support a parent, plan things so that one of them can deduct the parent's medical expenses. Here's how:

First step: File a multiple support declaration (Form 2120). Where several people contribute, this form designates the one who can take the exemption. If each pays at least 10% but less than half of the support, any one of them can take the exemption if the others agree.

Second step: The one claiming the exemption should pay doctor bills directly, and make clear (on the check) that his contribution is earmarked for medical expenses. Then he can deduct the parent's medical expenses on his tax return. Remember: Medical expenses can be deducted only for yourself, your spouse, and your dependents. You can't deduct medical expenses paid for anyone you can't properly claim as a dependent.

How to Get Tax Breaks When Supporting Elderly Parents

Strategies that save taxes when the family supports retired parents take planning but are worth considering for taxpayers who are in the higher income brackets.

Basic goal: Shift income to a low-bracket retired parent. A taxpayer who supports a parent gets a $1,000 exemption under the new tax law. And if he pays the parent's medical expenses, he can deduct them, too.

But if income can be shifted from the taxpayer to the parent, it will be taxed at the parent's lower rate. And the parent, if over the age of 65, will get a $2,000 exemption. Another $2,300 is protected from being taxed when the parent takes the standard deduction.

Ways to shift income:

• Put the parent on the company payroll (full- or part-time). Salary can be enough to cover basic living expenses and is now fully deductible as a business cost. A parent over 65 gets a double exemption ($2,000 under new law). The taxpayer loses his exemption for parent unless his payments other than salary still provide more than 50% of parent's total support. All amounts double if both parents are alive and capable of working. Important: They must really work for the business, and their pay must be in line with pay of other employees.

• Set up a business as a family partnership. Make an outright gift or lend the parent the money to buy in. The loan is repaid out of the parent's share of partnership profits. Good technique if parent is unable to work or if the business is one where capital is needed. Caution: A personal service business that doesn't need much capital will have to show that the parent actually contributes services.

• Set up a family corporation. This gets around requirement that parent participate actively in business. Transfer some dividend-paying stock to parent by gift or loan. But weigh cost and possible disadvantages of incorporating against probable tax savings.

• Give parent income-producing property. The income goes directly to the parent and is taxed at lower bracket. If property produces dividends, parent gets $100 annual exclusion in addition to personal exemption of $1,000 ($2,000 if over 65). Or give parent business property, and have company lease it back. Rental payments are deductible.

• Give property to a short-term trust for benefit of parent. Ownership reverts automatically when trust terminates. To make sure the taxpayer who makes the gift isn't taxed on the income, the trust must be irrevocable for at least ten years, or until the parent's death, or until some specified event occurs (parent is placed in a nursing home or taxpayer's income drops below a certain figure, etc.).

Caution: Gifts of partnership interest, corporate stock, or income-producing property to parents or to trust raise estate and gift tax problems, since parents are likely to die before children.

Gift tax problems can be minimized by careful use of annual gift tax exclusion. Taxpayer and spouse can jointly give $24,000 per year if both parents of each spouse are alive.

The estate tax problem is trickier, since property becomes part of estate when parent dies. Best solution is to limit gifts so that the total estate will not exceed the value of the estate tax credit—$175,625 after 1980.

Important to remember: If both parents are alive, some state laws provide that when one spouse dies, the survivor may claim one-third or one-half of the estate. This amount might increase the surviving spouse's assets to a point where the estate will be subject to tax.

Cutting College Costs

If your child is college or graduate school hunting, don't overlook Canada, which has 58 universities offering quality education at low cost.

Tuition fees in private U.S. universities now are soaring yearly, with concomitant but lesser increases each year in Canada.

• Universities in Ontario now charge undergraduate foreigners (including U.S. ones) a flat fee of $1,500 and $1,950 for graduate students.

• Alberta adds a $300 foreign student fee to normal tuition. (But check for changes.)

Other costs—travel, room and board, books and materials—tend to be less than in the U.S.

Among Canada's oldest and best universities (*E* = English, *F* = French, *B* = bilingual):

U. of British Columbia
Vancouver, B.C. *(E)*

U. of Alberta
Edmonton, Al. *(E)*

U. of Calgary
2920-24th Ave., N.W.
Calgary, Al. *(E)*

U. of Regina
Regina, Sask. *(E)*

U. of Manitoba
Fort Garry Campus
Winnipeg, Man. *(E)*

Laurentian Univ.
Sudbury
935 Ramsey Lake Rd.
Sudbury, Ont. *(E)*

U. of Ottawa
Ottawa, Ont. *(B)*

U. of Toronto
Toronto, Ont. *(E)*

U. of Waterloo
200 University Ave.
West
Waterloo, Ont. *(E)*
(Canada's M.I.T.)

U. of Western Ontario
1151 Richmond St.
London, Ont. *(E)*
(Excellent business
school)

Universite Laval
Quebec, Que. *(F)*

McGill University
P.O. Box 6070
Montreal, Que. *(E)*

**University of New
Brunswick**
Fredericton, N.B. *(E)*

Nova Scotia Agricultural College
Truro, N.S. *(E)*

Nova Scotia College of
Art & Design
6152 Coburg Rd.
Halifax, N.S. *(E)*

**Nova Scotia Technical
College
(Engineering)**
P.O. Box 1000
Halifax, N.S. *(E)*

**University of Prince
Edward Island**
P.O. Box 1358
Charlottetown, Prince
Edward Island *(E)*

**Memorial University
of Newfoundland**
Elizabeth Ave.
St. Johns, Nfld. *(E)*

Getting a Bigger Deduction for Sales Taxes

Don't be shortchanged on the sales tax deduction on your personal income tax. The deduction is an automatic formula based on income, without the need to prove how much was actually paid in sales tax. But there is a way to be sure you're getting the largest possible deduction.

Find the automatic deduction in the optional sales tax tables. The higher the income, the bigger the deduction. Include nontaxable income such as Social Security, untaxed long-term gains, municipal bond interest.

If you made a big purchase, such as a car, boat, or mobile home, deduct the actual sales tax paid on the big item in addition to the amount shown on the table under your income category.

Tax Savings When Parent Pays for Youngster's Car

Sales tax: If you buy the car in your own name and then give it to him, you'll get a sales tax deduction on your federal tax which will be worth more to you than to the child.

Interest deductions: If you buy the car on time, the interest deductions are yours even though you later give away the car.

Casualty losses: From a liability standpoint, you may be better off having the car in the youngster's name, but from both the tax and casualty loss standpoint, you might be better off having it in your own name. Then you'd be able to claim a casualty loss deduction. But you can't have it both ways. Since liability poses the far greater risk, you must pass up the casualty loss angle. Let the youngster get comprehensive and collision coverages, reasonable deductible, and let him carry any casualty loss risk remaining on his own. It might influence him to become a more careful driver.

Gift taxes: Gifts up to $3,000 per year per donee are exempt from tax. If your spouse consents, the exempt figure becomes $6,000. If it's a more expensive car—an $8,000 car, for example

—sell it to him for $2,000 and take back a $2,000 note payable next year. Make sure it provides for interest of at least 6%. You've made him a gift of $6,000 this year. No gift tax. Next year you burn the note. You've made him a gift of $2,000 plus interest, but you have next year's annual exclusion (exemption) to save you from gift tax. Handling it as a sale, though, could mean problems with sales tax.

Tax Treatment of Scholarships

Scholarship funds from an educational institution or a fellowship grant are generally not taxable. Among the exempt items: Tuition, matriculation and other fees, family allowances, room, board, and other living expenses, allowances for travel, research, clerical help, and equipment.

Limitations: Recipient must be a degree candidate, or the exemption is limited to $300 a month. Amounts paid for past, present, or future services, for example, teaching, are taxable. Employer-paid scholarships are taxable if the student must return to the employer when he or she finishes school.

Certain student loan programs erase all or part of an educational loan, if the student performs certain services for a period of time in certain geographical areas. Under current tax law the discharge of such a debt does not result in taxable income to the student.

Determining a Fair Price for a New Car

Start by figuring what that car costs the dealer. This can be done by subtracting the markup on the base sticker price (before options are added on) and subtracting the markup on options.

The markup on base sticker prices is generally as follows:

10% on economy cars (Chevette, Omni, Fiesta).

12% on subcompacts (Pinto, Monza).

15% on compacts (Nova, Volare, Fairmont).

16% on sporty cars (Camaro, Firebird).

18% on intermediates (Malibu, Cutlass, Granada).

20% on smaller luxury cars (Monte Carlo, Grand Prix, Thunderbird).

22% on full-size cars (Caprice, Galaxie).

25% on luxury cars (Cadillac, Lincoln).

25% on pickups and vans.

The markup option is as follows:

30% on appearance and convenience items (vinyl roof, air conditioning, power windows, radio).

20% on performance items (radial tires, five-speed transmission, heavy-duty suspension or cooling system).

After subtracting the markups to determine dealer cost, add $125 for dealer overhead. Add on freight charges (itemized on the sticker) and also $100 profit for the dealer (he'll still get an additional 2% rebate from the manufacturer). The final figure is what you should pay for the car you want. Shop around until you find a dealer who'll sell it for that price (give or take $100). Don't be pressured to take an options-loaded car from the dealer's inventory.

Source: *Road Test* magazine.

Option Choices on a New Car: How to Decide

The value of an optional feature depends on how, when, and where most of the driving will be done.

Important for everyone: Options that make the car safer, such as steel-belted radial tires. They hold the road better, provide better fuel economy and longer life. Another important safety feature: Day/night mirror.

Important but not essential:

• Disc brakes. Stand up to repeated hard use under big loads, but are not really necessary for city driving.

• Cruise control. Great advantage for driving long distances regularly. Sets pace and helps avoid speeding tickets.

• Air conditioning. Important for comfort and for car's subsequent resale value.

• Heavy-duty suspension system. Makes the car feel taut and firm and hold the road better. Little initial cost and little value on resale. Important for car owners who are going to carry heavy loads, or who love to drive and are sensitive to car's performance. Not important for those whose car use is limited mainly to trips to the supermarket.

• Power seats. Extremely useful feature for drivers who go long distances regularly. Permits moving the seat back. Allows arm position in relation to steering wheel to be manipulated and fine-tuned. In some ways a safety factor because it helps ward off fatigue. Quite expensive.

• Adjustable seat back. Some form of this is highly recommended. Wards off fatigue and thus is a safety element.

• Tilt steering wheel. Another aid in fine-tuning the driver's relation to car and therefore recommended as a safety factor. Important for large or short people.

• Electric door locks. Key unlocks all doors simultaneously. Button locks all doors at once, including trunk lid. A convenience. Makes it unnecessary to open each door from outside in bad weather. When driving through dangerous neighborhoods, provides immediate security with the touch of a button.

Options with problems:

• Sun roof. Redundant if a car has air conditioning, and not as comfortable. Disadvantages: Noise and buffeting as wind hits. Problem of water leakage.

• Power windows. Recommended for drivers who use toll highways regularly. (New Datsun 280ZX has dual control device that permits driver to control window without keeping finger on button.) Caution: Power windows can be dangerous to small children and pets.

General rules:

• Buy accessories that relate to the character of the car. A very lightweight car does not require power steering or power brakes. But the purchase of a heavy car without power steering (and such cars are still made) is a mistake many drivers regret making for the sake of economy.

231

- Consider where and how the car will be used. Distances. Neighborhoods. Weather.
- Decorative options. Important to the car's resale value. The plainest, unadorned model is not necessarily one that will save money in the long run. Chances are the used car buyer wants more pizzazz. Best to buy up scale rather than down to ensure optimum resalability.

Note: Don't buy a factory-installed AM/FM radio. They're priced too high and not very good. Instead, order the least expensive AM radio plus stereo speakers. Then buy and have installed a quality radio and speakers.

Choose the Best Car Engine

Commonsense rule: Concentrate on matching true driving needs to what's available. Don't choose an engine solely on the basis of fuel economy, which can be deceptive. Example: A buyer who finds a 1968 Cadillac in impeccable shape and working condition for $1,000 is getting a terrific value. A new, fuel-economical Volkswagon Rabbit at $6,000 would take ten years of driving before the $5,000 difference could be made up in fuel savings.

Main question to ask: How much and what kind of driving is done?

Diesel vs. gas: Diesels don't make sense for everyone, despite the fuel savings they represent.

Disadvantages:
- Except for the Mercedes (a special case), diesels cost more than gas engine cars. An Oldsmobile diesel costs at least $800 more. A Rabbit costs about $175 more. Reason: Demand for diesels far exceeds availability.
- They have an unpleasant smell.
- They are noisier.

Advantages:
- Greater fuel economy. Seven additional miles for every gallon of gas.
- In event of gas rationing, the crunch might not extend to diesel fuel (as was the case in 1973-74 fuel crisis, when it was readily available).
- Maintenance is lower.
- Resale value is greater.

Best customer for a diesel: Someone who drives a lot, goes long distances, and for whom fuel cost is a significant factor. Also, someone who won't be bothered by the odor. Diesel is a doubtful choice for the driver who doesn't travel heavily. Annual net saving on fuel will be very small. The payout for a heavier traveler (30,000 miles a year or so) comes more quickly, justifying the extra cost.

Large vs. small engine: The big-engine gas hog can be more economical. Depends on the work it's asked to do. An eight-cylinder engine moves weight with much less effort than a small-cylinder engine. They also run more smoothly, with fewer vibrations.

Front-wheel drive: Advantageous for everyone because it provides much better traction. The weight of the engine as it drives the front wheels also pushes them down on the road.

Paying for the Use of a 'Lemon'

When a buyer discovers that the car he's purchased has major defects and is, by all rights, a "lemon," he may revoke his acceptance and demand a new car if he acts promptly. If, as is usually the case, the seller undertakes to correct the defects, this may be taken into consideration in determining whether the buyer acted within a reasonable time in revoking his acceptance of the car. But the buyer is entitled to be paid for the fair value of the use of the car while the seller undertakes to correct the defects.

The same rule applies to any other item of defective equipment.

Used Cars That Mechanics Like Best

- Subcompacts: Pinto (despite fuel tank problems), Chevette, Datsun B-210.
- Compacts: Dart, Nova (V-8), Maverick (6-cyl., 200 or 250 cu. in.).

• Intermediates: Cutlass, Malibu, Buick Century/Regal (all with GM's 350 cu. in. V-8, Regal with V-6 as well), Torino with V-8.

• Full-size: Caprice/Impala with 283 or 350 cu. in. V-8, Olds 88 and 98 with 350 or 454 cu. in. V-8, LTD with 351 or 400 cu. in. V-8.

• Luxury: Lincoln Continental and Mark II, III, IV, V, Cadillac deVille.

Warning: There was much difference of opinion among the 126 mechanics replying. Manual transmission was preferred on smallest cars, automatic on others. Power options should be avoided—they create repair problems.

Source: *Changing Times,* Editors Park, MD.

Minimizing Car Breakdowns on the Road

If a patrol car stops, tell police the least expensive thing you can think of when they ask what's wrong with the car, because that is what they'll tell the garage. If the garage thinks you know what you're talking about, there's less chance of being cheated.

• Try to stay with the car while repairs are done: The mechanic needs only a minute to concoct an engine malfunction. Best to ask the mechanic to return the old part before putting in the new one. Prevents him from reinstalling the old unit.

• Ask the mechanic for an estimate of the job and ask him if he has the proper parts. If he doesn't have the parts or is uncertain about whether he can get them, you may save time and cash by picking them up yourself.

• The job will get done faster if you keep after the mechanic. Otherwise, the car may sit for several days and you may get charged for hours of labor that never occurred.

• Don't opt for the most expensive repair. If the car can be made to go with a less-than-perfect repair, do that and wait till you get home to have it fixed properly.

• One way to speed along the repair is to have a repair manual in the car. These books are published for virtually all cars and are available at dealers and some bookstores. Bring it out if the

mechanic looks at the car and starts talking about many hours of work and costly repairs.

• Insist that the bill itemize separately the charges for towing or road service, replacement parts, and labor.

Source: *Medical Economics.*

Smart Motorists' Guidelines to Intelligent Driving

• Park indoors on cold nights. Fuel efficiency for the first five miles of driving with a cold engine is half what it would be if kept warm overnight. (Cold oil in the engine is a heavy, gelatinous mass that is resistant to the movement of the engine. When warm, oil becomes slippery and parts move with less friction.)

• Turn off car engine when waiting instead of letting it idle. An engine running at idle speed for as little as one minute uses more gasoline than it takes to start it up again after it's shut off.

• Overheated car. When caught in traffic, if indicator needle moves up and red light comes on, car can probably make it to the next service station if these steps are followed: (1) Turn off air conditioner. (2) Turn on heater to draw heat away from engine. (3) Put transmission into neutral (when stopped) and race engine slightly. Note: Check water level as soon as possible. If it's adequate, thermostat may be malfunctioning.

• Don't use dealer financing plan to buy a car. Borrowing from a bank, a credit union, or against an insurance policy costs much less.

• Best time to buy a car: After the first severe winter weather of the year, especially snowstorms. Sales are slow then, and automobile dealers are very eager to move their stock.

• Testing a new car for leaks: Put some clean white paper (shelf paper is good) under the whole car at night. Don't worry about clear spots, which are likely moisture which has condensed around the air conditioner. Oily pink leaks are likely to be transmission fluid. Dark leaks are engine oil. Dry pink leaks are gasoline. Engine coolant leaks depend on what color the coolant is, either yellow-green or pink.

• Fan belt adjustment test: Press your thumb

down on the belt at the midpoint between the pulleys. You should be able to press the belt in about a half-inch by pressing down moderately. (If more or less, an adjustment is necessary.) Also, always carry extra belt in the trunk.

• Check tire tread by inserting a penny in the tread. If the top of Lincoln's head shows, replace the tire. The safety minimum is $\frac{1}{16}$ inch.

• Synthetic lubricants are a better buy in the long run than natural products. Advantages: Better reduction of friction and absorption of engine contaminants. Users report as much as 50,000 miles driven between oil changes. And there is little evidence of wear on engines that have logged 250,000 miles.

• Radial tires signal impending trouble before they blow out. Early warning signs: Difficult or erratic steering, rough ride under normal conditions, or a bulge on the tire.

• Sell your car yourself rather than trade it in. The dealer will only allow wholesale value on the car or even less.

Choosing a Moving Company

Before choosing a mover when relocating home or office, request performance records. All interstate moving companies are required to give them to you. How the ten busiest movers in the country rate:

	Low estimates[1]	Late pickups[2]	Late deliveries	Damages[3]
Allied	26.4%	1.4%	2.6%	14.8%
Atlas	29.4	1.1	9.2	23.1
Bekins	23.7	1.0	6.1	18.4
Global	24.1	0.3	7.5	8.8
Lyon	26.1	0.3	4.5	14.5
Mayflower	25.7	1.3	7.1	22.7
N. American	20.1	1.4	3.0	20.4
Red Ball	27.4	1.6	11.1	15.8
United	19.6	2.2	5.1	14.6
Wheaton	11.3	0.4	7.8	14.5

Heading: **Percentage of shipments with:**

[1]Cost underestimated at least 10%.
[2]Five or more days beyond schedule.
[3]Claims for $50 and up.
Source: Interstate Commerce Commission, 12th St. and Constitution Ave., N.W., Washington, DC 20423.

How to Buy Caviar

Caviar prices have gone up sharply and continue to rise. Tips for buying the best:

Caviar from sturgeon is top of the line and most expensive. Three grades (beluga, osetra, sevruga) all come from the same fish. Beluga is biggest grained and most expensive; color is black or gray. Osetra grains cost somewhat less and are almost the same size, brown to golden in color. Sevruga grains are much smaller and least expensive.

Freshest, best caviar is packed with mild salt, labeled Malossol. So is pressed caviar, which is top-grade caviar, too "ripe" to pack in whole grains. A best buy, it is very rich tasting, authentic (served widely both in Russia and Iran), and, unlike whole-grain, can be stored in a freezer. Bottom of the line: Strongly salted caviar that comes in jars.

How to serve: Figure $\frac{3}{4}$ of an ounce per person. Serve whole-grain right out of the tin atop crushed ice, pressed caviar at room temperature. Surround both with small plates of lemon wedges, chopped onions, chopped egg whites, sieved yolks. Spoon some caviar onto thin-sliced black bread, toast, or thin pancakes called blinys and let guests add whatever they want.

Don't shun red-colored salmon caviar, which is delicious and far less expensive. Best tasting are the smaller-size grains from silver salmon (rather than more common Ketovya or chum salmon caviar which is often artificially colored).

Buying a Piano

The best sound comes from a grand piano, but new ones cost from $6,000 to $15,000. A smaller spinet, console, or studio upright will provide satisfactory sound for most people and costs from $900 to $4,000. How to test a piano before purchase: Play it by running up and down the scales. High notes should be clean and crisp, low notes should resonate. If considering the purchase of a used piano, look for one ten years old or less. Don't buy one more than 20 years old. Have a piano tuner check out a used piano.

Get it tuned at least every six months, more frequently if it's new. It should be kept in a cool, dry room, away from direct sunlight and not close to radiators, air conditioners, or vents. Put it at least four inches away from the wall to allow the sound to get out. Get a professional cleaning every three years. Don't do it yourself. Dangers: Mothballs or spray inside the piano.

Executive Dressing

Best men's clothes for each body build: The pinstripe contributes to an illusion of height. The vertical line formed by the classic three-button jacket will enhance the illusion, as will pockets that point inward and upward. No cuffs on trousers.

Dark suits will make heavier men look lighter. Best for men of ordinary height is a single-breasted jacket with a center vent. A double-breasted jacket is suitable for taller men—of any weight. Pleats in trousers add bulk. Darts are better for comfort and a well-tailored look.

Thinner men can use pale, heavier-gauge fabrics to create a sense of bulk. Straight-legged trousers will give the legs a fuller appearance. Avoid tapered trousers which conform to the shape of the leg.

Quick test for jacket length: Stand with arms hanging straight at sides, hands curled inward into half-fists. Bottom of jacket should touch the palms.

Prolong the life of your clothes. (1) Hang jackets on wooden or plastic hangers that are curved to the approximate shape of the human back. (2) Remove all objects from pockets. Leave unbuttoned. (3) Keep some space between garments to avoid wrinkling. (4) Allow at least 24 hours between wearings. (5) Use pants hangers that clamp onto trouser bottoms. Remove belt before hanging up pants.

Best advice for males is still to emulate the boss: Conservative-looking suit, white shirt (pale pastels if your cohorts wear them), matching tie. Muted colors connote trust, upper-middle-class status. Black, navy, pinstripe, and chalk-striped suits exude power, competence, and authority.

Beware of loud pastels (gaudy); shades of pink (effeminate); gold or green-gray (unflattering); light blues, gray-beige (detracts from presence: you're more likely to be liked than respected). Also out: European cuts; turtlenecks, clashing colors that hint of sloppiness or academia, sports clothes (save them for sports). Buy clothes for more than one occasion (e.g., blazer with two pairs of slacks, one for business, one for evening wear). Avoid styles or colors that threaten to become overpopular.

Before Buying Air Conditioning

Check the Energy Efficiency Ratio (EER) of the unit. It should be 7.5 or more. A simple formula will show the size air conditioner needed to cool a room adequately.

$$\frac{W \times H \times I \times L \times E}{60} = \text{BTU/hr capacity needed}$$

W = width of room (in feet)
H = ceiling height
I = insulation factor (10 for a heated ceiling or attic above room; 18 for no insulation above, many or large windows)
L = length of room
E = exposure (16 for north, 17 for east, 18 for south and 20 for west)

Air conditioner mistake: Buying a bigger unit because it costs only a few dollars more. This wastes money in the long run.

Heating the House

• Have thermostats checked when furnace is serviced. Improper functioning wastes oil. Remove thermostat cover once a year and blow out dust and lint that can hinder operation.

• Radiators. The oldest are best. Cast-iron radiators even out the flow of heat from furnace, circulate air in rooms by convection. Leave them uncovered, undraped (drapes should end at the bottom of a window, or fall behind the radiators). Covers, if you insist on them for looks, should offer wide spaces for air flow in front and above radiators themselves. Avoid covers with solid tops. Paint radiators a flat black. Shiny silver cuts efficiency.

• Baseboard radiators should not be mounted at baseboard level. For best heating efficiency they should be about six inches off the floor.

• Furnace tips: Don't depend on oil-burner service people to keep it clean. Even if they do, they'll only handle cleaning once a year. That's not enough. Change the oil (or gas) burner nozzle for the spring and summer. A smaller nozzle cuts the burning rate 30%. Note: Gadgets that close the flue when the burner is not operating may seem a good idea but are rarely cost-effective at current prices ($400 installed).

Before You Buy Headache Remedies

Relief from incapacitating tension, vascular, and migraine headaches is possible without drugs, using a self-administered form of acupuncture known as acupressure.

The technique: Exert very heavy thumbnail pressure (painful pressure) successively on nerves lying just below the surface of the skin at key points in the hands and wrists. As with acupuncture, no one's sure why it works.

Pressure points to try:

• The triangle of flesh between the thumb and index finger on the back of your hands (thumb side of bone, near middle of the second metacarpal in the index finger).

• Just above the protruding bone on the thumb side of your wrist.

Before You Buy Sleeping Pills

Advice from Dr. Frank Zorick, clinical director of the sleep disorder center at Cincinnati Veterans Administration Hospital and the University of Cincinnati:

Nonprescription, over-the-counter sleeping pills are absolutely useless. Studies have shown "sugar pills" to be just as effective.

Doctor-prescribed sedatives are very useful in temporary situations where a particular emotional or physical upset is the cause of the insomnia. Problem: Tendency to become dependent on pills, and a worsening of the quality of sleep as more pills are used.

How to handle pills: Use for no more than a week or two. Expect that the first night or two after stopping the pills will be very disturbed sleep. That's perfectly normal.

Widely advertised insomnia cures like vibrating beds, prerecorded cassette tapes, and sleep masks might work—if they relax you.

Dr. Zorick's prescription for the occasional insomniac: Condition your sleep environment. Learn to associate your bed and your bedroom with sleep.

Pay attention to bedroom conditions, such as light, heat, noise. Shut off telephones if necessary. Keep temperature cool (around 68°). Make sure your mattress and your sleep clothing are comfortable.

If you don't fall asleep right away, get up, leave the bedroom, and go do something else. Don't lie awake thinking about it. Staying in bed for hours trying to get to sleep accentuates the problem. You begin to associate your bed and your bedroom with trying to get to sleep.

Stick to a regular bedtime schedule. Go to bed at the same time every night—weekdays and weekends. Some insomniacs have the idea they'll catch up on missed sleep on the weekends. You can't do it. Trying to do it simply disrupts your biological rhythms.

Exercise early in the day is okay. Late in the evening it's too stimulating. Exception to the rule: Sexual activity, within a comfortable relationship where no tension or anxiety exists, is helpful in inducing sleep.

Preventing a Heart Attack

1. Get an annual heart checkup:

• Complete blood workup, including tests of

cholesterol, triglycerides, sugar, and uric acid. All provide clues to heart troubles.

• Chest X rays—with emphasis on the heart.

• Two kinds of EKGs—one at rest and one under stress. The at-rest EKG should be done with a 12-lead technique (tiny wires that are attached to the skin). Don't settle for less than 12. The stress EKG is similar to the at-rest test, only now the patient is monitored during a physically stressful period—running on a treadmill or riding an exercise bike.

2. Don't smoke. That's the best advice. Nonsmokers clearly have the best chances.

3. Get your weight down. It's not as important as smoking. No question it's hard for many to lose weight. Weight Watchers has a good success record.

4. Get regular exercise—the kind that challenges the cardiovascular system—with the key word being "regular." Avoid strenuous competitive sports if you aren't in good shape. It's worse than no exercise at all. Any new exercise program should be reviewed by your physician.

5. If you suffer from hypertension (high blood pressure), have it treated by your physician.

Recognize the ailing heart:

Most heart attacks are accompanied by chest pain—but not always. In most instances, there aren't any specific early warning symptoms to have one's cardiovascular status evaluated on a periodic basis. Early warnings of an ailing heart may include irregularities in rhythm, such as a fluttering in the chest or skipped heartbeats. Don't wait for pain to send you to your physician. Any symptom should trigger a call to your doctor. If he is not immediately available, get to a hospital emergency room at once. If the pain is bad, rest and have someone else call.

The worst thing: To ignore the signs. Most victims do ignore the first signs. They want to deny the dreaded news, so they shrug it off. Some people are embarrassed about calling the doctor late at night, concerned that it is only indigestion or a muscle cramp.

Pain: Sometimes it's confined to the chest. It need not be very painful. It often is an uncomfortable pressure, a squeezing feeling in the center of the chest. The pain may radiate to the neck, shoulder, or arms. And it may come and go, disappearing overnight.

Other signs: Constant shortness of breath, even when you're not exerting yourself. Slowness in getting your heartbeat to slow down after some mild physical strain, and even a persistent swelling of the ankles.

Source: Dr. John P. McCann, Life Extension Institute, 1185 Ave. of Americas, New York 10036.

How to Handle Travel

Some 20% to 30% of all heart attacks occur just before or just after travel. Dr. Meyer Friedman, co-author of *Type A Behavior & Your Heart*, trains his patient/executives to contingency-plan for a business trip. Say he's going to New York for a conference on Monday, November 13:

• Monday, November 6. Executive starts cleaning desk in preparation for the trip. By the time he leaves work on Friday, the desk is clear except for the plane tickets.

• Sunday, November 12. He flies to New York. Goes straight to his hotel. Does not pick up the telephone. Takes a mild tranquilizer and goes to bed.

• Monday, November 13. Tranquilizer, conference, and back to the hotel before flying home.

Executives and High Blood Pressure

A high proportion of people have high blood pressure and don't know it. There are no symptoms obvious to the patient—until the effects of the hypertension cause disease (heart and other organs are damaged) over a period of time.

Hypertension test is simple: A one-minute blood-pressure check. Yet, since most people don't have periodic medical checkups, the number of hypertensive men, women, and children in all economic categories who fail to get diagnosed is staggering. The risk of hypertension increases with age. (Also, blacks and males have been found to be the most susceptible groups.)

Treatment: Usually very simple and very ef-

237

fective: Lose weight, stop smoking, and restrict salt. In more severe cases, daily drug-taking is required. Note: Cigarette smokers are most apt to suffer high blood pressure, cigar smokers less, and pipe smokers even less. But smoking in any form increases risk.

New kinds of treatment: Relaxation techniques such as biofeedback and meditation. In many cases, they can replace drugs.

Yoga: Five-Minute Office Routine

Most exercise programs aimed at improving physical and mental tone are too time-consuming for executives. Yoga is the exception. Practitioners find that ten minutes per day will do the trick. Here's a five-minute routine that you can do in your chair or standing beside your desk:

Chest expansion (2 minutes): Standing with heels together, slowly bring arms up so they are straight ahead of you, palms turned outward. (Feel elbows stretching.) Bring arms straight back on a line with shoulders and then upward, as high as you can. Then, slowly and carefully bend backward at the waist. Keep arms high, knees unbent, head back. Hold for a slow count of 5. Next, bend forward as far as you can (don't strain), holding arms high, head down, and neck relaxed. Hold for a count of 10. Straighten up a bit and extend left leg to the side. Bend forward at the waist, aiming forehead toward left knee. (Bend right leg slightly.) Hold for count of 10. Repeat, bending toward right. Straighten slowly, draw right leg in, unclasp hands, and relax. Repeat entire routine.

Head twist (2 minutes): Sitting at your desk, place elbows close together, put head between hands (hands over ears), and close eyes. Place clasped hands on lower part of back of your head. Slowly and gently push head forward until chin touches chest. Keeping arms still, turn head, resting chin in left hand and gripping back of head with right hand. Turn head very slowly as far to the left as you can. Hold for count of 20. Keep eyes closed. Don't move arms. Repeat, turning to the right.

Simple spinal twist (1 minute): Sitting, cross right leg over left. Then, while gripping back of chair seat with right hand, cross left arm over right knee and grasp left knee. Slowly twist head and trunk as far to the right as possible. Hold for count of 10. Resume original forward position, holding chair and knee. Relax and repeat once. Next, cross left leg over right, twist to left twice.

Back stretch (1 minute): Sitting toward chair's edge, extend legs outward, bend forward and hold upper calves firmly. Bending elbows outward, pull trunk down and relax all muscles, including neck, so head hangs down. Hold for count of 20. Straighten up slowly, rest a moment, then repeat holding lower calves or ankles.

Result: Fifteen minutes after you complete this set of exercises, you should feel a surge of mental and physical energy.
Source: *Yoga for Personal Living* by Richard L. Hittleman, Warner Books, New York.

How to Relax at the Office

Fully support your body by sitting back in a chair. Breathe in and tighten all the muscles in your body. Feel the tension in your body. Then release your breath, letting go completely. This should eliminate tenseness in all the muscles in your body. Repeat this sequence.

Then breathe in calmly two or three times in long and easy breaths. Resume breathing normally.

Close your eyes and begin relaxing the facial muscles, letting the jaw sag, and relaxing the muscles in the forehead. Feel the relaxation. Relax the neck muscles and then the leg muscles, resting your legs on the floor. Relax the shoulder muscles and finally release the whole body and sit there limp and peaceful and relaxed. Sit there for several minutes, feeling this relaxation and the absence of muscle tension.

After this brief period you will be refreshed and alert. Don't stand up too quickly or you may feel light-headed.

With practice this method should allow a person to relax easily. Use it to relieve tension or stress. Relaxing in tense, stressful situations greatly lessens the chance of becoming emotional when there are problems. Being able to relax and relieve tension conserves energy and produces more work and clearer thinking.

Understanding Your Doctor's Prescription

Doctors commonly use abbreviations for Latin phrases on prescriptions. Some of the most widely used and what they mean: ad lib (*ad libitum*)—take drug freely as needed; a.c. (*ante cibos*)—before meals; b.i.d. (*bis in die*)—twice a day; h.s. (*hora somni*)—at bedtime; p.o. (*per os*) —by mouth; q.4.h. (*quaque 4 hora*)—every 4 hours; q.i.d. (*quater in die*)—4 times a day.

Questions to Ask a Surgeon

To protect against unnecessary surgery, ask the physician important questions beforehand.
• What are the risks?
• What is the mortality rate for this operation?
• What is the likelihood of complications?
• How long will it take to recover?
• Are there ways to treat this condition medically?
• How many people have you seen with similar symptoms who have chosen not to have surgery?
• How many of these operations have you done in the past year?
Caution: Always get a second opinion.

Understanding Hospital Talk

A hospital patient may have considerable difficulty understanding some of the jargon used by nurses and other hospital personnel. Here is what some commonly used terms mean:
NPO: Sign placed by the bed of a patient who is not supposed to get anything to eat or drink.
Emisis basin: Basin brought to patients who are sick to their stomachs.
Ambulate: Take the patient for a walk.
Force fluids: Encourage intake of lots of liquid.
Void: Urinate.
IV: Intravenous.
OOB: Out of bed.
IPPB: Intermittent Positive Pressure Breathing machine to aid breathing.
HS: Medication before sleep.
BP: Blood pressure.
HR: Heart rate.

Before Undergoing a Vasectomy

According to the most recent studies, vasectomies have no effect on the production of testosterone or other hormones. The body still produces both sperm (which is reabsorbed by the body) and seminal fluid (which is ejaculated).

Vasectomies are considered so safe and simple that they're generally performed under local anesthetic in a doctor's office or in a clinic. The doctor makes one or two incisions in the scrotum through which each sperm-carrying tube (*vas deferens*) can be lifted, out, cut, and closed, thus blocking the passage of sperm. The operation takes 20 minutes. Cost: $100-$250 (depending on clinic or physician). The procedure is usually covered by Blue Shield or other private medical insurance. If it is performed on Friday afternoon, most men can go back to work on Monday. Best then to wear an athletic supporter and to avoid heavy labor for a week to ten days. There may be some discomfort for several days. Usually ice packs and aspirin provide all the relief that is needed.

Contraception is still necessary for the first ten to 12 ejaculations after a vasectomy—unless two samples of semen, generally taken a week or two apart, show no sperm.

Reversibility: Vasectomies can be reversed— sometimes. Although major surgery is involved, microsurgical vasovasotomy (reconnecting the tubes) is the technique when remarriage or another life change makes a man decide to father children again. Some doctors claim a 40%-50% success rate on vasectomy reversals (provided the wife is fertile, of course). This figure will probably rise as microsurgical techniques become more sophisticated.

Physical aftereffects:

• Sperm antibodies develop in about 50% of vasectomized men. One type immobilizes sperm. The other causes sperm to agglutinate (clump together). These antibodies may prevent restoration of fertility in men whose vasectomies have been reversed. But it is not yet known for what length of time these sperm antibodies are produced—or under what conditions the body stops producing them.

• Increased cholesterol and atherosclerotic placque. The results of an experiment on monkeys at the Oregon Primate Research Center, which concluded that vasectomies produced increased cholesterol and atherosclerotic plaque, were widely publicized. However, there were only five monkeys in the experimental group and the monkey diet contained twice the cholesterol found in an ordinary human diet. This study will have to be refined and repeated on a much larger scale before any firm conclusions can be drawn. Meanwhile, a low-cholesterol diet may be desirable for vasectomized men.

Source: Association for Voluntary Serilization, 708 Third Ave., New York 10017.

Health Hints

• Before buying vitamins: Check Vitamin A and D dosages, says the *Harvard Medical Health Letter.* Safe limits are 10,000 International Units for A, 400 for D. Signs of overdosage: Irritability, fever, bone pain (Vitamin A); lethargy, loss of appetite, kidney stones, or kidney failure (Vitamin D).

• Vitamin C and aspirin should not be taken together. Studies at the University of Southern Illinois indicate that combined heavy doses produce excessive stomach irritation which could lead to ulcers (especially for those with a history of stomach problems).

• Eye care: Use eyedrops sparingly, especially commercial brands. They relieve redness by constricting blood vessels so eyes will look whiter. If used frequently, varicose veins can develop and eyes will become permanently reddened.

• Contact-lens cautions: Avoid wearing lenses in the barber shop if hair sprays or other irritating vapors are in the air (including fumes from nail polish remover). Don't use any sprays (deodorant, hair, foot) after inserting lenses. Make sure there's no soap or shampoo on fingertips. (2) Wear lenses while shaving to avoid contaminating them with after-shave products applied with the hands.

• The best cold medicine may be no medicine at all. No capsule or pill can cure a cold or the flu. Over-the-counter remedies often prolong the discomfort and hinder the body's own inherent ability to fight off the virus. Recommended: Rest and drink fluids.

Losing Calories Through Sports

Tennis . . . . 210 cal./½ hr.
Bicycling (5 mph) . . . . 120 cal./½ hr.
Football . . . . 270 cal./½ hr.
Golf . . . . 150 cal./½ hr.
Skiing (normal speeds) . . . . . 330-480 cal./½ hr.
Long-distance running . . . . 330 cal./½ hr.
Swimming (less strenuous strokes, such as breaststroke) . . . . 330 cal./½ hr.
Swimming (crawl stroke) . . . . 420 cal./½ hr.
Source: *Take It Off With Frank!* by Dr. Frank Field, William Morrow & Co., New York.

Before You Sign Contract with Health Club

Inspect the club at the time of day you'd be most likely to attend. How crowded are the pool, sauna, exercise rooms? Make certain all facilities that are promised are available. Avoid clubs that require long-term contracts. Once a contract is signed and termination is desired, it's usually possible to avoid liability for the full term of the contract by notifying the club by registered mail, paying for services already rendered and a small cancellation fee. Check local consumer protection agency on rules. Don't be pushed into a hasty decision by a low-price offer. Specials are usually repeated.

Avoid the Morning-After Syndrome

Some hangover discomfort is caused by congeners (toxic chemicals formed during fermentation). Vodka has the lowest congener content, gin next. Blended scotch has four times the congener content of gin. Brandy, rum, and pure malt scotch have six times that amount; bourbon eight times.

Retard the absorption of alcohol by eating before and during drinking (especially foods containing fatty proteins, such as cheeses and milk).

Use water as a mixer. Carbonation speeds the absorption of alcohol.

If you get a hangover anyway, the only known cure is rest, aspirin and time. The endless list of other remedies—ranging from cucumber juice and salt to a Bloody Mary—have more to do with drinking mythology than with medical fact, although according to psychologists who have studied hangovers, if you believe in a cure, it may help.

Setting Personal Priorities

Mid-life crisis often results from confusion about where one is headed, and whether that is really the direction one wants to take. Instead of New Year's resolutions, what's needed is a year-round inventory to identify one's strengths, interests, goals, needs, and priorities. Only with that can you decide whether a decision (such as accepting more job responsibility, travel, or relocation) would be good or bad for you.

Ponder this: To whom do I owe what? How do job-related responsibilities (to stockholders, employees, customers) rank in priority with family responsibilities? Most big jobs preclude giving equal rank to both. Ask: Will I soon regret not spending more time with my family?

Consider responsibilities to yourself. Ask: Do I feel good about my work, the people in my life, myself? Do I waste valuable time and energy on things that don't really matter?

List a half-dozen activities you enjoy doing for pure fun. When is the last time you did them? If it's been too long, something's wrong.

Ask: Is the desire for "bigger, better, more" causing me to work harder without joy? What should I be doing differently in my work to be happier, more productive, less frustrated or bored? The answers will be an adventure in self-discovery.

To find them, examine personal needs (intellectual, emotional, spiritual, financial, and health). List your greatest strengths, the past achievements of which you're proudest, and your future goals.

A pattern will emerge.

Contradictions will become apparent; provide clues to what changes, if any, should be made.

Caution: Beware of unrealistic expectations that add stress. Examples: Trying to please everyone (some call it the formula for failure), and trying to change other people. Neither one can be done. You can only change yourself.

Also, despite media hype, it's rare to have all the good things in life—a luxury home, sports car, world travel, country club, Ivy League schools for the children, job satisfaction, peer approval, and perfect health. That's why priorities are needed.

Source: Professional Practice Consultants, 130 Cuttermill Rd., Great Neck, NY 11022.

PERSONNEL

MANAGEMENT

13 Key Questions for Job Applicants

Recruiting from Within

Screening without Discriminating

Alternatives to Retirement

Wonderful Working Women

The Four-Day Week

Fighting Absenteeism and Lateness

How to Fire with a Clear Conscience

17

PERSONNEL MANAGEMENT

Thirteen Best Questions to Ask Job Applicants

1. What did you do at your last job? What were your responsibilities?

2. What aspects of your last job did you like best? (People are usually prepared to discuss their accomplishments, not their attitudes.)

3. What aspects did you like least? (If these coincide with new job requirements, you immediately know enough to reject the candidate.)

4. Why did you leave your last job? (Watch out for excuses, where the applicant blames other people or circumstances for his own failures.)

5. If you could have made one suggestion to management, what would it have been? (Answer of "I don't know" certainly indicates lack of initiative, probably lack of intelligence and motivation, and not a very good attitude toward work.)

6. What have you done that you're proud of? (No proud accomplishments signals excessive modesty or limited abilities and attitude.)

7. Describe the best boss you ever had. (If the shoe fits, great.)

8. Describe the worst boss you ever had.

9. Would you tell me about the ups and downs of your health in recent years? (Ask, "How's your health?" and they'll always say "Fine.")

10. What do you consider your greatest strength? (If the answer is "good with people" and it's not a people job, there's a problem.)

11. What kinds of things bother you the most? (Again, compare with job realities. If it's a mismatch, better to find out now.)

12. What else should I know about your qualifications; about you? Is there anything else you want to tell me about yourself?

13. What else would you like to know about this job?

When Not to Trust the Test Scores

The most important single fact about the tests given to job candidates today is that business trusts them more than do the test experts.

Managers who hire on the basis of test scores alone are reading more into them than they should. Some things to know before a test is chosen or administered:

Tests are better at identifying desirable and undesirable traits than at predicting overall performance. For instance, a test can tell you Jones is a hard worker who may have trouble getting along with customers. But no test can tell you whether Jones will work out better than the other applicants you're considering. On average, tests are successful only 25% of the time in predicting relative performance of candidates. They're better at predicting how well employees do in training programs than on the job itself.

The first step in using tests profitably is giving the right test for the job. Here are the tests in general use today and what to expect from them:

• I.Q. tests can help you decide whether a candidate is intelligent enough for a demanding job. They can also warn you that the applicant is too smart for a dull job and will easily become bored.

• Work-sample tests (also known as performance tests) are helpful in evaluating typists and production-line workers, but not in choosing salespeople or executives.

• Aptitude tests are a measure of learning ability but do not disclose anything about the applicant's motivation, which is usually more important to know.

• Interest tests give insight into the kind of job an applicant will be happy in: Outdoor work, a desk job, solitary work, dealing with people. Colleges use them to help students choose careers.

• Personality tests are the closest thing to work-sample tests for executives. For instance, they indicate how a candidate will react to stress on the job. Caution: Personality tests of the "pencil and paper" kind, in which an applicant writes down answers to a series of questions, can be superficial and easy to fake, because applicants can figure out which answers will make them rate well. Best personality test is an in-depth psychological interview, a Rorschach (ink-blot) test, or a Thematic Apperception Test. Important: Personality tests were not intended for business purposes. They were designed as diagnostic tools for treating the mentally ill, and can disclose deep aspects of personality such as un-conscious sexual tendencies. Having this kind of information in company records can risk future legal problems for management.

The best approach to testing is intensive—and expensive. Companies like Sears, GE, and Bell Telephone have been experimenting with assessment centers, where groups of 10 to 15 candidates spend four days being evaluated. They are given a battery of tests plus some typical management problems to work on together. Experienced managers observe them and measure behavior rather than just personality or aptitude. Early findings indicate a strong correlation between assessment-center predictions and later performance on the job.

If your options are restricted to tests outside of assessment centers, by all means use them as a guide in making personnel decisions, not as the sole hiring basis.

Fringe benefits of testing: It can uncover qualifications and talents that may not be detected by interviewers or application forms. And it can compensate for prejudices of the interviewer and provide an impartial look at applicant's potential.

Source: *Managing Human Resources,* by Dr. Leonard R. Sayles and George Straus, Prentice-Hall, Englewood Cliffs, NJ.

Getting Honest Opinions from a Previous Employer

Many companies clam up in fear of legal repercussions. Four questions that may bring an informative response:

• Why did the employee leave the job?

• Would you rehire? (A pause before "yes" answer says more than words.)

• How would you rate the candidate in comparison with other candidates as to (whatever quality is important to caller)?

• When an answer sounds deliberately ambiguous: Why did you say that?

When the shoe is on the other foot, protect against lawsuits by routing queries about former workers to the personnel department. Don't worry that prospective employer won't be forewarned. Personnel department's terseness can be a clue that employee was less than satisfactory. Veterans in personnel work understand each other's tone and language.

Checking on Candidates for Top-Level Jobs

Top-level recruiting mistakes too often occur because reference checking is not given serious attention once the company thinks it has found a qualified candidate.

Instead, use the reference check to qualify the candidate, assess strengths and weaknesses, and project how they seem to mesh with company objectives. This can be more important than merely substantiating information on previous career and education.

The same person who interviews the candidate should conduct the reference audit, so the quality and tone of response can be tracked. Telephone queries are better than letters. Questions to ask:

• What were the applicant's responsibilities in order of importance?

• How would you rate the quality and volume of his/her work?

• How would you describe the candidate's general attitude?

• How would you characterize the relationship between the candidate and his/her staff?

• How well did the candidate work with other people?

• What are the candidate's strengths and outstanding successes?

• Was the candidate involved in any significant failures?

• What was found to be the most effective way to motivate the person?

• How would you compare the candidate's performance with that of others with similar responsibilities?

• How would you describe the candidate's success in training, developing, and motivating subordinates?

• What could he or she have done to produce even better results?

• What company did the applicant work for prior to joining yours and after leaving?

• What does he or she need to do for continued professional growth and development?
Source: Peter A. Rabinowitz, vice president of Bartholdi & Co., executive recruiters, in *The Personnel Administrator,* 30 Park Dr., Berea, OH 44017.

How to Deal with a Specialized Executive Recruiter

If a company doesn't do regular work with a recruiter in a special field, it should seek advice from larger companies in the field that may include customers or suppliers. Ask for at least two or three names of search firms the source has had good experiences with.

Interview a representative of each of the search firms that are being considered for the assignment. Meet the person who will head the search effort rather than the head of the firm or the outside contact person.

• Pay careful attention to the kind of questions they ask. If you are looking for a specialist rather than a generalist firm to do the search, they should ask sophisticated, detailed questions.

• Ask the recruiters the obvious questions: Whom they've worked for in the past, names of people as reference at other client companies, outstanding successes.

• Also ask if they have had assigments from management consulting firms that are acting on behalf of corporate clients. Those are usually evidence of top performance ability.

• Ask about instances of failures, and explanations of them. No firm hits every time. If recruiter claims a 100% success record, look for another.

• Have the prospective recruiter describe how the firm would approach this particular assignment. A specialist firm should make every effort, even at this preliminary stage, to get into details of the job.

• Inquire about their sources. Do they make use of a "kitchen cabinet," an informal group of contacts in the particular field that can provide them with leads to the right people for the client? No firm, no matter how expert, has enough in-house knowledge to handle every assignment.

Important: The recruiter should talk about salary early in the discussions. That's an indication that the recruiter is in close touch with what's going on in the field now.

Source: Herbert Halbrecht, Halbrecht Associates, 695 Summer St., Stamford, CT 06901.

Recruiting from Within

Considerations in developing a program to solicit new employees through referrals from present employees:

• Announce job openings to employees first. Give them a chance to apply on their own. Once the opening is known, the request for referrals should be made.

• Establish a definite policy on hiring (or not hiring) relatives of employees. Publicize and uphold it. Possibilities: (1) Allowing all relatives beyond immediate family (parent, spouse, child). (2) Allowing any relative but in different departments. (3) Requiring transfer of one if two people in the same department marry.

• If a bonus is to be paid for referrals, the amount and method should be uniform. It should be publicized in company newsletter, on bulletin boards, etc.

Advantages of employee referral program: No employment agency fees or advertising expense. Disadvantage: Possible unpleasantness that might result from the dismissal or rejection of a referred applicant.

Source: *Office Administrative Handbook,* edited by Clark Fetridge and Robert S. Minor, The Dartnell Corp., 4660 Ravenswood Ave., Chicago 60640.

What a Job Description Should Cover

Many organizations operate with either inadequate job descriptions or none at all. But a well-constructed job description simplifies perfor-

mance appraisals, prevents supervisors from making judgments based on inadequate measurements, and even helps orient new workers on the job.

Key components of a good job description:

• Position, title, and classification.

• Description of proposed duties and responsibilities. (Might include activities organized according to frequency.)

• List of the skills and special knowledge necessary for the job.

• Outline of working conditions, especially any that are out of the ordinary.

• Description of the type of supervision that the position requires and who gives it. Also, to what extent there is supervision of others.

• Qualifications: Education and work experience required.

• Full- or part-time. Permanent or temporary.

• Salary grades. Allowances.

• Nature of contact with other groups, such as the general public, other departments, government officials.

• Type of personal judgment, initiative, resourcefulness required.

Source: Larry G. McDougle, Indiana University of Kikomo, in *Supervisory Management,* 135 West 50 St., New York 10020.

Probationary Periods

If a newly hired employee isn't working out, don't let him/her stay beyond the probationary period (usually 30 days) unless it's clearly understood that you are extending the trial period, not conferring job security.

The difference: Under union contracts, an employee with seniority can't be fired without just cause. And if the employee can show that the work after the probationary period was no worse than it was before, the company is likely to lose the case in arbitration.

On the other hand, when dealing with a slow learner who might make good with a little more time, the union and the individual might agree to an extension of the probation period as an alternative to immediate dismissal.

If it's decided to dismiss a probationary em-

247

ployee, don't go into too many details about it. Normally, a dispute about the suitability of such an employee isn't subject to arbitration. However, if facts alleged are questionable, especially if they affect the employee's future employability, it may be necessary to prove them.

Screening Without Discriminating

Interviewing job applicants (especially women and minorities) without violating EEOC guidelines can be tricky. The questions you can't ask may seem to outnumber those you can. How to handle the interview:

Avoid assumptions. Instead of the leading question, "Your husband is probably tied down to his job here, isn't he?" ask "Could you relocate, given adequate notice?"

Substitute direct, job-related questions for those aimed at eliciting personal information that can no longer be asked. Example: "Do travel and working overtime present any problems for you?" instead of "Do you have children?" You may uncover more information about the applicant's personal life. There might, for example, be an elderly parent who would pose problems.

If the question doesn't fit all applicants being interviewed, don't ask it.

Don't set qualifications too high for a particular job. Requiring a high school diploma for a laboring job invites a complaint of race discrimination on the grounds that more minority people drop out of school.

Watch your employment agency carefully. Company can be held responsible if the agency discriminates.

The lack of previous job or educational background can also make evaluation difficult. Consider less obvious indicators of success. Has the applicant held volunteer posts? Have any of them involved leadership positions? What social or financial handicaps has the applicant overcome? Do his or her questions indicate curiosity and interest? How well does the applicant grasp what you're saying? How much extra training or education would the applicant need to qualify?

Unintentional Violation of Antidiscrimination Laws

Good intentions and affirmative action programs notwithstanding, it's easy to fall into traps that can lead to full-scale government investigations, class-action lawsuits, and big settlements to "wronged" employees for back pay.

Biggest pitfalls: Outmoded job descriptions, discriminatory pay scales, and hiring/promotion standards that stem from them. Government investigators looking into alleged equal pay law violations don't go by company descriptions. They interview employees on the job, decide whether the plaintiff(s) actually do substantially the same job as higher-paid employees in another job category at least 80% of the time. The company should check on this at frequent intervals.

In addition, you should be sure to take the the following steps:

• Update descriptions (and adjust pay scales) at least once a year. Spell out each job individually as it's actually being done, focusing on functions, percentage of working time spent on each, quantitative and qualitative output and performance requirements (units produced, documents typed, employees supervised, etc.).

• Avoid lumping "similar" but different jobs in a single category. Machine jobs vary substantially depending on equipment used. Secretaries don't just "handle" correspondence; they type form letters, take dictation, or answer routine correspondence themselves.

• Test hiring and promotion qualifications for relevance to the job as it's now being done.

Defense Against Unjust Discrimination Charges

Possible charge against the company: The percentage of women (or minority group) workers hired or promoted is less than the percentage of such people in the community from which the company hires.

Facts: The relevant community from which company hires can be the area immediately surrounding it, the city as a whole, the standard metropolitan statistical area, or the nation (rare, except for positions such as nuclear scientist, etc.). The government investigator may choose the area that has the largest percentage of the minority being examined, to build the strongest possible case against the company.

Defense: Employer should retain counsel skilled in constructing statistical marketing sample surveys. These same statistics can be used to show what percentage of employees live within that radius (three miles, five, ten or more) compared with racial or other breakdown of population in those areas. In some cases, just challenging the Office of Federal Contract Compliance Programs (OFCCP) figures as being loaded may be sufficient to halt the investigation.

Example: Theoretically, if a company had a facility in Grosse Pointe Farms (a wealthy Detroit suburb which is virtually 100% white) and could show that its employees all lived within a three-mile radius, the company could argue that it was in compliance. It was hiring only from the immediate geographic area and the racial makeup of its employees was an accurate reflection of the racial makeup of the area. Employer's defense: We can't hire from Detroit. People won't drive 27 miles to make $4 an hour.

Charge by investigator: Since employer has no women or minority employees, it obviously hasn't made sufficient effort to recruit them.

Defense No. 1. Employer shows that its work force has been static. Government cannot force employer to fire employees and replace them with minorities. The employer does have to agree that when job openings do occur, minority candidates will be considered in an effort to reach goals set forth in an affirmative action program.

Defense No. 2. The company shows that it has already actively made all efforts the OFCCP would have asked it to make, so it is in compliance. For instance:

• The company attempted to recruit for open positions through special interest groups, such as National Organization for Women, women's neighborhood groups, National Association for the Advancement of Colored People, and the state employment service. But no qualified women or minority candidates applied.

• The company advertises jobs regularly in minority newpapers. (This may be sufficient, regardless of who is subsequently hired.)

Important: Government can't require employer to change its work methods, such as suggesting that employees in the warehouse have to lift only 50 pounds instead of 100. (Then it would be able to hire more women.) Employer doesn't have to change any bona fide qualifications for the job so that more women or minorities would be eligible to be hired.

Source: Avrum M. Goldberg, Wald, Harkrader & Ross, 320 19 St., N.W., Washington, DC 20036.

Treatment of Pregnant Workers

The benefits that employees can claim under the Pregnancy Discrimination Act of 1979 are sweeping enough to require that managers be ready to field workers' questions. The act's major points:

• If the woman is temporarily unable to do part of her customary job (lifting, for instance), she must be excused from those chores. But that is only to the extent that other temporarily incapacitated employees, male or female, would be shown consideration. Critical issue: Can she perform the major functions of her job?

• The pregnant worker cannot be singled out for discriminatory treatment. A pregnant employee who asks for leave because she is not able to work does not have to submit medical proof unless that is a common company requirement for other disability leaves.

• There can be no automatic rule about how long after delivery a woman must wait before returning to work. Her job must be held open unless she stated in advance that she did not intend to resume work.

• Seniority and benefit accrual may be no less than for employees, male or female, on any other disability leave. For example, if time on leave is counted as time worked to compute vacation eligibility, it must also be counted for women on pregnancy leave.

• It is unlawful to require women taking leave to use up their vacation time first.

• State laws that happen to be less advantageous to women cannot be used to get around the federal law.

• The law does not require the employer to pay the cost of medical coverage for dependents of employees. But if a plan covers dependents for other medical conditions, it must also provide maternity coverage for wives of employees.

• Maximum recoverable amounts may be stated, provided payment for other medical or disabling conditions are similarly limited.

• A new benefit plan that excludes pre-existing conditions may also exclude pregnancies that occurred before adoption of the plan.

• Part of the cost of pregnancy coverage may be levied against the employee if that is the way the plan was designed. Thus, all employees pay part of the cost for all types of disabilities.

• Health insurance plans need not include abortion services unless the life of the woman would be endangered if the fetus were carried to term. However, medical services to correct difficulties resulting from any abortion must be included.

• Note: All leave, work assignment, and medical benefit questions must be resolved without regard to the female employee's marital status.

Wonderful Working Women

Government anti-bias laws are not the only reason to hire more female employees, recent survey findings show.

• The average male employee spends 52 minutes (11%) of each working day not working (coffee breaks, non-official conversation, lunch time beyond one hour) compared to 35 minutes (8%) for females.

• A "work effort scale" of energy expended at the job shows female employees' effort is 112% that of male employees. Single women, part-time employees, union members, and professionals rank highest.

The superiority of female employees didn't extend to wage rates, though. Average female worker's $4.34 hourly wage compares with $7 per hour for male employees.

Source: *Institute for Social Research Newsletter.*

Beliefs Managers Hold About Older Workers

Many managers believe the negative generalizations about older workers—and thus lose many opportunities. Many myths uncovered:

The young-tiger myth derives from belief that 30-year-old has more energy to burn and generally fiercer ambition. It overlooks the fact that an older worker may be able to focus energies better, and that there are other motivations besides the drive to get ahead.

The empty-vessel myth presumes that older workers have gone stale and are rigid and dogmatic, while 30-year-olds are receptive to new ideas, adaptable, etc. Actually, some research suggests that many employees begin to develop only after they go through a mid-life crisis. It may be simply a rough period passed through on the way to wisdom.

The resistance-to-change myth assumes that young people are less resistant and more receptive, but it's really an individual thing. With the benefit of experience, an older worker may be in the best position to suggest changes, or at least evaluate them.

The lack-of-creativity myth expects that the younger person will be more innovative and creative. Those expectations can tend to become self-fulfilling if the older worker's ideas are systematically ignored or not solicited.

Source: Benson Rosen of the University of North Carolina, in *The Effective Manager,* Warren, Gorham & Lamont, 210 South St., Boston 02111.

Alternatives to Forced Retirement

The extension of mandatory retirement to age 70 raises the question of how to deal with those older workers who may want to slow down but aren't yet ready to stop entirely. Some ways to mix thoughtful management with continued profit on salaries paid to the over-65s:

• Reduce the work week to help phase older employee into retirement. Salary can be reduced proportionately. It is important, though, that full benefits are paid when the worker does retire.

• Longer vacations, perhaps six to eight weeks per year. It sounds expensive, but may be worth it if overall productivity is at least maintained for the rest of the year.

• Unpaid or reduced-pay leaves and sabbaticals. Employee can spend time developing retirement interests, working in government exchange programs, teaching, getting involved in community work, etc. Success may prompt employee to retire early on a voluntary basis.

• Part-time status, possibly with two workers splitting what was formerly one job. Pay is reduced accordingly and the company also saves on fringes.

• Trial retirement with guarantee of re-employment, on a year-to-year contract basis. Another good method to help employee voluntarily decide to leave early.

• Retraining for a less demanding job in the company. This is often welcomed by a worker who's aware of slowing down; he picks up the new job more quickly than someone who doesn't know the company.

• Reducing the scope of current job and using the employee to train a replacement. For example, cut the salesperson's territory in half and bring in a successor candidate to take over the other half.

• Reassign the employee to special projects, troubleshooting, studies, training programs. Select a project that makes good use of the worker's accumulated experience.

Source: *The End of Mandatory Retirement: Implications for Management* by James L. Walker and Harriet L. Lazer, John Wiley & Sons, Inc., Somerset, NJ 08873.

Don't Hire Problems

A job applicant's finances are the company's business. The impact of a worker's money problems can extend beyond the individual job performance; it could affect company security.

What to look for during job interviews and pre-employment screening:

• Habitual borrowing from more than one personal finance company. A person who has borrowed from two personal loan companies has almost certainly failed to tell one of them the truth about unpledged assets.

• Monthly loan and time payments equal to more than half of visible monthly earnings. Anyone who is paying out more than 50% of income in time payments must often moonlight to meet those obligations. A second job often dilutes performance and can lead to on-the-job fatigue that causes accidents. And needed additional income could come from bribes or thefts.

At the least, too much continual debt not connected to some emergency need can indicate a lack of judgment.

But a poor credit rating should be judged in the light of recent information. Many young people get into heavy debt at least once in their lives because of lack of experience and today's easy access to credit. This often is not a continuing problem.

Important: The law requires that a job applicant give consent to a credit check. A bonding company will do a check if bond is required.

Source: *Managing Employee Honesty* by Charles R. Carson, Security World Publishing Co., Inc., Los Angeles 90034.

When Incentive Rates Should Be Examined

Make an hour-by-hour tally of production from each machine. If results show a consistent drop-off in production during last working hours of a shift, something may be wrong with base rates and incentives.

What one study showed: Employees slowed down as they approached base-rate obligations. Some believed they were not expected to produce more than the minimum during a shift. Others followed the lead of a few who expressed dissatisfaction with the incentive system by holding down production.

The solution: A revised incentive plan that allowed workers to earn 20% over base rates with normal effort. The slight increase in wage costs was more than compensated for by reduction in per-unit costs attributed to overhead.

Required Government Posters

Federal posters that are required to be displayed:

• Age discrimination poster for employers of 20 or more who are engaged in interstate commerce.

• Equal Employment Opportunity poster. Employers of 15 or more employees and government contractors and subcontractors regardless of number of employees.

• Fair Labor Standards Act poster. All employers engaged in interstate commerce.

• Handicapped discrimination poster. All government contractors and subs with contracts over $2,500.

• Occupational Safety and Health poster. All employers in industries affecting interstate commerce.

• Annual Summary OSHA Form 102. Employers of 11 or more. Posted only during month of February. Summarizes preceding year's occupational illnesses and injuries.

• Walsh-Healy Public Contracts Act Poster. Employers whose workers are directly involved in providing more than $10,000 worth of government-contracted goods or services.

• Davis-Bacon Public Contracts Act: Specifications of work contract as required by construction contractors for federally financed construction.

In addition, most states have poster requirements, too. Generally, they require posters on unemployment compensation, labor laws, minimum wages, workers compensation, fair employment practices.

Source: Columbus Industrial Association, 1515 West Lane Ave., Columbus, OH 43221.

Internal Communications

How to get more morale mileage and better understanding of company policies from the employee newsletter:

• Aim the publication at an external audience (shareholders, community leaders, elected officials, etc.), but disseminate it to employees and their families. Mail it to the home, giving the whole family the feeling of being made privy to information that would ordinarily be given only to officials or opinion makers. Include discussions of substance on economic trends.

Other topics of interest: New product development, new plant and equipment, sales and purchasing problems, how various departments function, how you're countering your competition, the company's role in community or regional economic development.

• Use traditional columns about personal lives of employees (promotions, births, marriages, etc.). And don't forget to include "how-to" and guideline stories geared to employees as consumers.

There are other measures that the company can take to make employees feel they have a stake in the business:

• Write and distribute an Annual Report to Employees (together with copies of your regular corporate annual report), informing them of the achievements you and they have made in the past year.

• Hold an annual jobholders' meeting at which the people who invest their working lives in the company can get an accounting of the progress of the business.

You Can Pay Students Less Than the Minimum Wage

Many businesses can get around the minimum wage law. Students can work as much as 20 hours a week at 85% of the minimum wage ($2.65/hr.), and as much as 40 hours a week during vacation periods.

A one-page form must be submitted to the government for the exemption to be allowed. Also, it must be shown that older workers won't be eliminated. Details may be obtained from local Labor Department offices or Wage & Hour Division, Labor Department, 200 Constitution Ave., N.W., Washington, DC 20210.

Trading Raises for Increased Time Off

Consider adding to vacation time as an alternative to a pay raise. Recent study shows that more time off may satisfy employees more than a small raise, and work out better for employer, too. (An additional week of vacation is equivalent to a 1.7% raise.)

In general, however, employees favor time off over money only when free time is offered in substantial chunks. A few minutes less work each day has little appeal. But additional days of annual vacation, paid holidays, or extended weekends (Monday mornings or Friday afternoons) are meaningful.

The trade-off won't work when vacations become too long. The preference reverts to money. Very few of those who were entitled to six weeks of vacation wanted the time all at once. The majority preferred three two-week periods.

But it isn't wise to trade off time for money too often. The result would be a company wage scale that compares unfavorably with what similar employees are earning elsewhere. The fact that the company gives long paid vacations would probably not overcome propaganda of a union organizer who accuses the company of paying less than the going rate.

Source: Study by Fred Best, Research Associate, National Commission for Manpower Policy, in *Monthly Labor Review,* U.S. Dept. of Labor, 200 Constitution Ave., N.W., Washington, DC 20210.

Special Pay Problems

The basic trouble is that benefits intended to maintain customary earnings come to be expected as a kind of bonus. The usual reason: Lax administration. How to control costs:

• Holiday pay. Limit it to those currently on the payroll. Exclude employees on leave of absence or temporary layoff. Problem: If workers are laid off just before a holiday they'll consider it a trick to avoid holiday pay. Solution: Pay for holidays that come soon after the layoff.

• Bereavement pay. The original idea was to compensate employees for time lost from work because of a death in the family. But careless application has resulted in the bereavement boodle: Paying for several extra days. Supervisor should be advised to tighten up here.

• Jury duty pay. Most companies pay only the difference between what employees get for court service and their regular salary. But management might also require that the employee show up for work on days when the jury is excused early. It may not seem to involve much money, but the rule that employees must work as much as they can sets the right tone for good personnel management.

• Sick leave pay. Perhaps the most costly of these benefits. Supervisors sometimes look the other way when employees claim sick pay to cover absence for other reasons. Best advice: A thoughtful (and financially able) employer might give a worker time off for such matters as court appearances, taking care of marital problems, etc. Such a policy would discourage the notion that sick leave pay is a benefit to be taken whether or not the worker is sick.

• Overtime distribution errors. They should be made good, whenever possible, by giving the bypassed employee the next overtime assignment, not by paying for time not worked. Exception: When overtime is erroneously offered to a person who does not normally share the available work, the bypassed worker may be entitled to money. If supervisors know their errors are costly, they won't make as many.

• Reporting pay (usually four hours). Commonly given to employees who show up and find no work available because of circumstances beyond management's control. The cost can be minimized by requiring employees to fill the time by working outside their regular classifications. Those who refuse the substitute work would forfeit reporting pay.

• Year-end bonuses. Should be given, where possible, as gifts, not as part of wages. If the bonus amount is based on hourly rates or the number of hours worked during the preceding year, it will come to be thought of as a form of wages, no matter what management calls it. A fixed sum for broad categories of work is the safer way. An accompanying note should explain that the decision was for that year alone, without implication for the future (when the profit picture might be different).

• Medical insurance premiums. Employees on extended leaves or on layoffs should pay them, subject to reimbursement by the company when they come back to work (if the company usually pays the premiums). This would avoid having to make payments for those who take other jobs and don't return.

Avoiding Extra Pay

Work during lunch does not necessarily require that a worker be paid overtime, "unless the employee has performed substantial job-related duties," according to a court decision. The key in the interpretation of the Fair Labor Standards Act is the magnitude and necessity of the off-duty chores. However, should an employee regularly forego all or part of lunchtime, overtime must be paid.

The law requires employees to be paid if they must stay at home, available to be called to work for a possible emergency. In these cases, it's better to ask employees to leave the telephone numbers where they can be reached if they leave home. Then the company doesn't have to pay them unless it calls them in.

Religious Time Off for Employees

The Civil Rights Act requires that employers make "reasonable accommodation" to the needs of the worker who, out of religious conviction, refuses to work certain days.

The old EEOC guideline said companies must yield unless it would cause "undue hardship." The Supreme Court has since strengthened managements's hand by saying in effect that employers need not sustain more than "minimal costs."

Strategies: If your only problem is with an occasional employee, try transferring him to a job that doesn't require weekend work. Or let him swap Saturday or Sunday shift with someone else. The occasional extra overtime cost to the company probably would be defined as "minimal." Avoid problems by making the switch.

But the burden shifts to the employees if there are so many of them who require accommodation to religious demands that costs to the company are more than minimal. The company can insist that workers who refuse to work Saturday or Sunday pay the premium-pay tab that would be necessary to get replacements.

Caution for the unionized employer: This advice doesn't hold for the company operating under a union contract. It would be an unfair labor practice under the NLRA to bargain separately with some employees to bypass contractual obligations that the employer pay time-and-a-half for weekend work. Seniority rights might also make transfers to other jobs impossible.

Questions to Ask Before Authorizing Overtime

Excessive overtime may be a tip-off to such plant problems as:

• Inadequate equipment. Consider investing in replacement or new machinery with greater capacity. Results to expect: Greater productivity and lower wage costs.

• Lax worker supervision. Look for this possibility when a particular group of employees consistently works overtime to meet normal output demands.

• Bad production scheduling could be the problem if a bottleneck area of production slows an entire operation.

• Need for another shift. Heavy and regular use of overtime may signal a real need for another shift. That would require a full supervisory crew and probably higher wages to compensate for less attractive hours. Make a detailed cost-benefit analysis to use as a guide before decision is made.

• Evaluate profitability of each product line. Some may not make enough money to make production at overtime rates worthwhile.

When Overtime Makes Sense

If overtime allows the company to meet substantial growth in demand and, at the same time, spread overhead over more units, it can still mean larger total profits despite lower margins. Possible added benefit: Overtime provides opportunity for volume purchases of raw materials or components at quantity discounts.

When to use overtime:

• For seasonal business. Allows use of a steady, trained work force instead of costly hiring and firing to staff peak periods.

• To avoid a second or third shift.

Cautions:

• Watch out for fatigue. Costs per unit can skyrocket as employees become overtired and output per worker declines. Keep a sharp eye on overall product costs.

• Establish an overtime policy and put it in writing for distribution to all employees. This will minimize disputes and help gain their cooperation. Note: If unionized, don't forget to confer with union representatives before announcing overtime policy.

Special values: Overtime provides an added source of compensation for regular workers. It helps to make up for low base wages and can aid in recruiting or keeping skilled workers. Another advantage: It can be eliminated in hard times.

Pros and Cons of Flexitime and Four-Day Week

Before plunging into the uncharted waters of alternate work schedules, be aware of some of the pros and cons.

Basic appeal to employees: It gives them more control over their lives.

From employer's point of view: It offers potential of reducing absenteeism, tardiness, and turnover, as well as improving morale and productivity.

Most common schedule rearrangements:

• Flexitime: Allows employees to choose, within limits, hours they will work. Usually scheduled around a core of common work time (say 9-3, or 9-12 and 1-3) when everyone is on tap. To fill out the eight hours, employee can come in early or stay late.

Lunch breaks can either be fixed or converted into flexible hours. Flexitime programs put great emphasis on role of supervisor, who must see that previous production standards are met and there is no falloff in productivity. When all goes well, supervisor and group exercise ingenuity in figuring out how to do the best job for employer with maximum flexibility for employees.

Employer benefits: Eliminates need for short-term absences and tardiness. Facility staffed over greater period of time without increases in overtime pay. Makes it easier to recruit good, high-quality workers.

Warning: Flexitime may raise collective bargaining issues, e.g., overtime pay (many contracts specify hours of the day beyond which overtime or night differentials apply), job classification (work group members probably will have to perform tasks falling outside scope of their strict job classification to get the work out), jury duty, voting time, minor illness. There is a question how each of these should be handled under Flexitime.

• Four-day, 40-hour week: Popular with unions, since it is seen as means to creating more jobs. Also popular with many employees, who vastly favor a three-day weekend (Friday is preferred day off).

Still, the four-day week is definitely not for everyone. Mothers don't like longer days, even if they are fewer in number. The four-day week is also not successful where work is too physically exhausting to permit ten-hour days. The four-day week is most successful in firms with high start-up and shut-down costs. It may gain momentum as more companies adopt it; a major objection of employees is that their schedule is different from the rest of the world's.

• Flexitime combined with four-day week: Still a new concept, but adoption of one in no way precludes adoption of the other. A creative Flexitime plan can permit optional four-day weeks by (1) allowing people to work extra "credit" hours on some days, and (2) having no required core hours on Fridays (or Mondays).

Results of Four-Day Week in 143 Companies

	Increased	Decreased	No Change
Costs	11%	38%	51%
Production	62	3	35
Profits	51	4	45

Main benefits: Improved employee relations (69% of companies, no change for 31%), reduced absenteeism, easier recruiting. Major disadvantage: The changeover made it more difficult to schedule work.

Source: American Management Associations, 135 W. 50 St., New York 10020.

Fighting Absenteeism and Lateness

• Insist that the worker talk to a supervisor when calling in sick. Don't permit leaving messages with a co-worker or secretary.

• One minute after starting time, have supervisor collect and hold all time cards that aren't punched yet, so the late worker can't avoid confronting his boss.

• When a worker is hired, tell him attendance record is on first page of his personnel file, and show it to him. Tell him, "That's the first thing we look at when we are considering raises and promotions."

• Don't say that workers absent more than X days will be disciplined—that practically invites them to miss one day less than that number.

• One company made Monday its payday, found a dramatic decline in Monday morning sick calls and stretched weekends.

Weather-Related Emergencies

Increased long-distance busing of school children may result in more plant and office absenteeism in the snow belt in winter.

Women with school-age children tend to stay home from work when schools close. This is something to think about if a decision has to be made about operating during a storm and the company work force consists mostly of women.

It's customary to ask radio stations to announce plant closings. But don't limit announcements to one or two big local stations. Minority employees often listen to ethnic stations. Failure to get word of a plant closing to them in time may obligate the company to pay workers just for reporting in.

Overstayed Lunch, Coffee Breaks

If employees are returning late from coffee and lunch breaks, encourage them to stay on the premises by making the lunchroom more attractive. And make the food in the vending machines appetizing.

But don't expect it to work if the improvements are made without consulting the workers. You might find that what attracted your employees to the luncheonette down the block wasn't the food but the atmosphere of freedom from the work environment.

When one company faced this problem, management consulted with the workers and found out that they would like an area cleared outside the plant, but still on company premises, where workers could throw a ball around or just chew the fat. They wanted at least the illusion of being away from work. It was easy to comply with the suggestion, and the problem was solved.

Sick-Leave Plans That Discourage Malingering

Paid sick leave should be thought of as income maintenance during occasional periods of illness. Long-term absence due to chronic conditions or serious physical disorders should be covered by insured plans that begin when paid sick leave is no longer available.

256

Recommendation: Eligibility should accumulate at the rate of about a day a month. The employee should be permitted to carry over unused sick leave from year to year, until 30 days are "in the bank." If accumulation is not permitted, workers will be tempted to call in sick whether ill or not, just to prevent the time from going to waste. And accumulation is a reward for long service.

Absences due to industrial accidents usually do not count against allowable sick leave. They're covered by Workmen's Compensation and other insured plans.

No matter how the plan is designed, some employees will use an occasional day of "sick leave" to take care of personal business. It may be better to permit limited use of sick leave for such personal business than to try to forbid it altogether. One way: After an employee has accumulated ten sick leave days, he may be permitted to use up to three for personal business when cleared in advance with supervision.

Advantages: Coordination of sick leave with personal leave rewards the employee with a good record. Moreover, it helps overcome the inclination of foremen and supervisors to overlook dissembling when they think the sick leave policy is too harsh. Limited use of sick leave for personal business may also help curb absenteeism. Reason: Leave is accumulated only during a month of perfect attendance on all perfect workdays. However: Personal leave time drawn from the sick leave bank cannot be added to vacations.

Verification is always a problem. It's not feasible to expect an employee to furnish proof of a one- or two-day illness. But a sick leave plan might contain a statement reserving the right of the management to ask for documentation after an employee has been out sick ten days in any calendar year. Note: Employers have the right to request verification at any point, with or without explicit warning. But a statement expressing an intention to question heavy use of sick leave sets a proper tone. It may also serve to dissuade would-be malingerers.

Record-keeping is important, too, not only to make sure employees are credited with allowable sick leave, but to pinpoint problems. Employees who never have sick leave to carry over from one year to the next may need counseling or prod-

ding. The formal sick leave plan should allow room for special consideration, on a case-by-case basis, if a long-service employee needs help after using up accumulated paid leave.

Source: Morris Stone, retired vice president, American Arbitration Association.

Six Ways to Reduce Workers' Compensation Costs

Important savings are possible on workers' compensation for employers who monitor claims. Premiums are set for each job classification by state agencies, so an employer can't change the basic rate. But the rate can be modified by the claims experience of the individual company. Some companies pay as much as one-third less than the basic rates. Others pay 50% more.

A common but wrong management policy is to put all claims through without question, sometimes because of union pressure. As a result, word gets around the company. Employees are tempted to claim compensation for injury that happens off the job.

What employers should do:

• Carefully investigate any claimed injury not verified by a supervisor. Especially suspicious: The worker does not report the injury until the next day.

• When the worker reports to medical unit, have the nurse take careful notes of when and how he was hurt. If a different version is told later to supervisor, or to a compensation referee, there's a better chance of getting the claim denied or the percentage of disability reduced.

• Challenge all questionable claims. Tell the worker the company won't put in the claim and will contest it if the worker pursues it himself. Be sure to appear at the hearing. Even if the worker wins, the grapevine spreads word that the company isn't a pushover. A deterrent effect is more important than the result of an individual case.

Make sure the insurance company diligently investigates all claims and rejects doubtful ones.

An aggressive safety program can also keep

257

claims down, with the active participation (not only lip service) of top management.

Appoint a management safety committee for each facility to review serious lost-time accidents, determine how they could have been prevented.
Source: Harold V. Hodnick, safety consultant, Reed, Shaw, Stenhouse, Inc., 3 Embarcadero Center, San Francisco 94111.

Exit Interview Technique

An essential element, but one missing from employee exit interviews: Honest feedback from the employee on what went wrong.

One aid: Write possible problem areas on index cards, one to each card. Cover job security, career advancement possibilities, training, relationship with supervisor, fair performance reviews, productive working environment, fringe benefits, clarity of responsibilities, and feeling of appreciation.

Ask the departing employee to place the cards in three piles, one for areas in which the company is strong, another for weak areas, and the third for partly successful. The proven advantages to this tactic: Employees are usually more willing to stack cards than to answer long, involved written questionnaires or oral inquiry. The interviewer can then explore areas as indicated by the card stacks.
Source: Martin Hills, Schering-Plough, Switzerland, in *Personnel Journal,* 1131 Olympic Blvd., Santa Monica, CA 90404.

How to Fire with a Clear Conscience

An employee should never be surprised at being fired. If need be, err on the side of painstaking deliberation rather than excessive haste.

Never fire someone in anger. Management should be satisfied that (a) training has been complete and clearly understood, (b) employee performance is unsatisfactory with very little chance of improvement, and (c) the employee

can't be salvaged by transfer to another job or another department.

If the best judgement is to fire, make a clean break. Keep the exit interview short (five to seven minutes). Be direct (indicate flatly that the job still isn't being done satisfactorily). Make the dismissal effective immediately. There is little to be gained by letting him stay around long. (A depressed or disgruntled employee can't work effectively. He also demoralizes others.) Refuse to be sidetracked into reconsidering or rehashing past errors.

Orient interview toward the employee's future. Indicate your respect for his special talents, the kind of position or environment in which you think he'd succeed. Encourage him to start job-hunting immediately. And offer such job-hunting assistance as can reasonably be provided.

Be generous with severance pay (normally, one week per six months' employment for creative, executive, professional staff).

Time the dismissal for late Friday afternoon so co-workers will have left and the employee can clear out without an audience. Any money due the employee (severance, unused vacation or sick pay) should be given at the end of that interview.

A good way to start the actual firing: "As you know from past conversations, we have certain job standards that have to be met. As I've mentioned from time to time over the past few weeks, you haven't been able to meet those standards. I don't believe it's because of any lack of effort on your part. But we're going to have to terminate your service. I really regret that. I wanted it to work out just as much as you did. But it hasn't, and we have to face up to reality. Here's your final check. This should give you a continuation of income until you find another job."

Using Independent Contractors Instead of Hiring Staff

Employers can realize important savings by using independent contractors rather than employees for the right kind of jobs. An independent contractor might cost 12%-15% less than an employee. No Social Security and no unemployment taxes have to be paid. And no medical insurance, vacations, or other fringe benefits.

But be very careful. IRS considers the use of independent contractors to be a tax loophole and it may claim that they are really employees. In that case, the employer could be liable for withholding taxes that had never been withheld, and for other payroll taxes, interest, and penalties.

The crucial test is control. If the employer closely supervises what the worker does and how and when he does it, then he is an employee. But if the person is free to do the work his own way on his own schedule, and if he is paid for the result rather than on an hourly, daily, or weekly basis, then he's probably a legitimate independent contractor.

Other factors supporting independent contractor status:

• The worker provides the tools, equipment, and motor vehicles.

• The worker acquired skills on his own, not through training provided by the company.

• Work is done off the company's premises.

• Worker selects, hires, and pays his own assistants.

Examples of independent contractors:

• Carpenter, plumber, or electrician who supplies his own tools, is paid for a completed job, and is not closely supervised while doing it.

• Salespeople who represent two or more manufacturers and are paid on commission only.

• Truck or taxi drivers who buy their own gas and take a percentage of the revenues collected.

• Free-lance magazine writers, commercial artists, draftsmen, designers, and the like.

Note: In borderline cases, it might be wise to ask IRS for a ruling.

Guaranteed trouble: An employee already on the payroll is shifted to independent contractor status without any real change in work schedules or pay arrangements.

The 1978 Revenue Act instructed IRS not to challenge companies on use of independent contractor status in the past or in 1979 if there is a reasonable basis for it, such as recognized industry practice, past court decisions, IRS rulings, or long-established practice of the company. Congress is planning to review the matter.

Reducing Unemployment Insurance Costs

• About 40% of unemployment claims can be successfully resisted, a recent survey finds.

Challenge every unjustified claim. Only people who are unemployed through no fault of their own, and are actively seeking work, are eligible. This excludes those who quit to accept other jobs which may not have panned out, those who were fired for cause, and those who chose not to return when called back from layoff.

• Some employers, in a misguided attempt to be "nice guys," conspire with employees to conceal the disqualifying truth. This can be very costly to the company.

Steps to take:

• Give a printed copy of work rules to all new employees to sign on their first day on the job. Reason: No benefits if a worker is fired for breaking rules as long as they're not unreasonable and employer can prove worker knew them.

• Have employees fill in "hours available for work" on job application form before hiring. They are ineligible for benefits if fired for refusing to work those hours.

• Rehire ex-employees who are still receiving benefits. This saves training time. (Note: If former employee refuses to be rehired, his right to further benefits can be cut off.)

• Study your company's experience to see whether high job turnover is concentrated in just a few areas. If that is the case, it may be that some jobs are more volatile than others. Rearranging work assignments might create steadier employment, fewer claims.

How Workers Who Leave Voluntarily Collect Unemployment Pay

• Unemployment pay is usually awarded to employees who quit because they don't want to go along when their company moves.

• Unemployment pay was allowed to an

employee on voluntary leave of absence. The company didn't promise there would be a job when the employee wanted to come back. Without re-employment rights, the court ruled that the employee qualified as unemployed. The company could have avoided this trap by accepting a resignation (thereby eliminating unemployment pay) and telling a valued employee his application for a job in the future would be given favorable consideration.

- Slow paychecks can be sufficient cause for workers to leave and collect unemployment compensation. In a recent case, the court approved such pay because checks were late four times in a few months.

Careful Way to Use Lie Detectors

Preventive security is always more effective than punishment after the fact. That's how polygraphs should be used. Suppose a theft has occurred in a plant or office. Carefully managed polygraph testing can eliminate the atmosphere of suspicion and tension about proving innocence. What to do:

- Tell employees that the money or merchandise loss could be the result of bookkeeping errors, shoplifting, or some other cause. It is not necessarily an inside theft. (If this seems true, of course.)
- Introduce the representative of the polygraph firm at a meeting of all employees. Explain that there has been a problem but that management is only concerned with what happens from that day forward, not with the past.
- Announce that the polygraph examiner will be on the premises to ask questions of those who voluntarily participate (95% usually do).
- Distribute questions with the exact wording the examiner will use.
- Tell employees that the same questions will be asked twice a year.
- Note that all new employees from that point on will be given polygraph exams before they are employed.

Any good security firm will refuse to work with a management that is simply trying to ferret out information from its employees.

Ethical examiners will not use a question that employees haven't reviewed ahead of time, so subjects know exactly what to expect. Questions are usually the same from one company to another. And the director of personnel (or other responsible representative of top management) must review the questions to be asked with the polygraph firm representative.

Important: Give the test across the board, from president to stock clerk, to keep employee acceptance of the program high.

Accuracy: Polygraph testing is 96% accurate with well-trained examiners.

Using the polygraph to prescreen job candidates is a very sensitive area right now. Use it only to identify:

- False data on application. About 85% of job candidates do lie in a minor way (about age, last salary, or reasons for leaving past job).
- Past dishonesty. Most test subjects usually admit if they've stolen small amounts. Once it's out of their systems, they test out all right.
- Use of dangerous drugs. Most companies aren't concerned about occasional social use of marijuana.
- Alcohol use. Concern is for drinking habits on the job.
- Physical condition. Serious chronic conditions could jeopardize health and life in job. Example: Man who's had coronary applying for a job loading trucks.

Key things to keep in mind when using a polygraph firm's services:

- Use firms affiliated with the American Polygraph Association (Box 74, Linthicum Heights, MD 21090).
- Ask for qualifications and experience of the examiner. Get names of clients. Check references.
- Review questions to be asked on test. The examiner should not ask for private information.
- Ask employees how examiner treated them and what was asked.
- If company judges that the examiner isn't conducting the tests properly or ethically, stop program immediately. Contact the APA or state attorney or attorney general.

Source: Lincoln M. Zonn, Zonn Corp., 3050 Biscayne Blvd., Miami 33137.

No-Smoking Rules

Under the federal government's drive to educate the public against smoking, employers will be subjected to official and unofficial pressure to participate. Some guidelines:

• First of all, the employment relationship doesn't give the employer the right to forbid smoking (except in hazardous situations) any more than it gives workers the right to insist that their bosses stop.

• Rules should be work-related: Prohibition should be enforced when there are combustible materials around, close working conditions, etc.

• Allow for regular smoke breaks. Smokers get edgy if they are forced to abstain for too long, and work will suffer.

• Smoke breaks must be in a safe place, away from the work area.

• If the company has always permitted smoking on the job because it didn't affect production, and safety is not an issue, there is no reason to change the policy.

Employee Health Records

Privacy of individual health records was guaranteed by a recent court case. The judge placed severe restrictions on how the National Institute of Occupational Safety and Health could use employees' health records to study the incidence of cancer among the personnel. The judge ordered the records to be shown only to those NIOSH staff members who were qualified and trained in public health.

POINTS OF LAW

If You Have to Go to Court

When You Don't Need a Lawyer

Some Essentials of Patent Law

Employment Contracts

Non-Compete Agreements

Sexual Harassment

Directors' Conflict of Interest

Keeping Records Confidential

18

POINTS OF LAW

If You Have to Go to Court

Selecting counsel: The best trial lawyers don't necessarily work for the biggest firms. Many of them are with smaller ones where chances for broad experience are greater. Choose the lawyer, not the firm. Trial law is a specialty. Seek out counsel with trial experience in the field. A local trial attorney who's familiar with the court where the case will be tried is usually best. If represented by a lawyer from out of town, most courts usually require local counsel, too.

Negotiating the fee: Avoid contingency arrangements. A fee based on time spent is safest, but get assurance that rates won't change during period of litigation without prior discussion. Costs quoted can be deceiving. A $40-per-hour fee for a lawyer fresh out of law school is no bargain. Better to pay much more for experienced senior partner who knows how to get work done in one-tenth the time. An hourly rate of $25 for law firm's paralegals is too high if they perform file clerk's job.

Questions to ask: Many law firms have more than one rate for attorney. Are you getting best price? Travel time: How much is charged for day spent away from office? How many hours count as a day? Are you charged for whole day if only part is used for your case? What if the trip is for more than one client? Is there a charge for weekends and holidays if lawyer doesn't work? Tourist or first-class travel? Who pays for lawyer's meals and entertainment? Disbursements: Are secretarial and messenger work handled as disbursement or overhead? How is duplicating of documents in law office charged?

Client's rights: Law firms are a business like any other. It's proper to demand good service, protest excessive costs, keep lawyers on their toes without compromising their professionalism. Ask for litigation plan in advance: Who will do what and when. Hold law firm to it. Counsel in charge of your case should stay with it from beginning to end, supervise internal administration (including billing) as well as represent your company in court.

• Get itemized monthly record of charges, with duplicates of all papers drawn up. Record should contain name of everyone in law office working on case, hourly rate, and time spent.

Watch for signs that people already familiar with your company's business are being rotated out and replaced by staff who must be educated at your expense.

• Question overtime closely. Someone's work is being done during regular office hours; why not yours?

Costly delays can pile up when trial lawyers on opposing sides exchange "professional courtesies" to accommodate personal or vacation schedules. Don't accept postponements unless they will clearly help the case.

• Be sure counsel knows enough about your business to handle any questions that may arise in the courtroom.

Trial lawyers tend to be cynical, need to be sold on merits of client's case. The more confident an attorney is that the client's right, the better his performance.

Source: Milton R. Wessel, Esq., New York University.

When to Sue an Attorney for Malpractice

The legal profession is entering its own malpractice crisis. The number of suits against attorneys being brought by clients is increasing and the availability of malpractice insurance is decreasing.

Ground rules for considering a suit against your lawyer:

• Where malpractice is charged in connection with litigation, the client must show that the litigation would have ended with a result more favorable to the client if it were not for the attorney's neglect.

• Where the attorney fell below the standards of skill and knowledge ordinarily possessed by attorneys under similar circumstances. Expert testimony is needed to support this charge. And the standard may be affected by specialization (which raises the standard of care required), custom, and locality. Locality and custom can't lower the standard, but they may be used as a defense to show that the procedure or law involved is unsettled.

The best ways to avoid malpractice charges:

• See that there is good communication between lawyer and client.

• Avoid a situation where a lawyer is handling serious matters for personal friends. The tendency is to deal with them more casually.

• The attorney should give an honest opinion of each case, good or bad. The client shouldn't press him for a guarantee as to the result.

• All fee arrangements should be in writing.

• The attorney should spell out the scope of his responsibilities, including appeals, and a limit should be placed on costs.

• The agreement should provide for periodic payments, unless the matter is one involving a contingent fee, and for withdrawal, if there is a default in payment.

When Not to Be Represented by a Company Lawyer

A company is free to throw its executives to the wolves when federal investigators come knocking. Court ruling (first ever on the subject) underscores the advice that executives should have their own lawyers on touchy matters of antitrust and similar business dealings, not rely on the company attorney.

With the lawyer-client privilege, the government can't force a lawyer to testify before a grand jury if his client tells him to keep mum. But the confusion comes when an executive consults with the company lawyer about possibly shady dealings. If the company later decides that it wants to cooperate with investigators, the individual who is the target of the probe can't stop the lawyer's testimony no matter how damning. The client is the corporation, not the executive.

In re *Backier*, USDC, So. Mich., 8/2/77.

When You Don't Need a Lawyer

• Compliance. Dealing with IRS, SEC, OSHA, EEOC, and other federal, state, and local agencies. What is needed here is the ability to read complex regulations carefully, determine how to follow them, and keep on top of the form-filling and filing. Much of this work needn't be done by lawyers. It can be done by finance-accounting-bookkeeping personnel with reports to staff lawyer.

• Contracts. Negotiating contracts is a business matter. It needs an experienced officer who knows the company's needs and what it can deliver, what it should agree to. Don't let the lawyers negotiate contracts; this is for the businessmen. After the handshake, have counsel prepare the agreement. All large contracts should be reviewed by a senior corporate officer who has not been involved in any of the negotiations.

When a Contract Is Unenforceable

A buyer may be able to get out of a contract if he can show that he was deceived by an intentional misstatement of an important fact.

Case: A prospective mall tenant was told that the property was 65% rented and what its share of the taxes (prorated among all tenants) would be. But in fact the property was only 30% rented. Result: Customer traffic was less and the tenant's share of the taxes turned out to be more than twice as high. The court held that the tenant did not have to live up to the terms of the lease.

Note: Courts take the view that it's normal business practice for salespeople to exaggerate. What made the difference in this case was the intent to deceive by misrepresenting important information.
242 So. 2d 801.

Good and Bad Divorce Lawyers

• Never ask your corporate lawyer to handle a divorce. In fact, avoid asking him for any specific advice. There is one question that you should ask him, however (and, even then, check out his answer independently): Who's the best divorce lawyer around?

Divorce and corporate law are completely different. Don't assume that any good lawyer can handle the unique problems divorce raises.

Similarly, don't use a general-purpose lawyer. Here, the problem may be worse: The corporate lawyer knows he doesn't know divorce law: The general lawyer thinks he does. And you will pay for that mistake.

Where to find a good divorce lawyer: Just ask around. The best names in the area will come up automatically.

Don't stop there. As good as the recommendation is, check him out personally. Interview him. See if you two can communicate. Do you understand him? Does he swamp you with details? Discuss fee arrangements. Tell him you'd like the arrangement in writing. Don't feel that the fee isn't negotiable; it frequently is.

Important: Make sure the lawyer understands that you want to be kept abreast of everything he does (every document and every conference on your case). It's not that you'll necessarily be able to make any legal contributions (although you may). It's just that you must deal with your peace of mind. Divorce is so mind-shattering that you don't want to make it even more disconcerting by feeling you don't know what is going on—a common complaint.

• Expect to be emotionally upset much of the time when dealing with the divorce proceeding. It's important, however, that your lawyer doesn't make you feel worse. If he does, consider someone else.

• Don't waste time (and money) putting a notice in the newspapers saying you're not responsible for your spouse's debts. That's ineffective. Better way: Send a certified letter to every creditor your spouse has dealings with. (Prepare a list of those credit cards before the divorce proceedings get under way.)

• Never let your spouse become a party to any agreement without her own lawyer providing advice. In many states, weakness becomes a strength; the law holds that any disagreement over interpretation must be construed in favor of the party who entered the agreement without any legal advice.

Understanding the New Bankruptcy Law

The first fundamental overhauling of bankruptcy law in 70 years consolidates Chapter X, XI, and XII rehabilitation proceedings into one form of business reorganization, and puts pressure on financially troubled companies and their creditors to work out arrangements with less court supervision. Joel B. Zweibel, partner in a major New York City law firm and an authority on secured transactions, cites some of the changes most important to smaller businesses.

• Provisions now favoring insolvent companies: It will be easier for financially troubled companies, or their trustees, to get back payments made within 90 days of filing a petition for relief. Exception: Payments made in the ordinary course, pursuant to usual business terms, and within 45 days of incurring the debt, will not be recoverable, no matter what the timing of the insolvency proceedings.

What this means: Suppliers to businesses with questionable liquidity should require, in the ordinary course of business, that payment be made within 45 days of creation of the debt.

An insolvent company suing a creditor for supplying incomplete or defective goods will now take its case to bankruptcy court rather than civil court. Impact: Cases will be heard by a bankruptcy judge before whom the reorganization is pending.

• Provisions now favoring the creditors: Under the old bankruptcy act, only financially troubled companies could seek an arrangement with their creditors under Chapter XI. Now, three creditors with a total of $5,000 or more in unsecured noncontingent claims may force a company to seek relief. If the company does not devise an acceptable reorganization plan, the creditors can then propose a plan themselves.

• The new code makes it easier for suppliers to recover goods sold to a company which declares itself insolvent. The suppliers must, however, demand return of the goods in writing within ten days after delivery.

• Provisions favoring large creditors over small ones: Under the old act, creditors voted for a committee to oversee their interests. Under the new code, the committee will be appointed and composed, as a rule, of the seven largest creditors. Thus, small-creditor representation in the reorganization proceedings may be diminished.

• Provisions favoring small creditors over large ones: Under the new code, an insolvent company may substitute collateral securing a loan. Example: A company has secured a bank loan with equipment. It declares bankruptcy, and says to the bank, "To get operating funds, we need to sell some equipment. Therefore, we now offer real estate as collateral for the loan." If the court finds that the substitute gives the bank adequate protection, the company may use, sell, or lease the original property. Thus, insolvent companies will be better able to stay in business, and the odds on small creditors' eventually recovering their debts should improve.

• Under the new code, a company's bank creditors and accounts receivable inventory lenders may not significantly reduce what the company owes them in the 90 days before a bankruptcy filing. Result: Large creditors will be less able to collect debts from an insolvent company at the expense of small creditors.

Essentials of Patent Law

Businessmen very often misunderstand what a patent really is and what it can and cannot do for them.

How to get a patent: The product must be new, useful, and not obvious to a person with ordinary skills. The U.S. patent office tends to minimize the "not obvious" restriction and grants patents for almost all inventions that fit the "new and useful" designation. Result: Patents are awarded for variations of the same product. So getting a patent does not usually mean other companies can be stopped from manufacturing nearly the same thing. Often all a patent protects is a manufacturer's specific technology. So, if a company holding a broader patent makes an accusation of infringement, the manufacturer can point to its own patent and arrive at a compromise settlement.

How to look at a patent: It's an asset, like

stocks. It may not mean much in court, but it can be traded on and used to obtain rights from others. It's usually not a fence protecting a field from incursions by others. Exception: A major technical breakthrough.

What's patentable: Machines, processes, compositions of matter, and articles of manufacture. It is not the idea that's patentable. The inventor has to offer practical plans for execution of the idea. When a patent isn't granted, the ruling can be appealed to the Court of Customs and Patent Appeals (which holds to the principle of granting patents wherever possible).

Pursuing a court fight to protect patent rights is expensive. Thus, most patent cases are settled out of court. Good reasons to sue: (1) To open up a needed market. (2) To protect a patent covering a genuine technical breakthrough, where the company should be entitled to keep the market. Warning: Unless these conditions exist, avoid litigation, particularly if the firm is small. Don't close the door on negotiation; compromise is usually a better strategy.

Where a strong patent is involved (the breakthrough type), go to court even against a major company. But play it safe. Get a thorough outside legal opinion first. If it shows the patent is strong, there is a 50-50 chance that a smaller company can prevail.

What the record shows: Courts have upheld the infringer and struck down the validity of the patent in a majority of cases (about 75%).

Guidelines for choosing a patent lawyer:
• Beware of types who promise that the patent system will solve all of the company's business problems.
• Get hard answers to these questions: What will the patent do for the company? What will it yield? How strong will the patent be?
• Ignore generalities about how the patent will protect the product. Get specifics.

Source: Mary Helen Sears, partner, Irons & Sears, attorneys, 1801 K St., N.W., Washington, DC 20006.

Employment Contracts

Employment contracts are usually good for the employees. But not always for the company.

That's because they're very difficult to enforce. Example:

Suppose an employee leaves after two years of a five-year contract. The court won't order the employee to work. The company has a theoretical claim for loss of services, but it would have to prove it couldn't replace him for the same money. Since damages are hard to prove, employers rarely sue.

Still, most employees honor the contract as a moral obligation. And the non-compete agreement puts some teeth in it for the company.

Situations where employees have enough clout to get contracts:
• In mergers, top officers of the acquired company ask for contracts. Acquiring company is usually glad to give them because it wants experienced management to stay.
• Experienced and mature executive going to a new company that courted him. He especially needs it if he's over 50.
• Chief executive doing a good job and the board wants to keep him happy.

When an executive is negotiating an employment contract for himself, keep in mind:
• The agreement not to compete if and when he leaves should be sharply limited in time and geographical area. (If it isn't, it may not be enforceable.)
• Try to get the non-compete agreement to end if the exec is let go at the end of the contract.
• Company will want the right to fire the exec "for cause." Useful provision: If there's a dispute on what constitutes "cause" for dismissal, it goes to arbitration and the exec collects his pay until it's settled.

Source: James Freund, partner, Skadden, Arps, Slate, Meagher & Flom, 919 Third Ave., New York 10022.

What to Spell Out in a Buy-Sell Agreement

Buy-sell agreements are essential in a closely held company to avoid crises when one stockholder dies, leaves, has financial difficulties, or goes bankrupt. Such agreements spell out what will happen to stock, thus avoiding distress sales by estate, outsiders getting control of company or becoming troublesome minority interest.

What to cover in an agreement:

• It takes effect when specified things happen to a stockholder (death, leaving the company, bankruptcy, retirement).

• The stockholder (or his estate) then has an option to sell his stock. Or there might be an obligation to sell within a period of time.

• The corporation, or the other stockholders (as a group), have either an option or an obligation to buy the stock.

• The price is determined by a formula specified in the agreement. Usually book value or a multiple of recent earnings (or a formula that combines the two). It's possible also to have the actual dollar price put in the agreement. Then it will have to be reviewed frequently to keep price up to date.

• If purchase is mandatory, the agreement price will usually be accepted as the value of the stock for estate tax purposes (whether payment is immediate or in installments).

• It's common practice to have the agreement funded by life insurance, so that the proceeds of the policy provide the money to buy the stock after death. Beneficiary is either the company or other stockholders, depending on who has the obligation to buy under the agreement.

One way to reduce the insurance premium cost: A "next death" policy. All stockholders are covered by a single policy that pays the proceeds one time, when the first person dies.

Buy-sell agreements are complicated and require considerable study and thought to prepare. That's because they'll go into effect at some unknown time in the future, when circumstances may be different. Some unforeseen problems that can arise:

• Stockholders might be committed to buying stock but may not have enough money to make the purchase.

• The company might be obligated to buy stock but not have enough surplus to do so. (Laws in many states provide that a corporation may not redeem shares except out of surplus.)

• If the corporation is owned by several members of the same family, there could be adverse tax consequences if the company buys the shares from one stockholder or from his estate. This can be avoided if the agreement provides that other family members, rather than the company, buy the stock.

Source: Jerry Cowan, partner, Frost & Jacobs, 511 Walnut St., Cincinnati 45202.

Points to Cover in Manufacturer's Contract with Distributor

• Which products. The manufacturer has no obligation to give the distributor the whole line. Be sure the contract states precisely which items the distributor will handle.

• Manufacturer prices. How much notice must the manufacturer give when changing prices? Who pays freight, taxes?

• Distributor prices. The manufacturer cannot dictate or control the distributor's resale prices.

• Territory exclusivity. The manufacturer will probably want to define a trading area, and prohibit the distributor from selling outside that area. (This can be legal.) There should be clear understandings as to whether the distributor has an exclusive on that territory or whether others may be appointed; if so, how many, what part of the total territory, etc.

• Reserved accounts. The manufacturer may reserve certain categories of accounts for itself, retaining the right to ship to them, even though they're within the distributor's territory, and prohibit the distributor from shipping to them. But manufacturer can't reserve certain named accounts and prevent distributor from shipping to them.

• Term of agreement. If it's for a fixed term, what obligations and rights do the parties have after it expires? (Examples: Manufacturer's obligation to continue service to distributor's customers, distributor's right to return goods.) If it's open-ended, be very clear what circumstances permit either party to cancel. The distributor should oppose any provision that allows the manufacturer to cancel "when he considers it in his best interests."

- Which state law governs if the manufacturer is in one state and the distributor in another?
- Warranties, product liability. How are these divided between the two? Particularly important if distributor modifies the product.

Source: *Industrial Distribution* magazine.

When Non-Compete Agreements Are Worthless

A non-compete agreement made by the seller of a business may be unenforceable if it is too broad-based.

The seller of a business agrees that he will not go into competition with the buyer. Courts have consistently held that this agreement is enforceable only if there is real consideration and if it is limited in time and area.

Buyer beware if the seller says, I want you to succeed so much that I'll never compete with you anywhere, as long as I live. This is worse than no agreement at all. It is unenforceable in court. The seller can open up across the street the very next day.

The agreement not to compete must be reasonably limited in time and area. What's reasonable depends on the type of business and its normal market area. For a single retail store, a non-compete agreement covering the county for ten years has stood up in many cases. For wholesalers and manufacturers, the time could be longer and the area larger. Possibly the whole country, maybe even several continents if there is already significant overseas business.

When a Note Is Sold to a Third Party

Situation: The company buys a machine on a time payment plan and the seller transfers buyer's installment note to a bank or finance company. Problem arises when the machine breaks down and the buyer, therefore, stops making payments. The finance company demands to be paid, saying it is not involved in any dispute between buyer and seller. The law says the buyer must pay the installments.

Solution: A buyer should insist that installment purchase contracts carry this provision:

Any holder of this contract is subject to all claims and defenses which the debtor could assert against the seller of goods or services obtained pursuant hereto.

Note: A long-established legal principle is that the third party who purchases a note is entitled to be paid. The debtor cannot refuse to pay because of a dispute with the original seller of the goods.

This rule, called the holder-in-due-course doctrine, no longer applies to consumer installment transactions. But it still applies to dealings between businesses—unless the suggested language is added to the contract.

Source: *UCC Law Journal*, Warren, Gorham & Lamont, 210 South St., Boston 02111.

Bypassing Discounters Without Violating the Law

Can a manufacturer refuse to sell to a dealer that discounts its products? It's very risky. And it's definitely illegal if it's done as part of an effort to fix retail prices. (The old fair trade laws were abolished by Congress in 1975.)

Steps the manufacturer may legally take in order to control the types of dealers that handle its products:

- It may give one dealer an exclusive right to sell in a geographic area and refuse to sell to other dealers.
- In some situations it may be legal to place restrictions on where dealers sell its products.
- And in some situations it may be legal for a manufacturer to prohibit its dealers from reselling to other dealers. But the manufacturer will almost surely be in trouble if it uses this provision only against dealers who resell to discounters.

The Supreme Court has held that restrictions on where products are sold and on reselling to other dealers might be permitted.

The court's reasoning: A manufacturer may legally take some steps which strengthen its dealer organization and make the manufacturer a more effective competitor with other brands. Sometimes it may do this even when it involves reducing competition among its own dealers. But it should be able to show that the result is to increase competition in the general marketplace for the product. (Note: The manufacturer in this case had a very small market share.)

Important to know: The court has not flashed a green light for restrictions on resale. It has merely held that they may be okay in some cases.
Continental TV v. *GTE Sylvania,* 433 U.S. 36 (1977), overruling *U.S.* v. *Arnold, Schwinn & Co.,* 388 U.S. 365 (1967).

Discrimination Suits

Persons who use Title VII antidiscrimination lawsuits solely to harass employers can be compelled to pay legal costs of defense. Three cases:

• An airline was awarded legal expenses from a claimant who forced the airline to continue litigating well after a time at which he must have realized, had he read the motion to dismiss, that his complaint was truly without basis.

• A country club demonstrated that it was exempt from strictures of Title VII. A federal judge ordered the claimant to withdraw his action, unless he wanted to dispute the defending party's defense.

• A baking company admitted that it had violated the law and agreed to a settlement. The claimant nevertheless continued the suit solely to increase "costs, expense, trouble, time, and effort" on the part of the company. Said the court: "The nothing-to-lose syndrome cannot be permitted to become an expensive drain on employers to satisfy the whim of spiteful ex-employees."

The U.S. Supreme Court has said that employers who succeed in antidiscrimination litigation might recover legal expenses from claimants only in rare circumstances. The federal district courts seem to be construing this liberally, finding many instances of lawsuits that were carried on long after it was obvious that the claims were futile.

In defending against a discrimination claim, counterclaim for legal expenses. Win or lose, this strategy may discourage frivolous dragging out of legal proceedings.
Davis v. *Braniff,* 19 FEP 811; *Brown* v. *Lakeside Country Club,* 19 FEP 796; *Christianburg* v. *EEOC,* 434 US 412.

Minority Stockholders' Right to See Books

Minority stockholders generally have a right to see corporate books and other documents. But they may have to go to court to enforce that right. Most corporate managements give little information to minority stockholders—especially in closely held companies that don't have to file reports with the SEC.

Who may see what: State laws vary. In most states those who have owned stock (even one share) for at least six months may ask for a look at the internal books. And a stockholder who owns 5% or more has inspection rights as soon as the stock is acquired. Holders may also ask to look at other documents as well as the financial books. They may be required to show a good reason for needing the information. Courts will not allow unjustified harassment or fishing expeditions.

Recent case: A small stockholder followed corporate affairs closely. He gathered evidence indicating financial irregularities. In addition, he was troubled by the failure to pay dividends. The court's ruling: Make the books available. The stockholder was acting in good faith and had shown a proper purpose.
373 N.E. 2d 421

Personal Liability for Corporate Contract

A corporate officer could be held personally liable on a contract he signs unless it's very clear that he acted for the company and not personally. He might have to pay damages if the company decides not to go through with the contract. Or if it gets into financial trouble.

What to do: Company name should appear

first, above the signature. (And don't forget the *Inc.*) Below it the word *By* followed by signature. And be sure to add title.

It's far-fetched, but possible, that the same problem could arise with a corporate check if the company stops payment or the check bounces. Executives have had to go to court to prove they weren't personally liable.

236 A. 2d 542; 251 A. 2d 722.

Sexual Harassment Charges

Claims of sexual harassment on the job usually take one of two forms:

• Allegations that a promotion was denied or employment was terminated because a woman rejected sexual overtures by a supervisor.

• Complaints that management took no action against rank-and-filers who made unwelcome sexual advances to women.

Two recent cases:

1. One company was cleared by a federal court because the unwelcome advances were made by a male co-worker who had no power to affect the woman's job tenure.

2. Management was held responsible for failing to investigate a woman's complaint that men were making loud, unpleasant remarks about her marital status.

How to avoid corporate responsibility:

• Include a statement in personnel policy booklets forbidding discourteous conduct toward any employee.

• Instruct supervisors to avoid social relationships with women in their departments.

• Investigate every complaint of sexual harassment.

18 EPD Par. 8698 and Par. 8700.

Facing a Conflict of Interest As a Corporate Director

Personal liability risk for a company director is greatest when the director has a personal interest in a specific transaction or contract because of involvement with the other party to the deal. Steps for protection against conflict-of-interest charge:

• Do not attend meeting in which the contract or transaction will be considered by the board. Give notice that you will be absent so that company can take steps to assure that there will be a quorum.

• If your presence is necessary for a quorum, disclose the nature of your involvement with the other party at the start of the meeting.

• Do not participate in discussion of the deal. Abstain from voting.

• Make sure that minutes of the meeting include your disclosure, nonparticipation in discussion, and abstention from voting.

Source: *Directors & Boards, The Journal of Corporate Action*, Information for Industry, Inc., 1621 Brookside Rd., McLean, VA 22101.

Before Accepting an Invitation to the Board of Directors

A position on a board of directors carries an increasing burden of legal liabilities. Advice: Look clearly at the company before accepting an invitation to become a director.

What to consider:

• Tender offers and takeover activities in which the company may be involved. Reason: When a board opposes a takeover, stockholder lawsuits are likely.

• Adequacy of company's management information system. Reason: Directors face charges of negligence if they fail to demand and consider all relevant and critical data before making decisions. Lack of knowledge is no defense.

• Compliance with ethical and legal standards. Insist on a detailed company ethics code with built-in enforcement provisions. And a sufficiently large internal auditing staff, plus the regular employment of outside auditors.

• Executive compensation and perquisites. These must be reasonable and defensible, as well as comparable to those accompanying similar positions in competing companies.

Other factors: (1) Company's insurance coverage of board members. (2) Specific and well-defined management development and succession policies. (3) An effective and efficient chief executive. (It's difficult to get rid of a CEO who's not doing a good job.)

Source: Myles L. Mace, professor emeritus of business administration, Harvard Business School, in *Harvard Business Review*.

Protecting Records from Federal Eyes

The Right to Financial Privacy Act protects bank records of individuals and partnerships (of five or fewer individuals). The protection is limited, however.

Where the problems are: The law doesn't apply to Internal Revenue Service subpoenas. Nor does the law apply to state investigators. And any federal agency can examine financial records for 90 days or more without telling the individual, if the agency can get a search warrant first.

The new law also does not apply if the target of inquiry is the financial institution itself, if the records are sought in judicial or administrative proceedings involving a bank and its customer, or if the federal government is considering or administrating a loan or loan guarantee to the individual or partnership.

There is also an exemption for national security matters.

How the law works: In matters where the law does apply, the government must notify the customer before asking a financial institution (bank, credit union, savings and loan, consumer finance company, or credit card issuer) to disclose personal records. The notice must name the records, the agency involved, and the purpose of the disclosure. Key point: The federal official wanting records can have the customer served with a subpoena giving notice that the material will be examined after ten days. Or the official can simply ask the customer to consent to an examination within ten days. The simple request can be refused without going to court. But a journey to federal district court would be needed to try to quash a subpoena. If the court refuses to deny access, the ruling cannot be appealed. It may, however, be contested in later proceedings. Persons believing that the statute has been violated may also sue the government and the institutions involved.

Source: C. Westbrook Murphy, of Wald, Harkrader & Ross, 1300 Nineteenth St. N.W., Washington, DC 20036.

PRODUCT DEVELOPMENT AND MARKETING

Before Investing in a New Product

Limiting Product Costs

Offering a New Product to Dealers

Competing With a National Brand

When a Big Budget Won't Pay Off

The Right Premium

How Much to Spend on R&D

Marketing in Hard Times

19

PRODUCT DEVELOPMENT AND MARKETING

Before Investing in a New Product

- What are the size and location of the potential market for the product? If the scope of the market isn't sufficient, stop right here.
- Does the product fit the company's production facilities or product assortment? If a company sells ashtrays direct to retail outlets, adding a line of matching cigarette lighters might complement the assortment that the sales force can offer customers. Developing other kinds of glass and ceramic gifts might fill in slack periods on the production line.
- Should the product be made by the company itself, or purchased outside for resale? Compare costs and possible profit margins, taking into consideration the distribution and timing.
- What financing is needed? Analyze potential return on investment, because that's what will determine the product's profitability.
- Are there obstacles to securing a patent, if one is needed? Can the product be designed to meet the applicable packaging, labeling, and quality standards?

- What is the anticipated market life?
- How will sales results be judged? What would be considered success or failure?
- Why should a customer buy from this company instead of the competition? What are the good points of the competitive unit? Is there a sample of the competitor's product on hand? What percentage of the market does the competition have?
- Does it fit into the distribution pattern?
- What effect does geographical location of the plant have on costs, suppliers, schedules, travel, shipping costs, etc.?
- If only one person in the company is "pushing" the new product, is he objective or does he have an emotional interest?
- What should be done once the product is released to support it?

What percentage of total manufacturing costs (parts, modules, components, etc.) will be in-house?

- What introductory incentives can be provided: Free offer, trial offer, special trade deal, coupons, co-op advertising? What else can be done to offer incentives?
- Can salespeople handle the new product on

their regular calls without making special calls?

• Will it energize the other products and refresh them, have a "halo effect"? Will it upgrade or cheapen the rest of the line?

• Is the idea fully developed? Should it be a single product or a line of products? Have the price, name, and positioning all been thought through? Potential customers could provide feedback to further develop the concept.

• Crucial questions: Is the new item really needed, or should an investment be made in current products? Should present products be treated like new ones? A new approach, new package, new uses, forms, line extensions? Sometimes $1 investment on a current line is more fruitful than $3 put into new products.
Source: Gerald Schoenfeld, Inc., 341 Madison Ave., New York 10017.

The Chances of New Product Success

Entrepreneurs and investors need to be aware of one of the realities of innovation. Roughly speaking, overall only one out of ten good new ideas will result in an actual product or service that will be a profitable success. Numbers vary depending upon how far along the idea is, and the market for which it is being developed. But experiences of managers in diverse fields are remarkably similar.

Publishers say candidly that only one out of ten new books (all of which they had high hopes for) ever catch on with enough readers to make money. The same is true on Broadway with new plays, and even with the research and development efforts of very successful companies.

The reason for failure may be bad research, but more influential may be the fact that consumer tastes are dynamic and fickle. Enormous gaps need to be bridged between the idea and a workable new technique or product.

An important point for investors and executives is to recognize that the ten-to-one odds are realistic. Approach each investment with proper conservatism and skepticism.
Source: Dr. Leonard R. Sayles, Columbia University Graduate School of Business.

Best Size for a Product Line

Once a company decides to market new products, it should develop as wide and varied a product line as possible.

That's the conclusion reached after an indepth analysis of the confidential data and experience of 1,800 manufacturers.

Reason: Products in the early and middle stages of the product cycle are changing so rapidly that missing out on one change could leave a company far behind its competitors.

In later, mature product stages, a company can take either one of two paths to profitability. They can specialize in a limited, narrow product line and enjoy the advantages of economies of scale in production and distribution. Or they can take a generalist route with a wide product line that provides something for every taste or need. Products in late life-cycle states have been on the market for a long time, are altered infrequently, and have little potential for dramatic growth.

A NARROW PRODUCT LINE IN EARLY OR MIDDLE STAGES IS UNPROFITABLE

	Narrow		Wide
Early	11	16	27
Middle	13	18	29
Late	23	18	23

The chart indicates breadth of the product line versus competitors' lines (when read horizontally) and the stage in the product's life cycle (vertically). Numbers in columns indicate return on investment.

Source: Dr. Sidney Schoeffler, Director, Strategic Planning Institute, 1 Broadway, Cambridge, MA 02142

Limiting Product Costs

Unnecessary product costs often go undetected because cost-cutting procedures usually tackle the problem piecemeal, reducing the price of just one part or one process.

As an alternative, put together a team of engineers, accountants, designers, and marketing people to think together creatively about the entire product function.

Don't put managers on the team who have the

277

power to kill an idea. Change implies criticism of the old. Managers frequently resist important changes because the solution is so simple that they are embarrassed not to have thought of it sooner themselves.

To make sure good cost-cutting ideas aren't sabotaged, team leaders must stay aware of personal impact of suggested changes as the team works on technical tasks:

• Comparing the cost of the current way of providing a necessary function with other means of providing that same use.

• Identifying and eliminating costs.

How the team works:

Develop basic information about the product. What is it? What does it do? Boil down the product's function to two words—one verb and one noun. Avoid words that restrict or bias thinking in terms of one material or tool. Example: Not "drills holes" but "removes material."

Analyze costs. Think about the product's basic function. Then cost that out in materials, parts, labor, etc. Identify secondary functions, not essential to the product's performance, and cost those out, too. Common discovery: Providing secondary functions costs a great deal more than producing the essential function. Questions to ask the team: Can nonessential features be dropped? Are there secondary functions that could be provided by the primary parts at no extra cost?

• The creative phase: Ask what else could serve this product's function. Let ideas flow. Don't allow criticism. Don't stop to evaluate each idea.

• The evaluation phase: Now ask: "Will it work?" Also: "What will it cost?" Weed out ideas that don't work or are too costly. Vendors might be asked to participate and contribute information on redesigning components, etc.

• Report test results, proposals, and recommendations for action to top management. Include estimate of the expected savings.

Top management must show support for the effort and willingness to implement useful recommendations. It must make clear to all lower managers that acceptance of a cost-cutting proposal is not a condemnation of anyone for past performance.

Follow-up is essential to ensure implementa-

tion, to resolve any hitches, and to measure the actual cost savings.

Source: *Production Engineering* magazine, 201 E. 42 St., New York 10017.

Traditional Pricing Strategies Reconsidered

• Unnecessary seasonal markdowns: Seasonal markdowns are, of course, traditional. But the seasons are changing—traceable to geographical population shifts (to the Sun Belt, for example). Air conditioning plays an especially major role. So does more long-distance travel, spurred by lower rates, longer weekends, and second homes (where so many traditions are defied). Many retailers kill sales by automatically marking down seasonal merchandise when the season has barely begun. Tests have shown that some summer lines will sell well even after the "sudden death" months of July and August. Most seasonal traditions are overdue for restudy.

• Odd-pricing above the even figure: It is also traditional to fix the odd price just under the even figure. (Example: $4.95 instead of $5.00). Try odd-pricing above the even figure. You may find that you can pick up additional margin this way. One manufacturer made this discovery by accident—freight rates compelled setting odd prices above the usual figure when shipping to various parts of the country. The company discovered to its surprise that the higher odd price had little negative impact on sales.

Before Cutting Price: How Much Extra Will You Have to Sell?

Running a sale will not necessarily increase profits—or even business. It's often done to liquidate aging inventory, increase share of market, or increase store traffic. But before cutting prices to increase profits, analyze how much of an increase in volume will be needed to offset the decreases while still maintaining the same bottom line.

How to figure the results:

• Assume the company has a 40% gross profit margin.

• As seen from Table I, if prices are decreased 15%, a 36% increase in sales dollar volume is necessary to maintain the same gross profit.

• In terms of physical units sold, there has to be a 60% increase in the physical unit traffic to maintain the same gross profit dollar amount.

• Assume that an item sells for $100, and ten items are normally sold. That gives a $1,000 gross sales volume. The gross profit is $40 per unit, or $400. If the price is dropped to $85 per item, the new gross profit per unit is $25.

Dividing the original gross profit ($400) by $25, we see that 16 units have to be sold to still earn a $400 gross profit. Sixteen units at $85 per unit is $1,360. Thus, the 60% increase in units and 36% increase in dollar volume are arrived at.

This calculation method can be followed for any gross profit percentage and dollar amount.

The new gross profit percent is the selling price divided by the gross profit dollar amount.

Important consideration: Can sales in units be increased as much as they have to be to yield a greater gross dollar profit?

Compare that to the decrease in unit volume that can be permitted to occur if prices are raised.

Table II shows that if the price is increased 15%, then a 17% drop in sales dollars can be tolerated, along with a 28% decrease in physical units. If the price is increased 15%, the gross profit becomes $55 per unit (instead of $40). At a $55 gross profit, only 7.2 units (instead of ten) have to be sold in order to maintain the same $400 gross profit.

A sale is best if it is more likely that the number of units sold will be increased by more than 60% than that the physical volume will go down 28% because of an increase in price. But if sales cannot be increased to that extent and it is equally likely that more than 28% of the sales will be lost if prices are raised, then no action should be considered either way.

A price increase is best if it appears im-

TABLE I
Using a 40% Regular Gross Profit

% Decrease in Price	New Selling Price Per Unit	$ Amount of Gross Profit	New Gross Profit %	Sales Needed to Earn $400 Gross Profit	% Increase in Total Sales Needed	No. Physical Units Needed to Be Sold to Earn $400 Gross Profit	% Increase in No. Physical Units Needed
0	$100	$40	40	$1,000	0	10.0	0
5	95	35	37	1,080	8	11.4	14
10	90	30	33	1,200	20	13.3	33
15	85	25	29	1,360	36	16.0	60
20	80	20	25	1,600	60	20.0	100
25	75	15	20	2,000	100	26.7	167
30	70	10	14	2,800	180	40.0	300

TABLE II
Using a 40% Regular Gross Profit

% Increase in Price	New Selling Price Per Unit	$ Amount of Gross Profit	New Gross Profit %	Sales Needed to Earn $400 Gross Profit	% Decrease in Total Sales Needed	No. Physical Units Needed to Be Sold to Earn $400 Gross Profit	% Decrease in No. Physical Units Needed
0	$100	$40	40	$1,000	0	10.0	0
5	105	45	43	930	7	8.9	11
10	110	50	45	890	11	8.1	19
15	115	55	48	830	17	7.2	28
20	120	60	50	800	20	6.7	33
25	125	65	52	770	23	6.2	38
30	130	70	54	740	26	5.7	43

probable that units sold can increase 60% and that as much as 28% of unit sales will be lost.

Note: Don't limit analysis to dollar volume. Results can be misleading.

Source: Edward Mendlowitz, CPA, Siegel & Mendlowitz, 310 Madison Ave., New York 10017.

Introducing a New Product to Dealers

Show retailers a full year's program of support in advertising and deals. That demonstrates long-term commitment and is evidence of prior planning.

Offer a short line and a wide variety of case-pack sizes. Reason: Dealers don't want to clutter shelves with lots of varieties of the same product. And they don't want to take up valuable space in storerooms with more stock than their turnover justifies.

Include advertising in the marketing plan, and offer a variety of point-of-purchase displays. Retailers may resent being pressured to use the only display available (often one that is impractically large).

Source: Gene Mahany, senior vice president, Needham, Harper & Steers, Chicago, in *Advertising Age.*

Competing Against a National Brand

• Use intimate knowledge of local market to tailor-make the marketing plans. Package potato chips in boxes if that's the way consumers in the area like to store them. Feature ski promotions in a big ski area. Make the most of enthusiasm for and loyalty to local sports teams and other home-town attractions.

• Take advantage of being smaller to make quick decisions. This can be a precious asset when competing with national companies that are outspending the regional company but can't fine-tune national media schedules. It's best to buy regional TV wherever possible. A network

spot might cost a national company twice as much per thousand.

• Be alert for market niches that the national brand is abandoning. If the market is still there, move in quickly to fill the void. Examples: Nalley's Foods found out that Kraft was dropping its imitation mayonnaise. It came out with a similar product of its own in nine days. International Rubber, a small Louisville, Ky., company which now makes the most expensive radial tires on the market, sells through the quality tire dealers who were piqued when Michelin abandoned its one-dealer-per-town franchise system.

• Don't scrimp on creative effort or execution for advertising, packaging, and promotion. A small company's product shouldn't look cheap. A quality image is particularly important for a food product.

• Monitor trade sources closely to keep track of what national giants are doing in the local market. Personal contacts with local distributors and dealers can yield valuable advice. They often know competitors' plans.

Source: *Advertising Age.*

When Big Marketing Budget Won't Pay Off

Save big-dollar marketing campaigns for products that have a large share of their particular markets. Money spent marketing products that have only low market shares is usually money uneconomically spent.

That finding comes from a continuing study run by Dr. Sidney Schoeffler, director of the Strategic Planning Institute. About 1,800 businesses contribute confidential financial data to this not-for-profit organization.

Don't be misled by the term "market share": It doesn't necessarily imply big, nationwide business. Market share can be measured locally or with a narrow product segment.

How much should a company spend on marketing its various product lines?

Dr. Schoeffler reports that companies with a low share (below 26%) of their product market will achieve the highest profits if they spend less than six cents of every sales dollar on marketing.

Companies with a 26%-63% share of their market are also best advised to spend less than six cents of every sales dollar on marketing.

But those middle-share companies aren't as adversely affected by increasing marketing costs to 11 cents per sales dollar as are the low-share companies.

The chart below shows the percentage of the sales dollar spent on marketing when read vertically and the company's own share of the market when read horizontally. The numbers in the columns indicate return on investment.

This adverse effect on profits is true for low-share companies no matter what the quality of their products, says Schoeffler. It's difficult for low market-share companies to act as leaders in new product innovation or in marketing.

Schoeffler points out that a few very smart companies with low market-share products have increased profits with heavy campaigns, but he adds that that kind of success is rare.

High-share companies, on the other hand, with more than 63% of their markets, can be as profitable with expensive marketing approaches (more than 11 cents of every sales dollar) as with inexpensive (less than six cents).

Large-share companies have many economies of scale working for them in production and marketing. They can afford to spend heavily on marketing without damaging profitability.

MARKETING COSTS/SALES

		Lo	6%	11%	Hi
	Lo				
			20	13	7
RELATIVE	26%				
MARKET			21	19	19
SHARE	63%				
			34	31	34
	Hi				

Source: Strategic Planning Institute, 1 Broadway, Cambridge, MA 02142.

Impact of Shelf-Pack Size

One manufacturer found that a sizable percentage of overstocks, understocks, and unbalanced stocks can very often be traced directly to shelf-pack sizes that urgently need updating.

Its retailers tended to stock their shelves with 12 of an item because the item was traditionally packed in dozens. The consequence was that retailers didn't reorder until all 12 had been sold—they did not want more than 12 on the shelf and neither did they want broken packs. The solution: A six-pack.

Of all marketing practices, shelf-packaging tends to be frozen most deeply by tradition. Maybe your company's shelf-pack size is overdue for a change.

If Dealer Contests Don't Work, Try This

Problem: The same outlets won each year. Smaller ones were discouraged and gave up trying. Effectively speaking, the company had no incentive program at all.

Solution: The company made each dealer compete with itself and set its goal as a percentage above its own prior year's sales. The size of the operation lost all meaning. Growth became all-important.

Result: A dramatic pickup in year-to-year sales. The cost of prizes went up, but increased volume more than made up for that.

Outside Market Research Helps

Four situations in which a company of any size could profit from talking to market research consultants:

• Marketing plans need technological information from resources in other industries.

• A merger or acquisition is being considered. Beyond the balance sheet, the company needs to know how product lines and markets will meld. Better to get an objective study.

• A company wants frank appraisal of its image as seen by competitors, customers, noncustomers, suppliers, etc. This kind of research typically turns up useful information about competitors, too.

- Pinpointed share-of-market data is needed. Senior management wants an independent check of marketing performance from an external research agency with no vested interest.
Source: *Industrial Marketing.*

Choosing the Right Premium

Premiums are especially valuable in generating new users for a product. And the selection of that premium is important. A bad premium can actually stifle sales.

What to look for in a premium:
- Easily recognized value and use.
- Distinctiveness and exclusivity. Items ordinarily stocked at retail lack promotional impact. Regular stock items offend dealers who object to giving away products that they can sell at a profit.
- Appropriateness. It should be right for the product being promoted. It should also be appealing to the target consumer.
- Visual appeal. Make it desirable for the dealer to display.
Source: *Sales Promotion Techniques—A Basic Guidebook,* American Association of Advertising Agencies, 200 Park Ave., New York 10017.

Selling a Product to the Premiums Market

Can the product work as a give-away (or a "bargain") item to bring customers into a store, help a manufacturer increase market share, or boost a salesperson's productivity?

What has worked: A 2¢ iron-on patch; a $9.95 camera; and a $49.95 wok. Generally, the manufacturer sells his goods at 50% off the retail price.

Why premium business can be profitable to a manufacturer:
- For a successful item, sales will be in quantities substantially larger than usual.

- Selling costs through specialized sales representatives are low.
- Advertising costs are low, too. Premiums are advertised in only a limited number of trade publications and two main trade shows.

To convert a product to a premium, consider:
- Simply removing the trade name and putting on a new label.
- Making a few inexpensive changes in the product to lower the price range.
- Adapting the product to some new use. Especially industrial product—or know-how—that can be transformed into a consumer item. Successful ideas: A manufacturer of industrial molded vinyl products used his expertise to create toys, dolls, and puppets for consumer firms. A manufacturer of heavy-duty fabric products for industry designed a knapsack as a consumer premium.

Be prepared for long lead times. Premium decisions are low priority in most firms, so it may take six to 18 months to firm up an order. Then the goods are wanted immediately.
- When the orders come in, the manufacturer must be able to handle a deluge. (One company recently planned on 25,000 orders and got 400,000.) Fast action is necessary, or business will fizzle.

Best advice from old hands:
- Three years is probably the optimum amount of time to decide whether premiums are good or bad business for the company.
- Don't expect to make a killing—or to get in and right out because it's slack on the production floor right now. Look for reasonable volume—remember, premiums are an addition to regular business.
- Consider putting one person in charge of developing the premium business.
Source: Carmela Maresca and Leslie Wolff, The Maresca/Wolff Organization, Inc., 120 E. 56 St., New York 10022.

How Much to Spend on R&D

Spending more than 3.7% of the sales dollar on research and development is generally not a good idea for any company interested in maximum profitability. It's an especially bad idea in heavily unionized companies.

The Strategic Planning Institute's analysis of the financial data and experiences of 1,800 member businesses indicates that spending more than 1.3% of the sales dollar on R&D isn't profitable in a company that can't use the results efficiently. The usual reason: Rigid union work rules.

What the institute's figures show:
• Return on investment drops to a range of 12% (for most-heavily unionized companies) to 16% (for least-unionized companies) when R&D expense goes above 3.7% of sales.

Business Strategy When the Economy Turns Down

Business should be prepared to deal with a recession. Some strategic moves to consider if a slowdown is detected, particularly a slowdown in the firm's own industry:

A company that has a big piece of its market (local market or national market) has a choice of strategies in a downturn. And it usually makes the wrong choice.

It usually tries to keep the factory running full tilt. To do this, it cuts prices, offers special deals, unpublished discounts—all in an effort to maintain volume.

Competitors often react out of panic. Faced with the threat of losing market share, they make radical and desperate moves. They try to match price cuts or even outdo the imitator. Result: A murderous price war in an already weak market, which soon makes a shambles of the industry price structure.

What to do instead: Hold prices as stable as possible. If a small competitor trims prices, resist following. Don't let a small firm lead the market on pricing.

Improve marketing. Strengthen service. Give more attention to customers' needs. Even consider some product improvement. Overall, such actions cost less than price cutting.

The competition usually has little choice but to tag along. If they're wise, they'll follow the leader in resisting price cutting.

At best, aim for holding the market slice. Don't try to increase it.

The conventional wisdom is to introduce new products and services when business is good. That's a mistake. When sales are booming, the wisest managers do nothing new. They ride the crest. Keep R&D going instead. Lay plans, but hold back new product introductions.

When sales are falling and the market is dull, it's the time to excite the market with new products and services. When staff sees a lag in sales, it gets discouraged. Bring out new products and services during this lagging period to boost its spirits. Salespeople who were fat and happy riding the crest are hungry now. They'll grab the new product and sell it hard.

PURCHASING AND INVENTORY

Calculating Real Cost

Phantom Price Increases

Price Index Strategy for Inflation

When the Warranty Clock Starts

Protecting Buyer's Rights

How to Control Incoming Shipments

The Efficient Warehouse

Buy Now—Negotiate Later

20 PURCHASING AND INVENTORY

When Saving a Dollar on Purchasing Is Better Than Earning a Dollar on Sales

Figuring the trade-off: The typical U.S. firm spends 40%-60% of its sales dollar on procurement. Its after-tax margin is about 5%-6% on sales. To calculate the trade-off in profits for an individual company between a cost savings on procurement and an increase in sales, use the chart below as a guide:

SALES GAIN NEEDED TO EQUAL A 2% PROCUREMENT COST SAVING

Margin on Sales (after taxes at 46%)	Sales Spent on Procurement		
	40%	50%	60%
3%	14.40%	18.00%	21.60%
4	10.80	13.50	16.20
5	8.64	10.80	12.96
6	7.20	9.00	10.80
7	6.17	7.77	9.26
8	5.40	6.75	8.10
9	4.80	6.00	7.20

How to use the chart: Assume purchasing's share of the sales dollar is 50% and the company's after-tax margin on sales is 5%. Locate the 50% on the top row of figures. Find the 5% profit margin in the far left column. The number at the intersection of the 5% profit margin row and 50% purchasing share column is 10.80. Interpretation: A 2% saving in procurement costs yields the same profit as a hefty 10.80% increase in company sales.

Warning: The purchasing leverage factor varies significantly, depending on the company's profit margin and its procurement share.

Leverage is highest when: (1) Purchasing's share of the sales dollar is high and (2) profit margins are low.

Source: *Purchasing World.*

Calculating Real Cost

Focus on total cost: The purchase order price itself is only part of the story. It actually tells less than the complete cost. Knowing what an item "sells for" is only one piece of information that goes into determining what it really costs the buyer.

Other factors: Cost of delivery, inventory, transportation, warehousing, payment terms, discounts, lead times, etc.

An unusually high price for any one of these factors can offset any savings gained on the original "price."

Indicated action: Analyze the price of all purchases from the point of view of total cost. Add up the factors leading to a buying decision; calculate how much each costs.

Example: If product A must be bought in lots of 1,000 (a six-month supply), figure the cost of unproductive capital for six months.

Then realize that the buyer can negotiate on each one of such points. But he must have the relative value of each in hand before he can effectively negotiate.

In all likelihood, the accounting system can't easily isolate this information. It's going to require accounting changes so all the real costs can be assembled—from marketing, manufacturing, finance, legal, etc.

A technique to explore: Find out from supplier at what volumes it produces most efficiently. If possible, have it produce at that volume. But request to be billed only when your firm actually consumes that product. Naturally, the supplier must have an accurate picture of your firm's future buying plans.

Then negotiate to share in the savings. Since the manufacturer is producing at economical production runs, it may be willing to slow up billing. Cash flow between buyer and seller can be a major area of negotiation.

The aim is to get away from short-term buying and move toward as-long-as-possible-term.

How to gain leverage: Centralize/coordinate as much purchasing as possible. One team should do all the long-term negotiating for all the real costs of the item. Local delivery schedules and other details can be worked out by branches and plants as their needs arise. Central office, for example, should figure whether it's cheaper to buy on 60-day consignment or push for a 5% price cut.

Source: John J. Davin, director of purchasing, GTE Products Corp., Stamford, CT.

How to Avoid Ethical Problems in Purchasing

The minute a buyer is perceived as being anything other than ethical, it starts costing the company money. Word travels fast among suppliers, even about subtle differences in ethical standards among different departments. Top managers can and should influence the signals that buyers transmit to suppliers.

• Make company policy unmistakably clear, preferably in writing. Frame and hang standards of purchasing behavior on the reception area wall where visiting salespeople can't fail to notice. No good salesperson is going to risk offending the customer.

• Talk about the problem frequently. Have outside experts address company meetings.

• Encourage employees to come to top management with ethical questions just as they would with knotty legal or financial matters.

• Use company audits to review purchasing practices. Internal auditors (or, when necessary, outside auditors) should examine purchasing files to see if there were vigorous competitive bids on large transactions. Rule of thumb: There should be at least three solid bids for any substantial piece of business. Goal: At least two good alternatives. Caution: Too many bids can be as bad as too few. Each bid requires staff time and analysis. And suppliers may lose interest if asked to bid against too many competitors.

• Stay aware of the life-style of everyone charged with spending company money.

• Also watch life-styles of nonpurchasing executives who have an influence on major buying decisions.

• Make sure that buyers' relations with suppliers are in balance. What to watch for: Buyer-supplier lunches are fine, even dinner, provided the supplier is not always the host.

Be suspicious of purchasing people who:

• Don't use their expense accounts or company facilities to reciprocate.

• Always seem to be lunching with the same supplier at his club.

• Don't seem comfortable in the role of host.

This could indicate that they are so used to taking hospitality (and perhaps more) that they can't accept the host's role.

Monitoring a Purchasing Department: Questions Management Should Ask

Do buyers keep track of suppliers' labor relations (union contracts, expiration dates, settlement outlook)? This is essential for planning.

Do the buyers know supplier capabilities and weaknesses? It's vital for them to know who the suppliers are, when those suppliers could be vulnerable to embargoes, import quotas, price increases, discontinuance of a line. Are they knowledgeable about their processes and production cycles, time needed for production setups, machining hours required? Which supplier has the special in-house capabilities or processing methods to accommodate rush or special orders, produce an item when other suppliers are down?

Do buyers have at least one top supplier in each line (one that will supply technical advice, assist with substitutions, handle prototype projects on a time and materials-cost basis)?

Do buyers keep vendors up to date on your company's new products and processes, tests and standards—enabling them to suggest substitutions, offer cost-cutting and product-improvement ideas?

Do buyers cultivate top-level people to turn to for special accommodation, frank discussion of labor, supply, other problems?

Do buyers know what discretion they can use in accepting minor spec changes, temporary or permanent substitutions?

Do buyers have alternate sources to turn to in event of an unexpected delay, sudden stock out, or inventory miscalculation?

How Suppliers Hide Price Increases

Vendors can mask markups by manipulating other elements of cost:

• Product service. Sell a replacement part rather than repairing it. Charge for services that were formerly free.

• Payment terms. Shorten payment terms. Cut or eliminate prompt-payment discount.

• Materials. Switch to cheaper substitutes.

• Packaging. Change the size of a package while increasing the price per unit more than the size increase warrants.

• Transportation. Tighten transportation allowance policy. Change f.o.b. terms. Eliminate or restrict freight equalization provisions. Adopt a more restrictive policy on lost or damaged shipments.

• Increase minimum-order quantities.

Source: *Purchasing Magazine*, 221 Columbus Ave., Boston 02116.

Phantom Price Increases

Don't believe and don't pay every posted price increase. Often the seller doesn't really expect to get the higher price but is merely establishing a list price in fear of controls. A major company's purchasing agent told about a recent conversation. Corrugated box salesman: "I've been sent here to tell you we're raising prices 8%." (General laughter.) "Well, if you won't go 8%, what can you do for me?" Purchasing agent: "I'll buy you lunch." Salesman: "That's the best offer I've had this week."

Before Agreeing to a Supplier's Price Increase

• Use the same engineering specs and send the part out for bids. Don't overlook smaller, new, local shops whose low overhead and desire for business could mean big savings.

• Switch to bulk purchases (and look for a lower price) instead of monthly as-needed orders. Even consider buying enough for the entire year at one time and storing it.

• Specify substitute material. The fact that it's an old idea doesn't make it less valuable.

• Negotiate for longer-term guarantees on prices in exchange for a longer-term commitment. If orders can't be placed at firm prices, put a limit on the escalation, especially on longer-term contracts.

Alternative: Make the product yourself.

Smart purchasing agents today aren't just buying specific products—they're buying "solutions" to problems. That isn't just a neat turn of phrase—it's a radical shift in buying philosophy. As an example: A company needs to move material around its factory. An intelligent buyer would shop around for various forklift trucks, overhead cranes, conveyors, etc. But the problem with that is that the buyer has to educate himself on each product, determine which to use when, etc. This is obviously a slow and inefficient process. A better way is to go to two or three of the largest materials-handling companies. Let them examine the company's present and future needs. Then let them compete on a systems approach and come up with the best technology that solves not only today's problems but tomorrow's also. In the long run, the cost will be lower and the operation more efficient.
Source: John Davin, vice president, GTE-Sylvania.

Every Price Is Negotiable

Negotiate all quoted prices—especially list prices, standard product prices, and discount schedules. They all represent averages designed to fit the average customer at some average time.

Investigate the company's order to find something other than average, something easier, more profitable, or more advantageous for the seller to handle. Then use that information to start negotiating for a discount. Examples:

• The supplier's price rate protects the seller from slow payers. But the company always pays on delivery. Make the point that prompt payers should not be penalized.

• Seller offers free engineering help during equipment installation. But the company has its own engineering staff; it just needs nuts and bolts, not free advice. Therefore, make it clear that the company should not be charged for services it doesn't need and won't use.

• The seller's price includes delivery. But the company plant is only one mile away. Obviously, then, transportation costs are either nonexistent or negligible and should not be charged.

• The quoted price is based on an average 100-item order. But the company always orders a minimum of 300 items per order. The company should be able to negotiate a volume discount.
Source: Dr. Chester L. Karrass, Center for Effective Negotiating, 2066 Westwood Blvd., Los Angeles 90026.

Things to Say When Negotiating a Price

• Is that price the best you can do?
• What if I buy six?
• This is what I need, but my budget is limited. What can you do for X dollars?
• It certainly is a great item, but why is it so expensive?

Inflation Strategy: Which Price Index to Use

When a supplier or customer insists on "indexing" the price of an item—that is, raising it proportionally to some price index—resist using the Consumer Price Index. It's much too volatile. For a more realistic index, use the Gross National Product Implicit Price Deflator, which is issued by the government every month (and reported regularly in *The Wall Street Journal*). To get on the mailing list, write *Economic Indicators*, Joint Economic Committee, Dirksen Senate Office Bldg., Washington, DC 20510.

If your company is the buyer, insist that the index clause include the possibility that the price will decline if the index declines.

Formula for Predicting the Price of Component Parts

Most price forecasters stick to predicting prices of raw materials. Rarely do they focus on components—the items most businesses really buy. Now a series of formulas devised by Dr. Louis J. Paradiso, economist and consultant, and Edgar A. Grunwald, retired managing editor of *Business Week*, provides the technique for an average manager to forecast prices of parts with reasonable accuracy.

How the technique works: Prices tend to follow specific leaders. Products primarily made of steel (metal containers, fasteners, valves, and fittings) follow the lead of finished steel products. Paints follow chemicals.

Using six leader items (finished steel products, chemicals, paper, nonmetallic mineral products, electrical machinery, and fuel power), managers can project price trends for 132 fabricated items.

To do this, managers must know how quickly or slowly followers respond to their leader—the time lag.

The Paradiso-Grunwald technique uses a series of charts to determine the time lag.

How to forecast hardware prices from finished steel (FSP), published monthly by the Bureau of Labor Statistics:

• The Paradiso-Grunwald formula is FSP × .6453 + 36.47. In 1978, the FSP index was 253.

• Multiply 253 by .6453 = 163.26.

• Add 36.47. Total: 199.73. That's the calculated 1978 price index for hardware.

• Use the same formula as above, but estimate the FSP for the period ahead. Assume that at the end of 1978 the forecast for the FSP was 273.

• Multiply 273 by .6453 = 176.17.

• Add 36.47. Total: 212.64. That is the 1979 hardware forecast.

The authors provide individual chapters on how to predict the price of each type of product from the six leader items. Movements of the leaders are signaled enough in advance to permit reasonably safe price estimates. The average accuracy of the formula approach has been within 0.6% of actual price movements over the past 11 years, according to the authors.

Paradiso and Grunwald employ index numbers because most managers use the government's producer price index for their basic data. This is available only in index form. Dollars and cents data must be converted into index form before use in these formulas, which are described in detail in *Industrial Products Forecaster—How to Predict the Prices,* McGraw-Hill, New York.

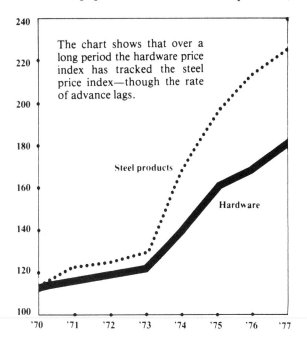

The chart shows that over a long period the hardware price index has tracked the steel price index—though the rate of advance lags.

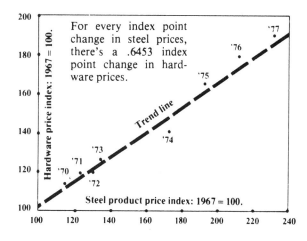

For every index point change in steel prices, there's a .6453 index point change in hardware prices.

Buying Secondhand Equipment

Have a lawyer check public records for any outstanding liens. They could endanger ownership rights to the equipment. Such a search isn't foolproof, however. A lien might have been filed in another county.

The seller will probably insist that the sale be

as is, with no warranties, express or implied. If the seller does not put this in writing, there is an implied warranty that the equipment is suitable for the intended use.

Don't forget the investment tax credit. Used equipment qualifies if its remaining useful life is at least three years. Depending on estimated life, the credit is 3.3%, 6.7%, or 10% of purchase cost up to $100,000 in any one year.

For items totaling up to $10,000 in any year, it may be okay to take additional first-year depreciation, too.

When the Warranty Clock Starts Running

The warranty period starts running when the equipment is delivered, even though the buyer may not accept it until much later, after all the necessary adjustments have been made. Warning: Where a serviceman has to come back repeatedly to tinker with a machine, watch the warranty deadline. Make sure the machine is put through all its paces before that to detect any defects. If necessary, file formal notice of a claim under the warranty before it expires. It's easy to withdraw the claim later if the equipment performs satisfactorily.
Source: 25 UCC Reporter 65.

Smart Purchasing

• Traveling requisition: Used for frequently ordered items, it works like an ordinary requisition form, but has permanent requisition data for a single item written in a space at the top and room for a series of requisitions at the bottom. The requisitioner fills it out and sends it to purchasing, which places the order. When the order is received, purchasing sends the form back to the requisitioner for use when additional supplies are needed.

• Requisition forms designed so the requisitioner (not purchaser) does most of the work: One part of the snap-out form is the requisition.

Another part becomes the purchase order when purchasing adds information and confirms it. Other parts go to accounting, inventory, etc. There could be parts that can serve as requests for quotes. The purchasing agent simply mails them to suitable vendors. When the requests are returned, one becomes a purchase order.

• Self-ordering: For some frequently used expendables, let the salesperson check inventory, order what is needed, and fill out the order form.

• Purchase department should see machinery repair and maintenance records. The cost of equipment after purchase should be a factor in all purchasing decisions.

• If there's a dispute about one bill from a steady supplier, pay other bills by earmarked checks that show which invoice is being paid. Otherwise the creditor will probably apply payments against the oldest invoices first, and courts will agree with that approach. Money for a bill that's being paid could be diverted to one that you didn't want to pay.

Protecting Buyer's Rights

• Detailed product specifications. Buyer can reject goods if there's any failure to conform to specs, no matter how minor (except for installment shipments). But if the defect is not covered by the specs, the difference between what was ordered and what was delivered must be material for rejection to be justified.

• Signature space. Have the seller sign there to acknowledge the order. Buyer now has a contract on his own terms, even if seller sends back a printed acknowledgment with different terms.

• Boiler-plate language covering important points often forgotten: Warranties, time to inspect, seller's liability for breach, etc. If this isn't done, seller's standard terms (often unacceptable) will govern unless objected to within ten days. If purchase order is tightly drafted and terms conflict with seller's acknowledgment, neither party's terms apply. In that case, the terms of the Uniform Commercial Code—which are basically fair—apply.
Source: William M. Sharpless, Esq., Green, Sharpless and Greenstein, 1 Rockefeller Plaza, New York 10020.

When Buyers Can be Held to Unsigned Order

Buyers don't have to sign a purchase contract for it to be valid under the Uniform Commercial Code.

Example: Buyer and seller work out a "rough" agreement; the seller writes out the details and sends a copy to the buyer. That is binding upon the buyer, unless he objects within ten days.

Exceptions: The rule applies to "merchants" and other businesspeople, but not to consumers. The dividing line can be hazy. Some state courts have ruled that farmers and unsophisticated "ma & pa" organizations are exempt, too.

Buyers' Alert: Read Seller's Acknowledgment Carefully

Background: The buyer sends purchase order. The seller sends back a printed acknowledgment and acceptance of the order. But his printed form changes some of the terms in his favor. It may, for example, weaken the warranties or the buyer's right to damages for defective goods.

Under the Uniform Commercial Code, these changes buried in the fine print are void. The code says the seller must spell things out for the buyer, make sure the changes are "brought home" to him. If they are prominently typed on the printed form or mentioned in a covering letter, then they are probably valid.

Here's the new development buyers should watch out for: The seller puts a printed legend on the acknowledgment form that says something like: "This acceptance is expressly conditioned upon buyer's assent to any additional or different terms contained in this form."

This language, or anything like it, is a red flag. The buyer should reply to the acknowledgment form, expressly refusing to assent to new terms. Sometimes it's simpler to tell the seller that the company won't accept delivery if the seller changes the form.

Source: Dean John E. Murray, Jr., University of Pittsburgh Law School, in *Purchasing World.*

Suing a Manufacturer When the Product Was Bought from a Dealer

Increasingly, buyers of defective industrial products sue the manufacturer, even though they bought from a middleman. Court cases have been running this way.

Background: Generally the law says: "I can't sue you unless I had some dealings with you." That is called "privity of contract." But there has long been an exception in consumer products, because advertising and "implied warranties" set up what amounts to a contractual relationship between the manufacturer and consumer, even when there is a dealer in the middle.

Now courts are following the same approach in industrial products:

• A hoist manufacturer sold a hoist to a truck dealer for installation on a truck that was then sold to a user. The user successfully sued the hoist maker.

• A chemical manufacturer sold resin to a textile converter and advertised its "shrink-resistance." He was successfully sued by the garment maker, who bought from the converter, not from the manufacturer.

Customer's Rights When Defective or Wrong Goods Arrive

Problem deliveries (wrong color, size, style, quantities, or defective goods) are inevitable. When the customer and supplier have a continuing relationship, the problems are usually worked out informally. But with a first-time supplier or in a single-purchase situation, the buyer should be aware of his rights under the law before negotiating.

• The worst thing to do is nothing. That's considered acceptance after a reasonable period (hours for some items, days or even weeks for others). The buyer has an obligation to let the seller know there's a problem and that the shipment is being rejected. Note: Signing the trucker's delivery doesn't mean acceptance of the goods. It merely shows buyer received something from the trucker.

• The buyer can take a reasonable time to inspect the shipment. It's usually a few hours or days, but it could be longer. (Example: Complex electronic equipment, where it takes weeks of testing and use to find out if it works properly.)

• The buyer has the right to accept part of a shipment and reject the rest—an important factor when goods are urgently needed. But that acceptance has to be at least one commercial unit (a case, a gross, a carload, or whatever is customary in the trade).

• The buyer can't destroy goods. He must keep them for a time and must follow reasonable instructions from seller about what to do with the goods. (Example: Ship them back or ship elsewhere at seller's expense.)

• The buyer must be prudent in care of the goods. If a computer is left out in the rain, or frozen food is allowed to thaw, the buyer could be liable for the damage. Special obligations for perishable goods: The buyer must notify the seller immediately. The buyer might have an obligation to take steps to resell the goods, charging the seller a sales commission.

Important: Using the goods or shipping them to a third party is considered acceptance.

When Goods Are Lost, Delayed, or Damaged in Transit

Both buyers and sellers must take the right steps to protect themselves if goods go astray during shipment.

The basic law says that the buyer is usually stuck with the hassles of tracing shipments, filing claims, and waiting for payment unless the contract provides otherwise. The Uniform Commercial Code provides that, if the contract does not cover the point, title and risk of loss pass from the seller to the buyer when the goods are made available for shipment at the seller's place of business. But that provision can be changed by agreement between the parties.

What buyers should do for their protection:

• Try to negotiate a contract provision that risk of loss does not pass to the buyer until the goods arrive at the purchaser's place of business. That way the seller has to deal with any problems that arise during shipment. (Where the order is small and the seller is a giant company, the buyer probably will not be able to negotiate these terms.)

• The buyer should cover this point in the printed language of the purchase order. Important: Buyer must be sure that the seller's acknowledgment does not try to countermand this. In that case there could be a battle.

• The buyer may get some protection by ordering goods shipped f.o.b. destination.

• If the buyer cannot shift the risk to the seller, it should be sure to have adequate insurance coverage. Common carriers usually have coverage only up to a few dollars per pound. Buy additional coverage for each shipment (expensive and a nuisance) or get blanket coverage of all arriving shipments.

What the seller should do: Have the acknowledgment of the purchase order specify that the risk of loss passes to the buyer as soon as goods are ready to ship. Be sure buyer accepts this and resist attempts to renegotiate it.

Source: William M. Sharpless, Esq., Green, Sharpless & Greenstein, 1 Rockefeller Plaza, New York, 10020.

Perils in Open-End Requirements Contracts

There is a danger that purchase contracts may not be binding if they don't specify a minimum order.

It's a common business arrangement: The seller agrees to supply the buyer with as much as the buyer requires of a certain item. Such a requirements contract may include some upper limit, but usually does not set a minimum.

Problem for the seller: Parties usually contemplate large quantities and a long-term relationship when the contract is signed. Contract price reflects expected high volume, so is lower than what the seller would charge for smaller orders. If the buyer finds cheaper source elsewhere, the seller not only loses the account, but also makes smaller profit than was projected on the quantities already shipped.

Problem for the buyer: Contract may not be enforceable against the seller if it's not binding on the buyer. If the seller finds another buyer willing to pay more, it may cut off shipments. This could be especially harmful to the buyer during supply shortages.

Solution for both: Contract should include a minimum quantity that the buyer commits to take, or a mutual promise that neither party will cut off relationship as long as the buyer's requirements continue. It might also include an escalator clause to protect the seller against a possible big cost increase.

ber 15. Or he says that conditions have changed and he must have a higher price. Either of these would constitute anticipatory repudiation by seller and would release the buyer from the contract, unless he chose to agree to the new terms. Once released, he is free to "cover" (buy equivalent goods elsewhere), and he may claim damages for difference and delay.

Warning: Only a clear and definite statement will repudiate the contract. Example: Seller says, "We're having some problems, we may be a little late." Buyer responds, "Do the best you can." That is not repudiation; the contract is still in force, and a buyer who refuses delivery is breaching contract.

Source: John E. Murray Jr., Dean, University of Pittsburgh Law School, in *Purchasing World.*

Late Delivery Not Always Breach of Contract

When the seller misses a delivery date, the buyer may be able to claim that it's a breach of contract. But not always. The answer depends on trade practices, past relationships, and other circumstances.

Example: Buyer and seller have dealt with each other for years. Deliveries have sometimes been as much as two weeks late, but the buyer never complained.

Result: This history defines their contractual rights and obligations. A delivery date stated by this seller to this buyer means "that date or up to two weeks later."

Similarly, trade practices can make delay acceptable. In some businesses lateness may be commonly accepted and even expected by buyers and sellers. In this case, "Delivery June 6" may mean "about June 6."

But what if the buyer really wants on-time delivery? He should write on the purchase order, "Time is of the essence; delivery must not be later than June 6."

In this case, delivery on the morning of June 7 is a breach of contract. (Caution: The words should be handwritten or typed; it may not work if printed as part of the form.)

Suppose the seller gives notice that delivery scheduled for June 6 will be made about Septem-

Buyer May Reject Goods Even After Long Delay

A buyer may be able to send defective goods back even after a long wait—if it can be shown that the delay was normal trade practice.

In one case, the buyer ordered carpet for a new building and had it delivered to a warehouse to await completion of construction. There were delays, and it wasn't until nine months later that the carpet was unwrapped and found to be defective. The seller refused to replace it.

The buyer sued and won. The court said that construction delays were common and the seller knew that it was normal trade practice to store carpet during construction.

Smart move: Avoid problems like these by immediate inspection of goods.

LaVilla Fair v. *Lewis Carpet,* Kansas Sup. Ct.

How to Control Incoming Shipments

Managers don't exercise the same close controls over incoming goods as in handling receipt of money. Result: The plant receiving dock becomes a trouble spot and often a cash drain.

• Problem: 10% of all shipments usually arrive without any documentation or with incorrect information. One solution: Notify all suppliers that the condition and timing of deliveries are important in (1) evaluating their service quality and (2) determining who gets future business.

• Problem: Even when a shipment arrives in order, there are often no internal records indicating anything was ordered, or the details don't match the shipment. (This happens most frequently when orders are issued orally to suppliers.) Suggestion: Limit the number of people authorized to place oral orders. Important: Set up a procedure to make sure written confirmation gets to the receiving dock. Management tip: Review a variety of incoming shipments and see what kind of instructions were issued for handling bonded items (imported or exported), reusable pallets, and other special situations, in order to provide clear-cut instructions for every contingency.

• Problem: As many as 15% to 20% of all shipments arrive 30 to 60 days ahead of schedule. Purchasing and receiving departments are usually under pressure to be alert to late shipments but fail to take account of early shipments. Too soon is as bad as too late. Early deliveries can tie up capital in excess inventory. Early shipping is a growing trend. The answer: Set penalties for early shipping that parallel the penalties in effect for late deliveries.

• Problem: Goods are ordered in units, but arrive in cartons. Or they come in cartons when ordered on skids. Result: Costly rearranging and repackaging by the customer and more time lost. Remedy: Get tough. Deduct from the supplier's invoice the cost of time and labor involved in rearranging and repackaging.

• Problem: Urgently needed parts or materials are held up for routine inspection or clerical procedures. A rush order notice should have been attached to get them directly to the production floor. Suggestions: (1) Maintain a list of hot items that are to be moved straight to the plant floor. (2) Specify exact procedures for bypassing usual inspection and other routines. (3) Make sure there is a control system to get special instructions to the receiving department whenever standard procedures are to be waived.

• Problem: A whole shipment is rejected because some items are defective when enough good items could have been salvaged from the shipment to keep production lines running. Better way: Establish categories of goods and recommended handling for each.

Example: Category I should be inspected, processed immediately, and either put into inventory or returned if defective or sub-par. Category II items are to be inspected immediately, but if the shipment is found to contain defective items, the acceptable portion is to be sent directly to the production floor. Category III items are low-priority and will be inspected during lulls.

• Problem: Inventory in limbo. That is the accountants' term for goods under warranty that have been returned for some reason by the customer but haven't been properly re-entered on the books. Since they have no accounting status, they can disappear without management being the wiser. Remedy: Set up procedures for identifying, segregating, and getting that inventory back on the books—fast.

• Problem: The order sheet specifies "arm" but the invoice says "support." Confusion grows even worse if the supplier has a subcontractor who uses yet another term. Receiving dock personnel shouldn't have to interpret. Remedy: Work out common nomenclature with suppliers in advance.

General recommendation: Establish a central checking point where all shipments are brought before routing to the appropriate receiving dock. This reduces time wasted in trucking to the wrong dock or plant area.

Cutting Costs of Inbound Freight

Cost-cutting efforts in transportation usually focus on outbound shipments. Inbound freight costs are often high because nobody has really tried to trim them. What to look at:

• Different shipping methods used by major suppliers. Check with the company's traffic department and/or local carriers to see if they recommend the same routing. If not, find out why not, and discuss it with the supplier.

• Methods of lowering the supplier's (and eventually the company's) transportation costs. Get a lower rate per unit by increasing size of shipments. A packaging change might also lower the rate.

• Descriptions that affect freight costs. Check inbound freight bills to find out if descriptions correctly describe products shipped. Differences in description of the same item can affect shipping costs by 80%.

• Number of carriers that handle inbound freight. Multisourcing in transportation is as expensive as it is in other purchases.

• Direct suppliers in the same area to ship to a common point where their separate loads can be consolidated and then reshipped at a significant saving.

• Frequency of shipments from major suppliers. If more often than weekly and if shipments are small, instruct them to accumulate enough weight to qualify for lower bulk rates.

• Make sure buyers and traffic people coordinate efforts. It makes little sense to save on the purchase if the transportation costs will be increased.

• F.o.b. terms. They determine: (1) Which company pays the freight charges. (2) Which company runs the risk of loss in case the shipment is damaged in transit. (3) What insurance covers the shipment. (4) Who pays for unloading the shipment if a claim is involved.

To help the company monitor inbound transportation costs, a traffic professional who knows all about transportation terminology, legal requirements, freight tariffs, and regulations can be a great asset.

Source: *Purchasing Magazine*, 221 Columbus Ave., Boston 02116.

Suing the Trucking Company for Damage to Shipment

A shipper may collect damages from a carrier that fails to use reasonable care in handling a shipment. What's reasonable depends on the particular cirumstances. Case: A trucking company advertised that it was properly equipped and skilled in handling shipments of wine. But it negligently left a trailerload of wine outside for two days in freezing weather, though it could have been delivered in three hours. Ruling: The trucker had to pay damages.

Note: The Interstate Commerce Act provides that if the carrier is liable the shipper may recover its full loss, including anticipated profit on the sale of the goods.

Source: 580 F 2d 240.

Extra Warehouse Space

High-ceiling warehouses usually have wasted space above the shipping area, just inside the loading bays. Build a mezzanine there. Some uses: Storing packing materials or office supplies, packing split cases, employee coffee-break area, lunchroom.

Tracking Down Inventory Errors

Particularly in small and medium-size manufacturing companies, it's those small pluses and minuses that add up to misleading on-hand inventory balances that, in turn, lead to erroneous judgments about buying, not buying, stocking, positioning, relocating, etc.

Here's how to solve that problem:

Start by studying any exception procedures, such as items that must be reworked in some way. Are they subtracted when taken out for reworking? Re-entered when they come back?

If not counted on the way out but counted on the way back in, inventory will be overstated.

If counted on the way out but not on the way back in, they will appear as receivables when they are actually in inventory.

Check items used for maintenance, whether they are made in-house or not. Because maintenance workers tend to be indirect rather than direct labor, disciplines often are not applied as they would be with production or sales people.

The same stringent procedures should be used not only for withdrawals, but for returns of unused supplies as well.

Watch for unplanned issues, such as replacements for parts that proved defective and had to be scrapped. It's important to record the re-issued parts that may be lost because they are issued against an original work order, whether or not the company overissues to allow for scrap.

Samples used by salesmen or purchasing agents soliciting special quotes from suppliers (especially in stylized industries) can amount to a hefty total in a year. These should be formally issued, without charge, not picked up casually.

Any variations from production norms caused by changes in procedures, average manufacturing time, lower scrap rates, and the like must be promptly factored into inventory record keeping. They will affect flow of materials through the plant and result in the drawing down of inventory in different ways than current process sheets call for. All of that influences purchasing decisions.

Look out for split-lot orders, which create opportunities for error all along the line.

Similarly, cancellations of original orders may get lost in the shuffle.

Color codes and numbering techniques are effective in separating the inventory pluses from the minuses.

The best discipline: Require that any transaction involving a change in inventory (plus or minus) have authorization.

The authorization can either be by a person or by the submission of a form. In either case, you have achieved (1) the discipline of authorization and (2) the documentation of any change.

Other fertile hunting ground: Research and development group; product, quality, and machine testing operations; training programs; and recall or warranty programs.

All of these involve use of product inventory, and much of that is typically underreported or unreported.

Don't forget unplanned receipts in the form of usable materials that can be salvaged from rejected production models. As unsalvageable items must be taken out of inventory, so must salvageable items be placed back in.

Source: Norman Kobert, P. O. Drawer 21396, Ft. Lauderdale, FL 33335.

The Efficient Warehouse

• Number all shelves, pallet racks, bins, etc. This is a lot of trouble in the beginning, but can improve your operation dramatically. A system used throughout the world is the "post office" location system, i.e., odd numbers on one side, evens on the other.

• Give all materials a designated position, or "home." In selecting that home, favor the order picker (who may visit the site 100 times to your one). Consider how products will be picked and packed. Generally, it's best to move from light-weight, fast-moving items, through medium- to slow-moving and heavy items. The idea is to get heavy items packed on the bottom and moved as short a distance as possible.

• Arrange by "families" in order of popularity. Families may be from same manufacturer; subfamilies can be arranged by usage (and might include similar products from different manufacturers).

• Products that are often used together should be stored side by side. Put substitutes nearby to avoid unnecessary backtracking.

• Within each shelving section, arrange materials to read like the pages of a book (i.e., left to right and top to bottom). Within a "family," arrange by alphabetical sequence according to manufacturer's trade names, and then by that company's stock numbers. Leave "holes" (non-allocated spaces) for future items to come into family groupings. One good way: Keep top and bottom shelves reserved for overstock or future growth. Plan for maximum on-hand quantity. Allow 4- to 5-inch clearances between pallets.

• Store goods in manufacturer's cartons (after removing all wires, bands, overwraps, etc.).

Source: Irving and Robert Footlik, Footlik & Associates, 2530 Crawford Ave., Evanston, IL 60201.

The Key Inventory Question: Why Stock This Item?

Here are three steps to take to identify and eliminate excess inventory:

1. Standardize. Find multiple uses for the same or similar items. Substitute and reduce the number in stock. Types of items to check in a standardization push: Paints, packing materials, hand tools, office supplies, couplings, valves, motors, pumps, fasteners. With ongoing analysis, it's almost always possible to replace many items with fewer items. But engineering and other departments must cooperate.

Five fast steps to inventory standardization:

• Compare all proposed new items with existing inventory items to determine possible substitutions from existing stocks.

• Analyze present inventories with suppliers from time to time in order to standardize some closely related items and eliminate others.

• Seek substitutes for materials, processes, or suppliers by studying specifications and designs.

• Establish time limits for when "special" items are to be discontinued in stock. Then stop reordering.

• Weigh all special designs against the potential cost savings of using standard items.

2. Commonality analysis. Consider the function of each inventory item. Instead of just re-evaluating different screws, broaden the analysis to include all types of fasteners (nuts, bolts, clamps, hooks and eyes, snaps, adhesives, rivets, pins, flaps, tabs).

Method: Make a value or functional analysis of what each inventory item does as opposed to what it is. Forget the number, the description, the size, and the cost. Just consider function. Renumbering by what an item does, establishing an identification code based on function, is one of the best ways to recognize commonality. Example: All items concerned with fastening get the number 9 in their code. Sorting by functional code will show up many duplications that can't be found any other way. Example: A support arm might be inventoried by six different item numbers, under such categories as "arm," "support," "davit," "weldment," "casting," or "weight balance." There may be four varieties of each and all 24 perform basically the same function. Codification will expose this.

It is more effective to make small savings on important inventory items than large savings on insignificant items. If it's impossible to work on the company's entire inventory, start with the significant areas first, then branch out.

Get support from the necessary departments (design, engineering) to substitute one item for another.

3. Obsolescence studies. Many companies outdate inventory on a purely tax basis. (Example: They take big writedowns in a good year.) Others have a once-a-year scrap sale. (That is not a good idea since it may or may not coincide with high scrap prices.)

Better idea: An ongoing obsolete or excess inventory analysis. Possibility: A computer program to show last usage, monthly usage, and no usage. Then products which have not had a call for three months, six months, or a year can be identified and perhaps eliminated.

Other ways to get rid of obsolete inventory:

• Postpone purchases of standard items by converting or modifying inventoried items for which there is no demand. Often a little more investment or reworking can convert excess inventory into something that is usable.

• Review scrap prices through the year and take advantage of high spots to unload excess inventory.

• Seek repurchase of some items by original suppliers, who may well know of other customers for them. This only works with suppliers who have a stake in maintaining the company's goodwill. It is worth trying, however, because the company can get a much higher price by selling material back to its manufacturer than by selling it for scrap.

Source: Norman Kobert, Norman Kobert & Assocs., P.O. Drawer 21396, Ft. Lauderdale, FL 33335. Author of *Inventory Strategies,* Boardroom Books, New York.

Inventory Control Priorities

The amount spent on inventory control should be in reasonable proportion to its profit potential. Basic problem: Identifying the profit contribution of every item would be a tremendous task.

The amount you spend for control should bear some relationship to contribution. A far less effective alternative: Spending an equivalent amount of effort on each item. One principle that has proved valid in many areas: A small percentage of causes is responsible for a major share of a

POLICY OPTIONS TO CONTROL INVENTORY

CLASSIFICATION	CONTROL OPTIONS
A (80% of sales, 20% of items)	Base ordering on Economic Order Quantities (EOQs).* Maintain perpetual inventory records. Establish reorder points (minimums) based on lead-time demands and safety stocks.
B (15% of sales, 20% of items)	Base ordering on 4- to 6-month supply. Maintain perpetual inventory records on some items. Reorder items when 2-month supply is on hand (e.g., assume that it takes 2 to 3 months to receive an ordered item).

*As the size of the order increases, the holding costs (interest expense on inventory investment, insurance, storage costs) increase, but ordering costs (selecting a supplier, receiving and inspecting goods, etc.) decrease. Any reduction in one set of costs is accompanied by an increase in the other. To find the Economic Order Quantity, find the lowest total cost for the sum of ordering and holding costs.
Source: *Business Controls Made Simple* by Glen Husack, *Boardroom Books,* New York.

given effect or result. This principle works for inventories, too. How to apply it:

• Arrange inventory items in descending order by annual dollar sales or usage. (If you already have a card system of some kind, this is quite easy. On separate slips of paper write down the item number or description and the dollar sales, then do the descending order sort.)

• Find the total dollar sales for all items.

• Classify the items as follows:

Class A—Items representing the top 80% of total dollar sales.

Class B—Items representing the next 15% of total dollar sales.

Class C—Items representing the remaining 5% of dollar sales.

In a typical company, the results will be something like this:

Class	Annual Dollar Sales	No. Inventory Items
A	80%	20%
B	15	20
C	5	60
	100%	100%

The items would fall in approximately the same categories if the distribution were made on the basis of gross profit contribution.

• Class A items include all those with annual sales of more than a certain amount (e.g., $600 is the cutoff point between A and B classes).

• Class B items include all those with annual sales falling in a middle range (e.g., between $300 and $600).

• Class C items include all those with annual sales below the B range (e.g., less than $300).

New items entering the inventory are categorized in accordance with their expected sales level.

Ledger cards make this system easy. If you don't have them:

• Identify all the fast-moving and high-value inventory items.

• Keep choosing until you have accounted for 20% of the items. These are your A items, which will probably account for 80% of the company's total dollar sales.

How to control the items in each of these groups? The right answer depends on the kind of business, the nature of the inventory, and the production schedule. Spend more time and effort controlling the 20% A items that account for 80% of the sales. That's 80% of the job. Don't disregard the B and C items, but give them far less emphasis than the A ones.

How to Keep Inventories Lean

Shorten the company's own internal lead time so material is required later in the production schedule. The later the commitment, the less probable that material orders will be affected by schedule changes.

Support the schedule as the number-one priority. Fight the tendency to overstock by ensuring that material is not received ahead of schedule.

Limit company liability by writing cancellation clauses into contracts. One recommended standard: Liability is limited to two months' requirements, regardless of the number of months contracted for.

Order less volume, but more frequently. It may be worth extra order-processing costs and even higher prices to stay liquid and lean.

Clean up records by writing off inventory that is either obsolete or in excess of current needs. **Source:** Ernest C. Huge, production and inventory management specialist, in *Purchasing World.*

Buy Now—Negotiate Later

"Buy now—negotiate later" is a rarely used technique. And for good reason.

But it works in the company's favor when:

• Work cannot be accurately estimated until some of it has been done.

• There is no time to negotiate.

• The buyer believes the seller's price is padded with costs that aren't likely to occur and won't appear in the final price.

• The seller's bargaining position will be worse later, because it has committed resources, and will be afraid to lose the contract.

• The seller's track record shows that it is unlikely to exploit the buyer.

• The seller is willing to commit to a reasonable "not-to-exceed" price.

Charitable Contribution from Inventory: Deduct Twice the Cost

A gift out of inventory might be the best charitable contribution a company can make.

Problem: How to value it for tax purposes? Before passage of the Tax Reform Act of 1976, a corporation couldn't claim a charitable deduc-

tion that was more than its basis in contributed inventory. Basis usually meant cost. That's tough on firms where fair market value was far higher, as in pharmaceuticals.

For contributions made after October 4, 1976, however, a corporation may deduct basis plus one-half of any appreciation in value. The deduction may not exceed twice the basis of the contributed property. The donee must be a public charity or a private operating foundation. It must furnish the donor with a statement that the donated inventory will be used for the purpose for which tax-exempt status has been granted.

Also, the charity (specifically limited to care of ill, needy, or infants) must certify that the property will not be sold. (This stepped-up basis for deductions doesn't apply to property which fails to meet the standards of the federal Food, Drug, and Cosmetics Act.)

How to Put an End to Overcharging by Vendors

In most instances, if a buyer spots an overcharge, all the supplier has to do is correct the billing. As a result, the seller has no strong incentive to eliminate overcharges. The time-consuming and often costly burden of checking rests with the buyer.

The buyer's defense:

1. Negotiate a contract clause which provides that if an overcharge is discovered by the buyer, the seller must immediately refund an amount determined by the percentage of the error to the entire billing, not just that portion discovered to be wrong.

For example: A $5,000 portion of a $40,000 bill is checked by the buyer and found to have a $500 (10%) overcharge. The 10% error is applied to the entire $40,000 on the assumption that the error rate was constant, so the seller must refund $4,000.

2. Have an outside auditor check all billings, with the seller agreeing to pay for the audit if the error rate exceeds a predetermined amount.

3. Agree on a error penalty. It might be a $2

penalty for every $1 of error made by the seller.

Negotiate these clauses as part of the contract. That's the time when the vendor is most likely to go along to avoid losing the sale.

Source: Chester Karrass, director of The Center for Effective Negotiating, 2066 Westwood Blvd., Los Angeles 90024.

Substitute Materials

The biggest reason to switch materials: Cost and/or energy savings.

Major substitutes:

• Plastics instead of metals. Advantages: Low density and light weight, handling ease, corrosion and chemical resistance, great strength when reinforced. New methods of molding complex shapes are pushing plastics into increasing number of metals' applications. The outlook is for a fast rate of substitution.

• Powder coatings instead of porcelain enameling. Ecology problems are the reason for the switch. The advantages of one-coat electrostatic powder coatings lie in the fact that there is no wasted material (epoxy powder can be recycled) and less pollution, since the messy pickling operation is eliminated.

• Embossed steel. It costs more, but the texture hides minor paint defects and is less subject to scratches and dents. Use of this product in refrigerator doors has reduced door return by 90% in one company's experience.

REAL ESTATE

Relocation Checklist

Before Signing Mortgage Papers

Real Estate Buyer Protection

When Property Tax Is in Doubt

Selling an Expensive House

Real Estate Profit Boosters

21

REAL ESTATE

Real Estate As Tax Shelter

The 1978 tax law knocked out most of the few tax shelters that the 1976 tax law did not. But real estate is still good. The high-bracket investor in income-producing real estate can deduct paper losses (resulting from depreciation) against ordinary income, so that the net cost is only 30%. Later, when he realizes a long-term capital gain, the tax bite won't be more than 28%.

Caution: There's one situation in which the tax on a sale can be higher than 28%. If accelerated depreciation was taken while the building was owned, part of the profit from a sale may be taxed as ordinary income.

Source: Martin Halpern, Laventhol & Horwath, CPAs, 919 Third Ave., New York 10022.

Tax Shelters in Foreclosed Properties

Distressed real estate can be that ideal but rare combination: A tax shelter as well as a good investment. But care and caution are essential.

How to find properties: Talk to your banker first. Many sound buildings get into trouble during recessions. Banks foreclose, but don't like to manage real estate and are often willing to sell on easy terms.

Terms to try to get:
• A bank sells foreclosed apartment building at a price equal to the total mortgage debt.
• The purchaser puts down 10% in cash. (Even this may be spread over three to four years if secured by letters of credit.)
• The balance is to be paid over 15-20 years.
• Very important: The bank should agree not to foreclose on the property for at least eight years, even though net cash flow from the property isn't enough to pay interest and amortization and mortgage payments aren't made in full. Allocate part of the purchase price as a consideration for this nonforeclosure provision.

Tax advantages: The amount allocated for the bank's agreement not to foreclose can be written off rapidly over the term of the agreement. And the interest due on the mortgage is deductible every year, even if it isn't paid. The interest is accrued, and is considered a binding obligation.

What to expect from a good deal: Deductible items over the eight years should total about four times the original cash investment.

It's probably best to take straight-line depreciation, not accelerated. Then, if the building doesn't work out and it's ultimately foreclosed, the release from the mortgage obligation produces a capital gain. (If accelerated depreciation were used, the release from the mortgage would produce ordinary income, to the extent that the accelerated depreciation exceeded straight-line. When on real estate, it's a tax preference item.)

The owner or owners should be actively involved in the management of the property. Otherwise, it could be considered a passive investor and then there's a limit to the amount of investment interest that can be deducted. But the owners can hire a managing agent to do the day-to-day work.

If the limitation on investment interest isn't a problem, then a leveraged sale-leaseback should be considered. The property is bought and leased back to someone who manages it and pays all expenses and taxes. Best way to do this: With no more than 10% down, and that 10% paid over several years with dollars that would normally be paid to IRS.

Another approach: Some real estate operators have good properties but don't need tax deductions. They may be willing to sell for 10% down, taking back a nonrecourse mortgage with a nonforeclosure covenant. Then they continue to manage the property under the terms of a management contract.

Advantage for both: The seller gets the cash that he wants from the down payment and from the monthly payments for his management services. The buyer gets tax deductions.

Disadvantage in real estate tax shelters offered by syndicators: Sales commissions and fees will usually add at least 25% to the investors' original purchase cost.

There's no reason why a group of investors can't find a good piece of property and organize their own tax-sheltered investment. They do need the help of a knowledgeable real estate broker and a lawyer experienced in both real estate and income taxes.

Source: Steven A. Burn, Esq., Royalty Controls Corp., 1234 Summer St., Stamford, CT 06905.

Buying Real Estate Seized for Taxes

Buying property sold for delinquent taxes can be a bargain. But often it only looks like a bargain. Beware of these traps:

- Back taxes can exceed potential value.
- Zoning restrictions may prevent development for profit.
- The previous owner may retain the right under state law to reclaim property by paying tax and penalties after it's bought. Result: Unclear title, which makes property hard to resell.
- Deteriorating neighborhoods should be avoided unless redevelopment plans are certain.
- The property should be investigated with utmost discretion to avoid alerting competitive bidders. Strategy: Don't have property appraised. Ask instead about similar property nearby.

The best deal could be vacant land (taxed at low rate) in an undeveloped area targeted for build-up.

Property lists: Sales are announced in advance but not necessarily in general newspapers. Contact city or county tax collector for details.

Screening Potential Real Estate Investments

Rules of thumb can be dangerous if relied on exclusively for real estate investments, but they do offer a quick and simple way to screen properties. Two rules: (1) Don't pay more than 6-7 times the gross annual rent, or ten times the net operating income, unless the going rate in the area is consistently higher. (2) Operating expenses eat up from 50% to 70% of gross rentals in an apartment building (leaving 30%-50% gross income), depending on geographic area. Major costs include vacancy and collection losses, repairs and maintenance, and management fees, before taxes and mortgage payments.

In-depth analysis of the area and property, plus expert legal and real estate advice, is still a must before any final decision is made.

Further information: *Real Estate Guidelines and Rules of Thumb* by Ronald Gettel, McGraw-Hill, New York.

Precaution When Selling Real Estate to a Corporation

A property owner entered into a contract to sell real estate to a corporation. Later, the buyer tried to renegotiate the terms, and then backed out. The seller threatened to sue. The buyer's response: "Go ahead and sue. You'll get the deposit but that's all. The corporation has no other assets."

What to do: Before contracting with a corporation, get a recent financial statement, verified by an independent source (accountant, banker, or credit reporting service). If this isn't possible, or if the corporation's assets are small, do two things: (1) Get the largest possible down payment or deposit. (2) Require that the officer sign the contract personally as well as signing as an officer of the corporation.

Source: *Real Estate Investing Letter,* United Media International, 306 Dartmouth St., Boston 02116.

Old Buildings That Are Worth Regenerating

Regeneration: A new buzzword in the real estate business that opens up investment opportunities for both companies and individuals.

It started in cities like New York, where the recurrent shortage of office space, combined with high construction costs, have made it worthwhile to renovate solid older buildings. Now the idea is catching on across the country where older buildings are in plentiful supply.

Building worth regenerating:

• Good natural lighting is a must. Ideally, the building should have at least 25 linear feet of windows for each 1,000 square feet of floor space. Be sure that the space between windows and the central corridor isn't too deep. That would mean a lot of inside offices (and low rents).

• Most important: The floor plan should fan out from the service core (elevators, fire stairs, and lavatories).

• If the service core is on the side of the building, watch out. That means long corridors and space that is hard to divide up for rental. This could be all right for owner occupancy or single-floor occupancy. But it limits the number of tenants (especially choice ones) when building is being developed primarily as an investment.

• Be particularly wary of spacious old buildings with center courts. It can be a very long walk around the courtyard.

Source: John Robert White, chief executive officer, Landauer Associates, Inc., 200 Park Ave., New York 10017.

Alternative to Renovating in Turnaround Neighborhood

The usual technique is to renovate the building, then wait to sell at a profit when neighborhood improvement is under way.

A better method might be to consider skipping the renovations. Resale will be at much lower price, but capital investment will also be lower. The profit in dollars may be as high as if property were renovated. And profit as a percentage of capital invested is likely to be much higher.

Use money that would have been spent on renovation to buy other properties in the same (or similar) neighborhood. Diversification reduces the risk of investment.

Caution: Check local laws carefully with professional advisors to be sure there are no requirements that owner must renovate.

Alternative to Demolishing Ravaged Property

What to do with a vandalized, burned-out building when the city demands that more money be spent to demolish it: Consider donating it to the city.

It may be possible to do this without the city's knowledge or consent, as long as it has some value. (And the land does even if the building doesn't.) Some state laws provide that a gift of something of value is presumed accepted, even if the receiver didn't know about it.

This way, the property owner avoids spending more money for demolition, and he gets a charitable deduction.

When to Watch the Real Estate Broker Closely

A company or individual listing property for sale with a real estate agent may find it's no longer listed after an offer is turned down. Reason: The agent is trying to make the commission by temporarily taking the property off the active list in hopes that the owner will give up and accept the offer. He may keep other agents from sending around prospects by removing the file or spreading word that the property has been sold.

Advice: Make sure property remains on the market until you're the one who takes it off.

Terms to Know Before Listing Property with a Broker

• Open listing: The owner reserves the right to sell the property himself or to retain brokers.

• Exclusive agency: No other broker will be retained as long as the agency continues (usually for a specified period), but this doesn't prevent the owner from selling the property himself.

• Exclusive right to sell: The broker gets his commission when the property is sold, whether by the broker, the owner, or anyone else.

• Multiple listing: Brokers combine to sell properties listed with any member of the brokers' pool. The brokers themselves split commissions between the listing and selling broker.

If no time is specified, the listing is good for a ''reasonable'' time. The owner can revoke the listing at any time before the broker has earned his commission, provided he acts in good faith and doesn't revoke when negotiations have been substantially completed.

If a time is specified, the agreement will then end. It would continue if the owner has waived the time limit by accepting the services of the broker, or if the owner has acted in bad faith (as by postponing agreement with a buyer until after the time limit). In some states, the owner can revoke only up to the time the broker has put money and effort into the listing contract.

If nothing is said, the broker will earn his commission on finding a buyer ready, willing, and able to buy on the terms specified.

Important: The owner, to protect himself, should ask for a provision under which payment of the commission will depend on closing the deal and full payment.

When the Buyer Should Pay the Broker a Commission

To get the biggest first payment possible on an installment sale, the seller should consider reducing the price by the amount of the broker's commission and having the buyer pay the broker.

Reason: IRS limits cash payment to 30% of sales price in the year of sale. If the seller gets more, the entire capital gain is taxed that year. If the 30% limit is observed, the tax is spread over the life of the installments. Example:

The installment sale price is $100,000, broker's fee $6,000. If seller pays fee, it comes out of his $30,000 (30% of total price), leaves him with $24,000 cash in first year. If seller reduces price to $94,000 and has buyer pay fee, seller gets 30% of $94,000, or $28,200 in first year. He is $4,200 ahead.

Buyers should suggest this approach when buying property on installment. It establishes a climate of mutual concern, and may get the seller to make other concessions for buyer's benefit.

Source: *Business Acquisitions Desk Book* by F.T. Davis, Jr., Institute for Business Planning, Inc., Englewood Cliffs, NJ 07632.

Relocation Checklist

Before selecting a new plant site, keep in mind the following dangers:

• Too hasty purchase of land or an option to buy land. Never sign on the dotted line without a ''subject to. . . .'' clause covering such things as soil condition. Always make test borings before making the final deal. Potential hazard: A com-

The Encyclopedia of Practical Business

pany constructing a building finds peat, running water, or an old garbage dump when work is started on the building's foundation. While it's possible to build on almost any kind of land, the cost of sinking footings or floating foundations may prove prohibitive.

• Underground remnants: Find out what structures used to be on that land. Certain industries (meatpacking plants and slaughterhouses, for instance) leave behind extensive underground plumbing. Concrete conduits might have to be dug out before a foundation can be built on the site.

• Buying in the wrong part of town. To a stranger unfamiliar with the area, many uneconomic sites appear attractive (often because they're offered at a good price). If the price is low, search for the reasons.

• Inadequate knowledge of zoning laws. Some item the company makes (or processes) might be unacceptable under the community's zoning ordinances. And sometimes they can be changed. It's best, of course, to know in advance. Any number of unlikely things can be covered in local zoning regulations. Another common mistake: Excess land in the parcel that the company buys with an eye to future expansion may be zoned for residential use only.

• Failure to investigate all covenants of industrial parks. A requirement for a 100-foot setback, for instance, might mean too little land is left for the plant itself. Or it could make the whole project too costly.

• Failure to consider possible transportation problems. Local road restrictions sometimes make it impossible for a company's trucks to meet load limits. Another trap for the unwary: Incorrectly assuming that a nearby railroad can be accessed by a spur. Sometimes there are regulations prohibiting that. Truckers, too, sometimes balk at having to go too far from the main access roads.

Where to get help: Local banks can often be of assistance, as can utilities. Both can usually be trusted. Some economic development agencies are also unbiased, although it's not a certainty. Remember, they are in business to promote the area. Also, seek out real estate agents who have a proven record of reliability.

Source: Charles F. Wilson, vice president, area development division, Continental Illinois National Bank & Trust Co., Chicago.

308

Minimizing Neighborhood Resistance to Construction

When local people try to stop a local company project, an effective public relations program can save more than it costs. One company donated money and labor to landscape local churches, sponsored Little League teams, participated in other civic activities, and built up a reputation for caring about the community.

The result was high credibility for the company's statements about the beneficial impact of its new structure on the neighborhood.

Other moves to consider:

• Start with an ad in a local paper. Spell out the nature of work, reasons, and timetable. Keep the press posted as work progresses.

• Send individual letters to local businessmen and printed newsletters to residents repeating the information in the advertisement. Follow up every month or so. Notify merchants in advance if work will restrict access to their shops or affect them in some other way, and for how long.

• Have a "hot line" phone number for neighborhood people to call for information or to report complaints and emergencies.

• Coordinate appropriate parts of work with local police and fire departments in advance.

• Kick the project off with a ground-breaking ceremony attended by community leaders. Have a lunch meeting with slides and speeches for business leaders and press.

• Use construction site as means to keep up friendly relations with the neighborhood. Post progress chart on a billboard. Give space to local charities to raise funds from passersby. Donate refreshments.

Investment Credit for Building Components

Don't overlook possible investment tax credits on building equipment, even though the building itself and structural components are not eligible. Examples: Elevators, escalators, fuse boxes, lighting fixtures, plumbing and heating equipment, refrigeration and air-conditioning equipment, safes, doors, burglar alarms, intercom systems. There is a full 10% investment credit if estimated life is seven years or more; 6⅔% if it's five to seven years; 3⅓% if it's three to five years.

Insist on getting a detailed cost breakdown from the contractors and subcontractors involved in order to identify the equipment cost and claim the tax credit.

Wraparound Mortgage Can Reduce Cost

A wraparound mortgage benefits both the borrower and the lender when interest rates are going up.

How it works: A borrower wants to buy property already mortgaged by current owner. The conventional course: Finance the total purchase price (less down payment) with a new mortgage, then pay off old mortgagee (and seller) with the proceeds. Wraparound method: The buyer's bank gives mortgage for difference between purchase price and amount remaining on old mortgage, but charges the buyer interest on combined amount at higher rate than old mortgage. The buyer makes regular payments to his own bank. The bank pays the holder of the old mortgage, and pockets the difference between the two interest rates.

For the buyer: Interest is usually lower than going rate because of bank's profit on the first mortgage.

What's in it for the seller: He gets asking price even though higher interest rates make financing difficult.

What's in it for the bank: Extra interest payments as long as the old mortgage is still outstanding.

Three possible obstacles to the wraparound method:

• The old mortgage may automatically terminate when the property is sold.

• The new bank has to bear the risk of waiting until the old mortgage is paid off; the bank may have to make the payments itself if the borrower gets into trouble.

• The legal mechanics are more complicated and more expensive (especially title insurance).

Before Signing Mortgage Papers

Because it is such a long-term contract, conditions that may seem minor when signing a mortgage loan contract can end up costing a lot of money during the life of the agreement.

Some typical mortgage clauses to negotiate before signing:

• Payment of points. Percentage of the amount of the loan paid to the lender at the start of the loan. Banks and thrift institutions have no statutory right to charge points. Their presence may reflect competitive local market conditions. And when rates are high, as they are now, points are inevitable in states with rate ceilings, such as New York. Try to negotiate on points.

• Prepayment penalties. Sometimes as much as six months' interest or a percentage of the balance due on the principal at the time the loan is paid off. With mortgages running for 25 or 30 years, chances of paying off early are relatively high. Another good place to negotiate:

• "Due on encumbrance" clause. This makes the first mortgage immediately due in full if the property is pledged as security on any other loan, including second mortgages. Not legal in some places and usually not enforced when it is legal. Request its deletion.

• "Due on sale" clauses. This requires full payment of the loan at the time that the property is sold.

• Escrow payments. A popular and very controversial practice among banks, this clause requires a prorated share of local taxes and insurance premiums with each monthly mortgage payment. The bank earns interest on the escrow funds throughout the year and only pays it out when taxes and premiums are due, usually annually. Escrow may amount to forced savings on which the borrower earns no interest.

Have a lawyer check state law to see if interest on escrow-account money is required. (It is, among others, in New York, Maryland, Massachusetts, and Connecticut.) If not, try to eliminate the escrow—paying taxes and insurance on your own.

Other alternatives to escrow:

1. A capitalization plan in which monthly tax and insurance payments are credited against

outstanding mortgage principal until they are paid out to the government or an insurer, thus lowering the amount of mortgage interest.

2. The lender may agree to waive escrow if borrower opens an interest-bearing savings account in the amount of the annual tax bill.

3. Option of closing out withheld escrow payments when borrower's equity reaches 40%. At that point, the bank figures, equity interest will be a powerful incentive to keep up tax payments.

Source: *The Consumer's Guide to Banks* by Gordon L. Weil, Stein & Day, Briarcliff Manor, NY.

Protect Mortgage 'Points' Deduction

"Points" paid to get a mortgage loan may not be immediately deductible. Interest must actually be paid to be deductible by cash-basis taxpayers, which most individuals are. In one case, the Tax Court held that, since the points were deducted from the loan proceeds, they weren't actually paid, thus no deduction that year. The deduction would have to be taken pro rata as the mortgage was repaid.

A typical real estate closing statement mixes up credits to buyer and amounts actually paid. Pay the points by single check to the lender. Don't lump it in with other payments.

How to Prove Your Property Is Assessed Too High

Make a habit of checking every property tax bill and revaluation. Unless it's done, odds are about even that you'll be overpaying. Assessment is an inexact science, and it's often practiced by assessors whose qualifications and available working time leave much to be desired. Here are four ways to get a reduction:

• Eliminate mechanical assessment errors. Local assessors' records on your property are public information. Review them for factual errors that affect assessed value—such as construc-

tion and quality ratings and mathematical errors in projection or extension of figures.

• Appeal any "discriminatory" assessments. Don't assume an assessment is fair because it's only 60% or 70% of market value. It isn't, if most other properties are assessed at 30% of market. List the properties most nearly comparable in the tax district; compare them for square-foot cost and land value assigned by the assessor, and recent sale prices. If the assessment is out of line, appeal—to the assessor, the local review board, or both.

• Challenge assessments covering property exempted from tax by law. (Check state and local manuals for exempt lists.)

• Ground rules for challenges: Do not request review of an assessment unless there are clear-cut grounds for reduction. Don't appear without adequate preparation. Most hearings are oral and informal. Make your presentation as simple as possible. Avoid trying to cover everything (hit the important issues). Use visual aids if you can. Provide review board members with written summaries of your statement. Make recommendations on what your assessment should be.

Real Estate Buyer Protection

Use photographs for protection when buying real estate. Take detailed pictures of building, fixtures, and grounds when the contract is signed. The contract should specify that the premises will be turned over at the closing as they are now—or the agreement is null and void.

If a dispute arises over interim damages or removal of items by the seller, the buyer has evidence to prove his case if he wants out.

The same photographs also support an insurance claim if the property is damaged shortly after title passes.

Mortgage Lender Can Lose the Right to Foreclose

Unless you're in the business of lending money and can spread the risk, don't lend to an individual or partnership on the strength of a real estate mortgage alone if the borrower appears to be in the deal on spec or for the tax shelter.

A lender who holds a mortgage may not be as secure as most would think. The debtor can sometimes default, yet keep possession and prevent the lender from taking the property.

The gambit: Using Chapter 12 of the Bankruptcy Act to avoid loss of property. A court might approve a repayment plan giving the mortgage holder less than full value, and after the debtor's discharge from bankruptcy, the holder has no claim for payment of the rest.

Chapter 12 was rarely used until technical changes in 1974. Now its use is broadening. Judges have wide latitude and have used it to prevent foreclosure. They have even enjoined secured creditors from going against those who have served as loan guarantors.

A mortgage lender on rental property may lose out if the owner goes bankrupt. The court probably won't let lender repossess the property right away, and rents collected during the proceedings may be distributed to other creditors. For protection, have agreement provide that, in case of default, all rents belong to the lender.

Raising Money on Property: Mortgaging vs. Sale-Leaseback

Selling property and leasing it back may be a better way to raise money than taking out a mortgage loan.

The biggest advantage is immediate cash amounting to 100% of current value of the property. A mortgage loan would probably produce only 75%.

The seller (lessee):
• Continues to use the property for term of lease, including renewal options.
• Pays rent which is fully deductible.
• Realizes taxable gain or loss on sale.
The buyer (lessor):
• Puts up the cash, maybe borrowing some of the amount needed.
• Receives taxable rental income.

• Takes depreciation deductions.
What happens when the lease runs out? Usually there is an option to repurchase the property.

Generally, this must provide for purchase at fair market value at the time. IRS will look very carefully at sale-leasebacks. It's sure trouble if there's an option to repurchase for $1.

In that case, IRS may claim it isn't really a sale, but a sham with no real change of ownership, really a disguised mortgage loan. Then the "rent" will not be deductible, only the part of it considered to be "interest" on the "loan."

When Property Tax Is in Doubt

It can be hard to determine a fair price for real estate when there's a chance property taxes may be reduced sharply.

In California, after the Proposition 13 vote, many sellers raised the asking prices to reflect the full amount of the expected reduction. But most buyers weren't willing to go along.

Here's one ingenious solution: A seller asks $115,000. Buyer thinks house is worth $100,000, even if property taxes don't go down. The sale is made at $115,000, with seller taking back a $15,000 second mortgage; but the second mortgage loan doesn't have to be repaid if the property tax reduction is knocked out by court decisions or new laws.
Source: *Real Estate Investing Letter,* 306 Dartmouth St., Boston 02116.

When Corporate Rent May Not Be Deductible

Corporations leasing property from their own shareholders may not be able to claim all the rent as a tax deduction. Reason: Rent paid to shareholders may be treated as a dividend to the shareholders rather than a business expense for the company if the IRS successfully challenges it.

Case: Two individuals leased land to a corporation of which they were the sole stockholders. The lease called for a fixed 20-year rental, after which land would go back to the landlords together with improvements. The company then constructed a building on the land, to be depreciated over 34 years.

Evidence showed that the rent paid was a fair amount for land and buildings. Court ruling:

• The portion of rent paid on land (55% of total) was tax-deductible.

• The corporation would not have signed the lease giving the building back to the landlords before it was fully depreciated, unless the landlords and shareholders were one and the same. So rent for the building (45% of the total) was not really an expense to the company, but a dividend to the company's owners.

Safway Steel Scaffolds Co. of Georgia v. *United States, 5th Cir., 3/9/79.*

taken as straight-line depreciation is taxed as ordinary income.

Example:

Original cost of building $100,000
Straight-line depreciation $35,000
or
Accelerated depreciation $55,000

How much of the $20,000 difference between accelerated and straight-line depreciation in this example will be recaptured and taxed as ordinary income depends on how long the building has been owned. If the building was acquired after 1969, all the difference will be recaptured.

Note: These rules are applicable to nonresidential buildings only. Rules are more liberal for income-producing residential property, especially for low-income housing.

A Depreciation Method That Can Boomerang

Some of the profit on the sale of commercial and industrial real estate may be taxed at high ordinary income rates rather than more favorable capital gains rates. Reason: If the accelerated depreciation was used by the owner, some of the depreciation deduction may be taxed as ordinary income when the building is sold. (This is called recapture.)

Example: Estimated useful life of a building is 40 years. Using straight-line depreciation, in which the same percentage is deducted each year over the life of the building, the owner deducts ¹⁄₄₀ (2½%) of the original cost from income each year. Alternatively, the owner could take accelerated depreciation, which might be as much as 3¾% in the first year, and would decline gradually in the second and later years.*

Taxable profit when the building is sold is the difference between the net proceeds of the sale and the original cost less all depreciation deducted during the period of ownership. Part or all of the difference between the amount that is actually deducted and the amount that would be

*Accelerated depreciation is permitted only on newly built buildings, not on used ones.

Inspection Checklist Before Buying a House

• Start in the basement, where defects are most obvious. Check walls for inward bulge, cracks or crumbling mortar, fresh patches, and high-water marks. Check floors for signs of leaks, seepage, or damp odor. Look for a hidden sump pump (which may be an indication of frequent flooding).

• Use a pocketknife to probe for termites or decay. If knife goes in easily, the wood is rotten. Other danger signs on joists: Marks of water seepage from kitchen or bathroom above. Pulling away from supporting masonry. Notches more than one-third into the joist for pipes. If joists are propped up, find out why.

• Check basement pipes for corrosion. Hot-water pipes should be copper, preferably insulated. Cold-water lines should be copper or plastic.

• Check fuse box for power adequacy (16-20 circuits with circuit breakers needed for an eight- to 12-room house).

• Study house from outside for sag, alignment of walls, missing mortar, broken bricks, cracks in walls. One tipoff to trouble: An extra-wide mortar joint on the stair steps may be a sign that the house is shifting.

312

• Siding. Aluminum is a plus. If siding is wooden, look for peeling that shows walls hold too much moisture. If windowsills are freshly painted and the rest of the house is not, paint may be covering rot.

• Check roof for broken/missing shingles, tar-paper bubbles, broken patches. Check metal sheathing around chimney and ventilators. Should be watertight and made of nonrusting material. Look for leaks or breaks in gutters. If possible, check attic for watermarks on underside of roof.

• In the house, check for warped doors that won't close, rattly doorknobs, creaky floor or stairs, loose tiling, inadequate plumbing, too many electric cords in an outlet. Check closets and storage space for adequacy. Water heater should be 30-40 gallons if gas, 60 if electric.

• Examine walls and ceilings for repaired cracks (may indicate structural problem) or patches (may indicate leaks from above).

Source: *How You Can Become Financially Independent by Investing in Real Estate* by Albert J. Lowry, Simon & Schuster, New York.

When Buying a Condominium

Make sure the board of directors sets up a contingency reserve for emergencies. It should be at least 3% of annual operating budget for newer buildings and 5% for older ones. If no reserve is set aside, there is danger of major assessment on little notice when an emergency arises.

Source: *The Condominium Community*, The Institute of Real Estate Management of the National Association of Realtors, 430 North Michigan Ave., Chicago 60611.

Real Estate Profit Boosters

• Travel expenses to and from a real estate investment can be deducted by the taxpayer. If detailed records are kept, deduct actual expenses. Other method: Deduct 20¢ a mile if using own car, plus meals and lodging if trip takes more than one day and spending isn't lavish.

• Taking back a second mortgage when you

sell a house can speed the sale and boost the price. Caution: Make both husband and wife jointly and severally liable for payments.

• Apartment landlords: The security deposit should be a different amount from the monthly rent. Experience shows that this discourages tenants from considering security the last month's rent and leaving apartment dirty or in bad condition. (Check local rent laws, though.)

Getting Your Money's Worth from a Building Contractor

• Get construction contracts in writing, down to the last detail.

• Make the contract specific. It should not say just "tile floor," but include the kind, color, quality, size, etc.

• Stipulate penalties for finishing the work late; bonuses for finishing early.

• Pay only on completion and acceptance of the project. (If necessary to pay for work in progress, keep payments well behind the work.)

• Make the contractor responsible for insurance indemnity, and for getting all the building permits.

• Get a guarantee from the contractor for the work.

• Check the work carefully while construction is underway. Problems found after a project is completed cost more than those caught early.

• If construction plans change after building has started, put the requirements and costs for those changes in writing.

• Before paying, make sure the contractor secures a release of subcontractor's liens.

Reducing Capital Gains Tax When House Is Sold

If you sell your home and then do not use the proceeds to buy another one, you are taxed on any gain realized from the sale (unless you're over 55 and gain is less than $100,000—and you can only do this once). Gain, in general, is the difference between your cost basis and the selling price, less selling expenses.

It's important, then, to understand: (1) How your cost basis is computed, and (2) what selling expenses are deductible. It's essential to keep an accurate record of those items which will help to reduce your tax liability.

Cost basis includes:

• Price paid in cash or property and by mortgage obligation assumed or mortgage to which property is subject.

• Attorney's fees and expenses in connection with the purchase contract and its closing or settlement; also the costs of searching, defending, or perfecting title.

• Costs of appraisal, recording of deed and mortgage, survey.

• Title search and title insurance.

• Cost of getting cash for purchase (mortgage broker's fees, lender's origination fee, title search and/or title insurance legal fees for drafting bond and morgage), but not "points."

• Architectural and engineering fees, plus termite inspection.

• Restoration of building or improvements prolonging its useful life or increasing its value which are in the nature of capital investment and long-term improvements. Example: Owner replaces the roof when house is sold.

• The cost of improvements outside the building(s), such as landscaping, grading, driveways, wells, ditches, walks, patio.

• Real estate taxes of the seller assumed by the buyer as part of the purchase price.

• Purchasing commissions.

• Insurance during construction.

• "Rent" paid while occupying under option to purchase and applied to purchase price on exercise of option.

Deductible selling expenses include:

• Broker's commission,

• Legal expenses and attorney's fees.

• Advertising.

• Sales tax, if applicable.

• Title abstract.

• "Points" paid by the seller to enable buyer to obtain financing.

• Fixing-up expenses if incurred within 90 days of the sale contract and paid within 30 days after sale.

Strategy When Selling a House to Finance a New One

Selling a house and buying a new one can be a tricky business, especially if the money from the old one is needed to finance the new.

When you're selling, the objective is to tie up the buyer as firmly as possible in the contract of sale. Ask your broker for the form of contract he proposes to present to prospective buyers so you can have your attorney check it beforehand.

The seller will probably give the buyer a right to a termite and engineering inspection. But give as little time as possible. The seller also has to allow time for the buyer to obtain a mortgage commitment. The agreement should give a reasonable time to obtain the commitment but limit the amount and term while providing a high enough interest rate to assure obtaining a commitment. Beyond these basic conditions, the objective is to deny the buyer any conditions or requirements that will enable him to get out of the contract. Resist any attempt on the part of the prospective buyer to put the down payment into an escrow account.

On the buying side: The strategy here is the direct opposite. The buyer wants as many "outs" as possible. He should insist on a large mortgage for a long term at a low interest rate (even though willing to take one for a smaller amount, shorter term, and higher interest rate). Allow plenty of time to get the commitment. Buyers want a title free from all encumbrances, easements, encroachments, pending highways or zoning changes (everything a good real estate attorney can think of to make the contract as open-ended as possible on the buyer's side and as close-ended as possible on the seller's side). Insist on an escrow of the down payment. If there are good real estate lawyers on both sides, you can expect compromises, even a standoff.

Never get into a sell-and-buy situation on a do-it-yourself basis. You might get stuck with one too many houses—or one too few.

If the move is company-sponsored, it should be of some help. Some companies will agree to buy the old house at a price if there's difficulty in selling it. Some will provide financing help on the purchase for those who haven't been able to sell.

Setting Price of a Home

Don't rely too heavily on a real estate broker's advice. A broker makes more on quick sales than big ones. A fast commission of $5,400 on a $90,000 sale is much more attractive than $6,000 on a $100,000 sale that takes months to make. Check out brokers carefully before giving an exclusive. Look into prices of recent sales in the community.

Getting a Higher Price for an Old House

An old house (built 1920-1950) can be sold as easily as a new one. The right strategy and a few improvements can raise the selling price significantly. That's the advice of Mary Weir of Rumson, NJ. She has bought, refurbished, and resold over 50 old houses. Her suggestions:

• Invest in a complete cleaning, repainting, or wallpapering. Recarpet or have the rugs and carpets professionally cleaned.

• Get rid of cat and dog odors that you may be used to but potential buyers will notice.

• With the trend to smaller families and working wives, it may be desirable to convert and advertise a four-bedroom house as two bedrooms, library, and den.

• The exterior of the house is crucial. It's the first thing a buyer sees. Clean and repair porch and remove clutter. Repaint porch furniture.

• Landscaping makes a great difference and can sell (or unsell) a house. Get expert advice on improving it.

• Good real estate agents are vital to a quick sale. There are one or two top people in every agency who will work hard to show houses and even arrange financing. Multiple listing lets these supersalespeople from different agencies work for the seller.

Selling an Expensive House

Improvements that do the most to increase the resale value of houses in the $100,000 or higher market (ranked in order):
• Separate family room.
• Fireplace.
• Separate dining room.
• Linen storage closet.
• Garbage disposal system.
• Wall-to-wall carpeting.
• Smoke and fire detector.
• Two-bowl vanity in bathroom.
• Double-glass windows.
• Hood (with fan) over range.
• Bathroom dressing area.
• Patio.
• Heavy-duty locks.
• Central air conditioning.
• Bathroom exhaust fan.
• Den/guest room.

Some features are less important in upgrading resale value of houses in the $85,000 to $100,000 range: Smoke and fire detector, two-bowl vanity, bathroom dressing area, patio and den/guest room.

Source: *Professional Builder* magazine, 205 East 42 St., New York 10017.

RETIREMENT AND ESTATE PLANNING

When to Stay Out of a Pension Plan

Exceeding the Keogh Plan Limit

Making a Secret Bequest

Where to Keep a Will

Checklist of Information for Heirs

Who Can Postpone Estate Tax

Minimizing Estate Taxes

Keeping Your Will Out of Court

22

RETIREMENT AND ESTATE PLANNING

When to Stay Out of the Company Pension Plan

Expecting to keep the job only a few years? Ask the company to exclude you from the pension plan so you can set up an Individual Retirement Account. This should be done if you will reach retirement age before qualifying for a pension, or if job will end before retirement age.

Many pension plans provide that benefits are lost if the employee leaves before working for ten years. If you don't expect to stay long enough to be vested, don't join the company plan.

Company Retirement Plan Plus Your Own IRA (or Keogh)

Any executive with a second source of employment income should not overlook the possible opportunity to make tax-deductible personal re-

tirement contributions. Keogh plans or Individual Retirement Accounts (IRAs) are allowed on some second incomes as well as for the self-employed and those not covered by employer plans.

The rules for making contributions that are deductible against income:

• Self-employed, including owners of businesses which are sole proprietorships, can establish Keogh plans. The plan must also cover employees and make contributions for them on same formula used for owner.

• Working partners are also eligible for contributions to Keogh plans set up by the partnership, not by the individuals. And the plan must also cover qualified employees on the same formula as the partners.

• Employees who aren't covered by pension or profit sharing plan are eligible to set up an IRA. Maximum annual contribution is $1,500 ($1,750 if there's a nonworking spouse). But it can't be more than 15% of gross compensation. It's also possible for an employer to sponsor an IRA for selected employees and make contributions (same limits) for each one.

• Covered by plan but with outside self-employment income: Outside consulting, selling, free-lance writing or other work qualifies, but income from a second job does not. Keogh plan contributions can be made up to 15% of the net self-employment income as shown on Schedule C of the federal income tax return. (But the contribution can't be more than $7,500.)

• Executives who receive directors' fees are eligible for Keogh plans on the fee income, even if it is for sitting on the board of their own company, which may have its own pension plan. Directors' fee must be paid separately, with no withholding or Social Security taken out.

Keogh and IRA plans are for employment income only. They can't be used for interest, dividends, or other investment income.

It's possible for an individual to have both a Keogh plan and an IRA. But in any one year contributions can be made to only one, not both. Self-employment income contributions, which would normally go into a Keogh plan, can be put into an IRA if desired. (However, once a Keogh is started, contributions may be required every year there is self-employment income.)

Investment alternatives: The law permits the money to be invested in four ways:

• Banks and savings and loan associations. The usual way is to buy eight-year certificates. But it's also possible to set up a trust account and have the bank invest in other things (for a fee).

• Mutual funds.

• Annuity or endowment contracts. If the contract includes life insurance (permitted for Keogh but not IRA), the portion paid for that coverage is not tax deductible.

• U.S. government Retirement Bonds.

Keogh and IRA money can be switched from one investment to another without penalty. And, of course, there's no tax on the earnings until the money is taken out after retirement.

Source: Michael F. Klein, CPA, partner, Price Waterhouse & Co., 153 East 53 St., New York 10022.

When Exceeding the Keogh Plan Maximum Is Okay

Self-employed businessmen can go beyond the $7,500 Keogh limit and set aside larger tax-deductible retirement contributions for themselves, while cutting down on contributions for younger employees.

How to do it: Instead of putting aside a certain percentage of everybody's salary, switch to a "defined benefit" plan. It establishes the benefit to be paid at retirement. Actuarial tables will determine how much must be set aside for each individual. Much more will be contributed for older employees.

With a defined benefit plan, it's permitted to exceed the usual $7,500 per year Keogh limits by substantial amounts. If the plan assumes retirement at 55 (the law now permits this), deductible contributions could be as high as $30,000 for officers in their 40s or 50s.

High Interest on Savings and No Tax till Retirement

Deferred annuities are worth considering at any age for cash savings that won't be needed until retirement, when the tax rate will be lower.

Money is placed with an insurance company. Interest is earned and compounded. But no income tax is paid until the interest is withdrawn. After a few years it's possible to make withdrawals that will be considered to be principal. Thus, there's no tax. (It could be dangerous to make repeated withdrawals on a regular schedule, though. IRS might tax them.)

Yield can equal the interest on bank savings certificates. The most common type guarantees a minimum rate for the first year or two. Then the guaranteed rate drops sharply. But the rate actually paid is considerably higher. Competition forces the insurance company to pay the going market rate or investors will cash in and take their money elsewhere.

Deferred annuities are excellent collateral to borrow against. And they can be converted at any time into a lifetime annuity or paid in installments. Conversion or withdrawal is usually required by age 75 or 80.

The best way to buy a deferred annuity: A single payment. Most insurance companies have a $5,000 minimum. It's also possible to buy them with regular monthly payments (on less attractive terms).

Be sure to examine several insurance company plans. And consider these negatives.

• They provide no protection against inflation.

• Some deduct commission from money invested. Others are no-load, meaning commission is buried in insurance company overhead.

• Many plans have penalties for withdrawal.

• Be sure the plan pays "excess interest" if the insurance company's earnings go up. Find out whether the excess interest rate is based on the insurance company's investment earnings on money invested the year the annuity is purchased or on its overall investment performance.

Using Discount Bonds to Build a Retirement Fund

Consider discount bonds for a retirement nest egg. They're a good idea for investors who expect to remain in high tax brackets to retirement.

Some high-quality discount bonds produce higher yields than savings accounts and they generate a nice capital gain when they mature.

Example: AT&T 3⅞s of 1990. When they are paid off, half of the capital gain between the current discounted selling price and the value at maturity is taxable. The other half is a tax preference item. But the total tax should be lower if the investor chooses a bond that matures in low-bracket retirement years.

There's a scarcity of high-quality deep-discount bonds. It might not be possible to find good bonds maturing when desired. Then try bonds with later maturity dates. They may be sold before maturity. The capital gain will be less, but there still may be a significant benefit.

Owning Property Jointly: Pros and Cons

When one spouse dies, ownership of jointly held property passes to the other automatically. It doesn't go through probate and no will is required for this transfer. (Joint ownership is known as the "poor man's will.")

Disadvantages: IRS assumes that the first

spouse to die originally paid for the property. Result: All of the property can be subject to estate tax. To counter that assumption, the executor of the estate must have documentary proof that the survivor put up part or all of the money for the property.

The person who puts up all the money to purchase a property can elect to report a taxable gift of half of it to his spouse. Then, at the death of either, only half of the value of the property is taxed in the estate.

A gift tax return must be filed covering the year the joint ownership was created. No gift tax may be due, but the gift will use up some of the combined lifetime gift-estate tax credit.

Limitations: Only available to property owned jointly by husband and wife. Can be used for stocks and other assets but does not apply to joint bank accounts. Applies only to gifts made after the 1976 Tax Reform Act. Advice: Joint ownership from before January 1, 1977 must be severed and recreated in order to benefit by this provision.

Checking Lost Social Security Benefits

Check Social Security account every year or so to make sure proper amounts have been credited. The government says it won't guarantee to make corrections if an error isn't caught within three years. Get Form SSA-7004C from Social Security office and give one to each employee in the pay envelope.

Keeping Company Death Benefits Out of the Estate

Many executive employment contracts provide for death benefits to be paid to the executive's beneficiary if the executive dies before retirement. If the benefit is included in his taxable estate, from 30% to 70% of it will be lost to federal taxes.

To keep the benefit out of an executive's estate, the employment contract should:

• Name both primary and contingent beneficiaries to keep down the value (to 5% or less) of any reversionary interest, i.e., any amount that might revert to the executive's estate because named beneficiaries die before he does. Internal Revenue Service tables are used to calculate the value of the reversionary benefit.

• The language should make it clear that the beneficiary is getting a present interest, not a future interest, in the death benefit.

• Make clear that the executive has absolutely no right to change the beneficiaries nor any other right over the payment under the contract.

• Provide that no amounts are to be paid to the executive during his lifetime or to his estate on his death, either directly or indirectly.

Contractual death benefits of this type require different handling than those payable under a qualified* pension, profit-sharing, or stock bonus plan. To exclude qualified plan benefits, make sure that beneficiaries other than the estate are named and that they aren't paid in a lump sum. The executive may retain the right to change the beneficiary without qualified benefits being included in his estate.

*An employee benefit arrangement that meets certain requirements of the tax code and is qualified by the Internal Revenue Service for favorable tax treatment.

Making a Secret Bequest

Sometimes a bequest (to a friend or a black-sheep relative) will upset family members. Thus, the estate owner wants to keep it secret. But that's a problem because the will must be probated in court, thus making all bequests public knowledge.

How to keep the secret: Take out a life insurance policy. The proceeds will be paid immediately on death without waiting for probate, and there will be no public announcement. (The executor will know about it and it will be subject to estate tax unless the policy is given to the person, too.) Note: The insurance company will probably require that the first beneficiary named be a family member. Get around that by changing the beneficiary after the policy is issued.

Or set up a trust now and provide instructions in the trust document and a letter to the trustee.

These papers remain private. The will discloses only how much money goes to the trust.

Source: Mintz, Girgan & Hanlon, insurance brokers, Grand Union Plaza, North Arlington, NJ 07032.

Revoking a Will

It sounds fairly simple to do, but many individuals who try to revoke their wills don't succeed, and others discover that their wills have been revoked—by law—against their wishes. How these unwanted consequences can occur:

• In the aftermath of a death, no one is sure that the will was revoked. Testator (person making the will) may have destroyed it alone or in the presence of a witness who also has died. Much time and effort can be wasted looking for a document that no longer exists. Worse yet, a serious mistake may be made. In some states, a copy of a will may be accepted when the original can't be found and there's no indication it was revoked.

• In many states, a will is automatically revoked—wholly or partly—whenever certain events occur in the lifetime of a testator, such as marriage, divorce, birth of a child, or death of a major beneficiary.

What to do:

• Write a separate document spelling out revocation. Keep it where will would have been.

• Check with a lawyer whenever a family event could trigger automatic revocation.

Source: *You & Your Will* by Paul P. Ashley, McGraw-Hill, New York.

Right and Wrong Places to Keep Your Will

The question of where to keep a will isn't as easy to answer as it sounds. It should be in a safe, private place. But it must also be available to the executor immediately upon the death of the testator (the one whose will it is). The answer depends partly on state law. Some ideas:

• If a bank is the estate executor, the natural choice is the bank vault. (If testator changes his mind and executes a new will naming another executor, remember to remove the will to another place.)

• A safe-deposit box is not a good place if no one else has access to it without a court order. Authorize executor's access in advance, if local law permits entry by two or more people and the death of one does not affect entry right of the other. Use a separate box for the will only, if the testator doesn't want the executor to see other private documents.

• Attorney's safe is a good choice only if it is fireproof and burglar resistant. Law firm's safe-deposit box in a bank vault is a better choice.

Whatever place is chosen, keep another copy of the will elsewhere. Make sure it is identical to the original but clearly marked "copy." It should not be signed. There is too great a risk that a signed copy might be thought to be the original. If the will is then changed, it could cause confusion and challenges.

Twenty Ways to Help Your Heirs Inherit

Make up (and periodically update) an inventory of important personal documents and names. Be sure your family knows its location. The inventory should include:

• Location of your will.
• Name and address of your attorney.
• Name and address of the accountant who prepares your tax return.
• Name and address of your banker.
• Name and address of your life and general insurance brokers.
• Location of your policies.
• Location of your safe-deposit box and its number. Where is the key?
• List of real estate you own and whereabouts of relevant papers.
• If you are active in real estate, name and address of your broker.
• Names of creditors (with amounts).
• Names and addresses of those who owe you money (with amounts).
• A list of credit cards with numbers.
• A list of charge accounts with numbers and company addresses.

• The location of stocks and bonds.
• Name and address of your stockbroker.
• Location of ownership certificates for autos, boats, motor homes, etc.
• Location of your birth certificate.
• Your Social Security number and that of your spouse.
• Location of your military discharge papers.
• Location of your marriage certificate.

Source: *Ideas & Trends,* Israeloff, Trattner & Co. P.C., CPAs, 11 Sunrise Plaza, Valley Stream, NY 11581.

Executor Should Have Tax-Return Work Sheets

Be sure an executor can find tax-return work sheets, bills, canceled checks, other supporting documents. And he should know who helped prepare the returns.

The last three years' tax returns can be challenged by IRS, which may raise questions that the executor can't answer without the records or access to the person who prepared the return. The executor will probably be responsible for filing the final return covering the year of death.

Information as to where records are located should not be in the will. Rather, include it in a separate communication to the executor in advance, or leave it among personal possessions.

Better Than Trust Fund for a Child

Consider setting up a custodial account. There are no legal or other fees, and minimum hassle. A custodian is named and handles the assets until the child becomes an adult at 18 or 21, depending on state law. Income from the assets is taxable to the child, not to parents or custodian. The custodian can be a parent or another person (it doesn't matter for income tax purposes). But if the custodian is a parent, the assets will be part of that parent's estate and thus subject to estate tax if the parent-custodian should die while the child is still a minor.

Estate Tax Break for Minor Children

Parents of minor children should change their wills to take advantage of the orphan's exclusion in the tax law. If parents die together (in a plane or auto crash, for instance), there's an additional estate tax deduction for assets passing to orphaned minor children. The deduction depends on the child's age (up to $100,000 for an infant).

Contesting IRS Valuation of an Estate

What to do when Internal Revenue Service claims additional estate tax because it puts a higher valuation on property: Find out how IRS arrived at the figure.

A written statement from the IRS as to how valuations were determined must be supplied to executor within 45 days of request. If there's an appraiser's report, IRS must supply that too.

Owners of a Closely Held Business Can Postpone Estate Tax

Problem: The owner of a business dies, leaving no other assets of any consequence. A large estate tax is owed, and the heirs may be under pressure to sell their interest in the business to raise money in order to pay the tax.

Solution: Tax laws provide that the estate tax can be postponed for five years and then paid in installments over the next ten years, although the IRS will charge interest on the installments.

To qualify: Sixty-five percent of the value of the gross estate consists of ownership interest in one or more closely held businesses (sole proprietorship, partnership, or corporation having 15 or fewer partners or stockholders).

IRS may grant an extension of time to pay the estate tax even though this test isn't met. But the executor must show good reasons for needing more time. Examples:

• The estate has no cash immediately available and the heirs cannot obtain any except by selling assets on a distress basis or borrowing at exorbitant rates.

• The size of the estate can't be calculated because of large pending lawsuits.

Tax-Free Gifts Make an Estate Smaller and Heirs Richer

Annual gifts up to $3,000 a year per recipient are not taxable. Married couples can give twice as much. Every year for the rest of your life, you and your spouse can jointly give $6,000 tax-free to each heir and reduce the tax on your estate by the same amount.

Tax savings are impressive even if you're widowed or divorced. An individual with four married children and ten grandchildren can give them $54,000 a year with no tax. Each year's gifts can lower the estate tax by $16,200 in the lowest bracket (30%) and $37,800 in the highest (70%).

Loophole for "deathbed" gifts: Money and property transferred during the last three years of life used to be taxable to the donor's estate unless executor could show these gifts were not made in contemplation of death. This was always hard to prove. But now, even a person who is known to have a terminal illness can make tax-free gifts within the $3,000 limit.

Avoiding tax on gifts over $3,000: Give a part interest each year. Or transfer property through an installment sale, taking back notes that are payable at annual intervals. You can cancel these notes as they fall due.

Gifts to reduce family's total income tax: Transfer income-producing assets to low-bracket members. (No gift tax if the $3,000 limit is observed.)

Reducing heir's income tax: Give assets to minor child by putting them into a trust that accumulates income during child's minority. Income will be taxable to trust and will not propel heir into higher bracket. (But a "throwback" may require additional tax when the income is distributed.)

Transferring money tax-free by means of loans: A parent can lend money to a child without charging interest and there will be no gift tax. IRS will consider this a loan provided there is a written agreement that money is a loan to be repaid by a given date or on demand.

Contract Between Parent and Child Can Eliminate Tax on Estate

A tax-wise way to transfer assets to the next generation is a private annuity arrangement between parent and child. The parent transfers assets to a son or daughter under a contractual agreement that a certain sum will be paid to the parent each year for life. Example:

A 58-year-old widow includes among her sizable assets a block of securities that originally cost, say, $50,000 and is now worth $200,000. She doesn't want to give them to her children, because she needs the dividend income.

• The widow transfers the securities to her son under an agreement that he will pay her $18,185 per year for life. (This figure comes from Treasury actuarial tables; it's based on her life expectancy of 23.2 years.)

• If they agree upon a figure that's less than $18,185, part of the amount transferred will be considered a taxable gift from the widow to her son. If they make the payments $15,000 per year, such an annuity would be worth $165,000. Thus, the remaining $35,000 would be a gift to the son in the year of the transaction.

Tax consequences to the mother: If Treasury tables are followed, she pays no gift tax. When she receives payments, they are taxed partly as ordinary income and partly as capital gains, and a small part (about 4%) is untaxed.

• Assuming that the son has no obligation to continue payments to her estate after her death, there is no estate tax upon any part of the $200,000 when she dies.

• Tax consequences to the son: None. He realizes no income when securities are transferred to him and neither income nor deductions when he makes the payments.

• If he sells the stock after his mother's death, his cost basis (for purposes of determining capital gain) is the total cumulative amount that he has paid his mother: $91,000 after five years, $182,000 after ten years, $423,000 after 23 years.

If he sells the stock while she is still alive, his cost basis is the total of payments made plus the actuarial value of future payments he's still obligated to make. (If he sells at a loss, it's past payments only.)

Points to consider:

• Although the stock has been removed from her estate, the money paid to the mother will be included in her estate if she saves it rather than spending it or giving it away.

• If the mother outlives her son, then the estate and the son's heirs will be obligated to make the payments.

• The mother may be concerned about depending on her son for the income she needs. It's a binding obligation, true, but he may lack self-discipline in money matters.

• If the mother lives beyond her life expectancy, the payments become a greater economic burden upon the son.

Source: Stanley H. Breitbard, CPA, Price Waterhouse & Co., 606 South Olive St., Los Angeles 90014.

Discount on Estate Taxes

Big savings on estate tax are possible, but there are traps to avoid.

How to get the savings: During his lifetime, a person buys certain Treasury bonds issued many years ago with interest rates of 4¼% or less. They may now be selling as much as 25% off face value. But the government accepts them at face value for estate taxes. Thus, $10,000 of estate taxes might be paid with bonds that cost approximately $7,500.

Only specific bonds are eligible. (Brokers, who call them "flower bonds," can tell you which ones.) And they must be owned before death. It's no good if the executor buys them.

This plan probably doesn't make sense for younger people unless they have a terminal illness. Demand for these bonds, because of the special estate tax feature, keeps the prices up at levels where they are less attractive as investments than other bonds.

Formerly, the estate had to pay a capital gains tax on the amount saved (the difference between cost and face value). This disadvantage has been removed by the Windfall Profit Tax Act of 1980; now the tax is assessed on the cost of the bonds.

One estate got hit with a double whammy. Thinking there were more flower bonds than needed for the estate tax, the executor sold the excess at a discount. Years later, after an audit, IRS demanded additional estate tax, and it also valued at face value the bonds that could have been used to pay estate tax.
Estate of Simmie v. *Comm'r.*, 69 TC 75, 3/6/78.

Tax Problems If Beneficiary Dies Before the Insured

Almost everyone with an estate within range of the federal estate tax* who also owns a significant amount of life insurance knows the one basic rule: To keep the insurance proceeds from being taxed as part of his estate, one must get rid of ownership of the policy and all incidents of ownership. Those "incidents" include the right to change the beneficiary or the right to borrow against the policy.

The standard solution: Transfer the policy to a beneficiary, usually insured's spouse.

What too many people ignore, however, is the possibility that the beneficiary may not survive the insured. Problems:

• If the policy winds up back under the insured's ownership, he again has the problem of keeping the assets out of his estate.

• If his spouse was the beneficiary and owner of the policy, the benefit of the marital deduction has been lost, unless he remarries.

• Any new transfer of the policy ownership runs a higher risk of being disqualified because of

*Exemption equivalent to $147,333 in 1979 rises to $175,625 after 1980; plus maximum marital deduction of the greater of $250,000 or 50% of adjusted gross estate.

the estate tax rule that makes gifts in excess of $3,000 made within three years of death includible in the estate of the donor.

One way to anticipate these problems: The beneficiary of the insurance puts the policy, along with other assets, in a trust for the benefit of the children. But the Internal Revenue Service has recently ruled that if the insured is named the trustee, he possesses incidents of ownership of the policy, which makes the proceeds includible in his estate. Alternatives to consider when the insurance policy is purchased:

• The beneficiary could make an outright gift of the insurance policy to someone other than the insured.

• The policy could be given to a separate trust with another person as trustee.

• A single trust could be set up for both the insurance policy and other property, with someone other than the insured as trustee.

Important When Making Plans for Estate

• Safe-deposit boxes taken out in corporate name don't get sealed upon the death of one of the principals. This might be very useful for closely held firms.

• Assets in someone else's name: The government rarely can prove that a taxpayer willfully intended to dodge taxes. The Internal Revenue Service wins by uncovering evidence of some "badge of fraud." One such badge, declared the court in a recent case, is a taxpayer's consistent practice of placing assets in the names of other persons.

• Beneficiaries should not be witnesses to the will. Nor should their spouses. If they do sign as witnesses, they may receive less than the will intended. Or, in some states, nothing at all.

• The executor can be held personally liable for mistakes in tracking down assets, paying taxes, debts, and funeral expenses, finding heirs, and distributing bequests, even if he relied on the professional accountants and lawyers he hired for those purposes.

325

• Estate-planning costs can be tax deductible. Don't overlook a tax deduction for fees paid to lawyers, accountants, or others involved in estate planning. Get separate bills showing fees for tax advice and analysis of tax consequences of various possible ways to handle property; these are deductible. The cost of preparing a will, however, is not deductible.

• Keep track of the witnesses to a will. When it is probated, it's often necessary to produce at least one of the witnesses in person. Periodically, check to be sure witnesses are still alive and able to testify.

When the Widow Inherits the Company

When the principal owner of a closely held corporation dies, he often leaves the controlling interest to his widow. She may be unable or unwilling to manage the business.

What you can do: Recapitalize the company in a tax-free exchange (swapping of securities—or other property—with the same value and tax basis). Give the widow nonvoting preferred in exchange for the voting common she inherited. She gets a safer security, perhaps paying better dividends. But voting control passes to the holders of the common stock, who are probably already in management positions.

How to Minimize Estate Taxes While Providing For the Spouse

If the estate will be more than $150,000, it could be a mistake to leave everything to the surviving spouse, even if it reduces or eliminates the estate tax.

Reason: That's only the first estate tax. It's also important to plan for the second estate tax, which comes when the surviving spouse then dies. And there's no marital deduction for that second estate.

New York attorney Marvin W. Weinstein, who specializes in taxes and estate planning, suggests using dual trusts in some cases, with one qualified and the other not qualified for the marital deduction.

This is important when the objective is to provide liberally for the surviving spouse, but at the same time reduce estate taxes on transfers to the next generation.

A marital trust is eligible for the marital deduction from the estate tax, but it has the disadvantage that the assets will be taxed in the surviving spouse's estate when he or she dies.

By contrast, a nonmarital trust isn't eligible for the marital deduction from the estate tax. The assets are moved to the next generation without being taxed in the survivor's estate. A typical nonmarital trust would be one in which a widow gets all of the income as long as she lives, but on her death the principal then passes to the children.

The two types of trusts differ in the degree of control of the assets that the widow has. And there are legal/technical requirements that an experienced trust lawyer should handle.

These procedures are unnecessary if the estate is less than $150,000, because there's no significant estate tax below that. But in estimating the value of the estate, don't forget life insurance. That's included in the estate unless one gives away the insurance policies and all the ownership rights. Also, the gift must be made at least three years before death.

Settle Arguments in Advance

Give the executor the power to decide who gets personal effects. It's often surprising how families can be torn apart by squabbling over personal items in the estate. Don't assume that they'll be able to work out a settlement amicably. Provide that if they agree, fine. But if they don't, give the executor absolute power to decide who gets what. And, if possible, two family members should take inventory of all personal possessions immediately after the death.

Source: Herbert Paul, partner, Touche Ross & Co.

Keep Your Will Out of Court

Discourage heirs from contesting the will by including in the will a no-contest clause. Any beneficiary who challenges the will forfeits the inheritance. It's not foolproof, though. This provision cannot disinherit a spouse or children entitled by state law to a certain share. And it wouldn't stop a challenge from somebody who was disinherited entirely.

Pricing a House Out of the Market

Listing your home at a price no one will pay can increase estate tax. It may be smart tax thinking, up to a point, to list your residence with a broker for sale at some astronomical value. Then you can feel safe that no one is going to buy the house, while you deduct depreciation and other expenses. But if you die while this property is listed that way, the strategy can backfire. For federal estate tax purposes, the Internal Revenue Service may use the valuation which you yourself

placed upon the property. The grounds for their sustaining the valuation: The decedent was the most knowledgeable person in the case of this particular residence, possibly having information not known to professional appraisers.

How to Trace Government Bonds

If an executor is aware that the decedent had owned United States savings bonds but their physical location is not known, and if no independent record had been kept of serial numbers, maturity dates, etc., there is a procedure available to enable the bonds to be listed properly in gross estate.

The Bureau of Public Debt, Division of Loans and Currency (536 South Clark St., Chicago 60605) has detailed records of such bonds. An executor can write to this bureau, providing the approximate month and date of purchase, the series and denominations of the bonds, and the names and addresses of the issuing agents. The executor may have trouble accumulating these data. But they will be necessary if he has to make application for replacement of lost certificates.

SAFETY

23

SAFETY

Seven Principles for Reducing Plant Hazards

• Housekeeping. Orderliness slashes accident potential. It lessens exposure of goods to fire, theft, and damage, and also helps minimize overstocking.

• Minimize manual handling. Substitute automatic or mechanical handling wherever possible. Ninety percent of injuries at a large chemical company occurred in the movement of large drums via forklifts and manual handling. Antidote: The company installed a gravity conveyor line and subsituted a lift-and-tip truck for manual handling. The accident rate plummeted. Annual drum-handling costs dropped by two-thirds. Another idea: Punch-press operators had to bend over to pick up parts from a tote pan on the floor. By building a holding table level with the mouth of the press, the company eliminated excessive handling, reduced back strain and employee fatigue. In addition, operating efficiency increased by 60%.

• Storage. Supplies and tools should be arranged to reduce unnecessary handling. A com-

puterized inventory system is an obvious answer. Short of that, racks and shelves should be checked regularly for defects and overloading.

• Clutter. Redesign work areas to eliminate obstructions. In one plant, fan housings scattered around each welder's station had to be lifted to a table for fitting, tacking, and finish-welding. Larger units were welded on the floor. The answer proved to be a Lazy Susan welding table, large enough to accommodate the bigger units and to allow welders to rotate work.

• Check scrap for clues to operating and potential safety problems. Example: A large volume of badly sealed packages from a polyethylene packaging line began turning up in the scrap pile because of a malfunctioning heating element in the sealing machine. Detection solved the problem before injuries or further machine damage occurred. And it stopped waste.

• Maintenance. Conditions that might cause accidents should be given immediate attention.

• Access roads, loading docks, and outside storage areas should be clearly marked. Set up a traffic pattern to prevent congestion.

Source: *Plant Engineering*, 1301 South Ave., Barrington, IL 60010.

Safety Questions About New Construction

First, contact the company's insurance carrier. Expert advice before construction can assure the company of adequate fire protection and may even save money.

Questions to ask:
• Are combustible building materials and extensive areas of combustible interior finish being planned?
• Are fire walls needed to separate hazards?
• Does the arrangement of the building introduce a hazard?
• Are water supplies and automatic sprinkler layouts adequate? Are fire pumps needed?
• Is public fire department service reliable?
• Do occupancy hazards and arrangements require any special protection?
• Are there any production facilities where a minor fire or accident could create widespread production stoppage?
• Are there combustion safeguards on boilers, ovens, or dryers?
• Do any planned storage arrangements involve hazardous high piling?
• Is the roof resistant to winds?
• Is there proper fire protection to protect structures during the construction period?
• Is the construction site within a known flood area? Are there nearby streams?
• What is the area's seismological history?

Source: *Occupational Hazards*, 614 Superior Ave. West, Cleveland 44113.

Warehouse Safety Checklist

• Specific safety program is in effect with the active participation of management.
• Supervisory personnel are safety-conscious.
• There is adequate on-the-job training.
• Aisles are clearly marked and rules for traffic flow enforced.
• Storage areas are clearly designated and merchandise stacked only in proper areas.
• Employees do not stand under suspended loads or jump off moving vehicles.

• No-smoking and no-trespassing signs are displayed and observed.
• Protective clothing (gloves, shoes, and safety glasses) is worn by employees.
• Motorized equipment is refueled outside the building.
• Hazardous materials are isolated and handled according to safety guidelines.
• Adequate fire protection is assured.

Source: *The ABC's of Warehousing* by the editors of *Distribution/Warehouse Cost Digest*, Marketing Publications, Inc., National Press Bldg., Washington, DC 20045.

Fire Safety

• A warning system should be set up in zones so fire can be found quickly. Include a master control panel in a central location. Another panel at the main entrance can help arriving firemen locate blaze quickly.
• Compartmentalize sections of the plant so they can be sealed off manually or automatically.
• Equip vents with smoke dampers and fire dampers held open by links that melt to close them when a specified temperature is reached.
• Place smoke detectors on each floor hooked up to elevator controls to prevent the doors from opening on the floor where fire is raging.
• Install automatic warning systems in all normally unattended areas such as crawl spaces and storage areas.
• Use dry chemical extinguishers rather than a sprinkler system in garage areas, since water from sprinklers can carry pools of burning gasoline, spreading fire and smoke.

Choosing a Fire Extinguisher

The right type of fire extinguisher, located in the best place, can stop a small fire from spreading as well as being the first line of defense against a big fire.

Choose extinguisher by category of hazard. Class A: Ordinary materials, like wood. Class B:

Liquids and gases, like oil, propane, etc. Class C: Electrical equipment (extinguishing agent must be nonconductive). Class D: Flammable metals.

Locate extinguishers where they are accessible (top should be no more than five feet off the floor), safe from obstruction, and close to exits. The distance from most hazardous areas to the extinguisher and back should be no more than 50 feet.

Replace all extinguishers that are activated by turning them upside down. They can explode when used. None have been produced since 1971 but many are still in service.

Source: *Journal of American Insurance*, Insurance Information Institute, 110 William St., New York 10038.

Smoke Detector Tip

• It's best to install two kinds of smoke detector, one using photoelectric detection and the other using ionization method. Ionization detectors are better at sensing a fire in its earliest stage, before much smoke is produced. Photoelectric detectors are better at detecting actual smoke. Have one detector powered by house current, the other by batteries.

• Replace smoke detector batteries annually. They wear out, making detector inoperable. Pick a special date for replacement, like a holiday. That way, it's easier to remember when it's time for a change.

Handling an OSHA Inspection

Although Occupational Safety and Health Administration inspectors have virtually free access to any workplace, a company does have certain rights during the inspection. Some basic points that can protect company's interest and also help achieve a smoother and less disruptive experience:

• Check the inspector's credentials. This can be done politely. His right to be there must be established. Never detain or deny access to someone with proper credentials, but others who may accompany him (i.e., an equipment expert) can be stopped. Ask for their business cards. Top management and/or the company's safety consultants should be alerted immediately.

• Exchange information before inspection. Try to determine the nature and scope of the inspection. Advise the inspector of work schedules. Ask permission to contact people involved along the route.

• Go along with the inspector (if possible take the company's safety consultant, too) and make detailed notes. These can be critical to the company's success in dealing with any resulting citations. Jot down all relevant conversations with the inspector, especially those that seem to indicate the reason for inspection. Also note the areas visited, people involved, condition of machinery, equipment, or materials examined, and practices observed. During and after inspection, gather as much information as possible about the inspector and his reasoning. Always maintain a cool, businesslike posture (carefully avoid any appearance of hostility). Try to find out why he feels a particular condition or practice constitutes a hazard, how seriously he rates a violation.

• Expect some disagreement. Stay calm. Arguing only aggravates the situation and may negatively influence the company's standing with OSHA. You can request that the area or practice in question be avoided until top management and/or safety consultants can be contacted in cases of dispute.

• Correct imminent hazard situations quickly. Post a notice. Deny entry by any person, without the inspector's permission, into any area judged an imminent hazard. The area then should be entered only for the purpose of making it safe. Notify top management and safety consultants immediately.

• Make a post-inspection report as soon as possible. Tape record or write down details while still fresh in your mind. (Tape recorders are not permitted on inspection tour itself.) And discuss the matter thoroughly with appropriate people.

• Appeal all citations that result from inspection, regardless of the company's view as to the citation's legitimacy or degree of severity. Two good reasons for this: (1) It allows for investigation of any mitigating circumstances that could affect the violation or the fine. (2) Even if the initial fine were to be inconsequential, a later similar violation will automatically carry a double fine; a third, four times the original fine; and the next one, an automatic fine that is ten times the original (no more than $10,000).

Source: James R. Hinson, director, technical services, Safety and Health Consultants, 1730 South Amphlett Blvd., San Mateo, CA 94040.

Preparing for an OSHA Hearing

When the company contests a safety violation citation from the Occupational Safety and Health Administration, the result is an administrative hearing. This is much like a trial. In preparation, the company should collect written records of the following:

• Accident experience and safety enforcement, including the company's nondisciplinary actions against employees for safety violations.

• Industry and company safety standards.

• Professional credentials of the person in the company responsible for safety, and the other experts who will advise legal counsel, and may also testify.

• Safety meetings: When and where held, who attended, subjects discussed.

• Details of training programs, especially for new employees.

• Protective and safety equipment provided to employees.

• Photographs of plant area where the violations were charged. Also helpful: Drawings and models for courtroom use.

Requiring Workers to Buy Own Safety Gear

An OSHA citation charging an employer with failing to provide safety footwear or shatterproof prescription glasses for employees does not mean that the employer must pay for them. Workers can be required to obtain the gear at their own expense.

The cost burden can be eased by making ar-

rangements with a local shoe store or optical center for a discount to workers who have a purchase authorization slip from the company. Payment may also be arranged by means of payroll deductions.

Some union negotiators try to impose the purchase obligation on management by stating falsely that it is already required by law. Court documents state clearly that it's up to the parties to decide who pays, as long as workers wear the protective devices when needed.

Safety-toe shoes and shatterproof eyeglasses are usually paid for by individuals because they are also used off the job. But it's common for employers to pay for protective devices that are not worn off the job and are put on only occasionally at work.

When a Worker Won't Use Safety Equipment

Employers face penalties if they don't insist that workers use safety equipment. Back up the order with supervision, discipline, and, if necessary, termination of an employee who violates rules even after receiving a warning.

One company was penalized when a worker repeatedly broke the rules and ignored the safety equipment. He had received only a mild reprimand. OSHA said that it wasn't enough.

Tough company policy may increase complaints from workers and unions. But arbitrators and courts generally concur that employers are justified in disciplining workers who consistently flout safety rules.

Handling Safety Walkouts

The Occupational Safety and Health Act does not permit the Department of Labor to compel reinstatement of workers who walk off their jobs because of alleged safety hazards.* But such discharges can be hazardous to management.

Two reasons:

F. Ray Marshall v. *Daniel Construction Co.,* 5th Circuit Court of Appeals, Docket No. 76-1465.

• The National Labor Relations Board regards refusal to perform abnormally dangerous work as protected activity on behalf of the entire work force. The authority to take action against the company that is lacking in OSHA is present in the Taft-Hartley Act.

• Discipline for refusing to obey work orders is subject to arbitration under virtually all union contracts.

Critical questions:

• Was the alleged danger to a person or to property?

Example: One employee refused to run a machine at its top-rated speed. Ruling: The only danger was that bearings would burn. No bodily harm would result. Discipline was upheld.

• Did the employee honestly believe his health or safety was in jeopardy? It's not enough merely to assert fear of an accident. There must be a rational basis for that fear.

Example: A man refused to clean the inside of a large vat unless another employee was within earshot. Although he was working with a non-toxic solvent, he was immune from punishment because there had been an incident in which a worker who was overcome by fumes escaped serious injury only because someone heard his cry for help.

• Was the job dangerous beyond normal expectations?

Example: A painter can't refuse to climb a ladder—unless there is some reason to think it isn't secure enough.

• Did the employee assert the accident hazard immediately? Delay is usually strong evidence that the worker was merely trying to evade an unpleasant chore.

If a worker believes a job is unsafe even though it isn't, his mental attitude may contribute to accidents. Best solution: Not discipline, but a transfer to work he can do more comfortably.

Variation on the unsafe work problem: Truck drivers and salespeople sometimes refuse to cross other unions' picket lines. Unless their own union contract permits refusal, they may be disciplined if there was no reason for them to fear bodily harm.

Examples: An arbitrator reversed the dismissal of a driver who refused to deliver cement to a struck building site. Evidence showed he was accosted by two burly pickets, one of whom was armed. Conversely, the discharge of a driver who refused to make a pickup at a customer's factory was upheld. His claim of fear was not persuasive. Reason: Other drivers from the same company had crossed the same picket line often without incident.

Source: Morris Stone, former vice presient, American Arbitration Association.

Before an OSHA Inspection

The maximum Occupational Safety and Health Administration fine is $10,000, plus cost of correcting violations. It's desirable, therefore, to go through an inspection drill before the inspectors from the OSHA show up.

The first step is to get a copy of OSHA standards for the company's operation (*Inspection Survey Guide, A Handbook of Guides and References to Safety and Health Standards for Federal Contracts Program,* Dept. of Labor, 200 Constitution Ave. N.W., Wash., DC 20210).

Next, conduct a strict internal inspection. The best way is to have a third party do it. The insurer will usually supply someone because of its financial interest in on-the-job safety checks.

One caution to bear in mind: Small size is no protection. Lobbying is already underway to expand OSHA force and require it to turn its attention to small plants where a disporportionate number of accidents occur.

Rules Must Be Detailed

The company is usually held responsible for a work-related accident unless the employee violated specific safety rules.

One elevator installer fell down a shaft because his special belt was not fastened to the safety line. The company's rules required belts to be fastened in dangerous situations. But it didn't define which situations were dangerous. Thus, it had to pay a fine.

Another case: An experienced electrician was killed when he cut into a live power line, violating the company's rule of testing first. Ruling:

The company was not at fault. Its rule was very specific. And the court noted that both the company and the union had good safety programs.

It May Pay to Challenge OSHA

Industry is becoming less accepting of expensive demands of the federal safety agency. And the courts are often responsive to industry's problems.

A case in point: Metal stamping presses produced loud noises. However, the company provided ear protectors for all employees working in the area; these reduced the noise level at the inner ear to an acceptable level. And no employees complained of hearing problems.

But the Occupational Safety and Health Administration demanded $30,000 worth of noise-control modifications to be made at the plant. On appeal, OSHA lost. The court held that the cost was economically impractical when balanced against the benefit to employees who already had ear protectors.

Turner Co., div. of Olin Corp., v. Secy. of Labor, 561 F. 2d 82.

SALES

MANAGEMENT

Secrets of the World's Best Salesman

Basic Sales Compensation Plan

Cutting Selling Costs

Ways to Break Out of a Selling Slump

How to Start a Sales Presentation

Selling By Phone

Recapturing Lost Customers

Using Salespeople for Intelligence

24
SALES MANAGEMENT

Secrets of the World's Best Salesman

Joe Girard is the world's greatest salesman, according to the *Guinness Book of World Records*. He has sold more automobiles than anyone else every year since 1966. He has written a book* (together with Stanley H. Brown) telling all he knows about selling. His down-to-earth advice for salespeople:

The thing to remember is that when customers come in, they are at least a little scared. They're scared of parting with money because it comes hard. They all think they're not going to get what they want at a price they ought to pay. But they need what you have to sell.

This means that every day of our working lives we're in a kind of war. That is, they think we are trying to put something over on them and we think they're wasting time.

• Your job is to get them over the desire to hide from you. That's the first thing, because

How to Sell Anything to Anybody, Simon & Schuster, New York.

you can't sell a scared person. Look into your own feelings: Are you sore because he interrupted a joke? Does he remind you of somebody you don't like? You've got a war on your hands with your customer, and a war with your own feelings. Don't forget why you're both here: To make a sale that is beneficial to both of you.

• The most important thing you can learn from Girard is his Law of 250. Everyone knows 250 people in his life. Just ask any wedding or funeral director. He'll tell you that is the average number of people who show up. Much of Girard's sales come from people telling other people about him. We're not talking about love or friendship; we're talking hard business. When you turn away one customer with an angry remark or a bad attitude, you're turning away the 250 prospects that he knows.

• Satisfied customers are the best bet for future sales. Girard guards his card file of customers with his life. Put down on those file cards everything you learn about a person: Kids, hobbies, travels, whatever you learn when you talk with a customer. Then when you are trying to sell, lead the prospect into subjects that take his mind off what you're trying to do, which is to trade him your product for money.

• Personalized mail is the best thing that anybody can receive from a salesperson. Have your own mailing pieces, each one a different color and in a different-shaped envelope. They can't readily be identified as advertising mail. But each one contains a very soft-sell message. Important: Don't send your mail out the same time bills go out (the first or 15th of the month).

• Use "bird dogs." Girard tells every customer who buys from him that he'll give him $25 if he sends someone who buys a car. He pays out $14,000 to bird dogs each year. That means about 550 sales from bird dogs or about one-third of his total. Bird dogs alone made him $75,000 in commissions. The rule is: Keep your promises and pay! Don't stall on paying a bird dog—even if there's a question about whether he did send in the customer.

• Take the customer's side if there are any service problems or other complaints after the product is delivered. This is the way to make a customer a believer—to turn a lemon into a peach.

Pros and Cons of Basic Sales Compensation Plans

Salary plan: Salespeople are paid a straight salary. Discretionary bonuses, sales contest prizes, or other short-term incentives may be added.

When to use: For prospecting, much account service, team effort.

Advantages:
• Regular income for salespeople.
• Relatively fixed sales costs for company.
• Develops loyalty.
• Gets nonselling chores done.
• Easy to administer, including reassignment of sales territories, quotas.
Disadvantages:
• Gives salespeople little financial incentive to put forth extra effort.
• Little distinction between the new and experienced, productive and nonproductive.

• Expensive.

Commission plan: Salespeople are paid in direct proportion to their sales. Now usually stabilized with some guarantee, monthly minimum, generous draw, security-oriented fringes.

When to use: New business, when market is unclear and quotas and customer assignments are difficult.

Advantages:
• Unit sales costs are proportional to net sales.
• Easy to understand and compute.
• Strongest possible incentive.
• Reduces company's selling costs.
Disadvantages:
• Apt to emphasize volume over profits.
• Doesn't generate company loyalty. Salespeople sell themselves instead of company.
• Tempts sales force to skim territory, neglect nonselling duties and service. Stresses short-term rather than long-term relations.
• Best-paid salespeople may resist managerial jobs and object to training others.
• Shifting territories, accounts, people, may cause trouble.
• Low earnings during recession cause big turnover.

Combination plan: All variations of straight salary plus other monetary incentives, e.g., commission on all sales, bonus on sales over quota, commission plus bonus. Offers management maximum incentive and control. Most common combination: 80% in salary and 20% incentive.

When to use: Programs can be tailor-made for salesperson, product, marketing situation.

Advantages:
• Gives sales force security plus wider range of earnings possibilities.
• Compensates salespeople for all selling, servicing, prospecting activities.
• Ratio of expense to sales can be controlled.
• Gives company latitude to motivate achievement of sales objectives.
Disadvantages:
• Often complex, difficult to understand.
• Causes turnover if balance between salary and incentives is wrong.
• Costly to administer.
• Can result in windfall earnings on some products and neglect of others.
• Tends to incorporate too many objectives.

Matching Sales Incentives to Marketing Goals

Most sales incentive planners start at the wrong end of the question, asking: "What shall I pay?" instead of asking, "What is it that I want these salespeople to accomplish?" It's really a question of marketing goals rather than one of compensation.

The salesperson's job is only part of an overall marketing plan. First, analyze business objectives. Then decide where the sales force fits in.

Specifically, what is the salesperson expected to produce? Quantify goals as much as possible. Example: Selling "X%" more of this product than that; generating "Y" new accounts, selling "Z%" more to existing accounts.

Things that are hard to quantify are better left out of an incentive plan. Give sales manager some discretion—perhaps as much as 20% to 30%—on how much of a salesperson's compensation should be incentive.

The basic objective of an incentive plan is to compensate salespeople for things you want them to do that are within their control. This varies greatly from marketing situation to marketing situation. Straight salary may be the best approach in totally uncharted waters. Incentive plans can be revised as experience builds. Straight salary may also be preferable in huge, complicated team sales extending over a period of years and in highly refined consumer packaged goods products where the market is analyzed to death and a salesman's role has little impact on end results.

Straight-commission salesmen are apt to be more entrepreneurial. This type of compensation is probably best where sales force is needed really to prospect for customers. It's becoming less prevalent among incentive plans, however, because it gives the company very little control over the sales staff. The same is true for combination plans where the base salary is too low and the commission too high in relation to total income. This tempts salespeople to skim off the cream by making easy sales instead of expending the time and effort necessary to build distribution and expand territory.

A quota plan offers a specific tool to build volume for a particular product during a limited time period. Example: You may want to stock distribution channels with a new product before a competitor moves in. The quota will get a salesman's attention, but be careful not to make rewards so compelling that he will push the new product at the expense of other imperatives, like expanding distribution and building good will.

Consider such concepts as putting 50% of the incentive on hot products and 50% on older products and more basic objectives.

Salespeople usually figure out quickly how to optimize an incentive plan in order to make the most money. If they can't figure it out, the plan is too complex to motivate them. No action will ensue from plans that offer too little reward or are paid too infrequently. For proper impact, incentive programs should total at least 15% of annual compensation. Quarterly payments are ideal because monthly bookkeeping would be onerous and each increment would be too small. Annual payments leave too much time between the accomplishment and the reward. At best, you want a plan so simple that a salesman can sit down and figure out what he made every week.

Forget rigid internal equities when it comes to compensating salespeople. It doesn't matter that a salesperson makes more than the sales manager or even the president of the company. If he is producing, the whole company and all of its employees are sharing in the wealth.

More important question: What is the going rate to attract good people and to keep the ones you have from joining the competition? If personal trade relationships are all-important, it's much better to risk overpaying your salesmen than to risk losing the business.

If convinced that overpayments are not justified, talk it out with salesman. The idea is to increase his base (security, fringe benefits rise accordingly) and play on the accumulated good will of that overpayment during past years. Encourage salesman to check out the market himself, explaining that management already has. In doing research, be sure not to just compare titles. The job responsibilities (and hence rewards) may vary tremendously from one company to another. Trade associations and magazines can often give rough guidelines, but it may be necessary to get a full analysis by compensation specialists.

Source: Frederick M. Crehan and Richard E. Penberthy, Hay Associates, New York.

Making the Big Sale

The sales staff that goes after the big-dollar sale that takes months to negotiate needs help from other departments. Reason: Many decision makers are usually involved on the customer side in big-ticket buys. The seller whose only contacts are with the prospective customer's purchasing department can encounter real trouble in completing the deal.

Whom to involve:

• Top company executives. They can open doors by dealing directly with top executives of the customer's company. An informal lunch often can provide entree to other decision makers within the company.

• Engineering staff. Use company engineers to discuss the technical merits of the product with the prospective customer's engineering staff. They will have an influence in the final buying decision.

• Product application experts: Have them meet staff members at the customer's company who will actually be using the product.

Cutting Selling Costs

How to cut the company's costs and still maintain the effectiveness of the sales force—four suggestions that work:

• Consolidate the sales force by switching to industry-wide (or vertical) coverage of the customers. The same salesmen sell the company's entire product line to a given industry rather than having a different sales force for each division. Where there is enough compatibility in the products to permit it, such consolidation saves salesmen's time, travel, and expense—and purchasing agents like it because it saves them time as well.

• Have salesmen work from their homes. It cuts trips back to the district sales office. Telephone-answering devices make it possible for them to keep in touch with home base and monitor calls several times a day.

• In cutting back on the expenses of travel, most firms have found that it may be counterproductive to make salesmen reduce their travel

by some specific percentage. Better to make sure that all trips are necessary, and that trips are planned to cover as much ground as possible when they are made.

• For shorter trips, bus or train is cheaper than air and may not take much longer. And in rural areas, salesmen can often set up special showings in hotels and get the customers to do the traveling.

Also, there is always the possibility of car pooling with salesmen from other companies—provided the product lines don't overlap but the territories and buyers do.

Mistakes Salespeople Make in Budgeting Their Time

• Overbudgeting. Not enough time to make all the calls they intended to make; some customers are overlooked.

• Spending too much time with small customers. There is a tendency to spend equal amounts of time with all customers no matter what their sales volume.

To avoid these mistakes, draw up a time-allocation schedule and stick to it. Here's how one time plan works:

First: List customers by sales volume. The top 15% generally provides 65% of the sales volume. The next 20% delivers 20%. The remaining 65% accounts for 15%. This breakdown generally applies to all types of industrial and consumer products.

Second: Calculate the total number of sales calls made during a year. (Don't include troubleshooting or prospecting calls in this figure.) Allocate them: Prime customers get 35% of the calls, middle group 25%, and the largest (bottom) group gets 40%.

Then the salesperson allocates by account. Example: To make sure that he sees his top 15% customers 24 times each year, he schedules those visits every two weeks.

Stay flexible. Customers can be moved from one group to another for reasons other than volume at discretion of salesman. Possible reasons: Large potential business, or customer is just starting out and needs more attention.

341

No customers are overlooked. The most important customers get enough regular attention to keep them from going to competitors. The salesperson knows how much time he has to schedule extra sales calls with prospects.

Source: *Investing Your Sales Time for Maximum Return*, a cassette-workbook program by Porter Henry Knowledge Resources, Inc., 633 Third Ave., New York 10017.

Streamlining Communications

Save salespeople's time and cut the cost of their telephone calls to the office by installing a special line to the sales manager. Limit the use of this line strictly to incoming calls from the field. This will eliminate person-to-person charges, wasted calls to the switchboard when the manager is out, and time wasted in tracking him down if he's just away from his desk. The sales staff will get right through if he's available, get no answer or a busy signal if he isn't.

Ways to Break Out of a Selling Slump

• Find a salesperson with worse problems and help out. Why it works: Being generous boosts morale and helps erase worry over troubles.

• Challenge another salesperson to an informal contest. Each puts up half the prize money and winner takes all.

• Talk with satisfied customers who are enthusiastic about company products. They might even provide ideas on other uses for company's products based on their own experiences.

• Keep so busy that there isn't time to worry about the slump. Schedule more customer calls each day, start work an hour earlier, and schedule every day's lunch with prospective customers.

• Get a nonselling friend to listen to your sales presentation. Warning: Don't reveal at the outset the reason for the trial run. What's needed are the reactions of a simulated customer, not those of an official critic.

• Spend time at the end of each day reviewing your performance. Record both mistakes and smart moves. Decide how the mistakes could have been avoided.

Source: *The Five Great Problems of Salesmen and How to Solve Them* by Percy H. Whiting, McGraw-Hill, New York.

Good Ways to Begin a Sales Presentation

The first 30 seconds of a sales pitch can be crucial. Some proven openings:

• Ask a question. Make it specific and related to solving a problem (reducing expenses, increasing production, improving work quality, saving time, eliminating waste). It helps to prediagnose a key problem. Example:

In walking through your offices earlier, I noticed some crowding in the filing area. Would you be interested in widening the aisles in front of your filing cabinets by almost two feet—without losing any filing capacity?

• Promise a benefit. Same idea as question, but make a statement instead. Example:

I've got an idea that will widen the aisles. Or, I think I can help you to. . . .

• Offer a free service. Can be a quick, on-the-spot action such as surveying lighting, inspecting the arrangement of work stations, etc.

Important: The opening should be the very first words in the presentation. Use it before personal introductions. The prospect is more interested in the help being offered or the problem being solved than in who is selling it. Example:

I think I have an idea that will widen those aisles. . . . My name is Jim Smith and I'm with. . . .

Source: Robert P. Levoy, Professional Practice Consultants, 130 Cuttermill Road., Great Neck, NY 11022.

Ad Inquiry Follow-ups

Make a salesperson more productive by having another staff member handle initial follow-up calls to prospective customers who sent in ad coupons requesting product information.

What this technique does: Pinpoints hot prospects deserving of prompt attention and a personal visit or phone contact by a salesperson.

How it works: The caller waits a few days after information has gone out, then calls to make certain that the information has been received. He uses that same phone call to collect other useful information, such as:

• If prospect would like to see a salesman or be placed on mailing list.

• How many people within the company are involved in the purchase of that product and who (and at what location) makes the final purchase decision.

• The specific time during the year when budget allocations are made for the product. Or is it covered by ongoing purchase allocation?

When a Prospect Is 'Too Busy to Talk'

Suggest a time limit of seven minutes and promise to stick to it. Place a stopwatch on the desk and end the presentation when time is up (whether finished or not). The prospect is impressed with a sharpened sales pitch that doesn't waste time. The salesperson's discipline conveys confidence in the product, suggests that the product sells itself and doesn't need puffery.

When Customer Says Price Is Too High

The most useful answers to price complaints:

• The tab is justified by quality of materials, superior workmanship, construction, durability, built-in convenience.

• Price is relative. Our price is actually lower than our competitor's when economies of quality and service are considered.

• Our company could produce a lower-priced product, but years of experience and constant research show that our present product is best for that job. A cheaper product will cost more in complaints, mishaps, breakdowns, etc.

• Our company produces a quality product at the lowest possible cost and sells that product at a fair markup.

• If a less expensive method of quality production were developed, our company would be the first to use it.

• Higher-priced, quality products are prestige- and profit-builders.

• A price is too high only if *your* customers balk. They won't. We're getting heavy reorders. And that's the key.

Closing the Sale

Some of the main reasons that salesmen have trouble closing: Overtalking, underlistening, failing to identify hidden influences, failing to close when there are positive signals.

To turn more prospects into customers, try these techniques:

• Eliminate nonstop presentations that bore the prospect. Gear all presentations to creating dialogue. Aim to elicit continuous questions, reactions, product/contract information from the prospect. Create openings for pertinent responses and attempt to make a closing.

• Ferret out undisclosed needs, hidden objections. Sew up details on specs, performance, delivery needs, and contract objectives. Find out what the prospect needs (and what the competitors may have offered). Then see what you can do to meet the competition.

• Identify all buying influences in the company. Aim to reach them. Ask the purchasing agent if he'd like engineers, maintenance supervisors, or others to see the product.

• Never try to close when a prospect has just voiced objections or shown he doesn't understand the proposal.

• Stay alert to buy signals and invitations to close. Obvious ones: "I wish I'd done this years ago"; "My production manager recommended something like this."

• Sometimes a nod of the head, a change in the tone of voice, or a move toward a pen are indications that a sale has been made. The salesperson who keeps talking beyond the ready-to-buy sign may unsell the customer.

• A prospect ripe for closing is likely to ask leading questions. The salesperson should be prepared to respond with another question that leads the customer to commitment. Examples:

CUSTOMER	SALESPERSON
How much does it cost?	In what quantity?
When could it be delivered?	When do you want delivery?
Can I get it in (a particular color or style)?	Do you want it in (that color or style)?
How much must I order to get a good price?	How much do you want to order?
What is the smallest trial order possible?	How small an order do you want?
When does a new model come out?	Do you want the newest model? This is it.

Classic closing techniques:
• Ask, "How much of this do you think you would use in a month?" or, "How soon would you need delivery?" While appearing to be information salesman needs to quote price and delivery, also serves as gauge of how ready prospect is to place order.
• Ask, "Which model would you prefer, the basic one or the one with attachments?" Such questions give the customer a choice between two models—either of which means a sale.

How to Handle Customers Who Are in the Wrong

Even when he's dead wrong, treat him as if he were right.
• Listen—carefully. Try to pick up what's on the customer's mind and then shape your reply accordingly.
• Change the subject. Most arguments stem from minor issues. Seize the first chance to move the conversation from the sticking point on to matters of importance.
• Acknowledge a good point. Let the buyer know when his position has merit. Then state your company's position.

• Restate the point. Helps to clarify and focus for better understanding.
If all else fails, have a rousing good argument. That may be what the customer really wants. Then get on with the sale.

Three Basic Buyer Personalities: How to Handle Each

• The dominant personality: Power- and winning-oriented. Buyer's tendency is to be closed-minded, anti-intellectual, and to view giving the order (or accepting a salesperson's advice) as a kind of defeat.
To close the sale: Never seem to demand surrender. Be direct and forceful. Lay out the facts, then appeal to his decisiveness.
• The detached type: Idea-oriented, impersonal, uncommunicative. Prefers order and predictability. Open to facts and logic. Takes pride in objectivity.
The best approach is low-pressure logic. Don't push, but demonstrate that the most intelligent action would be to buy now.
• The dependent personality: People-oriented. This buyer needs love and approval. Good listener. Compliant and easy to exploit. Loyal. Generally indecisive and can be pushed by someone he trusts.
To close the sale: Be forceful but friendly. Sales to this type of buyer can be lost by "getting right down to business." He wants to have coffee, chat, get to know the salesperson before committing himself to a deal.
Source: Alan H. Schoonmaker, Control Data Corporation, 8100 34 Ave. S., Minneapolis 55440.

Four Ways to Write a Follow-up Letter

• The benefit letter continues the sales pitch, reminds the prospect why he wants the product, what it can do for him.

• The transmittal letter accompanies something useful—sample, catalog, novelty; a more effective reminder of sales call than a business card clipped to a brochure.

• A cordial letter sells softly. It emphasizes a desire to help. Aimed at keeping contact alive.

• The list-cleaning letter asks for update on who's new at purchasing desk, where a prior contact has gone. Aimed at cutting seller's mailing costs, keeping track of old contacts, and getting to know new ones.

One letter is usually not enough. Develop a campaign of prewritten letter series, using six or so letters at two-week intervals, mixing letter types as appropriate.

Hiring Good Salespeople

What to look for in a resume, interview, and reference check:

• A stable job history—not less than two years at each previous place—except for good reason.

• Rank in the sales force. Above the middle is what you want.

• Measures of success: Progress up the ranks, upgrading in job changes, awards, other recognition, earnings (don't be afraid to ask for W-2 or tax returns).

What to look for in beginners: The most important qualities are resilience and persistence. Make sure the prospect knows exactly what's involved in the specific job. Define it carefully. If it requires ten calls a day on office managers, using a canned pitch, and making two sales out of ten tries, tell that to the candidate. Then ask for a playback to be certain that the applicant really understands the realities of the job.

The key ingredient of successful selling is willingness to overcome the pain of rejection and to go back for more. The best salespeople sell more because they simply make more calls. Everybody is afraid of rejection, but top sellers can handle it.

How to know that a person can endure the grind and succeed: Ask why the person wants to sell. Listen for answers that indicate competitive nature: Wants to do better than his brother, to make money to impress spouse, to surpass high school friends, or anything else that shows a desire to be above average.

The wanting-to-be-better-than-others is the key to effective selling.

Don't try to typecast a salesperson. Appearance and image are not the major factors for success. The seller should be an adequate representative of the company but not necessarily a perfect specimen of "the salesman type." Don't project personal judgment and feelings on the appearance of prospects if they are adequate by objective standards.

The ideal candidate isn't necessarily somebody who already has sold your company's kind of products somewhere else. Looking for the perfect fit will eliminate most good prospects, and somebody who can sell one kind of product or service well can learn enough about another product to do a good job on that one, too. Training in the details of selling a new product is usually cheaper and more effective than trying to find the perfect fit.

Big-ticket products such as industrial-process machinery or computers require a totally different approach to the sale—such as development of relationship with customer, frequent calls to learn the customer's needs. But the same amount of resilience and persistence is needed as would be the case for typewriters or encyclopedias.

Past success is fine, but watch out for too much. A salesperson who has earned $40,000 on past job won't be happy with $20,000 (if that's an accurate estimate of earning power on your sales force). It's obvious, but many employers forget that point when they're facing a star in another field. They assume the prospect will do as well for them. But he probably will get disappointing results and will leave.

Source: Malcolm Lazinsk, president of Fortune Personnel Agency, 505 Fifth Avenue, New York 10017.

Reasons to Hire Women As Salespeople

• Women, in general, have better developed verbal and social skills than men, give compliments easily, are good listeners.

• They tend to be more loyal, ethical, harder workers, and more conscientious than men.

• They have a natural, comfortable approach for sales presentations. They create a less suspicious sales atmosphere—which is important in these days, when advertising and sales credibility are under fire.

• They're better motivated to excel, to overcome prejudice, preconceptions.

• It's easier for women to get prospects on the phone and make appointments. Men will respond because they are "curious" to see what a saleswoman looks like.

Don't reject an inexperienced saleswoman. A varied work background may indicate desire for challenge, initiative, good motivations.

Source: David King, Careers for Women, Inc., 26 E. 11 St., New York 10003.

Before Promoting a Top Salesperson to Sales Manager

• Does the salesperson like paperwork? Or do it well?

• As a manager, will he understand and approve of management objectives? If he's too much the maverick, let him continue selling and look for another candidate.

• How does he handle complaints? As a manager, he must be a diplomat, soothing customers and sales reps.

• Does he get along with a broad range of people as well as with the customers? Management requires more understanding, broader interpersonal skills.

If you can say yes on all four counts, you're dealing with management material.

Source: *Research Institute Marketing for Sales Executives.*

Formula for Deciding If a Bigger Sales Staff Is Needed

To calculate whether or not it pays to hire an additional salesperson, use incremental break-even analysis.

The basic steps:

1. Add up direct costs (salary, bonus, commission, travel expenses, entertainment, and miscellaneous expenses). These direct costs are traceable directly to the salesperson. If he is eliminated, the direct costs are too.

2. Calculate the gross margin percentage (the difference between gross sales and the costs of manufacturing, expressed as a percentage of sales). Example:

Sales	$100,000
Manufacturing costs	80,000
Gross margin	$ 20,000
Gross margin percentage =	$20,000
	÷ $100,000
	× 100%
	= 20%

3. Determine the break-even volume. (In this example the direct costs are $30,000/yr.)

$$\text{Break-even volume} = \frac{\text{Direct Costs}}{\text{Gross Margin Percentage}}$$

Break-even volume =	$30,000
	÷ 20% or
	$150,000

With $150,000 in sales volume, the salesperson just covers the direct costs (20% of $150,000 is $30,000).

Question for management: Are there other ways of spending what it would cost to hire more salespeople that would have a better impact on sales and profits?

Caution: The additional business must be added business—not volume taken from other products, territories, or distributors of the company. The incremental volume must not require any increase in fixed costs (other than the additional salespersons) such as costs of plant, equipment, etc.

Source: *Checking Up On Your Sales Force*, The Sales Executive Club of New York, 122 E. 42 St., New York 10017.

Motivating Long-Time Reps

One way of rewarding manufacturers' representatives who are critical to company success and assuring their continued efforts: Give them company stock. Better than a simple monetary bonus, because it gives the rep an interest in seeing company continue to grow. The same type of stock program or same class of stock now available to regular employees could be expanded to reps. Shares available for them could be tied to their sales figures.

Most Important Qualities for Industrial Salespeople

Both ego and empathy, always thought of as desirable characteristics in salespeople, had a consistently negative relationship to nearly every measure of sales performance, according to a recent study of industrial salesmen. The authors think this may reflect the technical nature of industrial sales and the great number of sales calls required. Endurance was the trait that was related most positively to success.

Other characteristics of successful industrial salesmen:
• Physically impressive, energetic.
• Good work habits, persevering, willing to work long hours.
• Broad range of interests, but little involvement in civic and professional organizations.
• Not highly educated, but very capable intellectually.
• Maybe emotional and somewhat disorganized, but adaptable.
• Not overly sensitive or perceptive to the feelings of others.
• They view selling as a professional career.

Source: Lawrence M. Lamont, Washington and Lee University, and William J. Lundstrom, University of Mississippi, in *The Wharton Magazine*, University of Pennsylvania, Philadelphia 19104.

Selecting a Manufacturer's Rep

When shopping for a representative to sell your company's product, don't limit choices to those with experience in the same type of busi-

ness. Too strict adherence to such a guideline could rule out the younger, more eager, and energetic sales representative who could do the job just as well.

Don't worry about the number of lines a rep carries. The kind of lines carried is more important. Some lines have many items and require more work. Others have only a few items and need much less work.

Check the background of a sales rep by talking to a couple of sales managers of companies he now sells for. The trade association of manufacturer's representatives also keeps background materials on sales reps.

What to give a new rep:
• Lists of previous accounts and what they bought.
• Prospect lists (especially to a younger rep).
• Samples in compact, easy-to-carry case(s).
• Special markdowns or discounts on items.

Advice: Sales contests are rarely productive. Neither are many detailed reports from reps.

Source: Source: H. Keith Kittrell, United Association of Manufacturers' Representatives, 808 Broadway, Kansas City, MO 64105.

Pros and Cons of Selling Through Manufacturer's Reps

A manufacturer's representative:
• Gives manufacturer a predetermined sales cost. Costs are tied directly to goods shipped.
• Provides the manufacturer with local management. Good for a growing company whose staff is limited.
• Presents the manufacturer with a trained sales force. Training costs the manufacturer nothing because it is part of the package.
• Gives the manufacturer immediate access to the market.

Disadvantages:
• Reps tend to be generalists—not good when manufacturer needs sales representatives with a highly technical background.
• Reps are not useful when the manufacturer's product is so new or innovative that it re-

347

quires a highly developmental sales approach, including meetings to determine exactly what the needs are once the customer has agreed to buy the product or service.

• There could be a psychological reaction to a feeling of loss of control.

• Using a rep inhibits development of a company sales force. A perfect marriage would allow for internal sales personnel growth while working with a representative. Negotiate an arrangement where the internal sales force is restricted to certain territories at the beginning of the relationship with the rep.

Solving a Sales Problem: Replacing an Aging Sales Force

Innovative answer to the problem of efficiently replacing the sales force when senior members are retiring: Let salespeople train and ''pay'' their replacements. How it has worked for one large dealer (E.W. Curry Co., Pittsburgh):

• Hire juniors as field assistants for senior salespeople. Give them an intensive course in the company's paper flow and customer service procedures.

• Assign the junior to his senior salesperson/instructor. When the senior is beginning to reap some benefits from the arrangement (novice handling some calls on his own, handling some of the senior's phone calls at the office), and boosting his earnings, the senior is assessed 25% of the junior's salary.

• When the senior feels that he's getting 50% of the value of the junior's salary, he is assessed 50%. The junior is now spending half the time in the field, half in the office, with office time split between the senior's and the house accounts.

• A year after field work begins, the junior is ready to work full-time for the senior, maintaining several of the senior's existing accounts and canvassing for new ones. The senior pays all junior's salary, and all commissions go to the senior—his incentive for training the junior.

• When the junior is ready, he can start on his own in the senior's territory, subject to the senior's approval, with his own nucleus of accounts. He could take over the territory when the senior retires, or be asked to open a new territory.

How to Use a Sales Forecast

No sales forecast is complete without a battery of contingency plans to deal with its inaccuracies. Here's how to avoid getting locked into mediocre results because a vital forecast was incomplete.

Once committed to writing, sales forecasts tend to be treated as gospel. Executives often ''stick with the plan,'' hope for the best, and wind up wondering what went wrong.

Solution: Recognize the forecast for what it is: A best guess based on fallible assumptions. With effective contingency plans, even an inaccurate forecast can lead to highly profitable results.

• Isolate key assumptions and be aware of how major changes in them will affect the rest of the forecast.

• Plan in advance how to deal with major departures from projections, whether actual results are better or worse than the forecast.

• Monitor each key assumption as the results come in.

• If results fall short of expectations, be prepared to alter the plan immediately. But if sales are stronger than expected, be ready to seize the opportunity. The key is advance planning, being ready to move in either direction as soon as the results start to come in.

How Sales Offices Hurt Sales

They become places where salesmen go to *avoid* selling.

They make it too easy for the sales staff to sit around, drink coffee, fill out forms, and attend to other details that could be handled elsewhere.

It's generally much better to have the sales force out of the office, calling on trade and covering more territory.

And, for salesmen who pay their own expenses, the company office can result in loss of ''office at home'' deductions.

How to Keep Customers When a Product Is No Longer Unique

When competition duplicates a company's products, there are three ways to deal with the situation:

1. Cut prices.
2. Offer more (service, bonuses, discounts, free premiums).
3. Switch to systems selling.

In systems selling, the no-longer-unique product becomes part of a system composed of several products that are sold on how-they-solve-a-customer's-cost-problem basis rather than on how-they-operate, how-they-are-built, etc.

Guidelines to aid salespeople when they make the switch to systems selling:

• Increase the personalization of the relationship. Equipment sales are based on performance of the equipment; systems sales, on the performance of the systems seller.

• Increase customer's participation. Equipment sales are based on maximum sales representative participation and minimal customer participation. Systems sales are based on a high degree of active buyer-seller participation.

• Increase the professionalization of the relationship. Equipment sales are based on a traditional buyer-seller relationship. Systems selling positions the buyer as a client and the seller as a consultant.

Source: *Systems Selling Strategies* by Mark Hanan, James Cribbin, and Jack Donis, Amacom, 135 W. 50 St., New York 10020.

Legal Risk When the Salesman Lowers Price to Get Order

Common but illegal: A salesperson very close to a big order might offer a concession: A price discount, extra service without charge, absorbing freight, or allowing extra time to pay.

But that may violate the Robinson-Patman Act prohibition against price discrimination

favoring one customer over another. Offering a lower price to one customer is generally not allowed except in two situations:

• The lower price can be justified by lower cost of this particular order. Examples: An unusually large quantity permits seller to produce at lower cost. Or a long-term purchase contract enables seller to save through better long-range planning. Cost calculation must be realistic and include overhead, tooling, etc. Can't use marginal cost of producing this last order.

• The seller believes that he must offer a lower price or better terms to meet a competitor's offer that was legally made.

It's important that management and the sales force understand the law and the consequences of violating it. Congress is putting strong pressure on the Federal Trade Commission to step up enforcement of Robinson-Patman.

Illegal price discrimination can lead to investigation by the FTC and possibly a cease-and-desist order. That's not as innocuous as it sounds. The investigation is on the company's record, and the FTC may then watch all company operations more closely in the future.

Another danger: Even if the government doesn't take action, a competitor who feels damaged by price discrimination can sue for triple damages (plus legal fees).

The seller has a strong defense against a suit if it can prove that the lower price was justified by lower costs. But be aware that seller has the burden of proving lower costs. Courts are very skeptical if there was no study of costs until after the investigation started.

Meeting a competitor's lower price is a good defense, too. The seller must show a good-faith belief that competitor is willing to sell at the lower price. But calling the competitor to verify the price offered is not allowed, according to a recent Supreme Court decision.

U.S. v. *U.S. Gypsum,* U.S. Supreme Court, 6/29/78.

Generating Sales Leads by Mail

A key requirement for maximum sales: A planned promotional program that generates high-quality leads. With the cost of sales averaging $60 or more each, make sure that as high a percentage as possible result in sales commitments. What to do:

• Avoid promotions that will generate too many leads at once. Aim for a steady flow.

• Tailor the number of leads expected to size of the territory. Example: At a 5% return rate, a territory with ten salesmen making 20 new calls per month would mean a mailing of 4,000.

• Zero in on a specific area of a territory each time so leads are not scattered widely.

• Be sure your list includes those who influence the purchase as well as those with authority to buy. (Trade magazine subscription lists are a good source.)

• Remember, you'll generate more initial interest by promoting a less expensive bottom-of-the-line item. (Once your salesman calls, he can push for purchase of a higher-ticket item.)

• Test and retest copy, promotions, lists, media, timing. Don't be put off by cost. Higher-priced leads are usually the most valuable.

• Be sure the sales force is behind the program. Especially important are leads that aren't closed. Keep plugging away at them.

Source: Bob Stone of Rapp, Collins, Stone & Adler, Inc., Chicago, in *Advertising Age.*

Best Hours to Reach Prospects by Phone

• Chemists and engineers: 4-5 p.m.

• Contractors and builders: Before 9 a.m., at noon, or around 5 p.m.

• Dentists: 8:30-9:30 a.m.

• Druggists and grocers: 1-3 p.m.

• Executives: After 10:30 a.m.

• Housewives: 10-11:30 a.m.

• Lawyers: 11 a.m.-2 p.m. and 4-5 p.m. Avoids court hours.

• Physicians: 9-11 a.m. and 1-3 p.m. Those in suburbs can be called between 7 and 8 p.m.

• Professors and schoolteachers: After 4 p.m. or between 6 and 7 p.m.

• Salaried people: At home, 8-9 p.m.

• Stockbrokers: Before 10 a.m. or after 4 p.m. Eastern time. Avoids stock exchange hours.

• Insurance brokers and agents: 9-10 a.m., around noon, and at 4:30 p.m.

Source: *How to Increase Your Sales by Telephone* by Earl Prevette, C. & R. Anthony, Inc., 300 Park Ave. S., New York 10010.

Recapturing Lost Customers

• Write an earnest, friendly letter with a personal tone.

• Offer special discounts to people who haven't purchased in six months to a year.

• Submit questionnaires that don't require a signature asking why they no longer buy.

• Send different letters monthly for a full year before giving up.

Source: Luther Brock, in *Direct Marketing*, 224 7th Street, Garden City, NY 11530.

Selling by Phone from a Prepared Script

For maximum results: Deliver the sales message from a fixed, pretested script directed at the needs and cultural level of the audience for the service or product.

When testing a script, figure the percentage of positive responses as against turndowns. Then answer these questions:

• How many refused to listen, and why?

• How many prospects asked questions of the salesperson?

• What were the questions?

• Were objections raised? How many, and what kind?

• How many asked to receive additional information?

• Which sales points were well received?

Once the sales message is prepared, the representative must rehearse it so that approach to the customer does not sound canned or formal. Make certain that the message encourages response from the prospect early on. That helps the telephone seller develop a sense of rapport with the customer. (A hard sell is usually counterproductive.)

More telephone selling basics:

• Arm the telephone seller with additional material and data not in the basic message script so that he is prepared in advance to answer some of the more likely questions.

• Don't make unsupportable claims at any time. It's not necessary for the telephone seller to take risks if he's well prepared with information.
Source: Murray Roman, Communications Institute of America, Inc., 641 Lexingon Ave., New York 10022.

Better Sales Meetings

A cherished belief about sales meetings is that salespeople have to be entertained or cajoled into receiving the company's message. Actually, that's not true. They want to learn and will come to learn, but they must believe that management means business. And that there's something "in it" for them.

Here's what to do: Promote the meeting as if salespeople had to pay to get in. Stay away from management-centered theme and stress sales-benefit approach. Be frank, not tricky. Consider the meeting a quality product to be sold to the sales force. For an especially important meeting, use engraved invitations.

Create advance assignments to involve people in the meeting and to establish meeting objectives. There should be nothing secret about what the meeting is expected to accomplish. The best assignments are:

• Understandable. ("Read this and be prepared for a discussion about overcoming objections.")

• Interesting. ("Create a presentation for your most difficult product—you will be asked to sell it to the group.")

• Relevant. Don't ask for a compendium of customer complaints unless there are plans to include them as part of program.

Questionnaires should be used only if results are to be given and discussed at the meeting. There will be more honest and stimulating response by stating, "Do not sign."

Couch questions in a nonthreatening way. For example, ask, "What are the most frequent complaints you hear from your customers?" rather than, "What do you think is wrong with this company?"

One technique: Ask sales force in advance for a list of problems they encounter, plus problems that have been solved—and how. At the meeting, feature particularly resourceful solutions, or match up problems from one territory with solutions from another. If, in reading through responses, a general concern or a developing problem is spotted, assign someone on the staff to talk about it.

Eliminate the head table at large sales meetings. Top management should sit with salespeople at regular tables. This is the way to increase communication between management and the sales staff, and build close relationships.
Source: *Sales Management* magazine, 633 Third Ave., New York 10017.

Keynoting Sales Meetings

At meetings, the company president (or top official) should be the last, not the first, to address the group. The sales manager should be the keynoter. These are his people, his responsibility. He talks their language—the kind that emphasizes sales quotas and marketing support. The president's job, as last on the program, is to show why the new quotas are vital to corporate goals and new investments.
Source: Leif Juhl, Juhl Associates, Elkhart, IN.

How to Eliminate Price-Marking Errors

Marking prices on merchandise seems so easy that it often is delegated to low-level stockroom help. But carelessness can be costly.

The six most common errors:

• Unmarked items in display. Customers choose marked items, bypass others, to avoid delay at checkout. Slows inventory turnover, especially costly with dated products. Remedy: Spot checks by supervisor.

• Items marked in wrong spot. If price is on

351

bottom of item on low shelf, it can irritate customers, destroy benefits of specials. Remedy: Manager gives marker placement instructions listed by product, determined by shelf space.

• Mark obscures manufacturer's label. Reduces product's impact on shelf. May also conceal special instructions customer needs to use product properly, reduce repeat sales. Remedy: Again, instructions and frequent spot checks.

• Marking ink or label adhesive mars product, kills sales. Remedy: Buyer's or manager's responsibility to anticipate problem.

• Label illegible or incomplete. Blurred by multiple stampings, lists quantity price (e.g., 3/$1.00) but not unit price. Cashier is likely to misread or misfigure code. (Most errors favor the customer, not the store.) Remedy: Training and spot checks.

• Label too easily detached. It tempts dishonest customers to switch price tags. Remedies: Unbreakable plastic loops (cut with scissors at cashier); labels that disintegrate when removed, with seals that must be torn to remove; hidden marking elsewhere that switcher might overlook.
Source: *Pricemarking for Increased Profitability*, Monarch Marking Systems, Box 608, Dayton, OH 45401.

Sales Troubleshooters

Sales service coordinators can smooth communication between customers and the sales department. One sizable chemical company has four former field salespeople located in the home office who act as troubleshooters. Each of them has a region and specific customers, representatives, and sales managers to work with. What they do:

• Check the status of each order or shipment.
• Call on key accounts to identify service problems and product needs.
• Schedule early or preseason business (they don't actually write orders, however).
• Explain company service and distribution programs to the sales force.
• Sales service people report to company distribution rather than to marketing. Advantages: Impartiality when ironing out differences between sales and production, and greater credi-

bility with customers whose orders they are trying to expedite.
Source: *Sales Manager's Bulletin*, National Sales Development Institute, 24 Rope Ferry Rd., Waterford, CT 06386.

Writing a Customer Service Manual

What to include:
• Details on company's distribution organization, manufacturing facilities, and warehousing.
• Terms of sale, including sample contracts, shipping and billing procedures.
• Ordering procedure—how to write up an order and place it.
• Invoice description explaining why all items must be entered.
• What to do about stock shortages, damaged goods, and late deliveries.
• Definitions of technical terms: Back order, common carrier, f.o.b., freight allowance.
Source: *Sales Manager's Bulletin*, National Sales Development Institute, 24 Rope Ferry Rd., Waterford, CT 06386.

How to Take Advantage of Big Overseas Trade Opportunities

Don't assume that just because a product is a hot seller in this country, it will automatically appeal to European buyers. However, a well-designed, quality item that functions admirably may be ripe for foreign market development.

Where to start: Almost every country has a consulate in New York, Washington (and perhaps other major cities), each with a commercial attache or other commercial groups connected to it. If your city isn't large enough to have resident consulates, check the public library for directories that list the nearest one.

Then write a letter describing your product (with such details as size, shape, use, cost) and ask how to proceed. Since most of these offices are very busy, the answer may take a while.

The information they provide may be biased in their own favor, for example, encouraging your company to proceed when there is no real market or before it is really ready. But it's a start.

Another fertile source of information is trade associations. Whether the product is noodles or nuts and bolts, chances are some other manufacturer in the industry has experience in foreign markets. To avoid tipping your hand to a competitor, it's often possible to arrange a discussion on a related but noncompetitive basis, e.g., selling to the Communists.

Also check trade associations and local libraries for directories of foreign manufacturing companies that either make a similar product or might buy the product. This can suggest whether it would be best to seek customers through a joint venture with a fellow manufacturer abroad or to go it alone.

Once you are convinced of a potential market, it is extremely important to fine-tune the target with a local market study.

Example: Out of a spectrum of products, certain ones are going to be better suited for some foreign marketing than others. In Europe are a number of large international marketing research firms that can, for between $5,000 and $10,000, tell you quite precisely how well the product is suited to the market. They may suggest revisions in either product or marketing approach and can even provide a rundown on possible joint venture opportunities, types of financing available, etc.

Prime sources for finding a reliable research outfit: American embassies abroad. Most have commercial attaches and reliable consultants.

Also, some U.S. consulates are much more helpful than others, will find translators for you (English is spoken in most European countries except Spain) and might even send someone with you to see potential clients. Before signing on with a research house, ask for a list of previous American clients. Check all references carefully.

A detailed market study should include a list of current producers and manufacturers of products such as yours in the given country, together with an evaluation of their product quality, competitive pricing, etc.

This may turn up an ideal candidate for a joint venture—clearly the safest way to proceed, particularly for smaller companies.

Consulates can also suggest foreign sales agents who will act as a manufacturer's representative. This is, of course, the cheapest way to go. But it has two possible disadvantages:

1. The agent may represent so many other products that your company's gets lost.

2. You may risk losing the exclusivity of the product (patents are not nearly so well enforced abroad as they are here).

The trick is to keep the capital investment to a minimum. Even the largest companies are beginning to realize this makes sense. While the profit potential is much greater when you go it alone, so are the risks and the headaches.

Don't rush in with U.S. capital. Explore all possibilities for raising capital in the host country. Many have agencies that will provide free or highly advantageous financing to manufacturers who put up plants in less-developed areas.

The most common mistakes of Americans seeking foreign markets:

• Being in too big a hurry. Recognize that a market study which would take no more than a month here could easily require six months there. This is a necessary and prudent delay.

• Failure to adapt the product to the foreign market. Even though the U.S. is now moving toward the metric system, until recently some manufacturers were trying to palm off ounce- and pound-size packages in markets where they've always used liters and grams.

As always, it pays to have good tax and legal advice. Embassies can suggest good law firms abroad. Request one that has qualifications to practice law in the U.S. as well.

Source: Ronald Ady, director, Associated Consultants, 114 Liberty St., New York 10016.

Using an Export Management Company

The simplest way for a smaller company to make its first move into the overseas market is to use an export management company. It functions essentially as the manufacturer's exporting representative.

Its chief functions are to buy goods from the company, get them overseas, do paperwork and marketing, provide advice on changes needed in packaging, and it may help in financing, too.

A typical export management company has salespeople traveling to various parts of the world to sign up local sales representatives. The export manager usually works for several different manufacturers.

Advantages for the manufacturer: The management company makes it possible to expand into the export market with little expense, without adding staff and with little more complication than is involved in selling goods to a jobber in the U.S. The cutoff point is when the manufacturer's exports reach about $1 million a year. At that time it is usually better off having its own export department.

How to choose a good export management company:

• A list of export management companies is available from the nearest Department of Commerce field office. It provides a description of the type of product handled by each company.

• Look for a successful company with long-term clients who keep renewing contracts.

• Most important: Know what the export management company's area of specialization is. Avoid a company that attempts to cover all fields. The firm must know a particular geographic area and must be staffed with product specialists. Otherwise it can't adequately represent a client.

Since the manufacturer has no marketing costs, minimum overhead, and no credit costs, goods are usually sold to the export managing company at lower than wholesale prices in the U.S. Rule of thumb: The export managing companies usually work on margins of 5%-6%.

Some will insist on front-end money ($5,000 to $20,000), since it costs the export management firm a fair amount before it can export the first shipment of products.

Source: Dr. Lee Nehrt, director, World Trade Institute, 1 World Trade Center, New York 10048.

Manufacturers Can Limit Distributor Territory

A manufacturer can confine a distributor to a territory and also protect it against others selling in his area. That's the thrust of two important Supreme Court decisions.

Background: In the famous 1967 Schwinn case, the High Court said that any attempt by a manufacturer to restrict the distributors' sales areas was a clear antitrust violation. Two recent decisions went a long way toward reversing this ruling.

The way it stands now:

• In order to entice a distributor to take on a line, a manufacturer can assign a defined sales area. And the manufacturer can agree not to appoint any other distributor within a certain distance. But there should be a legitimate business reason for making that decision.

• If a manufacturer gives such an area to a distributor, it isn't required to do the same for other distributors.

• The manufacturer cannot absolutely prohibit a distributor from selling into another's area. But it can provide that the first distributor must pay part of the sales price to the second distributor.

• A manufacturer is permitted to drop distributors that carry competing lines, but not to single out one distributor for this treatment.

Source: David Fromson, legal counsel to Fluid Power Distributors Association, in *Industrial Distribution.*

Using Salespeople for Industrial Intelligence

Turn company salespeople into intelligence gatherers on competing companies. How? Let them know what kind of information is wanted—innovations in product design, research and development activities, release dates of new products, expansion plans, promotional programs, and so forth.

Where do they get data? From company customers. Competitors' salesmen give out exactly that kind of information—pricing, promotion, new products—in trying to woo customers to their side. Questioning customers as to just what the competition had to offer them under the guise of matching that offer is one way of extracting useful information.

Source: Dr. Robert H. Solomon, Stephen Austin State University, Texas, in *Industrial Marketing.*

When Salesman is Caught Between Customer and Boss

Here's useful advice for salespeople who are caught between crossed priorities—the customer and the sales manager. It's a continuing problem for management.

Faced with multiple objectives, the salesperson has to set priorities. Important as the customer may be, the first priority for the salesperson is keeping his job. So he must first deal with the expectations and demands of his boss.

If there is some sincere misunderstanding, a careful examination of the facts will help.

Example: You're a distributor/salesman and the customer is dissatisfied with an item distributed by your firm. Perhaps it's a long-time associate of your boss's—one who extended credit at a difficult time. Best bet: Assume a neutral, objective position—"just the facts"—but make sure that your boss knows about the dispute. The prime supplier knows how important this customer is in your area or industry.

It may pay to actually bring the supplier and customer together. This would put you in the role of catalyst, giving each of them a chance to meet and present his case to the other.

For both your boss's and your customer's sake (not to mention your own), remain passive during this confrontation, expressing no opinions. Your role is to present as many alternatives as possible, together with backup facts regarding probable consequences. The ultimate decision is still up to your boss.

Source: *Electrical Wholesaling.*

SECURITY

Burglarproofing Office and Home

Computer Crime

Coping with Corporate Theft

Anti-Shoplifting Strategies

How to Cut Warehouse Pilferage

Mailroom Security

Recognizing Con-Men Customers

Stock and Bond Theft

25

SECURITY

Burglarproofing Your Office

Every office should be ready for a robbery. Instructions to give all employees: As difficult as it seems, it's crucial that everyone remain calm. The robber may be more frightened than the victims. An unexpected shout or move could result in injury. Be as cooperative as possible. Let the thief get out the door (with his loot) so that no one is harmed. Make a point of designating some people in the office as identifiers—they should make a note of the thief's hair and eye color, height, weight, complexion, etc.

Office equipment has always been a target of thieves. Often the theft occurs during working hours. In a typical case, thieves monitor the janitorial services (schedules, clothing, equipment) and then plan their operation slightly ahead of the usual schedule. They'll wheel, say, a large trash container through a building and pick up typewriters, dictating machines, adding machines—stashing them in the trash container.

What to do: Maintenance people should always display distinctive identification badges. Limit them to one elevator or staircase. Desig-

nate one person (and a backup person) in the office to monitor the comings and goings of the maintenance staff.

Important: Avoid direct confrontation. If something is suspicious, a supervisor should call the police.

Bogus repairmen can pull a similar ploy. Require that all repairmen check in with a supervisor, who will then monitor all their comings and goings.

Other things to watch for:

• Phony messenger who wanders into the office—''casing'' your premises or maybe even looking for a quick pickup of some easy-to-carry-off office equipment (or a secretary's purse). Indicated action: Don't let messengers go beyond the reception area. If they come for a pickup, insist that they identify what is to be picked up. Don't leave packages for delivery in the reception area. Only give the package up after seeing the pickup authorization.

• The truck driver who drives his rig up to your loading dock and unloads some boxes. When the ''misunderstanding'' is cleared up, he'll reload —taking some of your material with him. Indicated action: Leave standing orders to check unexpected truck deliveries. Nothing is to be loaded or unloaded without specific authorization.

• The phony government inspector can be extremely dangerous, because he tends to be sophisticated—with little trouble he can get an indepth look at your operation. Indicated action: Don't rely on credentials alone—insist on positive identification via a call to his office. And have your secretary place the call after she checks the phone number to be sure it's not phony (tied into an accomplice).

Many managers set the safe on a so-called "day lock." That is, they complete the first two numbers in the combination so only the last number must be dialed. Sophisticated teams of thieves travel around looking for such safes. A team usually has three people. One is often a female (to distract personnel near the safe). When the safe watchers are distracted, the second member of the team signals that it's clear for the third person to approach the safe. Since the safe is "day locked," it can be opened quickly. The second person is the team's security person, or "muscle." He will intercede if the situation sours. He may be armed.

Prevention is simple: Don't use "day locks."

Some managers suppose they are staying protected by keeping the operating cash in file cabinets during business hours. The burglary teams are aware of this and learn the location when they "case" the office.

Burglarproofing Your Home

There's no such thing as a burglarproof house; at best, the homeowner or apartment dweller can make the premises more resistant to thieves. The cost of such resistance can be pennies—or several thousand dollars. Some practical—and economical—ideas to turn burglars away:

• Lights: You've heard it before, but you're probably still not doing it—leaving lights on when you leave the house. And even if you are leaving lights on, you're probably leaving only one—in the living room.

Some better ideas: Use several electronic timers that can be programmed to go on and off at various times during a 24-hour period. Avoid the simple ones that only make one on-off cycle a day. They are not versatile enough. Scatter them in various front and back rooms and upper and lower floors.

Put adequate lighting outside—illuminating doors or vulnerable windows, especially those entrances that aren't fully visible from the street or from a neighbor's house. Make sure those outside lights can't be easily turned off by the burglar. And this means they should be sufficiently inaccessible so that he can't just reach up and unscrew the bulb.

• Noise: Lights alone aren't very effective. Thieves who are "casing" affluent neighborhoods today assume that residents will leave some lights on. It's best to add noise to the burglar-resistance equipment.

Connect a radio to the timers. Even better: Make a tape of "household" noises. Include dog barking in inventory of sounds. Be sure the recorder and tape can rewind automatically, or the technique is too short-lived.

• Electronic alarms connected to an outside agency: They're theoretically fine. They often don't work. Worse: The resident who has bought one drops his guard and fails to institute the commonsense protection techniques outlined above. The best bet: Get a sign that warns of silent alarm and also use the commonsense approaches.

• Protecting valuables: At some point, the persistent burglar will break in. Here are some ways to keep him from finding some of your smaller valuables: If you must leave jewelry or cash in the house, put them in unobvious places. For example, in the freezer or refrigerator—well wrapped. In the attic under some old magazines. In a bag of potting soil. Use your imagination—the possibilities are endless (and can even be fun). Just remember where they are.

• Confronting the thief: If you enter a house and suspect a burglary has occurred (or is occurring), get right out and call police from a neighbor's home. A face-to-face meeting with the intruder is a bad idea; he may be dangerous when trapped. If the thief surprises you, be passive; follow his orders. Don't try to save your valuables or capture him.

• Weapons: In general, forget them. They're dangerous. The chances of being where the gun is when you confront a thief are rare.

Source: James Edward Keogh, private security consultant, author of *Burglarproof, A Complete Guide to Home Security,* McGraw-Hill, New York.

How to Stretch the Company's Security Dollars

Stretch security dollars by pretending to have more security than is actually present. The aim is to deceive criminals and discourage them from casing the premises.

Some suggestions:

• Set up dummy cameras. Mount a camera box and include a blinking red light. Attach the camera to an inexpensive oscillating fan motor and the camera will swing back and forth to cover the designated area.

• If there is a mezzanine, upper floor office, or a room to create a similar effect, give one or two of the windows an opaque finish. This simulated observation post is highly effective in discouraging would-be holdup men or thieves, especially if access to the upper floor is reasonably difficult.

• Box in the cashier's area and install a dummy pneumatic or similar transport system. Post a notice on the booth stating that all cash is routed after each transaction.

• Sound-activated silent alarms are easily simulated by installing unconnected dummy microphones throughout an area.

For night security in an empty area: Install a timer that turns on lights and voice recordings for at least five minutes at random intervals.

Corporate Theft: Uncovering and Coping With It

The time to take precautions against employee theft is always. But certain situations, when the risks are even greater than usual, deserve special attention:

• Labor relations are troubled and employees are embittered about working conditions, pay, other benefits.

• Some employees have serious personal problems, such as drinking or drugs, expensive illnesses at home, or gambling. Suggestion: Inform employees in job application that company may make credit checks from time to time without notifying the employee. Then run the check when personal problems are suspected.

• Stealing becomes so common that peer pressure escalates it, and honest employees are ridiculed and maybe even threatened.

• Supervisors are afraid to report the problem or get help in dealing with it, because they fear it will reflect adversely on them.

• The same person handles buying, receiving, and shipping. Remember: The most common thievery doesn't involve carrying things away. Rather, it's phantom shipments, paid for but never received (or a short count).

• Certain locations are especially vulnerable: Loading dock, cash handling departments, computer area.

• Some items have high value-to-size ratio, thus are portable, easy to hide.

Whenever there's major theft, experts agree it's essential to make a serious effort to identify the culprit. It's important to remove suspicion from the innocent, and also to make unmistakably clear that thievery won't be tolerated.

Another reason to nail the perpetrator: The bonding company won't pay off just because something disappeared. It'll insist on proof, preferably a signed confession.

It might be wise to bring in outside experts to do gumshoe work, interrogation of suspects, etc. Be aware that interrogation is a tricky business that involves legal hazards and employee-relations problems.

Once identified, the culprit should be fired. Purpose isn't punishment, rather deterring other employees from stealing. Usually the company should bring criminal charges, too, and attempt to get the authorities to prosecute. Probably it's best to go to district or county attorney rather than police. Police are usually less interested in business crime. Incredible but true: Law-enforcement people are so backlogged they may refuse to do anything unless the reported loss is over $10,000.

When a theft is suspected, first develop the

facts. Find out what's missing, value, etc. Next, find out how many people had access to the items. It helps to draw a diagram of the location, then map out who, in the normal course of business, passes through that location.

Trace everything back to the receiving department. What's missing may never have been there in the first place. The most common form of physical theft: Items that are never actually delivered or that arrive in smaller-than-ordered quantities.

Don't rush into action. Watch the flow of goods for a few weeks; carefully check on the paperwork and wait to see if some kind of pattern emerges.

Once a suspect has been spotted, however, don't ignore the discovery. This is a common temptation for managers who feel that reporting the problem (or their suspicions) to superiors may somehow reflect badly on them.

Before confronting the suspect(s), touch base both with the company counsel and with the chief financial officer to ascertain insurance coverage and procedures.

If the case is relatively simple, and you feel confident about the interrogation, be aware that it's best to have a third person present during the questioning. It avoids the possibility of the suspect recanting a confession. Consider having a secretary take notes, or use a tape recorder—but not surreptitiously.

In complicated cases or situations where the company has no one experienced in interrogation (such as security officer with some police or FBI background), it's probably best to hire professional experts. Names of competent private investigators can be obtained from a good law firm. They should be state licensed.

Source: Jules Kroll, Kroll Associates, 733 Third Ave., New York 10017.

Computer Crime

The company is vulnerable to computer rip-offs when:

• The computer generates negotiable instruments or is used to transfer credit, process loans, or obtain credit ratings.

• Employee relations in the data-processing area are handled ineptly.

• Key computer functions are not separated. Warning: Programmers should not also be computer operators. This is a likely situation in small businesses that make use of minicomputers, however.

• Nighttime EDP operations are too loosely supervised. Dangerous practice: Programmers who are never allowed to work on consoles during the day are allowed to debug on-line at night. After-hours processing should be subject to the same controls and procedures that apply during the normal work day.

• The company's auditors have little, if any, expertise or background in computer operations and are therefore not on the lookout for possible abuses.

Signals that an investigation should be launched:

• Such things as computer reports or carbons of continuous forms are found discarded in an outside trash bin.

• Frequent solo operation of EDP gear. Recommended rule: At least two people should be present.

• Transactions rejected by the system because they did not pass one or more control points are put aside, ignored, or deliberately overridden. Overrides should be explained in exception reports, and exceptions should be investigated and resolved promptly.

• There's a noticeable increase in employee complaints about overwithholding by the computer or about inaccuracies in year-end earnings statements.

• A surge in customer complaints about delays in crediting their accounts.

• Key forms, purchase orders, invoices, and checks are not numbered sequentially.

• The bill from the time-sharing service bureau is significantly higher than the computer time logs seem to justify. Or the computer use charges allocated to a department seem out of line. That means a possible unauthorized use of computer time.

• Payments are sent to new suppliers, whose names are not listed in directories.

Even managers with no technical or EDP-related backgrounds can recognize these danger signs and take corrective steps.

Retail Theft: Vulnerable Areas on and off the Selling Floor

Merchandisers shouldn't be willing to write off their theft losses as an inevitable cost of doing business.

Where to focus efforts: Both employee theft and professional shoplifting are directed, whenever possible, at areas where merchandise is available in quantity and where there is not adequate protection. That means: Stock room, access corridors to departments, and loading areas.

Access areas: Don't permit merchandise to be stored there while waiting to be displayed. If it's necessary for a short period, make someone responsible for observing the area until the merchandise is removed.

• You can't lock fire doors, but it is possible to install inexpensive signal devices that alert personnel when a door leading to a vulnerable area is opened.

• Security forces should respond to an alarm at the exit the door leads to (not the door itself), then conduct a search back to the door. If the door leads to a truck-parking zone, make that a checkpoint, too.

• Discourage loitering in access corridors so that it will be difficult for any outside accomplices to be used.

• Have guards patrol these areas at frequent, but not set, intervals.

• Install windows in doors leading to access areas. Keep the areas well lighted.

Stock room: Designate the minimum possible number of sales personnel authorized for entry. Keep doors locked.

• Conduct in-depth interviews with employees who transfer stock. Advise them of the need for security and the fact that management is aware of the opportunities for theft. Provide them with a feeling of job status and a sense of responsibility.

An electronic limited-access system that uses magnetic coded cards to unlock doors and log entries and exits is often useful.

Loading dock: Keep the loading area under surveillance by designated personnel during lunch or break time and slack periods to prevent thieves from making a getaway.

Selling floor: Conduct training sessions to install theft sense in salespeople. Train them to detect that something is amiss—and act on it often enough to give the store a "too tough" reputation on the street. Types to watch: (1) People whose elbows remain pressed against their sides are probably holding something under their clothing. (2) Those who seem to know where they're going but don't wish to be helped—and don't make a purchase. (3) People wearing bulky clothing, long coats, capes, or carrying large packages (these can have false bottoms that open to accommodate more merchandise).

The smart money is on merchandisers who deal with theft by arranging training sessions that include the services of a former professional thief. Contact local police for referrals. Some of the best advisers are rehabilitated convicts.

Destroying Old Records

Security for confidential financial, research, or marketing documents often breaks down when the time comes to dispose of those documents. One answer is to shred them, an easy office housecleaning solution for all waste paper, confidential or not. Shredded paper can be used as packaging material or sold for scrap.

First identify what has to be destroyed. The material itself will determine the size and kind of shredder installation that is needed.

Consider shredding sales reports and forecasts, bids and quotations, mailing lists, engineering drawings, new product proposals, personnel records, confidential correspondence and memos, accounts receivable lists, cost estimates, labor cost estimates, time studies, research and development reports, production reports, credit cards, purchase agreements, inventory reports, payroll data, canceled checks, bank statements, security holding statements. Don't overlook microfilm and punched tape.

Major resources for paper shredding:
• Industrial Shredder and Cutter Co., 607 South Ellsworth Ave., Salem, OH 44460. Expensive models can handle 15″ computer printouts, smaller models cannot.
• Shredmaster, Division of General Binding,

6831 N.W. 20th St., Fort Lauderdale, FL 33309. Most popular unit includes a 12 " feed with a funnel to shred computer printout forms 14 "-17 ", files, folders, even paper clips and staples.

- Electric Wastebasket Corp., 145 West 45th St., New York 10036.

Source: *Modern Office Procedures,* 614 Superior Ave. West, Cleveland 44113.

How Shoplifters Work

- Switching. The customer asks to examine rings in several trays and lulls a vulnerable salesperson to inattentiveness so a switch can be made. What to do: Employees should never take trays of valuables out and place them on the counter. Customers should be shown only one item at a time.
- Hand-offs. The shoplifter mingles with the crowd, turns a corner, and passes stolen merchandise to a partner. What to do: Suspect should be followed closely and detained immediately, before leaving the selling area.
- Smokescreen. An accused shoplifter reacts loudly and tries to draw attention to the incident in order to embarrass the employee. (Innocent people are frightened when faced with a police-related situation and usually do not react in a loud, aggressive manner.)
- Phony refunds. A common shoplifter ploy is to take something expensive and then return it for cash refund. Defense: If the customer can't produce a sales receipt, send the refund by mail. The shoplifter usually doesn't want to give a name and address.
- Smart clothing thieves always take the hangers. Thus, missing suits may not be noticed for days, or even weeks. And they always buy something, like a $40 shirt, so the salesman will remember them favorably. That way, they can return to the store without arousing suspicion.
- Heaviest shoplifting days: Friday, Saturday, and Sunday. Heaviest months: December, May, and September. Most vulnerable time: 3 p.m. to 6 p.m.
- Note: Although total retail shrinkage exceeds $6.2 billion annually, only one-third is stolen by outside shoplifters.

Antishoplifting Strategies

- Let shoppers know they are being watched. Tell them, ''I'll be with you in a moment.''
- Resist the temptation to watch a suspicious person quietly, then catch him in the act. Prevention is the key.
- Use self-adhesive tags which are perforated so they cannot be switched to another item without tearing.
- Employees should have a code word or sentence that can be used to alert each other to a possible shoplifter. Something as simple as ''Did Mr. Smith get his typewriter?'' could serve as an effective alarm system.
- Suspicious character: Approach him immediately and ask to be of service. If he's an amateur shoplifter he will either leave the store or make a quick purchase.
- Should you show a training film to discourage employee shoplifting? No, says Dayton, Ohio, security consultant S. J. Curtis. Films on shoplifting corrupt previously honest employees, and increase the incidence of stealing.

How to Reduce Warehouse Pilferage

- Don't allow customers inside the warehouse. Bring items to customers at the loading dock or over the counter.
- Place all responsibility for package shipments in the hands of one person.
- Use warehouse people, not drivers, to move goods to the truck.
- Set up a control system that aims to prevent collusion between drivers and warehouse people. Keep both groups apart as much as possible.
- Don't keep piles of pallets, ladders, or anything that can be climbed on outside the plant or warehouse.
- Control access to such tools as hammers and crowbars that can be used in a break-in.
- Check all documents and orders. Look for alterations, figures on carbons that don't match those on original copies, missing orders, etc.

Source: Robert B. Footlik, Footlik and Associates, 2530 Crawford Ave., Evanston, IL 60201, in *Electrical Wholesaling.*

Teenage Shoplifting

Kids are usually more nervous than adult thieves and tend to operate in groups to bolster their courage. They also are usually more obvious than their adult counterparts.

What to do:

• Focus closest scrutiny on counters and departments that stock items most popular with teenagers (records, clothes, cosmetics, magazines, etc.).

• Teenagers who score in a particular store return often, and go to the same area they stole from previously. Increase security measures in that particular area.

When a teenager is caught stealing, it may be best to offer the choice of arrest or the option of spreading the word in the neighborhood to stay away from the store because it's too tough to try to rip off.

Cash Register Theft

• Spot-check and balance cash registers during the day. Not always, but occasionally—on a random and surprise basis—so employees will worry about spot checks, never know when they will come.

• Warning signal: More cash in the drawer than the register tape shows. Significance: The employee who plans to steal from the register often starts by building up a cash surplus, a little at a time on each sale. A spot check may reveal a noticeable surplus in the drawer just before he's ready to pocket it.

• Place a large red star sticker on registers that are constantly short. Employees see the sticker as a warning that management suspects thievery at that register and plans to keep checking it from time to time.

Mailroom Security

• Lock heads of postage meters each night to prevent unauthorized use after hours.

• Run an occasional spot check on contents of mail bags for personal packages mailed at company expense.

• Check monthly postage against earlier figures to spot a sudden surge. It can be a tip-off that an employee has started running extra postage strips through meter. At the post office, they can be redeemed for 90% of face value.

Source: *Dartnell's Administrative Cost Control Survey & Guide* by Robert S. Minor and Paul R. Jacobs, The Dartnell Corp., Chicago.

Employee Theft: Hiding Places for Pilfered Goods

Employee theft usually involves a system to conceal pilfered goods on the premises until they can be safely transported. One sophisticated method: Hide stolen articles among standing inventory. Key to detection: Check inventory that is rarely audited. Examine:

• Warrantied items returned for repair.

• Service departments. Excellent storage areas for sidetracked merchandise.

• Sales items set aside for display.

Successful and consistent employee theft usually requires outside help. The shipping department is the favorite scene of such inside-outside operations.

Techniques:

• Arranging unauthorized pickups by bogus carriers.

• Enlisting authorized carriers to make unauthorized deliveries. It's important to check vehicles making deliveries to the company. Illegally ordered goods may be temporarily stored and then stolen later.

Other drop and retrieval areas to inspect:

• Trash cans and storage bins.

• Access corridors. Stolen goods are often moved there. Remove visual obstructions. Good light is important. Patrol regularly.

• Enclosed stairwells. Lock, renovate, or close them off.

• Unused cabinets. Lock them, convert to other use, or remove.

• Ceiling access ports. Use padlocks to seal.

• Air-conditioning vents. May have been altered internally to accommodate thieves or goods. Inspect regularly.

- Basement and subbasement. Remove sight obstructions. Check regularly.
- Laundry drop. Often located near the street. Reduce accessibility with a wire fence. Inspect laundry bundles periodically.
- Service elevator roof. Check regularly.

Controls Against White-Collar Crime

Poor control of invoicing and check disbursement makes large employee thefts easy. Steps you can take to guard against manipulation of the company's accounts:

- Never allow the bookkeeper to handle cash payments.
- Require two authorized signatures on disbursement checks.
- Stamp invoices once they are approved to avoid double processing and payments.
- Route canceled checks to controller for review of signatures.
- Reconcile bank statements at different times of month.
- Scrutinize interbank transfers for unusual transactions that could be covering thefts.

Source: *Security World* magazine, Box 272, Culver City, CA 90034.

Recognizing Conman Customers

Legitimate businessmen lose an estimated $80 million annually to customers who intend to go bankrupt. How they work: Conmen purchase merchandise on credit, then dispose of the goods and conceal the proceeds. Bankruptcy is claimed when creditors press for payment.

Signs of a bankruptcy fraud in the making:

- Customer comes under new management and new owner's identity remains obscure.
- Customer orders goods that are unrelated to the usual line.

- Order quantities soar and can't be explained by seasonal fluctuations.
- Financial statements requested from the account are unaudited and unverified.
- Payments lag while the customer's accounts receivable balance climbs and notes or postdated checks are sent in payment.
- Buyer from an unfamiliar firm places large orders for a wide range of goods at a trade show.
- Trade references don't check out or can't be located.
- New account's name is the same as that of a well-known company, except for a minor detail. (Even the address may be similar.)
- Rush orders, particularly during the busy season, are placed with above-average frequency. (Scam operators hope their credit limits can be exceeded without detection and/or that checks will be omitted, at least temporarily.)
- Potential customers who had previously resisted sales approaches now suddenly submit substantial orders.

Source: *White Collar Crime,* Chamber of Commerce of the United States, 1615 H St. N.W., Washington, DC 20006.

What a Contract with a Security Guard Service Should Cover

- Proof of security agency's insurance against dishonesty of guards and liability coverage for any improper actions. Require 30 days' notice from insurer in the event policy is canceled.
- Number of working hours per week before overtime goes into effect. Normal and overtime billing rates. Specify who is to bear the cost of overtime in situations where the agency may be responsible.

For example: When the relief guard doesn't show up so the duty guard has to stand a second shift.

- Complete description of all training requirements, including those the hiring company will have to provide. Specify who bears the cost of training (especially of replacements if the original guards leave through no fault of the company). Placing the burden on security agency is a good way to ensure their diligence in finding steady, reliable guards and assigning you the best.

- All duties that the security force is expected to perform.

- The right of the company to cancel the contract on 30 days' written notice if agency's performance is unsatisfactory. Also important: The right to have individual guards removed if performance is unsatisfactory.

- A schedule of inspections by agency supervisors to check on guards and discuss any problems with company management.

Source: *Security Management*, 2000 K St. N.W., Washington, DC 20006.

Fraudulent Use of Company Forms

Make sure your firm stocks only the number of copies absolutely required on numerically sequenced documents. A common temptation: One unused extra copy. Insiders quickly learn that the extra document can be used to authorize shipments. (One firm was recently ripped off for $1 million over a one-year period by a $250-a-week clerk using this technique.)

How to detect theft: The same document number used for two shipments.

Another mistake is the failure to destroy old forms when new forms are introduced.

How Companies Are Victimized by 'Idea Promoters'

The "innocent" letter or telephone call, in which you're told about some idea for a new product or a new way to market or make your present product, may be dangerous. In many cases, that communication isn't innocent at all; it could have been planned to entrap you. If you should ever adopt the idea, even years later, and even if the real thinking was was done totally independently by your own staff, the original "inventor" may press suit against you.

The charge: Violation of trade secrets.

His chance of success: If he has properly prepared his offense and you've not anticipated it with simple protective steps, prepare to lose—or at least to be forced into a protracted battle.

There are people—not many in number, but significant in their activity—who really work to ensnare companies. And there are instances of real inventors (with the paranoia of the breed) feeling they've been wronged by a company to which they've dropped hints of their idea.

It only takes one idea (which you may have pursued quite innocently) to make you the target of a suit; that's why precautionary measures are important.

You've only got to be able to prove that you haven't listened to an idea in confidence. The whole issue rests on the question of confidence. If an inventor can show that you did listen in confidence, your use of the idea would be violating the trade secrets law unless you met his terms.

How to prove your point: Establish a policy stating that no one in the company should listen to any outside idea before the inventor signs a release. Such releases are standard documents developed by lawyers which say, in effect, that once the document is signed, the only rights maintained by the inventor are those accorded him under the patent laws. Thus, if the idea isn't patented, he can no longer get protection under the trade secret laws. And you can take his idea without paying him. In fact, however, that very rarely happens.

Implementing the policy: How do you stop a person from telling you an idea? There are procedures that work well.

1. Ideas by letter: Limit letter-opening operations to one person or one quite small group. It could be an executive's secretary, but make sure all letter openers are aware of the procedure. Before forwarding an opened letter to the executive (middle managers and up), the secretary should quickly scan it. If it looks like an idea being presented, the letter opener should stop reading it and immediately return the letter to the sender with a note explaining that the letter wasn't read, that no idea can be presented to the company unless a confidentiality release has been signed first. Then ship the material back to him by registered mail, return receipt requested.

2. Phone: If the idea is given by telephone, in-

struct all personnel to tell the caller to stop, and explain that ideas cannot be listened to until the release is signed.

3. Visits: The same procedure should be followed when the inventor comes in person. Be especially wary of visitors who try this ploy: To ''prove'' they presented the idea, they will send a letter confirming the appointment ahead of time, be sure to sign the guest register, and then send another confirming letter after the meeting. That's done to establish presence. If it's obvious that a visitor is there to explain his idea, he must be told about the company's procedure.

The vital legal point: You must negate the confidentiality. If you fail to do so, you have, by default, accepted his idea in confidence. And his chances of winning in court are enhanced.

Stock and Bond Theft

Don't make the mistake of assuming such items as securities certificates are of no interest to thieves just because they're not easily cashed. Stolen certificates are often used as collateral on loans by forging required signatures. Until the loans are due and called years later, the lender is unaware the collateral is stolen and, therefore, worthless.

Rules for sending stock certificates to stockholders or bankers:

• Signatures of the certificate's owner (or owners) must correspond exactly with the name on the face of the certificate.

• Fill in the name of the brokerage firm or bank on the back of the certificate where it usually says, ''I do hereby irrevocably constitute and appoint _____.'' This makes the certificate nonnegotiable while en route to its destination. If the certificate is lost or stolen, it cannot be legally transferred by others (without the brokerage firm's consent).

• If you fill in the broker or bank's name, insure the shipment for only 4%, not 100%, of the market value of the securities. If the securities are lost, the corporation issuing replacements will require a Lost Securities Bond, for which the surety company charges a premium of not more than 4% on any one shipment.

Checkbook Cautions

• Treat checkbooks like cash. Sophisticated thieves steal blanks (usually from back of book, where they aren't noticed) and canceled checks (which they use to copy signature).

• It's dangerous to use printed signatures on checks. The bank may not be liable if a thief gets hold of blank checks and facsimile signature machine, and the company can't show that it has used adequate diligence.
Perini v. *First National Bank,* 553 F 2d 398.

Security Tips for Motorists

• A key caution: More than half of car owners leave all their keys with the car in parking lots and service stations—not just the ignition key.

• How car thieves steal cars in less than a minute: (1) Push a flat instrument (putty knife) down next to window (near lock)—tripping the lock in an instant. (2) Jam a hardened screw into the ignition lock; yank it out and insert a screwdriver and make contact with the now exposed wires, then zoom away. Protection: Park car in a supervised parking lot.

• In bad neighborhoods, keep doors locked, windows open no more than a crack, and at a red light, keep the car in gear for a fast takeoff. This is even more important if waiting in a parked car. When car is disabled, tie a white cloth to antenna, then wait inside car with doors locked and windows up. Be wary of accepting help from strangers. If another car ever tries to force you off the highway, forget the dents and scrapes—resist and keep blowing horn in short blasts to get attention and help. Head for a gas station or any other crowded place.

How to Outsmart Muggers

• Carry a second wallet—old, beat-up, with two or three singles and a couple of out-of-date credit cards in it. If accosted, hand it over without resistance.

367

• If assault seems imminent, don't take a chance on calling for help. Instead, yell "Fire!" When heads pop out of windows—as they're certain to—say, "Quick, call the cops. I caught him trying to set fire to your house." This gets around people's reluctance to get involved by making them think they already are.

Dealing With Organized Crime

Organized crime is deeply into the fabric of legitimate business. Every company comes into contact with organized crime somewhere, somehow. Possible points of contact are private garbage collection, vending machine companies, commercial laundries, small trucking firms, and some union locals.

Direct economic disadvantages of organized crime's penetration of legitimate business are not that substantial. Organized crime uses legitimate businesses to launder illegal receipts, not to generate cash. Thus, they usually compete in the legal marketplace like other businesses in order not to attract attention.

Physical danger stemming from criminal presence in the business world is not sizable. The potential profits from extorting legitimate businesses are usually not large enough to be worth the risk involved.

Not every street punk is a member of organized crime. The business that ignores approaches may suffer no consequences.

But a business can be hurt badly if it decides to borrow money from loan sharks. That's organized crime's traditional wedge into businesses. Declaring bankruptcy is preferable to being used as a front for illegal activities.

Source: Lawrence J. Lief, Industrial Security Analysts, 208 West 30 St., New York 10001.

Security for Rural Areas

Office buildings, plants, and warehouses in rural sections are more attractive and vulnerable to burglars because they tend to be isolated and police are slower to respond to distant alarms. A good rural security program requires the same general efficiency effort as city facilities, with some additions.

• A watchman with random route is the best protection. Guard checks in on a schedule, but not a predictable one (e.g., not on the hour, quarter hour, or half hour; better at odd times, like 10 past or 23 minutes before the hour, so his arrival at checkpoints can't be anticipated by a burglar). Failure to complete the tour in proper sequence or preset time sets off a delinquency signal. Extra advantage: Guard can summon help in the event of an attack or emergency simply by pushing a panic button.

• Guard dogs are excellent deterrents. However, they require special training, personnel to handle them, etc.

• Perimeter alarm system: A device that actuates lights, trips flares, can even set off a recording (e.g., barking dogs, message to intruder that he's under surveillance). This is an expensive and effective method to scare off burglars and vandals.

• Fencing and well-secured access roads: These don't prevent burglary, but they do limit possible use of vehicles to transport stolen merchandise. Thus, they discourage burglary attempts.

• Involved citizen: Consider an arrangement with a local resident who will be on the alert for signs of unusual activity at the building site (lights on at odd times, suspicious persons or vehicles, noise) and report it to the police. This often results in an arrest (the burglar is caught in the act rather than scared off).

Above all, let the word get around that the site is well guarded, and keep it well lit—burglars don't like to be in the spotlight.

Applying the Brakes to Arson

Ways to stop it:
• Limit visitor access to the plant.
• Evaluate entrance controls (fences, lighting, guards, alarms) for possible improvement.

• Practice good housekeeping. This means storing flammable liquids in safe areas, regularly hauling away combustible debris, and taking any other necessary steps to prevent spontaneous combustion.

• Install sprinklers throughout the plant and be sure that they are kept in working condition by inspecting regularly.

• Carefully screen potential employees, particularly people who will be concerned with security and maintenance.

• Discourage casual visitors.

Source: *Security World,* P.O. Box 272, Culver City, CA 92030.

TAXES

What Can Trigger a Tax Audit

The Most Vulnerable Deductions

Taking IRS to Court

Advance Rulings from IRS

Justifying High Salaries

Tax Rules on Deferred Compensation

Taking the Same Deduction Twice

Deductible Gambling Losses

26

TAXES

How IRS Can Mislead You

Every year the IRS advertises that it will "help" taxpayers prepare their forms. Case history: A taxpayer with a net operating loss was confused about the carryback adjustment and went to his local IRS office for advice. When the resultant tax return was audited, a tax deficiency was issued because the adjustment was incorrect. Tax court ruling: It may seem unfair, but erroneous advice by the IRS is not binding on the Commissioner of Internal Revenue. Imposition of the tax assessment was allowed to stand.

What Can Trigger a Tax Audit

- Information returns from banks, investments, or employers that show payments (dividends, interest, salaries, or fees) that differ from those reported.
- Unusually large deductions. The computer flags deductions that are much larger than the average amount taken by most taxpayers in the same income group. Suggestion: Provide some details on extra-large deductions. Big casualty loss? Describe the hurricane or flood, maybe even enclose newspaper clipping. Give dates and details of long illness or serious accident that produced large medical deductions.
- Unbelievable numbers. Such as claiming that you held real estate or IBM stock for 25 years and sold it at a loss. Or large deductions and losses that leave no money to live on. Business expenses that are out of line with the amount of gross income or the nature of the business.
- Large round numbers. These raise questions as to whether you just guessed (and exaggerated) without supporting documentation.
- Office at home. Getting close scrutiny because the rules were made much tougher in the 1976 tax law.
- Important: If IRS strikes gold in auditing a return, it will often go after other members of the family, partners, employees, other stockholders in the same Subchapter S corporation.

• Self-employed people are likely to have their returns audited if they take the standard deduction instead of itemizing personal nonbusiness deductions, especially if their business shows a high gross and a low net. IRS will suspect that personal deductions have been charged to the business.
IRS Manual 4137.2, 9/12/78.

If You Are Audited

Who should attend: Best to let your accountant attend the meeting with IRS. Accountants know more, can argue ambiguous points. (They will charge for their time, of course.) Persons being audited need not be present. In fact, it's often better if they are not. The danger is that taxpayer will give too much away. IRS counts on it, and instructs revenue agents: "The taxpayer may answer more honestly, because he does not know why questions are asked."
IRS Manual 3158-01, ¶4,015, May 1973.

Time Limits on IRS Right to Audit

If IRS is going to audit a return, a notice will usually be sent within 16 months of filing date. However, IRS has the legal right to examine any of the three most recent returns at any time. Exception: If income was understated by 25% or more, IRS can look back six years. If fraud was involved, there is no statute of limitation.

Kinds of IRS Agents

There are two types of IRS agents that the corporate executive may meet. The revenue agent customarily performs an examination, and matters can be discussed with him freely without the presence of professional advisors. But if the tax man identifies himself as a special agent, as he is

required to do, the executive should know he is assigned to cases where fraud is at least suspected. The executive should refuse to say or to supply anything until his lawyer is present.

But the executive should cooperate fully with a revenue agent. For one thing, anything refused to the agent probably can be obtained anyway, through the subpoena power, summons, or other procedures. In addition, delaying tactics or failure to cooperate with a revenue agent is considered by the courts to be a "badge of fraud," a deliberate attempt to evade taxes known to be due.

The executive should be cooperative, but not overly so. If he is too hospitable in entertaining or in gifts of the company's products, a bribery charge may be brought against him.
Source: Robert Holzman, *Business Tax Traps,* Boardroom Books, New York.

The Odds of Getting Audited

Percentages of tax returns audited by category in 1978:

	% audited
Individual (based on adjusted gross income)	
Under $10,000, standard	0.67
Under $10,000, itemized	2.90
$10,000 to $50,000	2.63
$50,000 and over	10.40
Business income	
Under $10,000	3.28
$10,000 to $30,000	2.03
$30,000 and over	6.68
Fiduciary	0.69
Corporation (based on assets)	
Under $100,000	3.83
$100,000 to $1,000,000	9.26
$1,000,000 to $10,000,000	26.97
$10,000,000 to $100,000,000	42.14
$100,000,000 and over	78.52
Estate taxes Gross estate	
Under $300,000	8.99
$300,000 and over	55.45
Gift tax	3.33

Source: *IRS Annual Report.*

Gauging Results of a Tax Audit

If the IRS examiner won't say anything after he's audited company books, tax trouble is likely. Reason: Examiners are under orders to clam up and report directly to a special agent, as soon as they suspect tax fraud. But if the books are okay, the examiner will probably give some comment or reassurance before leaving premises. What to do: If examiner leaves abruptly without comment, be prepared for a visit from a special agent. Have a tax lawyer present when the special agent arrives. Say nothing without the lawyer's okay.

Refusing a Second Audit

Examination of a corporation's tax returns can be time-consuming and onerous, as well as expensive in other ways. If the IRS chooses to examine the material a second time, the repeat audit must be requested in writing by the appropriate District Director of Internal Revenue. A revenue agent may be unwilling to ask his superior to write such a letter because he's not anxious to reveal that he wants to correct mistakes he might have made initially through ignorance or carelessness. The corporate executive must recognize this situation at once and decline to produce the records wtihout an authorizing letter. If the executive permits a revenue agent to start a second examination without any authorization, and later checks with counsel, he is deemed to have consented to the re-exam.
Source: Robert Holzman, *Business Tax Traps, Boardroom Books, New York.*

Deductions Most Likely to Be Challenged

- Expensive cars used in business. IRS is disallowing depreciation of the full cost of a Mercedes, Rolls, or Seville. There must be an allowance for estimated salvage value at the end of the car's useful life.
- Bank deposits. Agents seeking unreported income examine bank statements and ask for the source of all of the deposits.
- Dividend income. Agents compare form 1099 data (sent by the company to IRS) with dividends shown on the return. Agents pay special attention if dividends drop sharply from one year to the next. IRS will question the return if it does not show that the stock has been sold.
- Medical deductions. The IRS is questioning whether part of the medical expense was reimbursed by insurance or by the company directly. If so, the deduction must be reduced accordingly. If the reimbursement comes in a later year, it should be reported as income for that year.
- Medical deductions for drugs. If they're large and supported only by canceled checks to drug stores, look for a challenge (since drug stores also sell many other, nondeductible items.
- Change of address. It may flag the return for examination if no capital gain is reported on the sale of the former home. (Or alternatively, a statement that the capital gain is being deferred because a replacement home was purchased.)
- Sale of home. Agents may check whether depreciation was deducted in past years, when part of the home was used for office or business purposes. If so, the part of the gain equal to depreciation taken may be taxed as ordinary income.
- Travel and entertainment deductions are being scrutinized more carefully than ever.
- Scholarships and fellowships. Students who receive a scholarship and must perform services (example: graduate students who teach some classes) must report a portion of their income. (Since scholarships are nontaxable, students sometimes fail to report any income at all.)
- Separated and divorced parents. Agent will check whether both are claiming exemptions for children (only one is allowed to). And if one spouse claims a deduction for alimony paid, the other must report exactly the same amount of alimony received, which is taxable income. An agent may also ask to see separation agreement, since alimony is deductible only if it's required to be paid. Voluntary payments aren't deductible.
Source: Sidney Kess, CPA, partner, Main Lafrentz & Co., 280 Park Ave., New York 10017.

IRS Penalty When Deductions Are Disallowed

The Internal Revenue Service is getting much tougher on unsubstantiated deductions that appear on tax returns.

The danger to the company is that IRS may assess penalty (5% of tax underpayment) for intentional disregard of rules and regulations. Example: The cost of goods sold included cost of a car for personal use.

Added risk: The penalty can be applied to total additional tax assessed for the year, even if those assessments are based on factors other than the one that brought on the penalty. And these tax penalties are not deductible.

IR Code Sec. 6653 (a), TC Memos 1978-361, 373.

Tax Fraud: Who Gets Caught

Executives, lawyers, doctors, and other high income professionals are accused of tax fraud more often than the general population. Charges stem from IRS challenges that there was willful or intentional failure to file, understatement of income, or claiming of fraudulent deductions. About one out of every five charges brought by the IRS in a recent year involved a professional or business executive. The average claim for back taxes is nearly $70,000.

	Investigations	Convictions
Total	8,901	1,476
Of which:		
Business Owners	2,059	328
Other Executives	485	94
Company Officers	485	94
Attorneys	299	46
Managers	232	37
Dentists & Doctors	199	33
Non-CPA Accountants	164	40
CPAs	89	13

Less than 20% of IRS fraud investigations end in convictions. Other cases are dropped, Justice Department refuses to prosecute, or they end with acquittal or dismissal.

Taking IRS to Court: Which One?

If a taxpayer wants to battle the IRS, he has three choices of courts. Here's a rundown of which is best for different circumstances.

• Most people choose Tax Court. In that one, the disputed tax doesn't have to be paid until the tax is resolved. If the taxpayer's case is lost, interest must be paid from the date that the tax was originally due.

Tribunal hopping isn't possible. Once the case is submitted to the Tax Court, there can't be a change of mind. The litigation can't be submitted to any other court.

• Federal District Court is sometimes a good choice, because it's possible to ask for a jury trial there. There might be a better chance of winning with a jury. It depends on what type of case it is: One involving an emotional appeal is better with a jury. The tax must be paid first. Then, if IRS loses, it refunds the money with interest.

• Court of Claims is rarely used. There is no jury trial, the taxpayer must pay taxes before suing, and it is practically impossible to appeal from a Court of Claims decision.

Lawyers should check precedents in each court in cases of the same type to see if one has favored taxpayers.

• Small tax cases: If the amount involved is $5,000 or less, the taxpayer can handle it himself, without a lawyer, in the Tax Court's Small Case Division, with informal procedures. All it costs is a small filing fee and the time spent.

Why Taxpayers Lose in Tax Court

• A taxpayer has no constitutional or legal right to a jury trial in a U.S. Tax Court, according to the decision in a recent case.

The significance of the decision lies in the fact that most juries include several businesspeople. They will be more sympathetic to the problems of a fellow businessperson than a judge.

If the case is a type where jury trial seems to

favor your side, pay the tax deficiency, then file a refund claim. When it's rejected, sue for a refund in a U.S. District Court and specify that you want a jury trial.

Watson v. Comm'r., T.C. Memo, 1977-2167.

Advance Rulings from IRS

It's generally useful to ask the IRS for an advance ruling on the tax consequences of a proposed transaction. Especially valuable if it's a borderline case and if large amounts of money are involved. (Example: When two companies negotiate a merger, advance knowledge of the tax treatment is very important.)

If the IRS rules unfavorably, the transaction can be abandoned. Or it can be renegotiated on different terms.

Subjects on which the IRS won't give advance rulings:

- Excessive compensation.
- Whether a transaction has a good business purpose or whether it is being done only for tax avoidance.
- Depreciation rates.
- Whether a security is a stock or a bond.
- Whether redemption of stock will be treated as a dividend.
- Whether a family partnership will be recognized for tax purposes where capital is not a material factor.
- Whether business property gets ordinary income or capital gains treatment when sold.

Justifying Tax Deductions for Executive Salaries

A successful IRS challenge to the reasonableness of executive compensation hurts both the corporation (which loses the tax deduction) and the executives (who probably then have a hard time justifying any further increases).

- Each executive should be responsible for proving the extent and value of his services to the company. Keep track of little-publicized improvements, cost-cutting, salary offers from other companies.

- When an individual serves as an executive of two or more related companies, how much any one corporation can deduct as reasonable compensation for such a person must be established by credible records. Otherwise the Internal Revenue Service will decide how much each company can deduct.

If the companies are all 80% subsidiaries of a common parent, under most circumstances a consolidated federal income tax return may be filed. Then it doesn't matter how much each company deducts as long as the total for all companies is reasonable. But consolidated returns can't be filed by brother-sister corporations (where the same individuals own substantially the same proportions of each related company).

- Good strategy is an agreement that requires the executive to repay any amount disallowed the corporation as a tax deduction because it was excessive. He can then be paid a very generous salary without fear of tax loss to the corporation.

Justifying High Salaries When Company Is Losing Money

An executive is paid to make money for his company. If the corporation loses money, is he really worth his princely salary?

The Internal Revenue Service used that logic to throw out part of a president's salary as unreasonable in a year when a company experienced the loss that resulted from shutting down its manufacturing operations during an essential relocation of the plant. (Poor plant layout and inadequate space had resulted in costly and cumbersome operations.) The move, for which the president was largely responsible, laid a foundation for the highly profitable years which had been logged by the time the case reached court. Verdict: Deduction of the full salary was allowed in that loss year.

Roux Laboratories v. U.S., D.C., M.D., Fla.

Safe Deposit Dangers

• A man died, leaving a safe deposit box full of bearer bonds. Some were in his wife's name; some jointly owned. She didn't know about them and didn't have a key to the safe deposit box. IRS claimed that because she had no key she didn't own the bonds, and it collected estate tax on all the bonds. Moral: Make sure your wife knows about her property—and has a key to the safe deposit vault. (If there are things you don't want her to know about, get a second vault.)

• If cash is kept in the safe deposit box, it may be hit with extra taxes when the box is opened after death. IRS will assume the cash was unreported income and will assess both income tax and estate tax upon it. To avoid the tax: Keep documentary proof in the box, too, of where the cash came from. If shown to have been withdrawn from a checking account, it may be okay.

Tax Status of 24 Executive Fringes and Perks

• Special medical and dental expense reimbursement for executive and family. Tax status: Tax-free to executive; deductible by company. But the plan must cover all employees on a nondiscriminatory basis.

• Company payment or reimbursement of accident and health insurance. Tax status: Tax-free to executive; deductible by company.

• Medical examinations. Tax status: Tax-free to executive; deductible by company. If required as a condition of employment and paid by executive, deductible by him.

• Company gym. Tax status: Tax-free to executive; deductible by company.

• Group term life insurance. Tax status: Tax-free to executive up to $50,000 coverage; excess taxable on favored basis. Fully deductible by company.

• Split-dollar life insurance. Tax status: Tax-free to executive on basis of the "cost" of one-year term, less part of premium paid by the executive. Company gets no deduction for premiums paid but gets them back tax-free out of proceeds.

• Interest-free and low-interest loans. Tax status: Tax-free to executive; no tax consequences to company.

• Business and professional clubs. Tax status: Tax-free to executive; deductible by company.

• Country clubs, social, athletic, or sporting clubs. Tax status: Tax-free to executive and deductible by company if conducive to business.

• Meals furnished on company premises, including executive dining room. Tax status: Tax-free to executive and deductible by company if for company's convenience.

• Supper money. Tax status: Tax-free to executive; deductible by company.

• Lodging on company premises. Tax status: Tax-free to executive only if a condition of employment.

• Travel away from home. Tax status: Tax-free to executive and deductible by company if reasonable and necessary for business.

• Travel expenses of wife. Tax status: Taxable to executive unless wife's presence has bona fide business purpose. Deductible by company if ordinary and necessary.

• Local travel, parking, tolls. Tax status: Tax-free to executive and deductible by company if business-related, excluding commutation.

• Entertainment. Tax status: Business meals, employee recreation and social activities, business conventions generally are tax-free to executive and deductible by company if they are "ordinary and necessary." All other entertainment expenses are tax-free to the executive and deductible by the company only if directly related to business.

• Legal services. Tax status: Tax-free to executive and deductible by company if provided under qualified plan.

• Financial counseling. Tax status: Tax-free to executive if for tax advice or preparation of tax returns. Deductible by company.

• Education and training to improve existing job skills. Tax status: Tax-free to executive; deductible by firm.

• Company car, airplane, or boat. Tax status: Tax-free to executive to extent of business use and minimal personal use.

• Chauffeur. Tax status: Same as company vehicle.

• Death benefit. Tax status: Tax-free to executive's beneficiary up to $5,000. Deductible by company.

• Moving expenses. Tax status: Tax-free to executive and deductible by company subject to special limitations.

• Officer and director liability insurance. Tax status: Generally not taxable to executive; deductible by company.

Reminder: Fringes and perks—like salaries—are deductible only to the extent that they are "reasonable." If the Internal Revenue Service determines that the amount paid an executive is "unreasonably" high, the excess won't be deductible from the corporation's income tax and it will be taxable to the individual.

When Supper Money Is Taxable Income

Supper money paid in cash to late-working employees is not taxable to employees. But it is taxable to business proprietors, partners, and officers who are major stockholders of corporations. (No tax, though, to either employees or owners, if meals are served at work premises and are paid for directly by the company. That's different from making cash payments so that employees can eat elsewhere.)

Antos v. Comm'r., TC Memo 1976-89, affd. CA-9, 2/24/78.

Tax Rules on Deferred Compensation

• Compensation can be deferred to retirement, to any specified year, or spread over a number of years.

• It will be taxed as income (and deductible by the company) only when actually paid.

• Agreement can provide for payment sooner under specified conditions. Examples: It can be payable immediately if the executive becomes disabled, or to his beneficiaries on death.

• Deferred tax treatment does not depend on pay being subject to conditions, such as being

forfeited or reduced if the executive leaves the company. But such a provision is okay if the company asks for it and the executive agrees.

• Compensation can't be put into escrow or a special account subject to control of the executive. The company can establish a reserve or buy insurance, but funds must remain part of general company assets.

• Deferred compensation arrangements are allowed for owner-officers of closely held companies. But they are still subject to IRS scrutiny as to whether total compensation for the year (including both paid and deferred) is excessive.

The executive cannot say to the company, "Don't pay me now, I'll let you know when I want it." That's called constructive receipt and makes the amount taxable immediately.

Important to consider:

• Money paid in later years will probably be worth less because of inflation.

• Don't assume tax bracket will be lower after retirement. Executives now in the 50% bracket (maximum tax on earned income) could be in a higher bracket then if they have substantial income from investments.

Give Money to Charity and Keep Earning Interest on It

It's possible to give money to charity, take a deduction, and still receive interest on it for life.

It's called a charitable remainder trust. The trustees can agree to pay the donor a certain percentage, such as 5%, of the principal every year. Or a fixed number of dollars. Or the trustees may pool the gift with others and pay a pro rata share of the earnings of the combined fund. The payments continue as long as the donor lives.

The full contribution is not deductible. The deduction will be the actuarially determined value today of the money at some time in the future, when the charity gets full use of it. It depends on the giver's age. For a man of 55, it would be 42%. For a woman of 55, 34%.

If the property has appreciated, the calculation is based on current value, and there's no capital gains tax. But in the case of a gift of appreciated property, the deduction can't be more than 30% of adjusted gross income. The usual limit is 50%. (Any excess can be carried forward.)

Most charities have already set up the procedures and paid the lawyers; there shouldn't be any fees. But you can't change your mind. It must be a permanent transfer of ownership.

Give a House to Charity and Keep Living in It

It's possible to give a home to charity but continue to live in it for as long as either spouse lives. Then the charitable organization takes title and possession. It works for vacation houses or any other real estate, but not for personal property (paintings, jewelry, etc.).

The catch: The tax deduction for the charitable contribution is less than the full value of the property. It's some fraction of the value, determined by an actuarial calculation according to life expectancy. Since the charity won't get the property until sometime in the future, the present value of the gift is less than the full value of the property.

Example: Home is donated by 70-year-old man and 68-year-old wife, with provision that they keep the house as long as either one lives, then it goes to the charity. In the year of the gift, they would get a charitable deduction for 41.5% of the value of the house.

Tax Deduction When Property Is Abandoned

If unsalable machinery, supplies, intangibles, or even real estate carried on the books is abandoned, its unrecovered cost would be deducted on the federal income tax return for that year. Machinery can be abandoned for tax purposes when left in the yard to rot away. Shipping cartons and the like can be destroyed. Land can be deeded to the county. Patents and trademarks can be released to the public domain. An advan-

tage of this technique is that the property can be abandoned and the tax deduction claimed in any year the taxpayer chooses.

How Deducting Bad Debts Can Misfire

Seven mistakes the IRS is waiting for you to make:

1. A bad debt is not deductible if there was no reasonable prospect of payment when it was contracted—for instance if sale was made to an insolvent party.

2. The debt must be legally enforceable. No deduction is allowed, for instance, if interest is charged in excess of state's maximum rates.

3. No deduction unless the taxpayer is on an accrual basis and debt was reported as income in the same or previous year.

4. It isn't enough that debt is unpaid. The account must be uncollectable because of the debtor's financial inability to pay. The following are not bad debt deductions: Debt written off because enforcing it is too expensive; debt written off because customer is dissatisfied and it's "good business" not to demand payment.

5. There is no deduction unless creditor can cite an "identifiable event" that made the debt worthless. Some examples: Debtor's bankruptcy; his balance sheet showing no possibility of equity for creditors; destruction of debtor's plant by uninsured casualty; newspaper report that debtor has lost a government contract accounting for 80% of revenues; death or permanent incapacity of debtor's one truly indispensable presiding officer.

6. Debt is deductible only in the taxable year when the identifiable event took place. A company that does not hound debtors mercilessly may not discover the worthlessness of debt until it's too late to get a tax deduction.

7. Only business bad debts are fully deductible. Nonbusiness bad debts are short-term capital losses. Business bad debt must be connected with taxpayer's trade or business, not with outside investments.

Deducting partial bad debts:

Most taxpayers don't seem to know this privilege exists. Example of when you can use it: A credit agency or CPA with particular expertise in the matter concludes that chances of collecting are only 60%. If propertly documented for a particular debt (not total receivables), this could justify deducting 40% of the account as a partial bad debt. But no deduction is allowed if credit was extended to debtor after the debt became partially worthless.

A Way to Take Bigger Depreciation Deductions

A depreciation technique that can increase deductions by as much as 40%, increase flexibility in how depreciation is taken, and reduce paperwork: Asset Depreciation Range (ADR). It's widely used by sophisticated large companies but rarely by middle- and small-size businesses.

How it works: Instead of keeping cost and depreciation records on each piece of equipment, keep a single set of records for all equipment in a class acquired in any year. Examples of classes: Autos and trucks, data-processing equipment.

IRS allows firms using the ADR system to use estimated lives as much as 20% higher or lower than stated in IRS guidelines. If a guideline specifies ten years for a type of equipment, the company can reduce that by 20% and write off in eight years all property in that class acquired during the year.

Once estimated life is set, the company still has usual choice of depreciation methods: Straight line, declining balance, sum of the years digits, or any other IRS-approved method.

Caution: Once estimated useful life is chosen, it can't be changed for that batch of equipment. It can for a new batch next year, though.

Most companies like to set the life of equipment as short as possible so they can take more depreciation, increasing cash flow especially in the early years.

Some companies that are losing money or have other unusual situations may want to take less depreciation than the standard schedule allows. That is also possible under ADR.

Note: ADR cannot be used for general-purpose industrial or commmercial buildings. But it can be used for special-purpose buildings, such as cooling towers, storage bins, and fuel tanks.

Source: Leon M. Nad, tax partner, Price Waterhouse & Co., CPAs, 1251 Ave. of the Americas, New York 10020.

Deducting for Premature Obsolescence

Extra depreciation deductions are possible when assets become obsolete before the end of their normal lives. Write off all the remaining cost in one year by proving that the assets are out of date and continuing to use them would put the company at a competitive disadvantage. But it isn't enough to show that there's something newer, better, or cheaper on the market. The company must prove that the facility was abandoned because continuing use would, indeed, hurt its competitive position.

Fort Howard Paper v. *Comm'r.,* T.C. Memo. 1977-422, 12/14/77.

Understanding the Accumulated Earnings Tax

Income retained beyond the reasonable needs of the business can subject a corporation to accumulated earnings tax. One reason many corporations get clobbered: The officers who advise on internal matters often have misconceptions about how the tax really works.

• Fallacy #1: The way to avoid the tax (and still not subject shareholders to income tax on dividends) is to pay nontaxable stock dividends (i.e., the shares are diluted).

But the disbursement of shares alone fails to reduce the corporation's accumulated taxable income.

• Fallacy #2: If earnings and profits are very large, and the company wants to avoid paying taxable dividends to the shareholders, liquidate the company. Liquidating distributions reduce the corporation's accumulated taxable income.

That's fine if the corporation is completely liquidated by the end of the year. If it isn't, any undistributed earnings are surely vulnerable to the accumulated earnings tax, for a liquidating corporation has no expansion or other plans requiring the retention of earnings.

• Fallacy #3: If the corporation doesn't need to retain earnings for the needs of its business, diversify into some other business.

But earnings may be retained validly only for the needs of the business which had those earnings, not of a business in which the company isn't yet engaged.

• Fallacy #4: Earnings may safely be retained in order to acquire business assets that previously had been leased, or to finance operations without borrowing any more money from banks.

The IRS and the courts tend to assume that a corporation is going to continue past practices. So if it has used rented facilities in the past, there is a presumption that retained earnings are not really for the purpose of buying equipment.

• Fallacy #5: Earnings may be retained for realistic plans of expansion, to be put into operation as soon as the directors approve the plans.

But if there is strong dissension among the directors, the plan may never be approved.

• Fallacy #6: It would seem that the corporation's legitimate business needs for funds just about equaled its after-tax earnings for the year, so dividends couldn't be paid. But if the corporation already holds earnings and profits that hadn't been ploughed back into the business, they could have been used to finance the business needs, and dividends still would have to be paid in order to avoid the accumulated earnings tax.

President's Use of a Company Car Taxed as Dividend

In a very common situation, a company-owned car was used totally by the company president. In matters of this sort, the Internal Revenue Service often treats the fair market value of the personal use of the car as taxable income to the user. It's treated as a dividend if he's a major stockholder of the company or as compensation if he's not.

The remaining problem is what part of the value represents nontaxable business use and what part personal use. Here the president, a shareholder, argued that his personal use of the car was merely incidental. But he admitted he didn't own a personal car.

The court ruled that the full value was a taxable (and nondeductible) dividend to him. It wasn't deductible compensation, for there was no proof (like a reference in corporate minutes) that the use of the car had been intended to be compensation. A dividend, on the other hand, can be assumed, even if none was declared or intended.

Personal ownership of a car, any car, would have been helpful.

William D. Gardner et al., T.C. Memo, 1976-349, 11/16/76.

When (and Why) to Take the Same Deduction Twice

Sometimes there is real doubt about the year in which a deduction should be claimed on the federal income tax return. Bad debts are deductible only in the year when they become uncollectible. Casualties other than theft are deductible in the year of occurrence to the extent no recovery by insurance or otherwise is possible.

If you claim the deduction in one year and subsequently it is ascertained that you should have taken it in an earlier year, the deduction may be lost. That earlier year might now be closed by the statute of limitations.

In a case of genuine doubt, claim the deduction in each year. Then you'll be sure to have it allowed in the proper one. But seeking to evade taxes which you know are owing is fraud; and, as you know you're not entitled to the same deduction twice, your returns involve reducing tax by one deduction you know isn't proper.

What to do: Attach to each tax return a statement that says, because of uncertainty as to the year of deduction, you are claiming it twice only for that purpose and with the expectation of getting it only once.

What You Don't Have to Show a Tax Examiner

A court of appeals has affirmed a lower court's decision that you don't have to show the Internal Revenue Service everything.

The case: A "Big Eight" accounting firm was engaged to audit the consolidated financial statements of a major corporation, Johns-Manville, Inc. The accounting firm had no part in the preparation of J-M's federal income tax returns, nor in their review. But the IRS sought a court order to compel the accountants to turn over to the government various analyses prepared by J-M employees which the accountants used to verify financial statements for the SEC and other statements. The IRS admitted that the analyses had not been prepared for or used in connection with the tax returns, but they thought it might be helpful to have the data as a key to understanding how the audit of financial statements had been carried on by the accountants. Perhaps it would be convenient for federal tax examiners to see every piece of paper that might be informative in any way. But, the court ruled, mere convenience doesn't make an item producible under an IRS summons.

U.S. et al. v. Coopers & Lybrand et al., 10th Cir., 2/15/77.

How to Avoid Multiple State Taxes

When a person moves from one state to another, both states may try to collect income taxes while he's alive and death taxes afterward. So if an executive is transferred or moves for health or other reasons, he must be careful not to give any hint that he plans to return.

The same problem could arise if a person owns a house, a beach condominium, and a hunting

lodge in three different states. Expect all three of the states to try to tax the income and the estate if they can. The more wealth, the harder the states' agents will try.

What to do: Arrange all personal and financial affairs so legal residence is clear. Register to vote there, keep principal bank account and safe deposit box there, use that address on passport and federal income tax return. It's not enough to say that's where you live. The actions taken must show it to satisfy tax collectors.

Tax Obligation After Bankruptcy

Although the bankrupt company has losses for the year, a federal income tax return still has to be filed. In the case of a bankrupt corporation, the fiduciary (the receiver) must sign. If the president or other corporate officer signs it, as in the past, the IRS considers it no return. A tax return without a valid signature is not regarded as a tax return at all. Thus the statute of limitations never starts to run, and any elections made on the return do not count.

When Gambling Losses Are Tax-Deductible

Gambling gains are taxable, but the profits can be offset by gambling losses. Casinos and racetracks are required by law to report large payouts to the Internal Revenue Service. It is up to the individual, however, to establish the amount of any losses.

Here's how IRS says it can be done:
• Keep an accurate diary showing names, dates, types of bets, names of witnesses, and dollar amounts.
• Save verifiable documentation: Betting tickets, canceled checks, credit records, bank withdrawal slips. Also: Hotel bills, airline tickets, gasoline credit slips, and other records that show you were at those gambling locations.

• Get affidavits or testimony from responsible gambling officials attesting to your losses.
Rev. Proc. 77-29.

Tax Tips

• Medical deductions. If the doctor orders it, it may be deductible. Recent cases: A doctor wouldn't permit the executive to go to Europe unless he took along his wife, who was specially trained to deal with his heart illness; the wife's travel expenses were allowed as a medical deduction. The doctor told the patient to swim twice a day, and the tax court allowed him to deduct part of the cost of an indoor pool (a very expensive one) he installed.

• Facelifts and hair transplants are okay as medical deductions if the work is performed by a doctor, even though it may not be medically necessary. But wigs and toupees aren't deductible. (Possible exception: A woman loses all her hair in an illness or accident and the doctor recommends a wig to avoid emotional problems.)

• The last dollar of income could add $20 to the tax. That's because the tax table uses brackets rather than exact calculation. For a family of four, tax table income $37,500, the tax is $8,197. If income is $37,501, the tax is $8,217.

• Deductible commuting. Most commuting expenses aren't deductible, but if a person works at two jobs in the same day, the cost of traveling from first job to second job is deductible as a business expense. (He still can't deduct travel from home to the first job or from the second job back home.)

• When understating tax is okay. There's no penalty for understatement of tax if income came from a transfer where the legal issue was so complicated that there were legitimate differences of interpretation.

Otherwise, expect to pay 5% penalty on understated amount whether the difference is due to negligence or disregard of rules and regulations (even where there's no intent to defraud).
Carter, Jr. et al. v. Comm'r., T.C. Memo. 1977-322, 9/21/77.

• Sale-leaseback tax trap. A corporation sold some properties to an unrelated buyer and immediately leased them back, deducting the rent it paid the buyer. But the selling corporation agreed to pay all the property taxes, maintenance expense, liability for damages to the property, losses from possible government condemnation, etc. IRS held that the seller, retaining so many powers and obligations of ownership, hadn't made a real sale and couldn't deduct rent.
Sun Oil Co. et al. v. Comm'r., 3d Cir., 9/7/77.

• Tax danger in credit applications. When filing a credit statement for a loan, be sure that the income figures don't disagree with the tax returns. A revenue agent could interpret the difference as fraud. If the difference was the result of carelessness rather than fraud, your firm jeopardizes its relationship with the bank's loan officer and the loan review committee.

• Assets in someone else's name. The government rarely can prove that a taxpayer wilfully intended to dodge taxes. The Internal Revenue Service wins by uncovering evidence of some badge of fraud. One such badge, declared the court in a recent case, is a taxpayer's consistent practice of placing assets in the names of others.
Frank Costello et al., T.C. Memo. 1976-399.

• You can sue an IRS agent. When you file a federal income tax return or undergo an Internal Revenue Service audit, a tremendous amount of personal and confidential data is disclosed. In the new atmosphere of granting protection to persons against invasion of privacy, the Tax Reform Act of 1976 provided that any taxpayer damaged by an unlawful disclosure of such information can sue the government employee who wilfully or negligently disclosed information which, by law, is confidential. Minimum award: $1,000 for each instance of unauthorized disclosure. In addition to recompense for actual damage, punitive damages also are authorized when the unlawful disclosure is wilful or when it is the result of gross negligence.
I.R.C. Section 7217. Applies to unauthorized disclosure made on or after 1/1/77.

• The cost of laetrile, the controversial cancer medication, is deductible as a medical expense if a physician prescribes it and the taxpayer lives in a state where it's legal.

• Living together. In states where common law marriages are recognized, persons who are not legally married are able to file joint federal income tax returns.

• Home entertainment deductions for business guests may be hard to prove. If group is large enough, have outside caterer who provides food and service. Use caterer's bill as proof.

• Meals on one-day trip without an overnight stay are not deductible either by the employee or employer. If company reimburses the employee, it's taxable income to him.

• Deductible items charged to credit cards. Deduct for all items charged during taxable year even if not paid until after year ended.

• Individual Retirement Account. Once an IRA is started, Form 5329 must be attached to the tax return every year even if no further contributions are made. Penalty for neglecting this is $15 per day up to $5,000.

• Job-seeking expenses. It's okay to deduct travel and other expenses including meals with others, for purposes of seeking a new job in taxpayer's same business or profession.

• Publications. Medical and health publications are probably okay as a Schedule A medical deduction. Stock market letters and investment publications are a Schedule A miscellaneous deduction if you have investment income.

• Life insurance seized in taxes. If a person owes federal taxes, the IRS can attach the cash surrender value of any life insurance policies he owns. To protect against that, convert to term insurance; then there's no cash surrender value.

• Consider filing a protective refund claim even if the IRS has a policy on a particular issue that is adverse to that of the taxpayer. The action keeps the refund claim alive while issue is tried in the courts by other taxpayers.

• Cost of living is a deductible expense if business requires prolonged stay away from home, but at most up to one year.

• Deductible casualty losses are allowed only in the case of sudden or unusual events. Losses resulting from progressive deterioration of property are not deductible as casualties. Examples: The collapse of a pier due to exposure to salt water. In contrast, the loss of ornamental pine trees destroyed over a week by beetles is deductible.

• Charitable contributions. An accrual-basis corporation that pledges in one year and makes the contribution in the first 75 days of the following year can pick either year as the one for taking the deduction.

• Burglary or theft losses. Take a casualty loss deduction for estimated value of property at the time it was stolen. IRS won't allow deduction of the original purchase price but will cut it down to secondhand value. And it will resist large losses on jewelry and any claimed losses of cash. Take the total fair value of property stolen, subtract insurance reimbursement and $100 for each incident, then deduct the rest. (Don't subtract $100 if it's a business loss.)

• Storm damage. Loss incurred after the close of taxable year can be deducted on the same year's tax return if in a government-declared disaster area. If it's a large loss, volunteer some details, possibly including photos or newspaper clippings about the storm. This might make the difference in avoiding an audit.

• When repairs are not deductible. If the company acquires battered equipment that can't be used until repaired, the necessary initial repairs are considered part of the cost of the equipment. Thus, the repair cost is not deductible immediately but must be depreciated year by year.

• A lawsuit is an asset owned by the plaintiff, says IRS. Case: A taxpayer claimed a capital loss on stock considered worthless because the company had no assets. But that company had a lawsuit pending against another company. IRS and the court took the view that a suit wouldn't have been filed unless the company thought it might win. The lawsuit was a potential asset and the stock was not worthless.
TC Memo 1978-509, 12/26/78.

• Snow removal deductible. The owner of commercial property can deduct the cost of snow removal from the parking areas of his business premises. The practical problem: Getting proof. Snow removers usually insist on cash and don't always give receipts. Prepare receipts ahead of time and make sure the person who pays workers has them fill in signature and amounts.

• Consulting fees may not be deductible in the year they are paid. If the consultant works on a long-term project (e.g., property development, construction of new plant), the fees may be a capital item. They'd have to be deducted over the life of the project.

• Tax deadline is met if the envelope is

postmarked on the deadline day. But a metered date isn't good enough, since the taxpayer controls the postage meter and the IRS knows it.

• Ask IRS for immediate explanation if any form, communication, empty envelope, or indecipherable letter arrives. The taxpayer is held liable even though he doesn't get notice because of problems in postal delivery.

Donohue et al. v. *Commissioner,* T.C. Memo. 1978-224, 6/19/78.

When Local Taxes Are Not Deductible

With the passage of California's Proposition 13, and fears of taxpayer revolts elsewhere, some cities are increasing revenues by imposing new taxes but calling them something else. For example: To pay for a new water system, one city hit taxpayers with a "front door benefit charge," covering the cost of building the new water system, plus interest on money borrowed for construction, plus the cost of maintaining the new system.

The problem: "Local benefits taxes" are not deductible on IRS returns, because the revenues raised to pay for new water lines or curbs or other local improvements increase the value of taxpayers' property. One exception: Local benefits taxes assessed to pay for more than physical improvements. In the case of the city's "front door benefit charge," the portion of that local tax covering interest payments and maintenance costs was deductible on IRS returns.

What taxpayers should do: Insist that cities furnish them with a breakdown on exactly how all local benefits tax revenues are used.

Revenue Ruling 79-201.

TIME
MANAGEMENT

Why You're Busier Than Your Staff

Thieves of Executive Time

Scheduling

Cutting Telephone Time

Managing Meetings

Making Best Use of Subordinates

Office Visitors

Staying Organized

27

TIME MANAGEMENT

Thieves of Executive Time

If you're like most managers, you don't really know where your day goes. And if you tried to list the reasons why you fall behind in your work, you'd probably be writing down the wrong things. Time-management expert R. Alec Mackenzie* tells how to get more done.

Most important: Don't put the blame on outside factors. Instead, blame your own inability to control them.

The real time wasters:
- Attempting too much at once.
- Unrealistic time estimates.
- Procrastinating.
- Not listening.
- Not saying "no."
- Doing instead of delegating.
- Personal disorganization.
- Delegating responsibility without authority.
- Snap decisions.

A system that Mackenzie suggests:

A daily time log (but not the way most people

*President, R. Alec Mackenzie Associates, Greenwich, NY 12834; author of *New Time Management Methods.*

keep them). Common mistakes: (1) Filling in the sheet at the end of the day when one's memory can play tricks. (2) Listing what was done without analyzing the time spent in terms of the work accomplished. (3) Using a time log as a record of achievement instead of as a self-improvement tool.

Instead, enter everything that's done as soon as you stop, even for a brief interruption. Allow room on the sheet for comment on things that were done unnecessarily, work that could have been left to subordinates, things done poorly through lack of preparation, time spent on daydreaming, jobs that took more or less time than expected.

Spend the last 20 minutes of the day filling in a sheet for tomorrow. What you plan to do; how long it should take. Then compare what actually happens when tomorrow comes. How much of the plan can you follow? What goes wrong with the rest? Identify your own "thieves of time," then make daily plans you can stick to. (Don't skip this step just because tomorrow won't be a "typical" day. Most managers waste time in the same ways every day.

Why You're Busier Than Those Who Work for You

Too much of a boss's time can be work "imposed" on him by subordinates (and the boss). Example: An employee presents problem to a busy boss. The boss says, "Leave it with me. I'll get back to you." The subordinate is relieved of the problem and does nothing, waiting for instructions. The problem is on the boss's back along with other, similar ones. He runs out of time; subordinates run out of work to do. When employees start reminding the boss of answers he owes them, he realizes he has trapped himself into working for the people who are supposed to be working for him.

Stifle the impulse to say, "Leave it with me." Leave the burden on the subordinate's shoulders, where it probably belongs. Depending on how much you trust the employee's judgment, instruct him to: (1) Recommend the action to be taken and means of implementing it; (2) take action but advise you at once; or (3) act on his own and report routinely.

If you can't trust him to take one of these three courses, you may need a new subordinate.

Source: *Management Time: Who's Got the Monkey,* by William Oncken, Jr., and Donald L. Wall, in *Harvard Business Review.*

Getting Organized

• Most efficient desk: an L-shaped one with a back table.

• Get a second desk where you can work standing up. Switch to it when you sense that you're slowing down from tedium or fatigue.

• Arrange furniture so chair does not face door and there is no way to catch the eye of a would-be chatterer.

• How to clean up a cluttered desk: Arrange everything into four piles: (1) For immediate action; (2) to be handled within 24 hours; (3) to be handled within a month; (4) to be read when you get a chance. Then get everything off your desk except pile #1. (Keep pile #4 chronologically, with the latest on top. When it gets too big, remove some from the bottom and discard without

guilt. At least you're keeping the pile current.)

• Insist that all mail reach you in the original envelopes. Have them just slit open. This is the only way to make sure pieces don't get lost. (It also gives information only available on an envelope—particularly when a letter was mailed, as opposed to when it was dated.)

• If your reply is brief, write it on the incoming letter or memo. File a copy. Don't write when you can phone. Use the written word primarily to remind, confirm, or clarify.

• Handle each piece of paper only once. The matter itself will take the same amount of time, whether the paper is reviewed once or five times.

• Accumulate quick, easy, yes/no type work in a special "children's hour" folder. Set aside odd periods to work on it (while waiting for a meeting to start or while traveling).

• Don't keep records of information easily obtained elsewhere. To avoid unnecessary filing, never ask, "Is it possible we'll ever need this?" The real question: What would happen if you needed it and it wasn't there? The answer in most cases is that it wouldn't matter. (Files should contain a few fat folders, not many skinny ones. Less chance of misfiling.)

• Before filing a copy of an outgoing letter: Note on the copy when and if a reply is due. Then, if no answer is expected, the copy goes into the regular file. If a reply is expected, it is put in a dated suspense file. Result: Past-due follow-up is daily and automatic.

Scheduling

• Which tasks to perform first: Don't make the usual list based on what's needed fastest and what can wait. That often relegates the really important things to last place. Instead, list your projects in order of how much you will benefit from getting them done. Select the top two or three and concentrate on accomplishing them. Don't feel guilty about slighting the others.

• People who do their best work first thing in the morning should reserve this "prime time" for the most demanding task of the day. Let the mail wait. Let the phone calls wait.

• Set some appointments at odd times instead

of on the hour or half hour. Meeting at 2:50 or 3:20 makes others more prompt and puts across the message of careful time management.

• If possible, work during noon hour when interruptions are rare, because most others have gone to lunch. Go out to eat at 1 p.m. or later.

• When scheduling your day, schedule the interruptions as well. Set aside the specific times when you can be reached on routine matters. If calls come in at other hours, have your secretary say you'll call them back. (Even VIPs will accept this if you establish a reputation for returning calls when promised.)

Managing Meetings

• Instead of having a meeting, set up a conference call with the parties involved. You can arrange it locally as well as long-distance at surprisingly low rates.

• If you must have a meeting, don't use the conference room. A better site is an office filled with reminders of things to be done. To keep a meeting really short, make it a stand-up conference: People on their feet are inclined to talk less.

• Meetings that drag on without resolving conflicts: Adjourn the meeting until the next day. Resolution is bound to come much faster then at the second session.

• Staff meetings: Consider sending a deputy to stand in for you. Send along a list of points to be made and questions to be asked. Ask for a short report on the meeting and for the deputy's suggestions.

Cutting Telephone Time

• Preset time limit: "Yes, Tom. I can talk for three minutes."

• Foreshadow ending: "Bill, before we hang up . . ."

• When calling a long-winded party, time call for just before he goes out to lunch or leaves for the day. Gives him a reason to keep the call short.

• Never hold the phone waiting for someone who's on another line. Request an immediate callback instead.

• Make phone calls before 9 a.m. or after 3 p.m. At other hours, too many people are in meetings.

• Eliminate "hello" from telephone answering habits. It just wastes time and adds confusion. Answer by identifying yourself instead—it starts conversation with no lost motion.

• Don't return all calls the minute you get back to the office. Spot the crucial ones. Half the rest will be from people who've already solved their problems; the rest will get back to you soon enough.

• When a secretary places a call, tell her in advance: (1) If there's anyone else to ask for if the person wanted isn't there. (2) Whether to ask that the call be returned. (3) To find out the best time of day to place the call again.

• When asking someone to call back later, suggest the best time. This avoids repeated interruptions at inconvenient moments.

Staying Organized

• Time budget should include "quiet hours" when you have a chance to think without interruptions. Best time in the office is early morning before official hours begin. Otherwise, spend a few "office hours" at home. Have an answering machine cover telephone calls so you won't be interrupted.

• Why the best of us procrastinate: When we put off something important that we should be doing, it's usually because of nagging fears that we won't do it right. To handle these little anxieties, ask yourself, "What's the worst thing that could happen if I goof?" Often it will be simply embarrassment, or the need not to admit having made a mistake.

• If a task looks too hard or too big: Break it down into small, manageable "instant" things to do. The first one is to list—in writing—all the simple steps involved. Without such a list, you may never get started at all.

• The real reason for not taking work home: It gives you an excuse for not getting things done in the office.

• To find your coat on a crowded rack, tuck one sleeve over the hanger bar. To spot your car in a crowded parking lot, mark the antenna with brightly colored tape.

Making Best Use of Subordinates

• Have the secretary keep a list of things to be done so she can check on your progress. (Especially good for chief executives; it gives them someone to "report to.")

• To make sure a typist picks up all corrections, always make them in color.

• Excessive reporting by subordinates: Most memos contain information you don't need. One solution worth trying is "management by exception" (subordinates report only when results deviate from plan).

• More ways a secretary can help: Sit in at meetings; take minutes of action items and distribute to those concerned; follow up to make sure action items are actually completed; report to you if they aren't.

Office Visitors

• Let associates know that you're available if needed, but keep the door to your office physically closed.

• Impromptu business get-togethers can be kept brief by meeting visitor outside the office and conversing there.

• Tactful ways to end conversations at your desk: (1) Use an electric timer and blame brush-off on inanimate object. (2) Rest one hand on the telephone, even though it's not ringing. This conveys the message that there's a need to make an important call. (3) Turn your body to the side as though about to get up. (4) If that hint doesn't work, stand up and walk the person to the door, chatting casually.

INDEX

399

400